STUDENT'S SOLUTIONS MANUAL

NANCY BOUDREAU

Bowling Green University

STATISTICS FOR BUSINESS AND ECONOMICS

THIRTEENTH EDITION

James T. McClave

University of Florida

P. George Benson

College of Charleston

Terry Sincich

University of South Florida

Pearson

330 Hudson Street, NY NY 10013

The author and publisher of this book have used their best efforts in preparing this book. These efforts include the development, research, and testing of the theories and programs to determine their effectiveness. The author and publisher make no warranty of any kind, expressed or implied, with regard to these programs or the documentation contained in this book. The author and publisher shall not be liable in any event for incidental or consequential damages in connection with, or arising out of, the furnishing, performance, or use of these programs.

Reproduced by Pearson from electronic files supplied by the author.

ISBN-13: 978-0-13-451303-4
ISBN-10: 0-13-451303-7

Contents

Chapter 1
Statistics, Data, and Statistical Thinking

1.1   Statistics is a science that deals with the collection, classification, analysis, and interpretation of information or data. It is a meaningful, useful science with a broad, almost limitless scope of applications to business, government, and the physical and social sciences.

1.3   The four elements of a descriptive statistics problem are:

       1.   The population or sample of interest. This is the collection of all the units upon which the variable is measured.
       2.   One or more variables that are to be investigated. These are the types of data that are to be collected.
       3.   Tables, graphs, or numerical summary tools. These are tools used to display the characteristic of the sample or population.
       4.   Identification of patterns in the data. These are conclusions drawn from what the summary tools revealed about the population or sample.

1.5   The first major method of collecting data is from a published source. These data have already been collected by someone else and are available in a published source. The second method of collecting data is from a designed experiment. These data are collected by a researcher who exerts strict control over the experimental units in a study. These data are measured directly from the experimental units. The final method of collecting data is observational. These data are collected directly from experimental units by simply observing the experimental units in their natural environment and recording the values of the desired characteristics. The most common type of observational study is a survey.

1.7   A population is a set of existing units such as people, objects, transactions, or events. A variable is a characteristic or property of an individual population unit such as height of a person, time of a reflex, amount of a transaction, etc.

1.9   A representative sample is a sample that exhibits characteristics similar to those possessed by the target population. A representative sample is essential if inferential statistics is to be applied. If a sample does not possess the same characteristics as the target population, then any inferences made using the sample will be unreliable.

1.11   A population is a set of existing units such as people, objects, transactions, or events. A process is a series of actions or operations that transform inputs to outputs. A process produces or generates output over time. Examples of processes are assembly lines, oil refineries, and stock prices.

1.13   The data consisting of the classifications A, B, C, and D are qualitative. These data are nominal and thus are qualitative. After the data are input as 1, 2, 3, and 4, they are still nominal and thus qualitative. The only differences between the two data sets are the names of the categories. The numbers associated with the four groups are meaningless.

1.15   Both the variables current position and type of organization are qualitative. The variable 'years of experience' is quantitative.

1.17   a.   The experimental unit is a firm that had annual balance sheet data from 1973 to 2011 reported on Compustat.

        b.   The variable measured in this study is the DQ value.

        c.   This is an observational study. No variables were manipulated in this study.

1.19   a.   The population of interest is all U.S. residents with a listed phone number.

        b.   The variable of interest is the view of each U.S. resident as to whether the president is doing a good or bad job. It is qualitative.

        c.   The sample is the 2000 individuals selected for the poll.

        d.   The inference of interest is to estimate the proportion of all U.S. residents who believe the president is doing a good job.

        e.   The method of data collection is a survey.

        f.   It is not very likely that the sample will be representative of the population of all residents of the United States. By selecting phone numbers at random, the sample will be limited to only those people who have telephones. Also, many people share the same phone number, so each person would not have an equal chance of being contacted. Another possible problem is the time of day the calls are made. If the calls are made in the evening, those people who work in the evening would not be represented.

1.21   Since the data collected consist of the entire population, this would represent a descriptive study. Flaherty used the data to help describe the condition of the U.S. Treasury in 1861.

1.23   a.   This is a designed experiment because the college students were randomly assigned to a group.

        b.   The experimental unit is a college student.

        c.   The two variables are type of condition and type of disposal. Both type of condition and type of disposal are qualitative.

        d.   We could infer that in the population of all college students, those who could be placed in the *usefulness is salient* condition will recycle at a much higher rate (68%) than those who could be placed in the *control* condition (37%).

1.25   a.   The experimental unit for this study is a single-family residential property in Arlington, Texas.

        b.   The variables measured are the sale price and the Zillow estimated value. Both of these variables are quantitative.

        c.   If these 2,045 properties were all the single-family residential properties sold in Arlington, Texas in the past 6 months, then this would be considered the population.

        d.   If these 2,045 properties represent a sample, then the population would be all the singe-family residential properties sold in the last 6 months in Arlington, Texas.

        e.   No. The real estate market across the United States varies greatly. The prices of single-family residential properties in this small area are probably not representative of all properties across the United States.

1.27   a.   The population of interest is all individuals who took GMAT in the time period.

b.   The method of data collection was a survey.

c.   This is probably not a representative sample. The sample was self-selected. Not all of those who were selected for the study responded to all four surveys. Those who did respond to all 4 surveys probably have very strong opinions, either positive or negative, which may not be representative of all of those in the population.

1.29   a.   Length of maximum span can take on values such as 15 feet, 50 feet, 75 feet, etc. Therefore, it is quantitative.

b.   The number of vehicle lanes can take on values such as 2, 4, etc. Therefore, it is quantitative.

c.   The answer to this item is 'yes' or 'no,' which is not numeric. Therefore, it is qualitative.

d.   Average daily traffic could take on values such as 150 vehicles, 3,579 vehicles, 53,295 vehicles, etc. Therefore, it is quantitative.

e.   Condition can take on values 'good,' 'fair,' or 'poor, which are not numeric. Therefore, it is qualitative.

f.   The length of the bypass or detour could take on values such as 1 mile, 4 miles, etc. Therefore, it is quantitative.

g.   Route type can take on values 'interstate,' 'U.S.,' 'state,' 'county,' or 'city,' which are not numeric. Therefore, it is qualitative.

1.31   a.   The process being studied is the distribution of pipes, valves, and fittings to the refining, chemical, and petrochemical industries by the Wallace Company of Houston.

b.   The variables of interest are the speed of the deliveries, the accuracy of the invoices, and the quality of the packaging of the products.

c.   The sampling plan was to monitor a subset of current customers by sending out a questionnaire twice a year and asking the customers to rate the speed of the deliveries, the accuracy of the invoices, and the quality of the packaging minutes. The sample is the total numbers of questionnaires received.

d.   The Wallace Company's immediate interest is learning about the delivery process of its distribution of pipes, valves, and fittings. To do this, it is measuring the speed of deliveries, the accuracy of the invoices, and the quality of its packaging from the sample of its customers to make an inference about the delivery process to all customers. In particular, it might use the mean speed of its deliveries to the sampled customers to estimate the mean speed of its deliveries to all its customers. It might use the mean accuracy of its invoices from the sampled customers to estimate the mean accuracy of its invoices of all its customers. It might use the mean rating of the quality of its packaging from the sampled customers to estimate the mean rating of the quality of its packaging of all its customers.

e.   Several factors might affect the reliability of the inferences. One factor is the set of customers selected to receive the survey. If this set is not representative of all the customers, the wrong inferences could be made. Also, the set of customers returning the surveys may not be representative of all its customers. Again, this could influence the reliability of the inferences made.

1.33 a. The population of interest would be all accounting alumni of a large southwestern university.

      b. Age would produce quantitative data – the responses would be numbers.

          Gender would produce qualitative data – the responses would be 'male' or 'female'.

          Level of education would produce qualitative data – the responses could be categories such college degree, masters' degree, or PhD degree.

          Income would produce quantitative data – the responses would be numbers.

          Job satisfaction score would produce quantitative data. We would assume that a satisfaction score would be a number, where the higher the number, the higher the job satisfaction.

          Machiavellian rating score would produce quantitative data. We would assume that a rating score would be a number, where the higher the score, the higher the Machiavellian traits.

      c. The sample is the 198 people who returned the useable questionnaires.

      d. The data collection method used was a survey.

      e. The inference made by the researcher is that Machiavellian behavior is not required to achieve success in the accounting profession.

      f. Generally, those who respond to surveys are those with strong feelings (in either direction) toward the subject matter. Those who do not have strong feelings for the subject matter tend not to answer surveys. Those who did not respond might be those who are not real happy with their jobs or those who are not real unhappy with their jobs. Thus, we might have no idea what type of scores these people would have on the Machiavellian rating score.

1.35 a. Some possible questions are:

         1. In your opinion, why has the banking industry consolidated in the past few years? Check all that apply.

             a. Too many small banks with not enough capital.
             b. A result of the Savings and Loan scandals.
             c. To eliminate duplicated resources in the upper management positions.
             d. To provide more efficient service to the customers.
             e. To provide a more complete list of financial opportunities for the customers.
             f. Other. Please list.

         2. Using a scale from 1 to 5, where 1 means strongly disagree and 5 means strongly agree, indicate your agreement to the following statement: "The trend of consolidation in the banking industry will continue in the next five years."

            1 strongly disagree   2 disagree   3 no opinion   4 agree   5 strongly agree

      b. The population of interest is the set of all bank presidents in the United States.

      c. It would be extremely difficult and costly to obtain information from all bank presidents. Thus, it would be more efficient to sample just 200 bank presidents. However, by sending the questionnaires to only 200 bank presidents, one risks getting the results from a sample which is not representative of the population. The sample must be chosen in such a way that the results will be representative of the entire population of bank presidents in order to be of any use.

1.37   a.   The population of interest is the set of all people in the United States over 14 years of age.

      b.   The variable being measured is the employment status of each person. This variable is qualitative. Each person is either employed or not.

      c.   The problem of interest to the Census Bureau is inferential. Based on the information contained in the sample, the Census Bureau wants to estimate the percentage of all people in the labor force who are unemployed.

1.39   Suppose we want to select 900 intersections by numbering the intersections from 1 to 500,000. We would then use a random number table or a random number generator from a software program to select 900 distinct intersection points. These would then be the sampled markets.

      Now, suppose we want to select the 900 intersections by selecting a row from the 500 and a column from the 1000. We would first number the rows from 1 to 500 and number the columns from 1 to 1000. Using a random number generator, we would generate a sample of 900 from the 500 rows. Obviously, many rows will be selected more than once. At the same time, we use a random number generator to select 900 columns from the 1000 columns. Again, some of the columns could be selected more than once. Placing these two sets of random numbers side-by-side, we would use the row-column combinations to select the intersections. For example, suppose the first row selected was 453 and the first column selected was 731. The first intersection selected would be row 453, column 731. This process would be continued until 900 unique intersections were selected.

Chapter 2
Methods for Describing Sets of Data

2.1   First, we find the frequency of the grade A. The sum of the frequencies for all five grades must be 200. Therefore, subtract the sum of the frequencies of the other four grades from 200. The frequency for grade A is:

$$200 - (36 + 90 + 30 + 28) = 200 - 184 = 16$$

To find the relative frequency for each grade, divide the frequency by the total sample size, 200. The relative frequency for the grade B is $36/200 = .18$. The rest of the relative frequencies are found in a similar manner and appear in the table:

Grade on Statistics Exam	Frequency	Relative Frequency
A: 90 –100	16	.08
B: 80 – 89	36	.18
C: 65 – 79	90	.45
D: 50 – 64	30	.15
F: Below 50	28	.14
Total	200	1.00

2.3   a. $p_U = \dfrac{107}{174} = .615$

b. $p_S = \dfrac{57}{174} = .328$

c. $p_R = \dfrac{10}{174} = .057$

d. $.615(360) = 221.4$, $.328(360) = 118.1$, $.057(360) = 20.5$

e.   Using MINITAB, the pie chart is:

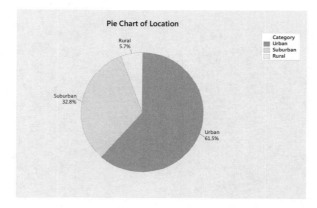

f.   61.5% of the STEM participants are from urban areas, 32.8% are from suburban areas, and 5.7% are from rural areas.

g.   Using MINITAB, the bar chart is:

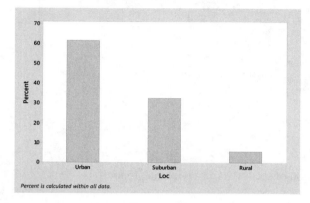

Both charts give the same information.

2.5   a.   The type of graph is a bar graph.

b.   The variable measured for each of the robots is type of robotic limbs.

c.   From the graph, the design used the most is the 'legs only' design.

d.   The relative frequencies are computed by dividing the frequencies by the total sample size. The total sample size is $n = 106$. The relative frequencies for each of the categories are:

Type of Limbs	Frequency	Relative Frequency
None	15	15/106 = .142
Both	8	8 /106 = .075
Legs ONLY	63	63/106 = .594
Wheels ONLY	20	20/106 = .189
Total	106	1.000

e.   Using MINITAB, the Pareto diagram is:

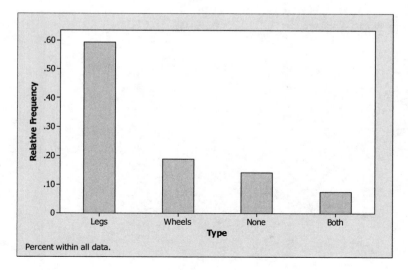

2.7   a.   Using MINITAB, the pie chart is:

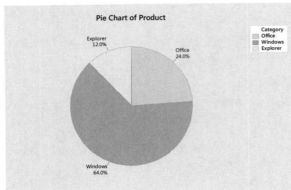

Explorer had the lowest proportion of security issues with the proportion $\dfrac{6}{50} = .12$.

    b.   Using MINITAB, the Pareto chart is:

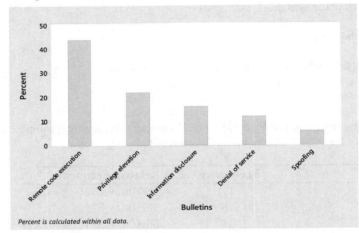

The security bulletin with the highest frequency is Remote code execution. Microsoft should focus on this repercussion.

2.9   Using MINITAB, the pie chart is:

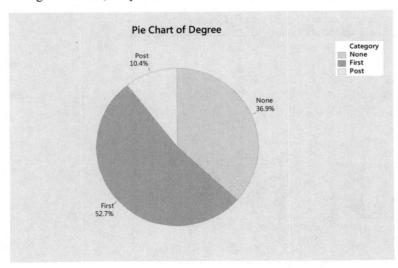

A little of half of the successful candidates had a First (Bachelor's) degree, while a little more than a third of the successful candidates had no degree. Only about 10% of the successful candidates had graduate degrees.

2.11   Using MINITAB, the Pareto diagram for the data is:

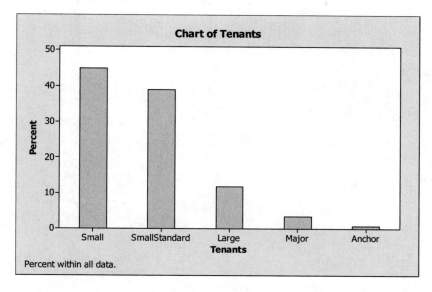

Most of the tenants in UK shopping malls are small or small standard. They account for approximately 84% of all tenants $\left([711+819]/1,821=.84\right)$. Very few (less than 1%) of the tenants are anchors.

2.13   a.   Using MINITAB, the pie chart of the data is:

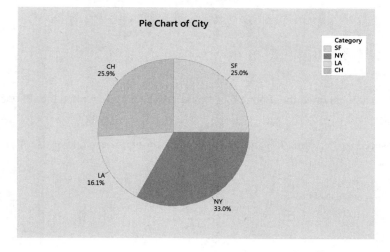

b.   Using MINITAB, the pie chart for San Francisco is:

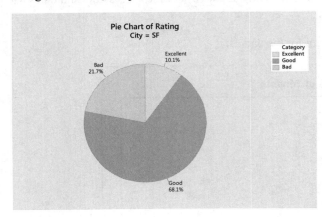

c.   Using MINITAB, the bar charts are:

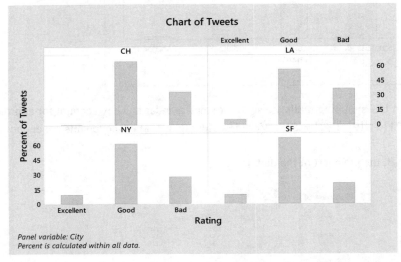

d.   In all cities, most customers rated the iPhone 6 as 'good', while very few rated the iPhone 6 as excellent.

2.15   a.   The variable measured by Performark is the length of time it took for each advertiser to respond back.

b.   The pie chart is:

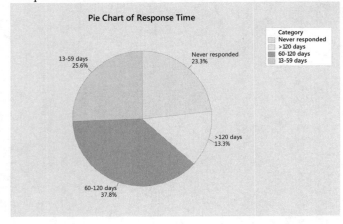

c.   Twenty-one percent or $.21 \times 17,000 = 3,570$ of the advertisers never respond to the sales lead.

d.   The information from the pie chart does not indicate how effective the 'bingo cards' are. It just indicates how long it takes advertisers to respond, if at all.

2.17   a.   Using MINITAB, bar charts for the 3 variables are:

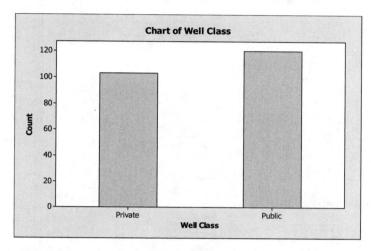

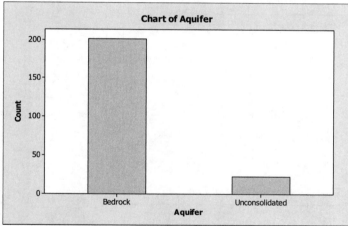

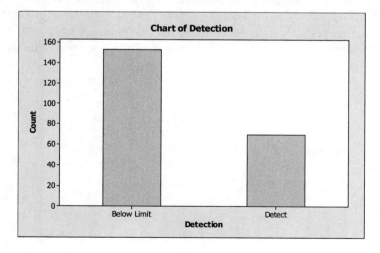

b.   Using MINITAB, the side-by-side bar chart is:

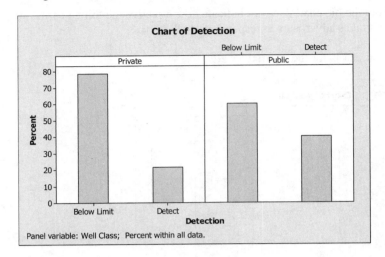

c.   Using MINITAB, the side-by-side bar chart is:

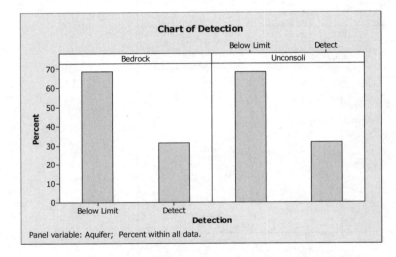

d.   From the bar charts in parts a-c, one can infer that most aquifers are bedrock and most levels of MTBE were below the limit ($\approx 2/3$).   Also the percentages of public wells verses private wells are relatively close. Approximately 80% of private wells are not contaminated, while only about 60% of public wells are not contaminated. The percentage of contaminated wells is about the same for both types of aquifers ($\approx 30\%$).

2.19   To find the number of measurements for each measurement class, multiply the relative frequency by the total number of observations, $n = 500$. The frequency table is:

Measurement Class	Relative Frequency	Frequency
.5 – 2.5	.10	500(.10) = 50
2.5 – 4.5	.15	500(.15) = 75
4.5 – 6.5	.25	500(.25) = 125
6.5 – 8.5	.20	500(.20) = 100
8.5 – 10.5	.05	500(.05) = 25
10.5 – 12.5	.10	500(.10) = 50
12.5 – 14.5	.10	500(.10) = 50
14.5 – 16.5	.05	500(.05) = 25
		500

Using MINITAB, the frequency histogram is:

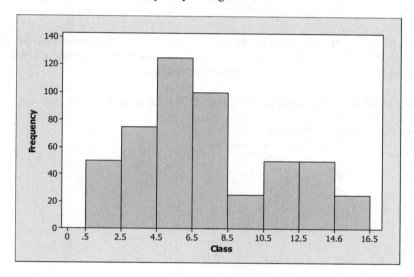

2.21   a.   This is a frequency histogram because the number of observations is graphed for each interval rather than the relative frequency.

b.   There are 14 measurement classes.

c.   There are 49 measurements in the data set.

2.23   a.   Since the label on the vertical axis is Percent, this is a relative frequency histogram. We can divide the percents by 100% to get the relative frequencies.

b.   Summing the percents represented by all of the bars above 100, we get approximately 12%.

2.25   a.   Using MINITAB, a dot plot of the data is:

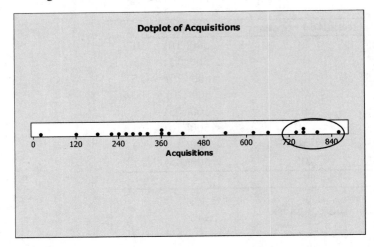

b.   By looking at the dot plot, one can conclude that the years 1996-2000 had the highest number of firms with at least one acquisition. The lowest number of acquisitions in that time frame (748) is almost 100 higher than the highest value from the remaining years.

2.27   a.   Using MINITAB, the frequency histograms for 2014 and 2010 SAT mathematics scores are:

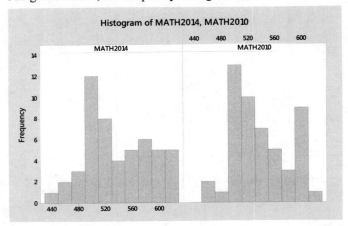

It appears that the scores have not changed very much at all. The graphs are very similar.

b.   Using MINITAB, the frequency histogram of the differences is:

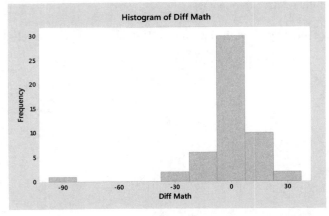

From this graph of the differences, we can see that there are more observations to the right of 0 than to the left of 0. This indicates that, in general, the scores have improved since 2010.

c.   From the graph, the largest improvement score is between 22.5 and 37.5. The actual largest score is 34 and it is associated with Wyoming.

2.29   Using MINITAB, the stem-and-leaf display is:

Stem-and-Leaf Display: Dioxide

```
Stem-and-leaf of Dioxide   N  = 16
Leaf Unit = 0.10

  5    0   12234
  7    0   55
 (2)   1   34
  7    1
  7    2   44
  5    2
  5    3   3
  4    3
  4    4   0000
```

The highlighted values are values that correspond to water specimens that contain oil. There is a tendency for crude oil to be present in water with lower levels of dioxide as 6 of the lowest 8 specimens with the lowest levels of dioxide contain oil.

2.31   Yes, we would agree with the statement that honey may be the preferable treatment for the cough and sleep difficulty associated with childhood upper respiratory tract infection. For those receiving the honey dosage, 14 of the 35 children (or 40%) had improvement scores of 12 or higher. For those receiving the DM dosage, only 9 of the 33 (or 24%) children had improvement scores of 12 or higher. For those receiving no dosage, only 2 of the 37 children (or 5%) had improvement scores of 12 or higher. In addition, the median improvement score for those receiving the honey dosage was 11, the median for those receiving the DM dosage was 9 and the median for those receiving no dosage was 7.

2.33   Using MINITAB, the histogram of the data is:

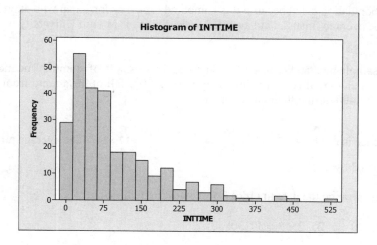

This histogram looks very similar to the one shown in the problem. Thus, there appears that there was minimal or no collaboration or collusion from within the company. We could conclude that the phishing attack against the organization was not an inside job.

2.35   Assume the data are a sample. The sample mean is:

$$\bar{x} = \frac{\sum x}{n} = \frac{3.2+2.5+2.1+3.7+2.8+2.0}{6} = \frac{16.3}{6} = 2.717$$

The median is the average of the middle two numbers when the data are arranged in order (since $n = 6$ is even). The data arranged in order are: 2.0, 2.1, 2.5, 2.8, 3.2, 3.7. The middle two numbers are 2.5 and 2.8. The median is:

$$\frac{2.5+2.8}{2} = \frac{5.3}{2} = 2.65$$

2.37   The mean and median of a symmetric data set are equal to each other. The mean is larger than the median when the data set is skewed to the right. The mean is less than the median when the data set is skewed to the left. Thus, by comparing the mean and median, one can determine whether the data set is symmetric, skewed right, or skewed left.

2.39   Assume the data are a sample. The mode is the observation that occurs most frequently. For this sample, the mode is 15, which occurs three times.

The sample mean is:

$$\bar{x} = \frac{\sum x}{n} = \frac{18+10+15+13+17+15+12+15+18+16+11}{11} = \frac{160}{11} = 14.545$$

The median is the middle number when the data are arranged in order. The data arranged in order are: 10, 11, 12, 13, 15, 15, 15, 16, 17, 18, 18. The middle number is the 6th number, which is 15.

2.41   a.   For a distribution that is skewed to the left, the mean is less than the median.

b.   For a distribution that is skewed to the right, the mean is greater than the median.

c.   For a symmetric distribution, the mean and median are equal.

2.43   a.   This statistic represents a population mean because it is computed for every freshman who attended the university in 2015. The average financial aid awarded to freshmen at Harvard University is $41,555.

b.   This statistic represents a sample median because it is computed for a sample of alumni. The median salary during early career for alumni of Harvard University is $61,400. Half of the alumni from Harvard make more than $61,400 during their early career.

2.45   a.   The mean years of experience is $\bar{x} = \frac{\sum x}{n} = \frac{30+15+10+\cdots+25}{17} = \frac{303}{17} = 17.824$. The average number of years of experience is 17.824 years.

b.   To find the median, we first arrange the data in order from lowest to highest:

3 5 6 9 10 10 10 15 20 20 25 25 25 30 30 30 30

Since there are an odd number of observations, the median is the middle number which is 20. Half of interviewees have less than 20 years of experience.

c.   The mode is 30. More interviewees had 30 years of experience than any other value.

2.47   a.   The mean permeability for group A sandstone slices is 73.62mD. The average permeability for group A sandstone is 73.62mD. The median permeability for group A sandstone is 70.45mD. Half of the sandstone slices in group A have permeability less than 70.45mD.

b.   The mean permeability for group B sandstone slices is 128.54mD. The average permeability for group B sandstone is 128.54mD. The median permeability for group B sandstone is 139.30mD. Half of the sandstone slices in group B have permeability less than 139.30mD.

c.   The mean permeability for group C sandstone slices is 83.07mD. The average permeability for group C sandstone is 83.07mD. The median permeability for group C sandstone is 78.650mD. Half of the sandstone slices in group C have permeability less than 78.65mD.

d.   The mode permeability score for group C sandstone is 70.9. More sandstone slices in group C had permeability scores of 70.9 than any other value.

e.   Weathering type B appears to result in faster decay because the mean, median, and mode values fore group B is higher than those for group C.

2.49   a.   The median is the middle number (18th) once the data have been arranged in order because $n = 35$ is odd. The honey dosage data arranged in order are:

4,5,6,8,8,8,9,9,9,9,10,10,10,10,10,10,<u>11</u>,11,11,11,12,12,12,12,12,12,13,13,14,15,15,15,15,16

The 18th number is the median = 11.

b.   The median is the middle number (17th) once the data have been arranged in order because $n = 33$ is odd. The DM dosage data arranged in order are:

3,4,4,4,4,4,4,6,6,6,7,7,7,7,7,8,<u>9</u>,9,9,9,9,10,10,10,11,12,12,12,12,12,13,13,15

The 17th number is the median = 9.

c.   The median is the middle number (19th) once the data have been arranged in order because $n = 37$ is odd. The No dosage data arranged in order are:

0,1,1,1,3,3,4,4,5,5,5,6,6,6,6,7,7,7,<u>7</u>,7,7,7,7,8,8,8,8,8,9,9,9,9,10,11,12,12

The 19th number is the median = 7.

d.   Since the median for the Honey dosage is larger than the other two, it appears that the honey dosage leads to more improvement than the other two treatments.

2.51   a.   Skewed to the right. There will be a few people with very high salaries such as the president and football coach.

b.   Skewed to the left. On an easy test, most students will have high scores with only a few low scores.

c.   Skewed to the right. On a difficult test, most students will have low scores with only a few high scores.

d.   Skewed to the right. Most students will have a moderate amount of time studying while a few students might study a long time.

e.   Skewed to the left. Most cars will be relatively new with a few much older.

f.   Skewed to the left. Most students will take the entire time to take the exam while a few might leave early.

2.53 For the 'Joint exchange offer with prepack' firms, the mean time is 2.6545 months, and the median is 1.5 months. Thus, the average time spent in bankruptcy for 'Joint' firms is 2.6545 months, while half of the firms spend 1.5 months or less in bankruptcy.

For the 'No prefiling vote held' firms, the mean time is 4.2364 months, and the median is 3.2 months. Thus, the average time spent in bankruptcy for 'No prefiling vote held' firms is 4.2364 months, while half of the firms spend 3.2 months or less in bankruptcy.

For the 'Prepack solicitation only' firms, the mean time is 1.8185 months, and the median is 1.4 months. Thus, the average time spent in bankruptcy for 'Prepack solicitation only' firms is 1.8185 months, while half of the firms spend 1.4 months or less in bankruptcy.

Since the means and medians for the three groups of firms differ quite a bit, it would be unreasonable to use a single number to locate the center of the time in bankruptcy. Three different 'centers' should be used.

2.55 a. Due to the 'elite' superstars, the salary distribution is skewed to the right. Since this implies that the median is less than the mean, the players' association would want to use the median.

b. The owners, by the logic of part **a**, would want to use the mean.

2.57 a. Range $= 4 - 0 = 4$ $4^2 + 2^2 + 1^2 + 0^2 + 1^2 = 22$

$$s^2 = \frac{\sum x^2 - \frac{\left(\sum x\right)^2}{n}}{n-1} = \frac{22 - \frac{8^2}{5}}{5-1} = 2.3 \qquad s = \sqrt{2.3} = 1.52$$

b. Range $= 6 - 0 = 6$

$$s^2 = \frac{\sum x^2 - \frac{\left(\sum x\right)^2}{n}}{n-1} = \frac{63 - \frac{17^2}{7}}{7-1} = 3.619 \qquad s = \sqrt{3.619} = 1.9$$

c. Range $= 8 - (-2) = 10$

$$s^2 = \frac{\sum x^2 - \frac{\left(\sum x\right)^2}{n}}{n-1} = \frac{154 - \frac{30^2}{10}}{10-1} = 7.111 \qquad s = \sqrt{7.111} = 2.67$$

d. Range $= 1 - (-3) = 4$

$$s^2 = \frac{\sum x^2 - \frac{\left(\sum x\right)^2}{n}}{n-1} = \frac{25.04 - \frac{(-6.8)^2}{17}}{17-1} = 1.395 \qquad s = \sqrt{1.395} = 1.18$$

2.59 a. $\sum x = 3 + 1 + 10 + 10 + 4 = 28 \qquad \sum x^2 = 3^2 + 1^2 + 10^2 + 10^2 + 4^2 = 226$

$$\bar{x} = \frac{\sum x}{n} = \frac{28}{5} = 5.6$$

$$s^2 = \frac{\sum x^2 - \frac{\left(\sum x\right)^2}{n}}{n-1} = \frac{226 - \frac{28^2}{5}}{5-1} = \frac{69.2}{4} = 17.3 \qquad s = \sqrt{17.3} = 4.1593$$

b. $\sum x = 8 + 10 + 32 + 5 = 55 \qquad \sum x^2 = 8^2 + 10^2 + 32^2 + 5^2 = 1213$

$$\bar{x} = \frac{\sum x}{n} = \frac{55}{4} = 13.75 \text{ feet}$$

$$s^2 = \frac{\sum x^2 - \frac{\left(\sum x\right)^2}{n}}{n-1} = \frac{1213 - \frac{55^2}{4}}{4-1} = \frac{456.75}{3} = 152.25 \text{ square feet}$$

$$s = \sqrt{152.25} = 12.339 \text{ feet}$$

c. $\sum x = -1 + (-4) + (-3) + 1 + (-4) + (-4) = -15$ $\sum x^2 = (-1)^2 + (-4)^2 + (-3)^2 + 1^2 + (-4)^2 + (-4)^2 = 59$

$$\bar{x} = \frac{\sum x}{n} = \frac{-15}{6} = -2.5$$

$$s^2 = \frac{\sum x^2 - \frac{\left(\sum x\right)^2}{n}}{n-1} = \frac{59 - \frac{(-15)^2}{6}}{6-1} = \frac{21.5}{5} = 4.3 \qquad\qquad s = \sqrt{4.3} = 2.0736$$

d. $\sum x = \frac{1}{5} + \frac{1}{5} + \frac{1}{5} + \frac{2}{5} + \frac{1}{5} + \frac{4}{5} = \frac{10}{5} = 2$ $\sum x^2 = \left(\frac{1}{5}\right)^2 + \left(\frac{1}{5}\right)^2 + \left(\frac{1}{5}\right)^2 + \left(\frac{2}{5}\right)^2 + \left(\frac{1}{5}\right)^2 + \left(\frac{4}{5}\right)^2 = \frac{24}{25} = .96$

$$\bar{x} = \frac{\sum x}{n} = \frac{2}{6} = \frac{1}{3} = .33 \text{ ounce}$$

$$s^2 = \frac{\sum x^2 - \frac{\left(\sum x\right)^2}{n}}{n-1} = \frac{\frac{24}{25} - \frac{2^2}{6}}{6-1} = \frac{.2933}{5} = .0587 \text{ square ounce} \quad s = \sqrt{.0587} = .2422 \text{ ounce}$$

2.61   This is one possibility for the two data sets.

Data Set 1: 0, 1, 2, 3, 4, 5, 6, 7, 8, 9
Data Set 2: 0, 0, 1, 1, 2, 2, 3, 3, 9, 9

The two sets of data above have the same range = largest measurement − smallest measurement = 9 − 0 = 9.

The means for the two data sets are:

$$\bar{x}_1 = \frac{\sum x}{n} = \frac{0+1+2+3+4+5+6+7+8+9}{10} = \frac{45}{10} = 4.5$$

$$\bar{x}_2 = \frac{\sum x}{n} = \frac{0+0+1+1+2+2+3+3+9+9}{10} = \frac{30}{10} = 3$$

The dot diagrams for the two data sets are shown below.

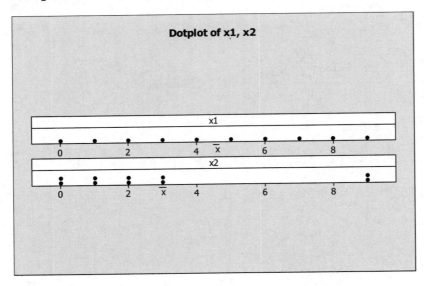

2.63   a.   Range $= 3 - 0 = 3$

$$s^2 = \frac{\sum x^2 - \frac{\left(\sum x\right)^2}{n}}{n-1} = \frac{15 - \frac{7^2}{5}}{5-1} = 1.3 \qquad\qquad s = \sqrt{1.3} = 1.14$$

b.   After adding 3 to each of the data points,

Range $= 6 - 3 = 3$

$$s^2 = \frac{\sum x^2 - \frac{\left(\sum x\right)^2}{n}}{n-1} = \frac{102 - \frac{22^2}{5}}{5-1} = 1.3 \qquad\qquad s = \sqrt{1.3} = 1.14$$

c.   After subtracting 4 from each of the data points,

Range $= -1 - (-4) = 3$

$$s^2 = \frac{\sum x^2 - \frac{\left(\sum x\right)^2}{n}}{n-1} = \frac{39 - \frac{(-13)^2}{5}}{5-1} = 1.3 \qquad\qquad s = \sqrt{1.3} = 1.14$$

d.   The range, variance, and standard deviation remain the same when any number is added to or subtracted from each measurement in the data set.

2.65   a.   The range of permeability scores for group A sandstone slices is
Range $= \max - \min = 122.4 - 55.2 = 67.2$.

b.   The variance of group A sandstone slices is $s^2 = \dfrac{\sum x^2 - \dfrac{\left(\sum x\right)^2}{n}}{n-1} = \dfrac{562,778 - \dfrac{7,362.3^2}{100}}{100-1} = 209.5292$.

The standard deviation is $s = \sqrt{209.5292} = 14.475$.

c.   Condition B has the largest range and the largest standard deviation. Thus, condition B has more variable permeability data.

2.67   a.   The range is 155. The statement is accurate.

b.   The variance is 722.036. The statement is not accurate. A more accurate statement would be: "The variance of the levels of supports for corporate sustainability for the 992 senior managers is 722.036."

c.   The standard deviation is 26.871. If the units of measure for the two distributions are the same, then the distribution of support levels for the 992 senior managers has less variation than a distribution with a standard deviation of 50. If the units of measure for the second distribution is not known, then we cannot compare the variation in the two distributions by looking at the standard deviations alone.

d.   The standard deviation best describes the variation in the distribution. The range can be greatly affected by extreme measures. The variance is measured in square units which is hard to interpret. Thus, the standard deviation is the best measure to describe the variation.

2.69   a.   The range is the largest observation minus the smallest observation or $6 - 1 = 5$.

$$\text{The variance is: } s^2 = \frac{\sum_i x_i^2 - \frac{\left(\sum_i x_i\right)^2}{n}}{n-1} = \frac{178 - \frac{62^2}{30}}{30-1} = 1.7195$$

$$\text{The standard deviation is: } s = \sqrt{s^2} = \sqrt{1.7195} = 1.311$$

b.   The largest observation is 6. It is deleted from the data set. The new range is: $5 - 1 = 4$.

$$\text{The variance is: } s^2 = \frac{\sum_i x_i^2 - \frac{\left(\sum_i x_i\right)^2}{n}}{n-1} = \frac{142 - \frac{56^2}{29}}{29-1} = 1.2094$$

$$\text{The standard deviation is: } s = \sqrt{s^2} = \sqrt{1.2094} = 1.100$$

When the largest observation is deleted, the range, variance and standard deviation decrease.

c.   The largest observation is 6 and the smallest is 1. When these two observations are deleted from the data set, the new range is: $5 - 1 = 4$.

$$\text{The variance is: } s^2 = \frac{\sum_i x_i^2 - \frac{\left(\sum_i x_i\right)^2}{n}}{n-1} = \frac{141 - \frac{55^2}{28}}{28-1} = 1.2209$$

$$\text{The standard deviation is: } s = \sqrt{s^2} = \sqrt{1.2209} = 1.1049$$

When the largest and smallest observations are deleted, the range, variance and standard deviation decrease.

2.71   a.   The unit of measurement of the variable of interest is dollars (the same as the mean and standard deviation). Based on this, the data are quantitative.

        b.   Since no information is given about the shape of the data set, we can only use Chebyshev's Rule.

$900 is 2 standard deviations below the mean, and $2100 is 2 standard deviations above the mean. Using Chebyshev's Rule, at least 3/4 of the measurements (or $3/4 \times 200 = 150$ measurements) will fall between $900 and $2100.

$600 is 3 standard deviations below the mean and $2400 is 3 standard deviations above the mean. Using Chebyshev's Rule, at least 8/9 of the measurements (or $8/9 \times 200 \approx 178$ measurements) will fall between $600 and $2400.

$1200 is 1 standard deviation below the mean and $1800 is 1 standard deviation above the mean. Using Chebyshev's Rule, nothing can be said about the number of measurements that will fall between $1200 and $1800.

$1500 is equal to the mean and $2100 is 2 standard deviations above the mean. Using Chebyshev's Rule, at least 3/4 of the measurements (or $3/4 \times 200 = 150$ measurements) will fall between $900 and $2100. It is possible that all of the 150 measurements will be between $900 and $1500. Thus, nothing can be said about the number of measurements between $1500 and $2100.

2.73   According to the Empirical Rule:

        a.   Approximately 68% of the measurements will be contained in the interval $\bar{x} - s$ to $\bar{x} + s$.

        b.   Approximately 95% of the measurements will be contained in the interval $\bar{x} - 2s$ to $\bar{x} + 2s$.

        c.   Essentially all the measurements will be contained in the interval $\bar{x} - 3s$ to $\bar{x} + 3s$.

2.75   Using Chebyshev's Rule, at least 8/9 of the measurements will fall within 3 standard deviations of the mean. Thus, the range of the data would be around 6 standard deviations. Using the Empirical Rule, approximately 95% of the observations are within 2 standard deviations of the mean. Thus, the range of the data would be around 4 standard deviations. We would expect the standard deviation to be somewhere between Range/6 and Range/4.

For our data, the range $= 760 - 135 = 625$.

The $\dfrac{\text{Range}}{6} = \dfrac{625}{6} = 104.17$ and $\dfrac{\text{Range}}{4} = \dfrac{625}{4} = 156.25$.

Therefore, I would estimate that the standard deviation of the data set is between 104.17 and 156.25.

It would not be feasible to have a standard deviation of 25. If the standard deviation were 25, the data would span $625/25 = 25$ standard deviations. This would be extremely unlikely.

2.77   a.   Because the distribution is skewed, we will use Chebyshev's Rule. At least 8/9 of the observations will be within 3 standard deviations of the mean:

$$\bar{x}_A \pm 3s_A \Rightarrow 73.62 \pm 3(14.48) \Rightarrow 73.62 \pm 43.44 \Rightarrow (30.18, 117.06)$$

b. Because the distribution is skewed, we will use Chebyshev's Rule. At least 8/9 of the observations will be within 3 standard deviations of the mean:

$$\bar{x}_A \pm 3s_A \Rightarrow 128.54 \pm 3(21.97) \Rightarrow 128.54 \pm 65.91 \Rightarrow (62.63, 194.45)$$

c. Because the distribution is skewed, we will use Chebyshev's Rule. At least 8/9 of the observations will be within 3 standard deviations of the mean:

$$\bar{x}_A \pm 3s_A \Rightarrow 83.07 \pm 3(20.05) \Rightarrow 83.07 \pm 60.15 \Rightarrow (22.92, 143.22)$$

d. Although all the intervals overlap, it appears that weathering group B results in faster decay because the sample mean is higher and the upper limit of the interval is much higher than the upper limit for the other two weathering types.

2.79   a. The interval $\bar{x} \pm 2s$ will contain at least 75% of the observations. This interval is
$\bar{x} \pm 2s \Rightarrow 3.11 \pm 2(.66) \Rightarrow 3.11 \pm 1.32 \Rightarrow (1.79, 4.43)$.

b. No. The value 1.25 does not fall in the interval $\bar{x} \pm 2s$. We know that at least 75% of all observations will fall within 2 standard deviations of the mean. Since 1.25 falls more than 2 standard deviations from the mean, it would not be a likely value to observe.

2.81   a. The sample mean is: $\bar{x} = \dfrac{\sum\limits_{i=1}^{n} x_i}{n} = \dfrac{18,482}{195} = 94.78$

The sample variance is: $s^2 = \dfrac{\sum\limits_{i=1}^{n} x^2 - \dfrac{\left(\sum\limits_{i=1}^{n} x_i\right)^2}{n}}{n-1} = \dfrac{1,756,550 - \dfrac{18,482^2}{195}}{195-1} = 24.9254$

The standard deviation is: $s = \sqrt{s^2} = \sqrt{24.9254} = 4.9925$

b. $\bar{x} \pm s \Rightarrow 94.78 \pm 4.99 \Rightarrow (89.79,\ 99.77)$

$\bar{x} \pm 2s \Rightarrow 94.78 \pm 2(4.99) \Rightarrow 94.78 \pm 9.98 \Rightarrow (84.80,\ 104.76)$

$\bar{x} \pm 3s \Rightarrow 94.78 \pm 3(4.99) \Rightarrow 94.78 \pm 14.97 \Rightarrow (79.81,\ 109.75)$

c. There are 143 out of 195 observations in the first interval. This is $(143/195) \times 100\% = 73.3\%$. There are 189 out of 195 observations in the second interval. This is $(189/195) \times 100\% = 96.9\%$. There are 191 out of 195 observations in the second interval. This is $(191/195) \times 100\% = 97.9\%$.

The percentages for the first 2 intervals are somewhat larger than we would expect using the Empirical Rule. The Empirical Rule indicates that approximately 68% of the observations will fall within 1 standard deviation of the mean. It also indicates that approximately 95% of the observations will fall within 2 standard deviations of the mean. Chebyshev's Theorem says that at least ¾ or 75% of the observations will fall within 2 standard deviations of the mean and at least 8/9 or 88.9% of the observations will fall within 3 standard deviations of the mean. It appears that our observed percentages agree with Chebyshev's Theorem better than the Empirical Rule.

2.83   Using MINITAB, the descriptive statistics are:

Descriptive Statistics: Q2

Variable	Q1	N	Mean	StDev	Minimum	Q1	Median	Q3	Maximum
Q2	No	1	2.0000	*	2.0000	*	2.0000	*	2.0000
	Undecided	5	4.800	0.447	4.000	4.500	5.000	5.000	5.000
	Yes	30	3.967	0.850	2.000	3.000	4.000	5.000	5.000

The data for those users who believe there should be national standards is close to being mound-shaped and symmetric. Therefore, we will use the Empirical Rule. Approximately 95% of the observations fall within 2 standard deviations of the mean. This interval is:

$$\bar{x} \pm 2s \Rightarrow 3.967 \pm 2(.85) \Rightarrow 3.967 \pm 1.70 \Rightarrow (2.267,\ 5.667)$$

2.85   a.   The interval $\bar{x} \pm 2s$ for the flexed arm group is $\bar{x} \pm 2s \Rightarrow 59 \pm 3(4) \Rightarrow 59 \pm 12 \Rightarrow (47,\ 71)$. The interval for the extended are group is $\bar{x} \pm 2s \Rightarrow 43 \pm 3(2) \Rightarrow 43 \pm 6 \Rightarrow (37,\ 49)$. We know that at least 8/9 or 88.9% of the observations will fall within 3 standard deviations of the mean using Chebyshev's Rule. Since these 2 intervals barely overlap, the information supports the researchers' theory. The shoppers from the flexed arm group are more likely to select vice options than the extended arm group.

   b.   The interval $\bar{x} \pm 2s$ for the flexed arm group is $\bar{x} \pm 2s \Rightarrow 59 \pm 2(10) \Rightarrow 59 \pm 20 \Rightarrow (39,\ 79)$. The interval for the extended are group is $\bar{x} \pm 2s \Rightarrow 43 \pm 2(15) \Rightarrow 43 \pm 30 \Rightarrow (13,\ 73)$. Since these two intervals overlap almost completely, the information does not support the researcher's theory. There does not appear to be any difference between the two groups.

2.87   Since we do not know if the distribution of the heights of the trees is mound-shaped, we need to apply Chebyshev's Rule. We know $\mu = 30$ and $\sigma = 3$. Therefore, $\mu \pm 3\sigma \Rightarrow 30 \pm 3(3) \Rightarrow 30 \pm 9 \Rightarrow (21,\ 39)$.

According to Chebyshev's Rule, at least $8/9 = .89$ of the tree heights on this piece of land fall within this interval and at most $1/9 = .11$ of the tree heights will fall above the interval. However, the buyer will only purchase the land if at least $\dfrac{1000}{5000} = .20$ of the tree heights are at least 40 feet tall. Therefore, the buyer should not buy the piece of land.

2.89   We know $\mu = 25$ and $\sigma = 1$. Therefore, $\mu \pm 2\sigma \Rightarrow 25 \pm 2(.1) \Rightarrow 25 \pm .2 \Rightarrow (24.8,\ 25.2)$

The machine is shut down for adjustment if the contents of two consecutive bags fall more than 2 standard deviations from the mean (i.e., outside the interval (24.8, 25.2)). Therefore, the machine was shut down yesterday at 11:30 (25.23 and 25.25 are outside the interval) and again at 4:00 (24.71 and 25.31 are outside the interval).

2.91   Using the definition of a percentile:

	Percentile	Percentage Above	Percentage Below
a.	75th	25%	75%
b.	50th	50%	50%
c.	20th	80%	20%
d.	84th	16%	84%

2.93   We first compute z-scores for each x value.

     a. $z = \dfrac{x - \mu}{\sigma} = \dfrac{100 - 50}{25} = 2$

     b. $z = \dfrac{x - \mu}{\sigma} = \dfrac{1 - 4}{1} = -3$

     c. $z = \dfrac{x - \mu}{\sigma} = \dfrac{0 - 200}{100} = -2$

     d. $z = \dfrac{x - \mu}{\sigma} = \dfrac{10 - 5}{3} = 1.67$

         The above z-scores indicate that the x value in part **a** lies the greatest distance above the mean and the x value of part **b** lies the greatest distance below the mean.

2.95   The mean score of U.S. eighth-graders on a mathematics assessment test is 282. This is the average score. The 25th percentile is 258. This means that 25% of the U.S. eighth-graders score below 258 on the test and 75% score higher. The 75th percentile is 308. This means that 75% of the U.S. eighth-graders score below 308 on the test and 25% score higher. The 90th percentile is 329. This means that 90% of the U.S. eighth-graders score below 329 on the test and 10% score higher.

2.97   A mean current salary of \$57,000 indicates that the average current salary of the University of South Florida graduates is \$57,000. At mid-career, half of the University of South Florida graduates had a salary less than \$48,000 and half had salaries greater than \$48,000. At mid-career, 90% of the University of South Florida graduates had salaries under \$131,000 and 10% had salaries greater than \$131,000.

2.99   Since the 90th percentile of the study sample in the subdivision was .00372 mg/L, which is less than the USEPA level of .015 mg/L, the water customers in the subdivision are not at risk of drinking water with unhealthy lead levels.

2.101   The average ROE is 13.93. The median ROE is 14.86, meaning 50% of firms have ROE below 14.86. The 5th percentile is -19.64 meaning 5% of firms have ROE below –19.64. The 25th percentile is 7.59 meaning 25% of firms have ROE below 7.59. The 75th percentile is 21.32 meaning 75% of firms have ROE below 21.32. The 95th percentile is 38.42 meaning 95% of firms have ROE below 38.42. The standard deviation is 21.65. Most observations will fall within 2s or 43.30 units of mean. The distribution will be somewhat skewed to the left as the 5th percentile value is much further from the median than the 95th percentile value.

2.103   a.   The z-score for Harvard is $z = 5.08$. This means that Harvard's productivity score was 5.08 standard deviations above the mean. This is extremely high and extremely unusual.

         b.   The z-score for Howard University is $z = -.85$. This means that Howard University's productivity score was .85 standard deviations below the mean. This is not an unusual z-score.

         c.   Yes. Other indicators that the distribution is skewed to the right are the values of the highest and lowest z-scores. The lowest z-score is less than 1 standard deviation below the mean while the highest z-score is 5.08 standard deviations above the mean.

Using MINITAB, the histogram of the z-scores is:

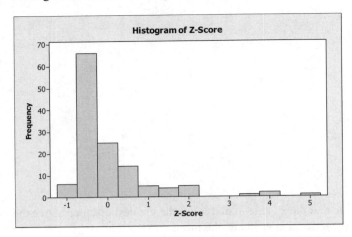

This histogram does imply that the data are skewed to the right.

2.105   Not necessarily. Because the distribution is highly skewed to the right, the standard deviation is very large. Remember that the z-score represents the number of standard deviations a score is from the mean. If the standard deviation is very large, then the z-scores for observations somewhat near the mean will appear to be fairly small. If we deleted the schools with the very high productivity scores and recomputed the mean and standard deviation, the standard deviation would be much smaller. Thus, most of the z-scores would be larger because we would be dividing by a much smaller standard deviation. This would imply a bigger spread among the rest of the schools than the original distribution with the few outliers.

2.107   The interquartile range is $IQR = Q_U - Q_L = 85 - 60 = 25$.

The lower inner fence $= Q_L - 1.5(IQR) = 60 - 1.5(25) = 22.5$.

The upper inner fence $= Q_U + 1.5(IQR) = 85 + 1.5(25) = 122.5$.

The lower outer fence $= Q_L - 3(IQR) = 60 - 3(25) = -15$.

The upper outer fence $= Q_U + 3(IQR) = 85 + 3(25) = 160$.

With only this information, the box plot would look something like the following:

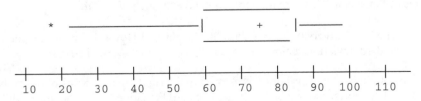

The whiskers extend to the inner fences unless no data points are that small or that large. The upper inner fence is 122.5. However, the largest data point is 100, so the whisker stops at 100. The lower inner fence is 22.5. The smallest data point is 18, so the whisker extends to 22.5. Since 18 is between the inner and outer fences, it is designated with a *. We do not know if there is any more than one data point below 22.5, so we cannot be sure that the box plot is entirely correct.

2.109   a.   Using MINITAB, the box plots for samples A and B are:

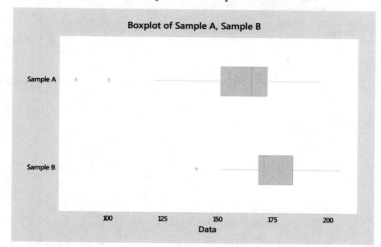

b.   In sample A, the measurement 84 is an outlier. This measurement falls outside the lower outer fence.

Lower outer fence = Lower hinge $-3(IQR) \approx 150 - 3(172 - 150) = 150 - 3(22) = 84$

Lower inner fence = Lower hinge $-1.5(IQR) \approx 150 - 1.5(22) = 117$

Upper inner fence = Upper hinge $+1.5(IQR) \approx 172 + 1.5(22) = 205$

In addition, 100 may be an outlier. It lies outside the inner fence.

In sample B, 140 and 206 may be outliers. The point 140 lies outside the inner fence while the point 206 lies right at the inner fence.

Lower outer fence = Lower hinge $-3(IQR) \approx 168 - 3(184 - 169) = 168 - 3(15) = 123$

Lower inner fence = Lower hinge $-1.5(IQR) \approx 168 - 1.5(15) = 145.5$

Upper inner fence = Upper hinge $+1.5(IQR) \approx 184 + 1.5(15) = 206.5$

2.111   a. $z = \dfrac{x - \bar{x}}{s} = \dfrac{400 - 353}{30} = 1.57$ Since the z-score is less than 2400 sags per week would not be considered unusual.

b. $z = \dfrac{x - \bar{x}}{s} = \dfrac{100 - 184}{25} = -3.36$ Since the absolute value of the z-score is greater than 3100 swells per week would be considered unusual.

2.113   a.   The average expenditure per full-time employee is $6,563. The median expenditure per employee is $6,232. Half of all expenditures per employee were less than $6,232 and half were greater than $6,232. The lower quartile is $5,309. Twenty-five percent of all expenditures per employee were below $5,309. The upper quartile is $7,216. Seventy-five percent of all expenditures per employee were below $7,216.

b. $IQR = Q_U - Q_L = \$7,216 - \$5,309 = \$1,907.$

c.   The interquartile range goes from the 25th percentile to the 75th percentile. Thus, $.5 = .75 - .25$ of the 1,751 army hospitals have expenses between $5,309 and $7,216.

2.115   a.   Using MINITAB, the boxplots for each type of firm are:

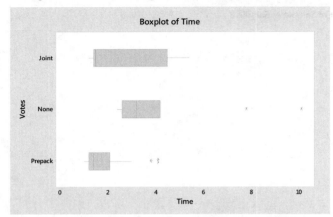

b.   The median bankruptcy time for No prefiling firms is about 3.2. The median bankruptcy time for Joint firms is about 1.5. The median bankruptcy time for Prepack firms is about 1.4.

c.   The range of the 'Prepack' firms is less than the other two, while the range of the 'None' firms is the largest. The interquartile range of the 'Prepack' firms is less than the other two, while the interquartile range of the 'Joint' firms is larger than the other two.

d.   No. The interquartile range for the 'Prepack' firms is the smallest which corresponds to the smallest standard deviation. However, the second smallest interquartile range corresponds to the 'None' firms. The second smallest standard deviation corresponds to the 'Joint' firms.

e.   Yes. There is evidence of two outliers in the 'Prepack' firms. These are indicated by the two *'s. There is also evidence of two outliers in the 'None' firms. These are indicated by the two *'s.

2.117   a.   Using MINITAB, the boxplot is:

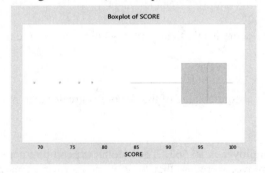

From the boxplot, there appears to be 4 outliers: 69, 73, 76, and 78.

b.   From Exercise 2.81, $\bar{x} = 94.78$ and $s = 4.99$. Since the data are skewed to the left, we will consider observations more than 2 standard deviations from the mean to be outliers. An observation with a z-score of 2 would have the value:

$$z = \frac{x - \bar{x}}{s} \Rightarrow 2 = \frac{x - 94.78}{4.99} \Rightarrow 2(4.99) = x - 94.78 \Rightarrow 9.98 = x - 94.78 \Rightarrow x = 104.76$$

An observation with a z-score of -2 would have the value:

$$z = \frac{x - \bar{x}}{s} \Rightarrow -2 = \frac{x - 94.78}{4.99} \Rightarrow -2(4.99) = x - 94.78 \Rightarrow -9.98 = x - 94.78 \Rightarrow x = 84.80$$

Observations greater than 104.76 or less than 84.80 would be considered outliers. Using this criterion, the following observations would be outliers: 69, 73, 76, and 78.

c.   Yes, these methods do not agree exactly. Using the boxplot, 4 observations were identified as outliers. Using the z-score method, 4 observations were also identified as outliers.

2.119   Using MINITAB, the boxplots of the data are:

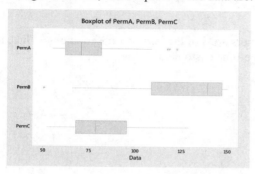

The descriptive statistics are:

Descriptive Statistics: PermA, PermB, PermC

Variable	N	Mean	StDev	Minimum	Q1	Median	Q3	Maximum	IQR
PermA	100	73.62	14.48	55.20	62.00	70.45	81.42	122.40	19.42
PermB	100	128.54	21.97	50.40	108.65	139.30	147.02	150.00	38.37
PermC	100	83.07	20.05	52.20	67.72	78.65	95.35	129.00	27.63

a.   For group A, the suspect outliers are any observations greater than
$Q_U + 1.5(IQR) = 81.42 + 1.5(19.42) = 110.55$ or less than $Q_L - 1.5(IQR) = 62 - 1.5(19.42) = 32.87$. There are 3 observations greater than 110.55: 117.3, 118.5, and 122.4.

b.   For group B, the suspect outliers are any observations greater than
$Q_U + 1.5(IQR) = 147.02 + 1.5(38.37) = 204.575$ or less than $Q_L - 1.5(IQR) = 108.65 - 1.5(38.37) = 51.095$. There is 1 observation less than 51.095: 50.4.

c.   For group C, the suspect outliers are any observations greater than
$Q_L + 1.5(IQR) = 95.35 + 1.5(27.63) = 136.795$ or less than $Q_L - 1.5(IQR) = 67.72 - 1.5(27.63) = 26.275$. No observations are greater than 136.795 or less than 26.275.

d.   For group A, if the outliers are removed, the mean will decrease, the median will slightly decrease, and the standard deviation will decrease. For group B, if the outlier is removed, the mean will increase, the median will slightly increase, and the standard deviation will decrease.

2.121   From the stem-and-leaf display in Exercise 2.34, the data are fairly mound-shaped, but skewed somewhat to the right.

The sample mean is $\bar{x} = \dfrac{\sum x}{n} = \dfrac{1493}{25} = 59.72$.

The sample variance is $s^2 = \dfrac{\sum x^2 - \dfrac{\left(\sum x\right)^2}{n}}{n-1} = \dfrac{96{,}885 - \dfrac{1493^2}{25}}{25-1} = 321.7933$.

The sample standard deviation is $s = \sqrt{321.7933} = 17.9386$.

The z-score associated with the largest value is $z = \dfrac{x - \bar{x}}{s} = \dfrac{102 - 59.72}{17.9386} = 2.36$.

This observation is a suspect outlier.

The observations associated with the one-time customers are 5 of the largest 7 observations. Thus, repeat customers tend to have shorter delivery times than one-time customers.

2.123   Using MINITAB, the scatterplot is:

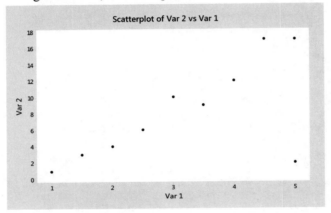

2.125.   From the scatterplot of the data, it appears that as the number of punishments increases, the average payoff decreases. Thus, there appears to be a negative linear relationship between punishment use and average payoff. This supports the researchers conclusion that 'winners don't punish'.

2.127   Using MINITAB, a scattergram of the data is:

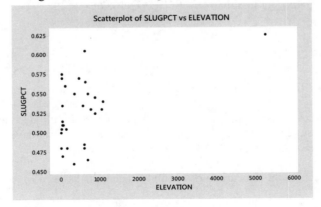

If we include the observation from Denver, then we would say there might be a linear relationship between slugging percentage and elevation. If we eliminated the observation from Denver, it appears that there might not be a relationship between slugging percentage and elevation.

2.129   Using MINITAB, the scatterplot of the data is:

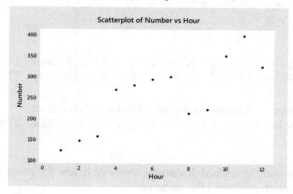

There appears to be a positive linear trend to the data. As the hours increase, the number of accidents tends to increase.

2.131   a.   Using MINITAB, a scatterplot of the data is:

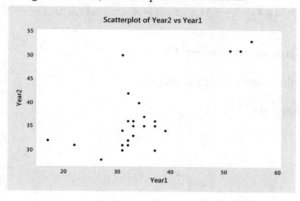

There is a moderate positive trend to the data. As the scores for Year1 increase, the scores for Year2 also tend to increase.

b.   From the graph, two agencies that had greater than expected PARS evaluation scores for Year2 were USAID and State.

2.133   a.   Using MINITAB, the scatterplot of the data is:

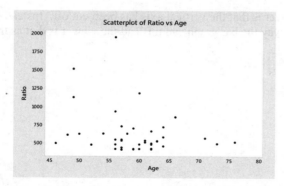

There appears to be a weak, negative relationship between a CEO's ratio of salary to worker pay and the CEO's age.

b.   Using MINITAB the descriptive statistics are:

Descriptive Statistics: Ratio

```
Variable    N    Mean   StDev   Minimum     Q1   Median      Q3   Maximum     IQR
Ratio      40   641.8   314.8     415.0  481.0    536.5   660.8    1951.0   179.8
```

Using the interquartile range, the highly suspect outliers are any observations greater than $Q_U + 3(IQR) = 660.8 + 3(179.8) = 1,200.2$ or less than $Q_L - 3(IQR) = 481.0 - 3(179.8) = -58.4$. There are 2 highly suspect outliers: 1,522 and 1,951.

Using the z-score, any observation greater than 3 standard deviations above or below the mean are highly suspect outliers. Three standard deviations above the mean is:

$$z = \frac{x - \bar{x}}{s} \Rightarrow 3 = \frac{x - 641.8}{314.8} \Rightarrow 3(314.8) = x - 641.8 \Rightarrow 944.4 = x - 641.8 \Rightarrow x = 1,586.2$$

Three standard deviations below the mean is:

$$z = \frac{x - \bar{x}}{s} \Rightarrow -3 = \frac{x - 641.8}{314.8} \Rightarrow -3(314.8) = x - 641.8 \Rightarrow -944.4 = x - 641.8 \Rightarrow x = -302.6$$

Using this method, there is one highly suspect outlier: 1,951.

c.   Removing the observation 1,951, the scatterplot of the data is:

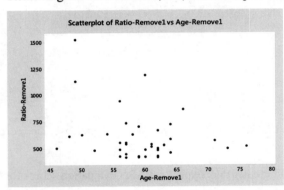

By removing the one highly suspect outlier, the relationship is still negative, but it is a stronger, negative relationship.

2.135   One way the bar graph can mislead the viewer is that the vertical axis has been cut off. Instead of starting at 0, the vertical axis starts at 12. Another way the bar graph can mislead the viewer is that as the bars get taller, the widths of the bars also increase.

2.137   a.   The graph might be misleading because the scales on the vertical axes are different. The left vertical axis ranges from 0 to $120 million. The right vertical axis ranges from 0 to $20 billion.

b.   Using MINITAB, the redrawn graph is:

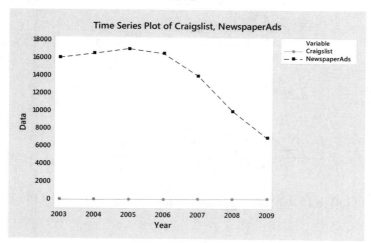

Although the amount of revenue produced by Craigslist has increased dramatically from 2003 to 2009, it is still much smaller than the revenue produced by newspaper ad sales.

2.139   The relative frequency histogram is:

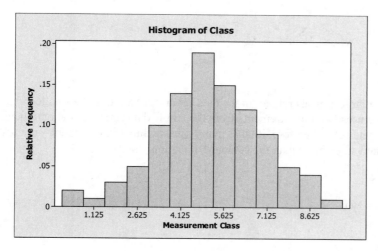

2.141   a. $z = \dfrac{x-\mu}{\sigma} = \dfrac{50-60}{10} = -1$ $z = \dfrac{70-60}{10} = 1$ $z = \dfrac{80-60}{10} = 2$

b. $z = \dfrac{x-\mu}{\sigma} = \dfrac{50-50}{5} = 0$ $z = \dfrac{70-50}{5} = 4$ $z = \dfrac{80-50}{5} = 6$

c $z = \dfrac{x-\mu}{\sigma} = \dfrac{50-40}{10} = 1$ $z = \dfrac{70-40}{10} = 3$ $z = \dfrac{80-40}{10} = 4$

d. $z = \dfrac{x-\mu}{\sigma} = \dfrac{50-40}{100} = .1$ $z = \dfrac{70-40}{100} = .3$ $z = \dfrac{80-40}{100} = .4$

2.143   a. $\sum x = 13 + 1 + 10 + 3 + 3 = 30$ $\sum x^2 = 13^2 + 1^2 + 10^2 + 3^2 + 3^2 = 288$

$$\bar{x} = \frac{\sum x}{n} = \frac{30}{5} = 6 \qquad s^2 = \frac{\sum x^2 - \frac{(\sum x)^2}{n}}{n-1} = \frac{288 - \frac{30^2}{5}}{5-1} = \frac{108}{4} = 27 \qquad s = \sqrt{27} = 5.20$$

b. $\sum x = 13 + 6 + 6 + 0 = 25$ $\sum x^2 = 13^2 + 6^2 + 6^2 + 0^2 = 241$

$$\bar{x} = \frac{\sum x}{n} = \frac{25}{4} = 6.25 \qquad s^2 = \frac{\sum x^2 - \frac{(\sum x)^2}{n}}{n-1} = \frac{241 - \frac{25^2}{4}}{4-1} = \frac{84.75}{3} = 28.25 \qquad s = \sqrt{28.25} = 5.32$$

c. $\sum x = 1 + 0 + 1 + 10 + 11 + 11 + 15 = 49$ $\sum x^2 = 1^2 + 0^2 + 1^2 + 10^2 + 11^2 + 11^2 + 15^2 = 569$.

$$\bar{x} = \frac{\sum x}{n} = \frac{49}{7} = 7 \qquad s^2 = \frac{\sum x^2 - \frac{(\sum x)^2}{n}}{n-1} = \frac{569 - \frac{49^2}{7}}{7-1} = \frac{226}{6} = 37.67 \qquad s = \sqrt{37.67} = 6.14$$

d. $\sum x = 3 + 3 + 3 + 3 = 12$ $\sum x^2 = 3^2 + 3^2 + 3^2 + 3^2 = 36$

$$\bar{x} = \frac{\sum x}{n} = \frac{12}{4} = 3 \qquad s^2 = \frac{\sum x^2 - \frac{(\sum x)^2}{n}}{n-1} = \frac{36 - \frac{12^2}{4}}{4-1} = \frac{0}{3} = 0 \qquad s = \sqrt{0} = 0$$

2.145   The range is found by taking the largest measurement in the data set and subtracting the smallest measurement. Therefore, it only uses two measurements from the whole data set. The standard deviation uses every measurement in the data set. Therefore, it takes every measurement into account—not just two. The range is affected by extreme values more than the standard deviation.

2.147   Using MINITAB, the scatterplot is:

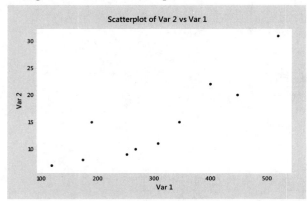

2.149   a.   Using MINITAB, the pie chart is:

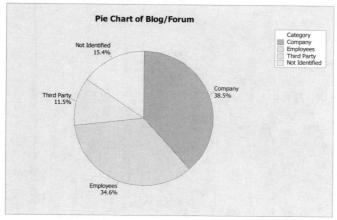

Companies and Employees represent (38.5 + 34.6 = 73.1) slightly more than 73% of the entities creating blogs/forums. Third parties are the least common entity.

b.   Using Chebyshev's Rule, at least 75% of the observations will fall within 2 standard deviations of the mean.

$$\bar{x} \pm 2s \Rightarrow 4.25 \pm 2(12.02) \Rightarrow 4.25 \pm 24.04 \Rightarrow (-19.79,\ 28.29) \text{ or } (0,\ 28.29)$$ since we cannot have a negative number blogs.

c.   We would expect the distribution to be skewed to the right. We know that we cannot have a negative number of blogs/forums. Even 1 standard deviation below the mean is a negative number. We would assume that there are a few very large observations because the standard deviation is so big compared to the mean.

2.151   a.   The relative frequency for each response category is found by dividing the frequency by the total sample size. The relative frequency for the category 'Global Marketing' is 235/2863 = .082. The rest of the relative frequencies are found in a similar manner and are reported in the table.

Area	*Number*	*Relative Frequencies*
Global Marketing	235	235/2863 = .082
Sales Management	494	494/2863 = .173
Buyer Behavior	478	478/2863 = .167
Relationships	498	498/2863 = .174
Innovation	398	398/2863 = .139
Marketing Strategy	280	280/2863 = .098
Channels/Distribution	213	213/2863 = .074
Marketing Research	131	131/2863 = .046
Services	136	136/2863 = .048
TOTAL	2,863	1.00

Relationships and sales management had the most articles published with 17.4% and 17.3%, respectively. Not far behind was Buyer Behavior with 16.7%. Of the rest of the areas, only innovation had more than 10%.

b.   Using MINITAB, the pie chart of the data is:

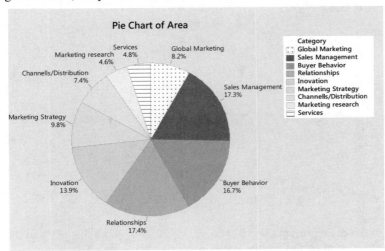

The slice for Marketing Research is smaller than the slice for Sales Management because there were fewer articles on Marketing Research than for Sales Management.

2.153   a.   Using MINITAB, the pie chart is:

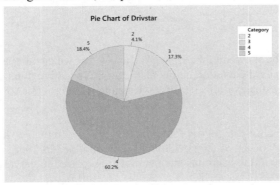

b.   The average driver's severity of head injury in head-on collisions is 603.7.

c.   Since the mean and median are close in value, the data should be fairly symmetric. Thus, we can use the Empirical Rule. We know that about 95% of all observations will fall within 2 standard deviations of the mean. This interval is $\bar{x} \pm 2s \Rightarrow 603.7 \pm 2(185.4) \Rightarrow 603.7 \pm 370.8 \Rightarrow (232.9, 974.5)$

Most of the head-injury ratings will fall between 232.9 and 974.5.

d.   The z-score would be: $z = \dfrac{x - \bar{x}}{s} = \dfrac{408 - 603.7}{185.4} = -1.06$

Since the absolute value is not very big, this is not an unusual value to observe.

2.155   a.   Using MINITAB, a Pareto diagram for the data is:

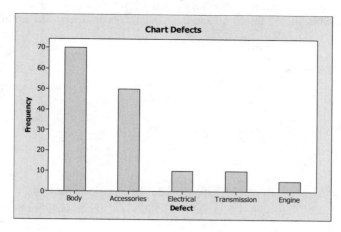

The most frequently observed defect is a body defect.

b.   Using MINITAB, a Pareto diagram for the Body Defect data is:

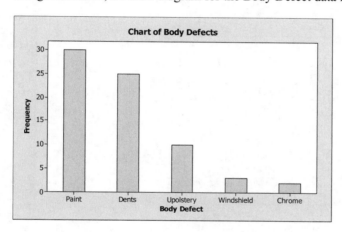

Most body defects are either paint or dents. These two categories account for
$(30 + 25) / 70 = 55 / 70 = .786$ of all body defects. Since these two categories account for so much of
the body defects, it would seem appropriate to target these two types of body defects for special
attention.

2.157   a.   The mean amount exported on the printout is 653. This means that the average amount of money per
market from exporting sparkling wine was $653,000.

b.   The median amount exported on the printout is 231. Since the median is the middle value, this means
that half of the 30 sparkling wine export values were above $231,000 and half of the sparkling wine
export values were below $231,000.

c.   The mean 3-year percentage change on the printout is 481. This means that in the last three years, the
average change is 481%, which indicates a large increase.

d.   The median 3-year percentage change on the printout is 156. Since the median is the middle value,
this means that half, or 15 of the 30 countries' 3-year percentage change values were above 156% and
half, or 15 of the 30 countries' 3-year percentage change values were below 156%.

e. The range is the difference between the largest observation and the smallest observation. From the printout, the largest observation is $4,852 thousand and the smallest observation is $70 thousand. The range is:

$$R = \$4,852 - \$70 = \$4,882 \text{ thousand}$$

f. From the printout, the standard deviation is $s = \$1,113$ thousand.

g. The variance is the standard deviation squared. The variance is:

$$s^2 = 1,113^2 = 1,238,769 \text{ million dollars squared}$$

h. We would expect an export amount to fall within 2 standard deviations of the mean or $\bar{x} \pm 2s \Rightarrow 653 \pm 2(1,113) \Rightarrow 653 \pm 2,226 \Rightarrow (-1,573,\ 2,879)$. Since the exports cannot be negative, the interval would be $(0,\ 2,879)$.

2.159　a.　Using MINITAB, a bar graph of the data is:

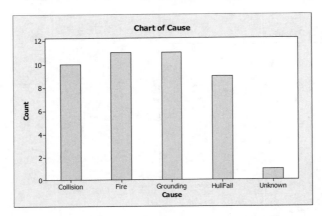

Fire and grounding are the two most likely causes of puncture.

b. Using MINITAB, the descriptive statistics are:

Descriptive Statistics: Spillage

Variable	N	Mean	StDev	Minimum	Q1	Median	Q3	Maximum
Spillage	42	66.19	56.05	25.00	32.00	43.00	77.50	257.00

The mean spillage amount is 66.19 thousand metric tons, while the median is 43.00. Since the median is so much smaller than the mean, it indicates that the data are skewed to the right. The standard deviation is 56.05. Again, since this value is so close to the value of the mean, it indicates that the data are skewed to the right.

Since the data are skewed to the right, we cannot use the Empirical Rule to describe the data. Chebyshev's Rule can be used. Using Chebyshev's Rule, we know that at least 8/9 of the observations will fall within 3 standard deviations of the mean.

$$\bar{x} \pm 3s \Rightarrow 66.19 \pm 3(56.05) \Rightarrow 66.19 \pm 168.15 \Rightarrow (-101.96,\ 234.34) \text{ or } (0,\ 234.34) \text{ since we cannot}$$
have negative spillage.

Thus, at least 8/9 of all oil spills will be between 0 and 234.34 thousand metric tons.

2.161   a.   Since no information is given about the distribution of the velocities of the Winchester bullets, we can only use Chebyshev's Rule to describe the data. We know that at least 3/4 of the velocities will fall within the interval:

$$\bar{x} \pm 2s \Rightarrow 936 \pm 2(10) \Rightarrow 936 \pm 20 \Rightarrow (916, 956)$$

Also, at least 8/9 of the velocities will fall within the interval:

$$\bar{x} \pm 3s \Rightarrow 936 \pm 3(10) \Rightarrow 936 \pm 30 \Rightarrow (906, 966)$$

   b.   Since a velocity of 1,000 is much larger than the largest value in the second interval in part **a**, it is very unlikely that the bullet was manufactured by Winchester.

2.163   a.   Using MINITAB, the time series plot is:

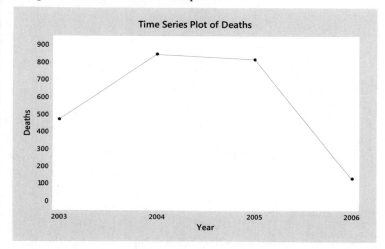

   b.   The time series plot is misleading because the information for 2006 is incomplete – it is based on only 2 months while all of the rest of the years are based on 12 months.

   c.   In order to construct a plot that accurately reflects the trend in American casualties from the Iraq War, we would want complete data for 2006 and information for the years 2007 through 2011.

2.165   a.   Since the mean is greater than the median, the distribution of the radiation levels is skewed to the right.

   b. $\bar{x} \pm s \Rightarrow 10 \pm 3 \Rightarrow (7, 13)$; $\bar{x} \pm 2s \Rightarrow 10 \pm 2(3) \Rightarrow (4, 16)$; $\bar{x} \pm 3s \Rightarrow 10 \pm 3(3) \Rightarrow (1, 19)$

Interval	Chebyshev's	Empirical
(7, 13)	At least 0	≈68%
(4, 16)	At least 75%	≈95%
(1, 19)	At least 88.9%	≈100%

Since the data are skewed to the right, Chebyshev's Rule is probably more appropriate in this case.

   c.   The background level is 4. Using Chebyshev's Rule, at least 75% or .75(50) ≈ 38 homes are above the background level. Using the Empirical Rule, ≈ 97.5% or .975(50) ≈ 49 homes are above the background level.

d. $z = \dfrac{x - \bar{x}}{s} = \dfrac{20 - 10}{3} = 3.333$

It is unlikely that this new measurement came from the same distribution as the other 50. Using either Chebyshev's Rule or the Empirical Rule, it is very unlikely to see any observations more than 3 standard deviations from the mean.

2.167   a.   Both the height and width of the bars (peanuts) change. Thus, some readers may tend to equate the area of the peanuts with the frequency for each year.

b.   Using MINITAB, the frequency bar chart is:

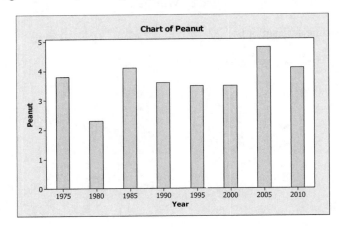

2.169   First we make some preliminary calculations.

Of the 20 engineers at the time of the layoffs, 14 are 40 or older. Thus, the probability that a randomly selected engineer will be 40 or older is 14/20 = .70. A very high proportion of the engineers is 40 or over.

In order to determine if the company is vulnerable to a disparate impact claim, we will first find the median age of all the engineers. Ordering all the ages, we get:

<u>29</u>, <u>32</u>, <u>34</u>, 35, <u>38</u>, 39, 40, 40, 40, <u>40</u>, <u>40</u>, 41, <u>42</u>, <u>42</u>, 44, <u>46</u>, 47, 52, <u>55</u>, 64

The median of all 20 engineers is $\dfrac{40 + 40}{2} = \dfrac{80}{2} = 40$

Now, we will compute the median age of those engineers who were not laid off. The ages underlined above correspond to the engineers who were not laid off. The median of these is $\dfrac{40 + 40}{2} = \dfrac{80}{2} = 40$.

The median age of all engineers is the same as the median age of those who were not laid off. The median age of those laid off is $\dfrac{40 + 41}{2} = \dfrac{81}{2} = 40.5$, which is not that much different from the median age of those not laid off. In addition, 70% of all the engineers are 40 or older. Thus, it appears that the company would not be vulnerable to a disparate impact claim.

2.171   There is evidence to support this claim. The graph peaks at the interval above 1.002. The heights of the bars decrease in order as the intervals get further and further from the peak interval. This is true for all bars except the one above 1.000. This bar is greater than the bar to its right. This would indicate that there are more observations in this interval than one would expect, suggesting that some inspectors might be passing rods with diameters that were barely below the lower specification limit.

Chapter 3
Probability

3.1   a.   Since the probabilities must sum to 1,

$$P(E_3) = 1 - P(E_1) - P(E_2) - P(E_4) - P(E_5) = 1 - .1 - .2 - .1 - .1 = .5$$

       b.

$$P(E_3) = 1 - P(E_1) - P(E_2) - P(E_4) - P(E_5) = 1 - P(E_3) - P(E_2) - P(E_4) - P(E_5)$$
$$\Rightarrow 2P(E_3) = 1 - .1 - .2 - .1 \Rightarrow 2P(E_3) = .6 \Rightarrow P(E_3) = .3$$

       c. $P(E_3) = 1 - P(E_1) - P(E_2) - P(E_4) - P(E_5) = 1 - .1 - .1 - .1 - .1 = .6$

3.3 $P(A) = P(1) + P(2) + P(3) = .05 + .20 + .30 = .55$

      $P(B) = P(1) + P(3) + P(5) = .05 + .30 + .15 = .50$

      $P(C) = P(1) + P(2) + P(3) + P(5) = .05 + .20 + .30 + .15 = .70$

3.5   a. $\dbinom{N}{n} = \dbinom{5}{2} = \dfrac{5!}{2!(5-2)!} = \dfrac{5 \cdot 4 \cdot 3 \cdot 2 \cdot 1}{2 \cdot 1 \cdot 3 \cdot 2 \cdot 1} = \dfrac{120}{12} = 10$

       b. $\dbinom{N}{n} = \dbinom{6}{3} = \dfrac{6!}{3!(6-3)!} = \dfrac{6 \cdot 5 \cdot 4 \cdot 3 \cdot 2 \cdot 1}{3 \cdot 2 \cdot 1 \cdot 3 \cdot 2 \cdot 1} = \dfrac{720}{36} = 20$

       c. $\dbinom{N}{n} = \dbinom{20}{5} = \dfrac{20!}{5!(20-5)!} = \dfrac{20 \cdot 19 \cdot 18 \cdots 3 \cdot 2 \cdot 1}{5 \cdot 4 \cdot 3 \cdot 2 \cdot 1 \cdot 15 \cdot 14 \cdot 13 \cdots 3 \cdot 2 \cdot 1} = \dfrac{2.432902008 \times 10^{18}}{1.569209242 \times 10^{14}} = 15{,}504$

3.7   a.   If we denote the marbles as B_1, B_2, R_1, R_2, and R_3, then the ten sample points are:

       (B_1, B_2) (B_1, R_1) (B_1, R_2) (B_1, R_3) (B_2, R_1) (B_2, R_2) (B_2, R_3) (R_1, R_2) (R_1, R_3) (R_2, R_3)

       b.   Each of the sample points would be equally likely. Thus, each would have a probability of 1/10 of occurring.

       c.   There is one sample point in A: (B_1, B_2). Thus, $P(A) = \dfrac{1}{10}$.

          There are 6 sample points in B: (B_1, R_1) (B_1, R_2) (B_1, R_3) (B_2, R_1) (B_2, R_2) (B_2, R_3). Thus, $P(B) = 6\left(\dfrac{1}{10}\right) = \dfrac{6}{10} = \dfrac{3}{5}$.

          There are 3 sample points in C: (R_1, R_2) (R_1, R_3) (R_2, R_3). Thus, $P(C) = 3\left(\dfrac{1}{10}\right) = \dfrac{3}{10}$.

3.9   Define the following events:

      C: {currently receive cable or satellite TV service at home}
      N: {never subscribed to cable/satellite TV service at home}
      U: {canceled the cable/satellite TV service}

a.   The sample points are C, N, and U.

b. $P(C) = \dfrac{1,521}{2,001} = .76$, $P(N) = \dfrac{180}{2,001} = .09$, $P(U) = \dfrac{300}{2,001} = .15$

c. $P(N) = .09$

d. $P(C \text{ or } U) = .76 + .15 = .91$

3.11   a.   The sample points of this experiment correspond to each of the 6 possible colors of the M&M's. Let Br = brown, Y = yellow, R = red, Bl = blue, O = orange, G = green. The six sample points are: Br, Y, R, Bl, O, and G

b.   From the problem, the probabilities of selecting each color are:

   $P(Br) = 0.13$, $P(Y) = 0.14$, $P(R) = 0.13$, $P(Bl) = 0.24$, $P(O) = 0.2$, $P(G) = 0.16$

c.   The probability that the selected M&M is brown is $P(Br) = 0.13$

d.   The probability that the selected M&M is red, green or yellow is:

   $P(R \text{ or } G \text{ or } Y) = P(R) + P(G) + P(Y) = 0.13 + 0.16 + 0.14 = 0.43$

e. $P(\text{not } Bl) = P(R) + P(G) + P(Y) + P(Br) + P(O) = 0.13 + 0.16 + 0.14 + 0.13 + 0.20 = 0.76$

3.13   Define the following events:

   W: {respondent works during summer vacation}
   N: {respondent does not work during summer vacation}
   U: {respondent is unemployed}

a. $P(W) = .61$

b. $P(\text{Not work}) = P(N) + P(U) = .22 + .17 = .39$

3.15   Define the following events:

   G: {Interviewee works for the government}
   Y: {Interviewee has at least 20 years of experience}

a. $P(G) = \dfrac{11}{17} = .647$

b. $P(Y) = \dfrac{9}{17} = .529$

3.17   Define the following events:

   R: {Recycle}

   For the *usefulness is salient* condition, $P(R) = \dfrac{26}{39} = .667$.

   For the *control* condition, $P(R) = \dfrac{14}{39} = .359$.

Those in the *usefulness is salient* condition recycled at almost twice the rate as those in the *control* condition.

3.19   a.   Define the following event:

C: {Slaughtered chicken passes inspection with fecal contamination}

$$P(C) = \frac{1}{100} = .01$$

b.   Based on the data, $P(C) = \frac{306}{32,075} = .0095 \approx .01$

Yes. The probability of a slaughtered chicken passing inspection with fecal contamination rounded off to 2 decimal places is .01.

3.21   a.   The probability that any network is selected on a particular day is 1/8. Therefore,

P(ESPN selected on July 11) = 1/8.

b.   The number of ways to select four networks for the weekend days is a combination of 8 networks taken 4 at a time. The number of ways to do this is $\binom{8}{4} = \frac{8!}{4!(8-4)!} = \frac{8 \cdot 7 \cdot 6 \cdot 5 \cdot 4 \cdot 3 \cdot 2 \cdot 1}{4 \cdot 3 \cdot 2 \cdot 1 \cdot 4 \cdot 3 \cdot 2 \cdot 1} = 70$.

c.   First, we need to find the number of ways one can choose the 4 networks where ESPN is one of the 4. If ESPN has to be chosen, then the number of ways of doing this is a combination of one thing taken one at a time or $\binom{1}{1} = \frac{1!}{1!(1-1)!} = \frac{1}{1 \cdot 1} = 1$. The number of ways to select the remaining 3 networks is a

combination of 7 things taken 3 at a time or $\binom{7}{3} = \frac{7!}{3!(7-3)!} = \frac{7 \cdot 6 \cdot 5 \cdot 4 \cdot 3 \cdot 2 \cdot 1}{3 \cdot 2 \cdot 1 \cdot 4 \cdot 3 \cdot 2 \cdot 1} = 35$. Thus, the total

number of ways of selecting 4 networks of which one has to be ESPN is 1(35) = 35.

Finally, the probability of selecting ESPN as one of the 4 networks for the weekend analysis is $35 / 70 = .5$.

3.23   Since one would be selecting 3 stocks from 15 without replacement, the total number of ways to select the 3 stocks would be a combination of 15 things taken 3 at a time. The number of ways would be

$$\binom{15}{3} = \frac{15!}{3!(15-3)!} = \frac{15 \cdot 14 \cdot 13 \cdots 3 \cdot 2 \cdot 1}{3 \cdot 2 \cdot 1 \cdot 12 \cdot 11 \cdot 10 \cdots 3 \cdot 2 \cdot 1} = \frac{1.307674368 \times 10^{12}}{2874009600} = 455$$

3.25   a.   There are a total of $3 \times 3 \times 3 = 27$ different combinations of Distance, Excess, and Association.

b.   There would be a total of 27 scenarios taken 2 at a time or
$\binom{27}{2} = \frac{27!}{2!(27-2)!} = \frac{27 \cdot 26 \cdot 25 \cdots 1}{2 \cdot 1 \cdot 25 \cdot 24 \cdot 23 \cdots 1} = \frac{27 \cdot 26}{2} = 351$ possible choices of two scenarios.

3.27   a.   The odds in favor of an Oxford Shoes win are $\frac{1}{3}$ to $1 - \frac{1}{3} = \frac{2}{3}$ or 1 to 2.

b. If the odds in favor of Oxford Shoes are 1 to 1, then the probability that Oxford Shoes wins is $\frac{1}{1+1} = \frac{1}{2}$.

c. If the odds against Oxford Shoes are 3 to 2, then the odds in favor of Oxford Shoes are 2 to 3. Therefore, the probability that Oxford Shoes wins is $\frac{2}{2+3} = \frac{2}{5}$.

3.29 a. The number of ways the 5 commissioners can vote is $2(2)(2)(2)(2) = 2^5 = 32$ (Each of the 5 commissioners has 2 choices for his/her vote – For or Against.)

b. Let F denote a vote 'For' and A denote a vote 'Against'. The 32 sample points would be:

FFFFF FFFFA FFFAF FFAFF FAFFF AFFFF FFFAA FFAFA FAFFA AFFFA
FFAAF FAFAF AFFAF FAAFF AFAFF AAFFF FFAAA FAFAA FAAFA FAAAF
AFFAA AFAFA AFAAF AAFFA AAFAF AAAFF FAAAA AFAAA AAFAA AAAFA
AAAAF AAAAA

Each of the sample points should be equally likely. Thus, each would have a probability of 1/32.

c. The sample points that result in a 2-2 split for the other 4 commissioners are:

FFAAF FAFAF AFFAF FAAFF AFAFF AAFFF FFAAA FAFAA FAAFA
AFFAA AFAFA AAFFA

There are 12 sample points.

d. Let V = event that your vote counts. $P(V) = 12/32 = 0.375$.

e. If there are now only 3 commissioners in the bloc, then the total number of ways the bloc can vote is $2(2)(2) = 2^3 = 8$. The sample points would be:

FFF   FFA   FAF   AFF   FAA   AFA   AAF   AAA

The number of sample points where your vote would count is 4: *FAF, AFF, FAA, AFA*

Let W = event that your vote counts in the bloc. $P(W) = 4/8 = 0.5$.

3.31 a. A: {*HHH, HHT, HTH, THH, TTH, THT, HTT*}
B: {*HHH, TTH, THT, HTT*}
$A \cup B$: {*HHH, HHT, HTH, THH, TTH, THT, HTT*}
A^c: {*TTT*}
$A \cap B$: {*HHH, TTH, THT, HTT*}

b. $P(A) = \frac{7}{8}$ $P(B) = \frac{4}{8} = \frac{1}{2}$ $P(A \cup B) = \frac{7}{8}$ $P(A^c) = \frac{1}{8}$ $P(A \cap B) = \frac{4}{8} = \frac{1}{2}$

c. $P(A \cup B) = P(A) + P(B) - P(A \cap B) = \frac{7}{8} + \frac{1}{2} - \frac{1}{2} = \frac{7}{8}$

d. No. $P(A \cap B) = \frac{1}{2}$ which is not 0.

3.33   a. $P(A) = P(E_1) + P(E_2) + P(E_3) + P(E_5) + P(E_6) = \dfrac{1}{5} + \dfrac{1}{5} + \dfrac{1}{5} + \dfrac{1}{20} + \dfrac{1}{10} = \dfrac{15}{20} = \dfrac{3}{4}$

b. $P(B) = P(E_2) + P(E_3) + P(E_4) + P(E_7) = \dfrac{1}{5} + \dfrac{1}{5} + \dfrac{1}{20} + \dfrac{1}{5} = \dfrac{13}{20}$

c. $P(A \cup B) = P(E_1) + P(E_2) + P(E_3) + P(E_4) + P(E_5) + P(E_6) + P(E_7)$

   $= \dfrac{1}{5} + \dfrac{1}{5} + \dfrac{1}{5} + \dfrac{1}{20} + \dfrac{1}{20} + \dfrac{1}{10} + \dfrac{1}{5} = 1$

d. $P(A \cap B) = P(E_2) + P(E_3) = \dfrac{1}{5} + \dfrac{1}{5} = \dfrac{2}{5}$

e. $P(A^c) = 1 - P(A) = 1 - \dfrac{3}{4} = \dfrac{1}{4}$

f. $P(B^c) = 1 - P(B) = 1 - \dfrac{13}{20} = \dfrac{7}{20}$

g. $P(A \cup A^c) = P(E_1) + P(E_2) + P(E_3) + P(E_4) + P(E_5) + P(E_6) + P(E_7)$

   $= \dfrac{1}{5} + \dfrac{1}{5} + \dfrac{1}{5} + \dfrac{1}{20} + \dfrac{1}{20} + \dfrac{1}{10} + \dfrac{1}{5} = 1$

h. $P(A^c \cap B) = P(E_4) + P(E_7) = \dfrac{1}{20} + \dfrac{1}{5} = \dfrac{5}{20} = \dfrac{1}{4}$

3.35   a. $P(A) = .50 + .10 + .05 = .65$

b. $P(B) = .10 + .07 + .50 + .05 = .72$

c. $P(C) = .25$

d. $P(D) = .05 + .03 = .08$

e. $P(A^c) = .25 + .07 + .03 = .35$ (Note: $P(A^c) = 1 - P(A) = 1 - .65 = .35$)

f. $P(A \cup B) = P(B) = .10 + .07 + .50 + .05 = .72$

g. $P(A \cap C) = 0$

h.   Two events are mutually exclusive if they have no sample points in common or if the probability of their intersection is 0.

   $P(A \cap B) = P(A) = .50 + .10 + .05 = .65$. Since this is not 0, A and B are not mutually exclusive.

   $P(A \cap C) = 0$.   Since this is 0, A and C are mutually exclusive.

   $P(A \cap D) = .05$.   Since this is not 0, A and D are not mutually exclusive.

$P(B \cap C) = 0.$ Since this is 0, B and C are mutually exclusive.

$P(B \cap D) = .05.$ Since this is not 0, B and D are not mutually exclusive.

$P(C \cap D) = 0.$ Since this is 0, C and D are mutually exclusive.

3.37   Define the following events:

L: {robot has legs only}
W: {robot has wheels only}
B: {robots have both legs and wheels}
N: {robots have neither legs nor wheels}

$$P(\text{legs or wheels}) = 1 - P(N) = 1 - \frac{15}{106} = 1 - .142 = .858$$

3.39   a.   The analyst makes an early forecast and is only concerned with accuracy is the event $(A \cap B)$.

b.   The analyst is not only concerned with accuracy is the event A^c.

c.   The analyst is from a small brokerage firm or makes an early forecast is the event $B \cup C$.

d.   The analyst makes a late forecast and is not only concerned with accuracy is the event $A^c \cap B^c$.

3.41   Define the following event:

A: {Store violates the NIST scanner accuracy standard}

Then $P(A^c) = 1 - P(A) = 1 - 52/60 = 8/60 = .133$

3.43   a. $P(A) = 1 - \left[P(\text{Online via personal computer}) + P(\text{Online via tablet or e-reader}) \right] = 1 - (.37 + .03) = .60$

b. $P(B) = 1 - \left[P(\text{Debit card}) + P(\text{Credit card}) \right] = 1 - (.09 + .07) = .84$

c. $P(A \cap B) = P(\text{Write check}) + P(\text{Checking account withdrawal}) + P(\text{Cash}) + P(\text{Mobile bill account})$
$= .22 + .10 + .07 + .08 = .44$

d. $P(A \cup B) = P(A) + P(B) - P(A \cap B) = .60 + .84 - .44 = 1$

3.45   First, define the following events:

F: {Fully compensated}
P: {Partially compensated}
N: {Non-compensated}
R: {Left because of retirement}

From the text, we know
$$P(F) = \frac{127}{244}, \quad P(P) = \frac{45}{244}, \quad P(N) = \frac{72}{244}, \text{ and } P(R) = \frac{7 + 11 + 10}{244} = \frac{28}{244}$$

a. $P(F) = \dfrac{127}{244}$

b. $P(F \cap R) = \dfrac{7}{244}$

c. $P(F^c) = 1 - P(F) = 1 - \dfrac{127}{244} = \dfrac{117}{244}$

d. $P(F \cup R) = P(F) + P(R) - P(F \cap R) = \dfrac{127}{244} + \dfrac{28}{244} - \dfrac{7}{244} = \dfrac{148}{244}$

3.47   Define the following events:

M_1: {Model 1}
M_2: {Model 2}

a. $P(5) = \dfrac{85}{160} = .531$

b. $P(5 \cup 0) = P(5) + P(0) - P(5 \cap 0) = .531 + \dfrac{35}{160} - 0 = .531 + .219 = .75$

c. $P(M_2 \cap 0) = \dfrac{15}{160} = .094$

3.49   Define the following events:

A: {Individual tax return is audited by the IRS}
B: {Corporation tax return is audited by the IRS}

a. $P(A) = \dfrac{1,242,479}{145,236,429} = .0086$

b. $P(A^c) = 1 - P(A) = 1 - .0086 = .9914$

c. $P(B) = \dfrac{25,905}{1,924,887} = .0135$

d. $P(B^c) = 1 - P(B) = 1 - .0135 = .9865$

3.51   A possible Venn Diagram would be:

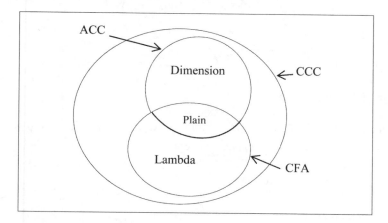

3.53   a. $P(A \mid B) = \dfrac{P(A \cap B)}{P(B)} = \dfrac{.1}{.2} = .5$

        b. $P(B \mid A) = \dfrac{P(A \cap B)}{P(A)} = \dfrac{.1}{.4} = .25$

        c.   Events A and B are said to be independent if $P(A \mid B) = P(A)$. In this case, $P(A \mid B) = .5$ and $P(A) = .4$. Thus, A and B are not independent.

3.55   a.   If two events are independent, then $P(A \cap B) = P(A)P(B) = .4(.2) = .08$.

        b.   If two events are independent, then $P(A \mid B) = P(A) = .4$.

        c. $P(A \cup B) = P(A) + P(B) - P(A \cap B) = .4 + .2 - .08 = .52$

3.57   a. $P(A) = P(E_1) + P(E_2) + P(E_3) = .2 + .3 + .3 = .8$

        $P(B) = P(E_2) + P(E_3) + P(E_5) = .3 + .3 + .1 = .7$

        $P(A \cap B) = P(E_2) + P(E_3) = .3 + .3 = .6$

        b. $P(E_1 \mid A) = \dfrac{P(E_1 \cap A)}{P(A)} = \dfrac{P(E_1)}{P(A)} = \dfrac{.2}{.8} = .25$

        $P(E_2 \mid A) = \dfrac{P(E_2 \cap A)}{P(A)} = \dfrac{P(E_2)}{P(A)} = \dfrac{.3}{.8} = .375$

        $P(E_3 \mid A) = \dfrac{P(E_3 \cap A)}{P(A)} = \dfrac{P(E_3)}{P(A)} = \dfrac{.3}{.8} = .375$

        The original sample point probabilities are in the proportion .2 to .3 to .3 or 2 to 3 to 3.
        The conditional probabilities for these sample points are in the proportion .25 to .375 to .375 or 2 to 3 to 3.

c.   (1) $P(B \mid A) = P(E_2 \mid A) + P(E_3 \mid A) = .375 + .375 = .75$ (from part **b**)

(2) $P(B \mid A) = \dfrac{P(A \cap B)}{P(A)} = \dfrac{.6}{.8} = .75$ (from part **a**)

The two methods do yield the same result.

d.   If A and B are independent events, $P(B \mid A) = P(B)$. From part **c**, $P(B \mid A) = .75$. From part **a**, $P(B) = .7$. Since $.75 \neq .7$, A and B are not independent events.

3.59   a. $P(A \cap C) = 0 \Rightarrow A$ and C are mutually exclusive.

$P(B \cap C) = 0 \Rightarrow B$ and C are mutually exclusive.

b. $P(A) = P(1) + P(2) + P(3) = .20 + .05 + .30 = .55$ $P(B) = P(3) + P(4) = .30 + .10 = .40$

$P(C) = P(5) + P(6) = .10 + .25 = .35$ $P(A \cap B) = P(3) = .30$

$P(A \mid B) = \dfrac{P(A \cap B)}{P(B)} = \dfrac{.30}{.40} = .75$

A and B are independent if $P(A \mid B) = P(A)$. Since $P(A \mid B) = .75$ and $P(A) = .55$, A and B are not independent.

Since A and C are mutually exclusive, they are not independent. Similarly, since B and C are mutually exclusive, they are not independent.

c.   Using the probabilities of sample points,
$P(A \cup B) = P(1) + P(2) + P(3) + P(4) = .20 + .05 + .30 + .10 = .65$

Using the additive rule,
$P(A \cup B) = P(A) + P(B) - P(A \cap B) = .55 + .40 - .30 = .65$

Using the probabilities of sample points,
$P(A \cup C) = P(1) + P(2) + P(3) + P(5) + P(6) = .20 + .05 + .30 + .10 + .25 = .90$

Using the additive rule,
$P(A \cup C) = P(A) + P(C) - P(A \cap C) = .55 + .35 - 0 = .90$

3.61   Define the following events:

A: {Company is a banking/investment company}
B: {Company is based in United States}

From the problem, we know that $P(A \cap B) = \dfrac{4}{20} = .20$ and $P(B) = \dfrac{9}{20} = .45$

$P(A \mid B) = \dfrac{P(A \cap B)}{P(B)} = \dfrac{.20}{.45} = .444.$

3.63   Define the following events:

B: {Diamond is a blood diamond}
R: {Diamond is a rough diamond}
S: {Rough diamond is processed in Surat, India}

From the Exercise, $P(B\mid R) = .25$, $P(S) = .9$, $P(B\mid S) = \dfrac{1}{3}$

a. $P(B^C\mid R) = 1 - P(B\mid R) = 1 - .25 = .75$

b. $P(B \cap S) = P(B\mid S)P(S) = \dfrac{1}{3}(.9) = .3$

3.65   Define the following events:

S: {Shopper used smartphone to make purchase}
M: {Shopper preferred mobile website}

From the Exercise, $P(S) = .41$, $P(M\mid S) = .38$

$P(M \cap S) = P(M\mid S)P(S) = .38(.41) = .1558$

3.67   Define the following events:

F: {Worker is fully compensated}
P: { Worker is partially compensated}
N: { Worker is non-compensated}
R: { Worker retired}

From the exercise, $P(F) = 127/244 = .520$, $P(P) = 45/244 = .184$, $P(R\mid F) = 7/127 = .055$, $P(R\mid P) = 11/45 = .244$, and $P(R\mid N) = 10/72 = .139$.

a. $P(R\mid F) = 7/127 = .055$

b. $P(R\mid N) = 10/72 = .139$

c.   The two events are independent if $P(R\mid F) = P(R)$.

$P(R) = \dfrac{7+11+10}{244} = \dfrac{28}{244} = .115$ and $P(R\mid F) = 10/72 = .055$. Since these are not equal, events *R* and *F* are not independent.

3.69   Define the following events:

I: {Invests in Market}
N: {No investment}

a. $P(I\mid \{IQ \ge 6\}) = \dfrac{P(I \cap \{IQ \ge 6\})}{P(IQ \ge 6)} = \dfrac{\dfrac{10,270+6,698+5,135+4,464}{158,044}}{\dfrac{31,943+17,958+12,145+9,531}{158,044}} = \dfrac{26,567}{71,577} = .371$

b. $P(I \mid IQ \le 5) = \dfrac{P(I \cap \{IQ \le 5\})}{P(IQ \le 5)} = \dfrac{\dfrac{44,651 - 26,567}{158,044}}{\dfrac{158,044 - 71,577}{158,044}} = \dfrac{18,084}{86,467} = .209$

c.   Yes, it appears that investing in the stock market is dependent on IQ. If investing in the stock market and IQ were independent, then $P(I \mid IQ \le 5) = P(I \mid IQ \ge 6) = P(I)$. Since

$P(I \mid IQ \le 5) \ne P(I \mid IQ \ge 6)$, then investing in the stock market and IQ are dependent.

3.71   Define the following events:

A: {Ambulance can travel to location A under 8 minutes}
B: {Ambulance can travel to location B under 8 minutes}
C: {Ambulance is busy}

We are given $P(A) = .58$, $P(B) = .42$, and $P(C) = .3$.

a. $P(A \cap C^c) = P(A \mid C^c)P(C^c) = .58(1 - .3) = .406$

b. $P(B \mid C^c)P(C^c) = .42(1 - .3) = .294$

3.73   Define the following events:

H: {Firefighter had no SOP for detecting/monitoring hydrogen cyanide in fire smoke}
C: {Firefighter had no SOP for detecting/monitoring carbon monoxide if fire smoke}

From the Exercise, $P(H) = .80$, $P(M) = .49$, $P(H \cup M) = .94$.

We know $P(H \cup M) = P(H) + P(M) - P(H \cap M) \Rightarrow P(H \cap M) = P(H) + P(M) - P(H \cup M)$

$P(H \cap M) = P(H) + P(M) - P(H \cup M) = .80 + .49 - .94 = .35$

3.75   Define the following event:

A: {The specimen labeled "red snapper" was really red snapper}

a.   The probability that you are actually served red snapper the next time you order it at a restaurant is $P(A) = 1 - .77 = .23$

b.   P(at least one customer is actually served red snapper)
= 1 − P(no customer is actually served red snapper)
$= 1 - P(A^c \cap A^c \cap A^c \cap A^c \cap A^c) = 1 - P(A^c)P(A^c)P(A^c)P(A^c)P(A^c)$
$= 1 - .77^5 = 1 - .271 = .729$

Note: In order to compute the above probability, we had to assume that the trials or events are independent. This assumption is likely to not be valid. If a restaurant served one customer a look-a-like variety, then it probably served the next one a look-a-like variety.

3.77   a. $P(E \mid H_p) = 1$

b. $P(E|H_d) = P\{6/9\} + P\{9/6\} = .21(.14) + .14(.21) = .0294 + .0294 = .0588$

c. $\dfrac{P(E|H_p)}{P(E|H_d)} = \dfrac{1}{.0588} = 17.0$ Since this value is greater than 1, this supports the prosecution.

3.79   a.   If the coin is balanced, then $P(H) = .5$ and $P(T) = .5$ on any trial. Also, we can assume that the results of any coin toss is independent of any other. Thus,

$$P(H \cap H \cap H \cap H \cap H \cap H \cap H \cap H \cap H \cap H)$$
$$= P(H)P(H)P(H)P(H)P(H)P(H)P(H)P(H)P(H)P(H)$$
$$= .5(.5)(.5)(.5)(.5)(.5)(.5)(.5)(.5) = .5^{10} = .0009766$$

$$P(H \cap H \cap T \cap T \cap H \cap T \cap T \cap H \cap H \cap H)$$
$$= P(H)P(H)P(T)P(T)P(H)P(T)P(T)P(H)P(H)P(H)$$
$$= .5(.5)(.5)(.5)(.5)(.5)(.5)(.5)(.5) = .5^{10} = .0009766$$

$$P(T \cap T \cap T \cap T \cap T \cap T \cap T \cap T \cap T \cap T)$$
$$= P(T)P(T)P(T)P(T)P(T)P(T)P(T)P(T)P(T)P(T)$$
$$= .5(.5)(.5)(.5)(.5)(.5)(.5)(.5)(.5) = .5^{10} = .0009766$$

   b.   Define the following events:

       A: {10 coin tosses result in all heads or all tails}
       B: {10 coin tosses result in mix of heads and tails}

$$P(A) = P(H \cap H \cap H \cap H \cap H \cap H \cap H \cap H \cap H \cap H)$$
$$+ P(T \cap T \cap T \cap T \cap T \cap T \cap T \cap T \cap T \cap T)$$
$$= .0009766 + .0009766 = .0019532$$

   c. $P(B) = 1 - P(A) = 1 - .0019532 = .9980468$

   d.   From the above probabilities, the chances that either all heads or all tails occurred is extremely rare. Thus, if one of these sequences really occurred, it is most likely sequence #2.

3.81   a. $P(B_1 \cap A) = P(A|B_1)P(B_1) = .3(.75) = .225$

   b. $P(B_2 \cap A) = P(A|B_2)P(B_2) = .5(.25) = .125$

   c. $P(A) = P(B_1 \cap A) + P(B_2 \cap A) = .225 + .125 = .35$

   d. $P(B_1|A) = \dfrac{P(B_1 \cap A)}{P(A)} = \dfrac{.225}{.35} = .643$

   e. $P(B_2|A) = \dfrac{P(B_2 \cap A)}{P(A)} = \dfrac{.125}{.35} = .357$

3.83   If A is independent of B_1, B_2, and B_3, then $P(A|B_1) = P(A) = .4$.

Then $P(B_1 | A) = \dfrac{P(A | B_1)P(B_1)}{P(A)} = \dfrac{.4(.2)}{.4} = .2.$

3.85   Define the following events:

E: {Expert makes the correct decision}
N: {Novice makes the correct decision}
M: {Matched condition}
E: {Similar distracter condition}
E: {Non-similar distracter condition}

a. $P(E^c | M) = 1 - .9212 = .0788$

b. $P(N^c | M) = 1 - .7455 = .2545$

c.   Since $P(N^c | M) = .2545 > P(E^c | M) = .0788,$ it is more likely that the participant is a Novice.

3.87   a.   Converting the percentages to probabilities,

$P(275 - 300) = .52, \quad P(305 - 325) = .39,$ and $P(330 - 350) = .09.$

b.   Using Bayes Theorem,

$$P(275 - 300 | CC) = \dfrac{P(275 - 300 \cap CC)}{P(CC)}$$

$$= \dfrac{P(CC | 275 - 300)P(275 - 300)}{P(CC | 275 - 300)P(275 - 300) + P(CC | 305 - 325)P(305 - 325) + P(CC | 330 - 350)P(330 - 350)}$$

$$= \dfrac{.775(.52)}{.775(.52) + .77(.39) + .86(.09)} = \dfrac{.403}{.403 + .3003 + .0774} = \dfrac{.403}{.7807} = .516$$

3.89   Define the following events:

S: {Shale}
D: {Dolomite}
G: {Gamma ray reading > 60}

From the exercise: $P(D) = \dfrac{476}{771} = .617, \quad P(S) = \dfrac{295}{771} = .383, \quad P(G | D) = \dfrac{34}{476} = .071,$ and $P(G | S) = \dfrac{280}{295} = .949.$

$P(D \cap G) = P(G | D)P(D) = .071(.617) = .0438$ and

$P(G) = P(G | D)P(D) + P(G | S)P(S) = .071(.617) + .949(.383) = .0438 + .3635 = .4073.$

Thus, $P(D | G) = \dfrac{P(D \cap G)}{P(G)} = \dfrac{.0438}{.4073} = .1075.$ Since this probability is so small, we would suggest that the area should not be mined.

3.91   Define the following events:

D: {Worker is drug user}

P: {Drug test is positive}

a. From the Exercise, $P(D)=.05,\ P(P|D^c)=.05,\ P(P^c|D)=.05.$

$$P(P)=P(P\cap D^c)+P(P\cap D)=P(P|D^c)P(D^c)+P(P|D)P(D)$$
$$=.05(1-.05)+(1-.05)(.05)=.0475+.0475=.095$$

$$P(D^c|P)=\frac{P(P\cap D^c)}{P(P)}=\frac{P(P|D^c)P(D^c)}{P(P)}=\frac{.05(1-.05)}{.095}=\frac{.0475}{.095}=.5$$

b. From the Exercise, $P(D)=.95,\ P(P|D^c)=.05,\ P(P^c|D)=.05.$

$$P(P)=P(P\cap D^c)+P(P\cap D)=P(P|D^c)P(D^c)+P(P|D)P(D)$$
$$=.05(1-.95)+(1-.05)(.95)=.0025+.9025=.905$$

$$P(D^c|P)=\frac{P(P\cap D^c)}{P(P)}=\frac{P(P|D^c)P(D^c)}{P(P)}=\frac{.05(1-.95)}{.905}=\frac{.0025}{.905}=.0028$$

3.93 a. If $\frac{P(T|E)}{P(T^c|E)}<1$, then $P(T|E)<P(T^c|E)$. Thus, the probability of more than two bullets given the evidence is greater than the probability of two bullets given the evidence. This supports the theory of more than two bullets were used in the assassination of JFK.

b. Using Bayes Theorem,

$$P(T|E)=\frac{P(T)P(E|T)}{P(T)P(E|T)+P(T^c)P(E|T^c)}\ \text{and}\ P(T^c|E)=\frac{P(T^c)P(E|T^c)}{P(T)P(E|T)+P(T^c)P(E|T^c)}.$$

Thus, $\dfrac{P(T|E)}{P(T^c|E)}=\dfrac{\frac{P(T)P(E|T)}{P(T)P(E|T)+P(T^c)P(E|T^c)}}{\frac{P(T^c)P(E|T^c)}{P(T)P(E|T)+P(T^c)P(E|T^c)}}=\dfrac{P(T)P(E|T)}{P(T^c)P(E|T^c)}.$

3.95 a. The two probability rules for a sample space are that the probability for any sample point is between 0 and 1 and that the sum of the probabilities of all the sample points is 1.

For this Exercise, all the probabilities of the sample points are between 0 and 1, and

$$\sum_{i=1}^{4}P(S_i)=P(S_1)+P(S_2)+P(S_3)+P(S_4)=.2+.1+.3+.4=1.0$$

b. $P(A)=P(S_1)+P(S_4)=.2+.4=.6$

3.97 a. If events A and B are mutually exclusive, then $P(A\cap B)=0.$

$$P(A \mid B) = \frac{P(A \cap B)}{P(B)} = \frac{0}{.3} = 0$$

    b.   No. If events A and B are independent, then $P(A \mid B) = P(A)$. However, from the Exercise we know $P(A) = .2$ and from part a, we know $P(A \mid B) = 0$. Thus, events A and B are not independent.

3.99 $P(A \cap B) = .4, \ P(A \mid B) = .8$

Since $P(A \mid B) = \dfrac{P(A \cap B)}{P(B)}$, substitute the given probabilities into the formula and solve for $P(B)$.

$$.8 = \frac{.4}{P(B)} \Rightarrow P(B) = \frac{.4}{.8} = .5$$

3.101   a. $P(A \cap B) = 0$

        $P(B \cap C) = P(2) = .2$

        $P(A \cup C) = P(1) + P(2) + P(3) + P(5) + P(6) = .3 + .2 + .1 + .1 + .2 = .9$

        $P(A \cup B \cup C) = P(1) + P(2) + P(3) + P(4) + P(5) + P(6) = .3 + .2 + .1 + .1 + .1 + .2 = 1$

        $P(B^c) = P(1) + P(3) + P(5) + P(6) = .3 + .1 + .1 + .2 = .7$

        $P(A^c \cap B) = P(2) + P(4) = .2 + .1 = .3$

        $P(B \mid C) = \dfrac{P(B \cap C)}{P(C)} = \dfrac{P(2)}{P(2) + P(5) + P(6)} = \dfrac{.2}{.2 + .1 + .2} = \dfrac{.2}{.5} = .4$

        $P(B \mid A) = \dfrac{P(B \cap A)}{P(A)} = \dfrac{0}{P(A)} = 0$

    b.   Since $P(A \cap B) = 0$, and $P(A)P(B) > 0$, these two would not be equal, implying A and B are not independent. However, A and B are mutually exclusive, since $P(A \cap B) = 0$.

    c. $P(B) = P(2) + P(4) = .2 + .1 = .3$. But $P(B \mid C)$, calculated above, is .4. Since these are not equal, B and C are not independent. Since $P(B \cap C) = .2$, B and C are not mutually exclusive.

3.103   Define the following events:

    E: {Industrial accident caused by faulty Engineering & Design}
    R: {Industrial accident caused by faulty Procedures & Practices}
    M: {Industrial accident caused by faulty Management & Oversight }
    T: {Industrial accident caused by faulty Training & Communication}

    a.   The sample points for this problem are: E, R, M, and T. Reasonable probabilities are:
        $P(E) = 27/83 = .3253, \ P(R) = 24/83 = .2892, \ P(M) = 22/83 = .2651,$ and $P(T) = 10/83 = .1205.$

b. $P(E) = 27/83 = .3253$. Approximately 32.53% of all industrial accidents are caused by faulty Engineering and Design.

c. P(Industrial accident caused by something other than procedures & practices)
$= 1 - P(R^c) = 1 - .2892 = .7108$. Approximately 71.08% of all industrial accidents are caused by something other than faulty procedures & practices.

3.105   Define the event:

B: {Small business owned by non-Hispanic white female}

From the problem, $P(B) = .27$

The probability that a small business owned by a non-Hispanic white is male-owned is
$P(B^c) = 1 - P(B) = 1 - .27 = .73$.

3.107   a.   This statement is false. All probabilities are between 0 and 1 inclusive. One cannot have a probability of 4.

b.   If we assume that the probabilities are the same as the percents (changed to proportions), then this is a true statement.

$$P(4 \text{ or } 5) = P(4) + P(5) = .6020 + .1837 = .7857$$

c.   This statement is true. There were no observations with one star. Thus, $P(1) = 0$.

d.   This statement is false. $P(2) = .0408$ and $P(5) = .1837$. $P(5) > P(2)$.

3.109   a.   Since we want to maximize the purchase of grill #2, grill #2 must be one of the 3 grills in the display. Thus, we have to pick 2 more grills from the 4 remaining grills. Since order does not matter, the number of different ways to select 2 grill displays from 4 would be a combination of 4 things taken 2 at a time. The number of ways is:

$$\binom{4}{2} = \frac{4!}{2!(4-2)!} = \frac{4 \cdot 3 \cdot 2 \cdot 1}{2 \cdot 1 \cdot 2 \cdot 1} = \frac{24}{4} = 6$$

Let Gi represent Grill i. The possibilities are:

$G_1 G_2 G_3$, $G_1 G_2 G_4$, $G_1 G_2 G_5$, $G_2 G_3 G_4$, $G_2 G_3 G_5$, $G_2 G_4 G_5$

b.   To find reasonable probabilities for the 6 possibilities, we divide the frequencies by the total sample size of 124. The probabilities would be:

$P(G_1 G_2 G_3) = 35/124 = .282$ $P(G_1 G_2 G_4) = 8/124 = .065$ $P(G_1 G_2 G_5) = 42/124 = .339$

$P(G_2 G_3 G_4) = 4/124 = .032$ $P(G_2 G_3 G_5) = 1/124 = .008$ $P(G_2 G_4 G_5) = 34/124 = .274$

c. $P($ display contained Grill #1$) = P(G_1 G_2 G_3) + P(G_1 G_2 G_4) + P(G_1 G_2 G_5) = .282 + .065 + .339 = .686$

3.111   a.   The international consumer is most likely to use the Certification mark on a label to identify a green product.

b.   Define the following events:

   A: {Certification mark on label}
   B: {Packaging}
   C: {Reading information about the product}
   D: {Advertisement}
   E: {Brand website}
   F: {Other}

   $$P(A \text{ or } B) = P(A) + P(B) = .45 + .15 = .60$$

c. $P(C \text{ or } E) = P(C) + P(E) = .12 + .04 = .16$

d. $P(\text{not } D) = P(A) + P(B) + P(C) + P(E) + P(F) = .45 + .15 + .12 + .04 + .18 = .94$

3.113   a. $P(A) = \dfrac{1,465}{2,143} = .684$

b. $P(B) = \dfrac{265}{2,143} = .124$

c.   No. There is one sample point that they have in common: Plaintiff trial win – reversed, Jury

d. $P(A^c) = 1 - P(A) = 1 - .684 = .316$

e. $P(A \cup B) = \dfrac{194 + 71 + 429 + 111 + 731}{2,143} = \dfrac{1,536}{2,143} = .717$

f. $P(A \cap B) = \dfrac{194}{2,143} = .091$

3.115   Define the following events:

A: {The watch is accurate}
N: {The watch is not accurate}

Assuming the manufacturer's claim is correct,

$P(N) = .05$ and $P(A) = 1 - P(N) = 1 - .05 = .95$.

The sample space for the purchase of four of the manufacturer's watches is listed below.

(A, A, A, A)   (N, A, A, A)   (A, N, N, A)   (N, A, N, N)
(A, A, A, N)   (A, A, N, N)   (N, A, N, A)   (N, N, A, N)
(A, A, N, A)   (A, N, A, N)   (N, N, A, A)   (N, N, N, A)
(A, N, A, A)   (N, A, A, N)   (A, N, N, N)   (N, N, N, N)

a.   All four watches not being accurate as claimed is the sample point *(N, N, N, N)*.

   Assuming the watches purchased operate independently and the manufacturer's claim is correct,

$$P(N,N,N,N) = P(N)P(N)P(N)P(N) = .05^4 = .00000625$$

b.   The sample points in the sample space that consist of exactly two watches failing to meet the claim are listed below.

(*A, A, N, N*)   (*N, A, A, N*)
(*A, N, A, N*)   (*N, A, N, A*)
(*A, N, N, A*)   (*N, N, A, A*)

The probability that exactly two of the four watches fail to meet the claim is the sum of the probabilities of these six sample points.

Assuming the watches purchased operate independently and the manufacturer's claim is correct,

$$P(A,A,N,N) = P(A)P(A)P(N)P(N) = .95(.95)(.05)(.05) = .00225625$$

All six of the sample points will have the same probability. Therefore, the probability that exactly two of the four watches fail to meet the claim when the manufacturer's claim is correct is

$$6(.00225625) = .0135$$

c.   The sample points in the sample space that consist of three of the four watches failing to meet the claim are listed below.

(*A, N, N, N*)   (*N, N, A, N*)
(*N, A, N, N*)   (*N, N, N, A*)

The probability that three of the four watches fail to meet the claim is the sum of the probabilities of the four sample points.

Assuming the watches purchased operate independently and the manufacturer's claim is correct,

$$P(A,N,N,N) = P(A)P(N)P(N)P(N) = .95(.05)(.05)(.05) = .00011875$$

All four of the sample points will have the same probability. Therefore, the probability that three of the four watches fail to meet the claim when the manufacturer's claim is correct is

$$4(.00011875) = .000475$$

If this event occurred, we would tend to doubt the validity of the manufacturer's claim since its probability of occurring is so small.

d.   All four watches tested failing to meet the claim is the sample point (*N, N, N, N*).
Assuming the watches purchased operate independently and the manufacturer's claim is correct,

$$P(N,N,N,N) = P(N)P(N)P(N)P(N) = .05(.05)(.05)(.05) = .00000625$$

Since the probability of observing this event is so small if the claim is true, we have strong evidence against the validity of the claim. However, we do not have conclusive proof that the claim is false. There is still a chance the event can occur (with probability .00000625) although it is extremely small.

3.117   Define the following events:

A: {Air pressure is over-reported by 4 psi or more}
B: {Air pressure is over-reported by 6 psi or more}
C: {Air pressure is over-reported by 8 psi or more}

a.   For gas station air pressure gauges that read 35 psi, $P(B) = .09$.

b.   For gas station air pressure gauges that read 55 psi, $P(C) = .09$.

c.   For gas station air pressure gauges that read 25 psi, $P(A^c) = 1 - P(A) = 1 - .16 = .84$.

d.   No. If air pressure is over-reported by 6 psi or more, then it is also over-reported by 4 psi or more. Thus, these 2 events are not mutually exclusive.

e.   The columns in the table are not mutually exclusive. All events in the last column (% Over-reported by 8 psi or more) are also part of the events in the first and second columns. All events in the second column are also part of the events in the first column. In addition, there is no column for the event 'Over-reported by less than 4 psi or not over-reported'.

3.119   Define the following events:

A: {Wheelchair user had an injurious fall}
B: {Wheelchair user had all five features installed in the home}
C: {Wheelchair user had no falls}
D: {Wheelchair user had none of the features installed in the home}

a. $P(A) = \dfrac{48}{306} = .157$

b. $P(B) = \dfrac{9}{306} = .029$

c. $P(C \cap D) = \dfrac{89}{306} = .291$

d. $P(A \mid B) = \dfrac{P(A \cap B)}{P(B)} = \dfrac{2/306}{9/306} = \dfrac{2}{9} = .222$

e. $P(A \mid D) = \dfrac{P(A \cap D)}{P(D)} = \dfrac{20/306}{109/306} = \dfrac{20}{109} = .183$

3.121   Define the following events:

S_1: {Salesman makes sale on the first visit}
S_2: {Salesman makes a sale on the second visit}

$P(S_1) = .4 \qquad P(S_2 \mid S_1^c) = .65$

The sample points of the experiment are:

$S_1 \cap S_2^c$, $S_1^c \cap S_2$, $S_1^c \cap S_2^c$

The probability the salesman will make a sale is:

$$P(S_1 \cap S_2^c) + P(S_1^c \cap S_2) = P(S_1) + P(S_2 \mid S_1^c)P(S_1^c) = .4 + .65(1 - .4) = .4 + .39 = .79$$

3.123 a. Suppose we let the four positions in a sample point represent in order (1) Raise a broad mix of crops, (2) Raise livestock, (3) Use chemicals sparingly, and (4) Use techniques for regenerating the soil, such as crop rotation. A farmer is either likely (L) to engage in an activity or unlikely (U). The possible classifications are:

LLLL   LLLU   LLUL   LULL   ULLL   LLUU   LULU   LUUL   ULLU   ULUL   UULL
LUUU   ULUU   UULU   UUUL   UUUU

  b. Since there are 16 classifications or sample points and all are equally likely, then each has a probability of 1/16.

$$P(UUUU) = \frac{1}{16}$$

  c. The probability that a farmer will be classified as likely on at least three criteria is

$$P(LLLL) + P(LLLU) + P(LLUL) + P(LULL) + P(ULLL) = 5\left(\frac{1}{16}\right) = \frac{5}{16}.$$

3.125 a. The tree diagram would be:

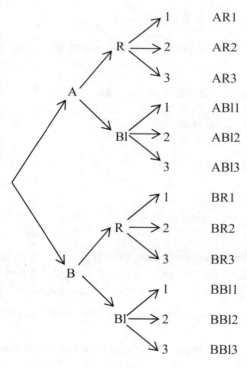

  b. No. If black color TVs are in higher demand then red TVs, then the probabilities involving black TVs should be higher than the probabilities involving the ref TVs with similar characteristics.

3.127 The probability of a false positive is $P(A \mid B)$.

3.129   Define the following events:

A: {Press is correctly adjusted}
B: {Press is incorrectly adjusted}
D: {part is defective}

From the exercise, $P(A) = .90$, $P(D \mid A) = .05$, and. We also know that event B is the complement of event A. Thus, $P(B) = 1 - P(A) = 1 - .90 = .10$.

$$P(B \mid D) = \frac{P(B \cap D)}{P(D)} = \frac{P(D \mid B)P(B)}{P(D \mid B)P(B) + P(D \mid A)P(A)} = \frac{.50(.10)}{.50(.10) + .05(.90)} = \frac{.05}{.05 + .045} = \frac{.05}{.095} = .526$$

3.131   Define the flowing events:

A: {Dealer draws a blackjack}
B: {Player draws a blackjack}

a.   For the dealer to draw a blackjack, he needs to draw an ace and a face card. There are

$$\binom{4}{1} = \frac{4!}{1!(4-1)!} = \frac{4 \cdot 3 \cdot 2 \cdot 1}{1 \cdot 3 \cdot 2 \cdot 1} = 4 \text{ ways to draw an ace and}$$

$$\binom{12}{1} = \frac{12!}{1!(12-1)!} = \frac{12 \cdot 11 \cdot 10 \cdots 1}{1 \cdot 11 \cdot 10 \cdot 9 \cdots 1} = 12 \text{ ways to draw a face card (there are 12 face cards in the deck).}$$

The total number of ways a dealer can draw a blackjack is $4 \cdot 12 = 48$.

The total number of ways a dealer can draw 2 cards is

$$\binom{52}{2} = \frac{52!}{2!(52-2)!} = \frac{52 \cdot 51 \cdot 50 \cdots 1}{2 \cdot 1 \cdot 50 \cdot 49 \cdot 48 \cdots 1} = 1326.$$

Thus, the probability that the dealer draws a blackjack is $P(A) = \dfrac{48}{1326} = .0362$.

b.   In order for the player to win with a blackjack, the player must draw a blackjack and the dealer does not. Using our notation, this is the event $B \cap A^C$. We need to find the probability that the player draws a blackjack $(P(B))$ and the probability that the dealer does not draw a blackjack given the player does $\left(P(A^c \mid B)\right)$. Then, the probability that the player wins with a blackjack is $P(A^c \mid B)P(B)$.

The probability that the player draws a blackjack is the same as the probability that the dealer draws a blackjack, which is $P(B) = .0362$.

There are 5 scenarios where the dealer will not draw a blackjack given the player does. First, the dealer could draw an ace and not a face card. Next, the dealer could draw a face card and not an ace. Third, the dealer could draw two cards that are not aces or face cards. Fourth, the dealer could draw two aces, and finally, the dealer could draw two face cards.

The number of ways the dealer could draw an ace and not a face card given the player draws a blackjack is

$$\binom{3}{1}\binom{36}{1} = \frac{3!}{1!(3-1)!} \cdot \frac{36!}{1!(36-1)!} = \frac{3\cdot2\cdot1}{1\cdot2\cdot1} \cdot \frac{36\cdot35\cdot34\cdots1}{1\cdot35\cdot34\cdot33\cdots1} = 3(36) = 108$$

(Note: Given the player has drawn blackjack, there are only 3 aces left and 36 non-face cards.)

The number of ways the dealer could draw a face card and not an ace given the player draws a blackjack is

$$\binom{11}{1}\binom{36}{1} = \frac{11!}{1!(11-1)!} \cdot \frac{36!}{1!(36-1)!} = \frac{11\cdot10\cdot9\cdots1}{1\cdot10\cdot9\cdot8\cdots1} \cdot \frac{36\cdot35\cdot34\cdots1}{1\cdot35\cdot34\cdot33\cdots1} = 11(36) = 396$$

The number of ways the dealer could draw neither a face card nor an ace given the player draws a blackjack is

$$\binom{36}{2} = \frac{36!}{2!(36-2)!} = \frac{36\cdot35\cdot34\cdots1}{2\cdot1\cdot34\cdot33\cdot32\cdots1} = 630$$

The number of ways the dealer could draw two aces given the player draws a blackjack is

$$\binom{3}{2} = \frac{3!}{2!(3-2)!} = \frac{3\cdot2\cdot1}{2\cdot1\cdot1} = 3$$

The number of ways the dealer could draw two face cards given the player draws a blackjack is

$$\binom{11}{2} = \frac{11!}{2!(11-2)!} = \frac{11\cdot10\cdot9\cdots1}{2\cdot9\cdot8\cdot7\cdots1} = 55$$

The total number of ways the dealer can draw two cards given the player draws a blackjack is

$$\binom{50}{2} = \frac{50!}{2!(50-2)!} = \frac{50\cdot49\cdot48\cdots1}{2\cdot1\cdot48\cdot47\cdot46\cdots1} = 1225$$

The probability that the dealer does not draw a blackjack given the player draws a   blackjack is

$$P(A^c \mid B) = \frac{108 + 396 + 630 + 3 + 55}{1225} = \frac{1192}{1225} = .9731$$

Finally, the probability that the player wins with a blackjack is

$$P(B \cap A^c) = P(A^c \mid B)P(B) = .9731(.0362) = .0352$$

3.133   First, we will list all possible sample points for placing a car (C) and 2 goats (G) behind doors #1, #2, and #3. If the first position corresponds to door #1, the second position corresponds to door #2, and the third position corresponds to door #3, the sample space is:

(*C G G*) (*G C G*) (*G G C*)

Now, suppose you pick door #1. Initially, the probability that you will win the car is 1/3 – only one of the sample points has a car behind door #1.

The host will now open a door behind which is a goat. If you pick door #1 in the first sample point ($C\,G\,G$), the host will open either door #2 or door #3. Suppose he opens door #3 (it really does not matter). If you pick door #1 in the second sample point ($G\,C\,G$), the host will open door #3. If you pick door #1 in the third sample point ($G\,G\,C$), the host will open door #2. Now, the new sample space will be:

$(C\,G)$ $(G\,C)$ $(G\,C)$

where the first position corresponds to door #1 (the one you chose) and the second position corresponds to the door that was not opened by the host.

Now, if you keep door #1, the probability that you win the car is 1/3. However, if you switch to the remaining door, the probability that you win the car is now 2/3. Based on these probabilities, it is to your advantage to switch doors.

The above could be repeated by selecting door #2 initially or door #3 initially. In either of these cases, again, the probability of winning the car is 1/3 if you do not switch and 2/3 if you switch. Thus, Marilyn was correct.

Chapter 4
Random Variables
and Probability Distributions

4.1   a.   The number of newspapers sold by New York Times each month can take on a countable number of values. Thus, this is a discrete random variable.

      b.   The amount of ink used in printing the Sunday edition of the New York Times can take on an infinite number of different values. Thus, this is a continuous random variable.

      c.   The actual number of ounces in a one gallon bottle of laundry detergent can take on an infinite number of different values. Thus, this is a continuous random variable.

      d.   The number of defective parts in a shipment of nuts and bolts can take on a countable number of values. Thus, this is a discrete random variable.

      e.   The number of people collecting unemployment insurance each month can take on a countable number of values. Thus, this is a discrete random variable.

4.3   Since there are only a fixed number of outcomes to the experiment, the random variable, x, the number of stars in the rating, is discrete.

4.5   The variable x, total compensation in 2015 (in $ millions), is a continuous random variable.

4.7   An economist might be interested in the percentage of the work force that is unemployed, or the current inflation rate, both of which are continuous random variables.

4.9   The manager of a clothing store might be concerned with the number of employees on duty at a specific time of day, or the number of articles of a particular type of clothing that are on hand.

4.11   a. $p(22) = .25$

      b. $P(x = 20 \text{ or } x = 24) = P(x = 20) + P(x = 24) = .15 + .20 = .35$

      c. $P(x \le 23) = P(x = 20) + P(x = 21) + P(x = 22) + P(x = 23) = .15 + .10 + .25 + .30 = .80$

4.13   a.   We know $\sum p(x) = 1$. Thus, $p(2) + p(3) + p(5) + p(8) + p(10) = 1$
        $\Rightarrow p(5) = 1 - p(2) - p(3) - p(8) - p(10) = 1 - .15 - .10 - .25 - .25 = .25$

      b. $P(x = 2 \text{ or } x = 10) = P(x = 2) + P(x = 10) = .15 + .25 = .40$

      c. $P(x \le 8) = P(x = 2) + P(x = 3) + P(x = 5) + P(x = 8) = .15 + .10 + .25 + .25 = .75$

4.15   a.   When a die is tossed, the number of spots observed on the upturned face can be 1, 2, 3, 4, 5, or 6. Since the six sample points are equally likely, each one has a probability of 1/6.

The probability distribution of x may be summarized in tabular form:

x	1	2	3	4	5	6
$p(x)$	$\dfrac{1}{6}$	$\dfrac{1}{6}$	$\dfrac{1}{6}$	$\dfrac{1}{6}$	$\dfrac{1}{6}$	$\dfrac{1}{6}$

b.   The probability distribution of x may also be presented in graphical form:

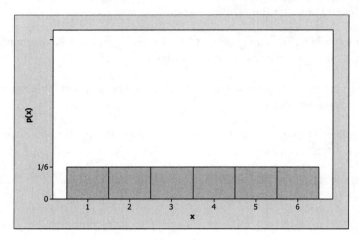

4.17   a.
$$\mu = E(x) = \sum xp(x) = -4(.02) + (-3)(.07) + (-2)(.10) + (-1)(.15) + 0(.3)$$
$$+ 1(.18) + 2(.10) + 3(.06) + 4(.02)$$
$$= -.08 - .21 - .2 - .15 + 0 + .18 + .2 + .18 + .08 = 0$$

$$\sigma^2 = E\left[(x-\mu)^2\right] = \sum (x-\mu)^2 p(x)$$
$$= (-4-0)^2(.02) + (-3-0)^2(.07) + (-2-0)^2(.10)$$
$$+ (-1-0)^2(.15) + (0-0)^2(.30) + (1-0)^2(.18)$$
$$+ (2-0)^2(.10) + (3-0)^2(.06) + (4-0)^2(.02)$$
$$= .32 + .63 + .4 + .15 + 0 + .18 + .4 + .54 + .32 = 2.94$$

$$\sigma = \sqrt{2.94} = 1.715$$

b.　Using MINITAB, the graph is:

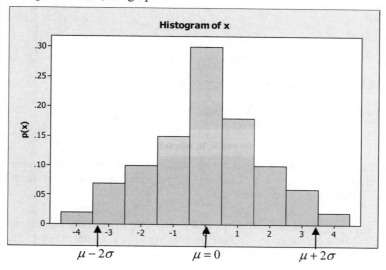

$$\mu \pm 2\sigma \Rightarrow 0 \pm 2(1.715) \Rightarrow 0 \pm 3.430 \Rightarrow (-3.430, 3.430)$$

c.　$P(-3.430 < x < 3.430) = p(-3) + p(-2) + p(-1) + p(0) + p(1) + p(2) + p(3)$
$$= .07 + .10 + .15 + .30 + .18 + .10 + .06 = .96$$

4.19　a.　It would seem that the mean of both would be 1 since they both are symmetric distributions centered at 1.

　　　b.　$P(x)$ seems more variable since there appears to be greater probability for the two extreme values of 0 and 2 than there is in the distribution of y.

　　　c.　For x: $\mu = E(x) = \sum xp(x) = 0(.3) + 1(.4) + 2(.3) + = 0 + .4 + .6 = 1$

$$\sigma^2 = E\left[(x-\mu)^2\right] = \sum (x-\mu)^2 \, p(x)$$
$$= (0-1)^2(.3) + (1-1)^2(.4) + (2-1)^2(.3) = .3 + 0 + .3 = .6$$

For y: $\mu = E(y) = \sum yp(y) = 0(.1) + 1(.8) + 2(.1) + = 0 + .8 + .2 = 1$

$$\sigma^2 = E\left[(y-\mu)^2\right] = \sum (y-\mu)^2 \, p(y)$$
$$= (0-1)^2(.1) + (1-1)^2(.8) + (2-1)^2(.1) = .1 + 0 + .1 = .2$$

The variance for x is larger than that for y.

4.21　a.　The probability distribution for x is found by converting the Percent column to a probability column by dividing the percents by 100. The probability distribution of x is:

x	$p(x)$
2	.0408
3	.1735
4	.6020
5	.1837

b. $P(x = 5) = p(5) = .1837$.

c. $P(x \le 2) = p(2) = .0408$.

d. $\mu = E(x) = \sum_{i=1}^{4} x_i p(x_i) = 2(.0408) + 3(.1735) + 4(.6020) + 5(.1837)$

$= .0816 + .5205 + 2.4080 + .9185 = 3.9286 \approx 3.93$

The average star rating for a car's drivers-side star rating is 3.93.

4.23   a.   In order for this to be a valid probability distribution, all probabilities must be between 0 and 1 and the sum of all the probabilities must be 1. For Section 1, all the probabilities are between 0 and 1. The sum of all the probabilities is $.05 + .25 + .25 + .45 = 1.00$.

b.   For Section 2, all the probabilities are between 0 and 1. The sum of all the probabilities is $.10 + .25 + .35 + .30 = 1.00$. For Section 3, all the probabilities are between 0 and 1. The sum of all the probabilities is $.15 + .20 + .30 + .35 = 1.00$.

c. $P(x > 30) = P(x = 40) + P(x = 50) + P(x = 60) = .25 + .25 + .45 = .95$

d.   For Section 2, $P(x > 30) = P(x = 40) + P(x = 50) + P(x = 60) = .25 + .35 + .30 = .90$. For Section 3, $P(x > 30) = P(x = 40) + P(x = 50) + P(x = 60) = .20 + .30 + .35 = .85$

4.25   a.   The possible values of x are 0, 2, 3, and 4.

b.   To find the probability distribution of x, we first find the frequency distribution of x. We then divide the frequencies by $n = 106$ to get the probabilities. The probability distribution of x is:

x	0	2	3	4
$f(x)$	35	58	5	8
$p(x)$	.3302	.5472	.0472	.0755

c. $\mu = E(x) = \sum xp(x) = 0(.3302) + 2(.5472) + 3(.0472) + 4(.0755) = 1.538$. For all social robots, the average number of legs on the robot is 1.538.

4.27   a.   The random variable x is a discrete random variable because it can take on only values 0, 1, 2, 3, 4, or 5 in this example.

b. $p(0) = \dfrac{5!(.65)^0 (.35)^{5-0}}{0!(5-0)!} = \dfrac{5 \cdot 4 \cdot 3 \cdot 2 \cdot 1(1)(.35)^5}{1 \cdot 5 \cdot 4 \cdot 3 \cdot 2 \cdot 1} = (.35)^5 = .0053$

$p(1) = \dfrac{5!(.65)^1 (.35)^{5-1}}{1!(5-1)!} = \dfrac{5 \cdot 4 \cdot 3 \cdot 2 \cdot 1(.65)^1 (.35)^4}{1 \cdot 4 \cdot 3 \cdot 2 \cdot 1} = 5(.65)(.35)^4 = .0488$

$p(2) = \dfrac{5!(.65)^2 (.35)^{5-2}}{2!(5-2)!} = \dfrac{5 \cdot 4 \cdot 3 \cdot 2 \cdot 1(.65)^2 (.35)^3}{2 \cdot 1 \cdot 3 \cdot 2 \cdot 1} = 10(.65)^2 (.35)^3 = .1811$

$$p(3) = \frac{5!(.65)^3(.35)^{5-3}}{3!(5-3)!} = \frac{5\cdot4\cdot3\cdot2\cdot1(.65)^3(.35)^2}{3\cdot2\cdot1\cdot2\cdot1} = 10(.65)^3(.35)^2 = .3364$$

$$p(4) = \frac{5!(.65)^4(.35)^{5-4}}{4!(5-4)!} = \frac{5\cdot4\cdot3\cdot2\cdot1(.65)^4(.35)^1}{4\cdot3\cdot2\cdot1\cdot1} = 5(.65)^4(.35)^1 = .3124$$

$$p(5) = \frac{5!(.65)^5(.35)^{5-5}}{5!(5-5)!} = \frac{5\cdot4\cdot3\cdot2\cdot1(.65)^5(.35)^0}{5\cdot4\cdot3\cdot2\cdot1\cdot1} = (.65)^5 = .1160$$

c. The two properties of discrete random variables are that $0 \le p(x) \le 1$ for all x and $\sum p(x)=1$. From above, all probabilities are between 0 and 1 and

$$\sum p(x) = .0053+.0488+.1811+.3364+.3124+.1160 = 1$$

d. $P(x \ge 4) = p(4)+p(5) = .3124+.1160 = .4284$

4.29 a. $p(1) = .23(.77)^{1-1} = .23(.77)^0 = .23$. The probability that one would encounter a contaminated cartridge on the first trial is .23.

b. $p(5) = .23(.77)^{5-1} = .23(.77)^4 = .0809$. The probability that one would encounter a the first contaminated cartridge on the fifth trial is .0809.

c. $P(x \ge 2) = 1-P(x \le 1) = 1-P(x=1) = 1-.23 = .77$. The probability that the first contaminated cartridge is found on the second trial or later is .77.

4.31 a. $$p(0) = \frac{\binom{20}{0}\binom{100-20}{3-0}}{\binom{100}{3}} = \frac{\frac{20!}{0!(20-0)!}\frac{80!}{3!(80-3)!}}{\frac{100!}{3!(100-3)!}} = \frac{\frac{20!}{0!20!}\frac{80!}{3!77!}}{\frac{100!}{3!97!}} = \frac{82,160}{161,700} = .508$$

b. $$p(1) = \frac{\binom{20}{1}\binom{100-20}{3-1}}{\binom{100}{3}} = \frac{\frac{20!}{1!(20-1)!}\frac{80!}{2!(80-2)!}}{\frac{100!}{3!(100-3)!}} = \frac{\frac{20!}{1!19!}\frac{80!}{2!78!}}{\frac{100!}{3!97!}} = \frac{63,200}{161,700} = .391$$

c. $$p(2) = \frac{\binom{20}{2}\binom{100-20}{3-2}}{\binom{100}{3}} = \frac{\frac{20!}{2!(20-2)!}\frac{80!}{1!(80-1)!}}{\frac{100!}{3!(100-3)!}} = \frac{\frac{20!}{2!18!}\frac{80!}{1!79!}}{\frac{100!}{3!97!}} = \frac{15,200}{161,700} = .094$$

d. $$p(3) = \frac{\binom{20}{3}\binom{100-20}{3-0}}{\binom{100}{3}} = \frac{\frac{20!}{3!(20-3)!}\frac{80!}{0!(80-0)!}}{\frac{100!}{3!(100-3)!}} = \frac{\frac{20!}{3!17!}\cdot1}{\frac{100!}{3!97!}} = \frac{1,140}{161,700} = .007$$

4.33   To find the probability distribution of x, we sum the probabilities associated with the same value of x. The probability distribution is:

x	8.5	9	9.5	10	10.5	11	12
$p(x)$	.462189	.288764	.141671	.069967	.025236	.011657	.000518

4.35   a.   Let x = the potential flood damages. Since we are assuming if it rains the business will incur damages and if it does not rain the business will not incur any damages, the probability distribution of x is:

x	0	300,000
$p(x)$	.7	.3

   b.   The expected loss due to flood damage is
   $$\mu = E(x) = \sum xp(x) = 0(.7) + 300,000(.3) = 0 + 90,000 = \$90,000$$

4.37   a.   The possible values of x are 30, 40, 50, or 60.

   b. $P(x = 30) = P(x = 30 \,|\, \text{Section 1})P(\text{Section 1}) + P(x = 30 \,|\, \text{Section 2})P(\text{Section 2})$
   $$+ P(x = 30 \,|\, \text{Section 3})P(\text{Section 3})$$
   $$= .05\left(\frac{1}{3}\right) + .10\left(\frac{1}{3}\right) + .15\left(\frac{1}{3}\right) = .10$$

   c. $P(x = 40) = P(x = 40 \,|\, \text{Section 1})P(\text{Section 1}) + P(x = 40 \,|\, \text{Section 2})P(\text{Section 2})$
   $$+ P(x = 40 \,|\, \text{Section 3})P(\text{Section 3})$$
   $$= .25\left(\frac{1}{3}\right) + .25\left(\frac{1}{3}\right) + .20\left(\frac{1}{3}\right) = .2333$$

   $P(x = 50) = P(x = 50 \,|\, \text{Section 1})P(\text{Section 1}) + P(x = 50 \,|\, \text{Section 2})P(\text{Section 2})$
   $$+ P(x = 50 \,|\, \text{Section 3})P(\text{Section 3})$$
   $$= .25\left(\frac{1}{3}\right) + .35\left(\frac{1}{3}\right) + .30\left(\frac{1}{3}\right) = .30$$

   $P(x = 60) = P(x = 60 \,|\, \text{Section 1})P(\text{Section 1}) + P(x = 60 \,|\, \text{Section 2})P(\text{Section 2})$
   $$+ P(x = 60 \,|\, \text{Section 3})P(\text{Section 3})$$
   $$= .45\left(\frac{1}{3}\right) + .30\left(\frac{1}{3}\right) + .35\left(\frac{1}{3}\right) = .3667$$

   Thus, the probability distribution of x is

x	30	40	50	60
$p(x)$	.1000	.2333	.3000	.3667

   d. $P(x \geq 50) = p(50) + p(60) = .3000 + .3667 = .6667$

4.39   Let x = bookie's earnings per dollar wagered. Then x can take on values $1 (you lose) and $-5 (you win). The only way you win is if you pick 3 winners in 3 games. If the probability of picking 1 winner in 1 game is .5, then $P(www) = p(w)p(w)p(w) = .5(.5)(.5) = .125$ (assuming games are independent).

Thus, the probability distribution for x is:

x	$p(x)$
$\$1$	.875
$\$-5$	.125

$$E(x) = \sum xp(x) = 1(.875) - 5(.125) = .875 - .625 = \$.25$$

4.41   a. x is discrete. It can take on only six values.

b.   This is a binomial distribution.

c. $p(0) = \binom{5}{0}(.7)^0(.3)^{5-0} = \frac{5!}{0!5!}(.7)^0(.3)^5 = \frac{5 \cdot 4 \cdot 3 \cdot 2 \cdot 1}{1 \cdot 5 \cdot 4 \cdot 3 \cdot 2 \cdot 1}(1)(.00243) = .00243$

$p(1) = \binom{5}{1}(.7)^1(.3)^{5-1} = \frac{5!}{1!4!}(.7)^1(.3)^4 = .02835$ $p(2) = \binom{5}{2}(.7)^2(.3)^{5-2} = \frac{5!}{2!3!}(.7)^2(.3)^3 = .1323$

$p(3) = \binom{5}{3}(.7)^3(.3)^{5-3} = \frac{5!}{3!2!}(.7)^3(.3)^2 = .3087$ $p(4) = \binom{5}{4}(.7)^4(.3)^{5-4} = \frac{5!}{4!1!}(.7)^4(.3)^1 = .36015$

$p(5) = \binom{5}{5}(.7)^5(.3)^{5-5} = \frac{5!}{5!0!}(.7)^5(.3)^0 = .16807$

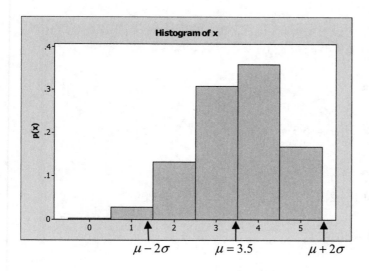

d. $\mu = np = 5(.7) = 3.5$ $\sigma = \sqrt{npq} = \sqrt{5(.7)(.3)} = 1.0247$

e. $\mu \pm 2\sigma \Rightarrow 3.5 \pm 2(1.0247) \Rightarrow 3.5 \pm 2.0494 \Rightarrow (1.4506, 5.5494)$

4.43   a. $P(x = 1) = \frac{5!}{1!4!}(.2)^1(.8)^4 = \frac{5 \cdot 4 \cdot 3 \cdot 2 \cdot 1}{1 \cdot 4 \cdot 3 \cdot 2 \cdot 1}(.2)^1(.8)^4 = 5(.2)^1(.8)^4 = .4096$

b. $P(x=2) = \dfrac{4!}{2!2!}(.6)^2(.4)^2 = \dfrac{4\cdot 3\cdot 2\cdot 1}{2\cdot 1\cdot 2\cdot 1}(.6)^2(.4)^2 = 6(.6)^2(.4)^2 = .3456$

c. $P(x=0) = \dfrac{3!}{0!3!}(.7)^0(.3)^3 = \dfrac{3\cdot 2\cdot 1}{1\cdot 3\cdot 2\cdot 1}(.7)^0(.3)^3 = 1(.7)^0(.3)^3 = .027$

d. $P(x=3) = \dfrac{5!}{3!2!}(.1)^3(.9)^2 = \dfrac{5\cdot 4\cdot 3\cdot 2\cdot 1}{3\cdot 2\cdot 1\cdot 2\cdot 1}(.1)^3(.9)^2 = 10(.1)^3(.9)^2 = .0081$

e. $P(x=2) = \dfrac{4!}{2!2!}(.4)^2(.6)^2 = \dfrac{4\cdot 3\cdot 2\cdot 1}{2\cdot 1\cdot 2\cdot 1}(.4)^2(.6)^2 = 6(.4)^2(.6)^2 = .3456$

f. $P(x=1) = \dfrac{3!}{1!2!}(.9)^1(.1)^2 = \dfrac{3\cdot 2\cdot 1}{1\cdot 2\cdot 1}(.9)^1(.1)^2 = 3(.9)^1(.1)^2 = .027$

4.45   a. $\mu = np = 25(.5) = 12.5$

$\sigma^2 = np(1-p) = 25(.5)(.5) = 6.25$ and $\sigma = \sqrt{\sigma^2} = \sqrt{6.25} = 2.5$

b. $\mu = np = 80(.2) = 16$

$\sigma^2 = np(1-p) = 80(.2)(.8) = 12.8$ and $\sigma = \sqrt{\sigma^2} = \sqrt{12.8} = 3.578$

c. $\mu = np = 100(.6) = 60$

$\sigma^2 = np(1-p) = 100(.6)(.4) = 24$ and $\sigma = \sqrt{\sigma^2} = \sqrt{24} = 4.899$

d. $\mu = np = 70(.9) = 63$

$\sigma^2 = np(1-p) = 70(.9)(.1) = 6.3$ and $\sigma = \sqrt{\sigma^2} = \sqrt{6.3} = 2.510$

e. $\mu = np = 60(.8) = 48$
$\sigma^2 = np(1-p) = 60(.8)(.2) = 9.6$ and $\sigma = \sqrt{\sigma^2} = \sqrt{9.6} = 3.098$

f. $\mu = np = 1,000(.04) = 40$

$\sigma^2 = np(1-p) = 1,000(.04)(.96) = 38.4$ and $\sigma = \sqrt{\sigma^2} = \sqrt{38.4} = 6.197$

4.47   a.   Let S = adult who does not work while on summer vacation.

b.   To see if x is approximately a binomial random variable we check the characteristics:

   1. n identical trials. Although the trials are not exactly identical, they are close. Taking a sample of reasonable size n from a very large population will result in trials being essentially identical.

2. Two possible outcomes. The adults can either not work on their summer vacation or they can work on their summer vacation. S = adult does not work on summer vacation and F = adult does work on summer vacation.

3. $P(S)$ remains the same from trial to trial. If we sample without replacement, then $P(S)$ will change slightly from trial to trial. However, the differences are extremely small and will essentially be 0.

4. Trials are independent. Again, although the trials are not exactly independent, they are very close.

5. The random variable x = number of adults who work on their summer vacation in $n = 10$ trials.

Thus, x is very close to being a binomial. We will assume that it is a binomial random variable.

c. For this problem, $p = .22$.

d. Using MINITAB $n = 10$ and $p = .22$, the probability is:

Probability Density Function
```
Binomial with n = 10 and p = 0.22

x   P( X = x )
3     0.224446
```

Thus, $P(x = 3) = .2244$.

e. Using MINITAB $n = 10$ and $p = .22$, the probability is:

Cumulative Distribution Function
```
Binomial with n = 10 and p = 0.22

x   P( X <= x )
2      0.616880
```
Thus, $P(x \le 2) = P(x = 0) + P(x = 1) + P(x = 2) = .6169$.

4.49 a. Let x = number of hotel guests who are delighted with their experience and would definitely recommend the hotel in 15 trials. To see if x is approximately a binomial random variable we check the characteristics:

1. n identical trials. Although the trials are not exactly identical, they are close. Taking a sample of reasonable size 15 from a very large population will result in trials being essentially identical.

2. Two possible outcomes. The hotel guests can either be delighted with their experience and would definitely recommend the hotel or not. S = hotel guest is delighted with his/her experience and would definitely recommend the hotel and F = hotel guest is not delighted with his/her experience and/or would not recommend the hotel.

3. $P(S)$ remains the same from trial to trial. If we sample without replacement, then $P(S)$ will change slightly from trial to trial. However, the differences are extremely small and will essentially be 0.

4. Trials are independent. Again, although the trials are not exactly independent, they are very close.

5. The random variable x = number of hotel guests who are delighted with their experience and would definitely recommend the hotel in $n = 15$ trials.

Thus, x is very close to being a binomial. We will assume that it is a binomial random variable.

b. $p = P(S)$

$= P(\text{hotel guest was delighted with experience}) P(\text{Hotel guest would definitely recommend the hotel})$

$= .15(.80) = .12$

c.   For $p = .10$, $P(x \geq 10) = 1 - P(x \leq 9) = 1 - 1 = 0$ using Table I, Appendix D.

4.51   a.   Let x = number of adults who participated in youth and/or high school sports who have an income greater than \$100,000 in 25 adults. Then x is a binomial random variable with $n = 25$ and $p = .15$. Using MINITAB, with $n = 25$ and $p = .15$, the probability is:

Cumulative Distribution Function
```
Binomial with n = 25 and p = 0.15

  x   P( X ≤ x )
 19            1
```

Thus, $P(x < 20) = P(x \leq 19) = 1.0000$.

b.   **Cumulative Distribution Function**
```
Binomial with n = 25 and p = 0.15

  x   P( X ≤ x )
 10    0.999505        1
```

Thus, $P(10 < x < 20) = P(x \leq 19) - P(x \leq 10) = 1.0000 - .9995 = .0005$.

c.   Let x = number of adults who did not participate in youth and/or high school sports who have an income greater than \$100,000 in 25 adults. Then x is a binomial random variable with $n = 25$ and $p = .09$. Using MINITAB, with $n = 25$ and $p = .09$, the probability is:

Cumulative Distribution Function
```
Binomial with n = 25 and p = 0.09

  x   P( X ≤ x )
 19     1.00000
```
Thus, $P(x < 20) = P(x \leq 19) = 1.0000$.

Cumulative Distribution Function
```
Binomial with n = 25 and p = 0.09

  x   P( X ≤ x )
 10     1.00000
```
Thus, $P(10 < x < 20) = P(x \leq 19) - P(x \leq 10) = 1.0000 - 1.0000 = 0.0000$.

4.53   a.   Let x = number of pairs correctly identified by an expert in 5 trials. Then x is a binomial random variable with $n = 5$ and $p = .92$. Using a MINITAB with $n = 5$ and $p = .92$, the probability is:

Probability Density Function
```
Binomial with n = 5 and p = 0.92

  x   P( X = x )
  5    0.659082
```
Thus, $P(x = 5) = .6591$.

b. Let y = number of pairs correctly identified by a novice in 5 trials. Then y is a binomial random variable with $n = 5$ and $p = .75$. Using MINITAB with $n = 5$ and $p = .75$, the probability is:

Probability Density Function
```
Binomial with n = 5 and p = 0.75

x   P( X = x )
5     0.237305
```

Thus, $P(x = 5) = .2373$.

4.55   Let x = number of major bridges in Denver that will have a rating of 4 or below in 2020 in 10 trials. Then x has an approximate binomial distribution with $n = 10$ and $p = .09$.

a. $P(x \geq 3) = 1 - P(x \leq 2) = 1 - P(x = 0) - P(x = 1) - P(x = 2)$

$$= 1 - \binom{10}{0}.09^0(.91)^{10-0} - \binom{10}{1}.09^1(.91)^{10-1} - \binom{10}{2}.09^2(.91)^{10-2}$$

$$= 1 - \frac{10!}{0!10!}.09^0.91^{10} - \frac{10!}{1!9!}.09^1.91^9 - \frac{10!}{2!8!}.09^2.91^8 = 1 - .3894 - .3851 - .1714 = .0541$$

b. Since the probability of seeing at least 3 bridges out of 10 with ratings of 4 or less is so small, we can conclude that the forecast of 9% of all major Denver bridges will have ratings of 4 or less in 2020 is too small. There would probably be more than 9%.

4.57   a. $\mu = np = 800(.85) = 680$, $\sigma = \sqrt{npq} = \sqrt{800(.85)(.15)} = \sqrt{102} = 10.100$

b. $z = \dfrac{x - \mu}{\sigma} = \dfrac{400 - 680}{10.1} = -27.72$

No. It would be extremely unlikely to observe less than half without traces of pesticide because the z-score associated with 400 is so far below the mean.

4.59   a. We must assume that the probability that a specific type of ball meets the requirements is always the same from trial to trial and the trials are independent. To use the binomial probability distribution, we need to know the probability that a specific type of golf ball meets the requirements.

b. For a binomial distribution, $\mu = np$ and $\sigma = \sqrt{npq}$.

In this example, n = two dozen = $2(12) = 24$, $p = .10$, and $q = 1 - .10 = .90$.
(Success here means the golf ball *does not* meet standards.)

$\mu = np = 24(.10) = 2.4$ and $\sigma = \sqrt{npq} = \sqrt{24(.10)(.90)} = 1.47$

c. In this situation, $n = 24$, p = Probability of success = Probability golf ball *does* meet standards = .90, and $q = 1 - .90 = .10$.

$E(y) = \mu = np = 24(.90) = 21.6$ and $\sigma = \sqrt{npq} = \sqrt{24(.10)(.90)} = 1.47$
(Note that σ is the same as in part **b**.)

4.61   a.   The random variable x is discrete since it can assume a countable number of values (0, 1, 2, ...).

b.   This is a Poisson probability distribution with $\lambda = 3$.

c.   In order to graph the probability distribution, we need to know the probabilities for the possible values of x. Using MINITAB with $\lambda = 3$:

Probability Density Function
```
Poisson with mean = 3

 x   P( X = x )
 0     0.049787
 1     0.149361
 2     0.224042
 3     0.224042
 4     0.168031
 5     0.100819
 6     0.050409
 7     0.021604
 8     0.008102
 9     0.002701
10     0.000810
```

Using MINITAB, the probability distribution of x in graphical form is:

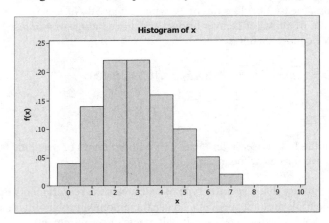

d. $\mu = \lambda = 3$

$\sigma^2 = \lambda = 3$ and $\sigma = \sqrt{3} = 1.7321$

4.63   a. $P(x=1) = \dfrac{\binom{r}{x}\binom{N-r}{n-x}}{\binom{N}{n}} = \dfrac{\binom{3}{1}\binom{5-3}{3-1}}{\binom{5}{3}} = \dfrac{\frac{3!}{1!2!}\frac{2!}{2!0!}}{\frac{5!}{3!2!}} = \dfrac{3(1)}{10} = .3$

b. $P(x=3) = \dfrac{\binom{r}{x}\binom{N-r}{n-x}}{\binom{N}{n}} = \dfrac{\binom{3}{3}\binom{9-3}{5-3}}{\binom{9}{5}} = \dfrac{\frac{3!}{3!0!}\frac{6!}{2!4!}}{\frac{9!}{5!4!}} = \dfrac{1(15)}{126} = .119$

c. $$P(x=2) = \frac{\binom{r}{x}\binom{N-r}{n-x}}{\binom{N}{n}} = \frac{\binom{2}{2}\binom{4-2}{2-2}}{\binom{4}{2}} = \frac{\frac{2!}{2!0!}\frac{2!}{0!2!}}{\frac{4!}{2!2!}} = \frac{1(1)}{6} = .167$$

d. $$P(x=0) = \frac{\binom{r}{x}\binom{N-r}{n-x}}{\binom{N}{n}} = \frac{\binom{2}{0}\binom{4-2}{2-0}}{\binom{4}{2}} = \frac{\frac{2!}{0!2!}\frac{2!}{2!0!}}{\frac{4!}{2!2!}} = \frac{1(1)}{6} = .167$$

4.65   a.   Using MINITAB with $\lambda = 1$, and the Poisson distribution, the probability is:

Cumulative Distribution Function
```
Poisson with mean = 1

x    P( X <= x )
2       0.919699
```

$P(x \le 2) = .919699$

b.   Using MINITAB with $\lambda = 2$, and the Poisson distribution, the probability is:

Cumulative Distribution Function
```
Poisson with mean = 2

x    P( X <= x )
2       0.676676
```

$P(x \le 2) = .676676$

c.   Using MINITAB with $\lambda = 3$, and the Poisson distribution, the probability is:

Cumulative Distribution Function
```
Poisson with mean = 3

x    P( X <= x )
2       0.423190
```

$P(x \le 2) = .42319$

d.   The probability decreases as λ increases. This is reasonable because λ is equal to the mean. As the mean increases, the probability that x is less than a particular value will decrease.

4.67   For this problem, $N = 100$, $n = 10$, and $x = 4$.

a.   If the sample is drawn without replacement, the hypergeometric distribution should be used. The hypergeometric distribution requires that sampling be done without replacement.

b.   If the sample is drawn with replacement, the binomial distribution should be used. The binomial distribution requires that sampling be done with replacement.

4.69 a. The characteristics of a binomial random variable are:

1. n identical trials. We are selecting 10 robots from 106. On the first trial, we are selecting 1 robot out of 106. On the next trial, we are selecting 1 robot out of 105. On the 10th trial, we are selecting 1 robot out of 97. These trials are not identical.

2. Two possible outcomes. A selected robot either has no legs or wheels or it has some legs or wheels. S = robot has no legs or wheels and F = robot has either legs and/or wheels. This condition is met.

3. $P(S)$ remains the same from trial to trial. For this example the probability of success does not stay constant. On the first trial, there are 106 robots of which 15 have neither legs nor wheels. Thus, $P(S)$ on the first trial is 15/106. If a robot with neither legs nor wheels is selected on the first trial, then $P(S)$ on the second trial would be 14/105. If a robot with neither legs nor wheels is not selected on the first trial, then $P(S)$ on the second trial would be 15/105. The value of $P(S)$ is not constant from trial to trial. This condition is not met.

4. Trials are independent. The trials are not independent. The type of robot selected on one trial affects the type of robot selected on the next trial. This condition is not met.

5. The random variable x = number of robots selected that do not have legs or wheels in 10 trials.

The necessary conditions for a binomial random variable are not met.

b. The characteristics of a hypergeometric random variable are:

1. The experiment consists of randomly drawing n elements without replacement from a set of N elements, r of which are successes and $(N - r)$ of which are failures. For this example there are a total of $N = 106$ robots, of which $r = 15$ have neither legs nor wheels and $N - r = 106 - 15 = 95$ have some legs and/or wheels. We are selecting $n = 10$ robots.

2. The hypergeometric random variable x is the number of successes in the draw of n elements. For this example, x = number of robots selected with no legs or wheels in 20 selections.

c. $\mu = \dfrac{nr}{N} = \dfrac{10(15)}{106} = 1.415$ and

$$\sigma = \sqrt{\frac{r(N-r)n(N-n)}{N^2(N-1)}} = \sqrt{\frac{15(106-15)10(106-10)}{106^2(106-1)}} = \sqrt{1.1107} = 1.0539$$

d. $P(x=2) = \dfrac{\binom{15}{2}\binom{106-15}{10-2}}{\binom{106}{10}} = \dfrac{\dfrac{15!}{2!(15-2)!}\dfrac{91!}{8!(91-8)!}}{\dfrac{106!}{10!(106-10)!}} = \dfrac{105(8.49869\times10^{12})}{3.18535\times10^{13}} = .2801$

4.71 a. For Poisson random variable x, $\lambda = 1$. $P(x=1) = \dfrac{1^1 e^{-1}}{1!} = .368$

b. $P(x=1) = \dfrac{1^1 e^{-1}}{1!} = .368$

c. $E(x) = \mu = \lambda = 1$, $\sigma = \sqrt{\lambda} = \sqrt{1} = 1$

4.73   Let x = number of "clean" cartridges selected in 5 trials. For this problem, $N = 158$, $n = 5$, and $r = 122$.

$$P(x = 5) = \frac{\binom{r}{x}\binom{N-r}{n-x}}{\binom{N}{n}} = \frac{\binom{122}{5}\binom{36}{0}}{\binom{158}{5}} = \frac{\frac{122!}{5!117!}\frac{36!}{0!36!}}{\frac{158!}{5!153!}} = .2693$$

4.75   Let x = number of times "total visitors" is selected in 5 museums. For this exercise, x has a hypergeometric distribution with $N = 30$, $n = 5$, $r = 8$ and $x = 0$.

$$P(x = 0) = \frac{\binom{8}{0}\binom{30-8}{5-0}}{\binom{30}{5}} = \frac{\frac{8!}{0!(8-0)!}\frac{22!}{5!(22-5)!}}{\frac{30!}{5!(30-5)!}} = .1848$$

4.77   Let x = number of times cell phone accesses color code "b" in 7 handoffs. For this problem, x has a hypergeometric distribution with $N = 85$, $n = 7$, and $r = 40$.

$$P(x = 2) = \frac{\binom{40}{2}\binom{85-40}{7-2}}{\binom{85}{7}} = \frac{\frac{40!}{2!(40-2)!}\frac{45!}{5!(45-5)!}}{\frac{85!}{7!(85-7)!}} = \frac{780(1,221,759)}{4,935,847,320} = .1931$$

4.79   Let x = number of flaws in a 4 meter length of wire. For this exercise, x has a Poisson distribution with $\lambda = .8$. The roll will be rejected if there is at least one flaw in the sample of a 4 meter length of wire.

$$P(x \geq 1) = 1 - P(x = 0) = 1 - \frac{.8^0 e^{-.8}}{0!} = 1 - .4493 = .5507$$

We have to assume that the flaws are randomly distributed throughout the roll of wire and that the 4 meter sample of wire is representative of the entire roll.

4.81   Let x = number of females promoted in the 72 employees awarded promotion, where x is a hypergeometric random variable. From the problem, $N = 302$, $n = 72$, and $r = 73$. We need to find if observing 5 females who were promoted was fair.

$$E(x) = \mu = \frac{nr}{N} = \frac{72(73)}{302} = 17.40$$

If 72 employees are promoted, we would expect that about 17 would be females.

$$V(x) = \sigma^2 = \frac{r(N-r)n(N-n)}{N^2(N-1)} = \frac{73(302-73)72(302-72)}{302^2(302-1)} = 10.084, \quad \sigma = \sqrt{10.084} = 3.176$$

Using Chebyshev's Theorem, we know that at least 8/9 of all observations will fall within 3 standard deviations of the mean. The interval from 3 standard deviations below the mean to 3 standard deviations above the mean is:

$$\mu \pm 3\sigma \Rightarrow 17.40 \pm 3(3.176) \Rightarrow 17.40 \pm 9.528 \Rightarrow (7.872, 26.928)$$

If there is no discrimination in promoting females, then we would expect between 8 and 26 females to be promoted within the group of 72 employees promoted. Since we observed only 5 females promoted, we would infer that females were not promoted fairly.

4.83   a. $P(y = 0) = P(n = 0) = \dfrac{1.1^0 e^{-1.1}}{0!} = .333$

   b. $P(y = 1) = P(n = 1 \cap x_1 = 1) = P(n = 1) P(x_1 = 1) = \dfrac{1.1^1 e^{-1.1}}{1!}(.4) = (.333)(.4) = .133$

4.85   Using Table II, Appendix D:

   a. $P(z > 1.46) = .5 - P(0 < z < 1.46) = .5 - .4279 = .0721$

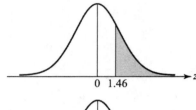

   b. $P(z < -1.56) = .5 - P(-1.56 < z < 0) = .5 - .4406 = .0594$

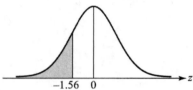

   c. $P(.67 \le z \le 2.41) = P(0 < z \le 2.41) - P(0 < z < .67)$
            $= .4920 - .2486 = .2434$

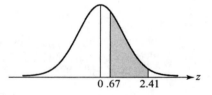

   d. $P(-1.96 \le z \le -.33) = P(-1.96 \le z < 0) - P(-.33 \le z < 0)$
            $= .4750 - .1293 = .3457$

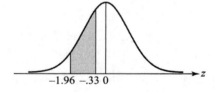

   e. $P(z \ge 0) = .5$

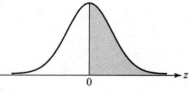

   f. $P(-2.33 < z < 1.50) = P(-2.33 < z < 0) + P(0 < z < 1.50)$
            $= .4901 + .4332 = .9233$

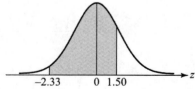

4.87   Using Table II, Appendix D:

a. $P(-1 \le z \le 1) = P(-1 \le z \le 0) + P(0 \le z \le 1)$
$= .3413 + .3413 = .6826$

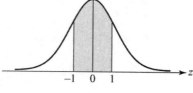

b. $P(-1.96 \le z \le 1.96) = P(-1.96 \le z \le 0) + P(0 \le z \le 1.96)$
$= .4750 + .4750 = .9500$

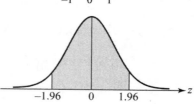

c. $P(-1.645 \le z \le 1.645) = P(-1.645 \le z \le 0) + P(0 \le z \le 1.645)$
$= .4500 + .4500 = .9000$
(using interpolation)

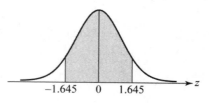

d. $P(-2 \le z \le 2) = P(-2 \le z \le 0) + P(0 \le z \le 2)$
$= .4772 + .4772 = .9544$

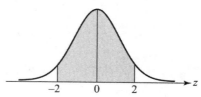

4.89   Using Table II of Appendix D:

a. $P(z \le z_0) = .2090$
$A = .5 - .2090 = .2910$
Looking up the area .2910 in the body of Table II
gives $z_0 = -.81$.   (z_0 is negative since the graph
shows z_0 is on the left side of 0.)

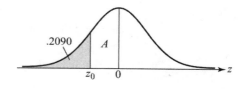

b. $P(z \le z_0) = .7090$
$P(z \le z_0) = P(z \le 0) + P(0 \le z \le z_0)$
$= .5 + P(0 \le z \le z_0) = .7090$

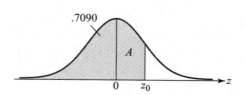

Therefore, $P(0 \le z \le z_0) = .7090 - .5 = .2090 = A$

Looking up the area .2090 in the body of Table II gives $z_0 \approx .55$.

c. $P(-z_0 \le z \le z_0) = .8472$

$P(-z_0 \le z \le z_0) = 2P(0 \le z \le z_0) = .8472$

Therefore, $P(0 \le z \le z_0) = .8472 / 2 = .4236$.

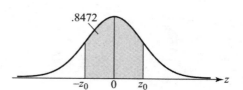

Looking up the area .4236 in the body of Table II gives $z_0 = 1.43$.

d. $P\left(-z_0 \leq z \leq z_0\right) = .1664$

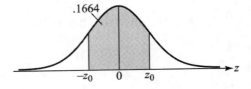

$P\left(-z_0 \leq z \leq z_0\right) = 2P\left(0 \leq z \leq z_0\right) = .1664$

Therefore, $P\left(0 \leq z \leq z_0\right) = .1664 / 2 = .0832.$

Looking up the area .0832 in the body of Table II gives $z_0 = .21.$

e. $P\left(z_0 \leq z \leq 0\right) = .4798$

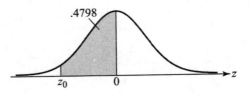

$P\left(z_0 \leq z \leq 0\right) = P\left(0 \leq z \leq -z_0\right)$

Looking up the area .4798 in the body of Table II gives $z_0 = -2.05.$

f. $P\left(-1 < z < z_0\right) = .5328$

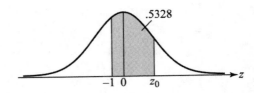

$P\left(-1 < z < z_0\right) = P\left(-1 < z < 0\right) + P\left(0 < z < z_0\right) = .5328$

$P\left(0 < z < 1\right) + P\left(0 < z < z_0\right) = .5328$

Thus, $P\left(0 < z < z_0\right) = .5328 - .3413 = .1915.$

Looking up the area .1915 in the body of Table II gives $z_0 = .50.$

4.91   a. $z = \dfrac{x - \mu}{\sigma} = \dfrac{20 - 30}{4} = -2.50$

b. $z = \dfrac{x - \mu}{\sigma} = \dfrac{30 - 30}{4} = 0$

c. $z = \dfrac{x - \mu}{\sigma} = \dfrac{27.5 - 30}{4} = -0.625$

d. $z = \dfrac{x - \mu}{\sigma} = \dfrac{15 - 30}{4} = -3.75$

e. $z = \dfrac{x - \mu}{\sigma} = \dfrac{35 - 30}{4} = 1.25$

f. $z = \dfrac{x - \mu}{\sigma} = \dfrac{25 - 30}{4} = -1.25$

4.93 a.
$$P(10 \le x \le 12) = P\left(\frac{10-11}{2} \le z \le \frac{12-11}{2}\right)$$

$$= P(-0.50 \le z \le 0.50) = A_1 + A_2 = .1915 + .1915 = .3830$$

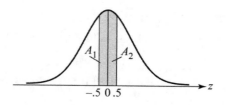

b.
$$P(6 \le x \le 10) = P\left(\frac{6-11}{2} \le z \le \frac{10-11}{2}\right) = P(-2.50 \le z \le -0.50)$$

$$= P(-2.50 \le z \le 0) - P(-0.50 \le z \le 0) = .4938 - .1915 = .3023$$

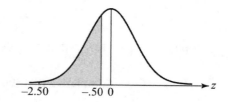

c.
$$P(13 \le x \le 16) = P\left(\frac{13-11}{2} \le z \le \frac{16-11}{2}\right) = P(1.00 \le z \le 2.50)$$

$$= P(0 \le z \le 2.50) - P(0 \le x \le 1.00) = .4938 - .3413 = .1525$$

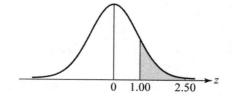

d.
$$P(7.8 \le x \le 12.6) = P\left(\frac{7.8-11}{2} \le z \le \frac{12.6-11}{2}\right)$$

$$= P(-1.60 \le z \le 0.80) = A_1 + A_2 = .4452 + .2881 = .7333$$

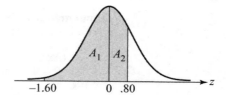

e.
$$P(x \ge 13.24) = P\left(z \ge \frac{13.24-11}{2}\right)$$

$$= P(z \ge 1.12) = A_2 = .5 - A_1 = .5000 - .3686 = .1314$$

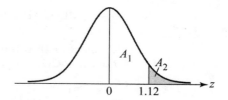

f.
$$P(x \ge 7.62) = P\left(z \ge \frac{7.62-11}{2}\right)$$

$$= P(z \ge -1.69) = A_1 + A_2 = .4545 + .5000 = .9545$$

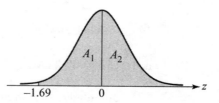

4.95 a. In order to approximate the binomial distribution with the normal distribution, the interval $\mu \pm 3\sigma \Rightarrow np \pm 3\sqrt{npq}$ should lie in the range 0 to n.

When $n = 25$ and $p = .4$,

$$np \pm 3\sqrt{npq} \Rightarrow 25(.4) \pm 3\sqrt{25(.4)(1-.4)} \Rightarrow 10 \pm 3\sqrt{6} \Rightarrow 10 \pm 7.3485 \Rightarrow (2.6515, 17.3485)$$

Since the interval calculated does lie in the range 0 to 25, we can use the normal approximation.

b. $\mu = np = 25(.4) = 10$ and $\sigma^2 = npq = 25(.4)(.6) = 6$

c. $P(x \geq 9) = 1 - P(x \leq 8) = 1 - .274 = .726$ (Table I, Appendix D)

d. $P(x \geq 9) \approx P\left(z \geq \dfrac{(9-.5)-10}{\sqrt{6}}\right)$

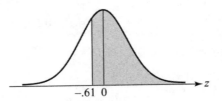

$= P(z \geq -.61) = .5000 + .2291 = .7291$
(Using Table II, Appendix D.)

4.97   a.   Using MINITAB with $\mu = 1.5$ and $\sigma = .2$, the probability is:

Cumulative Distribution Function
```
Normal with mean = 1.5 and standard deviation = 0.2

  x   P( X ≤ x )
1.6    0.691462
1.3    0.158655
```

$P(1.3 < x < 1.6) = P(x < 1.6) - P(x < 1.3) = .691462 - .158655 = .532807$

b.   Using MINITAB with $\mu = 1.5$ and $\sigma = .2$, the probability is:

Cumulative Distribution Function
```
Normal with mean = 1.5 and standard deviation = 0.2

  x   P( X ≤ x )
1.4    0.308538
```

$P(x > 1.4) = 1 - P(x < 1.4) = 1 - .308538 = .691462$

c.   Using MINITAB with $\mu = 1.5$ and $\sigma = .2$, the probability is:

Cumulative Distribution Function
```
Normal with mean = 1.5 and standard deviation = 0.2

  x   P( X ≤ x )
1.5    0.308538
```

$P(x < 1.5) = .5$

4.99   a.   Using MINITAB with $\mu = 105.3$ and $\sigma = 8$, the probability is:

Cumulative Distribution Function
```
Normal with mean = 105.3 and standard deviation = 8

  x   P( X <= x )
120    0.966932
```

$P(x > 120) = 1 - P(x \leq 120) = 1 - .966932 = .033068$

b.   Using MINITAB with $\mu = 105.3$ and $\sigma = 8$, the probabilities are:

Cumulative Distribution Function
Normal with mean = 105.3 and standard deviation = 8

```
   x   P( X <= x )
110     0.721566
100     0.253825
```

$$P(100 < x < 110) = P(x < 110) - P(x \le 100) = .721566 - .253825 = .467741$$

c. Using MINITAB with $\mu = 105.3$ and $\sigma = 8,$ the value of a is found:

Inverse Cumulative Distribution Function
Normal with mean = 105.3 and standard deviation = 8

```
P( X <= x )        x
      0.25   99.9041
```

Thus, $a = 99.9041$.

4.101 a. Using MINITAB with $\mu = 59$ and $\sigma = 5,$ the probability is:

Cumulative Distribution Function
Normal with mean = 59 and standard deviation = 5

```
  x   P( X <= x )
60      0.579260
```

$$P(x > 60) = 1 - P(x \le 60) = 1 - .57926 = .42074$$

b. Using MINITAB with $\mu = 43$ and $\sigma = 5,$ the probability is:

Cumulative Distribution Function
Normal with mean = 43 and standard deviation = 5

```
  x   P( X <= x )
60      0.999663
```

$$P(x > 60) = 1 - P(x \le 60) = 1 - .999663 = .000337$$

4.103 a. For $n = 700$ and $p = .25,$ $\mu = np = 700(.25) = 175.$

b. $\sigma = \sqrt{npq} = \sqrt{700(.25)(.75)} = \sqrt{131.25} = 11.4564$

c. $z = \dfrac{x - \mu}{\sigma} = \dfrac{200 - 175}{11.4564} = 2.18$

d. $P(x \le 200) = P\left(z \le \dfrac{(200 + .5) - 175}{11.4564}\right) = P(z \le 2.23) = .5 + .4871 = .9871$ using Table II, Appendix D

4.105 For $\mu = 13.93$ and $\sigma = 21.65,$ we want to find k such that $P(x > k) = .80.$

First, we find z_0 that corresponds to $P(z > z_0) = .80$ or $P(z_0 < z < 0) = .30.$ Using Table II, Appendix D, $z_0 = -.84.$

Thus, $z_0 = \dfrac{k-\mu}{\sigma} \Rightarrow -.84 = \dfrac{k-13.93}{21.65} \Rightarrow -18.186 = k - 13.93 \Rightarrow k = -4.256\%$

4.107   Let x = number of defects per million. Then x has an approximate normal distribution with $\mu = 3$. Using Table II, Appendix D,

$$P(3 - 1.5\sigma \le x \le 3 + 1.5\sigma) = P\left(\frac{3 - 1.5\sigma - 3}{\sigma} \le z \le \frac{3 + 1.5\sigma - 3}{\sigma}\right) = P(-1.5 \le z \le 1.5) = .4332 + .4332 = .8664$$

It is fairly likely that the goal will be met. Since the probability is .8664, the goal would be met approximately 86.64% of the time.

4.109   a. $\mu = np = 200(.12) = 24$, $\sigma = \sqrt{npq} = \sqrt{200(.12)(.88)} = \sqrt{21.12} = 4.5957$

$$P(x > 50) = P\left(z > \frac{(50 + .5) - 24}{4.5957}\right) = P(z > 5.77) \approx 0$$

If the true probability that a hotel guest was delighted with their stay and would recommend the hotel is .12, it would be extremely unlikely that more than 50 out of 200 guests were delighted with their stay and would recommend the hotel.

b.   In order for the claim to be true, the probability that a hotel guest was delighted with their stay and would recommend the hotel would have to be much larger than .12.

4.111   a.   Using Table II, Appendix D, with $\mu = 75$ and $\sigma = 7.5$,

$$P(x > 80) = P\left(z > \frac{80 - 75}{7.5}\right) = P(z > .67) = .5 - .2486 = .2514$$

Thus, 25.14% of the scores exceeded 80.

b. $P(x \le x_0) = .98$. Find x_0.

$P(x \le x_0) = P\left(z \le \dfrac{x_0 - 75}{7.5}\right) = P(z \le z_0) = .98$

$A_1 = .98 - .5 = .4800$

Looking up area .4800 in Table II, $z_0 = 2.05$.

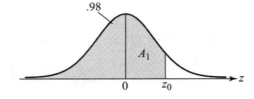

$z_0 = \dfrac{x_0 - 75}{7.5} \Rightarrow 2.05 = \dfrac{x_0 - 75}{7.5} \Rightarrow x_0 = 90.375$

4.113   b.   Let v = number of credit/debit card users out of 100 who carry Visa. Then v is a binomial random variable with $n = 100$ and $p_v = .59$.

$E(v) = np_v = 100(.59) = 59$

Let d = number of credit/debit card users out of 100 who carry Discover. Then d is a binomial random variable with $n = 100$ and $p_d = .02$.

$$E(d) = np_d = 100(.09) = 9$$

c. To see if the normal approximation is valid, we use:

$$\mu \pm 3\sigma \Rightarrow np_v \pm 3\sqrt{np_v q_v} \Rightarrow 100(.59) \pm 3\sqrt{100(.59)(.41)} \Rightarrow 59 \pm 3(4.918)$$
$$\Rightarrow 59 \pm 14.754 \Rightarrow (44.246,\ 73.754)$$

Since the interval lies in the range 0 to 100, we can use the normal approximation to approximate the probability.

$$P(v \ge 50) \approx P\left(z \ge \frac{(50-.5)-59}{4.918}\right) = P(z \ge -1.93) = .5 + .4732 = .9732$$

Let a = number of credit/debit card users out of 100 who carry American Express. Then a is a binomial random variable with $n = 100$ and $p_a = .13$. To see if the normal approximation is valid, we use:

$$\mu \pm 3\sigma \Rightarrow np_a \pm 3\sqrt{np_a q_a} \Rightarrow 100(.13) \pm 3\sqrt{100(.13)(.87)} \Rightarrow 13 \pm 3(3.363)$$
$$\Rightarrow 13 \pm 10.089 \Rightarrow (2.911,\ 23.089)$$

Since the interval lies in the range 0 to 100, we can use the normal approximation to approximate the probability.

$$P(a \ge 50) \approx P\left(z \ge \frac{(50-.5)-13}{3.363}\right) = P(z \ge 10.85) \approx .5 - .5 = 0$$

d. In order for the normal approximation to be valid, $\mu \pm 3\sigma$ must lie in the interval $(0, n)$. This check was done in part **c** for both portions of the question. The normal approximation was justified for both parts.

4.115 We have to find the probability of observing $x = .7$ or anything more unusual given the two different values of μ.

Without receiving executive coaching: Using Table II, Appendix D with $\mu = .75$ and $\sigma = .085$,

$$P(x \le .7) = P\left(z \le \frac{.7 - .75}{.085}\right) = P(z \le -.59) = .5 - .2224 = .2776.$$

After receiving executive coaching: Using Table II, Appendix D with $\mu = .52$ and $\sigma = .075$,

$$P(x \ge .7) = P\left(z \ge \frac{.7 - .52}{.075}\right) = P(z \ge 2.40) = .5 - .4918 = .0082.$$

Since the probability of observing $x \le .7$ for those not receiving executive coaching is much larger than the probability of $x \ge .7$ for those receiving executive coaching, it is more likely that the leader did not receive executive coaching.

4.117   a.   The proportion of measurements that one would expect to fall in the interval $\mu \pm \sigma$ is about .68.

        b.   The proportion of measurements that one would expect to fall in the interval $\mu \pm 2\sigma$ is about .95.

        c.   The proportion of measurements that one would expect to fall in the interval $\mu \pm 3\sigma$ is about 1.00.

4.119   If the data are normally distributed, then the normal probability plot should be an approximate straight line. Of the three plots, only plot **c** implies that the data are normally distributed. The data points in plot **c** form an approximately straight line. In both plots **a** and **b**, the plots of the data points do not form a straight line.

4.121   a.   For data that are normally distributed, the ratio IQR / s should be approximately 1.3. The ratio for contestants who played for a job, the ratio is $IQR / s = 7 / 4.324 = 1.62$. This number is close to 1.3. Therefore, the data are approximately normally distributed.

        b.   The ratio for contestants who played for a business partnership, the ratio is $IQR / s = 7 / 4.809 = 1.456$. This number is close to 1.3. Therefore, the data are approximately normally distributed.

4.123   a.   If the data are normal, then approximately 68% of the observations should fall within 1 standard deviation of the mean. For this data, the interval is $\bar{x} \pm s \Rightarrow 89.2906 \pm 3.1834 \Rightarrow (86.1072, 92.4740)$. There are 34 out of the 50 observations in this interval which is $34 / 50 = .68$ or 68%. This is exactly the 68%.

        If the data are normal, then approximately 95% of the observations should fall within 2 standard deviations of the mean. For this data, the interval is $\bar{x} \pm 2s \Rightarrow 89.2906 \pm 2(3.1834) \Rightarrow 89.2906 \pm 6.3668 \Rightarrow (82.9238, 95.6574)$. There are 48 out of the 50 observations in this interval which is $48 / 50 = .96$ or 96%. This is very close to the 95%.

        If the data are normal, then approximately 100% of the observations should fall within 3 standard deviations of the mean. For this data, the interval is $\bar{x} \pm 3s \Rightarrow 89.2906 \pm 3(3.1834) \Rightarrow 89.2906 \pm 9.5502 \Rightarrow (79.7404, 98.8408)$. There are 50 out of the 50 observations in this interval which is $50 / 50 = 1.00$ or 100%. This is exactly the 100%.

        Since these percents are very close to percentages for the normal distribution, this indicates that the data are approximately normal.

        The $IQR = Q_U - Q_L = 91.88 - 87.2725 = 4.6075$ and the standard deviation is $s = 3.1834$. If the data are normal, then $\dfrac{IQR}{s} \approx 1.3$. For this data, $\dfrac{IQR}{s} = \dfrac{4.6075}{3.1834} = 1.447$. This is fairly close to 1.3. This indicates that the data are approximately normal.

        b.   The data on the plot are fairly close to a straight line. This indicates that the data are approximately normal.

4.125   a.   Using MINITAB, a histogram of the data is:

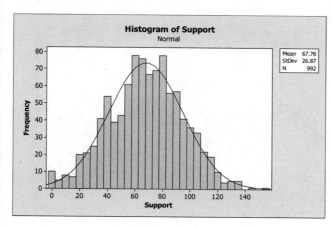

The data are fairly mound-shaped. This indicates that the data are probably from a normal distribution.

b.   Using MINITAB, the descriptive statistics are:

Descriptive Statistics: Support
Variable	N	Mean	StDev	Minimum	Q1	Median	Q3	Maximum
Support	992	67.755	26.871	0.000000000	49.000	68.000	86.000	155.000

If the data are normal, then approximately 68% of the observations should fall within 1 standard deviation of the mean. For this data, the interval is $\bar{x} \pm s \Rightarrow 67.755 \pm 26.871 \Rightarrow (40.884, 94.626)$. There are 665 out of the 992 observations in this interval which is $665 / 992 = .670$ or 67%. This is very close to the 68%.

If the data are normal, then approximately 95% of the observations should fall within 2 standard deviations of the mean. For this data, the interval is
$\bar{x} \pm 2s \Rightarrow 67.755 \pm 2(26.871) \Rightarrow 67.755 \pm 53.742 \Rightarrow (14.013, 121.497)$. There are 946 out of the 992 observations in this interval which is $946 / 992 = .954$ or 95.4%. This is very close to the 95%.

If the data are normal, then approximately 100% of the observations should fall within 3 standard deviations of the mean. For this data, the interval is
$\bar{x} \pm 3s \Rightarrow 67.755 \pm 3(26.871) \Rightarrow 67.755 \pm 80.613 \Rightarrow (-12.858, 148.368)$. There are 991 out of the 992 observations in this interval which is $991 / 992 = .999$ or 99.9%. This is very close to the 100%.

Since these percents are very close to percentages for the normal distribution, this indicates that the data are probably from a normal distribution.

c.   The $IQR = Q_U - Q_L = 86 - 49 = 37$ and the standard deviation is $s = 26.871$. If the data are normal, then $\dfrac{IQR}{s} \approx 1.3$. For this data, $\dfrac{IQR}{s} = \dfrac{37}{26.871} = 1.377$. This is very close to 1.3. This indicates that the data probably come from a normal distribution.

d.   Using MINITAB, the normal probability plot is:

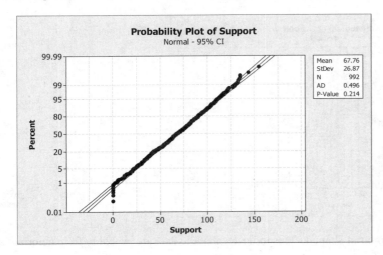

Except for the several 0's on the left of the plot, the data are very close to a straight line. This again indicates that the data probably come from a normal distribution.

4.127   Using MINITAB, a histogram of the data is:

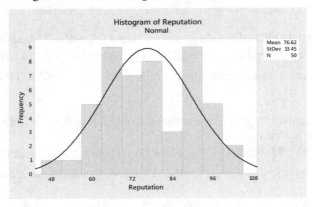

The data are not particularly mound-shaped. This indicates that the data may not be from a normal distribution.

Using MINITAB, the descriptive statistics are:

Descriptive Statistics: Reputation

Variable	N	Mean	StDev	Minimum	Q1	Median	Q3	Maximum
Reputation	50	76.62	13.45	47.00	64.75	76.00	89.50	100.00

If the data are normal, then approximately 68% of the observations should fall within 1 standard deviation of the mean. For this data, the interval is $\bar{x} \pm s \Rightarrow 76.62 \pm 13.45 \Rightarrow (63.17, 90.07)$. There are 30 out of the 50 observations in this interval which is $30/50 = .6$ or 60%. This is somewhat smaller than the 68% we would expect.

If the data are normal, then approximately 95% of the observations should fall within 2 standard deviations of the mean. For this data, the interval is $\bar{x} \pm s \Rightarrow 76.62 \pm 2(13.45) \Rightarrow 76.62 \pm 26.9 \Rightarrow (49.72, 103.52)$. There are 49 out of the 50 observations in this interval which is $49/50 = .98$ or 98%. This is somewhat larger than the 95% we would expect.

If the data are normal, then approximately 100% of the observations should fall within 3 standard deviations of the mean. For this data, the interval is $\bar{x} \pm s \Rightarrow 76.62 \pm 3(13.45) \Rightarrow 76.62 \pm 40.35 \Rightarrow (36.27, 116.97)$. All of the 100 observations are in this interval which is 100%. This equal to the 100% we would expect.

Since these percents are not very close to percentages for the normal distribution, this indicates that the data may not be from a normal distribution.

The $IQR = Q_U - Q_L = 89.5 - 64.75 = 24.75$ and the standard deviation is $s = 13.45$. If the data are normal, then $\dfrac{IQR}{s} \approx 1.3$. For this data, $\dfrac{IQR}{s} = \dfrac{24.75}{13.45} = 1.84$. This is somewhat larger than what we would expect if the data were normally distributed.

Using MINITAB, the normal probability plot is:

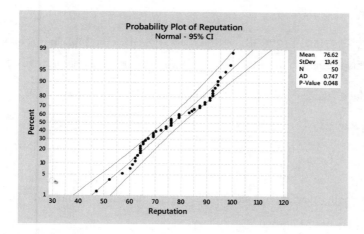

The data do not form a real straight line. This again indicates that the data probably do not come from a normal distribution.

4.129   We will look at the 4 methods or determining if the 3 variables are normal.

Distance:
First, we will look at A histogram of the data. Using MINITAB, the histogram of the distance data is:

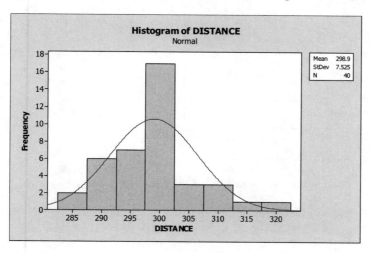

From the histogram, the distance data do not appear to have a normal distribution.

Next, we look at the intervals $\bar{x} \pm s,\ \bar{x} \pm 2s,\ \bar{x} \pm 3s$. If the proportions of observations falling in each interval are approximately .68, .95, and 1.00, then the data are approximately normal. Using MINITAB, the summary statistics are:

Descriptive Statistics: DISTANCE, ACCURACY, INDEX
```
Variable   N     Mean   StDev  Minimum    Q1  Median     Q3  Maximum
DISTANCE  40   298.95    7.53   283.20 294.60  299.05 302.00   318.90
```

$\bar{x} \pm s \Rightarrow 298.95 \pm 7.53 \Rightarrow (291.42,\ 306.48)$ 28 of the 40 values fall in this interval. The proportion is $28/40 = .70$. This is fairly close to the .68 we would expect if the data were normal.

$\bar{x} \pm 2s \Rightarrow 298.95 \pm 2(7.53) \Rightarrow 298.95 \pm 15.06 \Rightarrow (283.89,\ 314.01)$ 37 of the 40 values fall in this interval. The proportion is $37/40 = .925$. This is a fair amount below the .95 we would expect if the data were normal.

$\bar{x} \pm 3s \Rightarrow 298.95 \pm 3(7.53) \Rightarrow 298.95 \pm 22.59 \Rightarrow (276.36,\ 321.54)$ 40 of the 40 values fall in this interval. The proportion is $40/40 = 1.00$. This is equal to the 1.00 we would expect if the data were normal.

From this method, it appears that the distance data may not be normal.

Next, we look at the ratio of the *IQR* to *s*.

$IQR = Q_U - Q_L = 302 - 294.6 = 7.4$

$\dfrac{IQR}{s} = \dfrac{7.4}{7.53} = .983$. This is much smaller than the 1.3 we would expect if the data were normal. This method indicates the distance data may not be normal.

Finally, using MINTAB, the normal probability plot is:

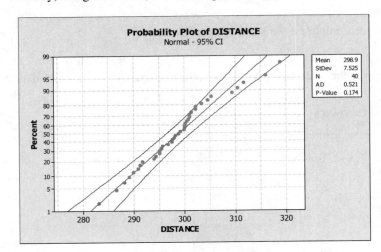

Since the data do not form a fairly straight line, the distance data may not be normal.

From the 4 different methods, all indications are that the distance data are not normal.

Accuracy:
First, we will look at a histogram of the data. Using MINITAB, the histogram of the accuracy data is:

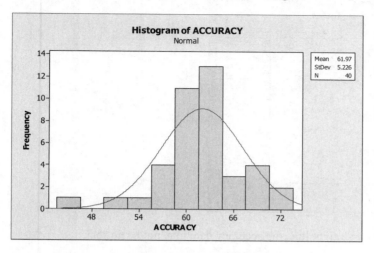

From the histogram, the accuracy data do not appear to have a normal distribution.

Descriptive Statistics: DISTANCE, ACCURACY, INDEX
```
Variable    N    Mean   StDev  Minimum     Q1  Median       Q3  Maximum
ACCURACY   40  61.970   5.226   45.400  59.400  61.950   64.075   73.000
```

$\bar{x} \pm s \Rightarrow 61.97 \pm 5.226 \Rightarrow (56.744, 67.196)$ 30 of the 40 values fall in this interval. The proportion is $30/40 = .75$. This is much greater than the .68 we would expect if the data were normal.

$\bar{x} \pm 2s \Rightarrow 61.97 \pm 2(5.226) \Rightarrow 61.97 \pm 10.452 \Rightarrow (51.518, 72.422)$ 37 of the 40 values fall in this interval. The proportion is $37/40 = .925$. This is a fair amount below the .95 we would expect if the data were normal.

$\bar{x} \pm 3s \Rightarrow 61.97 \pm 3(5.226) \Rightarrow 61.97 \pm 15.678 \Rightarrow (46.292, 77.648)$ 39 of the 40 values fall in this interval. The proportion is $39/40 = .975$. This is a fair amount lower than the 1.00 we would expect if the data were normal.

From this method, it appears that the accuracy data may not be normal.

Next, we look at the ratio of the IQR to s.

$IQR = Q_U - Q_L = 64.075 - 59.4 = 4.675$

$\dfrac{IQR}{s} = \dfrac{4.675}{5.226} = .895$. This is much smaller than the 1.3 we would expect if the data were normal. This method indicates the accuracy data may not be normal.

Finally, using MINTAB, the normal probability plot is:

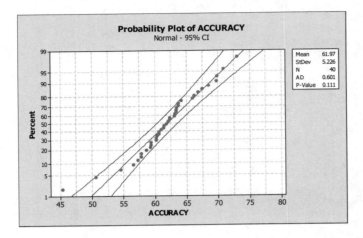

Since the data do not form a fairly straight line, the accuracy data may not be normal.

From the 4 different methods, all indications are that the accuracy data are not normal.

Index:
First, we will look at a histogram of the data. Using MINITAB, the histogram of the index data is:

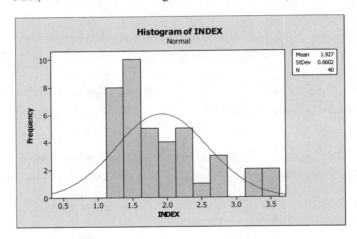

From the histogram, the index data do not appear to have a normal distribution.
Next, we look at the intervals $\bar{x} \pm s$, $\bar{x} \pm 2s$, $\bar{x} \pm 3s$. If the proportions of observations falling in each interval are approximately .68, .95, and 1.00, then the data are approximately normal. Using MINITAB, the summary statistics are:

Descriptive Statistics: DISTANCE, ACCURACY, INDEX

Variable	N	Mean	StDev	Minimum	Q1	Median	Q3	Maximum
INDEX	40	1.927	0.660	1.170	1.400	1.755	2.218	3.580

$\bar{x} \pm s \Rightarrow 1.927 \pm .660 \Rightarrow (1.267, \ 2.587)$ 30 of the 40 values fall in this interval. The proportion is $30 / 40 = .75$. This is much greater than the .68 we would expect if the data were normal.

$\bar{x} \pm 2s \Rightarrow 1.927 \pm 2(.660) \Rightarrow 1.927 \pm 1.320 \Rightarrow (.607, \ 3.247)$ 37 of the 40 values fall in this interval. The proportion is $37 / 40 = .925$. This is a fair amount below the .95 we would expect if the data were normal.

$\bar{x} \pm 3s \Rightarrow 1.927 \pm 3(.660) \Rightarrow 1.927 \pm 1.980 \Rightarrow (-.053,\ 3.907)$ 40 of the 40 values fall in this interval. The proportion is $40/40 = 1.000$. This is equal to the 1.00 we would expect if the data were normal.

From this method, it appears that the index data may not be normal.

Next, we look at the ratio of the *IQR* to *s*.

$IQR = Q_U - Q_L = 2.218 - 1.4 = .818$.

$\dfrac{IQR}{s} = \dfrac{.818}{.66} = 1.23$. This is fairly close to the 1.3 we would expect if the data were normal. This method indicates the index data may normal.

Finally, using MINTAB, the normal probability plot is:

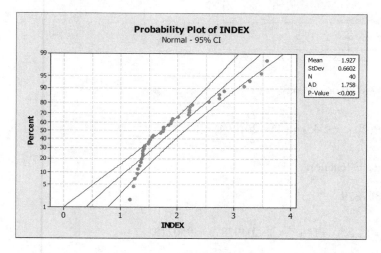

Since the data do not form a fairly straight line, the index data may not be normal.

From 3 of the 4 different methods, the indications are that the index data are not normal.

4.131   If the data are normally distributed, the distribution will be symmetric and the mean and median will be close in value. For this data set, the mean is much greater than the median, indicating the data are not normally distributed. In addition, the minimum value for the percentage of copper present in gold artifacts is 0. This value has a *z*-score of only $z = \dfrac{0 - 29.94}{28.37} = -1.06$. If the data were normally distributed, then the z-score associated with the minimum value should be around -2 to -3.Thus, it is very unlikely that the data are normally distributed.

4.133   a. $f(x) = \dfrac{1}{d-c} \qquad (c \le x \le d)$

$\dfrac{1}{d-c} = \dfrac{1}{45-20} = \dfrac{1}{25} = .04$

So, $f(x) = \begin{cases} .04 & (20 \le x \le 45) \\ 0 & \text{otherwise} \end{cases}$

b. $\mu = \dfrac{c+d}{2} = \dfrac{20+45}{2} = \dfrac{65}{2} = 32.5$ $\qquad$ $\sigma = \dfrac{d-c}{\sqrt{12}} = \dfrac{45-20}{\sqrt{12}} = 7.22$

c. Using MINITAB, the graph is:

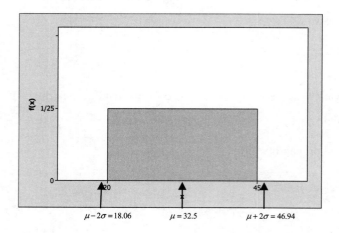

$\mu \pm 2\sigma \Rightarrow 32.5 \pm 2(7.22) \Rightarrow (18.06,\ 46.94)$

$P(18.06 < x < 46.94) = P(20 < x < 45) = (45-20)(.04) = 1$

4.135 $P(x \ge a) = e^{-a/\theta} = e^{-a/1}.$ Using a calculator:

a. $P(x > 1) = e^{-1/1} = e^{-1} = .367879$

b. $P(x \le 3) = 1 - P(x > 3) = 1 - e^{-3/1} = 1 - e^{-3} = 1 - .049787 = .950213$

c. $P(x > 1.5) = e^{-1.5/1} = e^{-1.5} = .223130$

d. $P(x \le 5) = 1 - P(x > 5) = 1 - e^{-5/1} = 1 - e^{-5} = 1 - .006738 = .993262$

4.137 $f(x) = \dfrac{1}{d-c} = \dfrac{1}{200-100} = \dfrac{1}{100} = .01$

$f(x) = \begin{cases} .01 & (100 \le x \le 200) \\ 0 & otherwise \end{cases}$

$\mu = \dfrac{c+d}{2} = \dfrac{100+200}{2} = \dfrac{300}{2} = 150$ $\qquad$ $\sigma = \dfrac{d-c}{\sqrt{12}} = \dfrac{200-100}{\sqrt{12}} = \dfrac{100}{\sqrt{12}} = 28.8675$

a. $\mu \pm 2\sigma \Rightarrow 150 \pm 2(28.8675) \Rightarrow 150 \pm 57.735 \Rightarrow (92.265,\ 207.735)$

$P(x < 92.265) + P(x > 207.735) = P(x < 100) + P(x > 200) = 0 + 0 = 0$

b.　$\mu \pm 3\sigma \Rightarrow 150 \pm 3(28.8675) \Rightarrow 150 \pm 86.6025 \Rightarrow (63.3975,\ 236.6025)$

$P(63.3975 < x < 236.6025) = P(100 < x < 200) = (200 - 100)(.01) = 1$

c.　From **a**, $\mu \pm 2\sigma \Rightarrow (92.265,\ 207.735)$.

$P(92.265 < x < 207.735) = P(100 < x < 200) = (200 - 100)(.01) = 1$

4.139　Let x = load of a cantilever beam. Then x has a uniform distribution on the interval from 100 to 115.

$$f(x) = \begin{cases} \dfrac{1}{115 - 100} = \dfrac{1}{15} & (100 \le x \le 115) \\ 0 & \text{otherwise} \end{cases}$$

a.　$P(x > 110) = (115 - 110)\left(\dfrac{1}{15}\right) = \dfrac{5}{15} = .333$

b.　$P(x < 102) = (102 - 100)\left(\dfrac{1}{15}\right) = \dfrac{2}{15} = .133$

c.　$P(x > L) = (115 - L)\left(\dfrac{1}{15}\right) = .100 \Rightarrow 115 - L = 1.5 \Rightarrow L = 113.5$

4.141　a.　Let x = temperature with no bolt-on trace elements. Then x has a uniform distribution.

$$f(x) = \dfrac{1}{d - c} \quad (c \le x \le d)$$

$$\dfrac{1}{d - c} = \dfrac{1}{290 - 260} = \dfrac{1}{30}$$

Therefore, $f(x) = \begin{cases} \dfrac{1}{30} & (260 \le x \le 290) \\ 0 & \text{otherwise} \end{cases}$

$$P(280 < x < 284) = (284 - 280)\dfrac{1}{30} = 4\left(\dfrac{1}{30}\right) = .133$$

Let y = temperature with bolt-on trace elements. Then y has a uniform distribution.

$$f(y) = \dfrac{1}{d - c} \quad (c \le y \le d)$$

$$\dfrac{1}{d - c} = \dfrac{1}{285 - 278} = \dfrac{1}{7}$$

Therefore, $f(y) = \begin{cases} \dfrac{1}{7} & (278 \le y \le 285) \\ 0 & otherwise \end{cases}$

$$P(280 < y < 284) = (284 - 280)\dfrac{1}{7} = 4\left(\dfrac{1}{7}\right) = .571$$

b. $P(x \le 268) = (268 - 260)\dfrac{1}{30} = 8\left(\dfrac{1}{30}\right) = .267$

$$P(y \le 268) = (268 - 260)(0) = 0$$

4.143   a. $P(x > 2) = e^{-2/2.5} = e^{-.8} = .449329$ (using a calculator)

b. $P(x < 5) = 1 - P(x \ge 5) = 1 - e^{-5/2.5} = 1 - e^{-2} = 1 - .135335 = .864665$ (using a calculator)

4.145   a.   For this problem, x has a uniform distribution on the interval from 0 to 1. Thus, $\mu = \dfrac{c+d}{2} = \dfrac{0+1}{2} = .5.$

b.   For this problem, $f(x) = \begin{cases} 1 & 0 \le x \le 1 \\ 0 & otherwise \end{cases}$ $P(x > .7) = (1 - .7)(1) = .3$

c.   With $n = 2$, the total possible connections is $\dbinom{2}{2} = \dfrac{2!}{2!(2-2)!} = 1.$ Thus, the density can be either 0 or 1.

Therefore, the uniform model would not be a good approximation for the distribution of network density.

4.147   a.   The amount dispensed by the beverage machine is a continuous random variable since it can take on any value between 6.5 and 7.5 ounces.

b.   Since the amount dispensed is random between 6.5 and 7.5 ounces, x is a uniform random variable.

$$f(x) = \dfrac{1}{d-c} \quad (c \le x \le d)$$

$$\dfrac{1}{d-c} = \dfrac{1}{7.5 - 6.5} = \dfrac{1}{1} = 1$$

Therefore, $f(x) = \begin{cases} 1 & (6.5 \le x \le 7.5) \\ 0 & otherwise \end{cases}$

The graph is as follows:

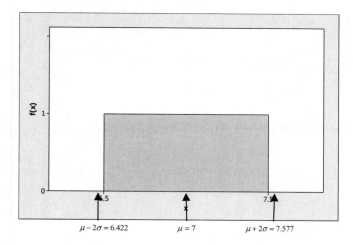

$$\mu - 2\sigma = 6.422 \qquad \mu = 7 \qquad \mu + 2\sigma = 7.577$$

c. $\mu = \dfrac{c+d}{2} = \dfrac{6.5+7.5}{2} = \dfrac{14}{2} = 7$

$\sigma = \dfrac{d-c}{\sqrt{12}} = \dfrac{7.5-6.5}{\sqrt{12}} = .2887$

$\mu \pm 2\sigma \Rightarrow 7 \pm 2(.2887) \Rightarrow 7 \pm .5774 \Rightarrow (6.422,\ 7.577)$

d. $P(x \geq 7) = (7.5-7)(1) = .5$

e. $P(x < 6) = 0$

f. $P(6.5 \leq x \leq 7.25) = (7.25-6.5)(1) = .75$

g.   The probability that the next bottle filled will contain more than 7.25 ounces is:

$P(x > 7.25) = (7.5-7.25)(1) = .25$

The probability that the next 6 bottles filled will contain more than 7.25 ounces is:

$$P\big[(x>7.25) \cap (x>7.25) \cap (x>7.25) \cap (x>7.25) \cap (x>7.25) \cap (x>7.25)\big]$$
$$= \big[P(x>7.25)\big]^6 = .25^6 = .0002$$

4.149   a.   Let x = product's lifetime at the end of its lifetime. Then x has an exponential distribution with $\mu = 500,000$.

$P(x < 700,000) = 1 - P(x \geq 700,000) = 1 - e^{-700000/5000000} = 1 - e^{-1.4} = 1 - .246597 = .753403$

b.   Let y = product's lifetime during its normal life. Then y has a uniform distribution.

$f(y) = \dfrac{1}{d-c}$ for $(c \leq y \leq d)$

$$\frac{1}{d-c} = \frac{1}{1,000,000 - 100,000} = \frac{1}{900,000}$$

Therefore, $f(y) = \begin{cases} \dfrac{1}{900,000} & (100,000 \le y \le 1,000,000) \\ 0 & \textit{otherwise} \end{cases}$

$$P(y < 700,000) = (700,000 - 100,000)\left(\frac{1}{900,000}\right) = .667$$

c. $P(x < 830,000) = 1 - P(x \ge 830,000) = 1 - e^{-830000/5000000} = 1 - e^{-1.66} = 1 - .190139 = .809861$
(Using a calculator)

$$P(y < 830,000) = (830,000 - 100,000)\left(\frac{1}{900,000}\right) = .811$$

4.151   Let x = number of inches a gouge is from one end of the spindle. Then x has a uniform distribution with $f(x)$ as follows:

$$f(x) = \begin{cases} \dfrac{1}{d-c} = \dfrac{1}{18-0} = \dfrac{1}{18} & 0 \le x \le 18 \\ 0 & \textit{otherwise} \end{cases}$$

In order to get at least 14 consecutive inches without a gouge, the gouge must be within 4 inches of either end. Thus, we must find:

$$P(x < 4) + P(x > 14) = (4-0)(1/18) + (18-14)(1/18) = 4/18 + 4/18 = 8/18 = .4444$$

4.153   Let x be a random variable with an exponential distribution with mean θ. Let k = median of the distribution. Then $P(x > k) = .5$. We now need to find k.

$$P(x > k) = .5 \Rightarrow e^{-k/\theta} = .5 \Rightarrow -k/\theta = \ln(.5)$$
$$\Rightarrow k = -\theta \ln(.5) = .693147\theta$$

4.155   a.   For $\theta = 250$, $P(x > a) = e^{-a/250}$

For $a = 300$ and $b = 200$, show $P(x > a + b) \ge P(x > a)P(x > b)$

$$P(x > 300 + 200) = P(x > 500) = e^{-500/250} = e^{-2} = .1353$$

$$P(x > 300)P(x > 200) = e^{-300/250}e^{-200/250} = e^{-1.2}e^{-.8} = .3012(.4493) = .1353$$

Since $P(x > 300 + 200) = P(x > 300)P(x > 200)$, then $P(x > 300 + 200) \ge P(x > 300)P(x > 200)$

Also, show $P(x > 300 + 200) \le P(x > 300)P(x > 200)$. Since we already showed that $P(x > 300 + 200) = P(x > 300)P(x > 200)$, then $P(x > 300 + 200) \le P(x > 300)P(x > 200)$.

b. Let $a = 50$ and $b = 100$. Show $P(x > a + b) \leq P(x > a)P(x > b)$

$P(x > 50 + 100) = P(x > 150) = e^{-150/250} = e^{-.6} = .5488$

$P(x > 50)P(x > 100) = e^{-50/250}e^{-100/250} = e^{-.2}e^{-.4} = .8187(.6703) = .5488$

Since $P(x > 50 + 100) = P(x > 50)P(x > 100)$, then $P(x > 50 + 100) \geq P(x > 50)P(x > 100)$

Also, show $P(x > 50 + 100) \leq P(x > 50)P(x > 100)$. Since we already showed that $P(x > 50 + 100) = P(x > 50)P(x > 100)$, then $P(x > 50 + 100) \leq P(x > 50)P(x > 100)$.

c. Show $P(x > a + b) \geq P(x > a)P(x > b)$

$P(x > a + b) = e^{-(a+b)/250} = e^{-a/250}e^{-b/250} = P(x > a)P(x > b)$

4.157 $p(x) = \binom{n}{x}p^x q^{n-x}$ for $x = 0, 1, 2, ..., n$

a. $P(x = 3) = p(3) = \binom{7}{3}.5^3.5^{7-3} = \frac{7!}{3!4!}.5^3.5^4 = 35(.125)(.0625) = .2734$

b. $P(x = 3) = p(3) = \binom{4}{3}.8^3.2^{4-3} = \frac{4!}{3!1!}.8^3.2^1 = 4(.512)(.2) = .4096$

c. $P(x = 1) = p(1) = \binom{15}{1}.1^1.9^{15-1} = \frac{15!}{1!14!}.1^1.9^{14} = 15(.1)(.228768) = .3432$

4.159 From Table I, Appendix D:

a. $P(x = 14) = P(x \leq 14) - P(x \leq 13) = .584 - .392 = .192$

b. $P(x \leq 12) = .228$

c. $P(x > 12) = 1 - P(x \leq 12) = 1 - .228 = .772$

d. $P(9 \leq x \leq 18) = P(x \leq 18) - P(x \leq 8) = .992 - .005 = .987$

e. $P(8 < x < 18) = P(x \leq 17) - P(x \leq 8) = .965 - .005 = .960$

f. $\mu = np = 20(.7) = 14$, $\sigma^2 = npq = 20(.7)(.3) = 4.2$, $\sigma = \sqrt{4.2} = 2.049$

g. $\mu \pm 2\sigma \Rightarrow 14 \pm 2(2.049) \Rightarrow 14 \pm 4.098 \Rightarrow (9.902, 18.098)$

$P(9.902 < x < 18.098) = P(10 \leq x \leq 18) = P(x \leq 18) - P(x \leq 9) = .992 - .017 = .975$

4.161 a. Poisson

    b.   Binomial

    c.   Binomial

4.163   a.   Discrete - The number of damaged inventory items is countable.

    b.   Continuous - The average monthly sales can take on any value within an acceptable limit.

    c.   Continuous - The number of square feet can take on any positive value.

    d.   Continuous - The length of time we must wait can take on any positive value.

4.165   a. $P(z \le 2.1) = A_1 + A_2 = .5 + .4821 = .9821$

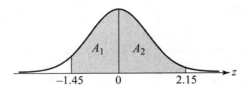

    b. $P(z \ge 2.1) = A_2 = .5 - A_1 = .5 - .4821 = .0179$

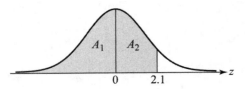

    c. $P(z \ge -1.65) = A_1 + A_2 = .4505 + .5000 = .9505$

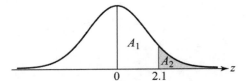

    d. $P(-2.13 \le z \le -.41) = P(-2.13 \le z \le 0) - P(-.41 \le z \le 0)$
$$= .4834 - .1591 = .3243$$

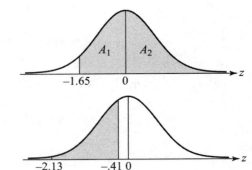

    e. $P(-1.45 \le z \le 2.15) = A_1 + A_2 = .4265 + .4842 = .9107$

    f. $P(z \le -1.43) = A_1 = .5 - A_2 = .5000 - .4236 = .0764$

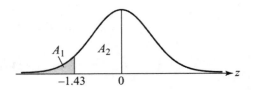

4.167　a.　For the probability density function, $f(x) = \dfrac{e^{-x/7}}{7}$, $x > 0$, x is an exponential random variable.

b.　For the probability density function, $f(x) = \dfrac{1}{20}$, $5 < x < 25$, x is a uniform random variable.

c.　For the probability function, $f(x) = \dfrac{e^{-.5[(x-10)/5]^2}}{5\sqrt{2\pi}}$, x is a normal random variable.

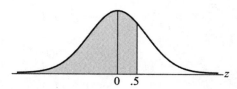

4.169　a.　$P(x \le 80) = P\left(z \le \dfrac{80-75}{10}\right) = P(z \le .5) = .5 + .1915 = .6915$

　　　　　　(Table II, Appendix D)

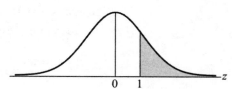

b.　$P(x \ge 85) = P\left(z \ge \dfrac{85-75}{10}\right) = P(z \ge 1) = .5 - .3413 = .1587$

　　　(Table II, Appendix D)

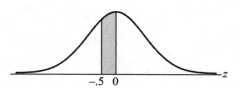

c.　$P(70 \le x \le 75) = P\left(\dfrac{70-75}{10} \le z \le \dfrac{75-75}{10}\right)$

　　　　　　　$= P(-.5 \le z \le 0) = P(0 \le z \le .5) = .1915$

　　　　　　(Table II, Appendix D)

d.　$P(x > 80) = 1 - P(x \le 80) = 1 - .6915 = .3085$　(Refer to part **a**.)

e.　$P(x = 78) = 0$, since a single point does not have an area.

f.　$P(x \le 110) = P\left(z \le \dfrac{110-75}{10}\right) = P(z \le 3.5)$

　　　　　$= .5 + .49977 = .99977$
　　　　　　(Table II, Appendix D)

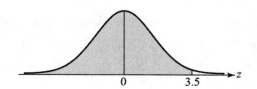

4.171　x is normal random variable with $\mu = 40$, $\sigma^2 = 36$, and $\sigma = 6$.

a.　$P(x \ge x_0) = .10$

So, $A = .5 - .10 = .4000$. Looking up the area .4000
In the body of Table II, Appendix D gives $z_0 = 1.28$.

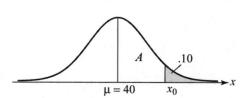

To find x_0, substitute the values into the z-score formula:

　　　$z_0 = \dfrac{x_0 - \mu}{\sigma} \Rightarrow 1.28 = \dfrac{x_0 - 40}{6} \Rightarrow x_0 = 1.28(6) + 40 = 47.68$

b. $P(\mu \le x \le x_0) = .40$

Looking up the area .4000 in the body of Table II, Appendix D gives $z_0 = 1.28$.

To find x_0, substitute the values into the z-score formula:

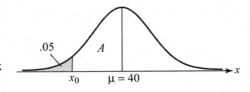

$$z_0 = \frac{x_0 - \mu}{\sigma} \Rightarrow 1.28 = \frac{x_0 - 40}{6} \Rightarrow x_0 = 1.28(6) + 40 = 47.68$$

c. $P(x < x_0) = .05$

So, $A = .5000 - .0500 = .4500$.

Looking up the area .4500 in the body of Table II, Appendix D gives $z_0 = -1.645$. (.45 is halfway between .4495 and .4505; therefore, we average the z-scores)

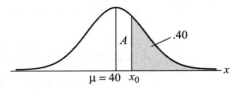

$$\frac{1.64 + 1.65}{2} = 1.645$$

z_0 is negative since the graph shows z_0 is on the left side of 0.

To find x_0, substitute the values into the z-score formula:

$$z_0 = \frac{x_0 - \mu}{\sigma} \Rightarrow -1.645 = \frac{x_0 - 40}{6} \Rightarrow x_0 = -1.645(6) + 40 = 30.13$$

d. $P(x > x_0) = .40$
So, $A = .5000 - .4000 = .1000$.

Looking up the area .1000 in the body of Table II, Appendix D gives $z_0 = .25$.

To find x_0, substitute the values into the z-score formula:

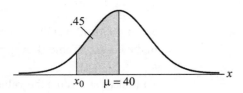

$$z_0 = \frac{x_0 - \mu}{\sigma} \Rightarrow .25 = \frac{x_0 - 40}{6} \Rightarrow x_0 = .25(6) + 40 = 41.5$$

e. $P(x_0 \le x < \mu) = .45$

Looking up the area .4500 in the body of Table II, Appendix D gives $z_0 = -1.645$. (.45 is halfway between .4495 and .4505; therefore, we average the z-scores)

$$\frac{1.64 + 1.65}{2} = 1.645$$

z_0 is negative since the graph shows z_0 is on the left side of 0.

To find x_0, substitute the values into the z-score formula:

$$z_0 = \frac{x_0 - \mu}{\sigma} \Rightarrow -1.645 = \frac{x_0 - 40}{6} \Rightarrow x_0 = -1.645(6) + 40 = 30.13$$

4.173 a. In order for this to be a valid probability distribution, all probabilities must be between 0 and 1 and the sum of all the probabilities must be 1. For this data, all the probabilities are between 0 and 1. If you sum all of the probabilities, the sum is 1.

b. $P(x \geq 10) = P(x = 10) + P(x = 11) + \cdots + P(x = 20)$
$$= .02 + .02 + .02 + .02 + .01 + .01 + .01 + .01 + .01 + .005 + .005 = .14$$

c. The mean of x is
$$\mu = E(x) = \sum xp(x) = 0(.17) + 1(.10) + 2(.11) + \cdots + 20(.005)$$
$$= 0 + .1 + .22 + .33 + \cdots + .1 = 4.655$$

The variance of x is
$$\sigma^2 = E(x - \mu)^2 = \sum (x - \mu)^2 p(x) = (0 - 4.655)^2(.17) + (1 - 4.655)^2(.1) + (2 - 4.655)^2(.11)$$
$$+ \cdots + (20 - 4.655)^2(.005)$$
$$= 3.6837 + 1.3359 + .7754 + \cdots + 1.1773 = 19.8560$$

d. From Chebyshev's Rule, we know that at least .75 of the observations will fall within 2 standard deviations of the mean. The standard deviation is $\sigma = \sqrt{19.8560} = 4.456$.

The interval is: $\mu \pm 2\sigma \Rightarrow 4.655 \pm 2(4.456) \Rightarrow 4.655 \pm 8.912 \Rightarrow (-4.257, 13.567)$. Since x cannot be negative, the interval is $(0, 13.567)$.

4.175 For this problem, $f(x) = \dfrac{1}{3600 - 0} = \dfrac{1}{3600}$. Thus,

$$f(x) = \begin{cases} \dfrac{1}{3600} & 0 \leq x \leq 3600 \\ 0 & \text{otherwise} \end{cases}$$

The last 15 minutes would represent the last $15(60) = 900$ seconds.
$$P(2700 < x < 3600) = (3600 - 2700)\frac{1}{3600} = \frac{900}{3600} = .25$$

4.177 Let $x =$ interarrival time between patients. Then x is an exponential random variable with a mean of 4 minutes.

a. $P(x < 1) = 1 - P(x \geq 1) = 1 - e^{-1/4} = 1 - e^{-.25} = 1 - .778801 = .221199$

b. Assuming that the interarrival times are independent,

P(next 4 interarrival times are all less than 1 minute)
$$= \left[P(x < 1) \right]^4 = .221199^4 = .002394$$

c. $P(x > 10) = e^{-10/4} = e^{-2.5} = .082085$

4.179   a.   We will check the 5 characteristics of a binomial random variable.

1.   The experiment consists of $n = 20$ identical trials.
2.   There are only 2 possible outcomes for each trial. Let $S =$ intruding object is detected and $F =$ intruding object is not detected.
3.   The probability of success (S) is the same from trial to trial. For each trial, $p = P(S) = .8$ and $q = 1 - p = 1 - .8 = .2$.
4.   The trials are independent.
5.   The binomial random variable x is the number of intruding objects in the 20 trials that are detected.

Thus, x is a binomial random variable.

b.   For this experiment, $n = 20$ and $p = .8$.

c.   Using Table I, Appendix D, with $n = 20$ and $p = .8$,

$$P(x = 15) = P(x \le 15) - P(x \le 14) = .370 - .196 = .174$$

d.   Using Table I, Appendix D, with $n = 20$ and $p = .8$,

$$P(x \ge 15) = 1 - P(x \le 14) = 1 - .196 = .804$$

e. $E(x) = np = 20(.8) = 16$.   For every 20 intruding objects, SBIRS will detect an average of 16.

4.181   a.   Let $x_1 =$ repair time for machine 1. Then x_1 has an exponential distribution with $\mu_1 = 1$ hour.

$$P(x_1 > 1) = e^{-1/1} = e^{-1} = .367879 \text{ (using a calculator)}$$

b.   Let $x_2 =$ repair time for machine 2. Then x_2 has an exponential distribution with $\mu_2 = 2$ hours.

$$P(x_2 > 1) = e^{-1/2} = e^{-.5} = .606531 \text{ (using a calculator)}$$

c.   Let $x_3 =$ repair time for machine 3. Then x_3 has an exponential distribution with $\mu_3 = .5$ hours.

$$P(x_3 > 1) = e^{-1/.5} = e^{-2} = .135335 \text{ (using a calculator)}$$

Since the mean repair time for machine 4 is the same as for machine 3, $P(x_4 > 1) = P(x_3 > 1) = .135335$.

d.   The only way that the repair time for the entire system will not exceed 1 hour is if all four machines are repaired in less than 1 hour. Thus, the probability that the repair time for the entire system exceeds 1 hour is:

P(Repair time entire system exceeds 1 hour)
$$= 1 - P\big((x_1 \le 1) \cap (x_2 \le 1) \cap (x_3 \le 1) \cap (x_4 \le 1)\big) = 1 - P(x_1 \le 1) P(x_2 \le 1) P(x_3 \le 1) P(x_4 \le 1)$$
$$= 1 - (1 - .367879)(1 - .606531)(1 - .135335)(1 - .135335)$$
$$= 1 - (.632121)(.393469)(.864665)(.864665) = 1 - .185954 = .814046$$

4.183 a. For $N = 209$, $r = 10$, and $n = 8$, $E(x) = \dfrac{nr}{N} = \dfrac{10(8)}{209} = .383$

      b. $P(x = 4) = \dfrac{\dbinom{8}{4}\dbinom{209-8}{10-4}}{\dbinom{209}{10}} = \dfrac{\dfrac{8!}{4!(8-4)!} \cdot \dfrac{201!}{6!(201-6)!}}{\dfrac{209!}{10!(209-10)!}} = .0002$

4.185 The information given in the problem states that $\bar{x} = 4.71$, $s = 6.09$, $Q_L = 1$, and $Q_U = 6$. To be normal, the data have to be symmetric. If the data are symmetric, then the mean would equal the median and would be half way between the lower and upper quartile. Half way between the upper and lower quartiles is 3.5. The sample mean is 4.71, which is much larger than 3.5. This implies that the data may not be normal. In addition, the interquartile range divided by the standard deviation will be approximately 1.3 if the data are normal. For this data,

$$\frac{IQR}{s} = \frac{Q_U - Q_L}{s} = \frac{6-1}{6.09} = .82$$

The value of .82 is much smaller than the necessary 1.3 to be normal. Again, this is an indication that the data are not normal. Finally, the standard deviation is larger than the mean. Since one cannot have values of the variable in this case less than 0, a standard deviation larger than the mean indicates that the data are skewed to the right. This implies that the data are not normal.

4.187 Let x equal the difference between the actual weight and recorded weight (the error of measurement). The random variable x is normally distributed with $\mu = 592$ and $\sigma = 628$.

      a. We want to find the probability that the weigh-in-motion equipment understates the actual weight of the truck. This would be true if the error of measurement is positive.

$$P(x > 0) = P\left(z > \frac{0 - 592}{628}\right) = P(z > -.94)$$
$$= .5000 + .3264 = .8264$$

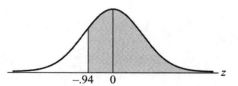

      b. $P(\text{overstate the weight}) = 1 - P(\text{understate the weight})$
$$= 1 - .8264 = .1736$$
$$(\text{Refer to part } \mathbf{a}.)$$

For 100 measurements, approximately $100(.1736) = 17.36$ or 17 times the weight would be overstated.

      c. $P(x > 400) = P\left(z > \dfrac{400 - 592}{628}\right) = P(z > -.31)$
$$= .5000 + .1217 = .6217$$

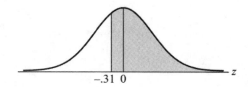

      d. We want $P(\text{understate the weight}) = .5$.
          To understate the weight, $x > 0$. Thus, we want to find μ so that $P(x > 0) = .5$.

$$P(x > 0) = P\left(z > \frac{0 - \mu}{628}\right) = .5$$

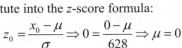

From Table II, Appendix D, $z_0 = 0$. To find μ, substitute into the z-score formula:

$$z_0 = \frac{x_0 - \mu}{\sigma} \Rightarrow 0 = \frac{0 - \mu}{628} \Rightarrow \mu = 0$$

Thus, the mean error should be set at 0.

We want P(understate the weight) = .4.

To understate the weight, $x > 0$. Thus, we want to find μ so that $P(x > 0) = .4$.

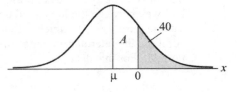

$A = .5 - .40 = .1$. Look up the area .1000 in the body of Table II, Appendix D, $z_0 = .25$.

To find μ, substitute into the z-score formula:

$$z_0 = \frac{x_0 - \mu}{\sigma} \Rightarrow .25 = \frac{0 - \mu}{628} \Rightarrow \mu = 0 - (.25)628 = -157$$

4. 189   a. $\mu = np = 25(.05) = 1.25$ $\sigma = \sqrt{npq} = \sqrt{25(.05)(.95)} = 1.09$

Since μ is not an integer, x could not equal its expected value.

b.   The event is $(x \geq 5)$. From Table I with $n = 25$ and $p = .05$:

$$P(x \geq 5) = 1 - P(x \leq 4) = 1 - .993 = .007$$

c.   Since the probability obtained in part **b** is so small, it is unlikely that 5% applies to this agency. The percentage is probably greater than 5%.

4.191   If the goal keeper stands in the middle of the goal and can reach any ball within 9 feet, then the only way a player can score is if he/she shoots the ball within 3 feet of either goal post.

a.   If a player aims at the right goal post, then the player will score if x is between -3 and 0. Using Table II, Appendix D, we get $P(-3 < x < 0) = P\left(\frac{-3 - 0}{3} < z < \frac{0 - 0}{3}\right) = P(-1 < z < 0) = .3413$.

b.   If a player aims at the center of the goal, then the player will score if x is greater than 9 or less than -9. Using Table II, Appendix D, we get

$$P(x < -9) + P(x > 9) = P\left(z < \frac{-9 - 0}{3}\right) + P\left(z > \frac{9 - 0}{3}\right) = P(z < -3) + P(z > 3)$$

$$= (.5 - .4987) + (.5 - .4987) = .0026$$

c. If a player aims halfway between the right goal post and the outer limit of the goal keeper's reach, then the player will score if x is between -1.5 and 1.5. Using Table II, Appendix D, we get

$$P(-1.5 < x < 1.5) = P\left(\frac{-1.5-0}{3} < z < \frac{1.5-0}{3}\right) = P(-.5 < z < .5) = .1915 + .1915 = .3830.$$

4.193 a. The properties of valid probability distributions are:

$$\sum p(x) = 1 \text{ and } 0 \le p(x) \le 1 \text{ for all } x.$$

For ARC a_1: $0 \le p(x) \le 1$ for all x and $\sum p(x) = .05 + .10 + .25 + .60 = 1.00$
Thus, this is a valid probability distribution.

For ARC a_2: $0 \le p(x) \le 1$ for all x and $\sum p(x) = .10 + .30 + .60 + 0 = 1.00$
Thus, this is a valid probability distribution.

For ARC a_3: $0 \le p(x) \le 1$ for all x and $\sum p(x) = .05 + .25 + .70 + 0 = 1.00$
Thus, this is a valid probability distribution.

For ARC a_4: $0 \le p(x) \le 1$ for all x and $\sum p(x) = .90 + .10 + 0 + 0 = 1.00$
Thus, this is a valid probability distribution.

b. For **Arc a_1**, $P(x > 1) = P(x = 2) + P(x = 3) = .25 + .6 = .85$

c. For **Arc a_2**, $P(x > 1) = P(x = 2) = .60$
For **Arc a_3**, $P(x > 1) = P(x = 2) = .70$
For **Arc a_4**, $P(x > 1) = 0$

d. For **Arc a_1**,
$$E(x) = \sum xp(x) = 0(.05) + 1(.10) + 2(.25) + 3(.60) = 0 + .10 + .50 + 1.80 = 2.40$$
The average capacity of Arc a_1 is 2.40.

For **Arc a_2**,
$$E(x) = \sum xp(x) = 0(.10) + 1(.30) + 2(.60) = 0 + .30 + 1.20 = 1.50$$
The average capacity of Arc a_2 is 1.50.

For **Arc a_3**,
$$E(x) = \sum xp(x) = 0(.05) + 1(.25) + 2(.70) + = 0 + .25 + 1.40 = 1.65$$
The average capacity of Arc a_3 is 1.65.

For **Arc a_4**,
$$E(x) = \sum xp(x) = 0(.90) + 1(.10) = 0 + .10 = .10$$
The average capacity of Arc a_4 is 0.10.

e.   For **Arc a_1,**
$$\sigma^2 = E\left[(x-\mu)\right]^2 = \sum(x-\mu)^2 p(x)$$
$$= (0-2.4)^2(.05)+(1-2.4)^2(.10)+(2-2.4)^2(.25)+(3-2.4)^2(.60)$$
$$= (-2.4)^2(.05)+(-1.4)^2(.10)+(-.4)^2(.25)+(.6)^2(.60)$$
$$= .288+.196+.04+.216 = .74$$

$$\sigma = \sqrt{.74} = .86$$

We would expect most observations to fall within 2 standard deviations of the mean or
$2.40 \pm 2(.86) \Rightarrow 2.40 \pm 1.72 \Rightarrow (.68,\ 4.12)$

For **Arc a_2,**
$$\sigma^2 = E\left[(x-\mu)\right]^2 = \sum(x-\mu)^2 p(x)$$
$$= (0-1.5)^2(.10)+(1-1.5)^2(.30)+(2-1.5)^2(.60)$$
$$= (-1.5)^2(.10)+(-.5)^2(.30)+(.5)^2(.60) = .225+.075+.15 = .45$$

$$\sigma = \sqrt{.45} = .67$$

We would expect most observations to fall within 2 standard deviations of the mean or
$1.50 \pm 2(.67) \Rightarrow 1.50 \pm 1.34 \Rightarrow (.16,\ 2.84)$

For **Arc a_3,**
$$\sigma^2 = E\left[(x-\mu)\right]^2 = \sum(x-\mu)^2 p(x)$$
$$= (0-1.65)^2(.05)+(1-1.65)^2(.25)+(2-1.65)^2(.70)$$
$$= (-1.65)^2(.05)+(-.65)^2(.25)+(.35)^2(.70) = .136125+.105625+.08575 = .3275$$

$$\sigma = \sqrt{.3275} = .57$$

We would expect most observations to fall within 2 standard deviations of the mean or
$1.65 \pm 2(.57) \Rightarrow 1.65 \pm 1.14 \Rightarrow (.51, 2.79)$

For **Arc a_4,**
$$\sigma^2 = E\left[(x-\mu)\right]^2 = \sum(x-\mu)^2 p(x) = (0-.1)^2(.90)+(1-.1)^2(.10)$$
$$= (-.1)^2(.90)+(.9)^2(.10) = .009+.081 = .090$$

$$\sigma = \sqrt{.09} = .30$$

We would expect most observations to fall within 2 standard deviations of the mean or
$.10 \pm 2(.30) \Rightarrow .10 \pm .60 \Rightarrow (-.50, .70)$

4.195   Let x = perception of light flicker. Then x has an approximate normal distribution with $\mu = 2.2$ and $\sigma = .5$.

$$P(x>3) = P\left(z > \frac{3-2.2}{.5}\right) = P(z>1.6) = .5 - P(0<z<1.6) = .5 - .4452 = .0548$$

4.197   Let x = demand for white bread. Then x is a normal random variable with $\mu = 7200$ and $\sigma = 300$:

a. $P(x \le x_0) = .94$. Find x_0.

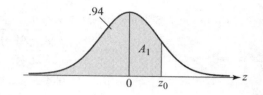

$$P(x \le x_0) = P\left(z \le \frac{x_0 - 7200}{300}\right) = P(z \le z_0) = .94$$

$A_1 = .94 - .50 = .4400$

Using Table II and area .4400, $z_0 = 1.555$.

$$z_0 = \frac{x_0 - 7200}{300} \Rightarrow 1.555 = \frac{x_0 - 7200}{300} \Rightarrow x_0 = 7666.5 \approx 7667$$

b.   If the company produces 7,667 loaves, the company will be left with more than 500 loaves if the demand is less than $7,667 - 500 = 7,167$.

$$P(x < 7167) = P\left(z < \frac{7167 - 7200}{300}\right) = P(z < -.11) = .5 - .0438 = .4562$$

(from Table II, Appendix D)

Thus, on 45.62% of the days the company will be left with more than 500 loaves.

4.199   a.   Let x = rating. Then x has a normal distribution with $\mu = 50$ and $\sigma = 15$. Using Table II, Appendix D,

$P(x > x_o) = .10.$ Find x_o.

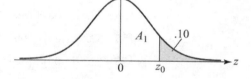

$$P(x > x_o) = P\left(z > \frac{x_o - 50}{15}\right) = P(z > z_o) = .10$$

$A_1 = .5 - .10 = .4000$

Looking up area .4000 in Table II, $z_o = 1.28$.

$$z_o = \frac{x_o - 50}{15} \Rightarrow 1.28 = \frac{x_o - 50}{15} \Rightarrow x_o = 50 + 1.28(15) = 69.2$$

b. $P(x > x_o) = .10 + .20 + .40 = .70.$ Find x_o.

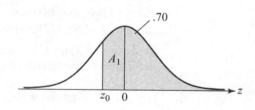

$$P(x > x_o) = P\left(z > \frac{x_o - 50}{15}\right) = P(z > z_o) = .70$$

$A_1 = .70 - .5 = .2000$

Looking up area .2000 in Table II, $z_o = -.52$.

$$z_o = \frac{x_o - 50}{15} \Rightarrow -.52 = \frac{x_o - 50}{15} \Rightarrow x_o = 50 - .52(15) = 42.2$$

4.201   We know from the Empirical Rule that almost all the observations are larger than $\mu - 2\sigma$. ($\approx 95\%$ are between $\mu - 2\sigma$ and $\mu + 2\sigma$). Thus $\mu - 2\sigma > 100$.

For the binomial, $\mu = np = n(.4)$ and $\sigma = \sqrt{npq} = \sqrt{n(.4)(.6)} = \sqrt{.24n}$

$$\mu - 2\sigma > 100 \Rightarrow .4n - 2\sqrt{.24n} > 100 \Rightarrow .4n - .98\sqrt{n} - 100 > 0$$

Solving for $\sqrt{n}$, we get:

$$\sqrt{n} = \frac{.98 \pm \sqrt{.98^2 - 4(.4)(-100)}}{2(.4)} = \frac{.98 \pm 12.687}{.8}$$

$$\Rightarrow \sqrt{n} = 17.084 \Rightarrow n = 17.084^2 = 291.9 \approx 292$$

4.203 a. Since there are 20 possible outcomes that are all equally likely, the probability of any of the 20 numbers is 1/20. The probability distribution of x is:

$$P(x = 5) = 1/20 = .05; \quad P(x = 10) = 1/20 = .05; \text{ etc.}$$

x	5	10	15	20	25	30	35	40	45	50	55	60	65	70	75	80	85	90	95	100
$p(x)$	.05	.05	.05	.05	.05	.05	.05	.05	.05	.05	.05	.05	.05	.05	.05	.05	.05	.05	.05	.05

b. $E(x) = \sum x p(x) = 5(.05) + 10(.05) + 15(.05) + 20(.05) + 25(.05) + 30(.05) + 35(.05)$
$+ 40(.05) + 45(.05) + 50(.05) + 55(.05) + 60(.05) + 65(.05) + 70(.05) + 75(.05)$
$+ 80(.05) + 85(.05) + 90(.05) + 95(.05) + 100(.05) = 52.5$

c. $\sigma^2 = E(x - \mu)^2 = \sum (x - \mu)^2 p(x) = (5 - 52.5)^2 (.05) + (10 - 52.5)^2 (.05)$
$+ (15 - 52.5)^2 (.05) + (20 - 52.5)^2 (.05) + (25 - 52.5)^2 (.05) + (30 - 52.5)^2 (.05)$
$+ (35 - 52.5)^2 (.05) + (40 - 52.5)^2 (.05) + (45 - 52.5)^2 (.05) + (50 - 52.5)^2 (.05)$
$+ (55 - 52.5)^2 (.05) + (60 - 52.5)^2 (.05) + (65 - 52.5)^2 (.05) + (70 - 52.5)^2 (.05)$
$+ (75 - 52.5)^2 (.05) + (80 - 52.5)^2 (.05) + (85 - 52.5)^2 (.05) + (90 - 52.5)^2 (.05)$
$+ (95 - 52.5)^2 (.05) + (100 - 52.5)^2 (.05)$
$= 831.25$

$\sigma = \sqrt{831.25} = 28.83$

Since the uniform distribution is not mound-shaped, we will use Chebyshev's theorem to describe the data. We know that at least 8/9 of the observations will fall with 3 standard deviations of the mean and at least 3/4 of the observations will fall within 2 standard deviations of the mean. For this problem, $\mu \pm 2\sigma \Rightarrow 52.5 \pm 2(28.83) \Rightarrow 52.5 \pm 57.66 \Rightarrow (-5.16, 110.16)$. Thus, at least 3/4 of the data will fall between −5.16 and 110.16. For our problem, all of the observations will fall within 2 standard deviations of the mean. Thus, x is just as likely to fall within any interval of equal length.

d. If a player spins the wheel twice, the total number of outcomes will be $20(20) = 400$. The sample space is:

5, 5	10, 5	15, 5	20, 5	25, 5...	100, 5
5,10	10,10	15,10	20,10	25,10...	100,10
5,15	10,15	15,15	20,15	25,15...	100,15
.	.	.	.	.	.
.	.	.	.	.	.
5,100	10,100	15,100	20,100	25,100...	100,100

Each of these outcomes are equally likely, so each has a probability of $1/400 = .0025$.

Now, let x equal the sum of the two numbers in each sample. There is one sample with a sum of 10, two samples with a sum of 15, three samples with a sum of 20, etc. If the sum of the two numbers exceeds 100, then x is zero. The probability distribution of x is:

x	$p(x)$	x	$p(x)$
0	.5250	55	.0250
10	.0025	60	.0275
15	.0050	65	.0300
20	.0075	70	.0325
25	.0100	75	.0350
30	.0125	80	.0375
35	.0150	85	.0400
40	.0175	90	.0425
45	.0200	95	.0450
50	.0225	100	.0475

e. We assumed that the wheel is fair, or that all outcomes are equally likely.

f. $\mu = E(x) = \sum xp(x) = 0(.5250) + 10(.0025) + 15(.0050) + 20(.0075) + \cdots + 100(.0475) = 33.25$

$\sigma^2 = E(x-\mu)^2 = \sum(x-\mu)^2 p(x) = (0-33.25)^2(.5250) + (10-33.25)^2(.0025)$
$\qquad + (15-33.25)^2(.0050) + (20-33.25)^2(.0075) + \cdots + (100-33.25)^2(.0475) = 1,471.3125$

$\sigma = \sqrt{1,471.3125} = 38.3577$

g. $P(x=0) = .525$

h. Given that the player obtains a 20 on the first spin, the possible values for x (sum of the two spins) are 0 (player spins 85, 90, 95, or 100 on the second spin), 25, 30, ..., 100. In order to get an x of 25, the player would spin a 5 on the second spin. Similarly, the player would have to spin a 10 on the second spin order to get an x of 30, etc. Since all of the outcomes are equally likely on the second spin, the distribution of x is:

x	$p(x)$	x	$p(x)$
0	.20	65	.05
25	.05	70	.05
30	.05	75	.05
35	.05	80	.05
40	.05	85	.05
45	.05	90	.05
50	.05	95	.05
55	.05	100	.05
60	.05		

i.   The probability that the players total score will exceed one dollar is the probability that x is zero.
$$P(x=0)=.20$$

j.   Given that the player obtains a 65 on the first spin, the possible values for x (sum of the two spins) are 0 (player spins 40, 45, 50, up to 100 on second spin), 70, 75, 80,..., 100. In order to get an x of 70, the player would spin a 5 on the second spin. Similarly, the player would have to spin a 10 on the second spin in order to get an x of 75, etc. Since all of the outcomes are equally likely on the second spin, the distribution of x is:

x	$p(x)$
0	.65
70	.05
75	.05
80	.05
85	.05
90	.05
95	.05
100	.05

The probability that the players total score will exceed one dollar is the probability that x is zero.
$$P(x=0)=.65$$

4.205   a.   Using Table II, Appendix D.

For $\sigma=1$:

$$P(-1<x<1)+P(4<x<6)+P(9<x<11)$$
$$=P\left(\frac{-1-5}{1}<z<\frac{1-5}{1}\right)+P\left(\frac{4-5}{1}<z<\frac{6-5}{1}\right)+P\left(\frac{9-5}{1}<z<\frac{11-5}{1}\right)$$
$$=P(-6<z<-4)+P(-1<z<1)+P(4<z<6)=0+.3413+.3413+0=.6826$$

For $\sigma=2$:

$$P(-1<x<1)+P(4<x<6)+P(9<x<11)$$
$$=P\left(\frac{-1-5}{2}<z<\frac{1-5}{2}\right)+P\left(\frac{4-5}{2}<z<\frac{6-5}{2}\right)+P\left(\frac{9-5}{2}<z<\frac{11-5}{2}\right)$$
$$=P(-3<z<-2)+P(-.5<z<.5)+P(2<z<3)$$
$$=(.4987-.4772)+(.1915+.1915)+(.4987-.4772)=.4260$$

For $\sigma=4$:

$$P(-1<x<1)+P(4<x<6)+P(9<x<11)$$
$$=P\left(\frac{-1-5}{4}<z<\frac{1-5}{4}\right)+P\left(\frac{4-5}{4}<z<\frac{6-5}{4}\right)+P\left(\frac{9-5}{4}<z<\frac{11-5}{4}\right)$$
$$=P(-1.5<z<-1)+P(-.25<z<.25)+P(1<z<1.5)$$
$$=(.4332-.3413)+(.0948+.0948)+(.4332-.3413)=.3734$$

b. For $\sigma = 1$, 764 of the 1100 flechettes hit a target. The proportion is $764/1100 = .6945$. This is a little higher than the probability that was computed in part *a*.

For $\sigma = 2$, 462 of the 1100 flechettes hit a target. The proportion is $462/1100 = .42$. This is very close to the probability that was computed in part *a*.

For $\sigma = 4$, 408 of the 1100 flechettes hit a target. The proportion is $408/1100 = .3709$. Again, this is very close to the probability that was computed in part *a*.

c. If the Army wants to maximize the chance of hitting the target that the prototype gun us aimed at, then σ should be set at 1. The probability of hitting the target is .6826.

If the Army wants to hit multiple targets with a single shot of the weapon, then σ should be set at 2. The probability of hitting at least one of the targets is .4260.

Chapter 5
Sampling Distributions

5.1   a–b. The different samples of $n = 2$ with replacement and their means are:

Possible Samples	$\bar{x}$	Possible Samples	$\bar{x}$
0, 0	0	4, 0	2
0, 2	1	4, 2	3
0, 4	2	4, 4	4
0, 6	3	4, 6	5
2, 0	1	6, 0	3
2, 2	2	6, 2	4
2, 4	3	6, 4	5
2, 6	4	6, 6	6

c.   Since each sample is equally likely, the probability of any 1 being selected is $\dfrac{1}{4}\left(\dfrac{1}{4}\right) = \dfrac{1}{16}$

d. $P(\bar{x} = 0) = \dfrac{1}{16}$

$P(\bar{x} = 1) = \dfrac{1}{16} + \dfrac{1}{16} = \dfrac{2}{16}$

$P(\bar{x} = 2) = \dfrac{1}{16} + \dfrac{1}{16} + \dfrac{1}{16} = \dfrac{3}{16}$

$P(\bar{x} = 3) = \dfrac{1}{16} + \dfrac{1}{16} + \dfrac{1}{16} + \dfrac{1}{16} = \dfrac{4}{16}$

$P(\bar{x} = 4) = \dfrac{1}{16} + \dfrac{1}{16} + \dfrac{1}{16} = \dfrac{3}{16}$

$P(\bar{x} = 5) = \dfrac{1}{16} + \dfrac{1}{16} = \dfrac{2}{16}$

$P(\bar{x} = 6) = \dfrac{1}{16}$

$\bar{x}$	$p(\bar{x})$
0	1/16
1	2/16
2	3/16
3	4/16
4	3/16
5	2/16
6	1/16

e.   Using MINITAB, the graph is:

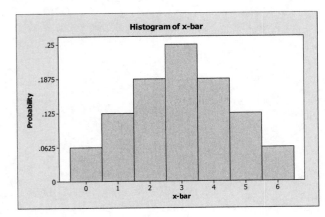

5.3   If the observations are independent of each other, then

$$P(1, 1) = p(1)p(1) = .2(.2) = .04 \qquad P(1, 2) = p(1)p(2) = .2(.3) = .06$$
$$P(1, 3) = p(1)p(3) = .2(.2) = .04$$

etc.

a.

Possible Sample	$\bar{x}$	$p(\bar{x})$	Possible Sample	$\bar{x}$	$p(\bar{x})$
1, 1	1	.04	3, 4	3.5	.04
1, 2	1.5	.06	3, 5	4	.02
1, 3	2	.04	4, 1	2.5	.04
1, 4	2.5	.04	4, 2	3	.06
1, 5	3	.02	4, 3	3.5	.04
2, 1	1.5	.06	4, 4	4	.04
2, 2	2	.09	4, 5	4.5	.02
2, 3	2.5	.06	5, 1	3	.02
2, 4	3	.06	5, 2	3.5	.03
2, 5	3.5	.03	5, 3	4	.02
3, 1	2	.04	5, 4	4.5	.02
3, 2	2.5	.06	5, 5	5	.01
3, 3	3	.04			

Summing the probabilities, the probability distribution of is:

$\bar{x}$	$p(\bar{x})$
1	.04
1.5	.12
2	.17
2.5	.20
3	.20
3.5	.14
4	.08
4.5	.04
5	.01

b.   Using MINITAB, the graph is:

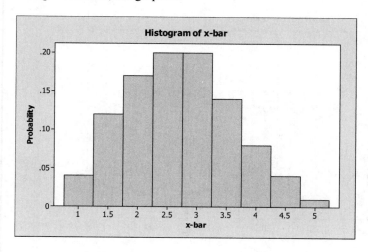

c. $P(\bar{x} \geq 4.5) = .04 + .01 = .05$

d.   No. The probability of observing $\bar{x} = 4.5$ or larger is small (.05).

5.5   a.   For a sample of size $n = 2,$ the sample mean and sample median are exactly the same. Thus, the sampling distribution of the sample median is the same as that for the sample mean (see Exercise 5.3**a**).

b.   The probability histogram for the sample median is identical to that for the sample mean (see Exercise 5.3**b**).

5.7   a.   Answers will vary. A statistical package was used to generate 500 samples of size 25 from a uniform distribution on the interval from 00 to 99. The sample mean was computed for each sample of size 25. Using MINITAB, a histogram of the sample means is:

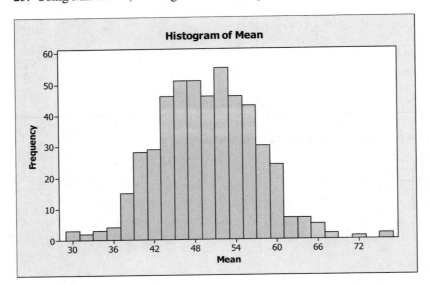

b.   The sample variances were computed for each of the 500 samples of size 25 used in part **a**. Using MINITAB, a histogram of the sample variances is:

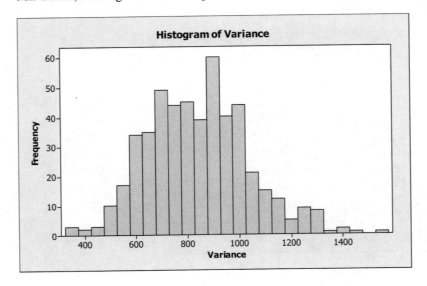

5.9   a. $\mu = \sum xp(x) = 2\left(\dfrac{1}{3}\right) + 4\left(\dfrac{1}{3}\right) + 9\left(\dfrac{1}{3}\right) = \dfrac{15}{3} = 5$

b.   The possible samples of size $n = 3$, the sample means, and the probabilities are:

Possible Samples	$\bar{x}$	$p(\bar{x})$	m	Possible Samples	$\bar{x}$	$p(\bar{x})$	m
2, 2, 2	2	1/27	2	4, 4, 4	4	1/27	4
2, 2, 4	8/3	1/27	2	4, 4, 9	17/3	1/27	4
2, 2, 9	13/3	1/27	2	4, 9, 2	5	1/27	4
2, 4, 2	8/3	1/27	2	4, 9, 4	17/3	1/27	4
2, 4, 4	10/3	1/27	4	4, 9, 9	22/3	1/27	9
2, 4, 9	5	1/27	4	9, 2, 2	13/3	1/27	2
2, 9, 2	13/3	1/27	2	9, 2, 4	5	1/27	4
2, 9, 4	5	1/27	4	9, 2, 9	20/3	1/27	9
2, 9, 9	20/3	1/27	9	9, 4, 2	5	1/27	4
4, 2, 2	8/3	1/27	2	9, 4, 4	17/3	1/27	4
4, 2, 4	10/3	1/27	4	9, 4, 9	22/3	1/27	9
4, 2, 9	5	1/27	4	9, 9, 2	20/3	1/27	9
4, 4, 2	10/3	1/27	4	9, 9, 4	22/3	1/27	9
				9, 9, 9	9	1/27	9

The sampling distribution of $\bar{x}$ is:

$\bar{x}$	$p(\bar{x})$
2	1/27
8/3	3/27
10/3	3/27
4	1/27
13/3	3/27
5	6/27
17/3	3/27
20/3	3/27
22/3	3/27
9	1/27
	27/27

$E(\bar{x}) = \sum \bar{x}p(\bar{x}) = 2\left(\dfrac{1}{27}\right) + \dfrac{8}{3}\left(\dfrac{3}{27}\right) + \dfrac{10}{3}\left(\dfrac{3}{27}\right) + 4\left(\dfrac{1}{27}\right) + \dfrac{13}{3}\left(\dfrac{3}{27}\right)$

$\qquad + 5\left(\dfrac{6}{27}\right) + \dfrac{17}{3}\left(\dfrac{3}{27}\right) + \dfrac{20}{3}\left(\dfrac{3}{27}\right) + \dfrac{22}{3}\left(\dfrac{3}{27}\right) + 9\left(\dfrac{1}{27}\right)$

$\qquad = \dfrac{2}{27} + \dfrac{8}{27} + \dfrac{10}{27} + \dfrac{4}{27} + \dfrac{13}{27} + \dfrac{30}{27} + \dfrac{17}{27} + \dfrac{20}{27} + \dfrac{22}{27} + \dfrac{9}{27} = \dfrac{135}{27} = 5$

Since $\mu = 5$ in part **a**, and $E(\bar{x}) = \mu = 5$, $\bar{x}$ is an unbiased estimator of μ.

c.   The median was calculated for each sample and is shown in the table in part **b**. The sampling distribution of *m* is:

m	*p(m)*
2	7/27
4	13/27
9	7/27
	27/27

$$E(m) = \sum mp(m) = 2\left(\frac{7}{27}\right) + 4\left(\frac{13}{27}\right) + 9\left(\frac{7}{27}\right) = \frac{14}{27} + \frac{52}{27} + \frac{63}{27} = \frac{129}{27} = 4.778$$

Then $E(m) = 4.778 \neq \mu = 5$. Thus, *m* is a biased estimator of μ.

d.   Use the sample mean, $\bar{x}$. It is an unbiased estimator.

5.11   Answers will vary. MINITAB was used to generate 500 samples of size *n* = 25 observations from a uniform population from 1 to 50. The first 10 samples along with the sample means and medians are shown in the table below:

Sample	Observations																									Mean	Median
1	28	27	11	19	50	30	47	26	9	33	50	15	21	41	31	41	35	32	32	17	6	32	39	34	21	29.08	31
2	8	4	32	32	3	45	18	9	40	3	42	21	44	50	42	14	24	10	36	6	15	47	26	48	28	25.88	26
3	6	20	27	1	50	14	21	37	46	23	1	34	42	47	24	46	8	29	18	28	40	39	49	33	23	28.24	28
4	45	12	26	13	40	17	11	43	8	35	20	8	44	48	13	46	49	17	47	27	5	45	9	21	36	27.4	26
5	40	38	25	37	47	2	17	40	32	6	22	30	23	2	18	22	14	6	22	3	43	47	16	35	35	24.88	23
6	17	8	43	27	21	5	18	45	31	15	2	38	22	18	7	9	3	35	23	45	24	39	38	35	37	24.20	23
7	40	1	22	29	6	8	22	20	36	18	45	16	29	9	6	3	49	34	24	40	27	5	49	11	30	23.16	22
8	25	3	44	34	29	6	33	32	43	6	43	24	49	14	37	8	46	44	1	12	36	18	30	25	4	25.84	29
9	7	33	36	41	30	13	17	19	14	36	20	39	41	20	15	38	12	37	14	9	19	2	37	15	8	22.88	19
10	4	46	49	49	45	49	24	3	25	22	27	28	23	17	14	6	35	5	20	34	4	41	9	15	3	23.88	23

Using MINITAB, side-by side histograms of the means and medians of the 500 samples are:

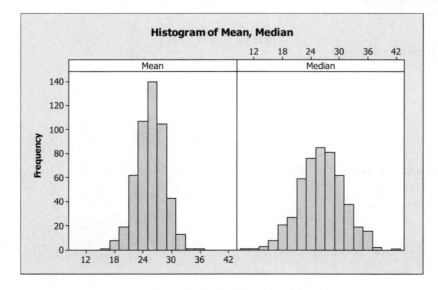

a. Yes, it appears that $\bar{x}$ and the median are unbiased estimators of the population mean. The centers of both distributions above appear to be around 25 to 26. In fact, the mean of the sampling distribution of $\bar{x}$ is 25.65 and the mean of the sampling distribution of the median is 25.73.

b. The sampling distribution of the median has greater variation because it is more spread out than the sampling distribution of $\bar{x}$.

5.13   a. Refer to the solution to Exercise 5.3. The values of s^2 and the corresponding probabilities are listed below:

$$s^2 = \frac{\sum x^2 - \frac{(\sum x)^2}{n}}{n-1}$$

For sample 1, 1; $s^2 = \dfrac{2 - \dfrac{2^2}{2}}{1} = 0$ For sample 1, 2: $s^2 = \dfrac{5 - \dfrac{3^2}{2}}{1} = .5$

The rest of the values are calculated and shown:

s^2	$p(s^2)$	s^2	$p(s^2)$
0.0	.04	0.5	.04
0.5	.06	2.0	.02
2.0	.04	4.5	.04
4.5	.04	2.0	.06
8.0	.02	0.5	.04
0.5	.06	0.0	.04
0.0	.09	0.5	.02
0.5	.06	8.0	.02
2.0	.06	4.5	.03
4.5	.03	2.0	.02
2.0	.04	0.5	.02
0.5	.06	0.0	.01
0.0	.04		

The sampling distribution of s^2 is:

s^2	$p(s^2)$
0.0	.22
0.5	.36
2.0	.24
4.5	.14
8.0	.04

b.
$$\sigma^2 = \sum (x-\mu)^2 \, p(x) = (1-2.7)^2 (.2) + (2-2.7)^2 (.3) + (3-2.7)^2 (.2)$$
$$+ (4-2.7)^2 (.2) + (5-2.7)^2 (.1) = 1.61$$

c. $E(s^2) = \sum s^2 p(s^2) = 0(.22) + .5(.36) + 2(.24) + 4.5(.14) + 8(.04) = 1.61$

d.   The sampling distribution of s is listed below, where $s = \sqrt{s^2}$:

s	p(s)
0.000	.22
0.707	.36
1.414	.24
2.121	.14
2.828	.04

e. $E(s) = \sum sp(s) = 0(.22) + .707(.36) + 1.414(.24) + 2.121(.14) + 2.828(.04) = 1.00394$

Since $E(s) = 1.00394$ is not equal to $\sigma = \sqrt{\sigma^2} = \sqrt{1.61} = 1.269$, s is a biased estimator of σ.

5.15   The sampling distribution is approximately normal only if the sample size is sufficiently large or if the population being sampled from is normal.

5.17   a. $\mu_{\bar{x}} = \mu = 100, \ \sigma_{\bar{x}} = \dfrac{\sigma}{\sqrt{n}} = \dfrac{\sqrt{100}}{\sqrt{4}} = 5$

b. $\mu_{\bar{x}} = \mu = 100, \ \sigma_{\bar{x}} = \dfrac{\sigma}{\sqrt{n}} = \dfrac{\sqrt{100}}{\sqrt{25}} = 2$

c. $\mu_{\bar{x}} = \mu = 100, \ \sigma_{\bar{x}} = \dfrac{\sigma}{\sqrt{n}} = \dfrac{\sqrt{100}}{\sqrt{100}} = 1$

d. $\mu_{\bar{x}} = \mu = 100, \ \sigma_{\bar{x}} = \dfrac{\sigma}{\sqrt{n}} = \dfrac{\sqrt{100}}{\sqrt{50}} = 1.414$

e. $\mu_{\bar{x}} = \mu = 100, \ \sigma_{\bar{x}} = \dfrac{\sigma}{\sqrt{n}} = \dfrac{\sqrt{100}}{\sqrt{500}} = .447$

f. $\mu_{\bar{x}} = \mu = 100, \ \sigma_{\bar{x}} = \dfrac{\sigma}{\sqrt{n}} = \dfrac{\sqrt{100}}{\sqrt{1000}} = .316$

5.19   In Exercise 5.18, it was determined that the mean and standard deviation of the sampling distribution of the sample mean are 20 and 2 respectively. Using Table II, Appendix D:

a. $P(\bar{x} < 16) = P\left(z < \dfrac{16 - 20}{2}\right) = P(z < -2) = .5 - .4772 = .0228$

b. $P(\bar{x} > 23) = P\left(z > \dfrac{23 - 20}{2}\right) = P(z > 1.50) = .5 - .4332 = .0668$

c. $P(\bar{x} > 25) = P\left(z > \dfrac{25 - 20}{2}\right) = P(z > 2.5) = .5 - .4938 = .0062$

d. $P(16 < \bar{x} < 22) = P\left(\dfrac{16 - 20}{2} < z < \dfrac{22 - 20}{2}\right) = P(-2 < z < 1) = .4772 + .3413 = .8185$

e. $P(\bar{x} < 14) = P\left(z < \dfrac{14 - 20}{2}\right) = P(z < -3) = .5 - .4987 = .0013$

5.21 By the Central Limit Theorem, the sampling distribution of $\bar{x}$ is approximately normal with $\mu_{\bar{x}} = \mu = 30$ and $\sigma_{\bar{x}} = \sigma / \sqrt{n} = 16 / \sqrt{100} = 1.6$. Using Table II, Appendix D:

a. $P(\bar{x} \geq 28) = P\left(z \geq \dfrac{28 - 30}{1.6}\right) = P(z \geq -1.25) = .5 + .3944 = .8944$

b. $P(22.1 \leq \bar{x} \leq 26.8) = P\left(\dfrac{22.1 - 30}{1.6} \leq z \leq \dfrac{26.8 - 30}{1.6}\right) = P(-4.94 \leq z \leq -2) = .5 - .4772 = .0228$

c. $P(\bar{x} \leq 28.2) = P\left(z \leq \dfrac{28.2 - 30}{1.6}\right) = P(z \leq -1.13) = .5 - .3708 = .1292$

d. $P(\bar{x} \geq 27.0) = P\left(z \geq \dfrac{27.0 - 30}{1.6}\right) = P(z \geq -1.88) = .5 + .4699 = .9699$

5.23 a. $E(\bar{x}) = \mu = 353$. The mean of the sampling distribution of $\bar{x}$ is 353.

b. $V(\bar{x}) = \dfrac{\sigma^2}{n} = \dfrac{30^2}{45} = 20$

c. By the Central Limit Theorem, the sampling distribution of $\bar{x}$ is approximately normal.

d. $P(\bar{x} > 400) = P\left(z > \dfrac{400 - 353}{\sqrt{20}}\right) = P(z > 10.51) \approx 0$. It is almost impossible to observe more than 400 sags in a week.

5.25 a. $\mu_{\bar{x}} = \mu = 68$. The average value of sample mean level of support is 68.

b. $\sigma_{\bar{x}} = \dfrac{\sigma}{\sqrt{n}} = \dfrac{27}{\sqrt{45}} = 4.0249$ The standard deviation of the distribution of the sample means is 4.0249.

c. Because the sample size is large ($n = 45 > 30$), the Central Limit Theorem says that the sampling distribution of $\bar{x}$ is approximately normal.

d. $P(\bar{x} > 65) = P\left(z > \dfrac{65 - 68}{4.0249}\right) = P(z > -.75) = .5 + .2734 = .7734$ (Using Table II, Appendix D)

5.27 By the Central Limit Theorem, the sampling distribution of $\bar{x}$ is approximately normal with $\mu_{\bar{x}} = \mu = 105.3$ and $\sigma_{\bar{x}} = \dfrac{\sigma}{\sqrt{n}} = \dfrac{8}{\sqrt{64}} = 1$.

$P(\bar{x} < 103) = P\left(z < \dfrac{103 - 105.3}{1}\right) = P(z < -2.3) = .5 - .4893 = .0107$ (Using Table II, Appendix D)

5.29 a. By the Central Limit Theorem, the sampling distribution of $\bar{x}$ is approximately normal with a mean $\mu_{\bar{x}} = \mu = .53$ and standard deviation $\sigma_{\bar{x}} = \dfrac{\sigma}{\sqrt{n}} = \dfrac{.193}{\sqrt{50}} = .0273$.

b. $P(\bar{x} > .58) = P\left(z > \dfrac{.58 - .53}{.0273}\right) = P(z > 1.83) = .5 - .4664 = .0336$

c. If Before Tensioning: $\mu_{\bar{x}} = \mu = .53$

$P(\bar{x} \geq .59) = P\left(z \geq \dfrac{.59 - .53}{.0273}\right) = P(z \geq 2.20) = .5 - .4861 = .0139$

If After Tensioning: $\mu_{\bar{x}} = \mu = .58$

$P(\bar{x} \geq .59) = P\left(z \geq \dfrac{.59 - .58}{.0273}\right) = P(z \geq 0.37) = .5 - .1443 = .3557$

Since the probability of getting a maximum differential of .59 or more Before Tensioning is so small, it would be very unlikely that the measurements were obtained Before Tensioning. However, since the probability of getting a maximum differential of .59 or more After Tensioning is not small, it would not be unusual that the measurements were obtained after tensioning. Thus, most likely, the measurements were obtained After Tensioning.

5.31 a. By the Central Limit Theorem, the sampling distribution of $\bar{x}$ is approximately normal with

$\mu_{\bar{x}} = \mu = 6$ and $\sigma_{\bar{x}} = \dfrac{\sigma}{\sqrt{n}} = \dfrac{10}{\sqrt{326}} = .5538.$

$P(\bar{x} > 7.5) = P\left(z > \dfrac{7.5 - 6}{.5538}\right) = P(z > 2.71) = .5 - .4966 = .0034$ (Using Table II, Appendix D)

b. We first need to find the probability of observing the current data or anything more unusual if the true mean is 6.

$P(\bar{x} \geq 300) = P\left(z \geq \dfrac{300 - 6}{.5538}\right) = P(z \geq 530.88) \approx .5 - .5 = 0$ (Using Table II, Appendix D)

Since the probability of observing a sample mean of 300 ppb or higher is essentially 0 if the true mean is 6 ppb, we would infer that the true mean PFOA concentration for the population of people who live near DuPont's Teflon facility is not 6 ppb but higher than 6 ppb.

5.33 a. From Exercise 2.33, the population of interarrival times is skewed to the right.

b. The population mean and standard deviation are:

$\mu = \dfrac{\sum x}{N} = \dfrac{25{,}504.84658}{267} = 95.52$

$\sigma^2 = \dfrac{\sum x^2 - \dfrac{\left(\sum x\right)^2}{N}}{N} = \dfrac{4{,}665{,}242.503 - \dfrac{\left(25{,}504.84658\right)^2}{267}}{267} = 8{,}348.027737$

$\sigma = \sqrt{8{,}348.027737} = 91.3675$

c. By the Central Limit Theorem, the sampling distribution of $\bar{x}$ will be approximately normal.

Theoretically, $\mu_{\bar{x}} = \mu = 95.52$ and $\sigma_{\bar{x}} = \dfrac{\sigma}{\sqrt{n}} = \dfrac{91.3675}{\sqrt{40}} = 14.4465$.

d. $P(\bar{x} < 90) = P\left(z < \dfrac{90 - 95.52}{14.4465}\right) = P(z < -.38) = .5 - .1480 = .3520$ (Using Table II, Appendix D.)

e &f. Answers will vary. A statistical package was used to randomly select 40 interarrival times from the Phishing data set and $\bar{x}$ was computed. This was repeated 50 times to simulate 50 students selecting 40 interarrival times and computing $\bar{x}$.

Using MINITAB, a histogram of the 50 $\bar{x}$ values is:

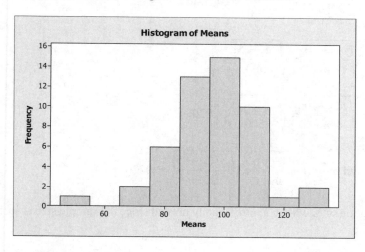

This shape is somewhat normal.

g. Using MINITAB, the mean and standard deviation of these 50 means is:

Descriptive Statistics: Means

Variable	N	Mean	StDev	Minimum	Q1	Median	Q3	Maximum
Means	50	96.09	14.08	52.73	86.36	95.65	105.23	130.23

The mean of these 50 means is 96.09. This is very close to $\mu_{\bar{x}} = 95.52$ found in part c. The standard deviation of these 50 means is 14.08. This is also very close to $\sigma_{\bar{x}} = \dfrac{\sigma}{\sqrt{n}} = \dfrac{91.54}{\sqrt{40}} = 14.4465$ found in part c.

5.35 For $n = 50$, we can use the Central Limit Theorem to decide the shape of the distribution of the sample mean bacterial counts. For the handrubbing sample, the sampling distribution of $\bar{x}$ is approximately normal with a mean of $\mu_{\bar{x}} = 35$ and standard deviation $\dfrac{\sigma}{\sqrt{n}} = \dfrac{59}{\sqrt{50}} = 8.344$. For the handwashing sample, the sampling distribution of $\bar{x}$ is approximately normal with a mean $\mu_{\bar{x}} = 69$ and standard deviation $\dfrac{\sigma}{\sqrt{n}} = \dfrac{106}{\sqrt{50}} = 14.991$.

For Handrubbing:

$$P(\bar{x} < 30 \mid \mu = 35) = P\left(z < \frac{30-35}{8.344}\right) = P(z < -.60) = .5 - .2257 = .2743 \text{ (using Table II, Appendix D)}$$

For Handwashing:

$$P(\bar{x} < 30 \mid \mu = 69) = P\left(z < \frac{30-69}{14.991}\right) = P(z < -2.60) = .5 - .4953 = .0047 \text{ (using Table II, Appendix D)}$$

Since the probability of getting a sample mean of less than 30 for the handrubbing is not small compared with that for the handwashing, the sample of workers probably came from the handrubbing group.

5.37   a. $\mu_{\hat{p}} = p = .1$ and $\sigma_{\hat{p}} = \sqrt{\dfrac{p(1-p)}{n}} = \sqrt{\dfrac{.1(1-.1)}{500}} = .0134$

b. $\mu_{\hat{p}} = p = .5$ and $\sigma_{\hat{p}} = \sqrt{\dfrac{p(1-p)}{n}} = \sqrt{\dfrac{.5(1-.5)}{500}} = .0224$

c. $\mu_{\hat{p}} = p = .7$ and $\sigma_{\hat{p}} = \sqrt{\dfrac{p(1-p)}{n}} = \sqrt{\dfrac{.7(1-.7)}{500}} = .0205$

5.39   a. $E(\hat{p}) = \mu_{\hat{p}} = p = .85$ and $\sigma_{\hat{p}} = \sqrt{\dfrac{p(1-p)}{n}} = \sqrt{\dfrac{.85(1-.85)}{250}} = .0226$

b.   The sampling distribution of $\hat{p}$ will be approximately normal since the sample size is sufficiently large.

c. $P(\hat{p} < .9) = P\left(z < \dfrac{.9-.85}{\sqrt{\dfrac{.85(1-.85)}{250}}}\right) = P(z < 2.21) = .5 + .4864 = .9864$ (Using Table II, Appendix D)

5.41   a.   Answers will vary. Using a statistical package, 500 samples of size 10 were generated from the population of (0,1). The histogram of the 500 sample proportions is:

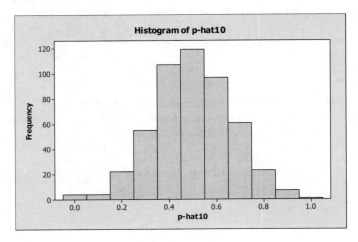

b. Using a statistical package, 500 samples of size 25 were generated from the population of (0,1). The histogram of the 500 sample proportions is:

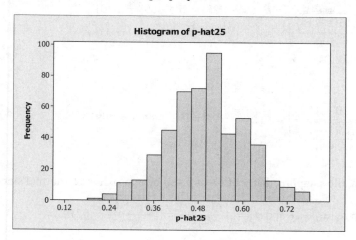

c. Using a statistical package, 500 samples of size 100 were generated from the population of (0,1). The histogram of the 500 sample proportions is:

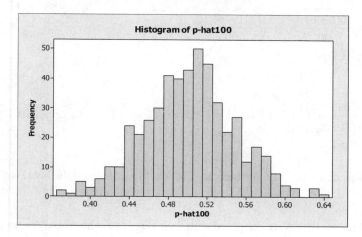

d. As the sample size increases, the spread of the values of $\hat{p}$ decreases. In the graph in part a, the spread of the values of $\hat{p}$ is from 0 to 1. In the graph in part b, the spread of the values of $\hat{p}$ is from .20 to .76. In the graph in part c, the spread of the values of $\hat{p}$ is from .37 to .64. In all graphs, the distributions are mound-shaped. As the sample size increases, the distribution becomes more peaked.

5.43 a. $E(\hat{p}) = p = .15$

b. $\sigma_{\hat{p}} = \sqrt{\dfrac{p(1-p)}{n}} = \sqrt{\dfrac{.15(1-.15)}{500}} = .0160$

c. The sampling distribution of $\hat{p}$ will be approximately normal since the sample size is sufficiently large.

d. $P(\hat{p} < .12) = P\left(z < \dfrac{.12 - .15}{\sqrt{\dfrac{.15(1-.15)}{500}}} \right) = P(z < -1.88) = .5 - .4699 = .0301$

(Using Table II, Appendix D)

e. $P(\hat{p} > .10) = P\left(z > \dfrac{.10 - .15}{\sqrt{\dfrac{.15(1-.15)}{500}}} \right) = P(z > -3.13) = .5 + .49913 = .99913$

5.45   By the Central Limit theorem, the sampling distribution of $\hat{p}$ will be approximately normal since the sample size is sufficiently large, with $\mu_{\hat{p}} = p = .6$ and $\sigma_{\hat{p}} = \sqrt{\dfrac{p(1-p)}{n}} = \sqrt{\dfrac{.6(1-.6)}{500}} = .0219.$

a. $P(.55 < \hat{p} < .65) = P\left(\dfrac{.55 - .6}{\sqrt{\dfrac{.6(1-.6)}{500}}} < z < \dfrac{.65 - .6}{\sqrt{\dfrac{.6(1-.6)}{500}}} \right) = P(-2.28 < z < 2.28) = .4887 + .4887 = .9774$

(Using Table II, Appendix D)

b. $P(\hat{p} > .75) = P\left(z > \dfrac{.75 - .6}{\sqrt{\dfrac{.6(1-.6)}{500}}} \right) = P(z > 6.85) \approx .5 - .5 = 0$ (Using Table II, Appendix D)

5.47   The probability that a guest was delighted with his/her stay and would recommend the hotel is $p = .15(.80) = .12.$

Let $\hat{p}$ = sample proportion of guests who were delighted with their stays and who would recommend the hotel. By the Central Limit theorem, the sampling distribution of $\hat{p}$ will be approximately normal since the sample size is sufficiently large, with $\mu_{\hat{p}} = p = .12$ and $\sigma_{\hat{p}} = \sqrt{\dfrac{p(1-p)}{n}} = \sqrt{\dfrac{.12(1-.12)}{100}} = .0325.$

$P\left(\hat{p} < \dfrac{10}{100} \right) = P(\hat{p} < .1) = P\left(z < \dfrac{.1 - .12}{\sqrt{\dfrac{.12(1-.12)}{100}}} \right) = P(z < -.62) = .5 - .2324 = .2676$

(Using Table II, Appendix D)

5.49   a. $E(\hat{p}) = \mu_{\hat{p}} = p = .92$

b.   By the Central Limit theorem, the sampling distribution of $\hat{p}$ will be approximately normal since the sample size is sufficiently large, with $\mu_{\hat{p}} = p = .92$ and $\sigma_{\hat{p}} = \sqrt{\dfrac{p(1-p)}{n}} = \sqrt{\dfrac{.92(1-.92)}{1000}} = .0086.$

$$P\left(\hat{p} < \frac{900}{1000}\right) = P(\hat{p} < .9) = P\left(z < \frac{.9 - .92}{\sqrt{\frac{.92(1-.92)}{1000}}}\right) = P(z < -2.33) = .5 - .4901 = .0099$$

(Using Table II, Appendix D)

5.51   Let $\hat{p}$ = sample proportion of Smartphone users who have a problem with apps not working on their cell phone. By the Central Limit theorem, the sampling distribution of $\hat{p}$ will be approximately normal since the sample size is sufficiently large, with $\mu_{\hat{p}} = p = .90$ and $\sigma_{\hat{p}} = \sqrt{\frac{p(1-p)}{n}} = \sqrt{\frac{.90(1-.90)}{75}} = .0346$.

$$P\left(\hat{p} < \frac{60}{75}\right) = P(\hat{p} < .8) = P\left(z < \frac{.8 - .9}{\sqrt{\frac{.9(1-.9)}{75}}}\right) = P(z < -2.89) = .5 - .4981 = .0019$$

(Using Table II, Appendix D)

Because this probability is so small, we would infer that the actual percentage of Smartphone users who have a problem with apps not working on their cell phone is not 90% but something less than 90%.

5.53   a.   "The sampling distribution of the sample statistic A" is the probability distribution of the variable A.

b.   "A" is an unbiased estimator of α if the mean of the sampling distribution of A is α.

c.   If both A and B are unbiased estimators of α, then the statistic whose standard deviation is smaller is a better estimator of α.

d.   No. The Central Limit Theorem applies only to the sample mean. If A is the sample mean, $\bar{x}$, and n is sufficiently large, then the Central Limit Theorem will apply. However, both A and B cannot be sample means. Thus, we cannot apply the Central Limit Theorem to both A and B.

5.55   By the Central Limit Theorem, the sampling distribution of $\bar{x}$ is approximately normal.

$$\mu_{\bar{x}} = \mu = 19.6 \; , \; \sigma_{\bar{x}} = \frac{3.2}{\sqrt{68}} = .388$$

a. $P(\bar{x} \le 19.6) = P\left(z \le \frac{19.6 - 19.6}{.388}\right) = P(z \le 0) = .5$ (Using Table II, Appendix D)

b. $P(\bar{x} \le 19) P\left(z \le \frac{19 - 19.6}{.388}\right) = P(z \le -1.55) = .5 - .4394 = .0606$ (Using Table II, Appendix D)

c. $P(\bar{x} \ge 20.1) = P\left(z \ge \frac{20.1 - 19.6}{.388}\right) = P(z \ge 1.29) = .5 - .4015 = .0985$ (Using Table II, Appendix D)

d. $P(19.2 \le \bar{x} \le 20.6) = P\left(\frac{19.2 - 19.6}{.388} < z < \frac{20.6 - 19.6}{.388}\right)$

$$= P(-1.03 \le z \le 2.58) = .3485 + .4951 = .8436$$ (Using Table II, Appendix D)

5.57 By the Central Limit theorem, the sampling distribution of $\hat{p}$ will be approximately normal since the sample size is sufficiently large with $\mu_{\hat{p}} = p = .8$ and $\sigma_{\hat{p}} = \sqrt{\dfrac{p(1-p)}{n}} = \sqrt{\dfrac{.8(1-.8)}{300}} = .0231$.

a. $P(\hat{p} < .83) = P\left(z < \dfrac{.83-.8}{\sqrt{\dfrac{.8(1-.8)}{300}}} \right) = P(z < 1.30) = .5 + .4032 = .9032$ (Using Table II, Appendix D)

b. $P(\hat{p} > .75) = P\left(z > \dfrac{.75-.8}{\sqrt{\dfrac{.8(1-.8)}{300}}} \right) = P(z > -2.17) = .5 + .4850 = .9850$ (Using Table II, Appendix D)

c. $P(.79 < \hat{p} < .81) = P\left(\dfrac{.79-.8}{\sqrt{\dfrac{.8(1-.8)}{300}}} < z < \dfrac{.81-.8}{\sqrt{\dfrac{.8(1-.8)}{300}}} \right) = P(-.43 < z < .43) = .1664 + .1664 = .3328$

(Using Table II, Appendix D)

5.59 Answers will vary. One hundred samples of size $n = 2$ were selected from a uniform distribution on the interval from 0 to 10. The process was repeated for samples of size $n = 5$, $n = 10$, $n = 30$, and $n = 50$. For each sample, the value of $\bar{x}$ was computed. Using MINITAB, the histograms for each set of 100 $\bar{x}$'s were constructed:

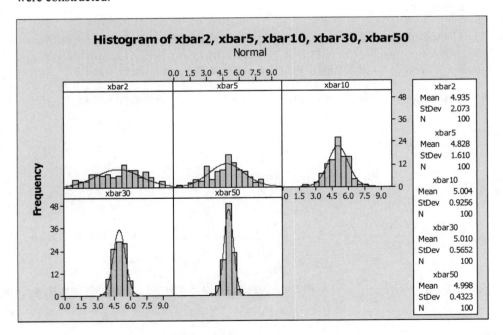

For small sizes of n, the sampling distributions of $\bar{x}$ are somewhat normal. As n increases, the sampling distributions of $\bar{x}$ become more normal.

5.61   Given: $\mu = 100$ and $\sigma = 10$

n	1	5	10	20	30	40	50
$\dfrac{\sigma}{\sqrt{n}}$	10	4.472	3.162	2.236	1.826	1.581	1.414

The graph of $\dfrac{\sigma}{\sqrt{n}}$ against n is given here:

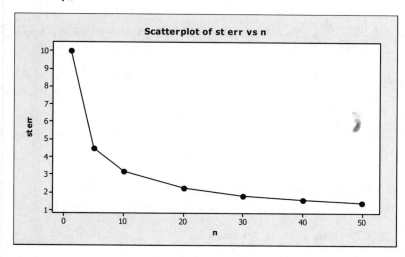

5.63   By the Central Limit Theorem, the sampling distribution of $\bar{x}$ is approximately normal with $\mu_{\bar{x}} = \mu = 19$

and $\sigma_{\bar{x}} = \dfrac{\sigma}{\sqrt{n}} = \dfrac{65}{\sqrt{100}} = 6.5.$

$$P(\bar{x} < 10) = P\left(z < \frac{10-19}{6.5}\right) = P(z < -1.38) = .5 - .4162 = .0838 \ \text{(using Table II, Appendix D)}$$

5.65   a.   By the Central Limit theorem, the sampling distribution of $\hat{p}$ will be approximately normal since the

sample size is sufficiently large, with $\mu_{\hat{p}} = p = .4$ and $\sigma_{\hat{p}} = \sqrt{\dfrac{p(1-p)}{n}} = \sqrt{\dfrac{.4(1-.4)}{50}} = .0693.$

$$P(\hat{p} > .6) = P\left(z > \frac{.6 - .4}{\sqrt{\dfrac{.4(1-.4)}{50}}}\right) = P(z > 2.89) = .5 - .4981 = .0019 \ \text{(Using Table II, Appendix D)}$$

b.   Since the probability of observing a value of $\hat{p}$ larger than .6 is so small ($p = .0019$) and we observed a value of $\hat{p} = .62,$ we would conclude that the true proportion of adult cell phone owners who download an "app" is not .4 but something larger than .4.

c.   If the value of $\hat{p} = .62$ was obtained at a convention for the International Association for the Wireless Telecommunications Industry, then it is probably not representative of the population of all adult cell phone owners. Those who attend such a convention would tend to be more "tech" savvy than the population of all adult cell phone owners. The value of $\hat{p} = .62$ would be larger than what we would expect from the general population.

5.67   a.   By the Central Limit Theorem, the sampling distribution of $\bar{x}$ is approximately normal with $\mu_{\bar{x}} = \mu$ and $\sigma_{\bar{x}} = \sigma / \sqrt{n} = \sigma / \sqrt{50}$.

b. $\mu_{\bar{x}} = \mu = 40$ and $\sigma_{\bar{x}} = \sigma / \sqrt{50} = 12 / \sqrt{50} = 1.6971$.

$$P(\bar{x} \geq 44) = P\left(z \geq \frac{44 - 40}{1.6971}\right) = P(z \geq 2.36) = .5 - .4909 = .0091 \text{ (using Table II, Appendix D)}$$

c. $\mu \pm 2\sigma / \sqrt{n} \Rightarrow 40 \pm 2(1.6971) \Rightarrow 40 \pm 3.3942 \Rightarrow (36.6058, \ 43.3942)$

$$P(36.6058 \leq \bar{x} \leq 43.3942) = P\left(\frac{36.6058 - 40}{1.6971} \leq z \leq \frac{43.3942 - 40}{1.6971}\right) \text{ (using Table II, Appendix D)}$$
$$= P(-2 \leq z \leq 2) = 2(.4772) = .9544$$

5.69   From Exercise 5.68, $\sigma = .001$. We must assume the Central Limit theorem applies (n is only 25). Thus, the distribution of $\bar{x}$ is approximately normal with $\mu_{\bar{x}} = \mu = .501$ and $\sigma_{\bar{x}} = \dfrac{\sigma}{\sqrt{n}} = \dfrac{.001}{\sqrt{25}} = .0002$. Using Table II, Appendix D,

$$P(\bar{x} < .4994) + P(\bar{x} > .5006) = P\left(z < \frac{.4994 - .501}{.0002}\right) + P\left(z > \frac{.5006 - .501}{.0002}\right)$$
$$= P(z < -8) + P(z > -2) = (.5 - .5) + (.5 + .4772) = .9772$$

5.71   a. $E(\hat{p}) = \mu_{\hat{p}} = p = .2$ and $\sigma_{\hat{p}} = \sqrt{\dfrac{p(1-p)}{n}} = \sqrt{\dfrac{.2(1-.2)}{250}} = .0253$

b. $E(\hat{p}) \pm 2\sigma_{\hat{p}} \Rightarrow .2 \pm 2(.0253) \Rightarrow .2 \pm .0506 \Rightarrow (.1494, \ .2506)$

c.   By the Central Limit Theorem, the sampling distribution of $\hat{p}$ will be approximately normal since the sample size is sufficiently large. Thus,

$$P(.1494 \leq \hat{p} \leq .2506) = P\left(\frac{.1494 - .2}{.0253} \leq z \leq \frac{.2506 - .2}{.0253}\right) = P(-2 \leq z \leq 2) = .4772 + .4772 = .9544$$

5.73   a.   Let $p_1 =$ probability of an error $= 1/100 = .01$ and $p_2 =$ probability of an error resulting in a significant problem $= 1/500 = .002$.

Let $\hat{p}_1 =$ proportion of errors. Then $E(\hat{p}_1) = \mu_{\hat{p}_1} = p_1 = .01$.

Let $\hat{p}_2 =$ proportion of significant errors. Then $E(\hat{p}_2) = \mu_{\hat{p}_2} = p_2 = .002$.

b. Since the distribution of $\hat{p}_2$ will be approximately normal by the Central Limit Theorem, we would expect the proportion of significant errors to fall within 2 standard deviations of the expected value. The interval would be:

$$\hat{p}_2 \pm 2\sigma_{\hat{p}_2} \Rightarrow .002 \pm 2\sqrt{\frac{.002(1-.002)}{60,000}} \Rightarrow .002 \pm .00036 \Rightarrow (.00164, .00236)$$

5.75 By the Central Limit Theorem, the sampling distribution of $\bar{x}$ is approximately normal with $\mu_{\bar{x}} = \mu = 40$ and $\sigma_{\bar{x}} = \dfrac{\sigma}{\sqrt{n}} = \dfrac{5}{\sqrt{100}} = .5$.

$$P(\bar{x} \geq 42) = P\left(z \geq \frac{42-40}{.5}\right) = P(z > 4) \approx .5 - .5 = 0 \quad \text{(Using Table II, Appendix D)}$$

Since this probability is so small, it is very unlikely that the sample was selected from the population of convicted drug dealers.

5.77 Answers will vary. We are to assume that the fecal bacteria concentrations of water specimens follow an approximate normal distribution. Now, suppose that the distribution of the fecal bacteria concentration at a beach is normal with a true mean of 360 and with a standard deviation of 40. If only a single sample was selected, then the probability of getting an observation at the 400 level or higher would be:

$$P(x \geq 400) = P\left(z \geq \frac{400-360}{40}\right) = P(z \geq 1) = .5 - .3413 = .1587 \quad \text{(Using Table II, Appendix D)}$$

Thus, even if the water is safe, the beach would be closed approximately 15.87% of the time.

On the other hand, if the mean was 440 and the standard deviation was still 40, then the probability of getting a single observation less than the 400 level would be:

$$P(x \leq 400) = P\left(z \leq \frac{400-440}{40}\right) = P(z \leq -1) = .5 - .3413 = .1587 \quad \text{(Using Table II, Appendix D)}$$

Thus, the beach would remain open approximately 15.78% of the time when it should be closed.

Now, suppose we took a random sample of 64 water specimens. The sampling distribution of $\bar{x}$ is approximately normal by the Central Limit Theorem with $\mu_{\bar{x}} = \mu$ and $\sigma_{\bar{x}} = \dfrac{\sigma}{\sqrt{n}} = \dfrac{40}{\sqrt{64}} = 5$.

If $\mu = 360$, $P(\bar{x} \geq 400) = P\left(z \leq \frac{400-360}{5}\right) = P(z \geq 8) \approx .5 - .5 = 0$. Thus, the beach would never be shut down if the water was actually safe if we took samples of size 64.

If $\mu = 440$, $P(\bar{x} \leq 400) = P\left(z \leq \frac{400-440}{5}\right) = P(z \leq -8) \approx .5 - .5 = 0$. Thus, the beach would never be left open if the water was actually unsafe if we took samples of size 64.

The single sample standard can lead to unsafe decisions or inconvenient decisions, but is much easier to collect than samples of size 64.

Copyright © 2018 Pearson Education, Inc.

Chapter 6
Inferences Based on a Single Sample: Estimation with Confidence Intervals

6.1   a.   For $\alpha = .10$, $\alpha/2 = .10/2 = .05$. $z_{\alpha/2} = z_{.05}$ is the z-score with .05 of the area to the right of it. The area between 0 and $z_{.05}$ is $.5 - .05 = .4500$. Using Table II, Appendix D, $z_{.05} = 1.645$.

b.   For $\alpha = .01$, $\alpha/2 = .01/2 = .005$. $z_{\alpha/2} = z_{.005}$ is the z-score with .005 of the area to the right of it. The area between 0 and $z_{.005}$ is $.5 - .005 = .4950$. Using Table II, Appendix D, $z_{.005} = 2.575$.

c.   For $\alpha = .05$, $\alpha/2 = .05/2 = .025$. $z_{\alpha/2} = z_{.025}$ is the z-score with .025 of the area to the right of it. The area between 0 and $z_{.025}$ is $.5 - .025 = .4750$. Using Table II, Appendix D, $z_{.025} = 1.96$.

d.   For $\alpha = .20$, $\alpha/2 = .20/2 = .10$. $z_{\alpha/2} = z_{.10}$ is the z-score with .10 of the area to the right of it. The area between 0 and $z_{.10}$ is $.5 - .10 = .4000$. Using Table II, Appendix D, $z_{.10} = 1.28$.

6.3   a.   For confidence coefficient .95, $\alpha = .05$ and $\alpha/2 = .05/2 = .025$. From Table II, Appendix D, $z_{.025} = 1.96$. The confidence interval is:

$$\bar{x} \pm z_{.025} \frac{\sigma}{\sqrt{n}} \Rightarrow 28 \pm 1.96 \frac{\sqrt{12}}{\sqrt{75}} \Rightarrow 28 \pm .784 \Rightarrow (27.216, \ 28.784)$$

b. $$\bar{x} \pm z_{.025} \frac{\sigma}{\sqrt{n}} \Rightarrow 102 \pm 1.96 \frac{\sqrt{22}}{\sqrt{200}} \Rightarrow 102 \pm .65 \Rightarrow (101.35, \ 102.65)$$

c. $$\bar{x} \pm z_{.025} \frac{\sigma}{\sqrt{n}} \Rightarrow 15 \pm 1.96 \frac{.3}{\sqrt{100}} \Rightarrow 15 \pm .0588 \Rightarrow (14.9412, \ 15.0588)$$

d. $$\bar{x} \pm z_{.025} \frac{\sigma}{\sqrt{n}} \Rightarrow 4.05 \pm 1.96 \frac{.83}{\sqrt{100}} \Rightarrow 4.05 \pm .163 \Rightarrow (3.887, \ 4.213)$$

e.   No. Since the sample size in each part was large (*n* ranged from 75 to 200), the Central Limit Theorem indicates that the sampling distribution of $\bar{x}$ is approximately normal.

6.5   a.   For confidence coefficient .95, $\alpha = .05$ and $\alpha/2 = .05/2 = .025$. From Table II, Appendix D, $z_{.025} = 1.96$. The confidence interval is:

$$\bar{x} \pm z_{\alpha/2} \frac{s}{\sqrt{n}} \Rightarrow 26.2 \pm 1.96 \frac{4.1}{\sqrt{70}} \Rightarrow 26.2 \pm .96 \Rightarrow (25.24, 27.16)$$

b.   The confidence coefficient of .95 means that in repeated sampling, 95% of all confidence intervals constructed will include μ.

    c.   For confidence coefficient .99, $\alpha = .01$ and $\alpha/2 = .01/2 = .005$. From Table II, Appendix D, $z_{.005} = 2.58$. The confidence interval is:

$$\bar{x} \pm z_{\alpha/2} \frac{s}{\sqrt{n}} \Rightarrow 26.2 \pm 2.58 \frac{4.1}{\sqrt{70}} \Rightarrow 26.2 \pm 1.26 \Rightarrow (24.94, 27.46)$$

    d.   As the confidence coefficient increases, the width of the confidence interval also increases.

    e.   Yes. Since the sample size is 70, the Central Limit Theorem applies. This ensures the distribution of $\bar{x}$ is normal, regardless of the original distribution.

6.7   A point estimator is a single value used to estimate the parameter, μ. An interval estimator is two values, an upper and lower bound, which define an interval with which we attempt to enclose the parameter, μ. An interval estimate also has a measure of confidence associated with it.

6.9   Yes. As long as the sample size is sufficiently large, the Central Limit Theorem says the distribution of $\bar{x}$ is approximately normal regardless of the original distribution.

6.11   For confidence coefficient .95, $\alpha = .05$ and $\alpha/2 = .05/2 = .025$. From Table II, Appendix D, $z_{.025} = 1.96$. The confidence interval is:

$$\bar{x} \pm z_{.025} \frac{\sigma}{\sqrt{n}} \Rightarrow 112 \pm 1.96 \frac{560}{\sqrt{2,617}} \Rightarrow 112 \pm 21.46 \Rightarrow (90.54, 133.46)$$

    We are 95% confidence that the true mean tipping point of all daily deal offerings in Korea is between 90.54 and 133.46.

6.13   a.   The point estimate of μ is $\bar{x} = 3.11$.

    b.   For confidence coefficient .98, $\alpha = .02$ and $\alpha/2 = .02/2 = .01$. From Table II, Appendix D, $z_{.01} = 2.33$. The confidence interval is:

$$\bar{x} \pm z_{.01} \frac{\sigma}{\sqrt{n}} \Rightarrow 3.11 \pm 2.33 \frac{.66}{\sqrt{307}} \Rightarrow 3.11 \pm .088 \Rightarrow (3.022, 3.198)$$

    c.   This statement is incorrect. Once the interval is constructed, there is no probability involved. The true mean is either in the interval or it is not. A better statement would be: "We are 98% confident that the true mean GPA will be between 3.022 and 3.198.

    d.   Since the sample size is so large $(n = 307)$, the Central Limit Theorem applies. Thus, it does not matter whether the distributions of grades is skewed or not.

6.15   a.   For confidence coefficient .90, $\alpha = .10$ and $\alpha/2 = .10/2 = .05$. From Table II, Appendix D, $z_{.05} = 1.645$. The confidence interval is:

$$\bar{x} \pm z_{.05} \frac{\sigma}{\sqrt{n}} \Rightarrow 2.42 \pm 1.645 \frac{2.84}{\sqrt{86}} \Rightarrow 2.42 \pm .504 \Rightarrow (1.916, 2.924)$$

    b.   We are 90% confidence that the true mean intention to comply score for the population of entry level accountants is between 1.916 and 2.924.

c. In repeated sampling, 90% of all similarly constructed confidence intervals will contain the true value of μ.

d. $\bar{x} \pm 2s \Rightarrow 2.42 \pm 2(2.84) \Rightarrow 2.42 \pm 5.68 \Rightarrow (-3.26, 8.10)$. This interval gives the range of the actual values of x, while the confidence interval in part a gives the range of values for the population mean.

6.17 a. The target parameter is the population mean salary of these 411 CEOs who participated in the *Forbes'* survey, μ.

b. Answers will vary. Using MINITAB, a sample of 50 CEOs was selected. The ranks of the 50 selected are:

3, 4, 6, 10, 17, 24, 41, 48, 50, 77, 78, 80, 88, 95, 98, 121, 125, 152, 155, 156, 162, 176, 184, 192, 197, 214, 215, 231, 240, 262, 268, 273, 279, 280, 295, 303, 306, 329, 337, 341, 346, 351, 372, 380, 398, 400, 414, 418, 433, 434

c. Using MINITAB, the descriptive statistics are:

Descriptive Statistics: Total Pay
```
Variable      N     Mean      StDev
Total Pay-R   50  13924013  9767808
```

The sample mean is $\bar{x} = \$13,924,013$.

d. Using MINITAB, the descriptive statistics for the entire data set is:

Descriptive Statistics: Total Pay
```
Variable     N      Mean       StDev
Total Pay   441  13879376  11357194
```

From the above, the standard deviation of the population is $11,357,194.

e. For confidence coefficient .99, $\alpha = .01$ and $\alpha / 2 = .01/2 = .005$. From Table II, Appendix D, $z_{.005} = 2.58$. The confidence interval is:

$$\bar{x} \pm z_{.005} \frac{\sigma}{\sqrt{n}} \Rightarrow 13,924,013 \pm 2.58 \frac{11,357,194}{\sqrt{50}} \Rightarrow 13,924,013 \pm 4,143,866.43$$
$$\Rightarrow (\$9,780,146.57, \$18,067,879.43)$$

f. We are 99% confident that the true mean salary of all 441 CEOs in the *Forbes'* survey is between $9,780,146.57 and $18,067,879.43.

g. From part d, the true mean salary of all 441 CEOs is $13,879,376. This value does fall within the 99% confidence interval that we found in part e.

6.19 a. An estimate of the true mean Mach rating score of all purchasing managers is $\bar{x} = 99.6$.

b. For confidence coefficient .95, $\alpha = .05$ and $\alpha / 2 = .05/2 = .025$. From Table II, Appendix D, $z_{.025} = 1.96$. The 95% confidence interval is:

$$\bar{x} \pm z_{\alpha/2} \frac{s}{\sqrt{n}} \Rightarrow 99.6 \pm 1.96 \frac{12.6}{\sqrt{122}} \Rightarrow 99.6 \pm 2.24 \Rightarrow (97.36, 101.84)$$

c.   We are 95% confident that the true Mach rating score of all purchasing managers is between 97.36 and 101.84.

d.   Yes, there is evidence to dispute this claim. We are 95% confident that the true mean Mach rating score is between 97.36 and 101.84. It would be very unlikely that the true means Mach scores is as low as 85.

6.21   To answer the question, we will first form 90% confidence intervals for each of the 2 SAT scores.

For confidence coefficient .90, $\alpha = .10$ and $\alpha / 2 = .10 / 2 = .05$. From Table II, Appendix D, $z_{.05} = 1.645$. The confidence interval for SAT-Mathematics scores is:

$$\bar{x} \pm z_{\alpha/2} \frac{s}{\sqrt{n}} \Rightarrow 19 \pm 1.645 \frac{65}{\sqrt{265}} \Rightarrow 19 \pm 6.57 \Rightarrow (12.43, \ 25.57)$$

We are 90% confident that the mean change in SAT-Mathematics score is between 12.43 and 25.57 points.

The confidence interval for SAT-Verbal scores is:

$$\bar{x} \pm z_{\alpha/2} \frac{s}{\sqrt{n}} \Rightarrow 7 \pm 1.645 \frac{49}{\sqrt{265}} \Rightarrow 7 \pm 4.95 \Rightarrow (2.05, \ 11.95)$$

We are 90% confident that the mean change in SAT-Verbal score is between 2.05 and 11.95 points.

The SAT-Mathematics test would be the most likely of the two to have 15 as the mean change in score. This value of 15 is in the 90% confidence interval for the mean change in SAT-Mathematics score. However, 15 does not fall in the 90% confidence interval for the mean SAT-Verbal test.

6.23   a.   For confidence coefficient .80, $\alpha = .20$ and $\alpha / 2 = .20 / 2 = .10$. From Table II, Appendix D, $z_{.05} = 1.28$. From Table III, with df $= n - 1 = 5 - 1 = 4$, $t_{.10} = 1.533$.

b.   For confidence coefficient .90, $\alpha = .10$ and $\alpha / 2 = .10 / 2 = .05$. From Table II, Appendix D, $z_{.05} = 1.645$. From Table III, with df $= n - 1 = 5 - 1 = 4$, $t_{.05} = 2.132$.

c.   For confidence coefficient .95, $\alpha = .05$ and $\alpha / 2 = .05 / 2 = .025$. From Table II, Appendix D, $z_{.025} = 1.96$. From Table III, with df $= n - 1 = 5 - 1 = 4$, $t_{.025} = 2.776$.

d.   For confidence coefficient .98, $\alpha = .02$ and $\alpha / 2 = .02 / 2 = .01$. From Table II, Appendix D, $z_{.01} = 2.33$. From Table III, with df $= n - 1 = 5 - 1 = 4$, $t_{.01} = 3.747$.

e.   For confidence coefficient .99, $\alpha = .01$ and $\alpha / 2 = .01 / 2 = .005$. From Table II, Appendix D, $z_{.005} = 2.575$. From Table III, with df $= n - 1 = 5 - 1 = 4$, $t_{.005} = 4.604$.

f.   Both the *t*- and *z*-distributions are symmetric around 0 and mound-shaped. The *t*-distribution is more spread out than the *z*-distribution.

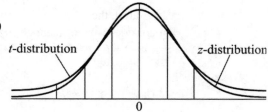

6.25   a. $P(-t_0 < t < t_0) = .95$ where $df = 10$

Because of symmetry, the statement can be written

$$P(0 < t < t_0) = .475 \text{ where } df = 10$$

$$\Rightarrow P(t \geq t_0) = .025 \Rightarrow t_0 = 2.228$$

b. $P(t \leq -t_0 \text{ or } t \geq t_0) = .05$ where $df = 10$

$$\Rightarrow 2P(t \geq t_0) = .05 \Rightarrow P(t \geq t_0) = .025 \Rightarrow t_0 = 2.228$$

c. $P(t \leq t_0) = .05$ where $df = 10$

Because of symmetry, the statement can be written

$$\Rightarrow P(t \geq -t_0) = .05 \Rightarrow t_0 = -1.812$$

d. $P(t \leq -t_0 \text{ or } t \geq t_0) = .10$ where $df = 20$

$$\Rightarrow 2P(t \geq t_0) = .10 \Rightarrow P(t \geq t_0) = .05 \Rightarrow t_0 = 1.725$$

e. $P(t \leq -t_0 \text{ or } t \geq t_0) = .01$ where $df = 5$

$$\Rightarrow 2P(t \geq t_0) = .01 \Rightarrow P(t \geq t_0) = .005 \Rightarrow t_0 = 4.032$$

6.27   First, we must compute $\bar{x}$ and s.

$$\bar{x} = \frac{\sum x}{n} = \frac{30}{6} = 5, \quad s^2 = \frac{\sum x^2 - \frac{(\sum x)^2}{n}}{n-1} = \frac{176 - \frac{(30)^2}{6}}{6-1} = \frac{26}{5} = 5.2, \quad s = \sqrt{5.2} = 2.2804$$

a.   For confidence coefficient .90, $\alpha = .10$ and $\alpha/2 = .10/2 = .05$. From Table III, Appendix D, with df $= n - 1 = 6 - 1 = 5$, $t_{.05} = 2.015$. The 90% confidence interval is:

$$\bar{x} \pm t_{.05} \frac{s}{\sqrt{n}} \Rightarrow 5 \pm 2.015 \frac{2.2804}{\sqrt{6}} \Rightarrow 5 \pm 1.88 \Rightarrow (3.12, \ 6.88)$$

b.   For confidence coefficient .95, $\alpha = .05$ and $\alpha/2 = .05/2 = .025$. From Table III, Appendix D, with df $= n - 1 = 6 - 1 = 5$, $t_{.025} = 2.571$. The 95% confidence interval is:

$$\bar{x} \pm t_{.025} \frac{s}{\sqrt{n}} \Rightarrow 5 \pm 2.571 \frac{2.2804}{\sqrt{6}} \Rightarrow 5 \pm 2.39 \Rightarrow (2.61, \ 7.39)$$

c.   For confidence coefficient .99, $\alpha = .01$ and $\alpha/2 = .01/2 = .005$. From Table III, Appendix D, with df $= n - 1 = 6 - 1 = 5$, $t_{.005} = 4.032$. The 99% confidence interval is:

$$\bar{x} \pm t_{.005} \frac{s}{\sqrt{n}} \Rightarrow 5 \pm 4.032 \frac{2.2804}{\sqrt{6}} \Rightarrow 5 \pm 3.75 \Rightarrow (1.25, \ 8.75)$$

d.   a)   For confidence coefficient .90, $\alpha = .10$ and $\alpha/2 = .10/2 = .05$. From Table III, Appendix D, with df $= n - 1 = 25 - 1 = 24$, $t_{.05} = 1.711$. The 90% confidence interval is:

$$\bar{x} \pm t_{.05} \frac{s}{\sqrt{n}} \Rightarrow 5 \pm 1.711 \frac{2.2804}{\sqrt{25}} \Rightarrow 5 \pm .78 \Rightarrow (4.22,\ 5.78)$$

b)   For confidence coefficient .95, $\alpha = .05$ and $\alpha/2 = .05/2 = .025$. From Table III, Appendix D, with df $= n-1 = 25-1 = 24$, $t_{.025} = 2.064$. The 95% confidence interval is:

$$\bar{x} \pm t_{.025} \frac{s}{\sqrt{n}} \Rightarrow 5 \pm 2.064 \frac{2.2804}{\sqrt{25}} \Rightarrow 5 \pm .94 \Rightarrow (4.06,\ 5.94)$$

c)   For confidence coefficient .99, $\alpha = .01$ and $\alpha/2 = .01/2 = .005$. From Table III, Appendix D, with df $= n-1 = 25-1 = 24$, $t_{.005} = 2.797$. The 99% confidence interval is:

$$\bar{x} \pm t_{.005} \frac{s}{\sqrt{n}} \Rightarrow 5 \pm 2.797 \frac{2.2804}{\sqrt{25}} \Rightarrow 5 \pm 1.28 \Rightarrow (3.72,\ 6.28)$$

Increasing the sample size decreases the width of the confidence interval.

6.29   a.   The target parameter is $\mu =$ mean trap spacing for the population of red spiny lobster fishermen fishing in Baja California Sur, Mexico.

b.   Using MINITAB, the descriptive statistics are:

Descriptive Statistics: Trap

Variable	N	Mean	StDev	Minimum	Q1	Median	Q3	Maximum
Trap	7	89.86	11.63	70.00	82.00	93.00	99.00	105.00

The point estimate of μ is $\bar{x} = 89.86$.

c.   For this problem, the sample size is $n = 7$. For a small sample size, the Central Limit Theorem does not apply. Therefore, we do not know what the sampling distribution of $\bar{x}$ is.

d.   For confidence coefficient .95, $\alpha = .05$ and $\alpha/2 = .05/2 = .025$. From Table III, Appendix D, with df $= n-1 = 7-1 = 6$, $t_{.025} = 2.447$. The 95% confidence interval is:

$$\bar{x} \pm t_{.025} \frac{s}{\sqrt{n}} \Rightarrow 89.86 \pm 2.447 \frac{11.63}{\sqrt{7}} \Rightarrow 89.86 \pm 10.756 \Rightarrow (79.104,\ 100.616)$$

e.   We are 95% confident that the true mean trap spacing for the population of red spiny lobster fishermen fishing in Baja California Sur, Mexico is between 79.104 and 100.616 meters.

f.   We must assume that the population of trap spacings is normally distributed and that the sample is a random sample.

6.31   a.   Using MINITAB, the descriptive statistics are:

Descriptive Statistics: Wheels

Variable	N	Mean	StDev	Minimum	Q1	Median	Q3	Maximum
Wheels	28	3.214	1.371	1.000	2.000	3.000	4.000	8.000

For confidence coefficient .99, $\alpha = .01$ and $\alpha/2 = .01/2 = .005$. From Table II, Appendix D, $z_{.005} = 2.58$. The confidence interval is:

$$\bar{x} \pm z_{.005} \frac{\sigma}{\sqrt{n}} \Rightarrow 67.755 \pm 2.58 \frac{1.371}{\sqrt{28}} \Rightarrow 3.214 \pm .668 \Rightarrow (2.546,\ 3.882)$$

b.   We are 99% confident that the true mean number of wheels used on all social robots is between 2.546 and 3.882.

c.   99% of all similarly constructed confidence intervals will contain the true mean.

6.33   a.   From the printout, the 95% confidence interval is $(7.639,\ 8.814)$.

b.   No. We are p5% confident that the true mean ratio of repair to replacement cost is between 7.639 and 8.814. The value is 7.0 is way below this range and would be very unlikely.

c.   We need to assume that the population of ratios of repair to replacement cost is normally distributed and that the sample was a random sample.

6.35   a.   Using MINITAB, the confidence interval is:

One-Sample T: Velocities
```
Variable       N      Mean     StDev   SE Mean         95% CI
Velocities    25   0.26208   0.04669   0.00934   (0.24281, 0.28135)
```

We are 95% confident that the true mean bubble rising velocity is between .24281 and .28135.

b.   No. The value of $\mu = .338$ is not in the interval and would be a very unlikely value for the mean. Thus, the data in the table were not generated at this sparging rate.

6.37   a.   Using MINITAB, the descriptive statistics are:

Descriptive Statistics: Skid
```
Variable    N   Mean   StDev   Minimum      Q1   Median      Q3   Maximum
Skid       20  358.5   117.8     141.0   276.0    367.5   438.0     574.0
```

For confidence coefficient .95, $\alpha = .05$ and $\alpha/2 = .05/2 = .025$. From Table III, Appendix D, with df $= n - 1 = 20 - 1 = 19$, $t_{.025} = 2.093$. The 95% confidence interval is:

$$\bar{x} \pm t_{.05} \frac{s}{\sqrt{n}} \Rightarrow 358.5 \pm 2.093 \frac{117.8}{\sqrt{20}} \Rightarrow 358.5 \pm 55.13 \Rightarrow (303.37,\ 413.63)$$

b.   We are 95% confident that the mean skidding distance is between 303.37 and 413.63 meters.

c.   In order for the inference to be valid, the skidding distances must be from a normal distribution. We will use the four methods to check for normality. First, we will look at a histogram of the data. Using MINITAB, the histogram of the data is:

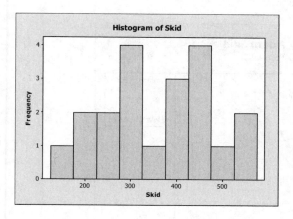

From the histogram, the data appear to be fairly mound-shaped. This indicates that the data may be normal.

Next, we look at the intervals $\bar{x} \pm s$, $\bar{x} \pm 2s$, $\bar{x} \pm 3s$. If the proportions of observations falling in each interval are approximately .68, .95, and 1.00, then the data are approximately normal.

$\bar{x} \pm s \Rightarrow 358.5 \pm 117.8 \Rightarrow (240.7, \ 476.3)$ 14 of the 20 values fall in this interval. The proportion is .70. This is very close to the .68 we would expect if the data were normal.

$\bar{x} \pm 2s \Rightarrow 358.5 \pm 2(117.8) \Rightarrow 358.5 \pm 235.6 \Rightarrow (122.9, \ 594.1)$ 20 of the 20 values fall in this interval. The proportion is 1.00. This is a larger than the .95 we would expect if the data were normal.

$\bar{x} \pm 3s \Rightarrow 358.5 \pm 3(117.8) \Rightarrow 358.5 \pm 353.4 \Rightarrow (5.1, \ 711.9)$ 20 of the 20 values fall in this interval. The proportion is 1.00. This is exactly the 1.00 we would expect if the data were normal.

From this method, it appears that the data may be normal.

Next, we look at the ratio of the *IQR* to *s*. $IQR = Q_U - Q_L = \ 438 - 276 = 162$.

$\dfrac{IQR}{s} = \dfrac{162}{117.8} = 1.37$ This is fairly close to the 1.3 we would expect if the data were normal. This method indicates the data may be normal.

Finally, using MINITAB, the normal probability plot is:

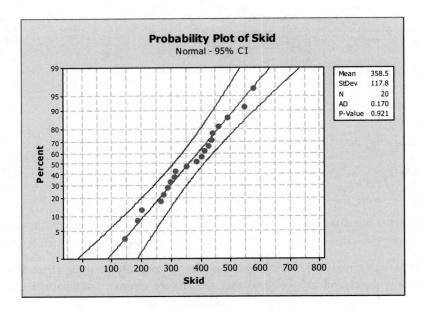

Since the data form a fairly straight line, the data may be normal.

From above, all the methods indicate the data may be normal. It appears that the assumption that the data come from a normal distribution is probably valid.

d.   No. A distance of 425 meters falls above the 95% confidence interval that was computed in part **a**. It would be very unlikely to observe a mean skidding distance of at least 425 meters.

6.39   a.   The population from which the sample was drawn is the Forbes 216 Biggest Private companies.

b.   Using MINITAB, the descriptive statistics are:

Descriptive Statistics: Revenue

Variable	N	Mean	StDev	Minimum	Q1	Median	Q3	Maximum
Revenue	15	7.43	7.36	2.30	3.10	4.40	9.70	31.00

For confidence coefficient .98, $\alpha = .02$ and $\alpha/2 = .02/2 = .01$. From Table III, Appendix D, with df $= n - 1 = 15 - 1 = 14$, $t_{.01} = 2.624$. The 98% confidence interval is:

$$\bar{x} \pm t_{.01} \frac{s}{\sqrt{n}} \Rightarrow 7.43 \pm 2.624 \frac{7.36}{\sqrt{15}} \Rightarrow 7.43 \pm 4.987 \Rightarrow (2.443, \ 12.417)$$

c.   We are 98% confident that the mean revenue is between $2.443 and $12.417 billion.

d.   The population must be approximately normally distributed in order for the procedure used in part **b** to be valid.

e.   Yes. The value of $5.0 billion dollars falls in the 98% confidence interval computed in part **b**. Therefore, we should believe the claim.

6.41   The sample size is large enough if both $n\hat{p} \geq 15$ and $n\hat{q} \geq 15$.

a.   When $n = 400$, $\hat{p} = .10$: $n\hat{p} = 400(.10) = 40$ and $n\hat{q} = 400(.90) = 360$

Since both numbers are greater than or equal to 15, the sample size is sufficiently large to conclude the normal approximation is reasonable.

b. When $n = 50$, $\hat{p} = .10$: $n\hat{p} = 50(.10) = 5$ and $n\hat{q} = 50(.90) = 45$

Since $n\hat{p}$ is less than 15, the sample size is not large enough to conclude the normal approximation is reasonable.

c. When $n = 20$, $\hat{p} = .5$: $n\hat{p} = 20(.5) = 10$ and $n\hat{q} = 20(.5) = 10$

Since both numbers are less than 15, the sample size is not large enough to conclude the normal approximation is reasonable.

d. When $n = 20$, $\hat{p} = .3$: $n\hat{p} = 20(.3) = 6$ and $n\hat{q} = 20(.7) = 14$

Since both numbers are less than 15, the sample size is not large enough to conclude the normal approximation is reasonable.

6.43　a. The sample size is large enough if both $n\hat{p} \geq 15$ and $n\hat{q} \geq 15$.
$n\hat{p} = 225(.46) = 103.5$ and $n\hat{q} = 225(.54) = 121.5$

Since both numbers are greater than or equal to 15, the sample size is sufficiently large to conclude the normal approximation is reasonable.

b. For confidence coefficient .95, $\alpha = .05$ and $\alpha/2 = .05/2 = .025$. From Table II, Appendix D, $z_{.025} = 1.96$. The 95% confidence interval is:

$$\hat{p} \pm z_{.025}\sqrt{\frac{pq}{n}} \Rightarrow \hat{p} \pm 1.96\sqrt{\frac{\hat{p}\hat{q}}{n}} \Rightarrow .46 \pm 1.96\sqrt{\frac{.46(.54)}{225}} \Rightarrow .46 \pm .065 \Rightarrow (.395, .525)$$

c. We are 95% confident the true value of p falls between .395 and .525.

d. "95% confidence interval" means that if repeated samples of size 225 were selected from the population and 95% confidence intervals formed, 95% of all confidence intervals will contain the true value of p.

6.45　a. $\hat{p} = \dfrac{x}{n} = \dfrac{125}{250} = .5$

b. For confidence coefficient .90, $\alpha = .10$ and $\alpha/2 = .10/2 = .05$. From Table II, Appendix D, $z_{.05} = 1.645$. The confidence interval is:

$$\hat{p} \pm z_{.05}\sqrt{\frac{\hat{p}\hat{q}}{n}} \Rightarrow .5 \pm 1.645\sqrt{\frac{.5(.5)}{250}} \Rightarrow .5 \pm .052 \Rightarrow (.448, .552)$$

c. We are 90% confident that the true proportion of all U.S. adults who would agree to participate in a store loyalty card program, despite the potential for information sharing is between .448 and .552.

d. "We are 90% confident" means that in repeated sampling, 90% of all intervals constructed in a similar manner will contain the true proportion.

6.47   a. $\hat{p} = \dfrac{x}{n} = \dfrac{818}{2,045} = .4$

   b.   By the Central Limit Theorem, the sampling distribution of $\hat{p}$ is approximately normal with $\mu_{\hat{p}} = p$

and $\sigma_{\hat{p}} = \sqrt{\dfrac{pq}{n}}$ if n is sufficiently large. The sample size is sufficiently large if $n\hat{p} \geq 15$ and $n\hat{q} \geq 15$.

For this exercise, $n\hat{p} = 2,045(.4) = 818$ and $n\hat{q} = 2,045(.6) = 1,227$. Since both values are greater than 15, the sample size is sufficiently large.

   c.   For confidence coefficient .95, $\alpha = .05$ and $\alpha/2 = .05/2 = .025$. From Table II, Appendix D, $z_{.025} = 1.96$. The confidence interval is:

$$\hat{p} \pm z_{.025}\sqrt{\dfrac{\hat{p}\hat{q}}{n}} \Rightarrow .4 \pm 1.96\sqrt{\dfrac{.4(.6)}{2,045}} \Rightarrow .4 \pm .021 \Rightarrow (.379, .421)$$

   d.   We are 95% confident that the true proportion of Arlington Texas homes with market values that are overestimated by more than 10% by Zillow is between .379 and .421.

   e.   No, the claim is not believable. The 95% confidence interval constructed in part c does not contain .3. Thus, .3 is not a likely value for p.

6.49   a.   The population of interest is all American adults.

   b.   The sample is the 1,000 adults surveyed.

   c.   The parameter of interest is the proportion of all American adults who think Starbucks coffee is overpriced, p.

   d.   The sample size is large enough if both $n\hat{p} \geq 15$ and $n\hat{q} \geq 15$.
        $n\hat{p} = 1,000(.73) = 730$ and $n\hat{q} = 1,000(.27) = 270$

Since both numbers are greater than or equal to 15, the sample size is sufficiently large to conclude the normal approximation is reasonable.

For confidence coefficient .95, $\alpha = .05$ and $\alpha/2 = .05/2 = .025$. From Table II, Appendix D, $z_{.025} = 1.96$. The 95% confidence interval is:

$$\hat{p} \pm z_{\alpha/2}\sqrt{\dfrac{pq}{n}} \Rightarrow \hat{p} \pm z_{\alpha/2}\sqrt{\dfrac{\hat{p}\hat{q}}{n}} \Rightarrow .73 \pm 1.96\sqrt{\dfrac{.73(.27)}{1000}} \Rightarrow .73 \pm .028 \Rightarrow (.702, .758)$$

We are 95% confident that the true proportion of all American adults who say Starbucks coffee is overpriced is between .702 and .758.

6.51 $\hat{p} = \dfrac{x}{n} = \dfrac{628}{766} = .820$

For confidence coefficient .90, $\alpha = .10$ and $\alpha/2 = .10/2 = .05$. From Table II, Appendix D, $z_{.05} = 1.645$. The confidence interval is:

$$\hat{p} \pm z_{.05} \sqrt{\frac{\hat{p}\hat{q}}{n}} \Rightarrow .82 \pm 1.645 \sqrt{\frac{.82(.18)}{766}} \Rightarrow .82 \pm .023 \Rightarrow (.797, .843)$$

We are 90% confident that the true probability of an expected cyberattack at a firm during the year is between .797 and .843.

6.53　　$\hat{p} = \dfrac{x}{n} = \dfrac{15}{100} = .15$

Suppose we form a 95% confidence interval for the true proportion of minority-owned franchises in Mississippi. For confidence coefficient .95, $\alpha = .05$ and $\alpha/2 = .05/2 = .025$. From Table II, Appendix D, $z_{.025} = 1.96$. The confidence interval is:

$$\hat{p} \pm z_{.025} \sqrt{\frac{\hat{p}\hat{q}}{n}} \Rightarrow .15 \pm 1.96 \sqrt{\frac{.15(.85)}{100}} \Rightarrow .15 \pm .07 \Rightarrow (.08, .22)$$

We are 95% confident that the true percentage of minority-owned franchises in Mississippi is between 8% and 22%. Since 20.5% falls in this interval, we would not conclude that the percentage of minority-owned franchises in Mississippi is less than the national value.

6.55　a.　In order for the large-sample estimation method to be valid, $n\hat{p} \ge 15$ and $n\hat{q} \ge 15$. For this exercise,

$\hat{p} = \dfrac{x}{n} = \dfrac{1}{333} = .003$, $n\hat{p} = 333(.003) = .999$, and $n\hat{q} = 333(.997) = 332.001$. Since one of these values is less than 15, the large-sample estimation method is not valid.

　　b.　$\tilde{p} = \dfrac{x+2}{n+4} = \dfrac{1+2}{333+4} = \dfrac{3}{337} = .009$

For confidence coefficient .95, $\alpha = .05$ and $\alpha/2 = .05/2 = .025$. From Table II, Appendix D, $z_{.025} = 1.96$. The confidence interval is:

$$\tilde{p} \pm z_{.025} \sqrt{\frac{\tilde{p}\tilde{q}}{n+4}} \Rightarrow .009 \pm 1.96 \sqrt{\frac{.009(.991)}{333+4}} \Rightarrow .009 \pm .010 \Rightarrow (-.001, .019)$$

We are 95% confident that the true proportion of all mountain casualties that require a femoral shaft splint is between 0 and .019. (We know the proportion cannot be negative, so the lower end point must be 0.)

6.57　a.　The parameter of interest is p, the proportion of all fillets that are red snapper.

　　b.　The estimate of p is $\hat{p} = \dfrac{x}{n} = \dfrac{22-17}{22} = .23$.

The sample size is large enough if both $n\hat{p} \ge 15$ and $n\hat{q} \ge 15$.

$n\hat{p} = 22(.23) = 5$ and $n\hat{q} = 22(.77) = 17$

Since $n\hat{p}$ is less than 15, the sample size is not large enough to conclude the normal approximation is reasonable.

c.   We will use Wilson's adjustment to form the confidence interval.

Using Wilson's adjustment, the point estimate of the true proportion of all fillets that are not red snapper is

$$\tilde{p} = \frac{x+2}{n+4} = \frac{5+2}{22+4} = \frac{7}{26} = .269$$

For confidence coefficient .95, $\alpha = .05$ and $\alpha/2 = .05/2 = .025$. From Table II, Appendix D, $z_{.025} = 1.96$. Wilson's adjusted 95% confidence interval is:

$$\tilde{p} \pm z_{\alpha/2} \sqrt{\frac{\tilde{p}\tilde{q}}{n}} \Rightarrow .269 \pm 1.96 \sqrt{\frac{.269(.731)}{22+4}} \Rightarrow .269 \pm .170 \Rightarrow (.099, .439)$$

d.   We are 95% confident that the true proportion of all fillets that are red snapper is between .099 and .439.

6.59 $\hat{p} = \dfrac{x}{n} = \dfrac{282,200}{332,000} = .85$

Suppose we form a 95% confidence interval for the true proportion of first class mail within the same city that is delivered on time between Dec. 10 and Mar. 3. For confidence coefficient .95, $\alpha = .05$ and $\alpha/2 = .05/2 = .025$. From Table II, Appendix D, $z_{.025} = 1.96$. The confidence interval is:

$$\hat{p} \pm z_{.025} \sqrt{\frac{\hat{p}\hat{q}}{n}} \Rightarrow .85 \pm 1.96 \sqrt{\frac{.85(.15)}{332,000}} \Rightarrow .85 \pm .001 \Rightarrow (.849, .851)$$

We are 95% confident that the true proportion of first class mail within the same city that is delivered on time between Dec. 10 and Mar. 3 is between .849 and .851 or between 84.9% and 85.1%. This interval does not contain the reported 95% of first class mailed delivered on time. It appears that the performance of the USPS is below the standard during this time period.

6.61   a.   An estimate of σ is obtained from: range $\approx 4s \Rightarrow s \approx \dfrac{\text{range}}{4} = \dfrac{34-30}{4} = 1$

To compute the necessary sample size, use $n = \left(\dfrac{z_{\alpha/2}\sigma}{ME}\right)^2$ where $\alpha = .10$ and $\alpha/2 = .10/2 = .05$. From Table II, Appendix D, $z_{.05} = 1.645$.

Thus, $n = \left(\dfrac{1.645(1)}{.2}\right)^2 = 67.65 \approx 68$

b.   A less conservative estimate of σ is obtained from range $\approx 6s \Rightarrow s \approx \dfrac{\text{range}}{6} = \dfrac{34-30}{6} = .6667$

Thus, $n = \left(\dfrac{z_{\alpha/2}\sigma}{ME}\right)^2 = \left(\dfrac{1.645(.6667)}{.2}\right)^2 = 30.07 \approx 31$

6.63   For confidence coefficient .90, $\alpha = .10$ and $\alpha/2 = .10/2 = .05$. From Table II, Appendix D, $z_{.05} = 1.645$.

We know $\hat{p}$ is in the middle of the interval, so $\hat{p} = \dfrac{.54 + .26}{2} = .4$.

The confidence interval is $\hat{p} \pm z_{.05}\sqrt{\dfrac{\hat{p}\hat{q}}{n}} \Rightarrow .4 \pm 1.645\sqrt{\dfrac{.4(.6)}{n}}$.

We know $.4 - 1.645\sqrt{\dfrac{.4(.6)}{n}} = .26$

$\Rightarrow .4 - \dfrac{.8059}{\sqrt{n}} = .26 \Rightarrow .4 - .26 = \dfrac{.8059}{\sqrt{n}} \Rightarrow \sqrt{n} = \dfrac{.8059}{.14} = 5.756 \Rightarrow n = 5.756^2 = 33.1 \approx 34$

6.65   a.   The width of a confidence interval is $W = 2(ME) = 2z_{\alpha/2}\dfrac{\sigma}{\sqrt{n}}$

For confidence coefficient .95, $\alpha = .05$ and $\alpha/2 = .05/2 = .025$. From Table II, Appendix D, $z_{.025} = 1.96$.

For $n = 16$, $W = 2z_{\alpha/2}\dfrac{\sigma}{\sqrt{n}} = 2(1.96)\dfrac{1}{\sqrt{16}} = 0.98$

For $n = 25$, $W = 2z_{\alpha/2}\dfrac{\sigma}{\sqrt{n}} = 2(1.96)\dfrac{1}{\sqrt{25}} = 0.784$

For $n = 49$, $W = 2z_{\alpha/2}\dfrac{\sigma}{\sqrt{n}} = 2(1.96)\dfrac{1}{\sqrt{49}} = 0.56$

For $n = 100$, $W = 2z_{\alpha/2}\dfrac{\sigma}{\sqrt{n}} = 2(1.96)\dfrac{1}{\sqrt{100}} = 0.392$

For $n = 400$, $W = 2z_{\alpha/2}\dfrac{\sigma}{\sqrt{n}} = 2(1.96)\dfrac{1}{\sqrt{400}} = 0.196$

b.

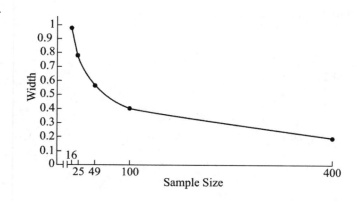

6.67 For confidence coefficient .90, $\alpha = .10$ and $\alpha/2 = .10/2 = .05$. From Table II, Appendix D, $z_{.05} = 1.645$. Since we have no estimate given for the value of p, we will use .5. The sample size is:

$$n = \frac{z_{\alpha/2}^2 pq}{(ME)^2} = \frac{1.645^2 (.5)(.5)}{.02^2} = 1,691.3 \approx 1,692$$

6.69 From Exercise 6.29, the standard deviation is 11.63. If the width of the interval is 5, then $ME = 5/2 = 2.5$. For confidence coefficient .95, $\alpha = .05$ and $\alpha/2 = .05/2 = .025$. From Table II, Appendix D, $z_{.025} = 1.96$.

$$n = \left(\frac{z_{\alpha/2}\sigma}{ME}\right)^2 = \left(\frac{1.96(11.63)}{2.5}\right)^2 = 83.14 \approx 84$$

6.71 From Exercise 6.48, $\hat{p} = .594$. For confidence coefficient .99, $\alpha = .01$ and $\alpha/2 = .01/2 = .005$. From Table II, Appendix D, $z_{.005} = 2.58$.

$$n = \frac{z_{\alpha/2}^2 pq}{(ME)^2} = \frac{2.58^2 (.594)(.406)}{.075^2} = 285.4 \approx 286$$

6.73 For confidence coefficient .99, $\alpha = .01$ and $\alpha/2 = .01/2 = .005$. From Table II, Appendix D, $z_{.005} = 2.575$. From the previous estimate, we will use $\hat{p} = 1/3$ to estimate p.

$$n = \frac{z_{\alpha/2}^2 pq}{(ME)^2} = \frac{2.575^2 (1/3)(2/3)}{.01^2} = 14,734.7 \approx 14,735$$

6.75 To compute the needed sample size, use $n = \left(\frac{z_{\alpha/2}\sigma}{ME}\right)^2$ where $\alpha = .05$ and $\alpha/2 = .05/2 = .025$. From Table II, Appendix D, $z_{.025} = 1.96$.

Thus, for $s = 10$, $n = \left(\frac{1.96(10)}{3}\right)^2 = 42.68 \approx 43$

For $s = 20$, $n = \left(\frac{1.96(20)}{3}\right)^2 = 170.72 \approx 171$

For $s = 30$, $n = \left(\frac{1.96(30)}{3}\right)^2 = 384.16 \approx 385$

6.77 To compute the necessary sample size, use $n = \left(\frac{z_{\alpha/2}\sigma}{ME}\right)^2$ where $\alpha = .10$ and $\alpha/2 = .10/2 = .05$. From Table II, Appendix D, $z_{.05} = 1.645$.

Thus, $n = \left(\dfrac{1.645(10)}{1}\right)^2 = 270.6 \approx 271$

6.79 a. To compute the needed sample size, use $n = \left(\dfrac{z_{\alpha/2}\sigma}{ME}\right)^2$ where $\alpha = .10$ and $\alpha/2 = .10/2 = .05$. From Table II, Appendix D, $z_{.05} = 1.645$.

Thus, $n = \left(\dfrac{1.645(2)}{.1}\right)^2 = 1{,}082.41 \approx 1{,}083$

b. As the sample size decreases, the width of the confidence interval increases. Therefore, if we sample 100 parts instead of 1,083, the confidence interval would be wider.

c. To compute the maximum confidence level that could be attained meeting the management's specifications,

$$n = \left(\frac{z_{\alpha/2}\sigma}{ME}\right)^2 \Rightarrow 100 = \left(\frac{z_{\alpha/2}(2)}{.1}\right)^2 \Rightarrow z_{\alpha/2}^2 = \frac{100(.01)}{4} = .25 \Rightarrow z_{\alpha/2} = .5$$

Using Table II, Appendix D, $P(0 \le z \le .5) = .1915$. Thus, $\alpha/2 = .5000 - .1915 = .3085$, $\alpha = 2(.3085) = .617$, and $1 - \alpha = 1 - .617 = .383$.

The maximum confidence level would be 38.3%.

6.81 $\sigma_{\bar{x}} = \dfrac{\sigma}{\sqrt{n}}\sqrt{\dfrac{N-n}{N}}$

a. $\sigma_{\bar{x}} = \dfrac{200}{\sqrt{1000}}\sqrt{\dfrac{2500-1000}{2500}} = 4.90$

b. $\sigma_{\bar{x}} = \dfrac{200}{\sqrt{1000}}\sqrt{\dfrac{5000-1000}{5000}} = 5.66$

c. $\sigma_{\bar{x}} = \dfrac{200}{\sqrt{1000}}\sqrt{\dfrac{10{,}000-1000}{10{,}000}} = 6.00$

d. $\sigma_{\bar{x}} = \dfrac{200}{\sqrt{1000}}\sqrt{\dfrac{100{,}000-1000}{100{,}000}} = 6.293$

6.83 a. $\hat{\sigma}_{\bar{x}} = \dfrac{s}{\sqrt{n}}\sqrt{\dfrac{N-n}{N}} = \dfrac{50}{\sqrt{2000}}\sqrt{\dfrac{10{,}000-2000}{10{,}000}} = 1.00$

b. $\hat{\sigma}_{\bar{x}} = \dfrac{50}{\sqrt{4000}}\sqrt{\dfrac{10{,}000-4000}{10{,}000}} = .6124$

c. $\hat{\sigma}_{\bar{x}} = \dfrac{50}{\sqrt{10,000}}\sqrt{\dfrac{10,000 - 10,000}{10,000}} = 0$

d.   As n increases, $\sigma_{\bar{x}}$ decreases.

e.   We are computing the standard error of $\bar{x}$. If the entire population is sampled, then $\bar{x} = \mu$. There is no sampling error, so $\sigma_{\bar{x}} = 0$.

6.85   The approximate 95% confidence interval for p is

$$\hat{p} \pm 2\hat{\sigma}_{\hat{p}} \Rightarrow \hat{p} \pm 2\sqrt{\dfrac{\hat{p}(1-\hat{p})}{n}}\sqrt{\dfrac{N-n}{N}} \Rightarrow .42 \pm 2\sqrt{\dfrac{.42(.58)}{1600}}\sqrt{\dfrac{6000 - 1600}{6000}} \Rightarrow .42 \pm .021 \Rightarrow (.399, .441)$$

6.87   a.   First, we must estimate p: $\hat{p} = \dfrac{x}{n} = \dfrac{759}{1,355} = .560$

For confidence coefficient .95, $\alpha = .05$ and $\alpha/2 = .05/2 = .025$. From Table II, Appendix D, $z_{.025} = 1.96$. Since $n/N = 1,355/1,696 = .799 > .05$, we must use the finite population correction factor. The 95% confidence interval is:

$$\hat{p} \pm z_{.025}\sqrt{\dfrac{\hat{p}\hat{q}}{n}\left(\dfrac{N-n}{N}\right)} \Rightarrow .560 \pm 1.96\sqrt{\dfrac{.560(.440)}{1,355}\left(\dfrac{1,696 - 1,355}{1,696}\right)} \Rightarrow .560 \pm .012 \Rightarrow (.548, .572)$$

b.   We used the finite correction factor because the sample size was very large compared to the population size.

c.   We are 95% confident that the true proportion of active NFL players who select a professional coach as the most influential in their career is between .548 and .572.

6.89   a.   First, we must calculate the sample mean:

$$\bar{x} = \dfrac{\sum\limits_{i=1}^{15} f_i x_i}{n} = \dfrac{3(108) + 2(55) + 1(500) + \cdots + 19(100)}{100} = \dfrac{15,646}{100} = 156.46$$

The point estimate of the mean value of the parts inventory is $\bar{x} = 156.46$.

b.   The sample variance and standard deviation are:

$$s^2 = \dfrac{\sum\limits_{i=1}^{15} f_i x_i^2 - \dfrac{\left(\sum f_i x_i\right)^2}{n}}{n-1} = \dfrac{3(108)^2 + 2(55)^2 + \cdots + 19(100)^2 - \dfrac{15,646^2}{100}}{100 - 1}$$

$$= \dfrac{6,776,336 - \dfrac{15,646^2}{100}}{99} = 43,720.83677$$

$$s = \sqrt{s^2} = \sqrt{43,720.83677} = 209.10$$

The estimated standard error is $\hat{\sigma}_{\bar{x}} = \dfrac{s}{\sqrt{n}}\sqrt{\dfrac{N-n}{N}} = \dfrac{209.10}{\sqrt{100}}\sqrt{\dfrac{500-100}{500}} = 18.7025$

c.   The approximate 95% confidence interval is:

$$\bar{x} \pm 2\hat{\sigma}_{\bar{x}} \Rightarrow \bar{x} \pm 2\left(\dfrac{s}{\sqrt{n}}\right)\sqrt{\dfrac{N-n}{N}} \Rightarrow 156.46 \pm 2(18.7025) \Rightarrow 156.46 \pm 37.405 \Rightarrow (119.055,\ 193.865)$$

We are 95% confident that the mean value of the parts inventory is between \$119.06 and \$193.87.

d.   Since the interval in part **c** does not include \$300, the value of \$300 is not a reasonable value for the mean value of the parts inventory.

6.91   For $N = 1,500$, $n = 35$, $\bar{x} = 1$, and $s = 124$, the 95% confidence interval is:

$$\bar{x} \pm 2\hat{\sigma}_{\bar{x}} \Rightarrow \bar{x} \pm 2\left(\dfrac{s}{\sqrt{n}}\right)\sqrt{\dfrac{N-n}{N}} \Rightarrow 1 \pm 2\left(\dfrac{124}{\sqrt{35}}\right)\sqrt{\dfrac{1,500-35}{1,500}} \Rightarrow 1 \pm 41.43 \Rightarrow (-40.43,\ 42.43)$$

We are 95% confident that the mean error of the new system is between -\$40.43 and \$42.43.

6.93   a. $\alpha/2 = .05/2 = .025$; $\chi^2_{.025,7} = 16.0128$ and $\chi^2_{.975,7} = 1.68987$

b. $\alpha/2 = .10/2 = .05$; $\chi^2_{.05,16} = 26.2962$ and $\chi^2_{.95,16} = 7.96164$

c. $\alpha/2 = .01/2 = .005$; $\chi^2_{.005,20} = 39.9968$ and $\chi^2_{.995,20} = 7.43386$

d. $\alpha/2 = .05/2 = .025$; $\chi^2_{.025,20} = 34.1696$ and $\chi^2_{.975,20} = 9.59083$

6.95   To find the 90% confidence interval for σ, we need to take the square root of the end points of the 90% confidence interval for σ^2 from Exercise 6.94.

a.   The 90% confidence interval for σ is: $\sqrt{4.537} \le \sigma \le \sqrt{8.809} \Rightarrow 2.13 \le \sigma \le 2.97$

b.   The 90% confidence interval for σ is: $\sqrt{.00024} \le \sigma \le \sqrt{.00085} \Rightarrow .016 \le \sigma \le .029$

c.   The 90% confidence interval for σ is: $\sqrt{641.86} \le \sigma \le \sqrt{1,809.09} \Rightarrow 25.34 \le \sigma \le 42.53$

d.   The 90% confidence interval for σ is: $\sqrt{.94859} \le \sigma \le \sqrt{12.6632} \Rightarrow .974 \le \sigma \le 3.559$

6.97   a.   The target parameter is σ^2 , the population variation in the internal oil content measurements for sweet potato chips.

b.   For confidence level .95, $\alpha = .05$ and $\alpha/2 = .05/2 = .025$. Using Table IV, Appendix D, with $df = n - 1 = 6 - 1 = 5$, $\chi^2_{.025,5} = 12.8325$ and $\chi^2_{.975,5} = .831211$. The 95% confidence interval is:

$$\dfrac{(n-1)s^2}{\chi^2_{.025}} \le \sigma^2 \le \dfrac{(n-1)s^2}{\chi^2_{.975}} \Rightarrow \dfrac{(6-1)11^2}{12.8325} \le \sigma^2 \le \dfrac{(6-1)11^2}{.831211} \Rightarrow 47.15 \le \sigma^2 \le 727.85$$

c.   "95% confidence" means that in repeated sampling, 95% of the intervals constructed in a similar manner will contain the true value of σ^2.

d.   We must assume that a random sample was selected and that the population of interest is approximately normal.

e.   The variance is measured in square millions of grams. This is difficult to relate to the data. The standard deviation is measured in millions of grams, the same units as the data.

f.   The 95% confidence interval for σ is: $\sqrt{47.15} \le \sigma \le \sqrt{727.85} \Rightarrow 6.87 \le \sigma \le 26.98$

We are 95% confident that the true standard deviation of internal oil content measurements for sweet potato chips is between 6.87 and 26.98.

6.99   a.   To find the confidence interval for σ, we first find the confidence interval for σ^2 and then take the square root of the endpoints. For confidence level .95, $\alpha = .05$ and $\alpha/2 = .05/2 = .025$. Using Table IV, Appendix D, with df $= n-1 = 55-1 = 54$, $\chi^2_{.025,54} \approx 71.4202$ and $\chi^2_{.975,54} \approx 32.3574$. The 95% confidence interval is:

$$\frac{(n-1)s^2}{\chi^2_{.025}} \le \sigma^2 \le \frac{(n-1)s^2}{\chi^2_{.975}} \Rightarrow \frac{(55-1)(.15)^2}{71.4202} \le \sigma^2 \le \frac{(55-1)(.15)^2}{32.3574} \Rightarrow .0170 \le \sigma^2 \le .0375$$

The 95% confidence interval for σ is: $\sqrt{.0170} \le \sigma \le \sqrt{.0375} \Rightarrow 0.130 \le \sigma \le 0.194$

We are 95% confident that the true standard deviation of the facial WHR values for all CEOs at publically traded Fortune 500 firms is between .130 and .194.

b.   In order for the interval to be valid, the distribution of WHR values should be approximately normally distributed. The distribution should look like:

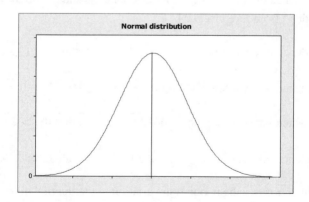

6.101   Using MINITAB, the descriptive statistics are:

Descriptive Statistics: Drug

Variable	N	Mean	StDev	Variance	Minimum	Median	Maximum
Drug	50	89.291	3.183	10.134	81.790	89.375	94.830

For confidence level .99, $\alpha = .01$ and $\alpha/2 = .01/2 = .005$. From Table IV, Appendix D, with df $= n-1 = 50-1 = 49$, $\chi^2_{.005,49} \approx 79.4900$ and $\chi^2_{.995,49} \approx 27.9907$. The 99% confidence interval is:

$$\frac{(n-1)s^2}{\chi^2_{.005}} \leq \sigma^2 \leq \frac{(n-1)s^2}{\chi^2_{.995}} \Rightarrow \frac{(50-1)(10.134)}{79.4900} \leq \sigma^2 \leq \frac{(50-1)(10.134)}{27.9907} \Rightarrow 6.247 \leq \sigma^2 \leq 17.740$$

We are 99% confident that the true population variation in drug concentrations for the new method is between 6.247 and 17.740.

6.103 Using MINITAB, the descriptive statistics are:

Descriptive Statistics: Spacing

Variable	N	Mean	StDev	Variance	Minimum	Median	Maximum
Spacing	7	89.86	11.63	135.14	70.00	93.00	105.00

For confidence level .99, $\alpha = .01$ and $\alpha/2 = .01/2 = .005$. Using Table IV, Appendix D, with $df = n-1 = 7-1 = 6$, $\chi^2_{.005,6} = 18.5476$ and $\chi^2_{.995,6} = .675727$. The 99% confidence interval is:

$$\frac{(n-1)s^2}{\chi^2_{.005}} \leq \sigma^2 \leq \frac{(n-1)s^2}{\chi^2_{.995}} \Rightarrow \frac{(7-1)(135.14)}{18.5476} \leq \sigma^2 \leq \frac{(7-1)(135.14)}{.675727} \Rightarrow 43.717 \leq \sigma^2 \leq 1,199.952$$

6.105 Using MINITAB, the descriptive statistics are:

Descriptive Statistics: Honey, DM

Variable	N	Mean	StDev	Variance	Minimum	Median	Maximum
Honey	35	10.714	2.855	8.151	4.000	11.000	16.000
DM	33	8.333	3.256	10.604	3.000	9.000	15.000

a. For confidence level .90, $\alpha = .10$ and $\alpha/2 = .10/2 = .05$. Using MINITAB with $df = n-1 = 35-1 = 34$, $\chi^2_{.05,34} = 48.6024$ and $\chi^2_{.95,34} = 21.6643$. The 90% confidence interval is:

$$\frac{(n-1)s^2}{\chi^2_{.05}} \leq \sigma^2 \leq \frac{(n-1)s^2}{\chi^2_{.95}} \Rightarrow \frac{(35-1)8.151}{48.6024} \leq \sigma^2 \leq \frac{(35-1)8.151}{21.6643} \Rightarrow 5.702 \leq \sigma^2 \leq 12.792$$

b. For confidence level .90, $\alpha = .10$ and $\alpha/2 = .10/2 = .05$. Using MINITAB with $df = n-1 = 33-1 = 32$, $\chi^2_{.05,32} = 46.1943$ and $\chi^2_{.95,32} = 20.0719$. The 90% confidence interval is:

$$\frac{(n-1)s^2}{\chi^2_{.05}} \leq \sigma^2 \leq \frac{(n-1)s^2}{\chi^2_{.95}} \Rightarrow \frac{(33-1)10.604}{46.1943} \leq \sigma^2 \leq \frac{(33-1)10.604}{20.0719} \Rightarrow 7.346 \leq \sigma^2 \leq 16.906$$

c. Since the confidence intervals overlap, the researchers cannot conclude that the variances of the two groups differ.

6.107 a. $P(t \leq t_0) = .05$ where $df = 20$. Thus, $t_0 = -1.725$.

b. $P(t \geq t_0) = .005$ where $df = 9$. Thus, $t_0 = 3.250$.

c. $P(t \leq -t_0 \text{ or } t \geq t_0) = .10$ where $df = 8$ is equivalent to $P(t \geq t_0) = .10/2 = .05$ where $df = 8$. Thus, $t_0 = 1.860$.

d. $P(t \leq -t_0 \text{ or } t \geq t_0) = .01$ where $df = 17$ is equivalent to $P(t \geq t_0) = .01/2 = .005$ where $df = 17$. Thus, $t_0 = 2.898$.

6.109   a.   For confidence coefficient .99, $\alpha = .01$ and $\alpha/2 = .01/2 = .005$. From Table II, Appendix D, $z_{.005} = 2.575$. The confidence interval is:

$$\bar{x} \pm z_{.005}\frac{s}{\sqrt{n}} \Rightarrow 32.5 \pm 2.575\frac{30}{\sqrt{225}} \Rightarrow 32.5 \pm 5.15 \Rightarrow (27.35,\ 37.65)$$

b.   The sample size is $n = \left(\dfrac{z_{\alpha/2}\sigma}{ME}\right)^2 = \left(\dfrac{2.575(30)}{.5}\right)^2 = 23{,}870.25 \approx 23{,}871$.

c.   For confidence level .99, $\alpha = .01$ and $\alpha/2 = .01/2 = .005$. Using MINITAB with $df = n-1 = 225-1 = 224$, $\chi^2_{.005,224} = 282.268$ and $\chi^2_{.995,224} = 173.238$. The 99% confidence interval is:

$$\frac{(n-1)s^2}{\chi^2_{.005}} \le \sigma^2 \le \frac{(n-1)s^2}{\chi^2_{.995}} \Rightarrow \frac{(225-1)(30)^2}{282.268} \le \sigma^2 \le \frac{(225-1)(30)^2}{173.238} \Rightarrow 714.215 \le \sigma^2 \le 1{,}163.717$$

d.   "99% confidence" means that if repeated samples of size 225 were selected from the population and 99% confidence intervals constructed for the population mean, then 99% of all the intervals constructed will contain the population mean.

6.111   a.   Using Table IV, Appendix D, with $df = n-1 = 10-1 = 9$, $\chi^2_{.025,9} = 19.0228$ and $\chi^2_{.975,9} = 2.70039$.

b.   Using Table IV, Appendix D, with $df = n-1 = 20-1 = 19$, $\chi^2_{.025,19} = 32.8523$ and $\chi^2_{.975,19} = 8.90655$.

c.   Using Table IV, Appendix D, with $df = n-1 = 50-1 = 49$, $\chi^2_{.005,49} \approx 79.4900$ and $\chi^2_{.995,49} = 27.9907$.

6.113   The parameters of interest for the problems are:

(1)   The question requires a categorical response. One parameter of interest might be the proportion, p, of all Americans over 18 years of age who think their health is generally very good or excellent.

(2)   A parameter of interest might be the mean number of days, μ, in the previous 30 days that all Americans over 18 years of age felt that their physical health was not good because of injury or illness.

(3)   A parameter of interest might be the mean number of days, μ, in the previous 30 days that all Americans over 18 years of age felt that their mental health was not good because of stress, depression, or problems with emotions.

(4)   A parameter of interest might be the mean number of days, μ, in the previous 30 days that all Americans over 18 years of age felt that their physical or mental health prevented them from performing their usual activities.

6.115   a.   The point estimate of p is $\hat{p} = .11..$

b.   The sample size is large enough if both $n\hat{p} \ge 15$ and $n\hat{q} \ge 15$.

$n\hat{p} = 150(.11) = 16.5$ and $n\hat{q} = 150(.89) = 133.5$

Since both numbers are greater than or equal to 15, the sample size is sufficiently large to conclude the normal approximation is reasonable.

For confidence coefficient .95, $\alpha = .05$ and $\alpha / 2 = .05 / 2 = .025$. From Table II, Appendix D, $z_{.025} = 1.96$. The confidence interval is:

$$\hat{p} \pm z_{.025}\sqrt{\frac{\hat{p}\hat{q}}{n}} \Rightarrow .11 \pm 1.645\sqrt{\frac{.11(.89)}{150}} \Rightarrow .11 \pm .05 \Rightarrow (.06,\ .16)$$

    c.   We are 95% confident that the true proportion of MSDSs that are satisfactorily completed is between .06 and .16.

6.117   For confidence coefficient .95, $\alpha = .05$ and $\alpha / 2 = .05 / 2 = .025$. From Table II, Appendix D, $z_{.025} = 1.96$. For this study,

$$n = \left(\frac{z_{\alpha/2}\sigma}{ME}\right)^2 = \left(\frac{1.96(5)}{1}\right)^2 = 96.04 \approx 97 \quad \text{The sample size needed is 97.}$$

6.119   First, we must estimate p: $\hat{p} = \dfrac{x}{n} = \dfrac{50}{72} = .694$. The 95% confidence interval is:

$$\hat{p} \pm 2\sqrt{\frac{\hat{p}\hat{q}}{n}\left(\frac{N-n}{N}\right)} \Rightarrow .694 \pm 2\sqrt{\frac{.694(.306)}{72}\left(\frac{251-72}{251}\right)} \Rightarrow .694 \pm .092 \Rightarrow (.602,\ .786)$$

We are 95% confident that the true proportion of all New Jersey Governor's Council business members that have employees with substance abuse problems is between .602 and .786.

6.121   For confidence coefficient .90, $\alpha = .10$ and $\alpha / 2 = .10 / 2 = .05$. From Table II, Appendix D, $z_{.05} = 1.645$. The 90% confidence interval is:

$$\bar{x} \pm z_{.05}\frac{s}{\sqrt{n}} \Rightarrow 6,563 \pm 1.645\frac{2,484}{\sqrt{1,751}} \Rightarrow 6,563 \pm 97.65 \Rightarrow (6,465.35,\ 6,660.65)$$

We are 90% confident that the true mean expenses per full-time equivalent employee of all U.S. Army hospitals is between $6,465.35 and $6,660.65.

6.123   There are a total of 96 channel catfish in the sample. The point estimate of p is $\hat{p} = \dfrac{x}{n} = \dfrac{96}{144} = .667$.

The sample size is large enough if both $n\hat{p} \geq 15$ and $n\hat{q} \geq 15$.

$n\hat{p} = 144(.667) = 96$ and $n\hat{q} = 144(.333) = 48$

Since both numbers are greater than or equal to 15, the sample size is sufficiently large to conclude the normal approximation is reasonable.

For confidence coefficient .90, $\alpha = .10$ and $\alpha / 2 = .10 / 2 = .05$. From Table II, Appendix D, $z_{.05} = 1.645$. The confidence interval is:

$$\hat{p} \pm z_{.05}\sqrt{\frac{\hat{p}\hat{q}}{n}} \Rightarrow .667 \pm 1.645\sqrt{\frac{.667(.333)}{144}} \Rightarrow .667 \pm .065 \Rightarrow (.602, .732)$$

We are 90% confident that the true proportion of channel catfish in the population is between .602 and .732.

6.125   a.   The 95% confidence interval for the mean surface roughness of coated interior pipe is (1.63580, 2.12620).

   b.   No. Since 2.5 does not fall in the 95% confidence interval, it would be very unlikely that the average surface roughness would be as high as 2.5 micrometers.

6.127   Using MINITAB, the descriptive statistics are:

Descriptive Statistics: Comp

Variable	N	Mean	StDev	Minimum	Q1	Median	Q3	Maximum
Comp	10	1368	463.13	720	1016	1352	1652	2112

For confidence coefficient .90, $\alpha = .10$ and $\alpha / 2 = .10 / 2 = .05$. From Table III, Appendix D, with df $= n - 1 = 10 - 1 = 9$, $t_{.05} = 1.833$. The 90% confidence interval is:

$$\bar{x} \pm t_{.05}\frac{s}{\sqrt{n}} \Rightarrow 1368 \pm 1.833\frac{463.13}{\sqrt{10}} \Rightarrow 1368 \pm 268.45 \Rightarrow (1,099.55, \ 1,636.45)$$

We are 90% confident that the true mean threshold compensation level for all major airlines is between $1,099.55 and $1,636.45.

6.129   a.   The point estimate of p is $\hat{p} = \dfrac{x}{n} = \dfrac{52}{60} = .867$.

   b.   For confidence coefficient .95, $\alpha = .05$ and $\alpha / 2 = .05 / 2 = .025$. From Table II, Appendix D, $z_{.025} = 1.96$. The confidence interval is:

$$\hat{p} \pm z_{.025}\sqrt{\frac{\hat{p}\hat{q}}{n}} \Rightarrow .867 \pm 1.96\sqrt{\frac{.867(.133)}{60}} \Rightarrow .867 \pm .086 \Rightarrow (.781, .953)$$

   c.   We are 95% confident that the true proportion of Wal-Mart stores in California that have more than 2 inaccurately priced items per 100 scanned is between .781 and .953.

   d.   If 99% of the California Wal-Mart stores are in compliance, then only 1% or .01 would not be. However, we found the 95% confidence interval for the proportion that are not in compliance is between .781 and .953. The value of .01 is not in this interval. Thus, it is not a likely value. This claim is not believable.

   e.   The sample size is large enough if both $n\hat{p} \geq 15$ and $n\hat{q} \geq 15$.

$$n\hat{p} = 60(.867) = 52 \text{ and } n\hat{q} = 60(.133) = 8$$

Since $n\hat{q}$ is less than 15, the sample size is not large enough to conclude the normal approximation is reasonable. Thus, the confidence interval constructed in part b may not be valid. Any inference based on this interval is questionable.

f. From above, the value of $\hat{p}$ is .867. For confidence coefficient .90, $\alpha = .10$ and $\alpha / 2 = .10 / 2 = .05$. From Table II, Appendix D, $z_{.05} = 1.645$.

$$n = \frac{z_{\alpha/2}^2 pq}{(ME)^2} = \frac{1.645^2 (.867)(.133)}{.05^2} = 124.8 \approx 125$$

6.131 a. $\hat{p} = \dfrac{x}{n} = \dfrac{1,298}{2,163} = .60$

b. For confidence coefficient .95, $\alpha = .05$ and $\alpha / 2 = .05 / 2 = .025$. From Table II, Appendix D, $z_{.025} = 1.96$. The confidence interval is:

$$\hat{p} \pm z_{.025} \sqrt{\frac{\hat{p}\hat{q}}{n}} \Rightarrow .60 \pm 1.96 \sqrt{\frac{.60(.40)}{2,163}} \Rightarrow .60 \pm .02 \Rightarrow (.58, .62)$$

c. We are 95% confident that the true proportion of all drivers who are using a cell phone while operating a motor passenger vehicle is between .58 and .62.

d. The margin of error would be $1.96 \sqrt{\dfrac{.60(.40)}{4,326}} = .015$

6.133 For confidence coefficient .95, $\alpha = .05$ and $\alpha / 2 = .05 / 2 = .025$. From Table II, Appendix D, $z_{.025} = 1.96$. From Exercise 6.132, a good approximation for p is .094. Also, $ME = .02$.

The sample size is $n = \dfrac{(z_{\alpha/2})^2 pq}{(ME)^2} = \dfrac{(1.96)^2 (.094)(.906)}{.02^2} = 817.9 \approx 818$

You would need to take $n = 818$ samples.

6.135 a. Answers will vary. Using a computer package, the 100 selected invoices are:

```
3590 1453 3726 2844 1767 1259 1091 1795 4431 4565 4586 1020 2135 1078 2659
4694 2572 4559 4601  965 4553 1052 3448  574 1360 3803 2247 1164 1862 2385
1255 4966  658 4007 4743 3746 3029 3723 3950  346 4744  312 4325  602 3137
4662  217  949 4580 4126 1794 2912   67 2514 3544 1596 2344 1603 3744 1886
 151 4258  183 1869 4509 4572 3875   34 3781 4993 1284 2177 4290   13 2717
1216 2052 4881 2220 3883  287 2977 3459 4639 2272 3620 4646 1544  919 3820
 121 2373 4684 2025 2254 4018 2304 3503 1634 2470
```

The observation numbers ending in 0 are highlighted above.

b. $\hat{p} = \dfrac{x}{n} = \dfrac{10}{100} = .10$

For confidence coefficient .90, $\alpha = .10$ and $\alpha / 2 = .10 / 2 = .05$. From Table II, Appendix D, $z_{.05} = 1.645$. The confidence interval is:

$$\hat{p} \pm z_{.05}\sqrt{\frac{\hat{p}\hat{q}}{n}} \Rightarrow .10 \pm 1.645\sqrt{\frac{.10(.90)}{100}} \Rightarrow .10 \pm .049 \Rightarrow (.051, .149)$$

c. Our sample proportion was $\hat{p} = .10$ which is equal to the true proportion. The confidence interval does contain .10.

6.137 Since the manufacturer wants to be reasonably certain the process is really out of control before shutting down the process, we would want to use a high level of confidence for our inference. We will form a 99% confidence interval for the mean breaking strength.

For confidence coefficient .99, $\alpha = .01$ and $\alpha/2 = .01/2 = .005$. From Table III, Appendix D, with $df = n - 1 = 9 - 1 = 8$ $t_{.005} = 3.355$. The 99% confidence interval is:

$$\bar{x} \pm t_{.005}\frac{s}{\sqrt{n}} \Rightarrow 985.6 \pm 3.355\frac{22.9}{\sqrt{9}} \Rightarrow 985.6 \pm 25.61 \Rightarrow (959.99, \ 1,011.21)$$

We are 99% confident that the true mean breaking strength is between 959.99 and 1,011.21. Since 1,000 is contained in this interval, it is not an unusual value for the true mean breaking strength. Thus, we would recommend that the process is not out of control.

6.139 a. As long as the sample is random (and thus representative), a reliable estimate of the mean weight of all the scallops can be obtained.

b. The government is using only the sample mean to make a decision. Rather than using a point estimate, they should probably use a confidence interval to estimate the true mean weight of the scallops so they can include a measure of reliability.

c. We will form a 95% confidence interval for the mean weight of the scallops. Using MINITAB, the descriptive statistics are:

Descriptive Statistics: Weight

Variable	N	Mean	StDev	Minimum	Q1	Median	Q3	Maximum
Weight	18	0.9317	0.0753	0.8400	0.8800	0.9100	9800	1.1400

For confidence coefficient .95, $\alpha = .05$ and $\alpha/2 = .05/2 = .025$. From Table III, Appendix A, with $df = n - 1 = 18 - 1 = 17$, $t_{.025} = 2.110$. The 95% confidence interval is:

$$\bar{x} \pm t_{.025}\frac{s}{\sqrt{n}} \Rightarrow .932 \pm 2.110\frac{.0753}{\sqrt{18}} \Rightarrow .932 \pm .037 \Rightarrow (.895, .969)$$

We are 95% confident that the true mean weight of the scallops is between .8943 and .9691. Recall that the weights have been scaled so that a mean weight of 1 corresponds to 1/36 of a pound. Since the above confidence interval does not include 1, we have sufficient evidence to indicate that the minimum weight restriction was violated.

Chapter 7
Inferences Based on a Single Sample:
Tests of Hypothesis

7.1   The null hypothesis is the "status quo" hypothesis, while the alternative hypothesis is the research hypothesis.

7.3   The "level of significance" of a test is α. This is the probability that the test statistic will fall in the rejection region when the null hypothesis is true.

7.5   The four possible results are:
1.   Rejecting the null hypothesis when it is true. This would be a Type I error.
2.   Accepting the null hypothesis when it is true. This would be a correct decision.
3.   Rejecting the null hypothesis when it is false. This would be a correct decision.
4.   Accepting the null hypothesis when it is false. This would be a Type II error.

7.7   When you reject the null hypothesis in favor of the alternative hypothesis, this does not prove the alternative hypothesis is correct. We are $100(1-\alpha)\%$ confident that there is sufficient evidence to conclude that the alternative hypothesis is correct.

        If we were to repeatedly draw samples from the population and perform the test each time, approximately $100(1-\alpha)\%$ of the tests performed would yield the correct decision.

7.9   Let p = proportion of American adults who pick professional football as their favorite sport. To see if the proportion of American adults who pick professional football as their favorite sport differs from .4, we test:

$$H_0 : p = .40$$
$$H_a : p \neq .40$$

7.11   Let p = student loan default rate in this year. To see if the student loan default rate is less than .12, we test:

$$H_0 : p = .12$$
$$H_a : p < .12$$

7.13   Let μ = mean caloric content of Virginia school lunches. To test the claim that after the testing period ended, the average caloric content dropped, we test:

$$H_0 : \mu = 863$$
$$H_a : \mu < 863$$

7.15   a.   Since the company must give proof the drug is safe, the null hypothesis would be the drug is unsafe. The alternative hypothesis would be the drug is safe.

        b.   A Type I error would be concluding the drug is safe when it is not safe. A Type II error would be concluding the drug is not safe when it is. α is the probability of concluding the drug is safe when it is not. β is the probability of concluding the drug is not safe when it is.

c.   In this problem, it would be more important for α to be small. We would want the probability of concluding the drug is safe when it is not to be as small as possible.

7.17   a.   A Type I error is rejecting the null hypothesis when it is true. In a murder trial, we would be concluding that the accused is guilty when, in fact, he/she is innocent.

            A Type II error is accepting the null hypothesis when it is false. In this case, we would be concluding that the accused is innocent when, in fact, he/she is guilty.

      b.   Both errors are serious. However, if an innocent person is found guilty of murder and is put to death, there is no way to correct the error. On the other hand, if a guilty person is set free, he/she could murder again.

      c.   In a jury trial, α is assumed to be smaller than β. The only way to convict the accused is for a unanimous decision of guilt. Thus, the probability of convicting an innocent person is set to be small.

      d.   In order to get a unanimous vote to convict, there has to be overwhelming evidence of guilt. The probability of getting a unanimous vote of guilt if the person is really innocent will be very small.

      e.   If a jury is prejudiced against a guilty verdict, the value of α will decrease. The probability of convicting an innocent person will be even smaller if the jury if prejudiced against a guilty verdict.

      f.   If a jury is prejudiced against a guilty verdict, the value of β will increase. The probability of declaring a guilty person innocent will be larger if the jury is prejudiced against a guilty verdict.

7.19   a. $p = P(z \geq 1.20) = .5 - .3849 = .1151$

      b. $p = P(z \leq -1.20) = .5 - .3849 = .1151$

      c. $p = P(z \leq -1.20) + P(z \geq 1.20) = 2(.1151) = .2302$

7.21   a.   Since the p-value $= .10$ is greater than $\alpha = .05$, H_0 is not rejected.

      b.   Since the p-value $= .05$ is less than $\alpha = .10$, H_0 is rejected.

      c.   Since the p-value $= .001$ is less than $\alpha = .01$, H_0 is rejected.

      d.   Since the p-value $= .05$ is greater than $\alpha = .025$, H_0 is not rejected.

      e.   Since the p-value $= .45$ is greater than $\alpha = .10$, H_0 is not rejected.

7.23 p-value $= p = P(z \geq 2.17) = .5 - P(0 < z < 2.17) = .5 - .4850 = .0150$ (using Table II, Appendix D)

       The probability of observing a test statistic of 2.17 or anything more unusual if the true mean is 100 is .0150. Since this probability is so small, there is evidence that the true mean is greater than 100.

7.25 p-value $= p = P(z \geq 2.17) + P(z \leq -2.17) = 2(.5 - .4850) = 2(.0150) = .0300$ (using Table II, Appendix D)

7.27   The smallest value of α for which the null hypothesis would be rejected is just greater than .06.

7.29   a.   The decision rule is to reject H_0 if $\bar{x} > 270$. Recall that $z = \dfrac{\bar{x} - \mu_0}{\sigma_{\bar{x}}}$.

Therefore, reject H_0 if $\bar{x} > 270$ can be written as reject H_0 if $z > \dfrac{\bar{x} - \mu_0}{\sigma_{\bar{x}}} = \dfrac{270 - 255}{63 / \sqrt{81}} = 2.14$.

The decision rule in terms of z is to reject H_0 if $z > 2.14$.

   b. $P(z > 2.14) = .5 - P(0 < z < 2.14) = .5 - .4838 = .0162$

7.31   a. $H_0 : \mu = .36$
$H_a : \mu < .36$

The test statistic is $z = \dfrac{\bar{x} - \mu_0}{\sigma_{\bar{x}}} \approx \dfrac{.323 - .36}{\sqrt{.034} / \sqrt{64}} = -1.61$

The rejection region requires $\alpha = .10$ in the lower tail of the z-distribution. From Table II, Appendix D, $z_{.10} = 1.28$. The rejection region is $z < -1.28$.

Since the observed value of the test statistic falls in the rejection region $(z = -1.61 < -1.28)$, H_0 is rejected. There is sufficient evidence to indicate the mean is less than .36 at $\alpha = .10$.

   b. $H_0 : \mu = .36$
$H_a : \mu \neq .36$

The test statistic is $z = -1.61$ (see part **a**).

The rejection region requires $\alpha / 2 = .10 / 2 = .05$ in the each tail of the z-distribution. From Table II, Appendix D, $z_{.05} = 1.645$. The rejection region is $z < -1.645$ or $z > 1.645$.

Since the observed value of the test statistic does not fall in the rejection region $(z = -1.61 < -1.645)$, H_0 is not rejected. There is insufficient evidence to indicate the mean is different from .36 at $\alpha = .10$.

7.33   a.   Let μ = true mean willingness to eat the brand of sliced apples. To determine if the true mean willingness to eat the brand of sliced apples exceeds 3, we test:

$H_0 : \mu = 3$
$H_a : \mu > 3$

The test statistic is $z = \dfrac{\bar{x} - \mu_0}{\dfrac{\sigma}{\sqrt{n}}} = \dfrac{3.69 - 3}{\dfrac{2.44}{\sqrt{408}}} = 5.71$.

The rejection region requires $\alpha = .05$ in the upper tail of the z-distribution. From Table II, Appendix D, $z_{.05} = 1.645$. The rejection region is $z > 1.645$.

Since the observed value of the test statistic falls in the rejection region $(z = 5.71 > 1.645)$, H_0 is rejected. There is sufficient evidence to indicate that the true mean willingness to eat the brand of sliced apples exceeds 3 at $\alpha = .05$.

b.   Even though the willingness to eat scores are not normally distributed, the test in part a is valid. Because the sample size is so large $(n = 408)$, the Central Limit Theorem applies.

7.35   Let $\mu =$ true mean facial width-to-height ratio. To determine if the true mean facial width-to-height ratio differs from 2.2, we test:

$H_0 : \mu = 2.2$
$H_a : \mu \neq 2.2$

The test statistic is $z = \dfrac{\bar{x} - \mu_0}{\dfrac{\sigma}{\sqrt{n}}} = \dfrac{1.96 - 2.2}{\dfrac{.15}{\sqrt{55}}} = -11.87$.

The p-value is $p = P(z \leq -11.87) + P(z \geq 11.87) \approx 0 + 0 = 0$.

Since the p-value is so small $(p \approx 0)$, H_0 will be rejected for any reasonable value of α. There is sufficient evidence to indicate the true mean facial width-to-height ratio differs from 2.2 for $\alpha > .001$.

7.37   a.   Let $\mu =$ true mean weight of golf tees. To determine if the process is not operating satisfactorily, we test:

$H_0 : \mu = .250$
$H_a : \mu \neq .250$

b.   Using MINITAB, the descriptive statistics are:

Descriptive Statistics: Tees

Variable	N	Mean	Median	StDev	Minimum	Maximum	Q1	Q3
Tees	40	0.25248	0.25300	0.00223	0.24700	0.25600	0.25100	0.25400

Thus, $\bar{x} = .25248$ and $s = .00223$.

c.   The test statistic is $z = \dfrac{\bar{x} - \mu_0}{\sigma_{\bar{x}}} \approx \dfrac{.25248 - .250}{.00223 / \sqrt{40}} = 7.03$.

d.   The p-value is $p = P(z \leq -7.03) + P(z \geq 7.03) \approx 0 + 0 = 0$.

e.   The rejection region requires $\alpha / 2 = .01 / 2 = .005$ in each tail of the z-distribution. From Table II, Appendix D, $z_{.005} = 2.575$. The rejection region is $z < -2.575$ or $z > 2.575$.

f.   Since the observed value of the test statistic falls in the rejection region $(z = 7.03 > 2.575)$, H_0 is rejected. There is sufficient evidence to indicate the process is performing in an unsatisfactory manner at $\alpha = .01$.

g. α is the probability of a Type I error. A Type I error, in this case, is to say the process is unsatisfactory when, in fact, it is satisfactory. The risk, then, is to the producer since he will be spending time and money to repair a process that is not in error.

β is the probability of a Type II error. A Type II error, in this case, is to say the process is satisfactory when it, in fact, is not. This is the consumer's risk since he could unknowingly purchase a defective product.

7.39   a.   Let μ = mean estimated time to read the report. To determine if the students, on average, overestimate the time it takes to read the report, we test:

$$H_0 : \mu = 48$$
$$H_a : \mu > 48$$

The test statistic is $z = \dfrac{\bar{x} - \mu_0}{\sigma_{\bar{x}}} \approx \dfrac{60 - 48}{41 / \sqrt{40}} = 1.85.$

The p-value is $p = P(z \geq 1.85) = .5 - .4678 = .0322$ (using Table II, Appendix D)

Since the p-value is less than $\alpha (p = .0322 < .10)$, H_0 is rejected. There is sufficient evidence to indicate the students, on average, overestimate the time it takes to read the report at $\alpha = .10$.

b.   Let μ = mean estimated number of pages of the report read. To determine if the students, on average, underestimate the number of report pages read, we test:

$$H_0 : \mu = 32$$
$$H_a : \mu < 32$$

The test statistic is $z = \dfrac{\bar{x} - \mu_0}{\sigma_{\bar{x}}} \approx \dfrac{28 - 32}{14 / \sqrt{42}} = -1.85.$

The p-value is $p = P(z \leq -1.85) = .5 - .4678 = .0322$ (using Table II, Appendix D)

Since the p-value is less than $\alpha (p = .0322 < .10)$, H_0 is rejected. There is sufficient evidence to indicate the students, on average, underestimate the number of report pages read at $\alpha = .10$.

c.   No. In both tests, the sample sizes are greater than 30. Thus, the Central Limit Theorem will apply. The distribution of $\bar{x}$ is approximately normal regardless of the population distribution.

7.41   To determine if the mean point-spread error is different from 0, we test:

$$H_0 : \mu = 0$$
$$H_a : \mu \neq 0$$

The test statistic is $z = \dfrac{\bar{x} - \mu_0}{\sigma_{\bar{x}}} \approx \dfrac{-1.6 - 0}{13.3 / \sqrt{240}} = -1.86$

The rejection region requires $\alpha / 2 = .01 / 2 = .005$ in each tail of the z-distribution. From Table II, Appendix D, $z_{.005} = 2.575$. The rejection region is $z < -2.575$ or $z > 2.575$.

Since the observed value of the test statistic does not fall in the rejection region $(z = -1.86 \not< -2.575)$, H_0 is not rejected. There is insufficient evidence to indicate that the true mean point-spread error is different from 0 at $\alpha = .01$.

7.43 a. To determine if the true mean forecast error for buy-side analysts is positive, we test:

$$H_0 : \mu = 0$$
$$H_a : \mu > 0$$

The test statistic is $z = \dfrac{\bar{x} - \mu_o}{\sigma_{\bar{x}}} \approx \dfrac{.85 - 0}{1.93 / \sqrt{3,526}} = 26.15.$

The observed p-value of the test is $p = P(z > 26.15) \approx 0$ (Using Table II, Appendix D)

Since the p-value is less than $\alpha(p \approx 0 < .01)$, H_0 is rejected. There is sufficient evidence to indicate that the true mean forecast error for buy-side analysts is positive at $\alpha = .01$. This means that the buy-side analysts are overestimating earnings.

b. To determine if the true mean forecast error for sell-side analysts is negative; we test:

$$H_0 : \mu = 0$$
$$H_a : \mu < 0$$

The test statistic is $z = \dfrac{\bar{x} - \mu_o}{\sigma_{\bar{x}}} \approx \dfrac{-.05 - 0}{.85 / \sqrt{58,562}} = -14.24 .$

The observed p-value of the test is $p = P(z < -14.24) \approx 0$ (using Table II, Appendix D)

Since the p-value is less than $\alpha(p \approx 0 < .01)$, H_0 is rejected. There is sufficient evidence to indicate that the true mean forecast error for sell-side analysts is negative at $\alpha = .01$. This means that the sell-side analysts are underestimating earnings.

7.45 a. Let $\mu =$ mean external tension level of all managers who engage in coopetition. To determine if the mean external tension level differs from 10.5, we test:

$$H_0 : \mu = 10.5$$
$$H_a : \mu \neq 10.5$$

The test statistic is $z = \dfrac{\bar{x} - \mu_0}{\sigma_{\bar{x}}} = \dfrac{10.82 - 10.5}{3.04 \big/ \sqrt{1,532}} = 4.12$.

The rejection region requires $\alpha / 2 = .05 / 2 = .025$ in each tail of the z-distribution. From Table II, Appendix D, $z_{.025} = 1.96$. The rejection region is $z < -1.96$ or $z > 1.96$.

Since the observed value of the test statistic falls in the rejection region $(z = 4.12 > 1.96)$, H_0 is rejected. There is sufficient evidence to indicate the true mean external tension level differs from 10.5 at $\alpha = .05$.

b. The 95% confidence interval is:

$$\bar{x} \pm z_{.025} \frac{\sigma}{\sqrt{n}} \Rightarrow 10.82 \pm 1.96 \frac{3.04}{\sqrt{1,532}} \Rightarrow 10.82 \pm .152 \Rightarrow (10.668, 10.972)$$

c. If the hypothesized value of the test statistic falls in the confidence interval, then H_0 is not rejected. If the hypothesized value of the test statistic does not fall in the confidence interval, then H_0 is rejected.

d. The observed value of $\bar{x}$ is very close to 10.5. Even though it is statistically significant, the mean external tension level may not be practically different from 10.5.

7.47   a. We should use the t-distribution in testing a hypothesis about a population mean if the sample size is small, the population being sampled from is normal, and the variance of the population is unknown.

b. Both distributions are mound-shaped and symmetric. The t-distribution is flatter than the z-distribution.

7.49   a. The rejection region requires $\alpha / 2 = .05 / 2 = .025$ in each tail of the t-distribution with $df = n - 1 = 14 - 1 = 13$. From Table III, Appendix D, $t_{.025} = 2.160$. The rejection region is $t < -2.160$ or $t > 2.160$.

b. The rejection region requires $\alpha = .01$ in the upper tail of the t-distribution with $df = n - 1 = 24 - 1 = 23$. From Table III, Appendix D, $t_{.01} = 2.500$. The rejection region is $t > 2.500$.

c. The rejection region requires $\alpha = .10$ in the upper tail of the t-distribution with $df = n - 1 = 9 - 1 = 8$. From Table III, Appendix D, $t_{.10} = 1.397$. The rejection region is $t > 1.397$.

d. The rejection region requires $\alpha = .01$ in the lower tail of the t-distribution with $df = n - 1 = 12 - 1 = 11$. From Table III, Appendix D, $t_{.01} = 2.718$. The rejection region is $t < -2.718$.

e. The rejection region requires $\alpha / 2 = .10 / 2 = .05$ in each tail of the t-distribution with $df = n - 1 = 20 - 1 = 19$. From Table III, Appendix D, $t_{.05} = 1.729$. The rejection region is $t < -1.729$ or $t > 1.729$.

f. The rejection region requires $\alpha = .05$ in the lower tail of the t-distribution with $df = n - 1 = 4 - 1 = 3$. From Table III, Appendix D, $t_{.05} = 2.353$. The rejection region is $t < -2.353$.

7.51   a. We must assume that a random sample was drawn from a normal population.

b. The hypotheses are:

$$H_0 : \mu = 1,000$$
$$H_a : \mu > 1,000$$

The test statistic is $t = 1.89$ and the p-value is $p = .038$.

Since the *p*-value is so small, there is evidence to reject H_0. There is evidence to indicate the mean is greater than 1000 for $\alpha > .038$.

c.   The hypotheses are:

$$H_0 : \mu = 1,000$$
$$H_a : \mu \neq 1,000$$

The test statistic is $t = 1.89$ and the *p*-value is $2(.038) = .076$.

There is no evidence to reject H_0 for $\alpha = .05$. There is insufficient evidence to indicate the mean is different than 1000 for $\alpha = .05$.

There is evidence to reject H_0 for $\alpha > .076$. There is evidence to indicate the mean is different than 1000 for $\alpha > .076$.

7.53   a.   Let μ = mean number of occupational accidents at all Turkish construction sites. To determine if the mean number of occupational accidents is less than 70, we test:

$$H_0 : \mu = 70$$
$$H_a : \mu < 70$$

b.   The rejection region requires $\alpha = .01$ in the lower tail of the *t*-distribution with df $= n - 1 = 3 - 1 = 2$. From Table III, Appendix D, $t_{.01} = 6.965$. The rejection region is $t < -6.965$.

c.   The test statistic is $t = \dfrac{\bar{x} - \mu_0}{s/\sqrt{n}} = \dfrac{64 - 70}{35.3/\sqrt{3}} = -.29$.

d.   Since the observed value of the test statistic does not fall in the rejection region $(t = -.29 \not< -6.956)$, H_0 is not rejected. There is insufficient evidence to indicate the mean number of occupational accidents at all Turkish construction sites is less than 70 at $\alpha = .01$.

e.   We must assume that a random sample was drawn from a normal population.

7.55   To determine if the mean level of radon exposure in the tombs is less than 6,000 Bq/m³, we test:

$$H_0 : \mu = 6,000$$
$$H_a : \mu < 6,000$$

From the printout, the test statistic is $t = -1.82$.

Since this is a one-tailed test, the *p*-value is $p = .096 / 2 = .0480$.

Since the *p*-value is less than $\alpha (p = .048 < .10)$, H_0 is rejected. There is sufficient evidence to indicate the mean level of radon exposure is less than 6,000 Bq/m³ at $\alpha = .10$.

7.57   a.   Using MINITAB, the calculations are:

One-Sample T: Velocity
```
Test of μ = 0.338 vs ≠ 0.338

Variable   N      Mean     StDev   SE Mean       90% CI            T      P
Velocity   25   0.26208   0.04669  0.00934  (0.24610, 0.27806)  -8.13  0.000
```

Let μ = mean bubble rising velocity. To determine if the mean bubble velocity differs from .338, we test:

$$H_0 : \mu = .338$$
$$H_a : \mu \neq .338$$

The test statistic is $t = -8.13$ and the p-value is $p = .000$.

Since the p-value is less than $\alpha(p = .000 < .10)$, H_0 is rejected. There is sufficient evidence to indicate the mean bubble velocity differs from .338 at $\alpha = .10$.

b.   No. Because the p-value is so small, it would be extremely unlikely that the data were generated at a sparging rate of 3.33 x 10^{-6}.

7.59   Using MINITAB, the descriptive statistics are:

One-Sample T: Skid
```
Test of mu = 425 vs < 425

Variable   N      Mean     StDev   SE Mean  95% Upper Bound     T      P
Skid       20   358.450   117.817  26.345        404.004     -2.53  0.010
```

To determine if the mean skidding distance is less than 425 meters, we test:

$$H_0 : \mu = 425$$
$$H_a : \mu < 425$$

The test statistics is $t = \dfrac{\bar{x} - \mu_o}{s/\sqrt{n}} = \dfrac{358.45 - 425}{117.817/\sqrt{20}} = -2.53$.

The rejection region requires $\alpha = .10$ in the lower tail of the t-distribution with.   From Table III, Appendix D, $t_{.10} = 1.328$.   The rejection region is $t < -1.328$.

Since the observed value of the test statistic falls in the rejection region $(t = -2.53 < -1.328)$, H_0 is rejected. There is sufficient evidence to indicate the true mean skidding distance is less than 425 meters at $\alpha = .10$. There is sufficient evidence to refute the claim.

7.61   Using MINITAB, the preliminary calculations are:

One-Sample T: Hardness
```
Test of μ = 76 vs > 76

Variable    N   Mean   StDev  SE Mean  95% Lower Bound    T      P
Hardness    3   82.00   2.65    1.53         77.54       3.93  0.030
```

Let μ = mean hardness of polyester composite mixture with 40% CKD weight ratio. To determine if using a 40% CKD weight ratio increases the mean hardness of polyester composite mixture, we test:

$H_0 : \mu = 76$

$H_a : \mu > 76$

The test statistic is $t = 3.93$ and the p-value is $p = .030$.

Since the p-value is small $(p = .030)$, H_0 is rejected. There is sufficient evidence to indicate that using a 40% CKD weight ratio increases the mean hardness of polyester composite mixture for any value of $\alpha > .03$.

7.63   Using MINITAB, the descriptive statistics for the 2 plants are:

Descriptive Statistics: AL1, AL2

Variable	N	Mean	StDev	Minimum	Q1	Median	Q3	Maximum
AL1	2	0.00750	0.00354	0.00500	*	0.00750	*	0.01000
AL2	2	0.0700	0.0283	0.0500	*	0.0700	*	0.0900

To determine if **plant 1** is violating the OSHA standard, we test:

$H_0 : \mu = .004$

$H_a : \mu > .004$

The test statistic is $t = \dfrac{\bar{x} - \mu_o}{s/\sqrt{n}} = \dfrac{.0075 - .004}{.00354/\sqrt{2}} = 1.40$.

The p-value is $p = P(t > 1.40)$. Using Minitab with df $= n - 1 = 2 - 1 = 1$, the p-value is $p = .197$. Since the p-value is not small, H_0 is not rejected. There is insufficient evidence to indicate the OSHA standard is violated by plant 1 for any value of $\alpha < .197$.

To determine if **plant 2** is violating the OSHA standard, we test:

$H_0 : \mu = .004$

$H_a : \mu > .004$

The test statistic is $t = \dfrac{\bar{x} - \mu_o}{s/\sqrt{n}} = \dfrac{.07 - .004}{.0283/\sqrt{2}} = 3.30$.

The p-value is $p = P(t > 1.40)$. Using Minitab with df $= n - 1 = 2 - 1 = 1$, the p-value is $p = .096$. Since the p-value is not small, H_0 is not rejected. There is insufficient evidence to indicate the OSHA standard is violated by plant 2 for any value of $\alpha < .096$.

If $\alpha > .096$, H_0 is rejected. There is sufficient evidence to indicate the OSHA standard is violated by plant 2 for any value of $\alpha > .096$.

7.65 a. $z = \dfrac{\hat{p} - p_0}{\sqrt{\dfrac{p_0 q_0}{n}}} = \dfrac{.83 - .9}{\sqrt{\dfrac{.9(.1)}{100}}} = -2.33$

b. The denominator in Exercise 7.64 is $\sqrt{\dfrac{.7(.3)}{100}} = .0458$ as compared to $\sqrt{\dfrac{.9(.1)}{100}} = .03$ in part **a**. Since the denominator in this problem is smaller, the absolute value of z is larger.

c. The rejection region requires $\alpha = .05$ in the lower tail of the z-distribution. From Table II, Appendix D, $z_{.05} = 1.645$. The rejection region is $z < -1.645$.

   Since the observed value of the test statistic falls in the rejection region $(z = -2.33 < -1.645)$, H_0 is rejected. There is sufficient evidence to indicate the population proportion is less than .9 at $\alpha = .05$.

d. The p-value $= p = P(z \le -2.33) = .5 - .4901 = .0099$ (from Table II, Appendix D). Since the p-value is less than $\alpha = .05$, H_0 is rejected.

7.67 Because p is the proportion of consumers who do not like the snack food, $\hat{p}$ will be:

$$\hat{p} = \frac{\text{Number of 0's in sample}}{n} = \frac{29}{50} = .58$$

First, check to see if the normal approximation will be adequate:

$$np_0 = 50(.5) = 25 \qquad\qquad nq_0 = 50(.5) = 25$$

Since both $np_0 \ge 15$ and $nq_0 \ge 15$, the normal distribution will be adequate.

a. $H_0 : p = .5$
   $H_a : p > .5$

   The test statistic is $z = \dfrac{\hat{p} - p_0}{\sigma_{\hat{p}}} = \dfrac{\hat{p} - p_0}{\sqrt{\dfrac{p_0 q_0}{n}}} = \dfrac{.58 - .5}{\sqrt{\dfrac{.5(1-.5)}{50}}} = 1.13.$

   The rejection region requires $\alpha = .10$ in the upper tail of the z-distribution. From Table II, Appendix D, $z_{.10} = 1.28$. The rejection region is $z > 1.28$.

   Since the observed value of the test statistic does not fall in the rejection region $(z=1.13 \ngtr 1.28)$, H_0 is not rejected. There is insufficient evidence to indicate the proportion of customers who do not like the snack food is greater than .5 at $\alpha = .10$.

b. $p - \text{value} = p = P(z \ge 1.13) = .5 - .3708 = .1292$ (using Table II, Appendix D)

7.69 a. $\hat{p} = \dfrac{225}{250} = .9$

b.   To determine if more than 80% of all customers would participate in a loyalty card program, we test:

$H_0 : p = .8$

$H_a : \mu > .8$

c.   The test statistic is $z = \dfrac{\hat{p} - p_0}{\sqrt{\dfrac{p_0 q_0}{n}}} = \dfrac{.9 - .8}{\sqrt{\dfrac{.8(.2)}{250}}} = 3.95.$

d.   The rejection region requires $\alpha = .01$ in the upper tail of the z-distribution. From Table II, Appendix D, $z_{.01} = 2.33$. The rejection region is $z > 2.33$.

e.   The p-value is $p = P(z > 3.95) = .5 - .49996 = .00004 \approx 0$ (Using Table II, Appendix D)

f.   Since the observed value of the test statistic falls in the rejection region $(z = 3.95 > 2.33)$, H_0 is rejected. There is sufficient evidence to indicate that more than 80% of all customers would participate in a loyalty card program at $\alpha = .01$.

g.   Since the p-value is less than $\alpha (p = 0 < .01)$, H_0 is rejected. There is sufficient evidence to indicate that more than 80% of all customers would participate in a loyalty card program at $\alpha = .01$.

7.71 $\hat{p} = \dfrac{x}{n} = \dfrac{785}{2,242} = .35013$

To determine if the true fraction of adult TV viewers who are subscription streamers differs from 1/3, we test:

$H_0 : p = 1/3$

$H_a : p \neq 1/3$

The test statistic is $z = \dfrac{.35013 - \frac{1}{3}}{\sqrt{\dfrac{\left(\frac{1}{3}\right)\left(1 - \frac{1}{3}\right)}{2,242}}} = 1.69.$

The rejection region requires $\alpha / 2 = .10 / 2 = .05$ in each tail of the z-distribution. From Table II, Appendix D, $z_{.05} = 1.645$. The rejection region is $z < -1.645$ or $z > 1.645$.

Since the observed value of the test statistic falls in the rejection region $(z = 1.69 > 1.645)$, H_0 is rejected. There is sufficient evidence to indicate the true fraction of adult TV viewers who are subscription streamers differs from 1/3 at $\alpha = .10$.

7.73   a.   To determine whether the true proportion of toothpaste brands with the ADA seal verifying effective decay prevention is less than .5, we test:

$H_0 : p = .5$

$H_a : p < .5$

b.   From the printout, the p-value is $p = .188$.

c.   Since the observed p-value is greater than $\alpha \left(p = .188 > .10 \right)$, H_0 is not rejected. There is insufficient evidence to indicate the true proportion of toothpaste brands with the ADA seal verifying effective decay prevention is less than .5 at $\alpha = .10$.

7.75 $\hat{p} = \dfrac{x}{n} = \dfrac{417 + 77}{845} = .585$

To determine if fewer than 60% of the coffee growers in southern Mexico are either certified or transitioning to become certified, we test:

$H_0 : p = .60$
$H_a : p < .60$

The test statistic is $z = \dfrac{\hat{p} - p_0}{\sigma_{\hat{p}}} = \dfrac{\hat{p} - p_0}{\sqrt{\dfrac{p_0 q_0}{n}}} = \dfrac{.585 - .60}{\sqrt{\dfrac{.60(1-.60)}{845}}} = -.89.$

The rejection region requires $\alpha = .05$ in the lower tail of the z-distribution. From Table II, Appendix D, $z_{.05} = 1.645$. The rejection region is.

Since the observed value of the test statistic does not fall in the rejection region $\left(z = -.89 \not< -1.645 \right)$, H_0 is not rejected. There is insufficient evidence to indicate that fewer than 60% of the coffee growers in southern Mexico are either certified or transitioning to become certified at $\alpha = .05$.

7.77   a.   Le $p =$ proportion of middle-aged women who exhibit skin improvement after using the cream. For this problem, $\hat{p} = \dfrac{x}{n} = \dfrac{24}{33} = .727.$

First we check to see if the normal approximation is adequate:

$np_0 = 33(.6) = 19.8, \ nq_0 = 33(.4) = 13.2$

Since $nq_0 = 13.2$ is less than 15, the assumption of normality may not be valid. We will go ahead and perform the test.

To determine if the cream will improve the skin of more than 60% of middle-aged women, we test:

$H_0 : p = .60$
$H_a : p > .60$

The test statistic is $z = \dfrac{\hat{p} - p_0}{\sqrt{\dfrac{p_0 q_0}{n}}} = \dfrac{.727 - .60}{\sqrt{\dfrac{.60(.40)}{33}}} = 1.49.$

The rejection region requires $\alpha = .05$ in the upper tail of the z-distribution. From Table II, Appendix D, $z_{.05} = 1.645$. The rejection region is $z > 1.645$.

Since the observed value of the test statistic does not fall in the rejection region $(z = 1.49 \not> 1.645)$, H_0 is not rejected. There is insufficient evidence to indicate the cream will improve the skin of more than 60% of middle-aged women at $\alpha = .05$.

b.   The p-value is $p = P(z \geq 1.49) = (.5 - .4319) = .0681$. (Using Table II, Appendix D.) Since the p-value is greater than $\alpha (p = .0681 > .05)$, H_0 is not rejected. There is insufficient evidence to indicate the cream will improve the skin of more than 60% of middle-aged women at $\alpha = .05$,

7.79   Answers will vary. The target population will be all households in the $75,000 income bracket in the United States. The experimental unit will be an individual household in the United States in the $75,000 income bracket. The variable to be measured is whether or not the household has a Smart TV with internet and video streaming access. Let p = proportion of be all households the $75,000 income bracket in the United States that have Smart TVs with internet and video streaming access. The hypotheses of interest are:

$H_0 : p = .29$

$H_a : p \neq .29$

The test statistic is $z = \dfrac{\hat{p} - p_0}{\sqrt{\dfrac{p_0 q_0}{n}}} = \dfrac{\hat{p} - .29}{\sqrt{\dfrac{.29(1 - .29)}{n}}}$.

One would have to obtain a list of households in the U.S. in the $75,000 income bracket. Once this list is obtained, one could take a random sample from this list to test the hypothesis.

7.81   To minimize the probability of a Type I error, we will select $\alpha = .01$.

First, check to see if the normal approximation is adequate:

$np_0 = 100(.5) = 50 \qquad nq_0 = 100(.5) = 50$

Since both $np_0 \geq .15$ and $nq_0 \geq .15$, the normal distribution will be adequate

$\hat{p} = \dfrac{x}{n} = \dfrac{56}{100} = .56$

To determine if more than half of all Diet Coke drinkers prefer Diet Pepsi, we test:

$H_0 : p = .5$

$H_a : p > .5$

The test statistic is $z = \dfrac{\hat{p} - p_0}{\sqrt{\dfrac{p_0 q_0}{n}}} = \dfrac{.56 - .5}{\sqrt{\dfrac{.5(.5)}{100}}} = 1.20$.

The rejection region requires $\alpha = .01$ in the upper tail of the z-distribution. From Table II, Appendix D, $z_{.01} = 2.33$. The rejection region is $z > 2.33$.

Since the observed value of the test statistic does not fall in the rejection region $(z = 1.20 \not> 2.33)$, H_0 is not rejected. There is insufficient evidence to indicate that more than half of all Diet Coke drinkers prefer Diet Pepsi at $\alpha = .01$.

Since H_0 was not rejected, there is no evidence that Diet Coke drinkers prefer Diet Pepsi.

7.83   a.   df $= n-1 = 16-1 = 15$; reject H_0 if $\chi^2 < 6.26214$ or $\chi^2 > 27.4884$

b.   df $= n-1 = 23-1 = 22$; reject H_0 if $\chi^2 > 40.2894$

c.   df $= n-1 = 15-1 = 14$; reject H_0 if $\chi^2 > 21.0642$

d.   df $= n-1 = 13-1 = 12$; reject H_0 if $\chi^2 < 3.57056$

e.   df $= n-1 = 7-1 = 6$; reject H_0 if $\chi^2 < 1.63539$ or $\chi^2 > 12.5916$

f.   df $= n-1 = 25-1 = 24$; reject H_0 if $\chi^2 < 13.8484$

7.85   a.
$$H_0 : \sigma^2 = 1$$
$$H_a : \sigma^2 > 1$$

The test statistic is $\chi^2 = \dfrac{(n-1)s^2}{\sigma_0^2} = \dfrac{(100-1)4.84}{1} = 479.16$.

The rejection region requires $\alpha = .05$ in the upper tail of the χ^2 distribution with df $= n-1 = 100-1 = 99$. From Table IV, Appendix D, $\chi^2_{.05} \approx 124.342$. The rejection region is $\chi^2 > 124.342$.

Since the observed value of the test statistic falls in the rejection region $(\chi^2 = 479.16 > 124.342)$, H_0 is rejected. There is sufficient evidence to indicate the variance is larger than 1 at $\alpha = .05$.

b.   In part **b** of Exercise 7.84, the test statistic was $\chi^2 = 29.04$. The conclusion was to reject H_0 as it was in this problem.

7.87   a.   To determine whether the population of institutional investors performs consistently, we test:
$$H_0 : \sigma^2 = 10^2 = 100$$
$$H_a : \sigma^2 < 100$$

b.   The rejection region requires $\alpha = .05$ in the lower tail of the χ^2 distribution with df $= n-1 = 200-1 = 199$. Using MINITAB, we get:

Inverse Cumulative Distribution Function
```
Chi-Square with 199 DF

P( X <= x )         x
        0.05   167.361
```

The rejection region is $\chi^2 < 167.361$.

c. For this problem, $\alpha = .05$. The probability of concluding the standard deviation is less than 10 when, in fact, it is equal to 10 is .05. If this test was repeated a large number of times, approximately 5% of the time we would conclude the standard deviation was less than 10 when it really was 10.

d. From the printout, $\chi^2 = 154.81$ and the p-value is $p = .009$.

e. Since the p-value is less than $\alpha (p = .009 < .05)$, H_0 is rejected. There is sufficient evidence to indicate the standard deviation is less than 10% at $\alpha = .05$.

f. We must assume that a random sample was selected from the target population and the population sampled from is approximately normal.

7.89 a. Let $\sigma^2 = $ weight variance of tees. To determine if the weight variance differs from .000004 (injection mold process is out-of-control), we test:

$$H_0 : \sigma^2 = .000004$$
$$H_a : \sigma^2 \neq .000004$$

b. Using MINITAB, the descriptive statistics are:

Descriptive Statistics: Tees

Variable	N	Mean	Median	StDev	Minimum	Maximum	Q1	Q3
Tees	40	0.25248	0.25300	0.00223	0.24700	0.25600	0.25100	0.25400

The test statistic is $\chi^2 = \dfrac{(n-1)s^2}{\sigma_0^2} = \dfrac{(40-1)(.00223)^2}{.000004} = 48.49$

The rejection region requires $\alpha / 2 = .01 / 2 = .005$ in each tail of the χ^2 distribution with $df = n - 1 = 40 - 1 = 39$. From Table IV, Appendix D, $\chi^2_{.005} \approx 66.7659$ and $\chi^2_{.995} \approx 20.7065$. The rejection region is $\chi^2 > 66.7659$ or $\chi^2 < 20.7065$.

Since the observed value of the test statistic does not fall in the rejection region $\left(\chi^2 = 49.49 \not> 66.7659 \text{ and } \chi^2 = 49.49 \not< 20.7065 \right)$, H_0 is not rejected. There is insufficient evidence to indicate the injection mold process is out-of-control at $\alpha = .01$.

c. We must assume that the distribution of the weights of tees is approximately normal. Using MINITAB, a histogram of the data is:

Copyright © 2018 Pearson Education, Inc.

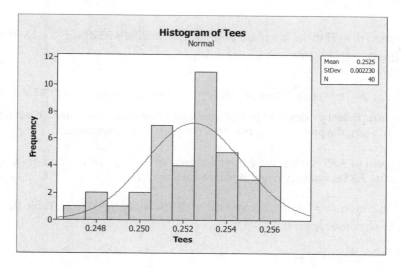

The data look fairly mound-shaped, so the assumption of normality seems to be reasonably satisfied.

7.91   Using MINITAB, the preliminary calculations are:

Descriptive Statistics: Force
```
Variable   N    Mean   StDev   Variance   Minimum     Q1   Median     Q3   Maximum
Force     12  163.22    4.99      24.87    158.20  159.95   161.70  165.80   175.60
```

To determine if the variance of the maximum strand forces that occur after anchorage failure is less than $25kN^2$, we test:

$$H_0 : \sigma^2 = 25$$
$$H_a : \sigma^2 < 25$$

The test statistic is $\chi^2 = \dfrac{(n-1)s^2}{\sigma_0^2} = \dfrac{(12-1)24.87}{25} = 10.94$.

The rejection region requires $\alpha = .10$ in the lower tail of the χ^2 distribution with df $= n - 1 = 12 - 1 = 11$. From Table IV, Appendix D, $\chi_{.90}^2 = 5.57779$. The rejection region is $\chi^2 < 5.57779$.

Since the observed value of the test statistic does not fall in the rejection region $\left(\chi^2 = 10.94 \not< 5.57779\right)$, H_0 is not rejected. There is insufficient evidence to indicate the variance of the maximum strand forces that occur after anchorage failure is less than $25kN^2$ at $\alpha = .10$.

7.93   To determine whether the true conduction time standard deviation is less than 7 seconds (variance less than 49), we test:

$$H_0 : \sigma^2 = 7^2$$
$$H_a : \sigma^2 < 7^2$$

The test statistic is $\chi^2 = \dfrac{(n-1)s^2}{\sigma_0^2} = \dfrac{(18-1)6.3^2}{7^2} = 13.77$.

The rejection region requires $\alpha = .01$ in the lower tail of the χ^2 distribution with df $= n-1 = 18-1 = 17$. From Table IV, Appendix D, $\chi^2_{.99} = 6.40776$. The rejection region is.

Since the observed value of the test statistic does not fall in the rejection region $\left(\chi^2 = 13.77 \not< 6.40776\right)$, H_0 is not rejected. There is insufficient evidence to indicate the true conduction time standard deviation is less than 7 seconds at $\alpha = .01$. Thus, the prototype system does not satisfy this requirement.

7.95   a.   Since the sample mean of 3.85 is not that far from the value of 3.5, a large standard deviation would indicate that the value 3.85 is not very many standard deviations from 3.5.

b.   The rejection region requires $\alpha = .01$ in the upper tail of the z-distribution. From Table II, Appendix D, $z_{.01} = 2.33$. The rejection region is $z > 2.33$.

The test statistic is $z = \dfrac{\bar{x} - \mu_o}{\sigma_{\bar{x}}} = \dfrac{3.85 - 3.5}{\sigma/\sqrt{137}}$.

To reject H_0, $z > 2.33$. Thus, we need to find σ so $z > 2.33$.

$$z = \frac{3.85 - 3.5}{\sigma/\sqrt{137}} > 2.33 \Rightarrow 3.85 - 3.5 > 2.33\frac{\sigma}{\sqrt{137}} \Rightarrow .35 > .199065\sigma \Rightarrow 1.758 > \sigma$$

Thus, the largest value of σ for which we will reject H_0 is 1.758.

c.   To determine if $\sigma < 1.758$, we test:

$H_0 : \sigma^2 = 1.758^2$
$H_a : \sigma^2 < 1.758^2$

The test statistic is $\chi^2 = \dfrac{(n-1)s^2}{\sigma_o^2} = \dfrac{(137-1)1.5^2}{1.758^2} = 99.011$.

The rejection region requires $\alpha = .01$ in the lower tail of the χ^2 distribution with df $= n-1 = 137-1 = 136$. Since there are no values in the table with df > 100, we will use MINITAB to compute the p-value of the test statistic.

Cumulative Distribution Function
```
Chi-Square with 136 DF

      x   P( X <= x )
 99.011     0.0072496
```

Since the p-value is less than $\alpha (p = 0.0072496 < .01)$, H_0 is rejected. There is sufficient evidence to indicate the standard deviation of the scores is less than 1.758 at $\alpha = .01$.

d.   Since the sample size is large $(n = 137)$, the Central Limit Theorem applies. The inference made in part b about the population mean is valid. However, the test for the population variance requires that the population from which the sample is drawn be normal. Therefore, the inference about the population standard deviation may not be valid.

7.97   a.   By the Central Limit Theorem, the sampling distribution of $\bar{x}$ is approximately normal with

$$\mu_{\bar{x}} = \mu = 500 \text{ and } \sigma_{\bar{x}} = \frac{\sigma}{\sqrt{n}} = \frac{100}{\sqrt{25}} = 20.$$

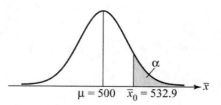

b. $\bar{x}_0 = \mu_0 + z_\alpha \sigma_{\bar{x}} = \mu_0 + z_\alpha \dfrac{\sigma}{\sqrt{n}}$ where $z_\alpha = z_{.05} = 1.645$ from

Table II, Appendix D.

Thus, $\bar{x}_0 = 500 + 1.645(20) = 532.9$

c.   The sampling distribution of $\bar{x}$ is approximately normal by the Central Limit Theorem with $\bar{x} = \mu = 550$ and

$$\sigma_{\bar{x}} = \frac{\sigma}{\sqrt{n}} = \frac{100}{\sqrt{25}} = 20.$$

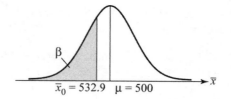

d. $\beta = P(\bar{x}_0 < 532.9 \text{ when } \mu = 550) = P\left(z < \dfrac{532.9 - 550}{100 / \sqrt{25}}\right) = P(z < -.86) = .5 - .3051 = .1949$

e. $Power = 1 - \beta = 1 - .1949 = .8051$

7.99   a.   The sampling distribution of $\bar{x}$ will be approximately normal (by the Central Limit Theorem) with

$$\mu_{\bar{x}} = \mu = 75 \text{ and } \sigma_{\bar{x}} = \frac{\sigma}{\sqrt{n}} = \frac{15}{\sqrt{49}} = 2.143.$$

b.   The sampling distribution of $\bar{x}$ will be approximately normal (by the Central Limit Theorem) with

$$\mu_{\bar{x}} = \mu = 70 \text{ and } \sigma_{\bar{x}} = \frac{\sigma}{\sqrt{n}} = \frac{15}{\sqrt{49}} = 2.143.$$

c.   First, find $\bar{x}_0 = \mu_0 - z_\alpha \sigma_{\bar{x}} = \mu_0 - z_\alpha \dfrac{\sigma}{\sqrt{n}}$ where $z_{.10} = 1.28$ from Table II, Appendix D.

Thus, $\bar{x}_0 = 75 - 1.28\dfrac{15}{\sqrt{49}} = 72.257.$

Now, find $\beta = P(\bar{x}_0 > 72.257 \text{ when } \mu = 70) = P\left(z > \dfrac{72.257 - 70}{15 / \sqrt{49}}\right) = P(z > 1.05) = .5 - .3531 = .1469$

d. $Power = 1 - \beta = 1 - .1469 = .8531$

7.101   a.   First, the sample is sufficiently large if both $np_0 \geq 15$ and $nq_0 \geq 15$.

$np_0 = 100(.7) = 70$ and $nq_0 \geq 100(1 - .7) = 30.$

Since both $np_0 \geq 15$ and $nq_0 \geq 15,$ the normal distribution will be adequate.

Thus, the sampling distribution of $\hat{p}$ will be approximately normal with $E(\hat{p}) = p = .7$ and

$$\sigma_{\hat{p}} = \sqrt{\frac{p_0 q_0}{n}} = \sqrt{\frac{.7(.3)}{100}} = .0458.$$

b. The sampling distribution of $\hat{p}$ will be approximately normal with $E(\hat{p}) = p = .65$ and

$$\sigma_{\hat{p}} = \sqrt{\frac{p_0 q_0}{n}} = \sqrt{\frac{.65(.35)}{100}} = .0477.$$

c. First, find $\hat{p}_{0,L} = p_0 - z_{\alpha/2}\sigma_{\hat{p}} = p_0 - z_{\alpha/2}\sqrt{\frac{p_0 q_0}{n}}$

where $z_{.05/2} = z_{.025} = 1.96$ from Table II, Appendix D.

Thus, $\hat{p}_{0,L} = .7 - 1.96\sqrt{\frac{.7(.3)}{100}} = .610$

$$\hat{p}_{0,U} = p_0 + z_{\alpha/2}\sigma_{\hat{p}} = p_0 + z_{\alpha/2}\sqrt{\frac{p_0 q_0}{n}} = .7 + 1.96\sqrt{\frac{.7(.3)}{100}} = .790$$

Now, find $\beta = P(.610 < \hat{p} < .79$ when $p = .65)$

$$= P\left(\frac{.610 - .65}{\sqrt{\frac{.65(.35)}{100}}} < z < \frac{.79 - .65}{\sqrt{\frac{.65(.35)}{100}}}\right) = P(-.84 < z < 2.94) = .2995 + .4984 = .7979$$

d. $\beta = P(.610 < \hat{p} < .79$ when $p = .71)$

$$= P\left(\frac{.610 - .71}{\sqrt{\frac{.71(.29)}{100}}} < z < \frac{.79 - .71}{\sqrt{\frac{.71(.29)}{100}}}\right) = P(-2.20 < z < 1.76) = .4861 + .4608 = .9469$$

7.103   a. We have failed to reject H_0 when it is not true. This is a Type II error.

To compute β, first find:

$$\bar{x}_0 = \mu_0 - z_\alpha \sigma_{\bar{x}} = \mu_0 - z_\alpha \frac{\sigma}{\sqrt{n}} \text{ where } z_{.05} = 1.645 \text{ from Table II, Appendix D.}$$

Thus, $\bar{x}_0 = 5.0 - 1.645\frac{.01}{\sqrt{100}} = 4.998355$

Then find:

$$\beta = P\left(\bar{x}_0 > 4.998355 \text{ when } \mu = 4.9975\right) = P\left(z > \frac{4.998355 - 4.9975}{.01/\sqrt{100}}\right)$$

$$= P\left(z > .86\right) = .5 - .3051 = .1949$$

b. We have rejected H_0 when it is true. This is a Type I error. The probability of a Type I error is $\alpha = .05$.

c. A departure of .0025 below 5.0 is $\mu = 4.9975$. Using **a**, $\beta = .1949$ when $\mu = 4.9975$. The power of the test is $1 - \beta = 1 - .1949 = .8051$.

7.105. To compute the power, we must first set up the rejection region in terms of $\hat{p}$. The rejection region requires $\alpha/2 = .01/2 = .005$ in each tail of the z-distribution. From Table II, Appendix D, $z_{.005} = 2.575$. The rejection region is $z > -2.575$ or $z > 2.575$.

Thus, $\hat{p}_{0,L} = p_0 - z_{\alpha/2}\sigma_{\hat{p}} = p_0 - z_{\alpha/2}\sqrt{\dfrac{p_0 q_0}{n}} = .5 - 2.575\sqrt{\dfrac{.5(.5)}{121}} = .5 - .117 = .383$ and

$$\hat{p}_{0,U} = p_0 + z_{\alpha/2}\sigma_{\hat{p}} = p_0 + z_{\alpha/2}\sqrt{\dfrac{p_0 q_0}{n}} = .5 + 2.575\sqrt{\dfrac{.5(.5)}{121}} = .5 + .117 = .617.$$

$$\text{Power} = P\left(\hat{p} < .383 \text{ or } \hat{p} > .617 \mid p_0 = .65\right) = P\left(z < \frac{\hat{p} - p_0}{\sigma_{\hat{p}}}\right) + P\left(z > \frac{\hat{p} - p_0}{\sigma_{\hat{p}}}\right)$$

$$= P\left(z < \frac{.383 - .65}{\sqrt{\dfrac{.65(.35)}{121}}}\right) + P\left(z > \frac{.617 - .65}{\sqrt{\dfrac{.65(.35)}{121}}}\right) = P\left(z < -6.16\right) + P\left(z > -.76\right) = (.5 - .5) + (.5 + .2764) = .7764$$

7.107 First, find $\bar{x}_0$ such that $P\left(\bar{x} < \bar{x}_0\right) = .05$.

$$P\left(\bar{x} < \bar{x}_0\right) = P\left(z < \frac{\bar{x}_0 - 10}{1.2/\sqrt{48}}\right) = P\left(z < z_0\right) = .05.$$

From Table II, Appendix D, $z_0 = -1.645$.

Thus, $z_0 = \dfrac{\bar{x}_0 - 10}{1.2/\sqrt{48}} \Rightarrow \bar{x}_0 = -1.645(.173) + 10 = 9.715.$

The probability of a Type II error is:

$$\beta = P\left(\bar{x} \geq 9.715 \mid \mu = 9.5\right) = P\left(z \geq \frac{9.715 - 9.5}{1.2/\sqrt{48}}\right) = P\left(z \geq 1.24\right) = .5 - .3925 = .1075$$

7.109 The smaller the p-value associated with a test of hypothesis, the stronger the support for the **alternative** hypothesis. The p-value is the probability of observing your test statistic or anything more unusual, given the null hypothesis is true. If this value is small, it would be very unusual to observe this test statistic if the null hypothesis were true. Thus, it would indicate the alternative hypothesis is true.

7.111   There is not a direct relationship between α and β. That is, if α is known, it does not mean β is known because β depends on the value of the parameter in the alternative hypothesis and the sample size. However, as α decreases, β increases for a fixed value of the parameter and a fixed sample size. Thus, if α is very small, β will tend to be large.

7.113   a. $H_0 : \mu = 80$
              $H_a : \mu < 80$

The test statistic is $t = \dfrac{\bar{x} - \mu_0}{s/\sqrt{n}} = \dfrac{72.6 - 80}{\sqrt{19.4}/\sqrt{20}} = -7.51.$

The rejection region requires $\alpha = .05$ in the lower tail of the t-distribution with df $= n - 1 = 20 - 1 = 19$. From Table III, Appendix D, $t_{.05} = 1.729$. The rejection region is $t < -1.729$.

Since the observed value of the test statistic falls in the rejection region $(t = -7.51 < -1.729)$, H_0 is rejected. There is sufficient evidence to indicate that the mean is less than 80 at $\alpha = .05$.

       b. $H_0 : \mu = 80$
             $H_a : \mu \neq 80$

The test statistic is $t = \dfrac{\bar{x} - \mu_0}{s/\sqrt{n}} = \dfrac{72.6 - 80}{\sqrt{19.4}/\sqrt{20}} = -7.51.$

The rejection region requires $\alpha/2 = .01/2 = .005$ in each tail of the t-distribution with df $= n - 1 = 20 - 1 = 19$. From Table III, Appendix D, $t_{.005} = 2.861$. The rejection region is $t < -2.861$ or $t > 2.861$.

Since the observed value of the test statistic falls in the rejection region $(t = -7.51 < -2.861)$, H_0 is rejected. There is sufficient evidence to indicate that the mean is different from 80 at $\alpha = .01$.

7.115   a. $H_0 : p = .35$
              $H_a : p < .35$

The test statistic is $z = \dfrac{\hat{p} - p_0}{\sqrt{\dfrac{p_0 q_0}{n}}} = \dfrac{.29 - .35}{\sqrt{\dfrac{.35(.65)}{200}}} = -1.78.$

The rejection region requires $\alpha = .05$ in the lower tail of the z-distribution. From Table II, Appendix D, $z_{.05} = 1.645$. The rejection region is $z < -1.645$.

Since the observed value of the test statistic falls in the rejection region $(z = -1.78 < -1.645)$, H_0 is rejected. There is sufficient evidence to indicate $p < .35$ at $\alpha = .05$.

       b. $H_0 : p = .35$
             $H_a : p \neq .35$

The test statistic is $z = -1.78$ (from **a**).

The rejection region requires $\alpha / 2 = .05 / 2 = .025$ in each tail of the z-distribution. From Table II, Appendix D, $z_{.025} = 1.96$. The rejection region is $z < -1.96$ or $z > 1.96$.

Since the observed value of the test statistic does not fall in the rejection region $(z = -1.78 \not< -1.96)$, H_0 is not rejected. There is insufficient evidence to indicate p is different from .35 at $\alpha = .05$.

7.117   a. $H_0 : \sigma^2 = 30$
$H_a : \sigma^2 > 30$

The test statistic is $\chi^2 = \dfrac{(n-1)s^2}{\sigma_0^2} = \dfrac{(41-1)(6.9)^2}{30} = 63.48$

The rejection region requires $\alpha = .05$ in the upper tail of the χ^2 distribution with $df = n - 1 = 41 - 1 = 40$. From Table IV, Appendix D, $\chi_{.05}^2 = 55.7585$. The rejection region is $\chi^2 > 55.7585$.

Since the observed value of the test statistic falls in the rejection region $(\chi^2 = 63.48 > 55.7585)$, H_0 is rejected. There is sufficient evidence to indicate the variance is larger than 30 at $\alpha = .05$.

b. $H_0 : \sigma^2 = 30$
$H_a : \sigma^2 \neq 30$

The test statistic is $\chi^2 = 63.48$ (from part a).

The rejection region requires $\alpha / 2 = .05 / 2 = .025$ in each tail of the χ^2 distribution with $df = n - 1 = 41 - 1 = 40$. From Table IV, Appendix D, $\chi_{.025}^2 = 59.3417$ and $\chi_{.975}^2 = 24.4331$. The rejection region is $\chi^2 < 24.4331$ or $\chi^2 > 59.3417$.

Since the observed value of the test statistic falls in the rejection region $(\chi^2 = 63.48 > 59.3417)$, H_0 is rejected. There is sufficient evidence to indicate the variance is not 30 at $\alpha = .05$.

7.119   To determine if the sample provides sufficient evidence to indicate that the true percentage of all firms that announced one or more acquisitions during the year 2000 is less than 30%, we test:

$H_0 : p = .30$
$H_a : p < .30$

The point estimate is $\hat{p} = \dfrac{x}{n} = \dfrac{748}{2{,}778} = .26926$.

The test statistic is $z = \dfrac{\hat{p} - p_o}{\sqrt{\dfrac{p_o q_o}{n}}} = \dfrac{.26926 - .30}{\sqrt{\dfrac{.30(.70)}{2{,}778}}} = -3.54$.

The rejection region requires $\alpha = .05$ in the lower tail of the z-distribution. From Table II, Appendix D, $z_{.05} = 1.645$. The rejection region is $z < -1.645$.

Since the observed value of the test statistic falls in the rejection region $(z = -3.54 < -1.645)$, H_0 is rejected. There is sufficient evidence to indicate that the true percentage of all firms that announced one or more acquisitions during the year 2000 is less than 30% at $\alpha = .05$.

7.121   a.   The rejection region requires $\alpha / 2 = .01 / 2 = .005$ in each tail of the χ^2 distribution with $df = n - 1 = 46 - 1 = 45$. Using MINITAB,

Inverse Cumulative Distribution Function
```
Chi-Square with 45 DF

P( X <= x )        x
     0.005   24.3110
```

Inverse Cumulative Distribution Function
```
Chi-Square with 45 DF

P( X <= x )        x
     0.995   73.1661
```

The rejection region is $\chi^2 < 24.3110$ or $\chi^2 > 73.1661$.

   b.   The test statistic is $\chi^2 = \dfrac{(n-1)s^2}{\sigma_o^2} = \dfrac{(46-1)11.9^2}{100} = 63.7245$.

   c.   Since the observed value of the test statistic does not fall in the rejection region $(\chi^2 = 63.7245 \not< 24.3110$ and $\chi^2 = 63.7245 \not> 73.1661)$, H_0 is not rejected. There is insufficient evidence to indicate the variance is different from 100 at $\alpha = .01$.

7.123   a.   To determine if the average high technology stock is riskier than the market as a whole, we test:

$$H_0 : \mu = 1$$
$$H_a : \mu > 1$$

   b.   The test statistic is $t = \dfrac{\bar{x} - \mu_0}{s / \sqrt{n}}$.

   The rejection region requires $\alpha = .10$ in the upper tail of the t-distribution with $df = n - 1 = 15 - 1 = 14$. From Table III, Appendix D, $t_{.10} = 1.345$. The rejection region is $t > 1.345$.

   c.   We must assume the population of beta coefficients of technology stocks is normally distributed.

   d.   The test statistic is $t = \dfrac{\bar{x} - \mu_0}{s / \sqrt{n}} = \dfrac{1.23 - 1}{.37 / \sqrt{15}} = 2.41$.

   Since the observed value of the test statistic falls in the rejection region $(t = 2.41 > 1.345)$, H_0 is rejected. There is sufficient evidence to indicate the mean high technology stock is riskier than the market as a whole at $\alpha = .10$.

e. From Table III, Appendix D, with $df = n-1 = 15-1 = 14$, $.01 < P(t \geq 2.41) < .025$. Thus, $.01 < p\text{-value} < .025$. The probability of observing this test statistic, $t = 2.41$, or anything more unusual is between .01 and .025. Since this probability is small, there is evidence to indicate the null hypothesis is false for $\alpha = .05$.

f. To determine if the variance of the stock beta values differs from .15, we test:

$$H_0 : \sigma^2 = .15$$
$$H_a : \sigma^2 \neq .15$$

The test statistic is $\chi^2 = \dfrac{(n-1)s^2}{\sigma_o^2} = \dfrac{(15-1).37^2}{.15} = 12.7773$.

The rejection region requires $\alpha / 2 = .05 / 2 = .025$ in each tail of the χ^2 distribution with $df = n-1 = 15-1 = 14$. From Table IV, Appendix D, $\chi^2_{.975} = 5.62872$ and $\chi^2_{.025} = 26.1190$. The rejection region is $\chi^2 < 5.62872$ or $\chi^2 > 26.1190$.

Since the observed value of the test statistic does not fall in the rejection region $(\chi^2 = 12.7773 \nless 5.62875$ and $\chi^2 = 12.7773 \ngtr 26.1190)$, H_0 is not rejected. There is insufficient evidence to indicate the variance of the stock beta values differs from .15 at $\alpha = .05$.

7.125 a. $\hat{p} = \dfrac{x}{n} = \dfrac{506}{755} = .67$

b. To determine if the true proportion of all internet-using adults who have paid to download music exceeds .7, we test:

$$H_0 : p = .7$$
$$H_a : p > .7$$

c. The test statistic is $z = \dfrac{\hat{p} - p_0}{\sigma_{\hat{p}}} = \dfrac{\hat{p} - p_0}{\sqrt{\dfrac{p_0 q_0}{n}}} = \dfrac{.67 - .7}{\sqrt{\dfrac{.7(1-.7)}{755}}} = -1.80$.

d. The rejection region requires $\alpha = .01$ in the upper tail of the z-distribution. From Table II, Appendix D, $z_{.01} = 2.33$. The rejection region is $z > 2.33$.

e. $p-\text{value} = p = P(z \geq -1.80) = .5 + .4641 = .9641$ (using Table II, Appendix D)

f. Since the observed value of the test statistic does not fall in the rejection region $(t = -1.80 \ngtr 2.33)$, H_0 is not rejected. There is insufficient evidence to indicate the true proportion of all internet-using adults who have paid to download music exceeds .7 at $\alpha = .01$.

g. Since the p-value is not less than $\alpha (p = .9641 \nless .01)$, H_0 is not rejected. There is insufficient evidence to indicate the true proportion of all internet-using adults who have paid to download music exceeds .7 at $\alpha = .01$.

7.127   a.   Let μ = mean Mach rating score for all purchasing managers. To determine if the mean Mach rating score is different from 85, we test:

$$H_0 : \mu = 85$$
$$H_a : \mu \neq 85$$

   b.   The rejection requires $\alpha / 2 = .10 / 2 = .05$ in each tail of the z-distribution. From Table II, Appendix D, $z_{.05} = 1.645$. The rejection region is $z < -1.645$ or $z > 1.645$.

   c.   The test statistic is $z = \dfrac{\bar{x} - \mu_o}{\sigma_{\bar{x}}} \approx \dfrac{99.6 - 85}{12.6 / \sqrt{122}} = 12.80$.

   d.   Since the observed value of the test statistic falls in the rejection region $(z = 12.80 > 1.645)$, H_0 is rejected. There is sufficient evidence to indicate that the true mean Mach rating score of all purchasing managers is not 85 at $\alpha = .10$.

7.129   a.   The hypotheses would be:

   H_0: Individual does not have the disease
   H_a: Individual does have the disease

   b.   A Type I error would be: Conclude the individual has the disease when in fact he/she does not. This would be a false positive test.

   A Type II error would be: Conclude the individual does not have the disease when in fact he/she does. This would be a false negative test.

   c.   If the disease is serious, either error would be grave. Arguments could be made for either error being more grave. However, I believe a Type II error would be more grave: Concluding the individual does not have the disease when he/she does. This person would not receive critical treatment, and may suffer very serious consequences. Thus, it is more important to minimize β.

7.131   To determine if the true standard deviation of the point-spread errors exceed 15 (variance exceeds 225), we test:

$$H_0 : \sigma^2 = 225$$
$$H_a : \sigma^2 > 225$$

The test statistic is $\chi^2 = \dfrac{(n-1)s^2}{\sigma_0^2} = \dfrac{(240-1)13.3^2}{225} = 187.896$.

The rejection region requires α in the upper tail of the χ^2 distribution with df $= n - 1 = 240 - 1 = 239$. The maximum value of df in Table IV is 100. Thus, we cannot find the rejection region using Table IV. Using a statistical package, the p-value associated with $\chi^2 = 187.896$ is $p = .9938$.

Since the p-value is so large, there is no evidence to reject H_0. There is insufficient evidence to indicate that the true standard deviation of the point-spread errors exceeds 15 for any reasonable value of α.

Since the observed standard deviation (13.3) is less than the hypothesized value of the standard deviation (15) under H_0, there is no way H_0 will be rejected for any reasonable value of α.

7.133 a. First, check to see if n is large enough:

$$np_0 = 132(.5) = 66 \text{ and } nq_0 = 132(.5) = 66$$

Since both $np_0 \geq 15$ and $nq_0 \geq 15$, the normal distribution will be adequate.

To determine if there is evidence to reject the claim that no more than half of all manufacturers are dissatisfied with their trade promotion spending, we test:

$$H_0 : p = .5$$
$$H_a : p > .5$$

The test statistic is $z = \dfrac{\hat{p} - p_0}{\sqrt{\dfrac{p_0 q_0}{n}}} = \dfrac{.36 - .5}{\sqrt{\dfrac{.5(.5)}{132}}} = -3.22.$

The rejection region requires $\alpha = .02$ in the upper tail of the z-distribution. From Table II, Appendix D, $z_{.02} = 2.05$. The rejection region is $z > 2.05$.

Since the observed value of the test statistic does not fall in the rejection region $(z = -3.22 \not> 2.05)$, H_0 is not rejected. There is insufficient evidence to reject the claim that no more than half of all manufacturers are dissatisfied with their trade promotion spending at $\alpha = .02$.

b. The observed significance level is p-value $= P(z \geq -3.22) \approx .5 + .5 = 1$. Since this p-value is so large, H_0 will not be rejected for any reasonable value of α.

c. First, we must define the rejection region in terms of $\hat{p}$.

$$\hat{p} = p_0 + z_\alpha \sigma_{\hat{p}} = .5 + 2.05\sqrt{\dfrac{.5(.5)}{132}} = .589$$

$$\beta = P(\hat{p} < .589 \mid p = .55) = P\left(z < \dfrac{.589 - .55}{\sqrt{\dfrac{.55(.45)}{132}}} \right) = P(z < .90) = .5 + .3159 = .8159$$

7.135 a. A Type II error is concluding the percentage of shoplifters turned over to police is 50% when in fact, the percentage is higher than 50%.

b. First, calculate the value of $\hat{p}$ that corresponds to the border between the acceptance region and the rejection region.

$$P(\hat{p} > p_o) = P(z > z_o) = .05. \quad \text{From Table II, Appendix D, } z_0 = 1.645.$$

$$\hat{p}_0 = p_o +1.645\sigma_{\hat{p}} = .5+1.645\sqrt{\frac{.5(.5)}{40}} = .5+.1300 = .6300$$

$$\beta = P(\hat{p} \le .6300 \text{ when } p = .55) = P\left(z \le \frac{.6300-.55}{\sqrt{\frac{.55(.45)}{40}}}\right) = P(z \le 1.02) = .5+.3461 = .8461$$

c.   If n increases, the probability of a Type II error would decrease.

First, calculate the value of $\hat{p}_0$ that corresponds to the border between the acceptance region and the rejection region.

$$P(\hat{p} > p_o) = P(z > z_o) = .05. \quad \text{From Table II, Appendix D, } z_0 = 1.645.$$

$$\hat{p}_0 = p_o +1.645\sigma_{\hat{p}} = .5+1.645\sqrt{\frac{.5(.5)}{100}} = .5+.082 = .582$$

$$\beta = P(\hat{p} \le .582 \text{ when } p = .55) = P\left(z \le \frac{.582-.55}{\sqrt{\frac{.55(.45)}{100}}}\right) = P(z \le 0.64) = .5+.2389 = .7389$$

7.137   a.   To determine if the production process should be halted, we test:

$$H_0 : \mu = 3$$
$$H_a : \mu > 3$$

where μ = mean amount of vinyl chloride in the air.

The test statistic is $z = \dfrac{\bar{x} - \mu_0}{\sigma_{\bar{x}}} = \dfrac{3.1-3}{.5/\sqrt{50}} = 1.41.$

The rejection region requires $\alpha = .01$ in the upper tail of the z-distribution. From Table II, Appendix D, $z_{.01} = 2.33$. The rejection region is $z > 2.33$.

Since the observed value of the test statistic does not fall in the rejection region, $(z = 1.41 \not> 2.33)$, H_0 is not rejected. There is insufficient evidence to indicate the mean amount of vinyl chloride in the air is more than 3 parts per million at $\alpha = .01$. Do not halt the manufacturing process.

b.   As plant manager, I do not want to shut down the plant unnecessarily. Therefore, I want $\alpha = P$(shut down plant when $\mu = 3$) to be small.

c.   The p-value is $p = P(z \ge 1.41) = .5 - .4207 = .0793$. Since the p-value is not less than $\alpha = .01$, H_0 is not rejected.

7.139   a.   No, it increases the risk of falsely rejecting H_0, i.e., closing the plant unnecessarily.

b.　First, find $\bar{x}_0$ such that $P(\bar{x} > \bar{x}_0) = P(z > z_0) = .05$.

From Table II, Appendix D, $z_0 = 1.645$.

$$z = \frac{\bar{x}_0 - \mu}{\sigma/\sqrt{n}} \Rightarrow 1.645 = \frac{\bar{x}_0 - 3}{.5/\sqrt{50}} \Rightarrow \bar{x}_0 = 3.116$$

Then, compute:

$$\beta = P(\bar{x}_0 \le 3.116 \text{ when } \mu = 3.1) = P\left(z \le \frac{3.116 - 3.1}{.5/\sqrt{50}}\right) = P(z \le .23) = .5 + .0910 = .5910$$

$$Power = 1 - \beta = 1 - .5910 = .4090$$

c.　The power of the test increases as α increases.

7.141　To determine if the diameters of the ball bearings are more variable when produced by the new process, test:

$$H_0 : \sigma^2 = .00156$$
$$H_a : \sigma^2 > .00156$$

The test statistic is $\chi^2 = \dfrac{(n-1)s^2}{\sigma_0^2} = \dfrac{99(.00211)}{.00156} = 133.90$.

The rejection region requires use of the upper tail of the χ^2 distribution with $df = n - 1 = 100 - 1 = 99$. We will use $df = 100 \approx 99$ due to the limitations of the table. From Table IV, Appendix D, $\chi^2_{.025} = 129.561 < 133.90 < 135.807 = \chi^2_{.010}$. The p-value of the test is between .010 and .025. The decision made depends on the desired α. For $\alpha < .010$, there is not enough evidence to show that the variance in the diameters is greater than .00156. For $\alpha \ge .025$, there is enough evidence to show that the variance in the diameters is greater than .00156.

7.143　a.　Let $\mu =$ mean daily amount of distilled water collected by the new system. To determine if the mean daily amount of distilled water collected by the new system is greater than 1.4, we test:

$$H_0 : \mu = 1.4$$
$$H_a : \mu > 1.4$$

b.　For this problem, $\alpha =$ probability of concluding the mean daily amount of distilled water collected by the new system is greater than 1.4 when, in fact, the mean daily amount of distilled water collected by the new system is not greater than 1.4. Since $\alpha = .10$, this means that H_0 will be rejected when it is true about 10% of the time.

c.　Using MINITAB, the descriptive statistics are:

Descriptive Statistics: Water

Variable	N	Mean	StDev	Minimum	Q1	Median	Q3	Maximum
Water	3	5.243	0.192	5.070	5.070	5.210	5.450	5.450

$\bar{x} = 5.243$ and $s = .192$.

d. The test statistic is $t = \dfrac{\bar{x} - \mu_0}{s/\sqrt{n}} = \dfrac{5.243 - 1.4}{.192/\sqrt{3}} = 34.67$.

e. Using MINITAB:

One-Sample T: Water
```
Test of mu = 1.4 vs > 1.4

Variable   N      Mean     StDev   SE Mean   95% Lower Bound      T       P
Water      3   5.24333   0.19218   0.11096           4.91935   34.64   0.000
```

The p-value is $p = 0.000$.

f. Since the p-value is less than $\alpha \left(p = .000 < .10 \right)$, H_0 is rejected. There is sufficient evidence to indicate daily amount of distilled water collected by the new system is greater than 1.4 at $\alpha = .10$.

7.145 a. To determine whether the true mean rating for this instructor-related factor exceeds 4, we test:

$$H_0 : \mu = 4$$
$$H_a : \mu > 4$$

The test statistic is $z = \dfrac{\bar{x} - \mu_0}{\sigma_{\bar{x}}} \approx \dfrac{4.7 - 4}{1.62/\sqrt{40}} = 2.73$.

The rejection region requires $\alpha = .05$ in the upper tail of the z-distribution. From Table II, Appendix D, $z_{.05} = 1.645$. The rejection region is $z > 1.645$.

Since the observed value of the test statistic falls in the rejection region $\left(z = 2.73 > 1.645 \right)$, H_0 is rejected. There is sufficient evidence to indicate that the true mean rating for this instructor-related factor exceeds 4 at $\alpha = .05$.

b. If the sample size is large enough, one could almost always reject H_0. Thus, we might be able to detect very small differences if the sample size is large enough. This would be statistical significance. However, even though statistical significance is found, it does not necessarily mean that there is practical significance. A statistical significance can sometimes be found between the hypothesized value of a mean and the estimated value of the mean, but, in practice, this difference would mean nothing. This would be practical significance.

c. Since the sample size is sufficiently large $\left(n = 40 \right)$, the Central Limit Theorem indicates that the sampling distribution of $\bar{x}$ is approximately normal. Also, since the sample size is large, s is a good estimator of σ. Thus, the analysis used is appropriate.

7.147 Using MINITAB, the descriptive statistics are:

Descriptive Statistics: Candy
```
Variable   N     Mean    StDev   Minimum      Q1   Median      Q3   Maximum
Candy      5   22.000    2.000    20.000   20.500   21.000   24.000   25.000
```

To give the benefit of the doubt to the students we will use a small value of α. (We do not want to reject H_0 when it is true to favor the students.) Thus, we will use $\alpha = .001$.

We must also assume that the sample comes from a normal distribution. To determine if the mean number of candies exceeds 15, we test:

$$H_0 : \mu = 15$$
$$H_a : \mu > 15$$

The test statistic is $z = \dfrac{\overline{x} - \mu_o}{\sigma / \sqrt{n}} = \dfrac{22 - 15}{2 / \sqrt{5}} = 7.83.$

The rejection region requires $\alpha = .001$ in the upper tail of the z-distribution. From Table II, Appendix D, $z_{.001} = 3.08$. The rejection region is $z > 3.08$.

Since the observed value of the test statistic falls in the rejection region $(z = 7.83 > 3.08)$, H_0 is rejected. There is sufficient evidence to indicate the mean number of candies exceeds 15 at $\alpha = .001$.

Chapter 8
Inferences Based on Two Samples: Confidence Intervals and Tests of Hypotheses

8.1   a. $\mu_1 \pm 2\sigma_{\bar{x}_1} \Rightarrow \mu_1 \pm 2\dfrac{\sigma_1}{\sqrt{n_1}} \Rightarrow 150 \pm 2\dfrac{\sqrt{900}}{\sqrt{100}} \Rightarrow 150 \pm 6 \Rightarrow (144,\ 156)$

     b. $\mu_2 \pm 2\sigma_{\bar{x}_2} \Rightarrow \mu_2 \pm 2\dfrac{\sigma_2}{\sqrt{n_2}} \Rightarrow 150 \pm 2\dfrac{\sqrt{1600}}{\sqrt{100}} \Rightarrow 150 \pm 8 \Rightarrow (142,\ 158)$

     c. $\mu_{\bar{x}_1-\bar{x}_2} = \mu_1 - \mu_2 = 150 - 150 = 0$ $\sigma_{\bar{x}_1-\bar{x}_2} = \sqrt{\dfrac{\sigma_1^2}{n_1} + \dfrac{\sigma_2^2}{n_2}} = \sqrt{\dfrac{900}{100} + \dfrac{1600}{100}} = \sqrt{\dfrac{2500}{100}} = 5$

     d. $(\mu_1 - \mu_2) \pm 2\sqrt{\dfrac{\sigma_1^2}{n_1} + \dfrac{\sigma_2^2}{n_2}} \Rightarrow (150 - 150) \pm 2\sqrt{\dfrac{900}{100} + \dfrac{1600}{100}} \Rightarrow 0 \pm 10 \Rightarrow (-10,\ 10)$

     e.   The variability of the difference between the sample means is greater than the variability of the individual sample means.

8.3   a.   For confidence coefficient .95, $\alpha = .05$ and $\alpha/2 = .05/2 = .025$. From Table II, Appendix D, $z_{.025} = 1.96$. The confidence interval is:

$$(\bar{x}_1 - \bar{x}_2) \pm z_{.025}\sqrt{\dfrac{\sigma_1^2}{n_1} + \dfrac{\sigma_2^2}{n_2}} \Rightarrow (5,275 - 5,240) \pm 1.96\sqrt{\dfrac{150^2}{400} + \dfrac{200^2}{400}} \Rightarrow 35 \pm 24.5 \Rightarrow (10.5,\ 59.5)$$

     We are 95% confident that the difference between the population means is between 10.5 and 59.5.

     b.   The test statistic is $z = \dfrac{(\bar{x}_1 - \bar{x}_2) - (\mu_1 - \mu_2)}{\sqrt{\dfrac{\sigma_1^2}{n_1} + \dfrac{\sigma_2^2}{n_2}}} = \dfrac{(5,275 - 5,240) - 0}{\sqrt{\dfrac{150^2}{400} + \dfrac{200^2}{400}}} = 2.8$.

     The p-value is $p = P(z \leq -2.8) + P(z \geq 2.8) = 2P(z \geq 2.8) = 2(.5 - .4974) = 2(.0026) = .0052$.

     Since the p-value is so small, there is evidence to reject H_0. There is evidence to indicate the two population means are different for $\alpha > .0052$.

     c.   The p-value would be half of the p-value in part b. The p-value $= p = P(z \geq 2.8) = .5 - .4974 = .0026$.

     Since the p-value is so small, there is evidence to reject H_0. There is evidence to indicate the mean for population 1 is larger than the mean for population 2 for $\alpha > .0026$.

     d.   The test statistic is $z = \dfrac{(\bar{x}_1 - \bar{x}_2) - (\mu_1 - \mu_2)}{\sqrt{\dfrac{\sigma_1^2}{n_1} + \dfrac{\sigma_2^2}{n_2}}} = \dfrac{(5,275 - 5,240) - 25}{\sqrt{\dfrac{150^2}{400} + \dfrac{200^2}{400}}} = .8$.

The *p*-value of the test is $p = P(z \le -.8) + P(z \ge .8) = 2P(z \ge .8) = 2(.5 - .2881) = 2(.2119) = .4238$.

Since the *p*-value is so large, there is no evidence to reject H_0. There is no evidence to indicate that the difference in the 2 population means is different from 25 for $\alpha \le .10$.

e.   We must assume that we have two independent random samples.

8.5   a.   No. Both populations must be normal.

       b.   No. Both populations variances must be equal.

       c.   No. Both populations must be normal.

       d.   Yes.

       e.   No. Both populations must be normal.

8.7   Some preliminary calculations are:

$$\bar{x}_1 = \frac{\sum x_1}{n_1} = \frac{11.8}{5} = 2.36 \qquad s_1^2 = \frac{\sum x_1^2 - \frac{(\sum x_1)^2}{n_1}}{n_1 - 1} = \frac{30.78 - \frac{(11.8)^2}{5}}{5 - 1} = .733$$

$$\bar{x}_2 = \frac{\sum x_2}{n_2} = \frac{14.4}{4} = 3.6 \qquad s_2^2 = \frac{\sum x_2^2 - \frac{(\sum x_2)^2}{n_2}}{n_2 - 1} = \frac{53.1 - \frac{(14.4)^2}{4}}{4 - 1} = .42$$

a. $s_p^2 = \dfrac{(n_1 - 1)s_1^2 + (n_2 - 1)s_2^2}{n_1 + n_2 - 2} = \dfrac{(5-1).773 + (4-1).42}{5 + 4 - 2} = \dfrac{4.192}{7} = .5989$

b. $H_0 : \mu_1 - \mu_2 = 0$
         $H_a : \mu_1 - \mu_2 < 0$

The test statistic is $t = \dfrac{(\bar{x}_1 - \bar{x}_2) - D_0}{\sqrt{s_p^2 \left(\frac{1}{n_1} + \frac{1}{n_2} \right)}} = \dfrac{(2.36 - 3.6) - 0}{\sqrt{.5989 \left(\frac{1}{5} + \frac{1}{4} \right)}} = \dfrac{-1.24}{.5191} = -2.39$.

The rejection region requires $\alpha = .10$ in the lower tail of the *t*-distribution with df $= n_1 + n_2 - 2 = 5 + 4 - 2 = 7$. From Table III, Appendix D, $t_{.10} = 1.415$. The rejection region is $t < -1.415$.

Since the test statistic falls in the rejection region $(t = -2.39 < -1.415)$, H_0 is rejected. There is sufficient evidence to indicate that $\mu_2 > \mu_1$ at $\alpha = .10$.

c.   A small sample confidence interval is needed because $n_1 = 5 < 30$ and $n_2 = 4 < 30$.

For confidence coefficient .90, $\alpha = .10$ and $\alpha / 2 = .10 / 2 = .05$. From Table III, Appendix D, with df $= n_1 + n_2 - 2 = 5 + 4 - 2 = 7$, $t_{.05} = 1.895$. The 90% confidence interval for $(\mu_1 - \mu_2)$ is:

$$\left(\bar{x}_1 - x_2\right) \pm t_{.05}\sqrt{s_p^2\left(\frac{1}{n_1}+\frac{1}{n_2}\right)} \Rightarrow \left(2.36-3.6\right)\pm1.895\sqrt{.5989\left(\frac{1}{5}+\frac{1}{4}\right)} \Rightarrow -1.24\pm.98 \Rightarrow (-2.22, -0.26)$$

d. The confidence interval in part **c** provides more information about $\left(\mu_1 - \mu_2\right)$ than the test of hypothesis in part **b**. The test in part **b** only tells us that μ_2 is greater than μ_1. However, the confidence interval estimates what the difference is between μ_1 and μ_2.

8.9   a. The *p*-value $= p = .1150$. Since the *p*-value is not small, there is no evidence to reject H_0 for $\alpha \le .10$. There is insufficient evidence to indicate the two population means differ for $\alpha \le .10$.

b. If the alternative hypothesis had been one-tailed, the *p*-value would be half of the value for the two-tailed test. Here, *p*-value $= .1150/2 = .0575$.

There is no evidence to reject H_0 for $\alpha = .05$. There is insufficient evidence to indicate the mean for population 1 is less than the mean for population 2 at $\alpha = .05$.

There is evidence to reject H_0 for $\alpha > .0575$. There is sufficient evidence to indicate the mean for population 1 is less than the mean for population 2 at $\alpha > .0575$.

8.11   a. $s_p^2 = \dfrac{\left(n_1-1\right)s_1^2 + \left(n_2-1\right)s_2^2}{n_1+n_2-2} = \dfrac{\left(17-1\right)3.4^2+\left(12-1\right)4.8^2}{17+12-2} = 16.237$

$H_0 : \mu_1 - \mu_2 = 0$
$H_a : \mu_1 - \mu_2 \ne 0$

The test statistic is $t = \dfrac{\left(\bar{x}_1 - \bar{x}_2\right)-0}{\sqrt{s_p^2\left(\frac{1}{n_1}+\frac{1}{n_2}\right)}} = \dfrac{\left(5.4-7.9\right)-0}{\sqrt{16.237\left(\frac{1}{17}+\frac{1}{12}\right)}} = -1.646$.

Since no α was given, we will use $\alpha = .05$. The rejection region requires $\alpha/2 = .05/2 = .025$ in each tail of the *t*-distribution with $df = n_1+n_2-2 = 17+12-2 = 27$. From Table III, Appendix D, $t_{.025} = 2.052$. The rejection region is $t < -2.052$ or $t > 2.052$.

Since the observed value of the test statistic does not fall in the rejection region $\left(t = -1.646 \nless -2.052\right)$, H_0 is not rejected. There is insufficient evidence to indicate $\mu_1 - \mu_2$ is different from 0 at $\alpha = .05$.

b. For confidence coefficient .95, $\alpha = .05$ and $\alpha/2 = .05/2 = .025$. From Table III, Appendix D, with $df = n_1+n_2-2 = 17+12-2 = 27$, $t_{.025} = 2.052$. The confidence interval is:

$$\left(\bar{x}_1 - \bar{x}_2\right)\pm t_{.025}\sqrt{s_p^2\left(\frac{1}{n_1}+\frac{1}{n_2}\right)} \Rightarrow \left(5.4-7.9\right)-2.052\sqrt{16.237\left(\frac{1}{17}+\frac{1}{12}\right)} \Rightarrow -2.50\pm3.12 \Rightarrow (-5.62,\ 0.62)$$

8.13   a. $s_p^2 = \dfrac{\left(n_1-1\right)s_1^2 + \left(n_2-1\right)s_2^2}{n_1+n_2-2} = \dfrac{\left(25-1\right)10.41^2+\left(25-1\right)7.12^2}{25+25-2} = \dfrac{3,817.5}{48} = 79.53125$

For confidence coefficient .95, $\alpha = .05$ and $\alpha / 2 = .05 / 2 = .025$. Using MINITAB with $df = n_1 + n_2 - 2 = 25 + 25 - 2 = 48$, $t_{.025} = 2.011$. The 95% confidence interval for $(\mu_1 - \mu_2)$ is:

$$(\bar{x}_1 - \bar{x}_2) \pm t_{\alpha/2} \sqrt{s_p^2 \left(\frac{1}{n_1} + \frac{1}{n_2} \right)} \Rightarrow (25.08 - 19.38) \pm 2.011 \sqrt{79.53125 \left(\frac{1}{25} + \frac{1}{25} \right)}$$

$$\Rightarrow 5.7 \pm 5.073 \Rightarrow (.627, \ 10.773)$$

b. Since 0 does not fall in the 95% confidence interval, there is evidence to indicate there is a difference in the mean response times between the two groups. Since the interval contains only positive numbers, it indicates that the mean response time for the group of students whose last names begin with the letters R-Z is shorter than the mean response time for the group of students whose last names begin with the letters A-I. This supports the researchers' *last name effect* theory.

8.15 a. Let μ_C = mean years of experience for commercial suppliers and μ_G = mean years of experience for government employees. To determine if the mean years of experience for commercial suppliers of DoD is less than that for government employees, we test:

$$H_0 : \mu_C = \mu_G$$
$$H_a : \mu_C < \mu_G$$

b. From the printout, the p-value is $p = .0447$. Since the p-value is less than $\alpha (p = .0447 < .05)$, H_0 is rejected. There is sufficient evidence to indicate the mean years of experience for commercial suppliers of DoD is less than that for government employees at $\alpha = .05$.

c. We have to assume that both samples are random samples, that the populations from which the samples were drawn were approximately normal, and that the population variances are the same.

Using MINITAB, histograms of the data are:

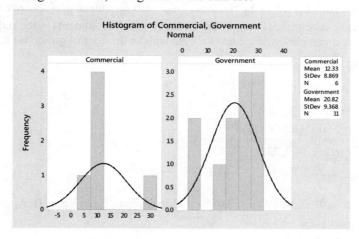

Neither population appears to be normally distributed. However, the spreads of the distributions appear to be the same. Thus, the assumption of equal variances appears to be met.

8.17 a. Let μ_1 = mean forecast error of buy-side analysts and μ_2 = mean forecast error of sell-side analysts. For confidence coefficient 0.95, $\alpha = .05$ and $\alpha / 2 = .05 / 2 = .025$. From Table II, Appendix D, $z_{.025} = 1.96$. The 95% confidence interval is:

$$\left(\overline{x}_1 - \overline{x}_2\right) \pm z_{.025}\sqrt{\frac{\sigma_1^2}{n_1} + \frac{\sigma_2^2}{n_2}} \Rightarrow \left(.85 - (-.05)\right) \pm 1.96\sqrt{\frac{1.93^2}{3,526} + \frac{.85^2}{58,562}} \Rightarrow .90 \pm .064 \Rightarrow (.836,\ .964)$$

We are 95% confident that the difference in the mean forecast error of buy-side analysts and sell-side analysts is between .836 and .964.

b.   Based on 95% confidence interval in part **a**, the buy-side analysts has the greater mean forecast error because our interval contains positive numbers.

c.   The assumptions about the underlying populations of forecast errors that are necessary for the validity of the inference are:

1.   The samples are randomly and independently sampled.
2.   The sample sizes are sufficiently large.

8.19   a.   None of the p-values for the 5 varieties of peach jam are less than $\alpha = .05$. Thus, we cannot conclude that the mean taste scores of the two protocols differ for any of the varieties at $\alpha = .05$.

b.   The p-values for the cheese varieties A, C, and D are less than $\alpha = .05$. Thus, we can conclude that the mean taste scores of the two protocols differ for cheese varieties A, C, and D at $\alpha = .05$.

c.   In all the tests, the sample sizes were greater than 30. Thus, the Central Limit Theorem applies, so we do not have to assume that the populations of taste test scores are normal.

8.21   Using MINITAB, the descriptive statistics are:

Descriptive Statistics: Control, Rude

Variable	N	Mean	StDev	Minimum	Q1	Median	Q3	Maximum
Rude	45	8.511	3.992	0.000	5.500	9.000	11.000	18.000
Control	53	11.81	7.38	0.00	5.50	12.00	17.50	30.00

Let $\mu_1 =$ mean performance level of students in the rudeness group and $\mu_2 =$ mean performance level of students in the control group. To determine if the true performance level for students in the rudeness condition is lower than the true mean performance level for students in the control group, we test:

$$H_0 : \mu_1 - \mu_2 = 0$$
$$H_a : \mu_1 - \mu_2 < 0$$

The test statistic is $z = \dfrac{\left(\overline{x}_1 - \overline{x}_2\right) - 0}{\sqrt{\dfrac{\sigma_1^2}{n_1} + \dfrac{\sigma_2^2}{n_2}}} \approx \dfrac{(8.511 - 11.81) - 0}{\sqrt{\dfrac{3.922^2}{45} + \dfrac{7.38^2}{53}}} = -2.81$

The rejection region requires $\alpha = .01$ in the lower tail of the z-distribution. From Table II, Appendix D, $z_{.01} = 2.33$. The rejection region is $z < -2.33$.

Since the observed value of the test statistic falls in the rejection region $\left(z = -2.81 < -2.33\right)$, H_0 is rejected. There is sufficient evidence to indicate the true mean performance level for students in the rudeness condition is lower than the true mean performance level for students in the control group at $\alpha = .01$.

8.23   Using MINITAB, the descriptive statistics are:

Descriptive Statistics: Honey, DM

Variable	N	Mean	StDev	Minimum	Q1	Median	Q3	Maximum
Honey	35	10.714	2.855	4.000	9.000	11.000	12.000	16.000
DM	33	8.333	3.256	3.000	6.000	9.000	11.500	15.000

Let μ_1 = mean improvement in total cough symptoms score for children receiving the Honey dosage and μ_2 = mean improvement in total cough symptoms score for children receiving the DM dosage. To test if honey may be a preferable treatment for the cough and sleep difficulty associated with childhood upper respiratory tract infection, we test:

$$H_0 : \mu_1 - \mu_2 = 0$$
$$H_a : \mu_1 - \mu_2 > 0$$

The test statistic is $z = \dfrac{(\bar{x}_1 - \bar{x}_2) - 0}{\sqrt{\dfrac{\sigma_1^2}{n_1} + \dfrac{\sigma_2^2}{n_2}}} \approx \dfrac{(10.714 - 8.333) - 0}{\sqrt{\dfrac{2.855^2}{35} + \dfrac{3.256^2}{33}}} = 3.20$

Since no α was given, we will use $\alpha = .05$. The rejection region requires $\alpha = .05$ in the upper tail of the z-distribution. From Table II, Appendix D, $z_{.05} = 1.645$. The rejection region is $z > 1.645$.

Since the observed value of the test statistic falls in the rejection region $(z = 3.20 > 1.645)$, H_0 is rejected. There is sufficient evidence to indicate that honey may be a preferable treatment for the cough and sleep difficulty associated with childhood upper respiratory tract infection at $\alpha = .05$.

8.25   a.   We cannot provide a measure of reliability because we have no measure of the variability or variance of the data.

b.   We would need the variances of the two samples.

c.   Let μ_1 = mean age for self-employed immigrants and μ_2 = mean age for the wage-earning immigrants. To determine if the mean age for self-employed immigrants is less than the mean age for wage-earning immigrants, we test:

$$H_0 : \mu_1 - \mu_2 = 0$$
$$H_a : \mu_1 - \mu_2 < 0$$

The rejection region requires $\alpha = .01$ in the lower tail of the z-distribution. From Table II, Appendix D, $z_{.01} = 2.33$. The rejection region is $z < -2.33$.

d.   We use the following to solve for σ:

$$z = \dfrac{(\bar{x}_1 - \bar{x}_2) - (\mu_1 - \mu_2)}{\sqrt{\dfrac{\sigma_1^2}{n_1} + \dfrac{\sigma_2^2}{n_2}}} = \dfrac{(44.88 - 46.79) - 0}{\sqrt{\dfrac{\sigma^2}{870} + \dfrac{\sigma^2}{84,875}}} \le -2.33$$

$$\Rightarrow -1.91 \le \sigma \sqrt{\dfrac{1}{870} + \dfrac{1}{84,875}}(-2.33) \Rightarrow \sigma \le 24.056$$

e.   The true value of σ is likely to be smaller than 24.056. This standard deviation would be too large for the ages of people.

8.27   a.   The rejection region requires $\alpha = .05$ in the upper tail of the t-distribution with $df = n_d - 1 = 12 - 1 = 11$. From Table III, Appendix D, $t_{.05} = 1.796$. The rejection region is $t > 1.796$.

b.   From Table III, with $df = n_d - 1 = 24 - 1 = 23$, $t_{.10} = 1.319$. The rejection region is $t > 1.319$.

c.   From Table III, with $df = n_d - 1 = 4 - 1 = 3$, $t_{.025} = 3.182$. The rejection region is $t > 3.182$.

d.   Using Minitab, with $df = n_d - 1 = 80 - 1 = 79$, $t_{.01} = 2.374$. The rejection region is $t > 2.374$.

8.29   Let μ_1 = mean of population 1 and μ_2 = mean of population 2.

a. $H_0 : \mu_d = 0$
       $H_a : \mu_d < 0$ where $\mu_d = \mu_1 - \mu_2$

b.   Some preliminary calculations are:

Pair	Population 1	Population 2	Difference, d
1	19	24	−5
2	25	27	−2
3	31	36	−5
4	52	53	−1
5	49	55	−6
6	34	34	0
7	59	66	−7
8	47	51	−4
9	17	20	−3
10	51	55	−4

$$\bar{d} = \frac{\sum_{i=1}^{n_d} d_i}{n_d} = \frac{-37}{10} = -3.7$$

$$s_d^2 = \frac{\sum_{i=1}^{n_d} d_i^2 - \frac{\left(\sum_{i=1}^{n_d} d_i\right)^2}{n_d}}{n_d - 1} = \frac{181 - \frac{(-37)^2}{10}}{10 - 1} = 4.9$$

The test statistic is $t = \dfrac{\bar{d}}{s_d / \sqrt{n_d}} = \dfrac{-3.7}{\sqrt{4.9}\big/\sqrt{10}} = -5.29$

The rejection region requires $\alpha = .10$ in the lower tail of the t-distribution with $df = n_d - 1 = 10 - 1 = 9$. From Table III, Appendix D, $t_{.10} = 1.383$. The rejection region is $t < -1.383$.

Since the observed value of the test statistic falls in the rejection region $(t = -5.29 < -1.383)$, H_0 is rejected. There is sufficient evidence to indicate the mean of population 1 is less than the mean for population 2 at $\alpha = .10$.

c. For confidence coefficient .90, $\alpha = .10$ and $\alpha / 2 = .10 / 2 = .05$. From Table III, Appendix D, with $df = n_d - 1 = 10 - 1 = 9$, $t_{.05} = 1.833$. The 90% confidence interval is:

$$\overline{d} \pm t_{\alpha/2} \frac{s_d}{\sqrt{n_d}} \Rightarrow -3.7 \pm 1.833 \frac{\sqrt{4.9}}{\sqrt{10}} \Rightarrow -3.7 \pm 1.28 \Rightarrow (-4.98, \ -2.42)$$

We are 90% confident that the difference in the two population means is between -4.98 and -2.42.

d. We must assume that the population of differences is normal, and the sample of differences is randomly selected.

8.31 a. Let μ_1 = mean starting BMI and μ_2 = mean ending BMI. To determine if the mean BMI at the end of the camp is less than the mean BMI at the start of camp, we test:

$$\begin{aligned} H_0 &: \mu_d = 0 \\ H_a &: \mu_d > 0 \end{aligned} \quad \text{where } \mu_d = \mu_1 - \mu_2$$

b. The data should be analyzed as a paired-difference t-test. Each camper had his/her BMI measured at the start of the camp and at the end. Therefore, these two sets of BMI's are not independent.

c. The test statistic is $z = \dfrac{(\overline{x}_1 - \overline{x}_2) - (\mu_1 - \mu_2)}{\sqrt{\dfrac{\sigma_1^2}{n_1} + \dfrac{\sigma_2^2}{n_2}}} = \dfrac{(34.9 - 31.6) - 0}{\sqrt{\dfrac{6.9^2}{76} + \dfrac{6.2^2}{76}}} = 3.10$.

d. The test statistic is $z = \dfrac{\overline{d}}{\sigma_d / \sqrt{n_d}} = \dfrac{3.3}{1.5 / \sqrt{76}} = 19.18$.

e. The test statistic using the paired-difference formula is much larger than the test statistic using the independent samples formula. The test statistic for the paired-difference provides more evidence to support the alternative hypothesis.

f. Since the p-value is less than $\alpha \left(p < .0001 < .01 \right)$, H_0 is rejected. There is sufficient evidence to indicate the mean BMI at the end of camp is less than the mean BMI at the start of camp.

g. No, the differences in the BMI values do not have to be normally distributed. The sample size is $n = 76$. Thus, the Central Limit Theorem applies and says that the sampling distribution of $\overline{d}$ will be approximately normally distributed.

h. For confidence coefficient .99, $\alpha = .01$ and $\alpha / 2 = .01 / 2 = .005$. From Table II, Appendix D, $z_{.005} = 2.58$. The 99% confidence interval is:

$$\overline{d} \pm z_{\alpha/2} \frac{\sigma_d}{\sqrt{n_d}} \Rightarrow 3.3 \pm 2.58 \frac{1.5}{\sqrt{76}} \Rightarrow 3.3 \pm .444 \Rightarrow (2.856, \ 3.744)$$

We are 99% confident that the true difference in the mean BMI scores between the start of camp and the end of camp is between 2.857 and 3.743.

8.33   a.   Since the data were collected as 'twin holes', it needs to be analyzed as paired differences.

   b.   The differences are calculated by finding the difference between the 1st hole and the second hole.

Location	1st hole	2nd hole	Difference
1	5.5	5.7	−0.2
2	11.0	11.2	−0.2
3	5.9	6.0	−0.1
4	8.2	5.6	2.6
5	10.0	9.3	0.7
6	7.9	7.0	0.9
7	10.1	8.4	1.7
8	7.4	9.0	−1.6
9	7.0	6.0	1.0
10	9.2	8.1	1.1
11	8.3	10.0	−1.7
12	8.6	8.1	0.5
13	10.5	10.4	0.1
14	5.5	7.0	−1.5
15	10.0	11.2	−1.2

   c. $\bar{d} = \dfrac{\sum_{1}^{n_d} d_i}{n_d} = \dfrac{2.1}{15} = 0.14$ $s_d^2 = \dfrac{\sum_{1}^{n_d} d_i^2 - \dfrac{\left(\sum_{1}^{n_d} d_i\right)^2}{n_d}}{n_d - 1} = \dfrac{22.65 - \dfrac{(2.1)^2}{15}}{15 - 1} = 1.597$ $s_d = \sqrt{1.597} = 1.2637$.

   d.   For confidence coefficient .90, $\alpha = .10$ and $\alpha / 2 = .10 / 2 = .05$. From Table III, Appendix D with $df = n_d - 1 = 15 - 1 = 14$, $t_{.05} = 1.761$. The 90% confidence interval is:

$$\bar{d} \pm t_{\alpha/2} \dfrac{s_d}{\sqrt{n_d}} \Rightarrow .14 \pm 1.761 \dfrac{1.2637}{\sqrt{15}} \Rightarrow .14 \pm .575 \Rightarrow (-.435, .715)$$

   e.   We are 90% confident that the true difference in the mean THM measurements between the 1st and 2nd hole is between -.435 and .715.

   Yes, the geologists can conclude that there is no evidence of a difference in the true mean THM measurements between the original holes and their twin holes because 0 falls in the interval at $\alpha = .10$.

8.35   a.   The data should be analyzed using a paired-difference experiment because that is how the data were collected. Response rates were observed twice from each survey using the 'not selling' introduction method and the standard introduction method. Since the two sets of data are not independent, they cannot be analyzed using independent samples.

   b.   Some preliminary calculations are:

$$s_p^2 = \dfrac{(n_1 - 1)s_1^2 + (n_2 - 1)s_2^2}{n_1 + n_2 - 2} = \dfrac{(29 - 1)(.12)^2 + (29 - 1)(.11)^2}{29 + 29 - 2} = .01325$$

   Let μ_1 = mean response rate for those using the 'not selling' introduction and μ_2 = mean response rate for those using the standard introduction. Using the independent-samples t-test to determine if the mean response rate for 'not selling' is higher than that for the standard introduction, we test:

$$H_0 : \mu_1 - \mu_2 = 0$$
$$H_a : \mu_1 - \mu_2 > 0$$

The test statistic is $t = \dfrac{(\bar{x}_1 - \bar{x}_2) - 0}{\sqrt{s_p^2 \left(\dfrac{1}{n_1} + \dfrac{1}{n_2} \right)}} = \dfrac{(.262 - .246) - 0}{\sqrt{.01325 \left(\dfrac{1}{29} + \dfrac{1}{29} \right)}} = .53$

The rejection region requires $\alpha = .05$ in the upper tail of the t-distribution with $df = n_1 + n_2 - 2 = 29 + 29 - 2 = 56$. From Table III, Appendix D, $t_{.05} \approx 1.671$. The rejection region is $t > 1.671$.

Since the observed value of the test statistic does not fall in the rejection region $(t = .53 \not> 1.671)$, H_0 is not rejected. There is insufficient evidence to indicate the mean response rate for 'not selling' is higher than that for the standard introduction at $\alpha = .05$.

c. Since p-value is less than $\alpha \left(p = .001 < .05 \right)$, H_0 is rejected. There is sufficient evidence to indicate the mean response rate for 'not selling' is higher than that for the standard introduction at $\alpha = .05$.

d. The two inferences in parts **b** and **c** have different results because using the independent samples t-test is not appropriate for this study. The paired-difference design is better. There is much variation in response rates from survey to survey. By using the paired difference design, we can eliminate the survey to survey differences.

8.37 Some preliminary calculations are:

Operator	Difference (Before - After)
1	5
2	3
3	9
4	7
5	2
6	−2
7	−1
8	11
9	0
10	5

$$\bar{d} = \frac{\sum d}{n_d} = \frac{39}{10} = 3.9 \qquad s_d^2 = \frac{\sum d^2 - \dfrac{\left(\sum d \right)^2}{n_E}}{n_d - 1} = \frac{319 - \dfrac{39^2}{10}}{10 - 1} = 18.5444 \qquad s_d = \sqrt{18.5444} = 4.3063$$

a.   To determine if the new napping policy reduced the mean number of customer complaints, we test:

$$H_0 : \mu_d = 0$$
$$H_a : \mu_d > 0$$

The test statistic is $t = \dfrac{\bar{d}-0}{\dfrac{s_d}{\sqrt{n_d}}} = \dfrac{3.9-0}{\dfrac{4.3063}{\sqrt{10}}} = 2.864$

The rejection region requires $\alpha = .05$ in the upper tail of the t-distribution with $df = n_d - 1 = 10 - 1 = 9$. From Table III, Appendix D, $t_{.05} = 1.833$. The rejection region is $t > 1.833$.

Since the observed value of the test statistic falls in the rejection region $(t = 2.864 > 1.833)$, H_0 is rejected. There is sufficient evidence to indicate the new napping policy reduced the mean number of customer complaints at $\alpha = .05$.

b.   In order for the above test to be valid, we must assume that

1. The population of differences is normal
2. The differences are randomly selected

c.   Variables that were not controlled that could lead to an invalid conclusion include time of day agents worked, day of the week agents worked, and how much sleep the agents got before working, among others.

8.39   Using MINITAB, the descriptive statistics are:

Descriptive Statistics: E-W, N-S, Diff

Variable	N	Mean	StDev	Minimum	Q1	Median	Q3	Maximum
E-W	5	7436	1484	5120	5991	7930	8633	8658
N-S	5	7719	1548	5274	6211	8317	8929	8936
Diff	5	-283.6	86.4	-387.0	-357.5	-286.0	-208.5	-154.0

Let μ_{EW} = mean solar energy amount generated by East-West oriented highways and μ_{NS} = mean solar energy amount generated by North-South oriented highways. For confidence coefficient .95, $\alpha = .05$ and $\alpha/2 = .05/2 = .025$. From Table III, Appendix D, with $df = n_d - 1 = 5 - 1 = 4$, $t_{.025} = 2.776$. The confidence interval is:

$$\bar{d} \pm t_{.025}\frac{s_d}{\sqrt{n_d}} \Rightarrow -283.6 \pm 2.776\frac{86.4}{\sqrt{5}} \Rightarrow -283.6 \pm 107.26 \Rightarrow (-390.86, -176.34)$$

We are 95% confident that the difference in the mean amount of solar energy generated by East-West oriented highways and North-South oriented highways is between -390.86 and -176.34 kilo-Watt hours. Since this interval contains only negative numbers, it supports the researchers conclusion that the two-layer solar panel energy generation is more viable for the north-south oriented highways as compared to east-west oriented roadways.

8.41   Using MINITAB, the descriptive statistics are:

Descriptive Statistics: Male, Female, Diff

Variable	N	Mean	Median	StDev	Minimum	Maximum	Q1	Q3
Male	19	5.895	6.000	2.378	3.000	12.000	4.000	8.000
Female	19	5.526	5.000	2.458	3.000	12.000	4.000	7.000
Diff	19	0.368	1.000	3.515	-5.000	7.000	-3.000	3.000

Let μ_1 = mean number of swims by male rat pups, μ_2 = mean number of swims by female rat pups, and $\mu_d = \mu_1 - \mu_2$. To determine if there is a difference in the mean number of swims required by male and female rat pups, we test:

$$H_0 : \mu_d = 0$$
$$H_a : \mu_d \neq 0$$

The test statistic is $t = \dfrac{\bar{d} - D_o}{\dfrac{s_d}{\sqrt{n_d}}} = \dfrac{.368 - 0}{\dfrac{3.515}{\sqrt{19}}} = 0.46$

The rejection region requires $\alpha / 2 = .10 / 2 = .05$ in each tail of the t-distribution with $df = n_d - 1 = 19 - 1 = 18$. From Table III, Appendix D, $t_{.05} = 1.734$. The rejection region is $t < -1.734$ or $t > 1.734$.

Since the observed value of the test statistic does not fall in the rejection region $(t = .46 \not> 1.734)$, H_0 is not rejected. There is insufficient evidence to indicate that there is a difference in the mean number of swims required by male and female rat pups at $\alpha = .10$. (using Minitab, the p-value $\approx .653$.)

Since the sample size is not large, we must assume that the population of differences is normally distributed and that the sample of differences is random. There is no indication that the sample differences are not from a random sample. However, because the number of swims is discrete, the differences are probably not normal.

8.43   a.   From the exercise, we know that x_1 and x_2 are binomial random variables with the number of trials equal to n_1 and n_2. From Chapter 7, we know that for large n, the distribution of $\hat{p}_1 = \dfrac{x_1}{n_1}$ is approximately normal. Since x_1 is simply $\hat{p}_1$ multiplied by a constant, x_1 will also have an approximate normal distribution. Similarly, the distribution of $\hat{p}_2 = \dfrac{x_2}{n_2}$ is approximately normal, and thus, the distribution of x_2 is approximately normal.

b.   The Central Limit Theorem is necessary to find the sampling distributions of $\hat{p}_1$ and $\hat{p}_2$ when n_1 and n_2 are large. Once we have established that both $\hat{p}_1$ and $\hat{p}_2$ have normal distributions, then the distribution of their difference will also be normal.

8.45   From Section 6.4, it was given that the distribution of $\hat{p}$ is approximately normal if $n\hat{p} \geq 15$ and $n\hat{q} \geq 15$.

a. $n_1 \hat{p}_1 = 12(.42) = 5.04 < 15$ and $n_1 \hat{q}_1 = 12(.58) = 6.96 < 15$

$n_2 \hat{p}_2 = 14(.57) = 7.98 < 15$ and $n_2 \hat{q}_2 = 14(.43) = 6.02 < 15$

Thus, the sample sizes are not large enough to conclude the sampling distribution of $(\hat{p}_1 - \hat{p}_2)$ is approximately normal.

b. $n_1 \hat{p}_1 = 12(.92) = 11.04 < 15$ and $n_1 \hat{q}_1 = 12(.08) = 0.96 < 15$

$n_2 \hat{p}_2 = 14(.86) = 12.04 < 15$ and $n_2 \hat{q}_2 = 14(.14) = 1.96 < 15$

Thus, the sample sizes are not large enough to conclude the sampling distribution of $(\hat{p}_1 - \hat{p}_2)$ is approximately normal.

c. $n_1 \hat{p}_1 = 30(.70) = 21 > 15$ and $n_1 \hat{q}_1 = 30(.30) = 9 < 15$

$n_2 \hat{p}_2 = 30(.73) = 21.9 > 15$ and $n_2 \hat{q}_2 = 30(.27) = 8.1 < 15$

Thus, the sample sizes are not large enough to conclude the sampling distribution of $(\hat{p}_1 - \hat{p}_2)$ is approximately normal.

d. $n_1 \hat{p}_1 = 100(.93) = 93 > 15$ and $n_1 \hat{q}_1 = 100(.07) = 7 < 15$

$n_2 \hat{p}_2 = 250(.97) = 242.5 > 15$ and $n_2 \hat{q}_2 = 250(.03) = 7.5 < 15$

Thus, the sample sizes are not large enough to conclude the sampling distribution of $(\hat{p}_1 - \hat{p}_2)$ is approximately normal.

e. $n_1 \hat{p}_1 = 125(.08) = 10 < 15$ and $n_1 \hat{q}_1 = 125(.92) = 115 > 15$

$n_2 \hat{p}_2 = 200(.12) = 24 > 15$ and $n_2 \hat{q}_2 = 200(.88) = 176 > 15$

Thus, the sample sizes are not large enough to conclude the sampling distribution of $(\hat{p}_1 - \hat{p}_2)$ is approximately normal.

8.47   a. $H_0 : p_1 - p_2 = 0$
$H_a : p_1 - p_2 > 0$

Will need to calculate the following:

$$\hat{p}_1 = \frac{320}{800} = .40 \qquad \hat{p}_2 = \frac{400}{800} = .50 \qquad \hat{p} = \frac{320 + 400}{800 + 800} = .45$$

The test statistic is $z = \dfrac{(\hat{p}_1 - \hat{p}_2) - 0}{\sqrt{\hat{p}\hat{q}\left(\dfrac{1}{n_1} + \dfrac{1}{n_2}\right)}} = \dfrac{(.40 - .50) - 0}{\sqrt{(.45)(.55)\left(\dfrac{1}{800} + \dfrac{1}{800}\right)}} = -4.02$

The rejection region requires $\alpha = .05$ in the upper tail of the z-distribution. From Table II, Appendix D, $z_{.05} = 1.645$. The rejection region is $z > 1.645$.

Since the observed value of the test statistic does not fall in the rejection region $(z = -4.02 \not> 1.645)$, H_0 is not rejected. There is insufficient evidence to indicate that $p_1 > p_2$ the proportions are unequal at $\alpha = .05$.

b. $H_0 : p_1 - p_2 = 0$
    $H_a : p_1 - p_2 \neq 0$

The test statistic is $z = -4.02$.
The rejection region requires $\alpha/2 = .01/2 = .005$ in each tail of the z-distribution. From Table II, Appendix D, $z_{.005} = 2.58$. The rejection region is $z < -2.58$ or $z > 2.58$.

Since the observed value of the test statistic falls in the rejection region $(z = -4.02 < -2.58)$, H_0 is rejected. There is sufficient evidence to indicate that the proportions are unequal at $\alpha = .01$.

c. $H_0 : p_1 - p_2 = 0$
    $H_a : p_1 - p_2 < 0$

Test statistic as above $z = -4.02$.

The rejection region requires $\alpha = .01$ in the lower tail of the z-distribution. From Table II, Appendix D, $z_{.01} = 2.33$. The rejection region is $z < -2.33$.

Since the observed value of the test statistic falls in the rejection region $(z = -4.02 < -2.33)$, H_0 is rejected. There is sufficient evidence to indicate that $p_1 < p_2$ at $\alpha = .01$.

d. For confidence coefficient .90, $\alpha = .10$ and $\alpha/2 = .10/2 = .05$. From Table II, Appendix D, $z_{.05} = 1.645$. The confidence interval is:

$$\left(\hat{p}_1 - \hat{p}_2\right) \pm z_{.05}\sqrt{\frac{\hat{p}_1\hat{q}_1}{n_1} + \frac{\hat{p}_2\hat{p}_2}{n_2}} \Rightarrow (.4 - .5) \pm 1.645\sqrt{\frac{(.4)(.6)}{800} + \frac{(.5)(.5)}{800}} \Rightarrow -.10 \pm .04 \Rightarrow (-.14, -.06)$$

We are 90% confident that the difference between p_1 and p_2 is between $-.14$ and $-.06$.

8.49   a. $\hat{p}_1 = \dfrac{x_1}{n_1} = \dfrac{29}{189} = .153$

b. $\hat{p}_2 = \dfrac{x_2}{n_2} = \dfrac{32}{149} = .215$

c. For confidence coefficient .90, $\alpha = .10$ and $\alpha/2 = .10/2 = .05$. From Table II, Appendix D, $z_{.05} = 1.645$. The 90% confidence interval is:

$$\left(\hat{p}_1 - \hat{p}_2\right) \pm z_{\alpha/2}\sqrt{\frac{\hat{p}_1\hat{q}_1}{n_1} + \frac{\hat{p}_2\hat{q}_2}{n_2}} \Rightarrow (.153 - .215) \pm 1.645\sqrt{\frac{.153(.847)}{189} + \frac{.215(.785)}{149}}$$
$$\Rightarrow -.062 \pm .070 \Rightarrow (-.132, \ .008)$$

d. We are 90% confident that the difference in the proportion of bidders who fall prey to the winner's curse between super-experienced bidders and less-experienced bidders is between $-.132$ and $.008$. Since this interval contains 0, there is no evidence to indicate that there is a difference in the proportion of bidders who fall prey to the winner's curse between super-experienced bidders and less-experienced bidders.

8.51   a.   Let p_1 =proportion of producers who are willing to offer windrowing services to the biomass market in Missouri and p_2 =proportion of producers who are willing to offer windrowing services to the biomass market in Illinois. The parameter of interest is $p_1 - p_2$.

   b.   To determine if the proportion of producers who are willing to offer windrowing services differs between Missouri and Illinois, we test:

$$H_0 : p_1 - p_2 = 0$$
$$H_a : p_1 - p_2 \neq 0$$

   c.   The test statistic is $z = -2.67$.

   d.   The rejection region requires $\alpha / 2 = .01 / 2 = .005$ in each tail of the z-distribution. From Table II, Appendix D, $z_{.005} = 2.58$. The rejection region is $z < -2.58$ and $z > 2.58$.

   e.   The p-value is $p = .008$.

   f.   Since the observed value of the test statistic falls in the rejection region $(z = -2.67 < -2.58)$, H_0 is rejected. There is sufficient evidence to indicate that the proportion of producers who are willing to offer windrowing services differs between Missouri and Illinois at $\alpha = .01$.

Since the p-value is less than $\alpha(p = .008 < .01)$, H_0 is rejected. This is the same conclusion as above.

8.53   a.   The first population of interest is all hospital patients admitted in January. The second population of interest is all hospital patients admitted in May.

   b. $\hat{p}_1 = \dfrac{x_1}{n_1} = \dfrac{32}{192} = .167$ $\hat{p}_2 = \dfrac{x_2}{n_2} = \dfrac{34}{403} = .084$

The point estimate for the difference in malaria admission rates in January and May is
$\hat{p}_1 - \hat{p}_2 = .167 - .084 = .083$.

   c.   For confidence coefficient .90, $\alpha = .10$ and $\alpha / 2 = .10 / 2 = .05$. From Table II, Appendix D, $z_{.05} = 1.645$. The 90% confidence interval is:

$$\left(\hat{p}_1 - \hat{p}_2\right) \pm z_{.05} \sqrt{\dfrac{\hat{p}_1 \hat{q}_1}{n_1} + \dfrac{\hat{p}_2 \hat{q}_2}{n_2}} \Rightarrow (.167 - .084) \pm 1.645 \sqrt{\dfrac{.167(.833)}{192} + \dfrac{.084(.916)}{403}}$$
$$\Rightarrow .083 \pm .050 \Rightarrow (.033, \ .133)$$

   d.   Since 0 is not contained in the confidence interval, we can conclude that a difference exists in the true malaria admission rates in January and May.

8.55   Let p_1 =proportion of salmonella in the region's water and p_2 =proportion of salmonella in the region's wildlife.

Some preliminary calculations are:

$$\hat{p}_1 = \frac{x_1}{n_1} = \frac{18}{252} = .071 \qquad \hat{p}_2 = \frac{x_2}{n_2} = \frac{20}{476} = .042 \qquad \hat{p} = \frac{x_1 + x_2}{n_1 + n_2} = \frac{18 + 20}{252 + 476} = \frac{38}{728} = .052$$

To determine if the prevalence of salmonella in the region's water differs from the prevalence of salmonella in the region's wildlife, we test:

$$H_0 : p_1 - p_2 = 0$$
$$H_a : p_1 - p_2 \neq 0$$

The test statistic is $z = \dfrac{(\hat{p}_1 - \hat{p}_2) - 0}{\sqrt{\hat{p}\hat{q}\left(\dfrac{1}{n_1} + \dfrac{1}{n_2}\right)}} = \dfrac{.071 - .042}{\sqrt{.052(.948)\left(\dfrac{1}{252} + \dfrac{1}{476}\right)}} = 1.68$

The rejection region requires $\alpha / 2 = .01 / 2 = .005$ in each tail of the z-distribution. From Table II, Appendix D, $z_{.005} = 2.58$. The rejection region is $z < -2.58$ and $z > 2.58$.

Since the observed value of the test statistic does not fall in the rejection region $(z = 1.68 \not> 2.58)$, H_0 is not rejected. There is insufficient evidence to indicate the prevalence of salmonella in the region's water differs from the prevalence of salmonella in the region's wildlife at $\alpha = .01$.

8.57   Let $p_1 =$ proportion of African American MBA students who begin their career as entrepreneurs and $p_2 =$ proportion of white MBA students who begin their career as entrepreneurs.

Some preliminary calculations:

$$\hat{p}_1 = \frac{x_1}{n_1} = \frac{209}{1,304} = .1603 \qquad\qquad \hat{q}_1 = 1 - \hat{p}_1 = 1 - .1603 = .8397$$

$$\hat{p}_2 = \frac{x_2}{n_2} = \frac{356}{7,120} = .05 \qquad\qquad \hat{q}_2 = 1 - \hat{p}_2 = 1 - .05 = .95$$

$$\hat{p} = \frac{x_1 + x_2}{n_1 + n_2} = \frac{209 + 356}{1,304 + 7,120} = .0671 \qquad\qquad \hat{q} = 1 - \hat{p} = 1 - .0671 = .9329$$

To determine if African American MBA students are more likely to begin their careers as an entrepreneur than white MAB students, we test:

$$H_0 : p_1 - p_2 = 0$$
$$H_a : p_1 - p_2 > 0$$

The test statistic is $z = \dfrac{(\hat{p}_1 - \hat{p}_2) - 0}{\sqrt{\hat{p}\hat{q}\left(\dfrac{1}{n_1} + \dfrac{1}{n_2}\right)}} = \dfrac{.1603 - .05}{\sqrt{.0671(.9329)\left(\dfrac{1}{1,304} + \dfrac{1}{7,120}\right)}} = 14.64$

Since no α was given, we will use $\alpha = .05$. The rejection region requires $\alpha = .05$ in the upper tail of the z-distribution. From Table II, Appendix D, $z_{.05} = 1.645$. The rejection region is $z > 1.645$.

Since the observed value of the test statistic falls in the rejection region $(z = 14.64 > 1.645)$, H_0 is rejected. There is sufficient evidence to indicate that the proportion of African American MBA students who begin their career as entrepreneurs is significantly greater than the proportion of white MBA students who begin their career as entrepreneurs.

8.59   Let p_1 = proportion of server-flow sites that are vulnerable to impersonation attacks and p_2 = proportion of client-flow sites that are vulnerable to impersonation attacks

Some preliminary calculations are:

$$\hat{p}_1 = \frac{20}{40} = .500 \quad \hat{p}_2 = \frac{41}{54} = .759 \quad \hat{p} = \frac{20+41}{40+54} = \frac{61}{94} = .649 \quad \hat{q} = 1-\hat{p} = 1-.649 = .351$$

To determine if a client-flow website is more likely to be vulnerable to an impersonation attack than a client-flow website, we test:

$$H_0 : p_1 - p_2 = 0$$
$$H_a : p_1 - p_2 < 0$$

The test statistic is $z = \dfrac{\hat{p}_1 - \hat{p}_2}{\sqrt{\hat{p}\hat{q}\left(\frac{1}{n_1}+\frac{1}{n_2}\right)}} = \dfrac{.500-.759}{\sqrt{.649(.351)\left(\frac{1}{40}+\frac{1}{54}\right)}} = -2.60$.

The p-value is $p = P(z < -2.60) = .5 - .4953 = .0047$ (Using Table II, Appendix D)

Since the p-value is so small, H_0 is rejected. There is sufficient evidence to indicate a client-flow website is more likely to be vulnerable to an impersonation attack than a client-flow website for any value of $\alpha > .0047$.

To determine how much more likely a client-flow website is more likely to be vulnerable to an impersonation attack than a server-flow website, we form a 95% confidence interval. For confidence level .95, $\alpha = .05$ and $\alpha/2 = .05/2 = .025$. From Table II, Appendix D, $z_{.05} = 1.96$. The 95% confidence interval is:

$$(\hat{p}_2 - \hat{p}_1) \pm z_{.05}\sqrt{\frac{\hat{p}_2(1-\hat{p}_2)}{n_2}+\frac{\hat{p}_1(1-\hat{p}_1)}{n_1}} \Rightarrow (.759-.500) \pm 1.96\sqrt{\frac{.759(1-.759)}{54}+\frac{.500(1-.500)}{40}}$$
$$\Rightarrow .259 \pm .192 \Rightarrow (.067, .451)$$

We are 95% confident that a client-flow website is more likely to be vulnerable to an impersonation attack than a server-flow website by anywhere from .067 to .451.

8.61   a.   For confidence coefficient .99, $\alpha = .01$ and $\alpha/2 = .01/2 = .005$. From Table II, Appendix D, $z_{.005} = 2.58$.

$$n_1 = n_2 = \frac{(z_{\alpha/2})^2(p_1q_1+p_2q_2)}{(ME)^2} = \frac{2.58^2(.4(1-.4)+.7(1-.7))}{.01^2} = \frac{2.99538}{.0001} = 29,953.8 \approx 29,954$$

b. For confidence coefficient .90, $\alpha = .10$ and $\alpha / 2 = .10 / 2 = .05$. From Table II, Appendix D, $z_{.05} = 1.645$. Since we have no prior information about the proportions, we use $p_1 = p_2 = .5$ to get a conservative estimate. For a width of .05, the margin of error is .025.

$$n_1 = n_2 = \frac{(z_{\alpha/2})^2 (p_1 q_1 + p_2 q_2)}{(ME)^2} = \frac{(1.645)^2 (.5(1-.5) + .5(1-.5))}{.025^2} = 2164.82 \approx 2165$$

c. From part **b**, $z_{.05} = 1.645$.

$$n_1 = n_2 = \frac{(z_{\alpha/2})^2 (p_1 q_1 + p_2 q_2)}{(ME)^2} = \frac{(1.645)^2 (.2(1-.2) + .3(1-.3))}{.03^2} = \frac{1.00123}{.0009} = 1112.48 \approx 1113$$

8.63 $\quad n_1 = n_2 = \dfrac{(z_{\alpha/2})^2 (\sigma_1^2 + \sigma_2^2)}{(ME)^2}$

For confidence coefficient .95, $\alpha = .05$ and $\alpha / 2 = .05 / 2 = .025$. From Table II, Appendix D, $z_{.025} = 1.96$.

$$n_1 = n_2 = \frac{1.96^2 (14 + 14)}{1.8^2} = 33.2 \approx 34$$

8.65 $\quad$ For confidence coefficient .95, $\alpha = .05$ and $\alpha / 2 = .05 / 2 = .025$. From Table II, Appendix D, $z_{.025} = 1.96$.

$$n_1 = n_2 = \frac{(z_{\alpha/2})^2 (\sigma_1^2 + \sigma_2^2)}{(ME)^2} = \frac{(1.96)^2 (9^2 + 9^2)}{2^2} = 155.6 \approx 156$$

8.67 a. The parameter of interest is $p_{\text{Server}} - p_{\text{Client}}$.

b. The desired confidence level is .95.

c. The desired sampling error is .15.

d. For confidence coefficient .95, $\alpha = .05$ and $\alpha / 2 = .05 / 2 = .025$. From Table II, Appendix D, c.

The required sample sizes are $n_1 = n_2 = \dfrac{(z_{\alpha/2})^2 (p_1 q_1 + p_2 q_2)}{(ME)^2} = \dfrac{(1.96)^2 (.5(.5) + .5(.5))}{(.15)^2} = 85.4 \approx 86$.

e. Assume that $n_1 = 2n_2$. Then $n_2 = \dfrac{(z_{\alpha/2})^2 (p_1 q_1 + a p_2 q_2)}{a(ME)^2} = \dfrac{(1.96)^2 (.5(.5) + 2(.5)(.5))}{2(.15)^2} = 64$ and

$n_1 = 2(64) = 128$.

8.69   For confidence coefficient .99, $\alpha = .01$ and $\alpha / 2 = .01 / 2 = .005$. From Table II, Appendix D, $z_{.005} = 2.575$.

Assume that $n_2 = 2n_1$. Then $n_1 = \dfrac{(z_{\alpha/2})^2 (2\sigma_1^2 + \sigma_2^2)}{2(ME)^2} = \dfrac{(2.575)^2 (2(.04) + .04)}{2(.05)^2} = 159.14 \approx 160$ and

$n_2 = 2(160) = 320$.

8.71   a.   For confidence coefficient .95, $\alpha = .05$ and $\alpha / 2 = .05 / 2 = .025$. From Table II, Appendix D,

$z_{.025} = 1.96$. From Exercise 8.56, $\hat{p}_1 = .184$ and $\hat{p}_2 = .177$.

$n_1 = n_2 = \dfrac{(z_{\alpha/2})^2 (p_1 q_1 + p_2 q_2)}{(ME)^2} = \dfrac{1.96^2 (.184(.816) + .177(.823))}{.015^2} = 5,050.7 \approx 5,051$

b.   The study would involve $5,051 \times 2 = 10,102$ patients. A study this large would be extremely time consuming and expensive.

c.   Since a difference of .015 is so small, the practical significance detecting a 0.015 difference may not be very worthwhile. A difference of .015 is so close to 0, that it might not make any difference.

8.73   a.   With $v_1 = 9$ and $v_2 = 6$, $F_{.05} = 4.10$.

b.   With $v_1 = 18$ and $v_2 = 14$, $F_{.01} \approx 3.57$. (Since $v_1 = 18$ is not given, we estimate the value between those for $v_1 = 15$ and $v_1 = 20$.)

c.   With $v_1 = 11$ and $v_2 = 4$, $F_{.025} \approx 8.80$. (Since $v_1 = 11$ is not given, we estimate the value by averaging those given for $v_1 = 10$ and $v_1 = 12$.)

d.   With $v_1 = 20$ and $v_2 = 5$, $F_{.10} = 3.21$.

8.75   a.   Reject H_0 if $F > F_{.10} = 1.74$. (From Table V, Appendix D, with $v_1 = 30$ and $v_2 = 20$.)

b.   Reject H_0 if $F > F_{.05} = 2.04$. (From Table VI, Appendix D, with $v_1 = 30$ and $v_2 = 20$.)

c.   Reject H_0 if $F > F_{.025} = 2.35$. (From Table VII.)

d.   Reject H_0 if $F > F_{.01} = 2.78$. (From Table VIII.)

8.77   a.   The rejection region requires $\alpha = .05$ in the upper tail of the F-distribution with $v_1 = n_1 - 1 = 25 - 1 = 24$ and $v_2 = n_2 - 1 = 20 - 1 = 19$. From Table VI, Appendix D, $F_{.05} = 2.11$. The rejection region is $F > 2.11$ (if $s_1^2 > s_2^2$).

b.   The rejection region requires $\alpha = .05$ in the upper tail of the F-distribution with $v_1 = n_2 - 1 = 15 - 1 = 14$ and $v_2 = n_1 - 1 = 10 - 1 = 9$. From Table VI, Appendix D, $F_{.05} \approx 3.01$. The rejection region is $F > 3.01$ (if $s_2^2 > s_1^2$).

c.   The rejection region requires $\alpha / 2 = .10 / 2 = .05$ in the upper tail of the F-distribution. If $s_1^2 > s_2^2$, $v_1 = n_1 - 1 = 21 - 1 = 20$ and $v_2 = n_2 - 1 = 31 - 1 = 30$. From Table VI, Appendix D, $F_{.05} = 1.93$. The rejection region is $F > 1.93$. If $s_1^2 < s_2^2$, $v_1 = n_2 - 1 = 30$ and $v_2 = n_1 - 1 = 20$. From Table VI, $F_{.05} = 2.04$. The rejection region is $F > 2.04$.

d.   The rejection region requires $\alpha = .01$ in the upper tail of the F-distribution with $v_1 = n_2 - 1 = 41 - 1 = 40$ and $v_2 = n_1 - 1 = 31 - 1 = 30$. From Table VIII, Appendix D, $F_{.01} = 2.30$. The rejection region is $F > 2.30$ (if $s_2^2 > s_1^2$).

e.   The rejection region requires $\alpha = .05$ and $\alpha / 2 = .05 / 2 = .025$ in the upper tail of the F-distribution. If $s_1^2 > s_2^2$, $v_1 = n_1 - 1 = 7 - 1 = 6$ and $v_2 = n_2 - 1 = 16 - 1 = 15$. From Table VII, Appendix D, $F_{.025} = 3.41$. The rejection region is $F > 3.41$. If $s_1^2 < s_2^2$, $v_1 = n_2 - 1 = 15$ and $v_2 = n_1 - 1 = 6$. From Table VII, Appendix D, $F_{.025} = 5.27$. The rejection region is $F > 5.27$.

8.79   a.   Using MINITAB, the descriptive statistics are:

Descriptive Statistics: Sample 1, Sample 2

Variable	N	Mean	Median	StDev	Minimum	Maximum	Q1	Q3
Sample 1	6	2.417	2.400	1.436	0.700	4.400	1.075	3.650
Sample 2	5	4.36	3.70	2.97	1.40	8.90	1.84	7.20

To determine if the variance for population 2 is greater than that for population 1, we test:

$$H_0 : \sigma_1^2 = \sigma_2^2$$
$$H_a : \sigma_1^2 < \sigma_2^2$$

The test statistic is $F = \dfrac{s_2^2}{s_1^2} = \dfrac{2.97^2}{1.436^2} = 4.28$

The rejection region requires $\alpha = .05$ in the upper tail of the F-distribution with $v_1 = n_2 - 1 = 5 - 1 = 4$ and $v_2 = n_1 - 1 = 6 - 1 = 5$. From Table VI, Appendix D, $F_{.05} = 5.19$. The rejection region is $F > 5.19$.

Since the observed value of the test statistic does not fall in the rejection region $(F = 4.29 \not> 5.19)$, H_0 is not rejected. There is insufficient evidence to indicate the variance for population 2 is greater than that for population 1 at $\alpha = .05$.

b.   The p-value is $p = P(F \geq 4.28)$. From Tables V and VI, with $v_1 = 4$ and $v_2 = 5$,

$$.05 < p = P(F \geq 4.28) < .10$$

There is no evidence to reject H_0 for $\alpha = .05$ but there is evidence to reject H_0 for $\alpha = .10$.

8.81   a.   Let σ_1^2 = variance of the years of experience for commercial suppliers and σ_2^2 = variance of the years of experience for government employees. To determine if the variability in years of experience differ between the two groups, we test:

$$H_0 : \sigma_1^2 = \sigma_2^2$$
$$H_a : \sigma_1^2 \neq \sigma_2^2$$

b.   From the printout, the test statistic is $F = .8963$.

c.   From the printout, the p-value is $p = .9617$.

d.   Since the p-value is not less than $\alpha (p = .9617 \not< .05)$, H_0 is not rejected. There is insufficient evidence to indicate the variability in years of experience differ between the two groups at $\alpha = .05$. This agrees with Exercise 8.15c.

8.83   Let σ_1^2 = variance at site 1 and σ_2^2 = variance of site 2. To determine if the variances at the two locations differ, we test:

$$H_0 : \sigma_1^2 = \sigma_2^2$$
$$H_a : \sigma_1^2 \neq \sigma_2^2$$

From the printout, the test statistic is $F = .844$ and the p-value is $p = .681$.

Since the p-value is not less than $\alpha (p = .681 \not< .05)$, H_0 is not rejected. There is insufficient evidence to indicate the variances at the two locations differ at $\alpha = .05$.

8.85   Using MINITAB, the descriptive statistics are:

Descriptive Statistics: Novice, Experienced

Variable	N	Mean	Median	StDev	Minimum	Maximum	Q1	Q3
Novice	12	32.83	32.00	8.64	20.00	48.00	26.75	39.00
Experien	12	20.58	19.50	5.74	10.00	31.00	17.25	24.75

a.   Let σ_1^2 = variance in inspection errors for novice inspectors and σ_2^2 = variance in inspection errors for experienced inspectors. Since we wish to determine if the data support the belief that the variance is lower for experienced inspectors than for novice inspectors, we test:

$$H_0 : \sigma_1^2 = \sigma_2^2$$
$$H_a : \sigma_1^2 > \sigma_2^2$$

The test statistic is $F = \dfrac{\text{Larger sample variance}}{\text{Smaller sample variance}} = \dfrac{s_1^2}{s_2^2} = \dfrac{8.64^2}{5.74^2} = 2.27$

The rejection region requires $\alpha = .05$ in the upper tail of the F-distribution with $v_1 = n_1 - 1 = 12 - 1 = 11$ and $v_2 = n_2 - 1 = 12 - 1 = 11$. Using MINITAB:

Inverse Cumulative Distribution Function
F distribution with 11 DF in numerator and 11 DF in denominator

P(X <= x)   x
    0.95   2.81793

The rejection region is $F > 2.82$.

Since the observed value of the test statistic does not fall in the rejection region $\left(F = 2.27 \not> 2.82\right)$, H_0 is not rejected. The sample data do not support her belief at $\alpha = .05$.

b. Using MINITAB:

Cumulative Distribution Function
```
F distribution with 11 DF in numerator and 11 DF in denominator

   x   P( X <= x )
2.27      0.905144
```

The p-value $= P\left(F \geq 2.27\right) = 1 - P\left(F < 2.27\right) = 1 - .905 = .095$.

8.87   For each scenario, we will compute the test statistic that would be used to test to see if there is a difference between the two variances.

For the first scenario, with $s_1 = 4$ and $s_2 = 2$, the test statistic is $F = \dfrac{\text{Larger sample variance}}{\text{Smaller sample variance}} = \dfrac{s_1^2}{s_2^2} = \dfrac{4^2}{2^2} = 4$.

For the second scenario, with $s_1 = 10$ and $s_2 = 15$, the test statistic is

$$F = \frac{\text{Larger sample variance}}{\text{Smaller sample variance}} = \frac{s_2^2}{s_1^2} = \frac{15^2}{10^2} = 2.25.$$

In both cases, the degrees of freedom for the tests are the same. Thus, the assumption required for the t-test for the first scenario, with $s_1 = 4$ and $s_2 = 2$, would be the most likely be violated because the value of the test statistic is larger.

8.89   a.   The 2 samples are randomly selected in an independent manner from the two populations. The sample sizes, n_1 and n_2, are large enough so that $\bar{x}_1$ and $\bar{x}_2$ each have approximately normal sampling distributions and so that s_1^2 and s_2^2 provide good approximations to σ_1^2 and σ_2^2. This will be true if $n_1 \geq 30$ and $n_2 \geq 30$.

     b.   1.   Both sampled populations have relative frequency distributions that are approximately normal.
             2.   The population variances are equal.
             3.   The samples are randomly and independently selected from the populations.

     c.   1.   The relative frequency distribution of the population of differences is normal.
             2.   The sample of differences are randomly selected from the population of differences.

     d.   The two samples are independent random samples from binomial distributions. Both samples should be large enough so that the normal distribution provides an adequate approximation to the sampling distributions of $\hat{p}_1$ and $\hat{p}_2$.

     e.   The two samples are independent random samples from populations which are normally distributed.

8.91   a.   Some preliminary calculations are:

$$s_p^2 = \frac{(n_1 - 1)s_1^2 + (n_1 - 1)s_2^2}{n_1 + n_2 - 2} = \frac{11(74.2) + 13(60.5)}{12 + 14 - 2} = 66.7792$$

$$H_0 : \mu_1 - \mu_2 = 0$$
$$H_a : \mu_1 - \mu_2 > 0$$

The test statistic is $t = \dfrac{(\bar{x}_1 - \bar{x}_2) - 0}{\sqrt{s_p^2\left(\dfrac{1}{n_1} + \dfrac{1}{n_2}\right)}} = \dfrac{(17.8 - 15.3) - 0}{\sqrt{66.7792\left(\dfrac{1}{12} + \dfrac{1}{14}\right)}} = .78$

The p-value is $p = P(t > .78)$. Using MINITAB, with $df = n_1 + n_2 - 2 = 12 + 14 - 2 = 24$,

Cumulative Distribution Function
```
Student's t distribution with 24 DF

   x   P( X ≤ x )
0.78     0.778492
```

The p-value is $p = P(t > .78) = 1 - .778 = .222$.

Since the p-value is not less than α $(p = .222 \not< .05)$, H_0 is not rejected. There is insufficient evidence to indicate that $\mu_1 > \mu_2$ at $\alpha = .05$.

b. For confidence coefficient .99, $\alpha = .01$ and $\alpha/2 = .01/2 = .005$. From Table III, Appendix D, with $df = n_1 + n_2 - 2 = 12 + 14 - 2 = 24$, $t_{.005} = 2.797$. The confidence interval is:

$$(\bar{x}_1 - \bar{x}_2) \pm t_{.005}\sqrt{s_p^2\left(\frac{1}{n_1} + \frac{1}{n_2}\right)} \Rightarrow (17.8 - 15.3) \pm 2.797\sqrt{66.7792\left(\frac{1}{12} + \frac{1}{14}\right)}$$
$$\Rightarrow 2.50 \pm 8.99 \Rightarrow (-6.49, 11.49)$$

c. For confidence coefficient .99, $\alpha = .01$ and $\alpha/2 = .01/2 = .005$. From Table II, Appendix D, $z_{.005} = 2.58$.

$$n_1 = n_2 = \frac{(z_{\alpha/2})(\sigma_1^2 + \sigma_2^2)}{(ME)^2} = \frac{(2.58)^2(74.2 + 60.5)}{2^2} = 224.15 \approx 225$$

8.93 a. For confidence coefficient .90, $\alpha = .10$ and $\alpha/2 = .10/2 = .05$. From Table II, Appendix D, $z_{.05} = 1.645$. The confidence interval is:

$$(\bar{x}_1 - \bar{x}_2) \pm z_{.05}\sqrt{\frac{s_1^2}{n_1} + \frac{s_2^2}{n_2}} \Rightarrow (12.2 - 8.3) \pm 1.645\sqrt{\frac{2.1}{135} + \frac{3.0}{148}}$$
$$\Rightarrow 3.90 \pm .31 \Rightarrow (3.59, 4.21)$$

b. Using MINITAB, some preliminary calculations are:

Two-Sample T-Test and CI
```
Sample    N    Mean   StDev   SE Mean
1        135   12.20   1.45    0.12
2        148    8.30   1.73    0.14

Difference = μ (1) - μ (2)
Estimate for difference:  3.900
99% CI for difference:  (3.409, 4.391)
T-Test of difference = 0 (vs ≠): T-Value = 20.60   P-Value = 0.000   DF = 278
```

$$H_0 : \mu_1 - \mu_2 = 0$$
$$H_a : \mu_1 - \mu_2 \neq 0$$

The test statistic is $z = 20.60$ and $p = .000$.

Since the p-value is less than $\alpha \left(p = .000 < .01 \right)$, H_0 is rejected. There is sufficient evidence to indicate that $\mu_1 \neq \mu_2$ at $\alpha = .01$.

c. For confidence coefficient .90, $\alpha = .10$ and $\alpha/2 = .10/2 = .05$. From Table II, Appendix D, $z_{.05} = 1.645$.

$$n_1 = n_2 = \frac{\left(z_{\alpha/2} \right)\left(\sigma_1^2 + \sigma_2^2 \right)}{\left(ME \right)^2} = \frac{\left(1.645 \right)^2 \left(2.1 + 3.0 \right)}{\left(.2 \right)^2} = 345.02 \approx 346$$

8.95   a. The parameter of interest is $p_{\text{Male}} - p_{\text{Female}}$. We must assume that the samples are independent.

b. The parameter of interest is $\mu_{\text{Crestor}} - \mu_{\text{Mevacor}}$. We must assume that the samples are independent.

c. The parameter of interest is μ_d. We must assume that the sample size is sufficiently large or that the population of differences is approximately normal.

d. The parameter of interest is $\sigma_{\text{High}}^2 / \sigma_{\text{Low}}^2$. We must assume that the samples are independent and from normal populations.

8.97   a. Let μ_1 = mean score for males and μ_2 = mean score for females. For confidence coefficient .90, $\alpha = .10$ and $\alpha/2 = .10/2 = .05$. From Table II, Appendix D, $z_{.05} = 1.645$. The 90% confidence interval is:

$$\left(\bar{x}_1 - \bar{x}_2 \right) \pm z_{\alpha/2} \sqrt{\frac{\sigma_1^2}{n_1} + \frac{\sigma_2^2}{n_2}} \Rightarrow \left(39.08 - 38.79 \right) \pm 1.645 \sqrt{\frac{6.73^2}{127} + \frac{6.94^2}{114}}$$
$$\Rightarrow 0.29 \pm 1.452 \Rightarrow \left(-1.162, \ 1.742 \right)$$

We are 90% confident that the difference in mean service-rating scores between males and females is between -1.162 and 1.742.

b. To determine if the service-rating score variances differ by gender, we test:

$$H_0 : \sigma_1^2 = \sigma_2^2$$
$$H_a : \sigma_1^2 \neq \sigma_2^2$$

The test statistic is $F = \dfrac{\text{larger sample variance}}{\text{smaller sample variance}} = \dfrac{s_2^2}{s_1^2} = \dfrac{6.94^2}{6.73^2} = 1.06$

The rejection region requires $\alpha / 2 = .10 / 2 = .05$ in the upper tail of the F-distribution with $v_2 = n_2 - 1 = 114 - 1 = 113$ and $v_1 = n_1 - 1 = 127 - 1 = 126$. Using MINITAB, we get:

Inverse Cumulative Distribution Function
```
F distribution with 113 DF in numerator and 126 DF in denominator

P( X <= x )         x
        0.95  1.35141
```

$F_{.05} = 1.35$. The rejection region is $F > 1.35$.

Since the observed value of the test statistic does not fall in the rejection region $(F = 1.06 \not> 1.35)$, H_0 is not rejected. There is insufficient evidence to indicate the service-rating score variances differ by gender at $\alpha = .10$.

c.   Since we did not reject H_0 in part b, the confidence interval in part **a** is valid. Because 0 falls in the 90% confidence interval, we are 90% confident that there is no difference in the mean service-rating scores between males and females.

8.99   Let μ_1 = the mean test score of students on the SAT reading test in classrooms that used educational software and μ_2 = the mean test score of students on the SAT reading test in classrooms that did not use the technology

a.   The parameter of interest is $\mu_1 - \mu_2$.

b.   The null and alternative hypotheses for the test are:

$$H_0 : \mu_1 - \mu_2 = 0$$
$$H_a : \mu_1 - \mu_2 > 0$$

c.   Since the p-value of the test is so large $(p = 0.62)$, we would not reject H_0 for any reasonable value of α. There is insufficient evidence to indicate that the mean test score of the students on the SAT reading test was significantly higher in classrooms using reading software products than in classrooms that 8.100

8.101   a.   Let μ_1 = mean driver chest injury rating and μ_2 = mean passenger chest injury rating. Because the data are paired, we are interested in $\mu_1 - \mu_2 = \mu_d$, the difference in mean chest injury ratings between drivers and passengers.

b.   The data were collected as matched pairs and thus, must be analyzed as matched pairs. Two ratings are obtained for each car – the driver's chest injury rating and the passenger's chest injury rating.

c.   Using MINITAB, the descriptive statistics are:

Descriptive Statistics: DrivChst, PassChst, diff

Variable	N	Mean	Median	StDev	Minimum	Maximum	Q1	Q3
DrivChst	98	49.663	50.000	6.670	34.000	68.000	45.000	54.000
PassChst	98	50.224	50.500	7.107	35.000	69.000	45.000	55.000
diff	98	-0.561	0.000	5.517	-15.000	13.000	-4.000	3.000

For confidence coefficient .99, $\alpha = .01$ and $\alpha/2 = .01/2 = .005$. From Table II, Appendix D, $z_{.005} = 2.58$. The 99% confidence interval is:

$$\bar{d} \pm z_{.005} \frac{s_d}{\sqrt{n_d}} \Rightarrow -0.561 \pm 2.58 \frac{5.517}{\sqrt{98}} \Rightarrow -0.561 \pm 1.438 \Rightarrow (-1.999, \ 0.877)$$

d. We are 99% confidence that the difference between the mean chest injury ratings of drivers and front-seat passengers is between -1.999 and 0.877. Since 0 is in the confidence interval, there is no evidence that the true mean driver chest injury rating exceeds the true mean passenger chest injury rating.

e. Since the sample size is large, the sampling distribution of $\bar{d}$ is approximately normal by the Central Limit Theorem. We must assume that the differences are randomly selected.

8.103 a. Let $\mu_1 =$ mean number of items recalled by those in the video only group and $\mu_2 =$ mean number of items recalled by those in the audio and video group. To determine if the mean number of items recalled by the two groups is the same, we test:

$$H_0 : \mu_1 - \mu_2 = 0$$
$$H_a : \mu_1 - \mu_2 \neq 0$$

b. $$s_p^2 = \frac{(n_1 - 1)s_1^2 + (n_2 - 1)s_2^2}{n_1 + n_2 - 2} = \frac{(20 - 1)1.98^2 + (20 - 1)2.13^2}{20 + 20 - 2} = 4.22865$$

The test statistic is $t = \dfrac{(\bar{x}_1 - \bar{x}_2) - D_o}{\sqrt{s_p^2 \left(\dfrac{1}{n_1} + \dfrac{1}{n_2} \right)}} = \dfrac{(3.70 - 3.30) - 0}{\sqrt{4.22865 \left(\dfrac{1}{20} + \dfrac{1}{20} \right)}} = \dfrac{0.4}{.65028} = 0.62$

c. The rejection region requires $\alpha/2 = .10/2 = .05$ in each tail of the t-distribution with $df = n_1 + n_2 - 2 = 20 + 20 - 2 = 38$. From Table III, Appendix D, $t_{.05} \approx 1.684$. The rejection region is $t < -1.684$ or $t > 1.684$.

d. Since the observed value of the test statistic does not fall in the rejection region $(t = 0.62 \not> 1.684)$, H_o is not rejected. There is insufficient evidence to indicate a difference in the mean number of items recalled by the two groups at $\alpha = .10$.

e. The p-value is $p = .542$. This is the probability of observing our test statistic or anything more unusual if H_0 is true. Since the p-value is not less than $\alpha = .10$, there is no evidence to reject H_0. There is insufficient evidence to indicate a difference in the mean number of items recalled by the two groups at $\alpha = .10$.

f. We must assume:

1. Both populations are normal
2. Random and independent samples
3. $\sigma_1^2 = \sigma_2^2$

8.105 a. Let p_1 = proportion of men who prefer to keep track of appointments in their head and

p_2 = proportion of women who prefer to keep track of appointments in their head. To determine if the proportion of men who prefer to keep track of appointments in their head is greater than that of women, we test:

$$H_0 : p_1 - p_2 = 0$$
$$H_a : p_1 - p_2 > 0$$

b. $\hat{p} = \dfrac{n_1 \hat{p}_1 + n_2 \hat{p}_2}{n_1 + n_2} = \dfrac{500(.56) + 500(.46)}{500 + 500} = .51$ and $\hat{q} = 1 - \hat{p} = 1 - .51 = .49$

The test statistic is $z = \dfrac{(\hat{p}_1 - \hat{p}_2) - 0}{\sqrt{\hat{p}\hat{q}\left(\dfrac{1}{n_1} + \dfrac{1}{n_2}\right)}} = \dfrac{(.56 - .46) - 0}{\sqrt{.51(.49)\left(\dfrac{1}{500} + \dfrac{1}{500}\right)}} = 3.16$

c. The rejection region requires $\alpha = .01$ in the upper tail of the z distribution. From Table II, Appendix D, $z_{.01} = 2.33$. The rejection region is $z > 2.33$.

d. The p-value is $p = P(z \geq 3.16) \approx .5 - .5 = 0$.

e. Since the observed value of the test statistic falls in the rejection region $(z = 3.16 > 2.33)$, H_0 is rejected. There is sufficient evidence to indicate the proportion of men who prefer to keep track of appointments in their head is greater than that of women at $\alpha = .01$.

8.107 a. The two populations are male and female smartphone users.

b. For financial transactions, $\hat{p}_{\text{Male}} = .48$ and $\hat{p}_{\text{Female}} = .60$.

c. For confidence coefficient .90, $\alpha = .10$ and $\alpha / 2 = .10 / 2 = .05$. From Table II, Appendix D, $z_{.05} = 1.645$. The 90% confidence interval is

$$(\hat{p}_1 - \hat{p}_2) \pm z_{\alpha/2}\sqrt{\dfrac{\hat{p}_1 \hat{q}_2}{n_1} + \dfrac{\hat{p}_2 \hat{q}_2}{n_2}} \Rightarrow (.48 - .60) \pm 1.645\sqrt{\dfrac{.48(1 - .48)}{251} + \dfrac{.60(1 - .60)}{284}}$$
$$\Rightarrow -.12 \pm .071 \Rightarrow (-.191, -.049)$$

d. Yes. Since the interval contains only negative numbers, we can conclude that men are less likely than women to conduct financial transactions on a smartphone.

e. For streaming content, $\hat{p}_{\text{Male}} = .42$ and $\hat{p}_{\text{Female}} = .35$.

f. To determine whether the proportions of men and women who watch streaming content on their phone differ, we test:

$$H_0 : p_1 - p_2 = 0$$
$$H_a : p_1 - p_2 \neq 0$$

$$\hat{p} = \frac{251(.42) + 284(.35)}{251 + 284} = .3828 \qquad \hat{q} = 1 - \hat{p} = 1 - .3828 = .6172$$

The test statistic is $z = \dfrac{\hat{p}_1 - \hat{p}_2}{\sqrt{\hat{p}\hat{q}\left(\dfrac{1}{n_1} + \dfrac{1}{n_2}\right)}} = \dfrac{.42 - .35}{\sqrt{.3828(.6172)\left(\dfrac{1}{251} + \dfrac{1}{284}\right)}} = 1.66$.

The rejection region requires $\alpha/2 = .10/2 = .05$ in each tail of the z-distribution. From Table II, Appendix D, $z_{.05} = 1.645$. The rejection region is $z < -1.645$ or $z > 1.645$.

Since the observed value of the test statistic falls in the rejection region $(z = 1.66 > 1.645)$, H_0 is rejected. There is sufficient evidence to indicate the proportions of men and women who watch streaming content on their phone differ at $\alpha = .10$.

8.109 a. Using MINITAB, the descriptive statistics are:

Descriptive Statistics: Purchasers, Nonpurchasers

Variable	N	Mean	Median	StDev	Minimum	Maximum	Q1	Q3
Purchase	20	39.80	38.00	10.04	23.00	59.00	32.25	48.75
Nonpurch	20	47.20	52.00	13.62	22.00	66.00	33.50	58.75

$$s_p^2 = \frac{(n_1 - 1)s_1^2 + (n_2 - 1)s_2^2}{n_1 + n_2 - 2} = \frac{(20-1)13.62^2 + (20-1)10.04^2}{20 + 20 - 2} = 143.153$$

Let μ_1 = mean age of nonpurchasers and μ_2 = mean age of purchasers.

To determine if there is a difference in the mean age of purchasers and nonpurchasers, we test:

$$H_0 : \mu_1 - \mu_2 = 0$$
$$H_a : \mu_1 - \mu_2 \neq 0$$

The test statistic is $t = \dfrac{(\bar{x}_1 - \bar{x}_2) - 0}{\sqrt{s_p^2\left(\dfrac{1}{n_1} + \dfrac{1}{n_2}\right)}} = \dfrac{(47.20 - 39.80) - 0}{\sqrt{143.153\left(\dfrac{1}{20} + \dfrac{1}{20}\right)}} = 1.956$

The rejection region requires $\alpha/2 = .10/2 = .05$ in each tail of the t-distribution with $df = n_1 + n_2 - 2 = 20 + 20 - 2 = 38$. From Table III, Appendix D, $t_{.05} \approx 1.684$. The rejection region is $t < -1.684$ or $t > 1.684$.

Since the observed value of the test statistic falls in the rejection region $(t = 1.956 > 1.684)$, H_0 is rejected. There is sufficient evidence to indicate the mean age of purchasers and nonpurchasers differ at $\alpha = .10$.

b. The necessary assumptions are:

1. Both sampled populations are approximately normal.
2. The population variances are equal.
3. The samples are randomly and independently sampled.

c. The *p*-value is $p = P(t \le -1.956) + P(t \ge 1.956) = (.5 - .4748) + (.5 - .4748) = .0504$. The probability of observing a test statistic of this value or more unusual if H_0 is true is .0504. Since this value is less than $\alpha = .10$, H_0 is rejected. There is sufficient evidence to indicate there is a difference in the mean age of purchasers and nonpurchasers.

d. For confidence coefficient .90, $\alpha = .10$ and $\alpha/2 = .10/2 = .05$. From Table III, Appendix D, with $df = 38$, $t_{.05} \approx 1.684$. The confidence interval is:

$$(\bar{x}_2 - \bar{x}_1) \pm t_{.05}\sqrt{s_p^2\left(\frac{1}{n_1} + \frac{1}{n_2}\right)} \Rightarrow (39.8 - 47.2) \pm 1.684\sqrt{143.153\left(\frac{1}{20} + \frac{1}{20}\right)}$$

$$\Rightarrow -7.4 \pm 6.37 \Rightarrow (-13.77, -1.03)$$

We are 90% confident that the difference in mean ages between purchasers and nonpurchasers is between −13.77 and −1.03.

8.111 a. Let p_1 = proportion of African-American drivers searched by the LAPD and p_2 = proportion of white drivers searched by the LAPD.

Some preliminary calculations are:

$$\hat{p}_1 = \frac{x_1}{n_1} = \frac{12,016}{61,688} = .195 \qquad \hat{p}_2 = \frac{x_2}{n_2} = \frac{5,312}{106,892} = .050$$

$$\hat{p} = \frac{x_1 + x_2}{n_1 + n_2} = \frac{12,016 + 5,312}{61,688 + 106,892} = \frac{17,328}{168,580} = .103$$

To determine if the proportions of African-American and white drivers searched differs, we test:

$$H_0 : p_1 - p_2 = 0$$
$$H_a : p_1 - p_2 \ne 0$$

The test statistic is $z = \dfrac{(\hat{p}_1 - \hat{p}_2) - 0}{\sqrt{\hat{p}\hat{q}\left(\frac{1}{n_1} + \frac{1}{n_2}\right)}} = \dfrac{.195 - .050}{\sqrt{.103(.897)\left(\frac{1}{61,688} + \frac{1}{106,892}\right)}} = 94.35$

The rejection region requires $\alpha/2 = .05/2 = .025$ in each tail of the *z*-distribution. From Table II, Appendix D, $z_{.025} = 1.96$. The rejection region is $z < -1.96$ or $z < -1.96$.

Since the observed value of the test statistic falls in the rejection region $(z = 94.35 > 1.96)$, H_0 is rejected. There is sufficient evidence to indicate the proportions of African-American drivers and white drivers searched differs at $\alpha = .05$.

b. Let p_1 = proportion of 'hits' for African-American drivers searched by the LAPD and p_2 = proportion of 'hits' for white drivers searched by the LAPD.

Some preliminary calculations are:

$$\hat{p}_1 = \frac{x_1}{n_1} = \frac{5,134}{12,016} = .427 \qquad\qquad \hat{p}_2 = \frac{x_2}{n_2} = \frac{3,006}{5,312} = .566$$

$$\hat{p} = \frac{x_1 + x_2}{n_1 + n_2} = \frac{5,134 + 3,006}{12,016 + 5,312} = \frac{8,140}{17,328} = .470$$

For confidence coefficient .95, $\alpha = .05$ and $\alpha/2 = .05/2 = .025$. From Table II, Appendix D, $z_{.025} = 1.96$. The 95% confidence interval is:

$$(\hat{p}_1 - \hat{p}_2) \pm z_{.025} \sqrt{\frac{\hat{p}_1 \hat{q}_1}{n_1} + \frac{\hat{p}_2 \hat{q}_2}{n_2}} \Rightarrow (.427 - .566) \pm 1.96 \sqrt{\frac{.427(.573)}{12,016} + \frac{.566(.434)}{5,312}}$$

$$\Rightarrow -.139 \pm .016 \Rightarrow (-.155, \ -.123)$$

We are 95% confident that the difference in 'hit' rates between African-American drivers and white drivers searched by the LAPD is between $-.155$ and $-.123$.

8.113   For probability .95, $\alpha = .05$ and $\alpha/2 = .05/2 = .025$. From Table II, Appendix D, $z_{.025} = 1.96$. Since we have no prior information about the proportions, we use $p_1 = p_2 = .5$ to get a conservative estimate.

$$n_1 = n_2 = \frac{(z_{\alpha/2})^2 (p_1 q_1 + p_2 q_2)}{ME^2} = \frac{(1.96)^2 (.5(1-.5) + .5(1-.5))}{.02^2} = \frac{1.9208}{.0004} = 4,802$$

8.115   Some preliminary calculations are:

$$s_1^2 = \frac{\sum x_1^2 - \frac{\left(\sum x_1\right)^2}{n_1}}{n_1 - 1} = \frac{10,251 - \frac{225^2}{5}}{5-1} = \frac{126}{4} = 31.5$$

$$s_2^2 = \frac{\sum x_2^2 - \frac{\left(\sum x_2\right)^2}{n_2}}{n_2 - 1} = \frac{10,351 - \frac{227^2}{5}}{5-1} = \frac{45.2}{4} = 11.3$$

Let σ_1^2 = variance for instrument A and σ_2^2 = variance for instrument B. Since we wish to determine if there is a difference in the precision of the two machines, we test:

$$H_0 : \sigma_1^2 = \sigma_2^2$$
$$H_a : \sigma_1^2 \neq \sigma_2^2$$

The test statistic is $F = \dfrac{\text{Larger sample variance}}{\text{Smaller sample variance}} = \dfrac{s_1^2}{s_2^2} = \dfrac{31.5}{11.3} = 2.79$

The rejection region requires $\alpha/2 = .10/2 = .05$ in the upper tail of the F-distribution with $v_1 = n_1 - 1 = 5 - 1 = 4$ and $v_2 = n_2 - 1 = 5 - 1 = 4$. From Table VI, Appendix D, $F_{.05} = 6.39$. The rejection region is $F > 6.39$.

Since the observed value of the test statistic does not fall in the rejection region $\left(F = 2.79 \not> 6.39\right)$, H_0 is not rejected. There is insufficient evidence of a difference in the precision of the two instruments at $\alpha = .10$.

8.117   For confidence coefficient .95, $\alpha = .05$ and $\alpha / 2 = .05 / 2 = .025$. From Table II, Appendix D, $z_{.025} = 1.96$.

$$n_1 = n_2 = \frac{\left(z_{\alpha/2}\right)^2 \left(\sigma_1^2 + \sigma_2^2\right)}{\left(ME\right)^2} = \frac{1.96^2 \left(35^2 + 80^2\right)}{10^2} = 292.9 \approx 293$$

8.119   **Attitude towards the Advertisement**:

The p-value is $p = .091$. There is no evidence to reject H_0 for $\alpha = .05$. There is no evidence to indicate the first ad will be more effective when shown to males for $\alpha = .05$. There is evidence to reject H_0 for $\alpha = .10$. There is evidence to indicate the first ad will be more effective when shown to males for $\alpha = .10$.

Attitude toward Brand of Soft Drink:

The p-value is $p = .032$. There is evidence to reject H_0 for $\alpha > .032$. There is evidence to indicate the first ad will be more effective when shown to males for $\alpha > .032$.

Intention to Purchase the Soft Drink:

The p-value is $p = .050$. There is no evidence to reject H_0 for $\alpha = .05$. There is no evidence to indicate the first ad will be more effective when shown to males for $\alpha = .05$. There is evidence to reject H_0 for $\alpha > .050$. There is evidence to indicate the first ad will be more effective when shown to males for $\alpha > .050$.

No, I do not agree with the author's hypothesis. The results agree with the author's hypothesis for only the attitude toward the Brand using $\alpha = .05$. If we want to use $\alpha = .10$, then the author's hypotheses are all supported.

8.121   a.   Let p_1 = proportion of 9th grade boys who gambled weekly or daily in first year and p_2 = proportion of 9th grade boys who gambled weekly or daily in second year. The researchers are interested in whether there is a difference in these two proportions, so the parameter of interest is $p_1 - p_2$.

Some preliminary calculations are:

$$\hat{p}_1 = \frac{x_1}{n_1} = \frac{4,684}{21,484} = .218 \qquad \hat{p}_2 = \frac{x_2}{n_2} = \frac{5,313}{23,199} = .229$$

$$\hat{p} = \frac{x_1 + x_2}{n_1 + n_2} = \frac{4,684 + 5,313}{21,484 + 23,199} = \frac{9,997}{44,683} = .224 \qquad \hat{q} = 1 - \hat{p} = 1 - .224 = .776$$

To determine if there is a difference in the proportions of 9th grade boys who gambled weekly or daily in the 2 years, we test:

$$H_0: p_1 - p_2 = 0$$
$$H_a: p_1 - p_2 \neq 0$$

The test statistic is $z = \dfrac{(\hat{p}_1 - \hat{p}_2) - 0}{\sqrt{\hat{p}\hat{q}\left(\dfrac{1}{n_1} + \dfrac{1}{n_2}\right)}} = \dfrac{(.218 - .229) - 0}{\sqrt{.224(.776)\left(\dfrac{1}{21,484} + \dfrac{1}{23,199}\right)}} = -2.79$

The rejection region requires $\alpha / 2 = .01 / 2 = .005$ in each tail of the z-distribution. From Table II, Appendix D, $z_{.005} = 2.58$. The rejection region is $z < -2.58$ or $z > 2.58$.

Since the observed value of the test statistic falls in the rejection region $(z = -2.79 < -2.58)$, H_0 is rejected. There is sufficient evidence to indicate a difference in the proportions of 9th grade boys who gambled weekly or daily in the 2 years at $\alpha = .01$.

b.   Yes. If samples sizes are large enough, differences can almost always be found. Suppose we compute a 99% confidence interval. For confidence coefficient .99, $\alpha = .01$ and $\alpha / 2 = .01 / 2 = .005$. From Table II, Appendix D, $z_{.005} = 2.58$. The 99% confidence interval is:

$$(\hat{p}_1 - \hat{p}_2) \pm z_{\alpha/2} \sqrt{\dfrac{\hat{p}_1\hat{q}_1}{n_1} + \dfrac{\hat{p}_2\hat{q}_2}{n_2}} \Rightarrow (.218 - .229) \pm 2.58\sqrt{\dfrac{.218(.782)}{21,484} + \dfrac{.229(.771)}{23,199}}$$

$$\Rightarrow -.011 \pm .010 \Rightarrow (-.021, \ -.001)$$

We are 99% confident that the difference in the proportions of 9th grade boys who gambled weekly or daily in the 2 years is between $-.021$ and $-.001$.

8.123   Let μ_1 = mean output for Design 1, μ_2 = mean output for Design 2, and $\mu_d = \mu_1 - \mu_2$. Some preliminary calculations are:

Working Days	Difference (Design 1 - Design 2)
8/16	−53
8/17	−271
8/18	−206
8/19	−266
8/20	−213
8/23	−183
8/24	−118
8/25	−87

$\bar{d} = \dfrac{\sum d}{n_d} = \dfrac{-1,397}{8} = -174.625$ $s_d^2 = \dfrac{\sum d^2 - \dfrac{\left(\sum d\right)^2}{n_d}}{n_d - 1} = \dfrac{289,793 - \dfrac{(-1,397)^2}{8}}{8 - 1} = 6,548.839$

$s_d = \sqrt{s_d^2} = \sqrt{6,548.839} = 80.925$

To determine if Design 2 is superior to Design 1, we test:

$H_0 : \mu_d = 0$

$H_a : \mu_d < 0$

The test statistic is $t = \dfrac{\bar{d} - \mu_o}{s_d / \sqrt{n_d}} = \dfrac{-174.625 - 0}{80.925 / \sqrt{8}} = -6.103$

Since no α value was given, we will use $\alpha = .05$. The rejection region requires $\alpha = .05$ in the lower tail of the t-distribution with $df = n_d - 1 = 8 - 1 = 7$. From Table III, Appendix D, $t_{.05} = 1.895$. The rejection region is $t < -1.895$.

Since the observed value of the test statistic falls in the rejection region $(t = -6.103 < -1.895)$, H_0 is rejected. There is sufficient evidence to indicate Design 2 is superior to Design 1 at $\alpha = .05$.

For confidence coefficient .95, $\alpha = .05$ and $\alpha / 2 = .05 / 2 = .025$. From Table III, Appendix D, with $df = n_d - 1 = 8 - 1 = 7$, $t_{.025} = 2.365$. A 95% confidence interval for μ_d is:

$$\bar{d} \pm t_{.025} \frac{s_d}{\sqrt{n_d}} \Rightarrow -174.625 \pm 2.365 \frac{80.925}{\sqrt{8}} \Rightarrow -174.625 \pm 67.666 \Rightarrow (-242.29, \ -106.96)$$

Since this interval does not contain 0, there is evidence to indicate Design 2 is superior to Design 1.

Chapter 9
Design of Experiments and
Analysis of Variance

9.1   Since only one factor is utilized, the treatments are the four levels (A, B, C, D) of the qualitative factor.

9.3   One has no control over the levels of the factors in an observational experiment. One does have control of the levels of the factors in a designed experiment.

9.5   a.   This is an observational experiment. The economist has no control over the factor levels or unemployment rates.

        b.   This is a designed experiment. The manager chooses only three different incentive programs to compare, and randomly assigns an incentive program to each of nine plants.

        c.   This is an observational experiment. Even though the marketer chooses the publication, he has no control over who responds to the ads.

        d.   This is an observational experiment. The load on the facility's generators is only observed, not controlled.

        e.   This is an observational experiment. One has no control over the distance of the haul, the goods hauled, or the price of diesel fuel.

9.7   a.   The experimental units are the firms with CPAs.

        b.   The response variable is the firm's likelihood of reporting sustainability policies.

        c.   There are two factors – firm size and firm type.

        d.   There are two levels of firm size – large and small. There are two levels of firm type – public and private.

        e.   The treatments are the combinations of the factor levels. There are $2 \times 2 = 4$ treatments – large/public, large/private, small/public, and small/private.

9.9   a.   The study is designed because the experimental units (study participants) were randomly assigned to the treatments (gift givers and gift receivers).

        b.   The experimental units are the study participants. The response variable is the level of appreciation measured on a scale from 1 to 7. There is one factor – role. There are two levels of role and thus, two treatments. The treatments are gift giver or gift receiver.

9.11   a.   There are 2 factors in this problem, each with 2 levels. Thus, there are a total of $2 \times 2 = 4$ treatments.

        b.   The 4 treatments are: (Within-store, home), (Within-store, in store), (Between-store, home), and (Between-store, in store).

9.13   a.   This is a designed experiment because the subjects are randomly assigned to groups and groups are randomly assigned to a decision rule.

b.   The experimental unit is a subject or person. The dependent variable is the number of words spoken by women on a certain topic per 1,000 total words spoken.

c.   There are 2 factors in this experiment – gender composition and decision rule. Gender composition has 6 levels: 0, 1, 2, 3, 4, or 5 women. Decision rule has 2 levels: unanimous or majority rule.

d.   There are a total of $6 \times 2 = 12$ treatments. They are: $(0, U)$, $(1, U)$, $(2, U)$, $(3, U)$, $(4, U)$, $(5, U)$, $(0, M)$, $(1, M)$, $(2, M)$, $(3, M)$, $(4, M)$, $(5, M)$.

9.15   a.   From Table VI with $\nu_1 = 4$ and $\nu_2 = 4$, $F_{.05} = 6.39$.

b.   From Table VIII with $\nu_1 = 4$ and $\nu_2 = 4$, $F_{.01} = 15.98$.

c.   From Table V with $\nu_1 = 30$ and $\nu_2 = 40$, $F_{.10} = 1.54$.

d.   From Table VII with $\nu_1 = 15$ and $\nu_2 = 12$, $F_{.025} = 3.18$.

9.17   a.   In the second dot diagram #2, the difference between the sample means is small relative to the variability within the sample observations. In the first dot diagram #1, the values in each of the samples are grouped together with a range of 4, while in the second diagram #2, the range of values is 8.

b.   For diagram #1,
$$\bar{x}_1 = \frac{\sum x_1}{n} = \frac{7+8+9+9+10+11}{6} = \frac{54}{6} = 9 \qquad \bar{x}_2 = \frac{\sum x_2}{n} = \frac{12+13+14+14+15+16}{6} = \frac{84}{6} = 14$$

For diagram #2,
$$\bar{x}_1 = \frac{\sum x_1}{n} = \frac{5+5+7+11+13+13}{6} = \frac{54}{6} = 9 \qquad \bar{x}_2 = \frac{\sum x_2}{n} = \frac{10+10+12+16+18+18}{6} = \frac{84}{6} = 14$$

c.   For diagram #1,
$$SST = \sum_{i=1}^{2} n_i (\bar{x}_i - \bar{x})^2 = 6(9-11.5)^2 + 6(14-11.5)^2 = 75 \qquad \left(\bar{x} = \frac{\sum x}{n} = \frac{54+84}{12} = 11.5 \right)$$

For diagram #2,
$$SST = \sum_{i=1}^{2} n_i (\bar{x}_i - \bar{x})^2 = 6(9 - 11.5)^2 + 6(14 - 11.5)^2 = 75$$

d.   For diagram #1,
$$s_1^2 = \frac{\sum x_1^2 - \frac{\left(\sum x_1 \right)^2}{n_1}}{n_1 - 1} = \frac{496 - \frac{54^2}{6}}{6-1} = 2 \qquad s_2^2 = \frac{\sum x_2^2 - \frac{\left(\sum x_2 \right)^2}{n_2}}{n_2 - 1} = \frac{1186 - \frac{84^2}{6}}{6-1} = 2$$

$$SSE = (n_1 - 1)s_1^2 + (n_2 - 1)s_2^2 = (6-1)2 + (6-1)2 = 20$$

For diagram #2,

$$s_1^2 = \frac{\sum x_1^2 - \frac{\left(\sum x_1\right)^2}{n_1}}{n_1 - 1} = \frac{558 - \frac{54^2}{6}}{6-1} = 14.4 \qquad s_2^2 = \frac{\sum x_2^2 - \frac{\left(\sum x_2\right)^2}{n_2}}{n_2 - 1} = \frac{1248 - \frac{84^2}{6}}{6-1} = 14.4$$

$$SSE = (n_1 - 1)s_1^2 + (n_2 - 1)s_2^2 = (6-1)14.4 + (6-1)14.4 = 144$$

e.   For diagram #1, $SS(\text{Total}) = SST + SSE = 75 + 20 = 95$

$$SST \text{ is } \frac{SST}{SS(\text{Total})} \times 100\% = \frac{75}{95} \times 100\% = 78.95\% \text{ of } SS(\text{Total})$$

For diagram #2, $SS(\text{Total}) = SST + SSE = 75 + 144 = 219$

$$SST \text{ is } \frac{SST}{SS(\text{Total})} \times 100\% = \frac{75}{219} \times 100\% = 34.25\% \text{ of } SS(\text{Total})$$

f.   For diagram #1, $MST = \frac{SST}{k-1} = \frac{75}{2-1} = 75$, $MSE = \frac{SSE}{n-k} = \frac{20}{12-2} = 2$, $F = \frac{MST}{MSE} = \frac{75}{2} = 37.5$

For diagram #2, $MST = \frac{SST}{k-1} = \frac{75}{2-1} = 75$, $MSE = \frac{SSE}{n-k} = \frac{144}{12-2} = 14.4$, $F = \frac{MST}{MSE} = \frac{75}{14.4} = 5.21$

g.   The rejection region for both diagrams requires $\alpha = .05$ in the upper tail of the F-distribution with $v_1 = k-1 = 2-1 = 1$ and $v_2 = n-k = 12-2 = 10$. From Table VI, Appendix D, $F_{.05} = 4.96$. The rejection region is $F > 4.96$.

For diagram #1, since the observed value of the test statistic falls in the rejection region $(F = 37.5 > 4.96)$, H_0 is rejected. There is sufficient evidence to indicate the samples were drawn from populations with different means at $\alpha = .05$.

For diagram #2, since the observed value of the test statistic falls in the rejection region $(F = 5.21 > 4.96)$, H_0 is rejected. There is sufficient evidence to indicate the samples were drawn from populations with different means at $\alpha = .05$.

h.   We must assume both populations are normally distributed with common variances.

9.19   Refer to Exercise 9.17, the ANOVA table is:

For diagram #1:

Source	df	SS	MS	F
Treatment	1	75	75	37.5
Error	10	20	2	
Total	11	95		

For diagram #2:

Source	df	SS	MS	F
Treatment	1	75	75	5.21
Error	10	144	14.4	
Total	11	219		

9.21   a.   Using MINITAB, the results are:

One-way ANOVA: T1, T2, T3
```
Source   DF     SS     MS     F     P
Factor    2  12.30   6.15  2.93  0.105
Error     9  18.89   2.10
Total    11  31.19

S = 1.449    R-Sq = 39.44%    R-Sq(adj) = 25.98%
```

b. $H_0 : \mu_1 = \mu_2 = \mu_3$
H_a : At least two treatment means differ

The test statistic is $F = 2.931$ and the p-value is $p = .105$.

Since the p-value is not less than $\alpha\left(p = .105 \not< .01\right)$, H_0 is not rejected. There is insufficient evidence to indicate a difference in the treatment means at $\alpha = .01$.

9.23   a.   There were 4 ANOVAs conducted. The response variable, treatments and hypotheses for each are:

1. Number of tweets for males; twitter skill level; $H_0 : \mu_1 = \mu_2 = \mu_3 = \mu_4 = \mu_5$ vs H_a : At least 1 μ_i differs .

2. Number of tweets for females; twitter skill level; $H_0 : \mu_1 = \mu_2 = \mu_3 = \mu_4 = \mu_5$ vs H_a : At least 1 μ_i differs .

3. Continue use for males; twitter skill level; $H_0 : \mu_1 = \mu_2 = \mu_3 = \mu_4 = \mu_5$ vs H_a : At least 1 μ_i differs .

4. Continue use for females; twitter skill level; $H_0 : \mu_1 = \mu_2 = \mu_3 = \mu_4 = \mu_5$ vs H_a : At least 1 μ_i differs .

b.   For male tweets, the p-value is $p = .331$. Since the p-value is not less than $\alpha\left(p = .331 \not< .05\right)$, H_0 is not rejected. There is insufficient evidence to indicate a difference in the mean number of tweets among the 5 levels of twitter skill at $\alpha = .05$.

For female tweets, the p-value is $p = .731$. Since the p-value is not less than $\alpha\left(p = .731 \not< .05\right)$, H_0 is not rejected. There is insufficient evidence to indicate a difference in the mean number of tweets among the 5 levels of twitter skill at $\alpha = .05$.

For male continuing usage, the p-value is $p = .062$. Since the p-value is not less than $\alpha\left(p = .062 \not< .05\right)$, H_0 is not rejected. There is insufficient evidence to indicate a difference in the mean continuing usage score among the 5 levels of twitter skill at $\alpha = .05$.

For female continuing usage, the p-value is $p = .006$. Since the p-value is less than $\alpha\left(p = .006 < .05\right)$, H_0 is rejected. There is sufficient evidence to indicate a difference in the mean continuing usage scores among the 5 levels of twitter skill at $\alpha = .05$.

9.25   a.   A completely randomized design was used for this study. The experimental units are the bus customers. The dependent variable is the performance score. There is one factor which is bus depot with 3 levels – Depot 1, Depot 2, and Depot 3. These factor levels are the treatments of the experiment.

b.   Yes. The *p*-value from the ANOVA *F*-test was $p = .0001$. For a 95% confidence level, $\alpha = .05$. Since the *p*-value is less than $\alpha \left(p = .0001 < .05 \right)$, H_0 is rejected. There is sufficient evidence to indicate the mean customer performance scores differed across the three bus depots at $\alpha = .05$.

9.27   a.   To determine if the mean LUST discount percentages across the seven states differ, we test:

$$H_0 : \mu_1 = \mu_2 = \cdots = \mu_7$$
$$H_a : \text{At least two treatment means differ}$$

b.   From the ANOVA table, the test statistic is $F = 1.60$ and the *p*-value is $p = 0.174$.

Since the observed *p*-value is not less than $\alpha \left(p = .174 \not< .10 \right)$, H_0 is not rejected. There is insufficient evidence to indicate a difference in the mean LUST discount percentages among the seven states at $\alpha = .10$.

9.29   a.   This was a completely randomized design.

b.   The experimental units are the college students. The dependent variable is the attitude toward tanning score and the treatments are the 3 conditions (view product advertisement with models with a tan, view product advertisement with models with no tan, and view product advertisement with no model).

c.   Let $\mu_1 = $ mean attitude score for those viewing product advertisement with models with a tan, $\mu_2 = $ mean attitude score for those viewing product advertisement with models without a tan, and $\mu_3 = $ mean attitude score for those viewing product advertisement with no models. To determine if the treatment mean scores differ among the three groups, we test:

$$H_0 : \mu_1 = \mu_2 = \mu_3$$

d.   These are just sample means. To determine if the population means differ, we have to determine how many standard deviations are between these sample means. In addition, the next time an experiment was conducted, the sample means could change.

e.   The hypotheses are:

$$H_0 : \mu_1 = \mu_2 = \mu_3$$
$$H_a : \text{At least two treatment means differ}$$

The test statistic is $F = 3.60$ and the *p*-value is $p = .03$. Since the *p*-value is less than $\alpha \left(p = .03 < .05 \right)$, H_0 is rejected. There is sufficient evidence to indicate a difference in the mean attitude scores among the three groups at $\alpha = .05$.

f.   We must assume that we have random samples from approximately normal populations with equal variances.

9.31   To determine if the mean recall percentages differ for student-drivers in the four groups, we test:

$H_0 : \mu_1 = \mu_2 = \mu_3 = \mu_4$
H_a : At least 1 μ_i differs

The test statistic is $F = 5.388$ and the p-value is $p = .004$.

Since the p-value is less than $\alpha \left(p < .004 < .01 \right)$, H_0 is rejected. There is sufficient evidence to indicate a difference in the mean recall percentages differ among the 4 groups at $\alpha = .01$.

9.33   To determine if the mean THICKNESS differs among the 4 types of housing, we test:

$H_0 : \mu_1 = \mu_2 = \mu_3 = \mu_4$
H_a : At least two treatment means differ

The test statistic is $F = 11.74$ and the p-value is $p = 0.000$. Since the observed p-value $\left(p = 0.000 \right)$ is less than any reasonable value of α, H_0 is rejected. There is sufficient evidence to indicate a difference in the mean thickness among the four levels of housing for any reasonable value of α.

To determine if the mean WHIPPING CAPACITY differs among the 4 types of housing, we test:

$H_0 : \mu_1 = \mu_2 = \mu_3 = \mu_4$
H_a : At least two treatment means differ

The test statistic is $F = 31.36$ and the p-value is $p = 0.000$. Since the observed p-value $\left(p = 0.000 \right)$ is less than any reasonable value of α, H_0 is rejected. There is sufficient evidence to indicate a difference in the mean whipping capacity among the four levels of housing for any reasonable value of α.

To determine if the mean STRENGTH differs among the 4 types of housing, we test:

$H_0 : \mu_1 = \mu_2 = \mu_3 = \mu_4$
H_a : At least two treatment means differ

The test statistic is $F = 1.70$ and the p-value is $p = 0.193$. Since the observed p-value $\left(p = 0.193 \right)$ is higher than any reasonable value of α, H_0 is not rejected. There is insufficient evidence to indicate a difference in the mean strength among the four levels of housing for any reasonable value of α.

Thus, the mean thickness and the mean percent overrun differ among the 4 housing systems.

9.35   The number of pairwise comparisons is equal to $k \left(k - 1 \right) / 2$.

a.   For $k = 3$, the number of comparisons is $3 \left(3 - 1 \right) / 2 = 3$.

b.   For $k = 5$, the number of comparisons is $5 \left(5 - 1 \right) / 2 = 10$.

c.   For $k = 4$, the number of comparisons is $4 \left(4 - 1 \right) / 2 = 6$.

d.   For $k = 10$, the number of comparisons is $10 \left(10 - 1 \right) / 2 = 45$.

9.37   A comparisonwise error rate is the error rate (or the probability of declaring the means different when, in fact, they are not different, which is also the probability of a Type I error) for each individual comparison. That is, if each comparison is run using $\alpha = .05$, then the comparisonwise error rate is .05.

9.39 $(\mu_1 - \mu_2)$: $(2,\ 15)$ Since all values in the interval are positive, μ_1 is significantly greater than μ_2.

$(\mu_1 - \mu_3)$: $(4,\ 7)$ Since all values in the interval are positive, μ_1 is significantly greater than μ_3.

$(\mu_1 - \mu_4)$: $(-10,\ 3)$ Since 0 is in the interval, μ_1 is not significantly different from μ_4.
 However, since the center of the interval is less than 0, μ_4 is larger than μ_1.

$(\mu_2 - \mu_3)$: $(-5,\ 11)$ Since 0 is in the interval, μ_2 is not significantly different from μ_3.
 However, since the center of the interval is greater than 0, μ_2 is larger than μ_3.

$(\mu_2 - \mu_4)$: $(-12,\ -6)$ Since all values in the interval are negative, μ_4 is significantly greater than μ_2.

$(\mu_3 - \mu_4)$: $(-8,\ -5)$ Since all values in the interval are negative, μ_4 is significantly greater than μ_3.

Thus, the largest mean is μ_4 followed by μ_1, μ_2, and μ_3.

9.41   Based on the results, there is no significant difference in the mean dot area between exposure times 8 and 14. Thus, exposure times 8 and 14 yield the highest mean dot area. The mean dot area for exposure time 12 is significantly less than that for any other exposure time.

9.43   Since all confidence intervals contain only positive values, this indicates that there is evidence that all population means are different. The largest mean is for Depot 1, then next highest is Depot 2, and the lowest is Depot 3.

9.45   a.   The treatments are the seven cheeses.

b.   The dependent variable is the color change index.

c.   Since the p-value is small $(p < .05)$, H_0 is rejected. There is sufficient evidence to indicate a difference in mean color change index among the seven cheeses for any value of $\alpha \geq .05$.

d.   There are a total of $\dfrac{k(k-1)}{2} = \dfrac{7(7-1)}{2} = 21$ pairwise-comparisons possible.

e.   Based on the results, the comparisons yield: $\mu_M > \mu_P > (\mu_G,\ \mu_{Ch}) > (\mu_{Em},\ \mu_{Ed}) > \mu_{Co}$.

9.47   The mean level of trust for the "no close" technique is significantly higher than that for "the visual close" and the "thermometer close" techniques. The mean level of trust for the "impending event" technique is significantly higher than that for the "thermometer close" technique. No other significant differences exist.

9.49   a.   The confidence interval for $(\mu_{CAGE} - \mu_{BARN})$ is $(-.1250,\ -.0323)$. Since 0 is not contained in this interval, there is sufficient evidence of a difference in the mean shell thickness between cage and barn egg housing systems. Since this interval is negative, this implies that the thickness is larger for the barn egg housing system.

b. The confidence interval for $(\mu_{CAGE} - \mu_{FREE})$ is $(-.1233, -.0307)$. Since 0 is not contained in this interval, there is sufficient evidence of a difference in the mean shell thickness between cage and free range egg housing systems. Since this interval is negative, this implies that the thickness is larger for the free range egg housing system.

c. The confidence interval for $(\mu_{CAGE} - \mu_{ORGANIC})$ is $(-.1050, -.0123)$. Since 0 is not contained in this interval, there is sufficient evidence of a difference in the mean shell thickness between cage and organic egg housing systems. Since this interval is negative, this implies that the thickness is larger for the organic egg housing system.

d. The confidence interval for $(\mu_{BARN} - \mu_{FREE})$ is $(-.0501, .0535)$. Since 0 is contained in this interval, there is insufficient evidence of a difference in the mean shell thickness between barn and free range egg housing systems. Since the center of the interval is greater than 0, the sample mean for barn is greater than that for free range.

e. The confidence interval for $(\mu_{BARN} - \mu_{ORGANIC})$ is $(-.0318, .0718)$. Since 0 is contained in this interval, there is insufficient evidence of a difference in the mean shell thickness between barn and organic egg housing systems. Since the center of the interval is greater than 0, the sample mean for barn is greater than that for organic.

f. The confidence interval for $(\mu_{FREE} - \mu_{ORGANIC})$ is $(-.0335, .0701)$. Since 0 is contained in this interval, there is insufficient evidence of a difference in the mean shell thickness between free range and organic egg housing systems. Since the center of the interval is greater than 0, the sample mean for free range is greater than that for organic.

g. We rank the housing system means as follows:

Housing System: Cage $<$ <u>Organic $<$ Free $<$ Barn</u>

We are 95% confident that the mean shell thickness for the cage housing system is significantly less than the mean thickness for the other three housing systems. There is no significant difference in the mean shell thicknesses among the barn, free range and organic housing systems.

9.51   a. $SSB = \sum_{i=1}^{b} \dfrac{B_i^2}{k} - CM$ where $CM = \dfrac{\left(\sum x_i\right)^2}{n} = \dfrac{49^2}{9} = 266.7778$

$SSB = \dfrac{17^2}{3} + \dfrac{15^2}{3} + \dfrac{17^2}{3} - 266.7778 = .8889$

$SSE = SS(Total) - SST - SSB = 30.2222 - 21.5555 - .8889 = 7.7778$

$MST = \dfrac{SST}{k-1} = \dfrac{21.5555}{2} = 10.7778$ $MSB = \dfrac{SSB}{b-1} = \dfrac{.8889}{2} = .4445$

$MSE = \dfrac{SSE}{n-k-b+1} = \dfrac{7.7778}{4} = 1.9445$

$F_T = \dfrac{MST}{MSE} = \dfrac{10.7778}{1.9445} = 5.54$ $F_B = \dfrac{MSB}{MSE} = \dfrac{.4445}{1.9445} = .23$

The ANOVA table is:

Source	df	SS	MS	F
Treatment	2	21.5555	10.7778	5.54
Block	2	.8889	.4445	.23
Error	4	7.7778	1.9445	
Total	8	30.2222		

b. $H_0 : \mu_1 = \mu_2 = \mu_3$

H_a : At least two treatment means differ

c. The test statistic is $F = \dfrac{MST}{MSE} = 5.54$

d. A Type I error would be concluding at least two treatment means differ when they do not.

A Type II error would be concluding all the treatment means are the same when at least two differ.

e. The rejection region requires $\alpha = .05$ in the upper tail of the F distribution with $v_1 = k - 1 = 3 - 1 = 2$ and $v_2 = n - k - b + 1 = 9 - 3 - 3 + 1 = 4$. From Table VI, Appendix D, $F_{.05} = 6.94$. The rejection region is $F > 6.94$.

Since the observed value of the test statistic does not fall in the rejection region $(F = 5.54 \not> 6.94)$, H_0 is not rejected. There is insufficient evidence to indicate at least two of the treatment means differ at $\alpha = .05$.

9.53 a. $SST = .2(500) = 100 \qquad SSB = .3(500) = 150$

$SSE = SS(Total) - SST - SSB = 500 - 100 - 150 = 250$

$$MST = \frac{SST}{k-1} = \frac{100}{4-1} = 33.3333 \qquad MSB = \frac{SSB}{b-1} = \frac{150}{9-1} = 18.75$$

$$MSE = \frac{SSE}{n-k-b+1} = \frac{250}{36-4-9+1} = \frac{250}{24} = 10.4167$$

$$F_T = \frac{MST}{MSE} = \frac{33.3333}{10.4167} = 3.20 \qquad F_B = \frac{MSB}{MSE} = \frac{18.75}{10.4167} = 1.80$$

To determine if differences exist among the treatment means, we test:

$H_0 : \mu_1 = \mu_2 = \mu_3 = \mu_4$

H_a : At least two treatment means differ

The test statistic is $F = 3.20$.

The rejection region requires $\alpha = .05$ in the upper tail of the F distribution with $v_1 = k - 1 = 4 - 1 = 3$ and $v_2 = n - k - b + 1 = 36 - 4 - 9 + 1 = 24$. From Table VI, Appendix D, $F_{.05} = 3.01$. The rejection region is $F > 3.01$.

Since the observed value of the test statistic falls in the rejection region $(F = 3.20 > 3.01)$, H_0 is rejected. There is sufficient evidence to indicate differences among the treatment means at $\alpha = .05$.

To determine if differences exist among the block means, we test:

$H_0 : \mu_1 = \mu_2 = \cdots = \mu_9$
H_a : At least two block means differ

The test statistic is $F = 1.80$.

The rejection region requires $\alpha = .05$ in the upper tail of the F distribution with $\nu_1 = b - 1 = 9 - 1 = 8$ and $\nu_2 = n - k - b + 1 = 36 - 4 - 9 + 1 = 24$. From Table VI, Appendix D, $F_{.05} = 2.36$. The rejection region is $F > 2.36$.

Since the observed value of the test statistic does not fall in the rejection region $(F = 1.80 \not> 2.36)$, H_0 is not rejected. There is insufficient evidence to indicate differences among the block means at $\alpha = .05$.

b. $SST = .5(500) = 250 \qquad SSB = .2(500) = 100$

$SSE = SS(Total) - SST - SSB = 500 - 250 - 100 = 150$

$MST = \dfrac{SST}{k-1} = \dfrac{250}{4-1} = 83.3333 \qquad MSB = \dfrac{SSB}{b-1} = \dfrac{100}{9-1} = 12.5$

$MSE = \dfrac{SSE}{n-k-b+1} = \dfrac{150}{36-4-9+1} = 6.25$

$F_T = \dfrac{MST}{MSE} = \dfrac{83.3333}{6.25} = 13.33 \qquad F_B = \dfrac{MSB}{MSE} = \dfrac{12.5}{6.25} = 2$

To determine if differences exist among the treatment means, we test:

$H_0 : \mu_1 = \mu_2 = \mu_3 = \mu_4$
H_a : At least two treatment means differ

The test statistic is $F = 13.33$.

The rejection region is $F > 3.01$ (same as above).

Since the observed value of the test statistic falls in the rejection region $(F = 13.33 > 3.01)$, H_0 is rejected. There is sufficient evidence to indicate differences exist among the treatment means at $\alpha = .05$.

To determine if differences exist among the block means, we test:

$H_0 : \mu_1 = \mu_2 = \cdots = \mu_9$
H_a : At least two block means differ

The test statistic is $F = 2.00$.

The rejection region is $F > 2.36$ (same as above).

Since the observed value of the test statistic does not fall in the rejection region $(F = 2.00 \not> 2.36)$, H_0 is not rejected. There is insufficient evidence to indicate differences exist among the block means at $\alpha = .05$.

c. $SST = .2(500) = 100$ $SSB = .5(500) = 250$

$SSE = SS(Total) - SST - SSB = 500 - 100 - 250 = 150$

$$MST = \frac{SST}{k-1} = \frac{100}{4-1} = 33.3333 \qquad MSB = \frac{SSB}{b-1} = \frac{250}{9-1} = 31.25$$

$$MSE = \frac{SSE}{n-k-b+1} = \frac{150}{36-4-9+1} = 6.25$$

$$F_T = \frac{MST}{MSE} = \frac{33.3333}{6.25} = 5.33 \qquad F_B = \frac{MSB}{MSE} = \frac{31.25}{6.25} = 5.00$$

To determine if differences exist among the treatment means, we test:

$H_0 : \mu_1 = \mu_2 = \mu_3 = \mu_4$
H_a : At least two treatment means differ

The test statistic is $F = 5.33$.

The rejection region is $F > 3.01$ (same as above).

Since the observed value of the test statistic falls in the rejection region $(F = 5.33 > 3.01)$, H_0 is rejected. There is sufficient evidence to indicate differences exist among the treatment means at $\alpha = .05$.
To determine if differences exist among the block means, we test:

$H_0 : \mu_1 = \mu_2 = \cdots = \mu_9$
H_a : At least two block means differ

The test statistic is $F = 5.00$.

The rejection region is $F > 2.36$ (same as above).

Since the observed value of the test statistic falls in the rejection region $(F = 5.00 > 2.36)$, H_0 is rejected. There is sufficient evidence to indicate differences exist among the block means at $\alpha = .05$.

d. $SST = .4(500) = 200$ $SSB = .4(500) = 200$

$SSE = SS(Total) - SST - SSB = 500 - 200 - 200 = 100$

$$MST = \frac{SST}{k-1} = \frac{200}{4-1} = 66.6667 \qquad MSB = \frac{SSB}{b-1} = \frac{200}{9-1} = 25$$

$$MSE = \frac{SSE}{n-k-b+1} = \frac{100}{36-4-9+1} = 4.1667$$

$$F_T = \frac{MST}{MSE} = \frac{66.6667}{4.1667} = 16.0 \qquad F_B = \frac{MSB}{MSE} = \frac{25}{4.1667} = 6.00$$

To determine if differences exist among the treatment means, we test:

$$H_0 : \mu_1 = \mu_2 = \mu_3 = \mu_4$$
H_a : At least two treatment means differ

The test statistic is $F = 16.0$.

The rejection region is $F > 3.01$ (same as above).

Since the observed value of the test statistic falls in the rejection region $(F = 16.0 > 3.01)$, H_0 is rejected. There is sufficient evidence to indicate differences among the treatment means at $\alpha = .05$.

To determine if differences exist among the block means, we test:

$$H_0 : \mu_1 = \mu_2 = \cdots = \mu_9$$
H_a : At least two block means differ

The test statistic is $F = 6.00$.

The rejection region is $F > 2.36$ (same as above).

Since the observed value of the test statistic falls in the rejection region $(F = 6.00 > 2.36)$, H_0 is rejected. There is sufficient evidence to indicate differences exist among the block means at $\alpha = .05$.

e. $\quad SST = .2(500) = 100 \qquad SSB = .2(500) = 100$

$SSE = SS(Total) - SST - SSB = 500 - 100 - 100 = 300$

$$MST = \frac{SST}{k-1} = \frac{100}{4-1} = 33.3333 \qquad MSB = \frac{SSB}{b-1} = \frac{100}{9-1} = 12.5$$

$$MSE = \frac{SSE}{n-k-b+1} = \frac{300}{36-4-9+1} = 12.5$$

$$F_T = \frac{MST}{MSE} = \frac{33.3333}{12.5} = 2.67 \qquad F_B = \frac{MSB}{MSE} = \frac{12.5}{12.5} = 1.00$$

To determine if differences exist among the treatment means, we test:

$$H_0 : \mu_1 = \mu_2 = \mu_3 = \mu_4$$
H_a : At least two treatment means differ

The test statistic is $F = 2.67$.

The rejection region is $F > 3.01$ (same as above).

Since the observed value of the test statistic does not fall in the rejection region $(F = 2.67 \not> 3.01)$, H_0 is not rejected. There is insufficient evidence to indicate differences exist among the treatment means at $\alpha = .05$.

To determine if differences exist among the block means, we test:

$$H_0 : \mu_1 = \mu_2 = \cdots = \mu_9$$
H_a : At least two block means differ

The test statistic is $F = 1.00$.

The rejection region is $F > 2.36$ (same as above).

Since the observed value of the test statistic does not fall in the rejection region $(F = 1.00 \not> 2.36)$, H_0 is not rejected. There is insufficient evidence to indicate differences among the block means at $\alpha = .05$.

9.55   a.   A randomized block design should be used to analyze the data because the same employees were measured at all three time periods. Thus, the blocks are the employees and the treatments are the three time periods.

       b.   There is still enough information in the table to make a conclusion because the *p*-values are given.

       c.   To determine if there are differences in the mean competence levels among the three time periods, we test:

$$H_0 : \mu_1 = \mu_2 = \mu_3$$
H_a : At least two treatment means differ

       d.   The *p*-value is $p = 0.001$. At a significance level > .001, we reject H_0. There is sufficient evidence to conclude that there is a difference in the mean competence levels among the three time periods for any value of $\alpha > .001$.

       e.   With 90% confidence, the mean competence before the training is significantly less than the mean competence 2-days after and 2-months after. There is no significant difference in the mean competence between 2-days after and 2-months after.

9.57   a.   The treatments were the 8 different activities.

       b.   The blocks were the 15 adults who participated in the study.

       c.   Since the *p*-value is less than $\alpha (p = .001 < .01)$, H_0 is rejected. There is sufficient evidence to indicate a difference in mean heart rate among the 8 activities at $\alpha = .01$.

       d.   The treadmill jogging had the highest mean heart rate. It was significantly greater than the mean heart rates of all the other activities. Brisk treadmill walking had the second highest mean heart rate. It was significantly less than the mean heart rate of treadmill jogging, but significantly greater than the mean heart rates of the other 6 activities. There was no significant difference in the mean heart rates among the treatments Wii aerobics, Wii muscle conditioning, Wii yoga, and Wii balance. The mean heart rates for these activities were significantly less than the mean heart rates for treadmill jogging and brisk treadmill walking, but greater than the mean heart rates of handheld gaming and rest. There was no significant difference in the mean heart rate between handheld gaming and rest. The mean heart rate for these two activities were significantly less than those for the other 6 activities.

9.59 a. To compare the mean item scores, we test:

$$H_0 : \mu_1 = \mu_2 = \cdots = \mu_5$$
$$H_a : \text{At least 2 of the treatment means differs}$$

b. Each of the 11 items was reviewed by each of the 5 systematic reviews. Since all reviews were made on each item, the observations are not independent. Thus, the randomized block ANOVA is appropriate.

c. The p-value for Review is $p = 0.319$. Since the p-value is not small, H_0 would not be rejected for any reasonable value of α. There is insufficient evidence to indicate a difference in the mean review scores among the 5 systematic reviews.

The p-value for Item is $p = 0.000$. Since the p-value is small, H_0 would be rejected for any reasonable value of α. There is sufficient evidence to indicate a difference in the mean scores among the 5 reviews.

d. None of the means are significantly different because all means are connected with the letter 'a'. This agrees with the conclusion drawn in part c about the treatment Review.

e. The experiment-wise error rate is .05. This means that the probability of declaring at least 2 means different when they are not different is .05.

9.61 Using SAS, the results are:

```
Dependent Variable: Y

                              Sum of
Source             DF         Squares     Mean Square   F Value    Pr > F

Model              11      5596.900000    508.809091     46.40     <.0001

Error              18       197.400000     10.966667

Corrected Total    29      5794.300000


          R-Square    Coeff Var    Root MSE     Y Mean

          0.965932    6.331923     3.311596    52.30000


Source             DF        Anova SS     Mean Square   F Value    Pr > F

SUBJECT             9      5486.300000    609.588889     55.59     <.0001
TRT                 2       110.600000     55.300000      5.04     0.0182

                     The ANOVA Procedure

           Tukey's Studentized Range (HSD) Test for Y

NOTE: This test controls the Type I experimentwise error rate, but it generally has a
      higher Type II error rate than REGWQ.


          Alpha                                  0.05
          Error Degrees of Freedom                 18
          Error Mean Square                   10.96667
          Critical Value of Studentized Range  3.60930
          Minimum Significant Difference        3.7797


     Means with the same letter are not significantly different.


          Tukey Grouping          Mean     N    TRT

                         A       54.600    10    High
                         A
                   B     A       52.400    10    Neutral
                   B
                   B             49.900    10    Low
```

To determine if there are differences in the mean ratings of the three candidates, we test:

$$H_0 : \mu_1 = \mu_2 = \mu_3$$
$$H_a : \text{At least 1 } \mu_i \text{ differs}$$

The test statistic is $F = 5.04$ and the p-value is $p = .0182$. Since the p-value is so small, H_0 is rejected. There is sufficient evidence to indicate there is a difference in the mean ratings among the three candidates.

Using Tukey's multiple comparison procedure, the mean rating for the high-performance morph candidate is significantly higher than the mean rating for the low-performance morph candidate. No other significant differences exist. The high-performance morph candidate and the neutral candidate received the highest mean rating.

9.63   Using MINITAB, the ANOVA table is:

Two-way ANOVA: Corrosion versus Time, System

```
Source  DF      SS       MS        F       P
Time     2   63.1050   31.5525   337.06  0.000
System   3    9.5833    3.1944    34.12  0.000
Error    6    0.5617    0.0936
Total   11   73.2500

S = 0.3060   R-Sq = 99.23%   R-Sq(adj) = 98.59%


                     Individual 95% CIs For Mean Based on
                     Pooled StDev
System    Mean    ------+---------+---------+---------+---
1        9.0667        (----*-----)
2        9.7333               (-----*----)
3       11.0667                             (----*-----)
4        8.7333    (----*-----)
                  ------+---------+---------+---------+---
                     8.80      9.60     10.40     11.20
```

To determine if there is a difference in mean corrosion rates among the 4 systems, we test:

$$H_0 : \mu_1 = \mu_2 = \mu_3 = \mu_4$$
$$H_a : \text{At least 2 of the treatment means differs}$$

The test statistic is $F = 34.12$ and the p-value is $p = .000$.

Since the p-value is so small, H_0 is rejected. There is sufficient evidence to indicate a difference in mean corrosion rates among the 4 systems at any reasonable value of α.

Using SAS, Tukey's multiple comparison results are:

```
          Tukey's Studentized Range (HSD) Test for CORROSION

NOTE: This test controls the Type I experimentwise error rate, but it generally has a higher Type
      II error rate than REGWQ.


                    Alpha                                0.05
                    Error Degrees of Freedom                6
                    Error Mean Square                0.093611
                    Critical Value of Studentized Range  4.89559
                    Minimum Significant Difference       0.8648

          Means with the same letter are not significantly different.
```

```
Tukey Grouping        Mean      N    SYSTEM

            A        11.0667    3     3

            B         9.7333    3     2
            B
       C    B         9.0667    3     1
       C
       C              8.7333    3     4
```

The mean corrosion rate for system 3 is significantly larger than all of the other mean corrosion rates. The mean corrosion rate of system 2 is significantly larger than the mean for system 4. If we want the system (epoxy coating) with the lowest corrosion rate, we would pick either system 1 or system 4. There is no significant difference between these two groups and they are in the lowest corrosion rate group.

9.65   a.   The ANOVA table is:

Source	df	SS	MS	F
A	2	.8	.4000	3.69
B	3	5.3	1.7667	16.31
AB	6	9.6	1.6000	14.77
Error	12	1.3	.1083	
Total	23	17.0		

df for A is $a-1=3-1=2$ df for B is $b-1=4-1=3$

df for AB is $(a-1)(b-1)=2(3)=6$ df for Error is $n-ab=24-3(4)=12$

df for Total is $n-1=24-1=23$

$$SSE = SS(Total) - SST - SSB = 17.0 - .8 - 5.3 - 9.6 = 1.3 \qquad MSA = \frac{SSA}{a-1} = \frac{.8}{3-1} = .40$$

$$MSB = \frac{SSB}{b-1} = \frac{5.3}{4-1} = 1.7667 \qquad MSAB = \frac{SSAB}{(a-1)(b-1)} = \frac{9.6}{(3-1)(4-1)} = 1.60$$

$$MSE = \frac{SSE}{n-ab} = \frac{1.3}{24-3(4)} = .1083 \qquad F_A = \frac{MSA}{MSE} = \frac{.4000}{.1083} = 3.69 \qquad F_B = \frac{MSB}{MSE} = \frac{1.7667}{.1083} = 16.31$$

$$F_{AB} = \frac{MSAB}{MSE} = \frac{1.6000}{.1083} = 14.77$$

b.   Sum of Squares for Treatment is $MST = SSA + SSB + SSAB = .8 = 5.3 + 2.6 = 15.7$

$$MST = \frac{SST}{ab-1} = \frac{15.7}{3(4)-1} = 1.4273 \qquad F_T = \frac{MST}{MSE} = \frac{1.4273}{.1083} = 13.18$$

To determine if the treatment means differ, we test:

$H_0 : \mu_1 = \mu_2 = \cdots = \mu_{12}$
$H_a :$ At least 2 of the treatment means differs

The test statistic is $F = 13.18$.

The rejection region requires $\alpha = .05$ in the upper tail of the F-distribution with $v_1 = ab - 1 = 3(4) - 1 = 11$ and $v_2 = n - ab = 24 - 3(4) = 12$. From Table VI, Appendix D, $F_{.05} \approx 2.75$. The rejection region is $F > 2.75$.

Since the observed value of the test statistic falls in the rejection region $(F = 13.18 > 2.75)$, H_0 is rejected. There is sufficient evidence to indicate the treatment means differ at $\alpha = .05$.

b. Yes. We need to partition the Treatment Sum of Squares into the Main Effects and Interaction Sum of Squares. Then we test whether factors A and B interact. Depending on the conclusion of the test for interaction, we either test for main effects or compare the treatment means.

d. Two factors are said to interact if the effect of one factor on the dependent variable is not the same at different levels of the second factor. If the factors interact, then tests for main effects are not necessary. We need to compare the treatment means for one factor at each level of the second.

e. To determine if the factors interact, we test:

H_0: Factors A and B do not interact to affect the response mean
H_a: Factors A and B do interact to affect the response mean

The test statistic is $F = \dfrac{MSAB}{MSE} = 14.77$

The rejection region requires $\alpha = .05$ in the upper tail of the F-distribution with $v_1 = (a-1)(b-1) = (3-1)(4-1) = 6$ and $v_2 = n - ab = 24 - 3(4) = 12$. From Table VI, Appendix D, $F_{.05} = 3.00$. The rejection region is $F > 3.00$.

Since the observed value of the test statistic falls in the rejection region $(F = 14.77 > 3.00)$, H_0 is rejected. There is sufficient evidence to indicate the two factors interact to affect the response mean at $\alpha = .05$.

f. No. Testing for main effects is not warranted because interaction is present. Instead, we compare the treatment means of one factor at each level of the second factor.

9.67 a. The treatments are the combinations of the levels of factor A and the levels of factor B. There are $2 \times 3 = 6$ treatments. The treatment means are:

$$\bar{x}_{11} = \frac{\sum x_{11}}{2} = \frac{3.1 + 4.0}{2} = 3.55 \quad \bar{x}_{12} = \frac{\sum x_{12}}{2} = \frac{4.6 + 4.2}{2} = 4.4 \quad \bar{x}_{13} = \frac{\sum x_{13}}{2} = \frac{6.4 + 7.1}{2} = 6.75$$

$$\bar{x}_{21} = \frac{\sum x_{21}}{2} = \frac{5.9 + 5.3}{2} = 5.6 \quad \bar{x}_{22} = \frac{\sum x_{22}}{2} = \frac{2.9 + 2.2}{2} = 2.55 \quad \bar{x}_{23} = \frac{\sum x_{23}}{2} = \frac{3.3 + 2.5}{2} = 2.9$$

Using MNIITAB, the graph is:

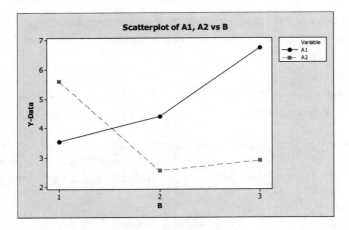

The treatment means appear to be different because the sample means are quite different. The factors appear to interact because the lines are not parallel.

b. $SST = SSA + SSB + SSAB = 4.4408 + 4.1267 + 18.0667 = 26.5742$

$$MST = \frac{SST}{ab-1} = \frac{26.5742}{2(3)-1} = 5.315 \qquad F_T = \frac{MST}{MSE} = \frac{5.315}{.246} = 21.62$$

To determine whether the treatment means differ, we test:

$H_0: \mu_1 = \mu_2 = \cdots = \mu_6$

$H_a:$ At least two treatment means differs

The test statistic is $F = \dfrac{MST}{MSE} = 21.62$

The rejection region requires $\alpha = .05$ in the upper tail of the F-distribution with $v_1 = ab-1 = 2(3)-1 = 5$ and $v_2 = n - ab = 12 - 2(3) = 6$. From Table VI, Appendix D, $F_{.05} = 4.39$. The rejection region is $F > 4.39$.

Since the observed value of the test statistic falls in the rejection region $(F = 21.62 > 4.39)$, H_0 is rejected. There is sufficient evidence to indicate that the treatment means differ at $\alpha = .05$. This supports the plot in **a**.

c.   Yes. Since there are differences among the treatment means, we test for interaction. To determine whether the factors A and B interact, we test:

$H_0:$ Factors A and B do not interact to affect the mean response

$H_a:$ Factors A and B do interact to affect the mean response

The test statistic is $F = \dfrac{MSAB}{MSE} = \dfrac{9.0033}{.24583} = 36.62$

The rejection region requires $\alpha = .05$ in the upper tail of the F-distribution with

$v_1 = (a-1)(b-1) = (2-1)(3-1) = 2$ and $v_2 = n-ab = 12-2(3) = 6$. From Table VI, Appendix D, $F_{.05} = 5.14$. The rejection region is $F > 5.14$.

Since the observed value of the test statistic falls in the rejection region $(F = 36.62 > 5.14)$, H_0 is rejected. There is sufficient evidence to indicate that factors A and B interact to affect the response mean at $\alpha = .05$.

    d.   No. Because interaction is present, the tests for main effects are not warranted.

    e.   The results of the tests in parts **b** and **c** support the visual interpretation in part **a**.

9.69   a. $SSA = .2(1000) = 200$, $SSB = .1(1000) = 100$, $SSAB = .1(1000) = 100$

$$SSE = SS(Total) - SSA - SSB - SSAB = 1000 - 200 - 100 - 100 = 600$$

$$SST = SSA + SSB + SSAB = 200 + 100 + 100 = 400 \qquad MSA = \frac{SSA}{a-1} = \frac{200}{3-1} = 100$$

$$MSB = \frac{SSB}{b-1} = \frac{100}{3-1} = 50 \qquad MSAB = \frac{SSAB}{(a-1)(b-1)} = \frac{100}{(3-1)(3-1)} = 25$$

$$MSE = \frac{SSE}{n-ab} = \frac{600}{27-3(3)} = 33.333 \qquad MST = \frac{SST}{ab-1} = \frac{400}{3(3)-1} = 50$$

$$F_A = \frac{MSA}{MSE} = \frac{100}{33.333} = 3.00 \qquad F_B = \frac{MSB}{MSE} = \frac{50}{33.333} = 1.50$$

$$F_{AB} = \frac{MSAB}{MSE} = \frac{25}{33.333} = .75 \qquad F_T = \frac{MST}{MSE} = \frac{50}{33.333} = 1.50$$

Source	df	SS	MS	F
A	2	200	100	3.00
B	2	100	50	1.50
AB	4	100	25	.75
Error	18	600	33.333	
Total	26	1000		

To determine whether the treatment means differ, we test:

$H_0 : \mu_1 = \mu_2 = \cdots = \mu_9$

H_a : At least two treatment means differs

The test statistic is $F = \dfrac{MST}{MSE} = 1.50$

Suppose $\alpha = .05$. The rejection region requires $\alpha = .05$ in the upper tail of the F-distribution with $v_1 = ab-1 = 3(3)-1 = 8$ and $v_2 = n-ab = 27-3(3) = 18$. From Table VI, Appendix D, $F_{.05} = 2.51$. The rejection region is $F > 2.51$.

Since the observed value of the test statistic does not fall in the rejection region $(F = 1.50 \not> 2.51)$, H_0 is not rejected. There is insufficient evidence to indicate the treatment means differ at $\alpha = .05$. Since there are no treatment mean differences, we have nothing more to do.

b. $SSA = .1(1000) = 100$, $SSB = .1(1000) = 100$, $SSAB = .5(1000) = 500$

$SSE = SS(Total) - SSA - SSB - SSAB = 1000 - 100 - 100 - 500 = 300$

$SST = SSA + SSB + SSAB = 100 + 100 + 500 = 700$ $MSA = \dfrac{SSA}{a-1} = \dfrac{100}{3-1} = 50$

$MSB = \dfrac{SSB}{b-1} = \dfrac{100}{3-1} = 50$ $MSAB = \dfrac{SSAB}{(a-1)(b-1)} = \dfrac{500}{(3-1)(3-1)} = 125$

$MSE = \dfrac{SSE}{n-ab} = \dfrac{300}{27-3(3)} = 16.667$ $MST = \dfrac{SST}{ab-1} = \dfrac{700}{9-1} = 87.5$

$F_A = \dfrac{MSA}{MSE} = \dfrac{50}{16.667} = 3.00$ $F_B = \dfrac{MSB}{MSE} = \dfrac{50}{16.667} = 3.00$

$F_{AB} = \dfrac{MSAB}{MSE} = \dfrac{125}{16.667} = 7.50$ $F_T = \dfrac{MST}{MSE} = \dfrac{87.5}{16.667} = 5.25$

Source	df	SS	MS	F
A	2	100	50	3.00
B	2	100	50	3.00
AB	4	500	125	7.50
Error	18	300	16.667	
Total	26	1000		

To determine if the treatment means differ, we test:

$H_0 : \mu_1 = \mu_2 = \cdots = \mu_9$
H_a : At least two treatment means differs

The test statistic is $F = \dfrac{MST}{MSE} = 5.25$

The rejection region requires $\alpha = .05$ in the upper tail of the F-distribution with $v_1 = ab - 1 = 3(3) - 1 = 8$ and $v_2 = n - ab = 27 - 3(3) = 18$. From Table VI, Appendix D, $F_{.05} = 2.51$. The rejection region is $F > 2.51$.

Since the observed value of the test statistic falls in the rejection region $(F = 5.25 > 2.51)$, H_0 is rejected. There is sufficient evidence to indicate the treatment means differ at $\alpha = .05$.

Since the treatment means differ, we next test for interaction between factors A and B. To determine if factors A and B interact, we test:

H_0: Factors A and B do not interact to affect the mean response
H_a: Factors A and B do interact to affect the mean response

The test statistic is $F = \dfrac{MS\,AB}{MSE} = 7.50$

The rejection region requires $\alpha = .05$ in the upper tail of the F-distribution with $v_1 = (a-1)(b-1) = (3-1)(3-1) = 4$ and $v_2 = n - ab = 27 - 3(3) = 18$. From Table VI, Appendix D, $F_{.05} = 2.93$. The rejection region is $F > 2.93$.

Since the observed value of the test statistic falls in the rejection region $(F = 7.50 > 2.93)$, H_0 is rejected. There is sufficient evidence to indicate the factors A and B interact at $\alpha = .05$. Since interaction is present, no tests for main effects are necessary.

c. $SSA = .4(1000) = 400$, $\quad SSB = .1(1000) = 100$, $\quad SSAB = .2(1000) = 200$

$SSE = SS(Total) - SSA - SSB - SSAB = 1000 - 400 - 100 - 200 = 300$

$SST = SSA + SSB + SSAB = 400 + 100 + 200 = 700 \qquad MSA = \dfrac{SSA}{a-1} = \dfrac{400}{3-1} = 50$

$MSB = \dfrac{SSB}{b-1} = \dfrac{100}{3-1} = 50 \qquad MSAB = \dfrac{MSAB}{(a-1)(b-1)} = \dfrac{200}{(3-1)(3-1)} = 50$

$MSE = \dfrac{SSE}{n-ab} = \dfrac{300}{27-3(3)} = 16.667 \qquad MST = \dfrac{SST}{ab-1} = \dfrac{700}{3(3)-1} = 87.5$

$F_A = \dfrac{MSA}{MSE} = \dfrac{200}{16.667} = 12.00 \qquad F_B = \dfrac{MSB}{MSE} = \dfrac{50}{16.667} = 3.00$

$F_{AB} = \dfrac{MSAB}{MSE} = \dfrac{50}{16.667} = 3.00 \qquad F_T = \dfrac{MST}{MSE} = \dfrac{87.5}{16.667} = 5.25$

Source	df	SS	MS	F
A	2	400	200	12.00
B	2	100	50	3.00
AB	4	200	50	3.00
Error	18	300	16.667	
Total	26	1000		

To determine if the treatment means differ, we test:

$H_0 : \mu_1 = \mu_2 = \cdots = \mu_9$
H_a : At least two treatment means differs

The test statistic is $F = \dfrac{MST}{MSE} = 5.25$

The rejection region requires $\alpha = .05$ in the upper tail of the F-distribution with $v_1 = ab - 1 = 3(3) - 1 = 8$ and $v_2 = n - ab = 27 - 3(3) = 18$. From Table VI, Appendix D, $F_{.05} = 2.51$. The rejection region is $F > 2.51$.

Since the observed value of the test statistic falls in the rejection region $(F = 5.25 > 2.51)$, H_0 is rejected. There is sufficient evidence to indicate the treatment means differ at $\alpha = .05$.

Since the treatment means differ, we next test for interaction between factors A and B. To determine if factors A and B interact, we test:

H_0: Factors A and B do not interact to affect the mean response
H_a: Factors A and B do interact to affect the mean response

The test statistic is $F = \dfrac{MS\,AB}{MSE} = 3.00$

The rejection region requires $\alpha = .05$ in the upper tail of the F-distribution with $v_1 = (a-1)(b-1) = (3-1)(3-1) = 4$ and $v_2 = n - ab = 27 - 3(3) = 18$. From Table VI, Appendix D, $F_{.05} = 2.93$. The rejection region is $F > 2.93$.

Since the observed value of the test statistic falls in the rejection region $(F = 3.00 > 2.93)$, H_0 is rejected. There is sufficient evidence to indicate the factors A and B interact at $\alpha = .05$. Since interaction is present, no tests for main effects are necessary.

d. $SSA = .4(1000) = 400$, $\quad SSB = .4(1000) = 400$, $\quad SSAB = .1(1000) = 100$

$SSE = SS(Total) - SSA - SSB - SSAB = 1000 - 400 - 400 - 100 = 100$

$SST = SSA + SSB + SSAB = 400 + 400 + 100 = 900$ $\qquad MSA = \dfrac{SSA}{a-1} = \dfrac{400}{3-1} = 200$

$MSB = \dfrac{SSB}{b-1} = \dfrac{400}{3-1} = 200$ $\qquad MSAB = \dfrac{SSAB}{(a-1)(b-1)} = \dfrac{100}{(3-1)(3-1)} = 25$

$MSE = \dfrac{SSE}{n-ab} = \dfrac{100}{27-3(3)} = 5.556$ $\qquad MST = \dfrac{SST}{ab-1} = \dfrac{900}{3(3)-1} = 112.5$

$F_A = \dfrac{MSA}{MSE} = \dfrac{200}{5.556} = 36.00$ $\qquad F_B = \dfrac{MSB}{MSE} = \dfrac{200}{5.556} = 36.00$

$F_{AB} = \dfrac{MSAB}{MSE} = \dfrac{25}{5.556} = 4.50$ $\qquad F_T = \dfrac{MST}{MSE} = \dfrac{112.5}{5.556} = 20.25$

Source	df	SS	MS	F
A	2	400	200	36.00
B	2	400	200	36.00
AB	4	100	25	4.50
Error	18	100	5.556	
Total	26	1000		

To determine if the treatment means differ, we test:

$H_0: \mu_1 = \mu_2 = \cdots = \mu_9$
H_a : At least two treatment means differs

The test statistic is $F = \dfrac{MST}{MSE} = 20.25$

The rejection region requires $\alpha = .05$ in the upper tail of the F-distribution with $v_1 = ab - 1 = 3(3) - 1 = 8$ and $v_2 = n - ab = 27 - 3(3) = 18$. From Table VI, Appendix D, $F_{.05} = 2.51$. The rejection region is $F > 2.51$.

Since the observed value of the test statistic falls in the rejection region $(F = 20.25 > 2.51)$, H_0 is rejected. There is sufficient evidence to indicate the treatment means differ at $\alpha = .05$.

Since the treatment means differ, we next test for interaction between factors A and B. To determine if factors A and B interact, we test:

H_0: Factors A and B do not interact to affect the mean response
H_a: Factors A and B do interact to affect the mean response

The test statistic is $F = \dfrac{MSAB}{MSE} = 4.50$

The rejection region requires $\alpha = .05$ in the upper tail of the F-distribution with $v_1 = (a-1)(b-1) = (3-1)(3-1) = 4$ and $v_2 = n - ab = 27 - 3(3) = 18$. From Table VI, Appendix D, $F_{.05} = 2.93$. The rejection region is $F > 2.93$.

Since the observed value of the test statistic falls in the rejection region $(F = 4.50 > 2.93)$, H_0 is rejected. There is sufficient evidence to indicate the factors A and B interact at $\alpha = .05$. Since interaction is present, no tests for main effects are necessary.

9.71   a.   There are 4 treatments for this experiment: (Male, STEM), (Male, non-STEM), (Female, STEM), (Female, non-STEM).

b.   If gender and discipline interact, then the effect of discipline on the mean satisfaction depends on gender.

c.   Yes. Because the lines are not parallel, this indicates that interaction exists.

d.   The ANOVA table would be:

Source	df
Gender	1
Discipline	1
G × D	1
Error	211
Total	214

e.   The test statistic is $F = 4.10$ and the p-value is $p = .04$. Since the p-value is so small, H_0 is rejected. There is sufficient evidence to indicate that gender and discipline interact to affect the mean satisfaction score for $\alpha > .04$.

9.73   a.   The two factors are type of statement and order of information. There are $2 \times 2 = 4$ treatments: concrete/statement first, concrete/behavior first, abstract/statement first, and abstract/behavior first.

b.   This indicates that the effect of type of statement on the level of hypocrisy depends on the order of the information.

c.   Using MINITAB, a plot of the means is:

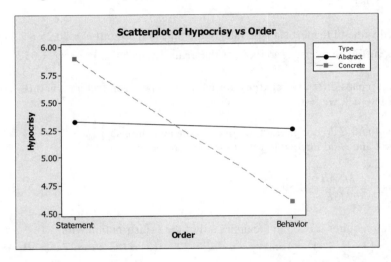

d.   Since the interaction between the type of statement and the order of information was significant, then the tests for main effects should not be performed. Multiple comparisons on some or all of the pairs of treatments should be performed next.

9.75   a. $df_{\text{Order}} = a - 1 = 2 - 1 = 1$, $df_{\text{Menu}} = b - 1 = 2 - 1 = 1$, $df_{\text{OxM}} = (a - 1)(b - 1) = (2 - 1)(2 - 1) = 1$,

$df_{\text{Error}} = n - ab = 180 - 2(2) = 176$

Source	df	F-value	p-value
Order	1	---	---
Menu	1	---	---
Order x Menu	1	11.25	<.001
Error	176		
Total	179		

b. Since the *p*-value is less than $\alpha\left(p < 0.001 < .05\right)$, H_0 is rejected. There is sufficient evidence to indicate order and menu interact to affect the amount willing to pay at $\alpha = .05$.

c. No, these results are not required to complete the analysis. Since the test for interaction was significant, there is no need to run the main effect tests.

d.

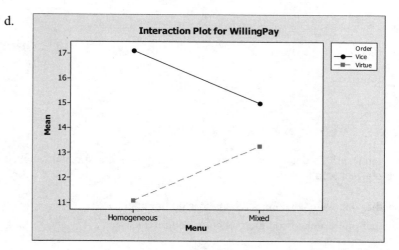

9.77 a. The treatments are the 4 combinations of size and distortion: (cut, extra-large), (no cut, extra-large), (cut, half-size), (not cut, half-size).

b. To determine if paper size and paper distortion interact, we test:

H_0: Paper size and paper distortion do not interact to affect attitude
H_a: Paper size and paper distortion interact to affect attitude

The test statistic is $F = 7.52$ and the *p*-value is $p < .010$. Since the *p*-value is so small, H_0 is rejected. There is sufficient evidence to indicate that paper size and paper distortion interact to affect attitude for $\alpha > .01$.

c. No. Because the interaction is significant, the test for main effects should not be conducted.

d. The mean attitude score for (cut, half-size) is significantly greater than the means for any of the other 3 treatments. No other differences exist.

9.79 Using MINITAB, a complete factorial design was fit to the data:

General Linear Model: RECALL versus CONTENT, BEFORE

```
Factor    Type    Levels  Values
CONTENT   fixed        3  NEUTRAL, SEX, VIOLENT
BEFORE    fixed        2  NO, YES

Analysis of Variance for RECALL, using Adjusted SS for Tests
```

Source	DF	Seq SS	Adj SS	Adj MS	F	P
CONTENT	2	123.265	120.004	60.002	20.01	0.000
BEFORE	1	6.458	6.393	6.393	2.13	0.145
CONTENT*BEFORE	2	7.472	7.472	3.736	1.25	0.289
Error	318	953.421	953.421	2.998		
Total	323	1090.617				

```
S = 1.73153    R-Sq = 12.58%    R-Sq(adj) = 11.21%

Grouping Information Using Tukey Method and 95.0% Confidence

CONTENT    N    Mean   Grouping
NEUTRAL   108   3.167   A
VIOLENT   108   2.090       B
SEX       108   1.731       B

Means that do not share a letter are significantly different.

Grouping Information Using Tukey Method and 95.0% Confidence

BEFORE    N    Mean   Grouping
NO       162   2.470   A
YES      162   2.188   A

Means that do not share a letter are significantly different.
```

First, we test for the interaction term. To determine if content group and whether one had watched the commercial before interact to affect recall, we test:

H_0 : Content and whether one watched commercial before do not interact

H_a : Content and whether one watched commercial before do interact

The test statistic is $F = 1.25$ and the p-value is $p = .289$. Since the p-value is not small, H_0 is not rejected. There is no evidence to indicate content and whether the commercial was viewed before interact to affect recall for any reasonable value of α.

Next, we test for the main effects.

To determine if the mean recall differs among the content groups, we test:

H_0 : $\mu_1 = \mu_2 = \mu_3$

H_a : At least two means differ

The test statistic is $F = 20.01$ and the p-value is $p = .000$. Since the p-value is very small, H_0 is rejected. There is evidence to indicate the mean recall differs among the different content groups for any reasonable value of α.

Tukey's multiple comparison on the content means yielded the following. The mean recall for those in the neutral content group was significantly higher than the mean recall of the other 2 groups. No other differences existed.

To determine if the mean recall differs between whether one watched the ad before or not, we test:

H_0 : $\mu_1 = \mu_2$

H_a : $\mu_1 \neq \mu_2$

The test statistic is $F = 2.13$ and the p-value is $p = .145$. Since the p-value is not small, H_0 is not rejected. There is no evidence to indicate the mean recall differs between whether one watched the ad before or not for any reasonable value of α.

These results agree with the researchers' conclusions.

9.81   a.   Low Load, Ambiguous: $\text{Total}_1 = n_1\bar{x}_1 = 25(18) = 450$

High Load, Ambiguous: $\text{Total}_2 = n_2\bar{x}_2 = 25(6.1) = 152.5$

Low Load, Common: $\text{Total}_3 = n_3\bar{x}_3 = 25(7.8) = 195$

High Load, Common: $\text{Total}_4 = n_4\bar{x}_4 = 25(6.3) = 157.5$

b. $CM = \dfrac{(\text{sum of all observations})^2}{n} = \dfrac{(450+152.5+195+157.5)^2}{100} = \dfrac{955^2}{100} = 9{,}120.25$

c.   Low Load total is $450+195 = 645$. High Load total is $152.5+157.5 = 310$.

$$SS(Load) = \frac{\sum_{i=1}^{a} A_i^2}{br} - CM = \frac{645^2}{2(25)} + \frac{310^2}{2(25)} - 9{,}120.25 = 10{,}242.5 - 9{,}120.25 = 1{,}122.25$$

Ambiguous total is $450+152.5 = 602.5$. Common total is $195+157.5 = 352.5$

$$SS(\text{Name}) = \frac{\sum_{j=1}^{b} B_j^2}{ar} - CM = \frac{602.5^2}{2(25)} + \frac{352.5^2}{2(25)} - 7{,}700.0625 = 9{,}745.25 - 9{,}120.25 = 625$$

$$SS(\text{Load} \times \text{Name}) = \frac{\sum_{i=1}^{a}\sum_{j=1}^{b} AB_{ij}^2}{r} - SS(\text{Load}) - SS(\text{Name}) - CM$$

$$= \frac{450^2}{25} + \frac{152.5^2}{25} + \frac{195^2}{25} + \frac{157.5^2}{25} - 1{,}122.25 - 625 - 9{,}120.25$$

$$= 11{,}543.5 - 1{,}122.25 - 625 - 9{,}120.25 = 676$$

d.   Low Load, Ambiguous: $s_1^2 = 15^2 = 225$ $(n_1-1)s_1^2 = (25-1)225 = 5{,}400$

High Load, Ambiguous: $s_2^2 = 9.5^2 = 90.25$ $(n_2-1)s_2^2 = (25-1)90.25 = 2{,}166$

Low Load, Common: $s_3^2 = 9.5^2 = 90.25$ $(n_3-1)s_3^2 = (25-1)90.25 = 2{,}166$

High Load, Common: $s_4^2 = 10^2 = 100$ $(n_4-1)s_4^2 = (25-1)100 = 2{,}400$

e. $SSE = (n_1-1)s_1^2 + (n_2-1)s_2^2 + (n_3-1)s_3^2 + (n_4-1)s_4^2 = 5{,}400 + 2{,}166 + 2{,}166 + 2{,}400 = 12{,}132$

f. $SS(\text{Total}) = SS(\text{Load}) + SS(\text{Name}) + SS(\text{Load x Name}) + SSE$

$$= 1{,}122.25 + 625 + 676 + 12{,}132 = 14{,}555.25$$

g.   The ANOVA table is:

Source	df	SS	MS	F
Load	1	1,122.25	1,122.25	8.88
Name	1	625.00	625.00	4.95
Load x Name	1	676.00	676.00	5.35
Error	96	12,132.00	126.375	
Total	99	14,555.25		

h.   Yes. We computed 5.35, which is almost the same as 5.34. The difference could be due to round-off error.

i.   To determine if interaction between Load and Name is present, we test:

H_0: Load and Name do not interact
H_a: Load and Name class do interact

The test statistic is $F = 5.35$.

The rejection region requires $\alpha = .05$ in the upper tail of the F-distribution with $\nu_1 = (a-1)(b-1) = (2-1)(2-1) = 1$ and $\nu_2 = n - ab = 100 - 2(2) = 96$. From Table VI, Appendix D, $F_{.05} \approx 3.96$. The rejection region is $F > 3.96$.

Since the observed value of the test statistic falls in the rejection region $(F = 5.35 > 3.96)$, H_0 is rejected. There is sufficient evidence to indicate that Load and Name interact at $\alpha = .05$.

Using MINITAB, a graph of the results is:

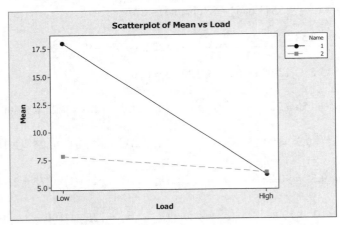

From the graph, the interaction is quite apparent. For Low load, the mean number of jelly beans taken for the ambiguous name is much higher than the mean number taken for the common name. However, for High load, there is essentially no difference in the mean number of jelly beans taken between the two names.

j.   We must assume that:
1.   The response distributions for each Load-Name combination (treatment) is normal.

2.   The response variance is constant for all Load-Name combinations.

3.   Random and independent samples of experimental units are associated with each Load-Name combination.

9.83   In a completely randomized design, independent random selection of treatments to be assigned to experimental units is required. In a randomized block design, the experimental units are first grouped into blocks such that within the blocks the experimental units are homogeneous and between the blocks the experimental units are heterogeneous. Once the experimental units are grouped into blocks, the treatments are randomly assigned to the experimental units within each block so that each treatment appears one time in each block.

9.85   When the overall level of significance of a multiple comparisons procedure is α, the level of significance for each comparison is less than α. This is because the comparisons within the experiment are not independent of each other.

9.87   a. $SST = SS\left(\text{Total}\right) - SS\left(\text{Block}\right) - SSE = 22.31 - 10.688 - .288 = 11.334$

$$MST = \frac{SST}{k-1} = \frac{11.334}{4-1} = 3.778, \quad df = k-1 = 4-1 = 3$$

$$MS\left(\text{Block}\right) = \frac{SS\left(\text{Block}\right)}{b-1} = \frac{10.688}{5-1} = 2.672, \quad df = b-1 = 5-1 = 4$$

$$MSE = \frac{SSE}{n-k-b+1} = \frac{.288}{20-4-5+1} = .024, \quad df = n-k-b+1 = 20-4-5+1 = 12$$

$$F_T = \frac{MST}{MSE} = \frac{3.778}{.024} = 157.42 \qquad F_B = \frac{MS\left(\text{Block}\right)}{MSE} = \frac{2.672}{.024} = 111.33$$

The ANOVA Table is:

Source	df	SS	MS	F
Treatment	3	11.334	3.778	157.42
Block	4	10.688	2.672	111.33
Error	12	0.288	0.024	
Total	19	22.310		

b.   To determine if there are differences among the treatment means, we test:

$H_0 : \mu_A = \mu_B = \mu_C = \mu_D$
$H_a :$ At least two treatment means differ

The test statistic is $F = \dfrac{MST}{MSE} = 157.42$

The rejection region requires $\alpha = .05$ in the upper tail of the F-distribution with $v_1 = k-1 = 4-1 = 3$ and $v_2 = n-k-b+1 = 20-4-5+1 = 12$. From Table VI, Appendix D, $F_{.05} = 3.49$. The rejection region is $F > 3.49$.

Since the observed value of the test statistic falls in the rejection region $\left(F = 157.42 > 3.49\right)$, H_0 is rejected. There is sufficient evidence to indicate differences among the treatment means at $\alpha = .05$.

c.   Since there is evidence of differences among the treatment means, we need to compare the treatment means. The number of pairwise comparisons is $\dfrac{k(k-1)}{2} = \dfrac{4(4-1)}{2} = 6$.

d.   To determine if there are differences among the block means, we test:

H_0: All block means are the same
H_a: At least two block means differ

The test statistic is $F = \dfrac{MS(\text{Block})}{MSE} = 111.33$

The rejection region requires $\alpha = .05$ in the upper tail of the F distribution with $v_1 = b-1 = 5-1 = 4$ and $v_2 = n-k-b+1 = 20-4-5+1 = 12$. From Table VI, Appendix D, $F_{.05} = 3.26$. The rejection region is $F > 3.26$.

Since the observed value of the test statistic falls in the rejection region $(F = 111.33 > 3.26)$, H_0 is rejected. There is sufficient evidence that the block means differ at $\alpha = .05$.

9.89   a.   A completely randomized design was used.

b.   There are 4 treatments: 3 robots/colony, 6 robots/colony, 9 robots/colony, and 12 robots/colony.

c.   To determine if there were differences in the mean energy expended (per robot) among the 4 colony sizes, we test:

$H_0 : \mu_1 = \mu_2 = \mu_3 = \mu_4$
$H_a :$ At least two means differ

d.   Since the p-value is less than $\alpha\,(p < .001 < .05)$, H_0 is rejected. There is sufficient evidence to indicate differences in mean energy expended per robot among the 4 colony sizes at $\alpha = .05$.

e.   The total number of comparisons conducted is $c = \dfrac{k(k-1)}{2} = \dfrac{4(4-1)}{2} = 6$.

f.   The mean energy expended by robots in the 12 robot colony is significantly smaller than the mean energy expended by robots in any of the other size colonies. There are no differences in the mean energy expended by robots in the 3 robot colony, the 6 robot colony, and the 9 robot colony.

9.91   a.   This is a complete 2×2 factorial design. The 2 factors are Color and Question. There are two levels of color – Blue and Red. There are two levels of question – difficult and simple. The 4 treatments are: blue/difficult, blue/simple, red/difficult, red/simple.

b.   Since the p-value is so small $(p < .03)$, H_0 is rejected. There is a significant interaction between color and question. The effect of color on the mean score is different at each level of question.

c. Using MINITAB, the graph is:

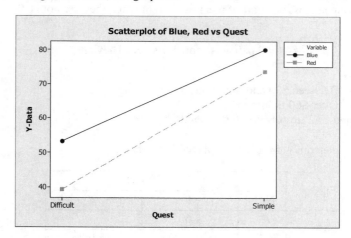

Since the lines are not parallel, it indicates that there is significant interaction between color and question.

9.93 a. Tukey's multiple comparison method is preferred over other methods because it controls experimental error at the chosen α level. It is more powerful than the other methods.

b. From the confidence interval comparing large-cap and medium-cap mutual funds, we find that 0 is in the interval. Thus, 0 is not an unusual value for the difference in the mean rates of return between large-cap and medium-cap mutual funds. This means we would not reject H_0. There is insufficient evidence of a difference in mean rates of return between large-cap and medium-cap mutual funds at $\alpha = .05$.

c. From the confidence interval comparing large-cap and small-cap mutual funds, we find that 0 is not in the interval. Thus, 0 is an unusual value for the difference in the mean rates of return between large-cap and small-cap mutual funds. This means we would reject H_0. There is sufficient evidence of a difference in mean rates of return between large-cap and small-cap mutual funds at $\alpha = .05$.

d. From the confidence interval comparing medium-cap and small-cap mutual funds, we find that 0 is in the interval. Thus, 0 is not an unusual value for the difference in the mean rates of return between medium-cap and small-cap mutual funds. This means we would not reject H_0. There is insufficient evidence of a difference in mean rates of return between medium-cap and small-cap mutual funds at $\alpha = .05$.

e. From the above, the mean rate of return for large-cap mutual funds is the largest, followed by medium-cap, followed by small-cap mutual funds. The mean rate of return for large-cap funds is significantly larger than that for small-cap funds. No other differences exist.

f. We are 95% confident of this decision.

9.95 a. To determine if the mean road rage score differs for the three income groups, we test:

$H_0 : \mu_1 = \mu_2 = \mu_3$
H_a : At least two treatment means differ

The test statistic is $F = 3.90$ and the p-value is $p < .01$. Since the p-value is less than $\alpha = .05$, H_0 is rejected. There is sufficient evidence to indicate the mean road rage score differs for the three income groups for $\alpha > .01$. Since the sample means increase as the income increases, it appears that road rage increases as income increases.

b. The probability of declaring at least one pair of means different when they are not is .01.

c. There are a total of $\dfrac{k(k-1)}{2} = \dfrac{3(3-1)}{2} = 3$ pair-wise comparisons. They are:

'Under $30 thousand' to 'Between $30 and $60 thousand'
'Under $30 thousand' to 'Over $60 thousand'
'Between $30 and $60 thousand' to 'Over $60 thousand'

d. Means for groups in homogeneous subsets are displayed in the table:

Income Group	N	Subsets	
		1	2
Under $30,000	379	4.60	
$30,000-$60,000	392		5.08
Over $60,000	267		5.15

e. Two of the comparisons in part **c** will yield confidence intervals that do not contain 0. They are:

'Under $30 thousand' to 'Between $30 and $60 thousand'
'Under $30 thousand' to 'Over $60 thousand'

9.97   a.   There are a total of $2 \times 4 = 8$ treatments.

b.   The interaction between temperature and type was significant. This means that the effect of type of yeast on the mean autolysis yield depends on the level of temperature.

c.   To determine if the main effect of type of yeast is significant, we test:

$H_0 : \mu_{Ba} = \mu_{Br}$
$H_a : \mu_{Ba} \neq \mu_{Br}$

To determine if the main effect of temperature is significant, we test:

$H_0 : \mu_1 = \mu_2 = \mu_3 = \mu_4$
$H_a :$ At least two treatment means differs

d.   The tests for the main effects should not be run since the test for interaction was significant. If interaction is significant, then these interaction effects could cover up the main effects. Thus, the main effect tests would not be informative.

e.   **Baker's yeast**:
The mean yield for temperature $54°$ is significantly lower than the mean yields for the other 3 temperatures. There is no difference in the mean yields for the temperatures $45°$, $48°$ and $51°$.

Brewer's yeast:
The mean yield for temperature $54°$ is significantly lower than the mean yields for the other 3 temperatures. There is no difference in the mean yields for the temperatures $45°$, $48°$ and $51°$.

9.99   a.   There is one factor in this problem which is Group. There are 5 treatments in this problem, corresponding to the 5 levels of Group: Casualties, Survivors, Implementers/casualties,

Implementers/survivors, and Formulators. The response variable is the ethics score. The experimental units are the employees enrolled in an Executive MBA program.

b.   To determine if there are any differences among the mean ethics scores for the five groups, we test:

$H_0 : \mu_1 = \mu_2 = \mu_3 = \mu_4 = \mu_5$
H_a : At least two means differ

c.   The test statistic is $F = 9.85$ and the p-value is $p = .000$. Since the p-value (0.000) is less than any reasonable significance level α, H_0 is rejected. There is sufficient evidence to indicate a difference in the mean ethics scores among the five groups of employees for any reasonable value of α.

d.   We will check the assumptions of normality and equal variances. Using MINITAB, the histograms are:

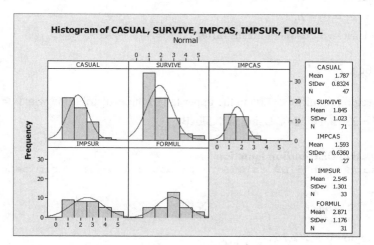

The data for some of the 5 groups do not look particularly mound-shaped, so the assumption of normality is probably not valid.
Using MINITAB, the boxplots are:

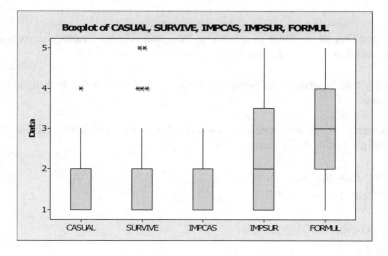

The spreads of responses do not appear to be about the same. The groups Implementers/survivors and Formulators have more variability than the other three groups. Thus, the assumption of constant variance is probably not valid.
The assumptions required for the ANOVA F-test do not appear to be reasonably satisfied.

e. The Bonferroni method is preferred over other multiple comparisons methods because it does not require equal sample sizes. The five groups of employees do not have the same sample sizes. In addition, it is more powerful than Scheffe's method.

f. The number of pairwise comparisons for this analysis is $c = \dfrac{k(k-1)}{2} = \dfrac{5(5-1)}{2} = \dfrac{20}{2} = 10$.

g. The mean ethics scores for both Groups 4 and 5 are significantly higher than the mean ethics scores for Groups 1, 2, and 3. There is no difference in the mean ethics scores between Group 4 and Group 5. There is no difference in the mean ethics scores among Groups 1, 2 and 3.

9.101   a. To determine if the mean level of trust differs among the six treatments, we test:

$H_0 : \mu_1 = \mu_2 = \cdots = \mu_6$
$H_a :$ At least two treatment means differ

b. The test statistic is $F = 2.21$.

The rejection region requires $\alpha = .05$ in the upper tail of the F-distribution with $\nu_1 = k - 1 = 6 - 1 = 5$ and $\nu_2 = n - k = 230 - 6 = 224$. Using MINITAB,

Inverse Cumulative Distribution Function
```
F distribution with 5 DF in numerator and 231 DF in denominator

P( X <= x )           x
       0.95    2.25436
```

The rejection region is $F > 2.25$.

Since the observed value of the test statistic does not fall in the rejection region $(F = 2.21 \ngtr 2.25)$, H_0 is not rejected. There is insufficient evidence to indicate that at least two mean trusts differ at $\alpha = .05$.

c. We must assume that all six samples are drawn from normal populations, the six population variances are the same, and that the samples are independent.

d. I would classify this experiment as designed. Each subject was randomly assigned to receive one of the six scenarios.

9.103   a. We will select size as the quantitative variable and color as the qualitative variable. To determine if the mean size of diamonds differ among the 6 colors, we test:

$H_0 : \mu_1 = \mu_2 = \mu_3 = \mu_4 = \mu_5 = \mu_6$
$H_a :$ At least two means differ

b. Using MINITAB, the ANOVA table is:

One-way ANOVA: Carats versus Color
```
Analysis of Variance for Carats
Source     DF        SS        MS         F         P
Color       5     0.7963    0.1593      2.11     0.064
Error     302    22.7907    0.0755
Total     307    23.5869
```
```
                                  Individual 95% CIs For Mean
                                  Based on Pooled StDev
Level      N      Mean     StDev  ----------+---------+---------+------
D         16    0.6381    0.3195  (-------------*------------)
E         44    0.6232    0.2677     (-------*-------)
F         82    0.5929    0.2648   (-----*-----)
G         65    0.5808    0.2792  (------*------)
H         61    0.6734    0.2643           (------*------)
I         40    0.7310    0.2918              (-------*--------)
                                  ----------+---------+---------+------
Pooled StDev =    0.2747                   0.60      0.70      0.80
```
The test statistic is $F = 2.11$ and the p-value is $p = .064$.

Since the p-value is less than α $(p = .064 < .10)$, H_0 is rejected. There is sufficient evidence to indicate the mean sizes of diamonds differ among the 6 colors at $\alpha = .10$.

b.   We will check the assumptions of normality and equal variances. Using MINITAB, the histograms are:

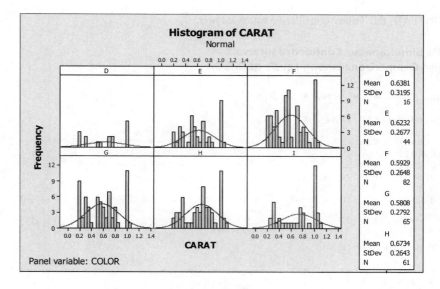

The data for the 6 colors do not look particularly mound-shaped, so the assumption of normality is probably not valid. However, departures from this assumption often do not invalidate the ANOVA results.

Using MINITAB, the box plots are:

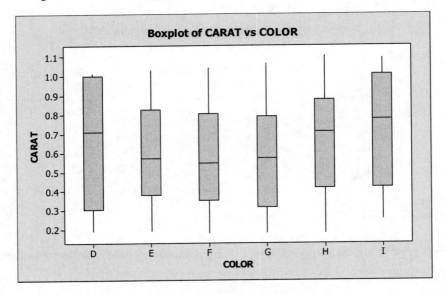

The spreads of all the colors appear to be about the same, so the assumption of constant variance is probably valid.

d.   Using MINITAB, the Tukey confidence intervals are:

Tukey 95% Simultaneous Confidence Intervals
All Pairwise Comparisons among Levels of COLOR

```
Individual confidence level = 99.53%

COLOR = D subtracted from:

COLOR    Lower    Center    Upper    ---------+---------+---------+---------+
E      -0.2435   -0.0149   0.2136        (-------------*-------------)
F      -0.2591   -0.0452   0.1688      (------------*-------------)
G      -0.2758   -0.0574   0.1611     (------------*-------------)
H      -0.1846    0.0353   0.2552         (-------------*-------------)
I      -0.1387    0.0929   0.3244            (--------------*-------------)
                                       ---------+---------+---------+---------+
                                          -0.16      0.00      0.16      0.32


COLOR = E subtracted from:

COLOR    Lower    Center    Upper    ---------+---------+---------+---------+
F      -0.1765   -0.0303   0.1160         (--------*--------)
G      -0.1952   -0.0424   0.1104        (--------*---------)
H      -0.1046    0.0503   0.2051            (---------*---------)
I      -0.0632    0.1078   0.2788               (----------*---------)
                                       ---------+---------+---------+---------+
                                          -0.16      0.00      0.16      0.32


COLOR = F subtracted from:

COLOR    Lower    Center    Upper    ---------+---------+---------+---------+
G      -0.1422   -0.0122   0.1178        (-------*-------)
H      -0.0518    0.0805   0.2129           (-------*-------)
I      -0.0129    0.1381   0.2890              (---------*-------)
                                       ---------+---------+---------+---------+
                                          -0.16      0.00      0.16      0.32
```

```
COLOR = G subtracted from:

COLOR    Lower   Center   Upper   ---------+---------+---------+---------+
H       -0.0469  0.0927  0.2322                   (--------*--------)
I       -0.0071  0.1502  0.3075                       (--------*---------)
                                   ---------+---------+---------+---------+
                                        -0.16     0.00      0.16      0.32

COLOR = H subtracted from:

COLOR    Lower   Center   Upper   ---------+---------+---------+---------+
I       -0.1017  0.0576  0.2168                   (---------*---------)
                                   ---------+---------+---------+---------+
                                        -0.16     0.00      0.16      0.32
```

All of the confidence intervals contain 0. Thus, at 95% confidence, there is no evidence that the mean sizes of the diamonds are different among the different colors. This disagrees with the test of hypothesis because the test was run using $\alpha = .10$.

9.105   a.   The treatments are the $3 \times 3 = 9$ combinations of PES and Trust. The nine treatments are: (BC, Low), (PC, Low), (NA, Low), (BC, Med), (PC, Med), (NA, Med), (BC, High), (PC, High), and (NA, High).

   b. $df(\text{Trust}) = b - 1 = 3 - 1 = 2$;

$$SSE = SS(\text{Total}) - SS(\text{PES}) - SS(\text{Trust}) - SS(P \times T) = 301.55 - 4.35 - 15.20 - 3.50 = 278.50$$

$$MS(\text{PES}) = \frac{SS(\text{PES})}{df(\text{PES})} = \frac{4.35}{2} = 2.175 \qquad MS(\text{Trust}) = \frac{SS(\text{Trust})}{df(\text{Trust})} = \frac{15.20}{2} = 7.600$$

$$MS(\text{PT}) = \frac{SS(\text{PT})}{df(\text{PT})} = \frac{3.50}{4} = .875 \qquad MSE = \frac{SSE}{df(\text{Error})} = \frac{278.50}{191} = 1.458$$

$$F_{PES} = \frac{MS(\text{PES})}{MSE} = \frac{2.175}{1.458} = 1.49 \qquad F_{Trust} = \frac{MS(\text{Trust})}{MSE} = \frac{7.600}{1.458} = 5.21$$

$$F_{P \times T} = \frac{MS(P \times T)}{MSE} = \frac{.875}{1.458} = .600$$

The ANOVA table is:

Source	df	SS	MS	F
PES	2	4.35	2.175	1.49
Trust	2	15.20	7.600	5.21
PES × Trust	4	3.50	.875	0.60
Error	191	278.50	1.458	
Total	199	301.55		

   c.   To determine if PES and Trust interact, we test:

   H_0: PES and Trust do not interact to affect the mean tension
   H_a: PES and Trust do interact to affect the mean tension

The test statistic is $F = 0.60$.

The rejection region requires $\alpha = .05$ in the upper tail of the F-distribution with $v_1 = (a-1)(b-1) = (3-1)(3-1) = 4$ and $v_2 = n - ab = 215 - 3(3) = 191$. From Table VI, Appendix D, $F_{.05} \approx 2.37$. The rejection region is $F > 2.37$.

Since the observed value of the test statistic does not fall in the rejection region $(F = 0.60 \ngtr 2.37)$, H_0 is not rejected. There is insufficient evidence to indicate that PES and Trust interact at $\alpha = .05$.

d.   The plot of the treatment means is:

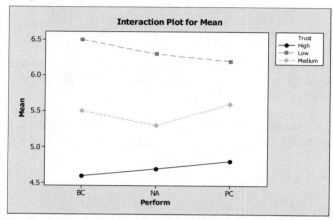

The three lines corresponding to the Trust levels are almost parallel. This indicates that PES and Trust do not interact. This agrees with the result in part **c**.

e.   Since the interaction is not significant, the tests for the main effects should be run.

9.107   a.   This is a 2×2 factorial experiment.

b.   The two factors are the tent type (treated or untreated) and location (inside or outside). There are $2 \times 2 = 4$ treatments. The four treatments are (treated, inside), (treated, outside), (untreated, inside), and (untreated, outside).

c.   The response variable is the number of mosquito bites received in a 20 minute interval.

d.   There is sufficient evidence to indicate interaction is present. This indicates that the effect of the tent type on the number of mosquito bites depends on whether the person is inside or outside.

9.109   a.   Using MINITAB, the results are:

Two-Sample T-Test and CI: PAH2, Site
```
Two-sample T for PAH2

Site          N    Mean    StDev   SE Mean
Development   7   1.0743   0.0565   0.021
IndustryA     8   0.9981   0.0464   0.016


Difference = μ (Development) - μ (IndustryA)
Estimate for difference:  0.0762
95% CI for difference:  (0.0169, 0.1355)
T-Test of difference = 0 (vs ≠): T-Value = 2.83   P-Value = 0.016   DF = 11
```

To determine if the mean PAH2 ratio at the development site is different than the corresponding mean at Industry A, a two-sample t-test yields a test statistic of $t = 2.83$ and a p-value of $p = .016$. This indicates that the mean PAH2 ratio at the development site is significantly different than the corresponding mean at Industry A.

Two-Sample T-Test and CI: PAH2, Site
```
Two-sample T for PAH2

Site           N    Mean    StDev   SE Mean
Development     7   1.0743   0.0565    0.021
IndustryB       5   1.0980   0.0669    0.030


Difference = μ (Development) - μ (IndustryB)
Estimate for difference:   -0.0237
95% CI for difference:   (-0.1106, 0.0632)
T-Test of difference = 0 (vs ≠): T-Value = -0.65   P-Value = 0.539   DF = 7
```

To determine if the mean PAH2 ratio at the development site is different than the corresponding mean at Industry B, a two-sample t-test yields a test statistic of $t = -.65$ and a p-value of $p = .539$. This indicates that the mean PAH2 ratio at the development site is not significantly different than the corresponding mean at Industry B.

b. Since so many t-tests were performed that are not independent of each other, the overall significance level is inflated. The probability of declaring two means different when in fact they are not different is much higher than the value of α used for each individual test.

c. A more efficient analysis would be to run an analysis of variance, comparing all treatments at the same time.

Using MINITAB for PAH1, the results are:

One-way ANOVA: PAH1 versus Site
```
Null hypothesis          All means are equal
Alternative hypothesis   At least one mean is different
Significance level       α = 0.05

Equal variances were assumed for the analysis.

Factor Information

Factor   Levels  Values
Site          4  Development, IndustryA, IndustryB, IndustryC


Analysis of Variance

Source  DF   Adj SS    Adj MS  F-Value  P-Value
Site     3  0.02041  0.006802     2.61    0.083
Error   18  0.04697  0.002610
Total   21  0.06738


Model Summary

        S    R-sq  R-sq(adj)  R-sq(pred)
0.0510835  30.29%     18.67%       0.00%
```

To determine if there is a difference in mean PAH1 among the 4 locations, we test:

$H_0 : \mu_1 = \mu_2 = \mu_3 = \mu_4$

H_a : At least two treatment means differ

The test statistic is $F = 2.61$ and the p-value is $p = .083$. Since the p-value is not small, H_0 is not rejected. There is insufficient evidence to indicate there is a difference in mean PAH1 among the 4 locations for any $\alpha < .083$.

Using MINITAB for PAH1, the results are:

One-way ANOVA: PAH2 versus Site
```
Null hypothesis         All means are equal
Alternative hypothesis  At least one mean is different
Significance level      α = 0.05

Equal variances were assumed for the analysis.

Factor Information

Factor   Levels  Values
Site         4   Development, IndustryA, IndustryB, IndustryC

Analysis of Variance

Source  DF   Adj SS    Adj MS   F-Value  P-Value
Site     3  0.03977  0.013255     4.45    0.017
Error   18  0.05366  0.002981
Total   21  0.09343

Model Summary

        S    R-sq  R-sq(adj)  R-sq(pred)
0.0546000  42.56%     32.99%      14.59%
```

Tukey Pairwise Comparisons
```
Grouping Information Using the Tukey Method and 95% Confidence

Site          N    Mean  Grouping
IndustryB     5  1.0980  A
IndustryC     2  1.0875  A B
Development   7  1.0743  A B
IndustryA     8  0.9981    B

Means that do not share a letter are significantly different.
```

To determine if there is a difference in mean PAH2 among the 4 locations, we test:

$H_0 : \mu_1 = \mu_2 = \mu_3 = \mu_4$

H_a : At least two treatment means differ

The test statistic is $F = 4.45$ and the p-value is $p = .017$. Since the p-value is small, H_0 is rejected. There is sufficient evidence to indicate there is a difference in mean PAH2 among the 4 locations for any $\alpha > .017$.

The mean PAH2 for Industry A is significantly greater than the mean PAH2 for Industry A. No other significant differences exist.

Chapter 10
Categorical Data Analysis

10.1   a.   The rejection region requires $\alpha = .05$ in the upper tail of the χ^2 distribution with $df = k - 1 = 3 - 1 = 2$. From Table IV, Appendix D, $\chi^2_{.05} = 5.99147$. The rejection region is $\chi^2 > 5.99147$.

   b.   The rejection region requires $\alpha = .10$ in the upper tail of the χ^2 distribution with $df = k - 1 = 5 - 1 = 4$. From Table IV, Appendix D, $\chi^2_{.10} = 7.77944$. The rejection region is $\chi^2 > 7.77944$.

   c.   The rejection region requires $\alpha = .01$ in the upper tail of the χ^2 distribution with $df = k - 1 = 4 - 1 = 3$. From Table IV, Appendix D, $\chi^2_{.01} = 11.3449$. The rejection region is $\chi^2 > 11.3449$.

10.3   The sample size n will be large enough so that, for every cell, the expected cell count, E_i, will be equal to 5 or more.

10.5   Some preliminary calculations are:

If the probabilities are the same, $p_{1,0} = p_{2,0} = p_{3,0} = p_{4,0} = .25$

$E_1 = np_{1,0} = 205(.25) = 51.25 = E_2 = E_3 = E_4$

   a.   To determine if the multinomial probabilities differ, we test:

$H_0 : p_1 = p_2 = p_3 = p_4 = .25$
$H_a :$ At lease one of the probabilities differs from .25

The test statistic is

$$\chi^2 = \sum \frac{[n_i - E_i]^2}{E_i} = \frac{(43 - 51.25)^2}{51.25} + \frac{(56 - 51.25)^2}{51.25} + \frac{(59 - 51.25)^2}{51.25} + \frac{(47 - 51.25)^2}{51.25} = 3.293$$

The rejection region requires $\alpha = .05$ in the upper tail of the χ^2 distribution with $df = k - 1 = 4 - 1 = 3$. From Table IV, Appendix D, $\chi^2_{.05} = 7.81473$. The rejection region is $\chi^2 > 7.81473$.

Since the observed value of the test statistic does not fall in the rejection region $\left(\chi^2 = 3.293 \ngtr 7.81473 \right)$, H_0 is not rejected. There is insufficient evidence to indicate the multinomial probabilities differ at $\alpha = .05$.

   b.   The Type I error is concluding the multinomial probabilities differ when, in fact, they do not.

The Type II error is concluding the multinomial probabilities are equal, when, in fact, they are not.

c.   For confidence coefficient .95, $\alpha = .05$ and $\alpha / 2 = .05 / 2 = .025$. From Table II, Appendix D, $z_{.025} = 1.96$.

$$\hat{p}_3 = 59 / 205 = .288$$

The confidence interval is:

$$\hat{p}_3 \pm z_{.025} \sqrt{\frac{\hat{p}\hat{q}}{n}} \Rightarrow .288 \pm 1.96 \sqrt{\frac{.288(.712)}{205}} \Rightarrow .288 \pm .062 \Rightarrow (.226, \ .350)$$

10.7   a.   The data are categorical because they are measured using categories, not meaningful numbers. The possible categories are legs only, wheels only, both legs and wheels, and neither legs nor wheels.

b.   Let p_1 = proportion of social robots with legs only, p_2 = proportion of social robots with wheels only, p_3 = proportion of social robots with both legs and wheels, and p_4 = proportion of social robots with neither legs nor wheels. To determine if the design engineer's claim is incorrect, we test:

$H_0 : p_1 = .50, \ p_2 = .30, \ p_3 = .10,$ and $p_4 = .10$
$H_a :$ At least one of the probabilities differs from the hypothesized value

c.   If the claim is true, $E_1 = np_{1,0} = 106(.50) = 53$, $E_2 = np_{2,0} = 106(.30) = 31.8$, $E_3 = np_{3,0} = 106(.10) = 10.6$, and $E_4 = np_{4,0} = 106(.10) = 10.6$.

d.   The test statistic is $\chi^2 = \sum \frac{[n_i - E_i]^2}{E_i} = \frac{(63 - 53)^2}{53} + \frac{(20 - 31.8)^2}{31.8} + \frac{(8 - 10.6)^2}{10.6} + \frac{(15 - 10.6)^2}{10.6} = 8.730$

e.   The rejection region requires $\alpha = .05$ in the upper tail of the χ^2 distribution with $df = k - 1 = 4 - 1 = 3$. From Table IV, Appendix D, $\chi_{.05}^2 = 7.81473$. The rejection region is $\chi^2 > 7.81473$.

Since the observed value of the test statistic falls in the rejection region $\left(\chi^2 = 8.730 > 7.81473 \right)$, H_0 is rejected. There is sufficient evidence to indicate that at least one of the probabilities differs from its hypothesized value at. $\alpha = .05$.

10.9   a.   Let p_1 = proportion using total visitors, p_2 = proportion using paying visitors, p_3 = proportion using big shows, p_4 = proportion using funds raised, and p_5 = proportion using members.

To determine if one performance measure is used more often than any of the others, we test:

$H_0 : p_1 = p_2 = p_3 = p_4 = p_5 = .20$
$H_a :$ At least one of the probabilities differs from the hypothesized value

From the printout, the test statistic is $\chi^2 = 1.66667$ and the p-value is $p = 0.797$.

Since the p-value is not less than $\alpha \left(p = .797 \nless .10 \right)$, H_0 is not rejected. There is insufficient evidence to indicate that one performance measure is used more often than any of the others at $\alpha = .10$.

b. For confidence coefficient .90, $\alpha = .10$ and $\alpha / 2 = .10 / 2 = .05$. From Table II, Appendix D, $z_{.05} = 1.645$.

$\hat{p}_1 = 8 / 30 = .267$

The confidence interval is:

$$\hat{p}_1 \pm z_{.05} \sqrt{\frac{\hat{p}\hat{q}}{n}} \Rightarrow .267 \pm 1.645 \sqrt{\frac{.267(.733)}{30}} \Rightarrow .267 \pm .133 \Rightarrow (.134, .400)$$

We are 90% confident that the proportion of museums world-wide that use total visitors as their performance measure is between .134 and .400.

10.11 Some preliminary calculations are:

If the probabilities are the same, $p_{1,0} = p_{2,0} = p_{3,0} = 1/3$

$E_1 = np_{1,0} = 505(1/3) = 168.333 = E_2 = E_3$

To determine if in the population of posts to a travel destination website there are no differences in the percentages of posts classified into the three destination image categories, we test:

$H_0 : p_1 = p_2 = p_3 = 1/3$
$H_a :$ At lease one of the probabilities differs from 1/3

The test statistic is

$$\chi^2 = \sum \frac{[n_i - E_i]^2}{E_i} = \frac{(338 - 168.333)^2}{168.333} + \frac{(112 - 168.333)^2}{168.333} + \frac{(55 - 168.333)^2}{168.333} = 266.17$$

The rejection region requires $\alpha = .10$ in the upper tail of the χ^2 distribution with $df = k - 1 = 3 - 1 = 2$. From Table IV, Appendix D, $\chi^2_{.10} = 6.25139$. The rejection region is $\chi^2 > 6.25139$.

Since the observed value of the test statistic falls in the rejection region $\left(\chi^2 = 266.17 > 6.25139 \right)$, H_0 is rejected. There is sufficient evidence to indicate there are differences in the percentages of posts classified into the three destination image categories at $\alpha = .10$.

10.13 Let $p_1 =$ proportion users using both hands/both thumbs, $p_2 =$ proportion of users using right hand/right thumb, $p_3 =$ proportion of users suing left hand/left thumb, $p_4 =$ proportion of users using both hands/right index finger, $p_5 =$ proportion of users using left hand/right index finger and $p_6 =$ proportion of users using other. Some preliminary calculations: $E_1 = E_2 = E_3 = E_4 = E_5 = E_6 = np_{i,0} = 859(1/6) = 143.167$.

To determine if the proportions of mobile device users in the six texting style categories differ, we test:

$H_0 : p_1 = p_2 = p_3 = p_4 = p_5 = p_6 = 1/6$
$H_a :$ At least one of the probabilities differs from the hypothesized value

The test statistic is

$$\chi^2 = \sum \frac{[n_i - E_i]^2}{E_i} = \frac{(396-143.167)^2}{143.167} + \frac{(311-143.167)^2}{143.167} + \frac{(70-143.167)^2}{143.167} + \frac{(39-143.167)^2}{143.167}$$

$$+ \frac{(18-143.167)^2}{143.167} + \frac{(25-143.167)^2}{143.167} = 756.436$$

The rejection region requires $\alpha = .10$ in the upper tail of the χ^2 distribution with $df = k - 1 = 6 - 1 = 5$. From Table IV, Appendix D, $\chi^2_{.10} = 9.23635$. The rejection region is $\chi^2 > 9.23635$.

Since the observed value of the test statistic falls in the rejection region $\left(\chi^2 = 756.436 > 9.23635 \right)$, H_0 is rejected. There is sufficient evidence to indicate that the proportions of mobile device users in the six texting style categories differ at $\alpha = .10$.

10.15 Let p_1 = proportion of mail only users, p_2 = proportion of Internet only users, and p_3 = proportion of both mail and Internet. Some preliminary calculations:

$$E_1 = E_2 = E_3 = np_{i,0} = 440(1/3) = 146.667$$

To determine if the professor's beliefs are correct, we test:

$H_0 : p_1 = p_2 = p_3 = 1/3$
H_a : At least one of the probabilities differs from the hypothesized value

The test statistic is $\chi^2 = \sum \frac{[n_i - E_i]^2}{E_i} = \frac{(262-146.667)^2}{146.667} + \frac{(43-146.667)^2}{146.667} + \frac{(135-146.667)^2}{146.667} = 164.895$

The rejection region requires $\alpha = .01$ in the upper tail of the χ^2 distribution with $df = k - 1 = 3 - 1 = 2$. From Table IV, Appendix D, $\chi^2_{.01} = 9.21034$. The rejection region is $\chi^2 > 9.21034$.

Since the observed value of the test statistic falls in the rejection region $\left(\chi^2 = 164.895 > 9.21034 \right)$, H_0 is rejected. There is sufficient evidence to indicate that the proportions mail only, Internet only, and both mail and Internet users differ at $\alpha = .01$.

10.17 To determine if the number of overweight trucks per week is distributed over the 7 days of the week in direct proportion to the volume of truck traffic, we test:

$H_0 : p_1 = .191, \ p_2 = .198, \ p_3 = .187, \ p_4 = .180, \ p_5 = .155, \ p_6 = .043, \ p_7 = .046$
H_a : At least one of the probabilities differs from the hypothesized value

$E_1 = np_{1,0} = 414(.191) = 79.074 \qquad E_2 = np_{2,0} = 414(.198) = 81.972 \qquad E_3 = np_{3,0} = 414(.187) = 77.418$

$E_4 = np_{4,0} = 414(.180) = 74.520 \qquad E_5 = np_{2,0} = 414(.155) = 64.170 \qquad E_6 = np_{3,0} = 414(.043) = 17.802$

$E_7 = np_{3,0} = 414(.046) = 19.044$

The test statistic is

$$\chi^2 = \sum \frac{[n_i - E_i]^2}{E_i} = \frac{(90 - 79.074)^2}{79.074} + \frac{(82 - 81.972)^2}{81.972} + \frac{(72 - 77.418)^2}{77.418} + \frac{(70 - 74.520)^2}{74.520}$$

$$+ \frac{(51 - 64.170)^2}{64.170} + \frac{(18 - 17.802)^2}{17.802} + \frac{(31 - 19.044)^2}{19.044} = 12.374$$

The rejection region requires $\alpha = .05$ in the upper tail of the χ^2 distribution with $df = k - 1 = 7 - 1 = 6$. From Table IV, Appendix D, $\chi^2_{.05} = 12.5916$. The rejection region is $\chi^2 > 12.5916$.

Since the observed value of the test statistic does not fall in the rejection region $\left(\chi^2 = 12.374 \not> 12.5916\right)$, H_0 is not rejected. There is insufficient evidence to indicate the number of overweight trucks per week is distributed over the 7 days of the week is not in direct proportion to the volume of truck traffic at $\alpha = .05$.

10.19   a. $df = (r - 1)(c - 1) = (5 - 1)(5 - 1) = 16$. From Table IV, Appendix D, $\chi^2_{.05} = 26.2962$. The rejection region is $\chi^2 > 26.2962$.

   b. $df = (r - 1)(c - 1) = (3 - 1)(6 - 1) = 10$. From Table IV, Appendix D, $\chi^2_{.10} = 15.9871$. The rejection region is $\chi^2 > 15.9871$.

   c. $df = (r - 1)(c - 1) = (2 - 1)(3 - 1) = 2$. From Table IV, Appendix D, $\chi^2_{.01} = 9.21034$. The rejection region is $\chi^2 > 9.21034$.

10.21   a.   To convert the frequencies to percentages, divide the numbers in each column by the column total and multiply by 100. Also, divide the row totals by the overall total and multiply by 100. The column totals are 25, 64, and 78, while the row totals are 96 and 71. The overall sample size is 165. The table of percentages are:

		Column		
	1	**2**	**3**	**Totals**
Row 1	$\frac{9}{25} \times 100 = 36\%$	$\frac{34}{64} \times 100 = 53.1\%$	$\frac{53}{78} \times 100 = 67.9\%$	$\frac{96}{167} \times 100 = 57.5\%$
2	$\frac{16}{25} \times 100 = 64\%$	$\frac{30}{64} \times 100 = 46.9\%$	$\frac{25}{78} \times 100 = 32.1\%$	$\frac{71}{167} \times 100 = 42.5\%$

b.   Using MINITAB, the graph is:

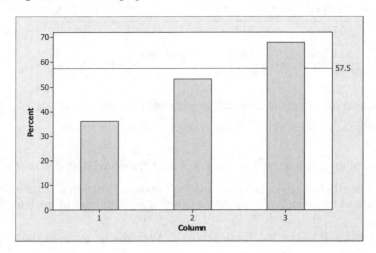

c.   If the rows and columns are independent, the row percentages in each column would be close to the row total percentages. This pattern is not evident in the plot, implying the rows and columns are not independent. In Exercise 10.20, we did not have enough evidence to say the rows and columns were not independent. If the sample sizes were bigger, we would have been able to reject H_0.

10.23   a-b.   To convert the frequencies to percentages, divide the numbers in each column by the column total and multiply by 100. Also, divide the row totals by the overall total and multiply by 100.

	B			
	B$_1$	**B$_2$**	**B$_3$**	**Totals**
A$_1$	$\dfrac{40}{134} \times 100 = 29.9\%$	$\dfrac{72}{163} \times 100 = 44.2\%$	$\dfrac{42}{142} \times 100 = 29.6\%$	$\dfrac{154}{439} \times 100 = 35.1\%$
A$_2$ **Row**	$\dfrac{63}{134} \times 100 = 47.0\%$	$\dfrac{53}{163} \times 100 = 32.5\%$	$\dfrac{70}{142} \times 100 = 49.3\%$	$\dfrac{186}{439} \times 100 = 42.4\%$
A$_3$	$\dfrac{31}{134} \times 100 = 23.1\%$	$\dfrac{38}{163} \times 100 = 23.3\%$	$\dfrac{30}{142} \times 100 = 21.1\%$	$\dfrac{99}{439} \times 100 = 22.6\%$

c.   Using MINITAB, the graph of A$_1$ is:

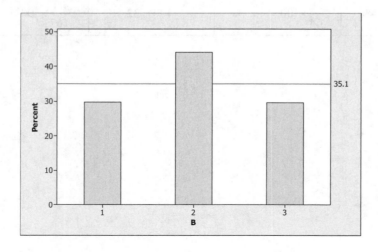

The graph supports the conclusion that the rows and columns are not independent. If they were, then the height of all the bars would be essentially the same.

    d.   Using MINITAB, the graph of A_2 is:

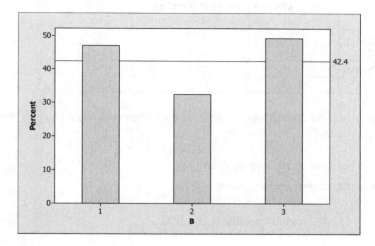

The graph supports the conclusion that the rows and columns are not independent. If they were, then the height of all the bars would be essentially the same.

    e.   Using MINITAB, the graph of A_3 is:

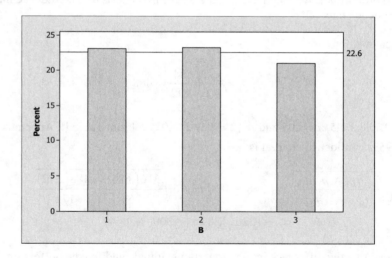

The graph does not support the conclusion that the rows and columns are not independent. All the bars would be essentially the same.

10.25   a.   Yes, it appears that the male and female tourists differ in their responses to purchasing photographs, postcards, and paintings. The values in the 'Always' and 'Rarely or Never' categories are quite different. The percentages are insufficient to draw a conclusion because the sample sizes must be taken into account.

b. The counts are found by changing the percentages to proportions and multiplying the proportions by the sample sizes in each gender. The counts are:

	Male Tourist	Female Tourist	Total
Always	240	476	716
Often	405	527	932
Occasionally	525	493	1018
Rarely or Never	330	204	534
Total	1500	1700	3200

c. To determine whether male and female tourists differ in their responses to purchasing photographs, postcards, or paintings, we test:

H_0 : Gender and purchasing are independent

H_a : Gender and purchasing are dependent

d. The test statistic is $\chi^2 = 112.433$ and the p-value is $p = .000$.

e. Since the p-value is less than $\alpha (p = .000 < .01)$, H_0 is rejected. There is sufficient evidence to indicate male and female tourists differ in their responses to purchasing photographs, postcards, or paintings at $\alpha = .01$.

10.27 a. To compare the two proportions, we could use either a test of hypothesis or a confidence interval. I will use a 95% confidence interval.

Some preliminary calculations are:

$$\hat{p}_{M1} = \frac{x_{M1}}{n_M} = \frac{24}{76} = .316 \qquad\qquad \hat{p}_{F1} = \frac{x_{F1}}{n_F} = \frac{84}{172} = .488$$

For confidence coefficient .95, $\alpha = .05$ and $\alpha / 2 = .05 / 2 = .025$. From Table II, Appendix D, $z_{.025} = 1.96$. The 95% confidence interval is:

$$\left(\hat{p}_{M1} - \hat{p}_{F1} \right) \pm z_{.025} \sqrt{\frac{\hat{p}_{M1}\hat{q}_{M1}}{n_M} + \frac{\hat{p}_{F1}\hat{q}_{F1}}{n_F}} \Rightarrow (.316 - .488) \pm 1.96 \sqrt{\frac{.316(.684)}{76} + \frac{.488(.512)}{172}}$$

$$\Rightarrow -.172 \pm .128 \Rightarrow (-.300, \ -.044)$$

We are 95% confident that the difference in the proportions of male and female professionals who believe their salaries are too low is between $-.300$ and $-.044$. Since 0 is not in this interval, there is evidence that the two proportions are different.

b. Some preliminary calculations are:

$$\hat{p}_{M2} = \frac{x_{M2}}{n_M} = \frac{38}{76} = .500 \qquad\qquad \hat{p}_{F2} = \frac{x_{F2}}{n_F} = \frac{69}{172} = .401$$

For confidence coefficient .95, $\alpha = .05$ and $\alpha / 2 = .05 / 2 = .025$. From Table II, Appendix D, $z_{.025} = 1.96$. The 95% confidence interval is:

$$\left(\hat{p}_{M2}-\hat{p}_{F2}\right)\pm z_{.025}\sqrt{\frac{\hat{p}_{M2}\hat{q}_{M2}}{n_M}+\frac{\hat{p}_{F2}\hat{q}_{F2}}{n_F}} \Rightarrow \left(.500-.401\right)\pm 1.96\sqrt{\frac{.5(.5)}{76}+\frac{.401(.599)}{172}}$$

$$\Rightarrow .099\pm .134 \Rightarrow \left(-.035,\ .233\right)$$

We are 95% confident that the difference in the proportions of male and female professionals who believe their salaries are equitable/fair is between -.035 and .233. Since 0 is in this interval, there is no evidence that the two proportions are different.

c. Some preliminary calculations are:

$$\hat{p}_{M3}=\frac{x_{M3}}{n_M}=\frac{14}{76}=.184 \qquad\qquad \hat{p}_{F3}=\frac{x_{F3}}{n_F}=\frac{19}{172}=.110$$

For confidence coefficient .95, $\alpha = .05$ and $\alpha/2 = .05/2 = .025$. From Table II, Appendix D, $z_{.025}=1.96$. The 95% confidence interval is:

$$\left(\hat{p}_{M3}-\hat{p}_{F3}\right)\pm z_{.025}\sqrt{\frac{\hat{p}_{M3}\hat{q}_{M3}}{n_M}+\frac{\hat{p}_{F3}\hat{q}_{F3}}{n_F}} \Rightarrow \left(.184-.110\right)\pm 1.96\sqrt{\frac{.184(.816)}{76}+\frac{.110(.890)}{172}}$$

$$\Rightarrow .074\pm .099 \Rightarrow \left(-.025,\ .173\right)$$

We are 95% confident that the difference in the proportions of male and female professionals who believe they are well paid is between $-.025$ and .173. Since 0 is in this interval, there is no evidence that the two proportions are different.

d. Yes. Since there were differences between the proportions of males and females for one of the 3 levels, there is probably evidence that the opinions of males and females are different.

e. Some preliminary calculations are:

$$\hat{E}_{11}=\frac{R_1 C_1}{n}=\frac{108(76)}{248}=33.097 \qquad\qquad \hat{E}_{12}=\frac{R_1 C_2}{n}=\frac{108(172)}{248}=74.903$$

$$\hat{E}_{21}=\frac{R_2 C_1}{n}=\frac{107(76)}{248}=32.790 \qquad\qquad \hat{E}_{22}=\frac{R_2 C_2}{n}=\frac{107(172)}{248}=74.210$$

$$\hat{E}_{31}=\frac{R_3 C_1}{n}=\frac{33(76)}{248}=10.113 \qquad\qquad \hat{E}_{33}=\frac{R_3 C_3}{n}=\frac{33(172)}{248}=22.887$$

To determine if the opinion on the fairness of a travel professional's salary differ for males and females, we test:

H_0: Opinion and Gender are independent
H_a: Opinion and Gender are dependent

The test statistic is

$$\chi^2 = \sum\sum \frac{\left[n_{ij}-\hat{E}_{ij}\right]^2}{\hat{E}_{ij}} = \frac{(24-33.097)^2}{33.097}+\frac{(84-74.903)^2}{74.903}+\frac{(38-32.790)^2}{32.790}$$

$$+\frac{(69-74.210)^2}{74.210}+\frac{(14-10.113)^2}{10.113}+\frac{(19-22.887)^2}{22.887}=6.953$$

The rejection region requires $\alpha = .10$ in the upper tail of the χ^2 distribution with $df = (r-1)(c-1) = (3-1)(2-1) = 2$. From Table IV, Appendix D, $\chi_{.10}^2 = 4.60517$. The rejection region is $\chi^2 > 4.60517$.

Since the observed value of the test statistic falls in the rejection region $\left(\chi^2 = 6.953 > 4.60517\right)$, H_0 is rejected. There is sufficient evidence to indicate that the opinions on the fairness of a travel professional's salary differ for males and females at $\alpha = .10$.

f.   For confidence coefficient .90, $\alpha = .10$ and $\alpha/2 = .10/2 = .05$. From Table II, Appendix D, $z_{.05} = 1.645$. The 90% confidence interval is:

$$\left(\hat{p}_{M1} - \hat{p}_{F1}\right) \pm z_{.05} \sqrt{\frac{\hat{p}_{M1}\hat{q}_{M1}}{n_M} + \frac{\hat{p}_{F1}\hat{q}_{F1}}{n_F}} \Rightarrow (.282 - .511) \pm 1.645 \sqrt{\frac{.282(.718)}{103} + \frac{.511(.489)}{174}}$$

$$\Rightarrow -.229 \pm .096 \Rightarrow (-.325, \; -.133)$$

We are 90% confident that the difference in the proportions of male and female professionals who believe their salaries are too low is between -.325 and -.133. Since 0 is not in this interval, there is evidence that the two proportions are different.

10.29   a.   To determine if package design and sound pitch combination influences the consumer's opinion on product taste, we test:

H_0: Package design/sound pitch and taste are independent
H_a: Package design/sound pitch and taste are dependent

b. $\hat{E}_{11} = \dfrac{R_1 C_1}{n} = \dfrac{42(40)}{80} = 21$ $\hat{E}_{12} = \dfrac{R_1 C_2}{n} = \dfrac{42(40)}{80} = 21$

$\hat{E}_{21} = \dfrac{R_2 C_1}{n} = \dfrac{38(40)}{80} = 19$ $\hat{E}_{22} = \dfrac{R_2 C_2}{n} = \dfrac{38(40)}{80} = 19$

c.   The test statistic is

$$\chi^2 = \sum\sum \frac{\left[n_{ij} - \hat{E}_{ij}\right]^2}{\hat{E}_{ij}} = \frac{(35-21)^2}{21} + \frac{(7-21)^2}{21} + \frac{(5-19)^2}{19} + \frac{(33-19)^2}{19} = 39.30$$

d.   Since the p-value is so small $(p \approx 0)$, H_0 is rejected. There is sufficient evidence to indicate that package design and sound pitch combination influences the consumer's opinion on product taste for any reasonable value of α.

10.31   Using MINITAB, the contingency table analysis is:

Tabulated statistics: Position, Nationality
```
Using frequencies in Fr

Rows: Position    Columns: Nationality

            1     2     3     4    All

1         126    75    35    93    329
2          72    36    10    27    145
3          30     9     4     6     49
4         372   180    51   174    777
All       600   300   100   300   1300

Cell Contents:        Count

Pearson Chi-Square = 21.242, DF = 9, P-Value = 0.012
Likelihood Ratio Chi-Square = 21.327, DF = 9, P-Value = 0.011
```

To determine if a firm's position on off-shoring depends on the firm's nationality, we test:

H_0 : Position and Nationality are independent

H_a : Position and Nationality are dependent

From the printout, the test statistic is $\chi^2 = 21.242$ and the p-value is $p = .012$. Since the p-value is less than $\alpha\left(p = .012 < .05\right)$, H_0 is rejected. There is sufficient evidence to indicate a firm's position on off-shoring depends on the firm's nationality at $\alpha = .05$.

10.33   Some preliminary calculations are:

$$\hat{E}_{11} = \frac{R_1 C_1}{n} = \frac{396(335)}{859} = 154.435 \quad \hat{E}_{21} = \frac{R_2 C_1}{n} = \frac{311(335)}{859} = 121.286 \quad \hat{E}_{31} = \frac{R_3 C_1}{n} = \frac{70(335)}{859} = 27.299$$

$$\hat{E}_{41} = \frac{R_4 C_1}{n} = \frac{39(335)}{859} = 15.210 \quad \hat{E}_{51} = \frac{R_5 C_1}{n} = \frac{18(335)}{859} = 7.020 \quad \hat{E}_{61} = \frac{R_6 C_1}{n} = \frac{25(335)}{859} = 9.750$$

$$\hat{E}_{12} = \frac{R_1 C_2}{n} = \frac{396(524)}{859} = 241.565 \quad \hat{E}_{22} = \frac{R_2 C_2}{n} = \frac{311(524)}{859} = 189.714 \quad \hat{E}_{32} = \frac{R_3 C_2}{n} = \frac{70(524)}{859} = 42.701$$

$$\hat{E}_{42} = \frac{R_4 C_2}{n} = \frac{39(524)}{859} = 23.790 \quad \hat{E}_{52} = \frac{R_5 C_2}{n} = \frac{18(524)}{859} = 10.980 \quad \hat{E}_{62} = \frac{R_6 C_2}{n} = \frac{25(524)}{859} = 15.250$$

To determine if the proportions of mobile device users in the six texting style categories depend on whether a male or female are texting, we test:

H_0 : Texting style and sex are independent

H_a : Texting style and sex are dependent

The test statistic is:

$$\chi^2 = \sum\sum \frac{\left[n_{ij} - \hat{E}_{ij}\right]^2}{\hat{E}_{ij}} = \frac{(161-154.435)^2}{154.435} + \frac{(235-241.565)^2}{241.565} + \cdots + \frac{(14-15.250)^2}{15.250} = 4.209$$

The rejection region requires $\alpha = .10$ in the upper tail of the χ^2 distribution with $df = (r-1)(c-1) = (6-1)(2-1) = 5$. From Table IV, Appendix D, $\chi^2_{.10} = 9.23635$. The rejection region is $\chi^2 > 9.23635$.

Since the observed value of the test statistic does not fall in the rejection region $\left(\chi^2 = 4.209 \not> 9.23635\right)$, H_0 is not rejected. There is insufficient evidence to indicate the proportions of mobile device users in the six texting style categories depend on whether a male or female are texting at $\alpha = .10$.

10.35   The contingency table for this data is

		Condition		
		Useful	Control	Totals
Recycle	**Recycled**	26	14	40
	Garbage	13	25	38
	Totals	39	39	78

Some preliminary calculations are:

$$\hat{E}_{11} = \frac{R_1 C_1}{n} = \frac{40(39)}{78} = 20 \qquad \hat{E}_{12} = \frac{R_1 C_2}{n} = \frac{40(39)}{78} = 20$$

$$\hat{E}_{21} = \frac{R_2 C_1}{n} = \frac{38(39)}{78} = 19 \qquad \hat{E}_{22} = \frac{R_2 C_2}{n} = \frac{38(39)}{78} = 19$$

To determine if students in the *usefulness is salient* condition will recycle as a higher rate than students in the *control* condition, we test:

H_0: Condition and recycling are independent
H_a: Condition and recycling are dependent

The test statistic is

$$\chi^2 = \sum\sum \frac{\left[n_{ij} - \hat{E}_{ij}\right]^2}{\hat{E}_{ij}} = \frac{(26-20)^2}{20} + \frac{(14-20)^2}{20} + \frac{(13-19)^2}{19} + \frac{(25-19)^2}{19} = 7.39$$

The rejection region requires $\alpha = .05$ in the upper tail of the χ^2 distribution with $df = (r-1)(c-1) = (2-1)(2-1) = 1$. From Table IV, Appendix D, $\chi^2_{.05} = 3.84146$. The rejection region is $\chi^2 > 3.84146$.

Since the observed value of the test statistic falls in the rejection region $\left(\chi^2 = 7.39 > 3.84146\right)$, H_0 is rejected. There is sufficient evidence to indicate students in the *usefulness is salient* condition will recycle as a higher rate than students in the *control* condition at $\alpha = .05$.

10.37   Using MINITAB, the results are:

Tabulated statistics: Instruction, Strategy
```
Rows: Instruction   Columns: Strategy

              Guess    Other     TTBC      All

Cue               5        6       13       24
              20.83    25.00    54.17   100.00
              35.71    35.29    76.47    50.00

Pattern           9       11        4       24
              37.50    45.83    16.67   100.00
              64.29    64.71    23.53    50.00

All              14       17       17       48
              29.17    35.42    35.42   100.00
             100.00   100.00   100.00   100.00

Cell Contents:      Count
                    % of Row
                    % of Column
```

Pearson Chi-Square = 7.378, DF = 2, P-Value = 0.025
Likelihood Ratio Chi-Square = 7.668, DF = 2, P-Value = 0.022

To determine if the choice of heuristic strategy depends on type of instruction, we test:

H_0: Heuristic strategy and type of instruction are independent
H_a: Heuristic strategy and type of instruction are dependent

From the printout, the test statistic is $\chi^2 = 7.378$ and the p-value is $p = .025$.

Since the p-value is less than $\alpha(p = .025 < .05)$, H_0 is rejected. There is sufficient evidence to indicate the choice of heuristic strategy depends on type of instruction at $\alpha = .05$.

Since the p-value is not less than $\alpha(p = .025 \nless .01)$, H_0 is not rejected. There is insufficient evidence to indicate the choice of heuristic strategy depends on type of instruction at $\alpha = .01$.

10.39   a.   Using MINITAB, the results for the First Trial are:

Chi-Square Test: Switch Boxes, No Switch
```
Expected counts are printed below observed counts
Chi-Square contributions are printed below expected counts

          Switch
          Boxes  No Switch  Total
   1         10         17     27
            6.50      20.50
           1.885      0.598

   2          3         24     27
            6.50      20.50
           1.885      0.598

   3          5         22     27
            6.50      20.50
           0.346      0.110

   4          8         19     27
            6.50      20.50
           0.346      0.110

Total        26         82    108
Chi-Sq = 5.876, DF = 3, P-Value = 0.118
```

To determine if the likelihood of switching boxes depends on condition for the first trial, we test:

H_0: Likelihood of switching boxes and condition are independent
H_a: Likelihood of switching boxes and condition are dependent

From the printout above, the test statistic is $\chi^2 = 5.876$ and the p-value is $p = 0.118$. Since the p-value is not small, H_0 is not rejected. There is insufficient evidence to indicate that the likelihood of switching boxes depends on condition for the first trial for any value of $\alpha < .118$.

Using MINITAB, the results for the Last Trial are:

Chi-Square Test: Switch Boxes, No Switch
```
Expected counts are printed below observed counts
Chi-Square contributions are printed below expected counts

          Switch
          Boxes  No Switch   Total
    1        23          4      27
         18.75       8.25
         0.963      2.189

    2        12         15      27
         18.75       8.25
         2.430      5.523

    3        21          6      27
         18.75       8.25
         0.270      0.614

    4        19          8      27
         18.75       8.25
         0.003      0.008

Total       75         33     108
Chi-Sq = 12.000, DF = 3, P-Value = 0.007
```

To determine if the likelihood of switching boxes depends on condition for the last trial, we test:

H_0: Likelihood of switching boxes and condition are independent
H_a: Likelihood of switching boxes and condition are dependent

From the printout above, the test statistic is $\chi^2 = 12.00$ and the p-value is $p = 0.007$. Since the p-value is small, H_0 is rejected. There is sufficient evidence to indicate that the likelihood of switching boxes depends on condition for the last trial for any value of $\alpha > .007$.

b. Using MINITAB, the results from the Empty condition are:

Chi-Square Test: Switch Boxes, No Switch
```
Expected counts are printed below observed counts
Chi-Square contributions are printed below expected counts

          Switch
          Boxes  No Switch   Total
    1        10         17      27
         16.50      10.50
         2.561      4.024

    2        23          4      27
         16.50      10.50
         2.561      4.024

Total       33         21      54
Chi-Sq = 13.169, DF = 1, P-Value = 0.000
```

To determine if the likelihood of switching boxes depends on trial number for the Empty condition, we test:

H_0: Likelihood of switching boxes and trial number are independent
H_a: Likelihood of switching boxes and trial number are dependent

From the printout above, the test statistic is $\chi^2 = 13.169$ and the p-value is $p = 0.000$. Since the p-value is so small, H_0 is rejected. There is sufficient evidence to indicate that the likelihood of switching boxes depends on trial number for the Empty condition for any value of $\alpha > .000$.

Using MINITAB, the results from the Vanish condition are:

Chi-Square Test: Switch Boxes, No Switch

```
Expected counts are printed below observed counts
Chi-Square contributions are printed below expected counts

        Switch
        Boxes   No Switch   Total
    1       3          24      27
         7.50       19.50
        2.700        1.038

    2      12          15      27
         7.50       19.50
        2.700        1.038

Total      15          39      54
Chi-Sq = 7.477, DF = 1, P-Value = 0.006
```

To determine if the likelihood of switching boxes depends on trial number for the Vanish condition, we test:

H_0: Likelihood of switching boxes and trial number are independent
H_a: Likelihood of switching boxes and trial number are dependent

From the printout above, the test statistic is $\chi^2 = 7.477$ and the p-value is $p = 0.006$. Since the p-value is so small, H_o is rejected. There is sufficient evidence to indicate that the likelihood of switching boxes depends on trial number for the Vanish condition for any value of $\alpha > .006$.

Using MINITAB, the results from the Steroids condition are:

Chi-Square Test: Switch Boxes, No Switch

```
Expected counts are printed below observed counts
Chi-Square contributions are printed below expected counts

        Switch
        Boxes   No Switch   Total
    1       5          22      27
        13.00       14.00
        4.923        4.571

    2      21           6      27
        13.00       14.00
        4.923        4.571

Total      26          28      54
Chi-Sq = 18.989, DF = 1, P-Value = 0.000
```

To determine if the likelihood of switching boxes depends on trial number for the Steroids condition, we test:

H_0: Likelihood of switching boxes and trial number are independent
H_a: Likelihood of switching boxes and trial number are dependent

From the printout above, the test statistic is $\chi^2 = 18.989$ and the *p*-value is $p = .000$. Since the *p*-value is so small, H_0 is rejected. There is sufficient evidence to indicate that the likelihood of switching boxes depends on trial number for the Steroids condition for any value of $\alpha > .000$.

Using MINITAB, the results from the Steroids2 condition are:

Chi-Square Test: Switch Boxes, No Switch
```
Expected counts are printed below observed counts
Chi-Square contributions are printed below expected counts

          Switch
          Boxes  No Switch   Total
     1       8        19       27
         13.50     13.50
          2.241     2.241

     2      19         8       27
         13.50     13.50
          2.241     2.241

  Total     27        27       54
  Chi-Sq = 8.963,  DF = 1,  P-Value = 0.003
```

To determine if the likelihood of switching boxes depends on trial number for the Steroids2 condition, we test:

H_0: Likelihood of switching boxes and trial number are independent
H_a: Likelihood of switching boxes and trial number are dependent

From the printout above, the test statistic is $\chi^2 = 8.963$ and the *p*-value is $p = .003$. Since the *p*-value is so small, H_0 is rejected. There is sufficient evidence to indicate that the likelihood of switching boxes depends on trial number for the Steroids2 condition for any value of $\alpha > .003$.

c.   Of all the tests performed, only one was not significant. There was no evidence that the likelihood of switching boxes depended on condition for the first trial. All other tests indicated that the variables were dependent. Thus, both condition and trial number influence a subject to switch.

10.41   a.   If all the categories are equally likely, then $p_{1,0} = p_{2,0} = p_{3,0} = p_{4,0} = p_{5,0} = .2$.

$$E_1 = E_2 = E_3 = E_4 = E_5 = np_{i,0} = 150(.20) = 30$$

To determine if the categories are not equally likely, we test:

$H_0 : p_1 = p_2 = p_3 = p_4 = p_5 = .2$
$H_a :$ At lease one of the probabilities differs from .2

The test statistic is $\chi^2 = \sum \dfrac{\left[n_i - E_i\right]^2}{E_i} = \dfrac{(28-30)^2}{30} + \dfrac{(35-30)^2}{30} + \dfrac{(33-30)^2}{30} + \dfrac{(25-30)^2}{30} = 2.133$

The rejection region requires $\alpha = .10$ in the upper tail of the χ^2 distribution with $df = k - 1 = 5 - 1 = 4$. From Table IV, Appendix D, $\chi^2_{.10} = 7.77944$. The rejection region is $\chi^2 > 7.77944$.

Since the observed value of the test statistic does not fall in the rejection region $\left(\chi^2 = 2.133 \not> 7.77944\right)$, H_0 is not rejected. There is insufficient evidence to indicate the categories are not equally likely at $\alpha = .10$.

b. $\hat{p}_2 = \dfrac{35}{150} = .233$

For confidence coefficient .90, $\alpha = .10$ and $\alpha/2 = .10/2 = .05$. From Table II, Appendix D, $z_{.05} = 1.645$. The confidence interval is:

$$\hat{p}_2 \pm z_{.05}\sqrt{\dfrac{\hat{p}_2\hat{q}_2}{n_2}} \Rightarrow .233 \pm 1.645\sqrt{\dfrac{.233(.767)}{150}} \Rightarrow .233 \pm .057 \Rightarrow (.176,\ .290)$$

10.43 a. Since there are 10 income groups, we would expect 10% or $1,072(.10) = 107.2$ givers in each of the income categories.

b. The null hypothesis for testing whether the true proportions of charitable givers in each income group are the same is:

$H_0: p_1 = p_2 = \cdots = p_{10} = .10$

c. Some preliminary calculations are: $E_1 = E_2 = \cdots = E_{10} = np_{i,0} = 1,072(.10) = 107.2$

$$\chi^2 = \sum \dfrac{[n_i - E_i]^2}{E_i} = \dfrac{(42 - 107.2)^2}{107.2} + \dfrac{(93 - 107.2)^2}{107.2} + \ldots + \dfrac{(127 - 107.2)^2}{107.2} = 93.15$$

d. The rejection region requires $\alpha = .10$ in the upper tail of the χ^2 distribution with $df = k - 1 = 10 - 1 = 9$. From Table IV, Appendix D, $\chi^2_{.10} = 14.6837$. The rejection region is $\chi^2 > 14.6837$.

e. Since the observed value of the test statistic falls in the rejection region $\left(\chi^2 = 93.15 > 14.6837\right)$, H_0 is rejected. There is sufficient evidence to indicate that the true proportions of charitable givers in each income group are not all the same at $\alpha = .10$.

10.45 a. The sample proportion of negative tone news stories that are deceptive is $111/170 = .653$.

b. The sample proportion of neutral tone news stories that are deceptive is $61/110 = .555$.

c. The sample proportion of positive tone news stories that are deceptive is $11/31 = .355$.

d. Yes, it appears that the proportion of news stories that are deceptive depends on the story tone. The proportion that is deceptive for negative tone stories is .653, while the proportion that is deceptive for positive tone stories is only .355. These proportions look much different.

e. To determine if the authenticity of a news story depends on tone, we test:

H_0: Authenticity and tone are independent
H_a: Authenticity and tone are dependent

f.   The test statistic is $\chi^2 = 10.427$ and the p-value is $p = .005$.

Since the p-value is less than $\alpha (p = .005 < .05)$, H_o is rejected. There is sufficient evidence to indicate authenticity of a news story depends on tone at $\alpha = .05$.

10.47   a.   Some preliminary calculations are:

$$E_1 = np_{1,0} = 1,000(.65) = 650 \quad E_2 = np_{2,0} = 1,000(.08) = 80 \quad E_3 = np_{3,0} = 1,000(.05) = 50$$

$$E_4 = np_{4,0} = 1,000(.03) = 30 \quad E_5 = np_{5,0} = 1,000(.025) = 25 \quad E_6 = np_{6,0} = 1,000(.165) = 165$$

To determine if the data disagree with the percentages reported by *Search Engine Land*, we test:

$H_0 : p_1 = .65, p_2 = .08, p_3 = .05, p_4 = .03, p_5 = .025, p_6 = .165$
$H_a :$ At lease one of the probabilities differs from the hypothesized values

The test statistic is

$$\chi^2 = \sum \frac{[n_i - E_i]^2}{E_i} = \frac{(648 - 650)^2}{650} + \frac{(91 - 80)^2}{80} + \frac{(45 - 50)^2}{50}$$
$$+ \frac{(40 - 300)^2}{300} + \frac{(21 - 25)^2}{25} + \frac{(155 - 165)^2}{165} = 6.60$$

The rejection region requires $\alpha = .05$ in the upper tail of the χ^2 distribution with $df = k - 1 = 6 - 1 = 5$. From Table IV, Appendix D, $\chi^2_{.05} = 11.0705$. The rejection region is $\chi^2 > 11.0705$.

Since the observed value of the test statistic does not fall in the rejection region $(\chi^2 = 6.60 \ngtr 11.0705)$, H_0 is not rejected. There is insufficient evidence to indicate the data disagree with the percentages reported by *Search Engine Land* at $\alpha = .05$.

b.   Some preliminary calculations are:

$$\hat{p}_1 = \frac{x_1}{n} = \frac{648}{1000} = .648$$

For confidence coefficient .95, $\alpha = .05$ and $\alpha / 2 = .05 / 2 = .025$. From Table II, Appendix D, $z_{.025} = 1.96$. The 95% confidence interval is:

$$\hat{p}_1 \pm z_{.025} \sqrt{\frac{\hat{p}_1 \hat{q}_1}{n}} \Rightarrow .648 \pm 1.96 \sqrt{\frac{.648(.352)}{1,000}} \Rightarrow .648 \pm .030 \Rightarrow (.618, \ .678)$$

We are 95% confident that the proportion of all internet searches that use the Google search engine is between .618 and .678. Expressing the confidence interval using percentages is $(61.8\%, \ 67.8\%)$.

10.49   Some preliminary calculations are: $E_1 = E_2 = E_3 = E_4 = np_{1,0} = 83(.25) = 20.75$

To determine if there are differences in the percentages of incidents in the four cause categories, we test:

$H_0 : p_1 = p_2 = p_3 = p_4 = .25$

H_a : At lease one of the probabilities differs from its hypothesized value

The test statistic is

$$\chi^2 = \sum \frac{[n_i - E_i]^2}{E_i} = \frac{(27-20.75)^2}{20.75} + \frac{(24-20.75)^2}{20.75} + \frac{(22-20.75)^2}{20.75} + \frac{(10-20.75)^2}{20.75} = 8.036$$

The rejection region requires $\alpha = .05$ in the upper tail of the χ^2 distribution with $df = k - 1 = 4 - 1 = 3$. From Table IV, Appendix D, $\chi^2_{.05} = 7.81473$. The rejection region is $\chi^2 > 7.81473$.

Since the observed value of the test statistic falls in the rejection region $(\chi^2 = 8.036 > 7.81473)$, H_0 is rejected. There is sufficient evidence to indicate there are differences in the percentages of incidents in the four cause categories at $\alpha = .05$.

10.51   Some preliminary calculations are:

$$\hat{E}_{11} = \frac{R_1 C_1}{n} = \frac{32(32)}{96} = 10.667 \qquad \hat{E}_{21} = \frac{R_2 C_1}{n} = \frac{32(32)}{96} = 10.667 \qquad \hat{E}_{31} = \frac{R_3 C_1}{n} = \frac{32(32)}{96} = 10.667$$

$$\hat{E}_{12} = \frac{R_1 C_2}{n} = \frac{32(64)}{96} = 21.333 \qquad \hat{E}_{22} = \frac{R_2 C_2}{n} = \frac{32(64)}{96} = 21.333 \qquad \hat{E}_{32} = \frac{R_3 C_2}{n} = \frac{32(64)}{96} = 21.333$$

To determine if the proportion of subjects who selected menus consistent with the theory depends on goal condition, we test:

H_0: Goal condition and Consistent with theory are independent

H_a: Goal condition and Consistent with theory are dependent

The test statistic is

$$\chi^2 = \sum\sum \frac{[n_{ij} - \hat{E}_{ij}]^2}{\hat{E}_{ij}} = \frac{(15-10.667)^2}{10.667} + \frac{(17-21.333)^2}{21.333} + \frac{(14-10.667)^2}{10.667} + \frac{(18-21.333)^2}{21.333}$$
$$+ \frac{(3-10.667)^2}{10.667} + \frac{(29-21.333)^2}{21.333} = 12.469$$

The rejection region requires $\alpha = .01$ in the upper tail of the χ^2 distribution with $df = (r-1)(c-1) = (3-1)(2-1) = 2$. From Table IV, Appendix D, $\chi^2_{.01} = 9.21034$. The rejection region is $\chi^2 > 9.21034$.

Since the observed value of the test statistic falls in the rejection region $(\chi^2 = 12.469 > 9.21034)$, H_0 is rejected. There is sufficient evidence to indicate that the proportion of subjects who selected menus consistent with the theory depends on goal condition at $\alpha = .01$.

10.53   Some preliminary calculations are:

$$\hat{E}_{11} = \frac{R_1 C_1}{n} = \frac{57(60)}{171} = 20 \qquad \hat{E}_{21} = \frac{R_2 C_1}{n} = \frac{58(60)}{171} = 20.35 \qquad \hat{E}_{31} = \frac{R_3 C_1}{n} = \frac{56(60)}{171} = 19.65$$

$$\hat{E}_{12} = \frac{R_1 C_2}{n} = \frac{57(111)}{171} = 37 \qquad \hat{E}_{22} = \frac{R_2 C_2}{n} = \frac{58(111)}{171} = 37.65 \qquad \hat{E}_{32} = \frac{R_3 C_2}{n} = \frac{56(111)}{171} = 36.35$$

To determine if the option choice depends on emotion state, we test:

H_0: Option choice and emotion state are independent
H_a: Option choice and emotion state are dependent

The test statistic is

$$\chi^2 = \sum\sum \frac{\left[n_{ij} - \hat{E}_{ij}\right]^2}{\hat{E}_{ij}} = \frac{(45-20)^2}{20} + \frac{(12-37)^2}{37} + \frac{(8-20.35)^2}{20.35} + \frac{(50-37.65)^2}{37.65}$$

$$+ \frac{(75-19.65)^2}{19.65} + \frac{(49-36.35)^2}{36.35} = 72.234$$

The rejection region requires $\alpha = .10$ in the upper tail of the χ^2 distribution with $df = (r-1)(c-1) = (3-1)(2-1) = 2$. From Table IV, Appendix D, $\chi^2_{.10} = 4.60517$. The rejection region is $\chi^2 > 4.60517$.

Since the observed value of the test statistic falls in the rejection region $\left(\chi^2 = 72.234 > 4.60517\right)$, H_0 is rejected. There is sufficient evidence to indicate that the option choice depends on emotion state at $\alpha = .10$.

10.55   a.   The contingency table is:

Altitude	Flight Response		Totals
	Low	High	
< 300	85	105	190
300-600	77	121	198
≥ 600	17	59	76
Totals	179	285	464

b.   Some preliminary calculations are:

$$\hat{E}_{11} = \frac{R_1 C_1}{n} = \frac{190(179)}{464} = 73.297 \qquad \hat{E}_{12} = \frac{R_1 C_2}{n} = \frac{190(285)}{464} = 116.703$$

$$\hat{E}_{21} = \frac{R_2 C_1}{n} = \frac{198(179)}{464} = 76.384 \qquad \hat{E}_{22} = \frac{R_2 C_2}{n} = \frac{198(285)}{464} = 121.616$$

$$\hat{E}_{31} = \frac{R_3 C_1}{n} = \frac{76(179)}{464} = 29.319 \qquad \hat{E}_{32} = \frac{R_3 C_2}{n} = \frac{76(285)}{464} = 46.681$$

To determine if flight response of the geese depends on the altitude of the helicopter, we test:

H_0: Flight response and Altitude of helicopter are independent
H_a: Flight response and Altitude of helicopter are dependent

The test statistic is

$$\chi^2 = \sum\sum \frac{\left[n_{ij} - \hat{E}_{ij}\right]^2}{\hat{E}_{ij}} = \frac{(85 - 73.297)^2}{73.297} + \frac{(105 - 116.703)^2}{116.703} + \frac{(77 - 76.384)^2}{76.384}$$

$$+ \frac{(121 - 121.616)^2}{121.616} + \frac{(17 - 29.319)^2}{29.319} + \frac{(59 - 46.681)^2}{46.681} = 11.477$$

The rejection region requires $\alpha = .01$ in the upper tail of the χ^2 distribution with $df = (r-1)(c-1) = (3-1)(2-1) = 2$. From Table IV, Appendix D, $\chi^2_{.01} = 9.21034$. The rejection region is $\chi^2 > 9.21034$.

Since the observed value of the test statistic falls in the rejection region $\left(\chi^2 = 11.477 > 9.21034\right)$, H_0 is rejected. There is sufficient evidence to indicate that the flight response of the geese depends on the altitude of the helicopter at $\alpha = .01$.

c.   The contingency table is:

	Flight Response		
Lateral Distance	**Low**	**High**	**Totals**
< 1000	37	243	280
1000-2000	68	37	105
2000-3000	44	4	48
≥ 3000	30	1	31
Totals	179	285	464

d.   Some preliminary calculations are:

$$\hat{E}_{11} = \frac{R_1 C_1}{n} = \frac{280(179)}{464} = 108.017 \qquad \hat{E}_{12} = \frac{R_1 C_2}{n} = \frac{280(285)}{464} = 171.983$$

$$\hat{E}_{21} = \frac{R_2 C_1}{n} = \frac{105(179)}{464} = 40.506 \qquad \hat{E}_{22} = \frac{R_2 C_2}{n} = \frac{105(285)}{464} = 64.494$$

$$\hat{E}_{31} = \frac{R_3 C_1}{n} = \frac{48(179)}{464} = 18.517 \qquad \hat{E}_{32} = \frac{R_3 C_2}{n} = \frac{48(285)}{464} = 29.483$$

$$\hat{E}_{41} = \frac{R_4 C_1}{n} = \frac{31(179)}{464} = 11.959 \qquad \hat{E}_{42} = \frac{R_4 C_2}{n} = \frac{31(285)}{464} = 19.041$$

To determine if flight response of the geese depends on the lateral distance of the helicopter, we test:

H_0: Flight response and Lateral distance of the helicopter are independent
H_a: Flight response and Lateral distance of the helicopter are dependent

The test statistic is

$$\chi^2 = \sum\sum \frac{\left[n_{ij} - \hat{E}_{ij}\right]^2}{\hat{E}_{ij}} = \frac{(37-108.017)^2}{108.017} + \frac{(243-171.983)^2}{171.983} + \frac{(68-40.506)^2}{40.506} + \frac{(37-64.494)^2}{64.494}$$

$$+ \frac{(44-18.517)^2}{18.517} + \frac{(4-29.494)^2}{29.494} + \frac{(30-11.959)^2}{11.959} + \frac{(1-19.041)^2}{19.041} = 207.814$$

The rejection region requires $\alpha = .01$ in the upper tail of the χ^2 distribution with $df = (r-1)(c-1) = (4-1)(2-1) = 3$. From Table IV, Appendix D, $\chi^2_{.01} = 11.3449$. The rejection region is $\chi^2 > 11.3449$.

Since the observed value of the test statistic falls in the rejection region $\left(\chi^2 = 207.814 > 11.3449\right)$, H_0 is rejected. There is sufficient evidence to indicate that the flight response of the geese depends on the lateral distance of the helicopter at $\alpha = .01$.

e.   Using SAS, the contingency table for altitude by response with the column percents is:

```
                        Table of ALTGRP by RESPONSE

            ALTGRP       RESPONSE

            Frequency|
            Percent  |
            Row Pct  |
            Col Pct  |LOW     |HIGH    | Total
            ---------+--------+--------+
            <300     |     85 |    105 |   190
                     |  18.32 |  22.63 | 40.95
                     |  44.74 |  55.26 |
                     |  47.49 |  36.84 |
            ---------+--------+--------+
            300-600  |     77 |    121 |   198
                     |  16.59 |  26.08 | 42.67
                     |  38.89 |  61.11 |
                     |  43.02 |  42.46 |
            ---------+--------+--------+
            600+     |     17 |     59 |    76
                     |   3.66 |  12.72 | 16.38
                     |  22.37 |  77.63 |
                     |   9.50 |  20.70 |
            ---------+--------+--------+
            Total         179      285     464
                        38.58    61.42  100.00

            Statistics for Table of ALTGRP by RESPONSE

   Statistic                        DF       Value      Prob
   ------------------------------------------------------------
   Chi-Square                        2      11.4770    0.0032
   Likelihood Ratio Chi-Square       2      12.1040    0.0024
   Mantel-Haenszel Chi-Square        1      10.2104    0.0014
   Phi Coefficient                          0.1573
   Contingency Coefficient                  0.1554
   Cramer's V                               0.1573
                   Sample Size = 464
```

From the row percents, it appears that the lower the plane, the lower the response. For altitude <300m, 55.26% of the geese had a high response. For altitude 300-600m, 61.11% of the geese had a high response. For altitude 600+m, 77.63% of the geese had a high response. Thus, instead of setting a minimum altitude for the planes, we need to set a maximum altitude. For this data, the lowest response is at an altitude of < 300 meters.

Using SAS, the contingency table for lateral distance by response with the column percents is:

```
                        The FREQ Procedure

                    Table of LATGRP by RESPONSE

            LATGRP      RESPONSE

            Frequency |
            Percent   |
            Row Pct   |
            Col Pct   |LOW     |HIGH    | Total
            ----------+--------+--------+
            <1000     |     37 |    243 |    280
                      |   7.97 |  52.37 |  60.34
                      |  13.21 |  86.79 |
                      |  20.67 |  85.26 |
            ----------+--------+--------+
            1000-2000 |     68 |     37 |    105
                      |  14.66 |   7.97 |  22.63
                      |  64.76 |  35.24 |
                      |  37.99 |  12.98 |
            ----------+--------+--------+
            2000-3000 |     44 |      4 |     48
                      |   9.48 |   0.86 |  10.34
                      |  91.67 |   8.33 |
                      |  24.58 |   1.40 |
            ----------+--------+--------+
            3000+     |     30 |      1 |     31
                      |   6.47 |   0.22 |   6.68
                      |  96.77 |   3.23 |
                      |  16.76 |   0.35 |
            ----------+--------+--------+
            Total           179      284      464
                          38.58    61.42   100.00

              Statistics for Table of LATGRP by RESPONSE

            Statistic                  DF      Value      Prob
            ------------------------------------------------------
            Chi-Square                  3    207.0812   <.0001
            Likelihood Ratio Chi-Square 3    227.5212   <.0001
            Mantel-Haenszel Chi-Square  1    189.2843   <.0001
            Phi Coefficient                    0.6692
            Contingency Coefficient            0.5562
            Cramer's V                         0.6692
                        Sample Size = 464
```

From the row percents, it appears that the greater the lateral distance, the lower the response. For a lateral distance of 3000+m only 3.23% of the geese had a high response. Thus, the further away the plane is laterally, the lower the response. For this data, the lowest response is when the plane is further than 3000 meters.

Thus, the recommendation would be a maximum height of 300 m and a minimum lateral distance of 3000 m.

10.57   a. $\chi^2 = \sum \dfrac{[n_i - E_i]^2}{E_i} = \dfrac{(26-23)^2}{23} + \dfrac{(146-136)^2}{136} + \dfrac{(361-341)^2}{341} + \dfrac{(143-136)^2}{136} + \dfrac{(13-23)^2}{23} = 9.647$

b.   From Table IV, Appendix D, with $df = 5$, $\chi^2_{.05} = 11.0705$

c.   No. Since the observed value of the test statistics does not fall in the rejection region $\left(\chi^2 = 9.647 \not> 11.0705 \right)$, H_0 is not rejected. There is insufficient evidence to indicate the salary distribution is non-normal for $\alpha = .05$.

d.   The p-value is $p = P\left(\chi^2 \geq 9.647 \right)$. Using MINITAB,

Cumulative Distribution Function
```
Chi-Square with 5 DF

      x   P( X <= x )
  9.647      0.914122
```
The p-value is $p = P\left(\chi^2 \geq 9.647 \right) = 1 - .914122 = .085878$.

Chapter 11
Simple Linear Regression

11.1 a.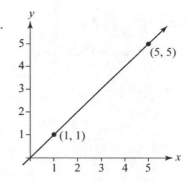

b.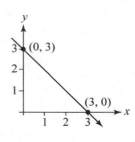

c.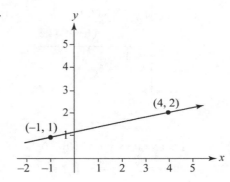

d.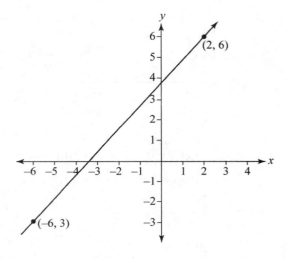

11.3   The two equations are: $4 = \beta_0 + \beta_1(-2)$ and $6 = \beta_0 + \beta_1(4)$

Subtracting the first equation from the second, we get

$$6 = \beta_0 + 4\beta_1$$
$$-(4 = \beta_0 - 2\beta_1)$$
$$\overline{}$$
$$2 = 6\beta_1 \Rightarrow \beta_1 = \frac{1}{3}$$

Substituting $\beta_1 = \frac{1}{3}$ into the first equation, we get:

$$4 = \beta_0 + \frac{1}{3}(-2) \Rightarrow \beta_0 = 4 + \frac{2}{3} = \frac{14}{3}$$

The equation for the line is $y = \dfrac{14}{3} + \dfrac{1}{3}x$.

11.5   To graph a line, we need two points. Pick two values for x, and find the corresponding y values by substituting the values of x into the equation.

a.   Let $x = 0 \Rightarrow y = 4 + (0) = 4$
       and $x = 2 \Rightarrow y = 4 + (2) = 6$

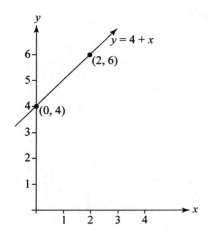

b.   Let $x = 0 \Rightarrow y = 5 - 2(0) = 5$

       and $x = 2 \Rightarrow y = 5 - 2(2) = 1$

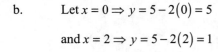

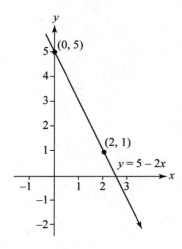

c.   Let $x = 0 \Rightarrow y = -4 + 3(0) = -4$
       and $x = 2 \Rightarrow y = -4 + 3(2) = 2$

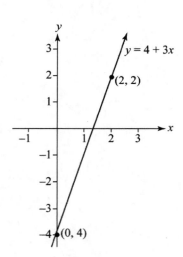

d.   Let $x = 0 \Rightarrow y = -2(0) = 0$
       and $x = 2 \Rightarrow y = -2(2) = -4$

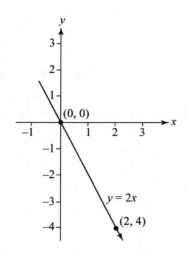

e. Let $x = 0 \Rightarrow y = 0$
and $x = 2 \Rightarrow y = 2$

f. Let $x = 0 \Rightarrow y = .5 + 1.5(0) = .5$
and $x = 2 \Rightarrow y = .5 + 1.5(2) = 3.5$

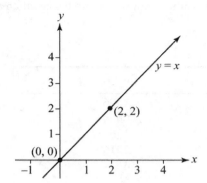

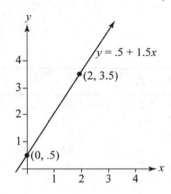

11.7   A deterministic model does not allow for random error or variation, whereas a probabilistic model does. An example where a deterministic model would be appropriate is:

Let y = cost of a 2×4 piece of lumber and
x = length (in feet)

The model would be $y = \beta_1 x$. There should be no variation in price for the same length of wood.

An example where a probabilistic model would be appropriate is:

Let y = sales per month of a commodity and
x = amount of money spent advertising

The model would be $y = \beta_0 + \beta_1 x + \varepsilon$. The sales per month will probably vary even if the amount of money spent on advertising remains the same.

11.9   No. The random error component, ε, allows the values of the variable to fall above or below the line.

11.11   a. The dependent variable is the ratio of salary to worker pay. The independent variable is the CEO's age.

b. A probabilistic model is more appropriate than a deterministic model because not all CEOs with the same age have the same ratio of salary to worker pay. There is error present.

c. The model is $y = \beta_0 + \beta_1 x + \varepsilon$.

11.13   a. The dependent variable is the opening weekend box-office revenue. The independent variable is the movie's tweet rate.

b. A probabilistic model is more appropriate than a deterministic model because not all movies with the same tweet rate have the same opening weekend box-office revenue. There is error present.

c. The model is $y = \beta_0 + \beta_1 x + \varepsilon$.

11.15   From Exercise 11.14, $\hat{\beta}_0 = 7.10$ and $\hat{\beta}_1 = -.78$.

The fitted line is $\hat{y} = 7.10 - .78x$. To obtain values for $\hat{y}$, we substitute values of x into the equation and solve for $\hat{y}$.

a.

x	y	$\hat{y} = 7.10 - .78x$	$(y - \hat{y})$	$(y - \hat{y})^2$
7	2	1.64	.36	.1296
4	4	3.98	.02	.0004
6	2	2.42	−.42	.1764
2	5	5.54	−.54	.2916
1	7	6.32	.68	.4624
1	6	6.32	−.32	.1024
3	5	4.76	.24	.0576
			$\sum(y-\hat{y}) = 0.02$	$SSE = \sum(y-\hat{y})^2 = 1.2204$

b.

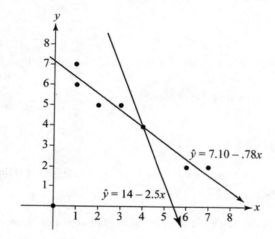

c.

x	y	$\hat{y} = 14 - 2.5x$	$(y - \hat{y})$	$(y - \hat{y})^2$
7	2	−3.5	5.5	30.25
4	4	4	0	0
6	2	−1	3	9
2	5	9	−4	16
1	7	11.5	−4.5	20.25
1	6	11.5	−5.5	30.25
3	5	6.5	−1.5	2.25
			$\sum(y-\hat{y}) = -7$	$SSE = 108.00$

11.17   a.   Using MINITAB, the scattergram of the data is:

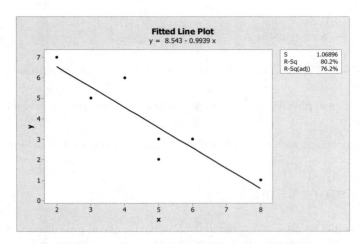

b.   Looking at the scattergram, x and y appear to have a negative linear relationship.

c.   Some preliminary calculations are:

$$\sum x = 33 \qquad \sum y = 27 \qquad \sum xy = 104 \qquad \sum x^2 = 179$$

$$SS_{xy} = \sum xy - \frac{\left(\sum x\right)\left(\sum y\right)}{n} = 104 - \frac{(33)(27)}{7} = -23.2857143$$

$$SS_{xx} = \sum x^2 - \frac{\left(\sum x\right)^2}{n} = 179 - \frac{(33)^2}{7} = 23.4285714$$

$$\hat{\beta}_1 = \frac{SS_{xy}}{SS_{xx}} = \frac{-23.2857143}{23.4285714} = -.99390244$$

$$\bar{x} = \frac{\sum x}{7} = \frac{33}{7} = 4.714285714 \qquad \bar{y} = \frac{\sum y}{7} = \frac{27}{7} = 3.857142857$$

$$\hat{\beta}_0 = \bar{y} - \hat{\beta}_1\bar{x} = 3.857142857 - (-.99390244)(4.714285714) = 8.542682931 \approx 8.5427$$

The least squares line is $\hat{y} = 8.5427 - .9939x$.

d.   The least squares line is plotted in part **a**. It appears to fit the data well.

11.19   a.   The straight-line model would be: $y = \beta_o + \beta_1 x + \varepsilon$

b.   From the printout, the least squares line is: $\hat{y} = -70.692 + 1.132x$.

c.   Since range of observed values for the 2010 Math SAT scores (x) does not include 0, the y-intercept has no meaning.

d.   The slope of the least squares line is $\hat{\beta}_1 = 1.132$. In terms of this problem, for each additional point increase in the 2010 Math SAT score, the mean 2014 Math SAT score is estimated to increase by

1.132. This interpretation is meaningful for values of x within the observed range. The observed range of x is 462 to 611.

11.21 a. The least squares line is $\hat{y} = 6.68 + .0048x$.

b. From the printout, $SSE = .5374$. No. The least squares line has the minimum squared error.

c. $\hat{\beta}_0 = 6.68$. Since the range of pipe diameters does not include 0, $\hat{\beta}_0$ has no practical interpretation.

$\hat{\beta}_1 = .0048$. For every 1 mm increase in pipe diameter, the mean ratio is estimated to increase by .0048.

d. For $x = 800$, $\hat{y} = 6.68 + .0048(800) = 10.5$

e. This prediction is not reliable because 800 is not in the observed range of pipe diameters. We do not know what the relationship between pipe diameter and the ratio looks like outside the observed range.

11.23 a. Using MINITAB, the results are:

Regression Analysis: MillionaireBirths versus TotalBirths
```
The regression equation is
MillionaireBirths = - 14.1 + 0.628 TotalBirths

Predictor        Coef  SE Coef      T      P
Constant       -14.138    8.121  -1.74  0.157
TotalBirths     0.6277   0.2435   2.58  0.061

S = 3.32256    R-Sq = 62.4%    R-Sq(adj) = 53.0%

Analysis of Variance

Source           DF      SS     MS      F      P
Regression        1   73.34  73.34   6.64  0.061
Residual Error    4   44.16  11.04
Total             5  117.50
```

The least squares prediction equation is $\hat{y} = -14.138 + .6277x$.

b. $\hat{\beta}_0 = -14.138$. Since 0 is not in the observed range of total US births, $\hat{\beta}_0$ has no meaning.

$\hat{\beta}_1 = .6277$. For each additional one million births, the mean number of software millionaire birthdays is estimated to increase by .6277.

c. For $x = 35$, $\hat{y} = -14.138 + .6277(35) = 7.8315$.

d. Using MINITAB, the results are:

Regression Analysis: MillionaireBirths versus CEOBirths
```
The regression equation is
MillionaireBirths = 2.72 + 0.306 CEOBirths

Predictor        Coef  SE Coef      T      P
Constant       2.7227   0.8513   3.20  0.033
CEOBirths     0.30626  0.04592   6.67  0.003
```

```
S = 1.55683    R-Sq = 91.7%    R-Sq(adj) = 89.7%

Analysis of Variance

Source          DF     SS      MS      F      P
Regression      1    107.81  107.81  44.48  0.003
Residual Error  4      9.69    2.42
Total           5    117.50
```

The least squares prediction equation is $\hat{y} = 2.7227 + .3063x$.

e. $\hat{\beta}_0 = 2.7227$. The estimate of the mean number of software millionaire birthdays is 2.7227 when the number of CEO birthdays is 0.

 $\hat{\beta}_1 = .3063$. For each additional CEO birthday, the mean number of software millionaire birthdays is estimated to increase by .3063.

f.   For $x = 10$, $\hat{y} = 2.7227 + .3063(10) = 5.7857$.

11.25   a.   The straight line model would be: $E(y) = \beta_0 + \beta_1 x$

b.   Some preliminary calculations are:

$$\sum x = 11,958 \qquad \sum y = 2,478.8 \qquad \sum xy = 739,647.16 \qquad \sum x^2 = 3,577,052.56 \qquad \sum y^2 = 154,676.28$$

$$\bar{x} = \frac{\sum x}{n} = \frac{11,958}{40} = 298.95 \qquad\qquad \bar{y} = \frac{\sum y}{n} = \frac{2,478.8}{40} = 61.97$$

$$SS_{xy} = \sum xy - \frac{(\sum x)(\sum y)}{n} = 739,647.16 - \frac{11,958(2,478.8)}{40} = -1,390.1$$

$$SS_{xx} = \sum x^2 - \frac{(\sum x)^2}{n} = 3,577,052.56 - \frac{11,958^2}{40} = 2,208.46$$

$$\hat{\beta}_1 = \frac{SS_{xy}}{SS_{xx}} = \frac{-1,390.1}{2,208.46} = -0.629443141 \approx -0.629$$

$$\hat{\beta}_0 = \bar{y} - \hat{\beta}_1\bar{x} = 61.97 - (-0.629443141)(298.95) = 250.142027 \approx 250.14$$

The least squares line is $\hat{y} = 250.14 - 0.629x$.

c.   Since 0 is not in the observed range of x (distance), $\hat{\beta}_0$ has no meaning.

d. $\hat{\beta}_1 = -0.629$. For each additional yard in a golfer's average driving distance, the mean driving accuracy is estimated to decrease by 0.629%.

e.   The estimate of the slope will help determine if the golfer's concern is valid since it tells us the change in driving accuracy per unit change in driving distance.

11.27 Some preliminary calculations are:

$$\sum x = 6,980.65 \qquad \sum y = 576.3 \qquad \sum xy = 396,603.225 \qquad \sum x^2 = 4,933,198.773 \qquad \sum y^2 = 35,626.09$$

$$\bar{x} = \frac{\sum x}{n} = \frac{6,980.65}{23} = 303.5065 \qquad\qquad \bar{y} = \frac{\sum y}{n} = \frac{576.3}{23} = 25.0565$$

$$SS_{xy} = \sum xy - \frac{\left(\sum x\right)\left(\sum y\right)}{n} = 396,603.225 - \frac{6,980.65(576.3)}{23} = 221,692.4165$$

$$SS_{xx} = \sum x^2 - \frac{\left(\sum x\right)^2}{n} = 4,933,198.773 - \frac{6,980.65^2}{23} = 2,814,525.972$$

$$\hat{\beta}_1 = \frac{SS_{xy}}{SS_{xx}} = \frac{221,692.4165}{2,814,525.972} = 0.07876723 \approx 0.0788$$

$$\hat{\beta}_0 = \bar{y} - \hat{\beta}_1\bar{x} = 25.0565 - (.07876723)(303.5065) = 1.1501335 \approx 1.1501$$

The fitted regression line is $\hat{y} = 1.1501 + .0788x$. We would estimate that the movie's opening weekend revenue would increase by $(.0788)(100) = 7.88$ million dollars as the tweet rate increases by 100.

11.29 a. Answers will vary. Suppose that the dependent variable is academic reputation score and the independent variable is average financial aid.

   b. Using MINITAB, the results are:

Regression Analysis: Academic Rep Score versus Avg Financial Aid
```
Analysis of Variance

Source          DF   Adj SS   Adj MS   F-Value   P-Value
Regression       1     3802   3802.5     37.73     0.000
Error           48     4838    100.8
Total           49     8640

Model Summary

       S    R-sq   R-sq(adj)   R-sq(pred)
 10.0392   44.01%     42.84%       40.42%

Coefficients

Term                    Coef    SE Coef   T-Value   P-Value    VIF
Constant               49.81       4.56     10.93     0.000
Avg Financial Aid   0.001006   0.000164      6.14     0.000   1.00

Regression Equation

Academic Rep Score = 49.81 + 0.001006 Avg Financial Aid
```

The least squares line is $\hat{y} = 49.81 + .001006x$.

$\hat{\beta}_0 = 49.81$. Since the range of average financial aid does not include 0, $\hat{\beta}_0$ has no practical interpretation.

$\hat{\beta}_1 = .001006$. For every one dollar increase in average financial aid, the mean academic reputation score is estimated to increase by .001006.

11.31   The graph in **b** would have the smallest s^2 because the width of the data points is the smallest.

11.33   a. $s^2 = \dfrac{SSE}{n-2} = \dfrac{8.34}{26-2} = .3475$

b.   We would expect most of the observations to be within $2s = 2\sqrt{.3475} \approx 1.179$ of the least squares line.

11.35   a. $s^2 = \dfrac{SSE}{n-2} = \dfrac{1.04}{28-2} = .04$ and $s = \sqrt{.04} = .2$

b.   We would expect most of the observations to be within $2s$ or of the $2(.2) = .4$ units of the fitted regression line.

11.37   a.   From the printout, $s = .22$.

b.   We would expect approximately 95% of the observed values of y (ratio of repair to replacement cost of commercial pipe) to fall within $2s$ or $2(.22) = .44$ units of their least squares predicted values.

11.39   a.   The straight line model would be: $y = \beta_0 + \beta_1 x + \varepsilon$.

b.   From the printout, the least squares prediction equation is: $\hat{y} = 119.9 + 0.3456x$.

c.   The assumptions are:
i. The mean of the probability distribution of the random component ε is 0.
ii. The variance of the probability distribution of ε is constant for all settings of the independent variable x.
iii. The probability distribution of ε is normal.
iv. The values of ε associated with any two observed values of y are independent.

d. $s = 635.187$

e.   About 95% of the observed values of y (total area) will fall within $2s$ or $2(635.187) = 1,270.374$ units of their least squares predicted values.

11.41   a.   Using MINITAB, the results of fitting the regreeeion line are:

Regression Analysis: AACC versus AAFEMA
```
The regression equation is
AACC = 0.249 + 0.00542 AAFEMA

Predictor      Coef     SE Coef      T       P
Constant     0.24885    0.02922    8.52   0.000
AAFEMA       0.005416   0.003245   1.67   0.102

S = 0.149176   R-Sq = 5.5%   R-Sq(adj) = 3.5%
```

```
Analysis of Variance

Source              DF      SS        MS       F      P
Regression          1    0.06200   0.06200  2.79   0.102
Residual Error     48    1.06817   0.02225
Total              49    1.13016
```

The estimate of σ^2 is $MSE = .02225$.

b.   The estimate of σ is $s = .149176$.

c.   The standard deviation in part b can be interpreted practically. The standard deviation is measured in the same units as the data. The variance is measured in square units and is very difficult to interpret.

d.   The range of the values of the average annual number of public corruption convictions is from .06 to .71 or range $= .71 - .06 = .65$. Two standard deviations is $2(.149) = .298$. Adding and subtracting 2 standard deviations from the mean would give a width of $2(.298) = .596$. Thus, knowing the state's average annual FEMA relief does not help very much in the prediction of a state's average annual number of public convictions compared with prediction without using the state's average annual FEMA relief.

11.43   Answers will vary. Suppose the dependent variable is again academic reputation score. Let the independent variable be average net cost. Using MINITAB, the results are:

Regression Analysis: Academic Rep Score versus Avg Net Cost
```
Analysis of Variance

Source        DF   Adj SS   Adj MS   F-Value   P-Value
Regression     1    239.6    239.6     1.37     0.248
Error         48   8400.6    175.0
Total         49   8640.2

Model Summary

       S    R-sq   R-sq(adj)   R-sq(pred)
 13.2292   2.77%      0.75%        0.00%

Coefficients

Term                 Coef    SE Coef   T-Value   P-Value   VIF
Constant            69.86       5.91     11.81     0.000
Avg Net Cost     0.000295   0.000252      1.17     0.248   1.00


Regression Equation

Academic Rep Score = 69.86 + 0.000295 Avg Net Cost
```

From this analysis, the standard deviation is $s = 13.23$. From the analysis in Exercise 11.29 with the independent variable as average financial aid, the standard deviation was $s = 10.04$. Since the standard deviation using average financial aid as the independent variable is smaller than the standard deviation using average net cost as the independent variable, average financial aid is a more accurate predictor for academic reputation score.

11.45   a.   For confidence coefficient .95, $\alpha = .05$ and $\alpha / 2 = .05 / 2 = .025$. From Table III, Appendix D, with $df = n - 2 = 10 - 2 = 8$, $t_{.025} = 2.306$. The 95% confidence interval for β_1 is:

$$\hat{\beta}_1 \pm t_{.025}s_{\hat{\beta}_1} \Rightarrow \hat{\beta}_1 \pm t_{.025}\frac{s}{\sqrt{SS_{xx}}} \Rightarrow 31 \pm 2.306\frac{3}{\sqrt{35}} \Rightarrow 31 \pm 1.17 \Rightarrow (29.83, 32.17)$$

For confidence coefficient .90, $\alpha = .10$ and $\alpha/2 = .10/2 = .05$. From Table III, Appendix D, with $df = 8$, $t_{.05} = 1.860$. The 90% confidence interval for β_1 is:

$$\hat{\beta}_1 \pm t_{.05}s_{\hat{\beta}_1} \Rightarrow 31 \pm 1.860\frac{3}{\sqrt{35}} \Rightarrow 31 \pm .94 \Rightarrow (30.06, 31.94)$$

b. $s^2 = \dfrac{SSE}{n-2} = \dfrac{1960}{14-2} = 163.33$, $s = \sqrt{s^2} = 12.7802$

For confidence coefficient, .95, $\alpha = .05$ and $\alpha/2 = .05/2 = .025$. From Table III, Appendix D, with $df = n - 2 = 14 - 2 = 12$, $t_{.025} = 2.179$. The 95% confidence interval for β_1 is:

$$\hat{\beta}_1 \pm t_{.025}s_{\hat{\beta}_1} \Rightarrow \hat{\beta}_1 \pm t_{.025}\frac{s}{\sqrt{SS_{xx}}} \Rightarrow 64 \pm 2.179\frac{12.7802}{\sqrt{30}} \Rightarrow 64 \pm 5.08 \Rightarrow (58.92, 69.08)$$

For confidence coefficient .90, $\alpha = .10$ and $\alpha/2 = .10/2 = .05$. From Table III, Appendix D, with $df = 12$, $t_{.05} = 1.782$. The 90% confidence interval for β_1 is:

$$\hat{\beta}_1 \pm t_{.05}s_{\hat{\beta}_1} \Rightarrow 64 \pm 1.782\frac{12.7802}{\sqrt{30}} \Rightarrow 64 \pm 4.16 \Rightarrow (59.84, 68.16).$$

c. $s^2 = \dfrac{SSE}{n-2} = \dfrac{146}{20-2} = 8.1111$, $s = \sqrt{s^2} = 2.848$.

For confidence coefficient .95, $\alpha = .05$ and $\alpha/2 = .05/2 = .025$. From Table III, Appendix D, with $df = n - 2 = 20 - 2 = 18$, $t_{.025} = 2.101$. The 95% confidence interval for β_1 is:

$$\hat{\beta}_1 \pm t_{.025}s_{\hat{\beta}_1} \Rightarrow \hat{\beta}_1 \pm t_{.025}\frac{s}{\sqrt{SS_{xx}}} \Rightarrow -8.4 \pm 2.101\frac{2.848}{\sqrt{64}} \Rightarrow -8.4 \pm .75 \Rightarrow (-9.15, -7.65)$$

For confidence coefficient .90, $\alpha = .10$ and $\alpha/2 = .10/2 = .05$. From Table III, Appendix D, with $df = 18$, $t_{.05} = 1.734$. The 90% confidence interval for β_1 is:

$$\hat{\beta}_1 \pm t_{.05}s_{\hat{\beta}_1} \Rightarrow -8.4 \pm 1.734\frac{2.848}{\sqrt{64}} \Rightarrow -8.4 \pm .62 \Rightarrow (-9.02, -7.78)$$

11.47   From Exercise 11.46, $\hat{\beta}_1 = .82$, $s = 1.1922$, $SS_{xx} = 28$, and $n = 7$.

For confidence coefficient .80, $\alpha = .20$ and $\alpha/2 = .20/2 = .10$. From Table III, Appendix D, with $df = n - 2 = 7 - 2 = 5$, $t_{.10} = 1.476$. The 80% confidence interval for β_1 is:

$$\hat{\beta}_1 \pm t_{.10}s_{\hat{\beta}_1} \Rightarrow .82 \pm 1.476\frac{1.1922}{\sqrt{28}} \Rightarrow .82 \pm 1.476(.2253) \Rightarrow .82 \pm .33 \Rightarrow (.49, 1.15)$$

For confidence coefficient .98, $\alpha = .02$ and $\alpha / 2 = .02 / 2 = .01$. From Table III, Appendix D, with df = 5, $t_{.01} = 3.365$. The 98% confidence interval for β_1 is:

$$\hat{\beta}_1 \pm t_{.01}s_{\hat{\beta}_1} \Rightarrow .82 \pm 3.365\frac{1.1922}{\sqrt{28}} \Rightarrow .82 \pm 3.365(.2253) \Rightarrow .82 \pm .76 \Rightarrow (.06, \ 1.58)$$

11.49   a.   To determine if the average state Math SAT score in 2011 has a positive relationship with the average state Math SAT score in 2001, we test:

$$H_0 : \beta_1 = 0$$
$$H_a : \beta_1 > 0$$

b.   From the printout in Exercise 11.19, the p-value is $p = 0.000$. This is the p-value for a 2-tailed test. The p-value for this one-tailed test is $0.000/2 = 0.000$. Since the p-value is less than $\alpha = .05$, H_0 is rejected. There is sufficient evidence to indicate the average state Math SAT score in 2011 has a positive relationship with the average state Math SAT score in 2001 at $\alpha = .05$.

c.   For confidence coefficient .95, $\alpha = .05$ and $\alpha / 2 = .05 / 2 = .025$. From Table III, Appendix D, with $df = n - 2 = 51 - 2 = 49$, $t_{.025} \approx 2.011$. The 95% confidence interval is:

$$\hat{\beta}_1 \pm t_{.025}s_{\hat{\beta}_1} \Rightarrow 1.188 \pm 2.011(.050) \Rightarrow 1.188 \pm .101 \Rightarrow (1.087, \ 1.289)$$

We are 95% confident that for each additional point on the 2001 average state Math SAT score, the increase in the mean 2011 average state Math SAT score is between 1.087 and 1.289.

11.51   a.   The sign of β_1 should be positive. As the number of daughters increase, the AAUW score should be higher.

b.   For confidence coefficient .95, $\alpha = .05$ and $\alpha / 2 = .05 / 2 = .025$. From Table II, Appendix D, $z_{.025} = 1.96$. The 95% confidence interval is:

$$\hat{\beta}_1 \pm z_{.025}s_{\hat{\beta}_1} \Rightarrow .27 \pm 1.96(.74) \Rightarrow .27 \pm 1.4504 \Rightarrow (-1.1804, \ 1.7204)$$

c.   Since 0 falls in the confidence interval found in part a, there is no evidence to reject H_0. There is insufficient evidence to indicate the number of daughters is linearly related to the AAUW score at $\alpha = .05$.

11.53   To determine if the cost ratio increases linearly with pipe diameter, we test:

$$H_0 : \beta_1 = 0$$
$$H_a : \beta_1 > 0$$

The test statistic is $t = 14.87$ and the p-value is $p = .000 / 2 = .000$.

Since the p-value is less than $\alpha(p = .000 < .05)$, H_0 is rejected. There is sufficient evidence to indicate that the cost ratio increases linearly with pipe diameter at $\alpha = .05$.

From the printout, the 95% confidence interval for the increase in cost ratio for every 1 millimeter increase in pipe diameter is $(.004077, .005494)$.

11.55   **a.**   From Exercise 11.23 a, $\hat{\beta}_1 = .6277$ and $s_{\hat{\beta}_1} = .2435$.

For confidence coefficient .95, $\alpha = .05$ and $\alpha / 2 = .05 / 2 = .025$. From Table III, Appendix D, with $df = n - 2 = 6 - 2 = 4$, $t_{.025} = 2.776$. The confidence interval is:

$$\hat{\beta}_1 \pm t_{.025} s_{\hat{\beta}_1} \Rightarrow .6277 \pm 2.776(.2435) \Rightarrow .6277 \pm .6760 \Rightarrow (-.0483, \, 1.3037)$$

We are 95% confident that for each additional one million US births, the mean number of software millionaire birthdays will change from -.0483 to 1.3037. Since 0 is in this interval, there is no evidence of a linear relationship between total US births and the number of software millionaire birthdays.

b.   From Exercise 11.23 d, $\hat{\beta}_1 = .3063$ and $s_{\hat{\beta}_1} = .0459$.

For confidence coefficient .95, $\alpha = .05$ and $\alpha / 2 = .05 / 2 = .025$. From Table III, Appendix D, with $df = n - 2 = 6 - 2 = 4$, $t_{.025} = 2.776$. The confidence interval is:

$$\hat{\beta}_1 \pm t_{.025} s_{\hat{\beta}_1} \Rightarrow .3063 \pm 2.776(.0459) \Rightarrow .3063 \pm .1274 \Rightarrow (.1789, \, .4337)$$

We are 95% confident that for each CEO birthdays, the mean number of software millionaire birthdays will increase from .1789 to .4337. Since 0 is not in this interval, there is evidence of a linear relationship between the number of CEO birthdays and the number of software millionaire birthdays.

c.   No, you cannot conclude that the number of software millionaires born in a decade is linearly related to the total number of people born in the U.S. because 0 is contained in the 95% confidence interval for β_1.

Yes, you can conclude that the number of software millionaires born in a decade is linearly related to the number of CEOs born in a decade because 0 is not contained in the 95% confidence interval for β_1.

11.57   **a.**   To determine if driving accuracy decreases linearly as driving distance increases, we test:

$$H_0: \beta_1 = 0$$
$$H_a: \beta_1 < 0$$

b.   From Exercise 11.25:

$$\sum y = 2{,}478.8 \qquad \sum y^2 = 154{,}676.28 \qquad SS_{xy} = -1{,}390.1 \qquad SS_{xx} = 2{,}208.46 \qquad \hat{\beta}_1 = -0.629443141$$

$$SS_{yy} = \sum y^2 - \frac{\left(\sum y\right)^2}{n} = 154{,}676.28 - \frac{2{,}478.8^2}{40} = 1{,}065.044$$

$$SSE = SS_{yy} - \hat{\beta}_1 SS_{xy} = 1{,}065.044 - (-.629443141)(-1{,}390.1) = 190.0550891$$

$$s^2 = MSE = \frac{SSE}{n-2} = \frac{190.0550891}{40-2} = 5.001449713 \qquad s = \sqrt{5.001449713} = 2.23639212$$

$$s_{\hat{\beta}_1} = \frac{s}{\sqrt{SS_{xx}}} = \frac{2.23639212}{\sqrt{2,208.46}} = .04759$$

The test statistic is $t = \dfrac{\hat{\beta}_1}{s_{\hat{\beta}_1}} = \dfrac{-.6294}{.04759} = -13.23$.

Using Table III, with $df = n - 2 = 40 - 2 = 38$, the p-value is approximately 0.000.

c.   Since the p-value is less than $\alpha = .01$, H_0 is rejected. There is sufficient evidence to indicate driving accuracy decreases linearly as driving distance increases at $\alpha = .01$.

11.59   To determine if the simple linear regression model is statistically useful for predicting Democratic vote share, we test:

$$H_0 : \beta_1 = 0$$
$$H_a : \beta_1 \neq 0$$

From Exercies 11.28, the test statistic is $t = .42$ and the p-value is $p = .676$.

Since the p-value is not less than $\alpha (p = .676 \not< .10)$, H_0 is not rejected. There is insufficient evidence to indicate the simple linear regression model is statistically useful for predicting Democratic vote share at $\alpha = .10$.

11.61   Using MINITAB, the results are:

Regression Analysis: Academic Rep Score versus Early Career Pay
```
Analysis of Variance

Source        DF   Adj SS   Adj MS   F-Value   P-Value
Regression     1    887.3    887.3      5.49     0.023
Error         48   7752.9    161.5
Total         49   8640.2

Model Summary

      S     R-sq   R-sq(adj)
12.7090   10.27%       8.40%

Coefficients

Term                    Coef    SE Coef   T-Value   P-Value
Constant                51.9       10.6      4.88     0.000
Early Career Pay    0.000441   0.000188      2.34     0.023

Regression Equation

Academic Rep Score = 51.9 + 0.000441 Early Career Pay
```

To determine if there is a positive linear relationship between academic reputation score and early career median salary, we test:

$$H_0 : \beta_1 = 0$$
$$H_a : \beta_1 > 0$$

The test statistic is $t = 2.34$ and the p-value is $p = .023 / 2 = .0115$.

Since the p-value is less than $\alpha\left(p = .0115 < .05\right)$, H_0 is rejected. There is sufficient evidence to indicate there is a positive linear relationship between academic reputation score and early career median salary at $\alpha = .05$.

If we use $\alpha = .01$, the conclusion changes. Since the p-value is not less than $\alpha\left(p = .0115 \not< .01\right)$, H_0 is not rejected. There is insufficient evidence to indicate there is a positive linear relationship between academic reputation score and early career median salary at $\alpha = .01$.

11.63   a.   Using MINITAB, the results are:

Regression Analysis: SLUGPCT versus ELEVATION
```
The regression equation is
SLUGPCT = 0.515 + 0.000021 ELEVATION

Predictor         Coef      SE Coef       T       P
Constant      0.515140     0.007954   64.76   0.000
ELEVATION    0.00002074   0.00000719    2.89   0.008


S = 0.0369803    R-Sq = 23.6%    R-Sq(adj) = 20.7%

Analysis of Variance

Source          DF         SS         MS       F       P
Regression       1    0.011390   0.011390    8.33   0.008
Residual Error  27    0.036924   0.001368
Total           28    0.048314
```

To determine if a positive linear relationship exists between elevation and slugging percentage, we test:

$$H_0 : \beta_1 = 0$$
$$H_a : \beta_1 > 0$$

The test statistic is $t = 2.89$ and the p-value is $p = .008 / 2 = .004$. Since the p-value is less than $\alpha\left(p = .004 < .01\right)$, H_0 is rejected. There is sufficient evidence to indicate that a positive linear relationship exists between elevation and slugging percentage at $\alpha = .01$.

b.   The scatterplot for the data is:

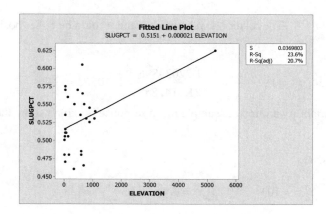

The data point for Denver is very far from the rest. This point looks to be an outlier. It is much different than all of the rest of the points.

c.   Removing the data point for Denver, the Minitab output is:

Regression Analysis: SLUGPCT versus ELEVATION
```
The regression equation is
SLUGPCT = 0.515 + 0.000020 ELEVATION

Predictor          Coef      SE Coef       T       P
Constant        0.51537      0.01066   48.33   0.000
ELEVATION    0.00002012   0.00002034    0.99   0.332


S = 0.0376839    R-Sq = 3.6%    R-Sq(adj) = 0.0%

Analysis of Variance

Source            DF         SS         MS      F       P
Regression         1   0.001389   0.001389   0.98   0.332
Residual Error    26   0.036922   0.001420
Total             27   0.038311
```

To determine if a positive linear relationship exists between elevation and slugging percentage, we test:

$$H_0 : \beta_1 = 0$$
$$H_a : \beta_1 > 0$$

The test statistic is $t = .99$ and the p-value is $p = .332 / 2 = .166$. Since the p-value is not less than $\alpha\left(p = .166 \not< .01\right)$, H_0 is not rejected. There is insufficient evidence to indicate that a positive linear relationship exists between elevation and slugging percentage when Denver is removed form the data at $\alpha = .01$. Since there was a linear relationship with Denver in the data set and no linear relationship with Denver removed from the data set, it supports the "thin air" theory.

11.65   a.   If $r = .7$, there is a positive relationship between x and y. As x increases, y tends to increase. The slope is positive.

b.   If $r = -.7$, there is a negative relationship between x and y. As x increases, y tends to decrease. The slope is negative.

c.   If $r = 0$, there is a 0 slope. There is no relationship between x and y.

d.   If $r^2 = .64$, then r is either .8 or $-.8$. The relationship between x and y could be either positive or negative.

11.67   a.   From Exercises 11.14 and 11.34, $r^2 = 1 - \dfrac{SSE}{SS_{yy}} = 1 - \dfrac{1.22033896}{21.7142857} = 1 - .0562 = .9438$

94.38% of the total sample variability around the sample mean response is explained by the linear relationship between y and x.

b.   Some preliminary calculations are:

$$\sum x = 33 \qquad \sum y = 27 \qquad \sum xy = 104 \qquad \sum x^2 = 179 \qquad \sum y^2 = 133$$

$$SS_{xy} = \sum xy - \frac{(\sum x)(\sum y)}{n} = 104 - \frac{33(27)}{7} = -23.2857143$$

$$SS_{xx} = \sum x^2 - \frac{(\sum x)^2}{n} = 179 - \frac{33^2}{7} = 23.4285714$$

$$\hat{\beta}_1 = \frac{SS_{xy}}{SS_{xx}} = \frac{-23.2857143}{23.4285714} = -.99390244$$

$$SS_{yy} = \sum y^2 - \frac{(\sum y)^2}{n} = 133 - \frac{27^2}{7} = 28.8571429$$

$$SSE = SS_{yy} - \hat{\beta}_1 SS_{xy} = 28.8571429 - (-.99390244)(-23.2857143) = 5.71341462$$

$$r^2 = 1 - \frac{SSE}{SS_{yy}} = 1 - \frac{5.71341462}{28.8571429} = 1 - .1980 = .802$$

80.2% of the total sample variability around the sample mean response is explained by the linear relationship between y and x.

11.69   a. $r^2 = .18$. 18% of the total sample variability around the sample mean number of points scored by a team that has a first-down is explained by the linear relationship between the number of points scored by a team that has a first-down and the number of yards from the opposing goal line.

   b. $r = \sqrt{.18} = -.424$. The value of r will be negative because the sign of the estimate of β_1 is negative.

11.71   a.   The linear model would be: $E(y) = \beta_0 + \beta_1 x$

   b. $r = .68$. There is a moderate positive linear relationship between RMP and SET.

   c.   Since $r = .68$ is positive, the slope of the line will also be positive.

   d.   The p-value is $p = .001$. Since this value is so small, we would reject H_0. There is sufficient evidence of a linear relationship between RMP and SET for any value of $\alpha > .001$.

   e. $r^2 = .68^2 = .4624$. 46.24% of the total sample variability around the sample mean SET values is explained by the linear relationship between SET and RMP.

11.73   a. $r = .983$. There is a strong positive linear relationship between the number of females in managerial positions and the number of females with college degrees.

   b. $r = .074$. There is a very weak positive linear relationship between the number of females in managerial positions and the number of female high school graduates with no college degree.

   c. $r = .722$. There is a moderately strong positive linear relationship between the number of males in managerial positions and the number of males with college degrees.

   d. $r = .528$. There is a moderately weak positive linear relationship between the number of males in managerial positions and the number of male high school graduates with no college degree.

11.75   a.   From the printout in Exercise 11.23a, $r^2 = 62.4\%$. 62.4% of the total sample variability around the sample mean number of software millionaire birthdays is explained by the linear relationship between the number of software millionaire birthdays and the total number of U.S. births.

      b.   From the printout in Exercise 11.23d, $r^2 = 91.7\%$. 91.7% of the total sample variability around the sample mean number of software millionaire birthdays is explained by the linear relationship between the number of software millionaire birthdays and the number of CEO birthdays.

      c.   Yes. There is a very strong positive linear relationship between the number of sotware millionaire birthdays and the number of CEO birthdays. As the number of software millionaire birthdays increase, the number of CEO birthdays also increases.

11.77   Some preliminary calculations are:

$$\sum x = 6,167 \qquad \sum x^2 = 1,641,115 \qquad \sum xy = 34,764.5 \qquad \sum y = 135.8 \qquad \sum y^2 = 769.72$$

$$SS_{xy} = \sum xy - \frac{\sum x \sum y}{n} = 34,764.5 - \frac{6167(135.8)}{24} = -130.44167$$

$$SS_{xx} = \sum x^2 - \frac{\left(\sum x\right)^2}{n} = 1,641,115 - \frac{(6,167)^2}{24} = 56,452.95833$$

$$SS_{yy} = \sum y^2 - \frac{\left(\sum y\right)^2}{n} = 769.72 - \frac{135.8^2}{24} = 1.3183333$$

$$\hat{\beta}_1 = \frac{SS_{xy}}{SS_{xx}} = \frac{-130.44167}{56,452.95833} = -0.002310625$$

$$SSE = SS_{yy} - \hat{\beta}_1 SS_{xy} = 1.3183333 - (-0.002310625)(-130.44167) = 1.016931516$$

$$r^2 = \frac{SS_{yy} - SSE}{SS_{yy}} = \frac{1.3183333 - 1.016931516}{1.3183333} = .2286$$

22.86% of the total sample variability around the sample mean sweetness index is explained by the linear relationship between the sweetness index and the amount of water soluble pectin.

$r = -\sqrt{.2286} = -.478$ (The value of r is negative because $\hat{\beta}_1$ is negative.)

Since this value is not close to one, there is a rather weak negative linear relationship between the sweetness index and the amount of water soluble pectin.

11.79   a.   To determine if the true population correlation coefficient relating NRMSE and bias is positive, we test:

$$H_0 : \rho = 0$$
$$H_a : \rho > 0$$

The test statistic is $t = \dfrac{r\sqrt{n-2}}{\sqrt{1-r^2}} = \dfrac{.2838\sqrt{3,600-2}}{\sqrt{1-.2838^2}} = \dfrac{17.02327}{.9588835} = 17.75$.

The p-value is $p = P(t > 17.75)$. Using MINITAB with $df = n - 2 = 3,600 - 2 = 3,598$, $p = P(t > 17.75) \approx 0$. Since the p-value is so small, H_0 is rejected. There is sufficient evidence to indicate the true population correlation coefficient relating NRMSE and bias is positive for any reasonable value of α.

b.   No. Even though there is a significant positive linear relationship between NRMSE and bias, the relationship is very weak. The relationship is highly significant because the sample size is so large.

11.81   To determine whether average earnings and height are positively correlated for those in the different occupations, we test:

$$H_0 : \rho = 0$$
$$H_a : \rho > 0$$

The test statistic is $t = \dfrac{r\sqrt{n-2}}{\sqrt{1-r^2}}$

We will use $\alpha = .01$ for all tests. The rejection region requires $\alpha = .01$ in the upper tail of the t-distribution. Since all of the sample sizes are over 100, the rejection regions will all be approximately the same. Using $df = \infty$ and Table III, Appendix D, $t_{.01} \approx 2.33$. The rejection region is $t > 2.33$.

For Sales, the test statistic is $t = \dfrac{r\sqrt{n-2}}{\sqrt{1-r^2}} = \dfrac{.41\sqrt{117-2}}{\sqrt{1-.41^2}} = 4.82$

For Managers, the test statistic is $t = \dfrac{r\sqrt{n-2}}{\sqrt{1-r^2}} = \dfrac{.35\sqrt{455-2}}{\sqrt{1-.35^2}} = 7.95$

For Blue Collar Workers, the test statistic is $t = \dfrac{r\sqrt{n-2}}{\sqrt{1-r^2}} = \dfrac{.32\sqrt{349-2}}{\sqrt{1-.32^2}} = 6.29$

For Service Workers, the test statistic is $t = \dfrac{r\sqrt{n-2}}{\sqrt{1-r^2}} = \dfrac{.31\sqrt{265-2}}{\sqrt{1-.31^2}} = 5.29$

For Professional/Technical Workers, the test statistic is $t = \dfrac{r\sqrt{n-2}}{\sqrt{1-r^2}} = \dfrac{.30\sqrt{453-2}}{\sqrt{1-.30^2}} = 6.68$

For Clerical Workers, the test statistic is $t = \dfrac{r\sqrt{n-2}}{\sqrt{1-r^2}} = \dfrac{.25\sqrt{358-2}}{\sqrt{1-.25^2}} = 4.87$

For Crafts/Forepersons, the test statistic is $t = \dfrac{r\sqrt{n-2}}{\sqrt{1-r^2}} = \dfrac{.24\sqrt{250-2}}{\sqrt{1-.24^2}} = 3.89$

Since the observed value of the test statistic falls in the rejection region for all occupations, H_0 is rejected. There is sufficient evidence to indicate the average earnings and height for those in all occupations are positively correlated at $\alpha = .01$.

We cannot conclude that a person taller than oneself will earn a higher salary. These correlation coefficients indicate that although there is a significant correlation, the correlations are all fairly weak. There is a trend, but there is also much variation that is not explained.

11.83   a.,b.   The scattergram is:

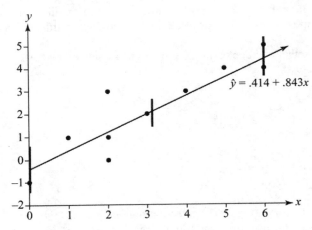

$\hat{y} = .414 + .843x$

c. $SSE = SS_{yy} - \hat{\beta}_1 SS_{xy} = 33.6 - .84318766(32.8) = 5.94344473$

$$s^2 = \frac{SSE}{n-2} = \frac{5.94344473}{10-2} = .742930591 \qquad s = \sqrt{.742930591} = .8619 \qquad \bar{x} = \frac{31}{10} = 3.1$$

The form of the confidence interval is $\hat{y} \pm t_{\alpha/2}\, s \sqrt{\dfrac{1}{n} + \dfrac{(x_p - \bar{x})^2}{SS_{xx}}}$

For $x_p = 6$, $\hat{y} = -.414 + .843(6) = 4.64$

For confidence coefficient .95, $\alpha = .05$ and $\alpha / 2 = .05 / 2 = .025$. From Table III, Appendix D, with $df = n - 2 = 10 - 2 = 8$, $t_{.025} = 2.306$. The confidence interval is:

$$4.64 \pm 2.306(.8619) \sqrt{\frac{1}{10} + \frac{(6-3.1)^2}{38.9}} \Rightarrow 4.64 \pm 1.12 \Rightarrow (3.52,\ 5.76)$$

d.   For $x_p = 3.2$, $\hat{y} = -.414 + .843(3.2) = 2.28$

The confidence interval is:

$$2.28 \pm 2.306(.8619) \sqrt{\frac{1}{10} + \frac{(3.2-3.1)^2}{38.9}} \Rightarrow 2.28 \pm .63 \Rightarrow (1.65,\ 2.91)$$

For $x_p = 0$, $\hat{y} = -.414 + .843(0) = -.41$

The confidence interval is:

$$-.41 \pm 2.306(.8619)\sqrt{\frac{1}{10}+\frac{(0-3.1)^2}{38.9}} \Rightarrow -.41 \pm 1.17 \Rightarrow (-1.58, .76)$$

e. The width of the confidence interval for the mean value of y depends on the distance x_p is from $\bar{x}$. The width of the interval for $x_p = 3.2$ is the smallest because 3.2 is the closest to $\bar{x} = 3.1$. The width of the interval for $x_p = 0$ is the widest because 0 is the farthest from $\bar{x} = 3.1$.

11.85   a. $\hat{\beta}_1 = \dfrac{SS_{xy}}{SS_{xx}} = \dfrac{28}{32} = .875 \qquad \hat{\beta}_0 - \bar{y} - \hat{\beta}_1\bar{x} = 4 - .875(3) = 1.375$

The least squares line is $\hat{y} = 1.375 + .875x$.

b.   The least squares line is:

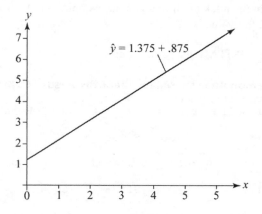

c. $SSE = SS_{yy} - \hat{\beta}_1 SS_{xy} = 26 - .875(28) = 1.5$

d. $s^2 = \dfrac{SSE}{n-2} = \dfrac{1.5}{10-2} = .1875$

e. $s = \sqrt{.1875} = .4330$

For $x_p = 2.5$, $\hat{y} = 1.375 + .875(2.5) = 3.5625$

For confidence coefficient .95, $\alpha = .05$ and $\alpha/2 = .05/2 = .025$. From Table III, Appendix D, with $df = n - 2 = 10 - 2 = 8$, $t_{.025} = 2.306$. The confidence interval is:

$$\hat{y} \pm t_{\alpha/2}\, s\sqrt{\frac{1}{n}+\frac{(x_p-\bar{x})^2}{SS_{xx}}} \Rightarrow 3.5625 \pm 2.306(.4330)\sqrt{\frac{1}{10}+\frac{(2.5-3)^2}{32}} \Rightarrow 3.5625 \pm .3279 \Rightarrow (3.2346, 3.8904)$$

f.   For $x_p = 4$, $\hat{y} = 1.375 + .875(4) = 4.875$

For confidence coefficient .95, $\alpha = .05$ and $\alpha/2 = .05/2 = .025$. From Table III, Appendix D, with $df = n - 2 = 10 - 2 = 8$, $t_{.025} = 2.306$. The prediction interval is:

$$\hat{y} \pm t_{\alpha/2}\, s\sqrt{1+\frac{1}{n}+\frac{\left(x_p-\bar{x}\right)^2}{SS_{xx}}} \Rightarrow 4.875 \pm 2.306(.4330)\sqrt{1+\frac{1}{10}+\frac{(4-3)^2}{32}} \Rightarrow 4.875 \pm 1.062$$

$$\Rightarrow (3.813,\ 5.937)$$

11.87   a.   The 95% confidence interval for $E(y)$ is $(4{,}783,\ 6{,}792)$. We are 95% confident that the true mean total catch is between 4,783 and 6,792 kilograms when the search function is 25.

      b.   The 95% prediction interval for y is $(2{,}643,\ 8{,}933)$. We are 95% confident that the true actual total catch is between 2,643 and 8,933 kilograms when the search function is 25.

11.89   Answers may vary. One possible answer is:

      For run 1, the 90% confidence interval for $x = 220$ is $(5.64898,\ 5.83848)$. We are 90% confident that the mean sweetness index of all orange juice samples will be between 5.64898 and 5.83848 parts per million when the pectin value is 220.

11.91   a.   Using MINITAB, the results are:

Regression Analysis: MillionaireBirths versus CEOBirths
```
The regression equation is
MillionaireBirths = 2.72 + 0.306 CEOBirths

Predictor      Coef   SE Coef     T      P
Constant     2.7227    0.8513  3.20  0.033
CEOBirths    0.30626  0.04592  6.67  0.003

S = 1.55683    R-Sq = 91.7%    R-Sq(adj) = 89.7%

Analysis of Variance

Source           DF       SS      MS      F      P
Regression        1   107.81  107.81  44.48  0.003
Residual Error    4     9.69    2.42
Total             5   117.50
```

Predicted Values for New Observations
```
New
Obs     Fit  SE Fit       95% CI              95% PI
  1  10.379   0.862  (7.987, 12.771)   (5.439, 15.320)
Values of Predictors for New Observations

New
Obs  CEOBirths
  1       25.0
```

      The 95% prediction interval is $(5.439,\ 15.320)$. We are 95% confident that the actual number of software millionaire birthdays in the decade will be between 5.439 and 15.320 when the number of CEO birthdays is 25.

      b.   The smaple mean number of CEO birthdays per decade is $\bar{x} = \dfrac{\sum x}{n} = \dfrac{74}{6} = 12.333$. The narrowest prediction interval is when the value of x used for the prediction is equal to $\bar{x}$. The further the value of x is from $\bar{x}$, the wider the prediction interval. Thus, the interval when $x = 11$ will be narrower than the interval when $x = 25$.

11.93   a.   From Exercises 11.30 and 11.62, $\hat{\beta}_0 = 5.221$, $\hat{\beta}_1 = -.114$, $SS_{xx} = 6,906.6087$, and $s = .8573$.

For $x_p = 15$, $\hat{y} = 5.2207 - .11402(15) = 3.5104$

For confidence coefficient .99, $\alpha = .01$ and $\alpha/2 = .01/2 = .005$. From Table III, Appendix D, with $df = n - 2 = 23 - 2 = 21$, $t_{.005} = 2.831$. The confidence interval is:

$$\hat{y} \pm t_{\alpha/2} s \sqrt{\frac{1}{n} + \frac{\left(x_p - \bar{x}\right)^2}{SS_{xx}}} \Rightarrow 3.5104 \pm 2.831(.8573)\sqrt{\frac{1}{23} + \frac{(15 - 22.8696)^2}{6,906.6087}} \Rightarrow 3.5104 \pm .5558$$

$$\Rightarrow (2.9546, \ 4.0662)$$

We are 99% confident that the mean mass of all spills will be between 2.9546 and 4.0662 when the elapsed time is 15 minutes.

     b.   For $x_p = 15$, $\hat{y} = 5.2207 - .11402(15) = 3.5104$

For confidence coefficient .99, $\alpha = .01$ and $\alpha/2 = .01/2 = .005$. From Table III, Appendix D, with $df = n - 2 = 23 - 2 = 21$, $t_{.005} = 2.831$. The prediction interval is:

$$\hat{y} \pm t_{\alpha/2} s \sqrt{1 + \frac{1}{n} + \frac{\left(x_p - \bar{x}\right)^2}{SS_{xx}}} \Rightarrow 3.5104 \pm 2.831(.8573)\sqrt{1 + \frac{1}{23} + \frac{(15 - 22.8696)^2}{6,906.6087}} \Rightarrow 3.5104 \pm 2.4898$$

$$\Rightarrow (1.0206, \ 6.0002)$$

We are 99% confident that the actual mass of a spill will be between 1.0206 and 6.0002 when the elapsed time is 15 minutes.

     c.   The prediction interval for the actual value is larger than the confidence interval for the mean. This will always be true. The prediction interval for the actual value contains 2 errors. First, we must locate the true mean of the distribution. Once this mean is located, the actual values of the variables can still vary around this mean. There is variance in locating the mean and then variance of the actual observations around the mean.

11.95   a.   Using MINITAB, the results of the regression analysis are:

Regression Analysis: QuitRate versus AvgWage
```
The regression equation is
QuitRate = 4.86 - 0.347 AvgWage

Predictor         Coef      SE Coef          T          P
Constant        4.8615       0.5201       9.35      0.000
AvgWage        -0.34655      0.05866      -5.91      0.000

S = 0.4862      R-Sq = 72.9%      R-Sq(adj) = 70.8%

Analysis of Variance

Source           DF           SS          MS          F          P
Regression        1       8.2507      8.2507      34.90      0.000
Residual Error   13       3.0733      0.2364
Total            14      11.3240
```

To determine if the average hourly wage rate contributes information to predict quit rates, we test:

$$H_0 : \beta_1 = 0$$
$$H_a : \beta_1 \neq 0$$

The test statistic is $t = \dfrac{\hat{\beta}_1 - 0}{s_{\hat{\beta}_1}} = -5.91$ and the p-value is $p = 0.000$.

Since the p-value is less than $\alpha(p = 0.000 < .05)$, H_0 is rejected. There is sufficient evidence to indicate that the average hourly wage rate contributes information to predict quit ratio at $\alpha = .05$.

Since the slope is negative $\left(\hat{\beta}_1 = -.34655\right)$, the model suggests that x and y have a negative relationship. As the average hourly wage rate increases, the quit rate tends to decrease.

b. Some preliminary calculations are:

$$\sum x = 129.05 \quad \sum x^2 = 1,178.9601 \quad \bar{x} = \frac{\sum x}{n} = \frac{129.05}{15} = 8.6033 \quad \hat{y} = 4.8615 - 0.34655(9) = 1.743$$

$$SS_{xx} = \sum x^2 - \frac{\left(\sum x\right)^2}{n} = 1,178.9601 - \frac{(129.05)^2}{15} = 68.699933$$

For confidence level .95, $\alpha = .05$ and $\alpha / 2 = .05 / 2 = .025$. From Table III, Appendix D, with $df = n - 2 = 15 - 2 = 13$, $t_{.025} = 2.160$. The 95% prediction interval is:

$$\hat{y} \pm t_{\alpha/2} s \sqrt{1 + \frac{1}{n} + \frac{\left(x_p - \bar{x}\right)^2}{SS_{xx}}} \Rightarrow 1.743 \pm 2.160(.4862)\sqrt{1 + \frac{1}{15} + \frac{(9 - 8.6033)^2}{68.699933}}$$

$$\Rightarrow 1.743 \pm 1.086 \Rightarrow (0.657,\ 2.829)$$

We are 95% confident that the actual quit rate when the average hourly wage is $9.00 is between 0.657 and 2.829.

c. The 95% confidence interval is:

$$\hat{y} \pm t_{\alpha/2} s \sqrt{\frac{1}{n} + \frac{\left(x_p - \bar{x}\right)^2}{SS_{xx}}} \Rightarrow 1.743 \pm 2.160(.4862)\sqrt{\frac{1}{15} + \frac{(9 - 8.6033)^2}{68.699933}}$$

$$\Rightarrow 1.743 \pm 0.276 \Rightarrow (1.467,\ 2.019)$$

We are 95% confident that the mean quit rate when the average hourly wage is $9.00 is between 1.467 and 2.019.

11.97   **Step 1:** The hypothesized model is $y = \beta_0 + \beta_1 x + \varepsilon$.

Step 2: The estimates of the unknown parameters are $\hat{\beta}_0 = -32.35$ and $\hat{\beta}_1 = 4.82$.

Since 0 is not in the range of observed values of the monthly price of naphtha, $\hat{\beta}_0$ has no practical interpretation. For each additional unit increase in the monthly price of naphtha, the mean monthly price of recycled colored plastic bottles is estimated to increase by 4.82.

Step 3: We assume that the error terms are normally and independently distributed with a mean of 0 and constant variance. Not enough information was provided in the exercise to estimate the variance of the error terms.

Step 4: To determine if there is a linear relationship between the monthly price of recycled colored plastic bottles and the monthly price of naphtha, we test:

$$H_0 : \beta_1 = 0$$
$$H_a : \beta_1 \neq 0$$

The test statistic is $t = 16.60$.

The p-value is $P(t > 16.60) + P(t < -16.60)$ where the t-distribution has $df = n - 2 = 120 - 2 = 118$. Using MINITAB, $P(t > 16.60) + P(t < -16.60) = .000 + .000 = .000$.

Since the p-value is so small, H_0 is rejected for any reasonable value of α. There is sufficient evidence to indicate a linear relationship exists between the monthly price of recycled colored plastic bottles and the monthly price of naphtha.

$r^2 = .69$. 69% of the total sample variation of monthly prices of recycled colored plastic bottles around their sample mean is explained by the linear relationship between the monthly price of recycled colored plastic bottles and the monthly price of naphtha.

$r = .83$. The correlation indicates a fairly strong positive linear relationship. This confirms our conclusion that monthly naphtha prices and monthly prices of recycled colored plastic bottles are positively linearly related.

11.99   a.   Using MINITAB, the results are:

Regression Analysis: Corrupt versus GDP
```
Analysis of Variance

Source        DF   Adj SS   Adj MS   F-Value   P-Value
Regression     1   3345.8   3345.76    45.33     0.000
Error         11    811.9     73.81
Total         12   4157.7


Model Summary

      S     R-sq   R-sq(adj)   R-sq(pred)
8.59141   80.47%      78.70%       70.72%


Coefficients

Term           Coef    SE Coef   T-Value   P-Value   VIF
Constant      25.89       3.09      8.37     0.000
GDP        0.000985   0.000146      6.73     0.000   1.00


Regression Equation
Corrupt = 25.89 + 0.000985 GDP
```

To determine if the model is adequate, we test:

$$H_0 : \beta_1 = 0$$
$$H_a : \beta_1 \neq 0$$

The test statistic is $t = 6.73$ and the p-value is $p = .000$. Since the p-value is so small, H_0 is rejected. There is sufficient evidence to indicate the model is adequate for predicting corruption level for any reasonable value of α.

In addition, $r^2 = .8047$. 80.47% of the sample variation in the corruption levels is explained by the linear relationship between the corruption levels and the GDP per capita. Thus, we would recommend that the model be used for thr predicition of corruption levels.

b.   Using MINITAB, the results are:

Regression Analysis: Corrupt versus PolR
```
Analysis of Variance

Source          DF  Adj SS  Adj MS  F-Value  P-Value
Regression       1  2527.6  2527.6    17.06    0.002
  PolR           1  2527.6  2527.6    17.06    0.002
Error           11  1630.0   148.2
  Lack-of-Fit    4   807.3   201.8     1.72    0.250
  Pure Error     7   822.8   117.5
Total           12  4157.7
```

```
Model Summary

      S    R-sq  R-sq(adj)  R-sq(pred)
12.1732  60.79%     57.23%      41.39%
```

```
Coefficients

Term         Coef  SE Coef  T-Value  P-Value   VIF
Constant    66.06     7.34     9.00    0.000
PolR        -6.25     1.51    -4.13    0.002  1.00
```

```
Regression Equation

Corrupt = 66.06 - 6.25 PolR
```

To determine if the model is adequate, we test:

$$H_0 : \beta_1 = 0$$
$$H_a : \beta_1 \neq 0$$

The test statistic is $t = -4.13$ and the p-value is $p = .002$. Since the p-value is so small, H_0 is rejected. There is sufficient evidence to indicate the model is adequate for predicting corruption level for any reasonable value of α.

In addition, $r^2 = .6079$. 60.79% of the sample variation in the corruption levels is explained by the linear relationship between the corruption levels and the degree of freedom in political rights. Thus, we would recommend that the model be used for thr predicition of corruption levels.

c.   The relationship between corruption levels and the GDP per capita is positive. The relationship between corruption levels and the degree of freedom in political rights is negative. Because the r^2 for the model using GDP per capita to predict corruption levels is greater than the the r^2 for the model using the degree of freedom in political rights to predict corruption levels, using GDP per capita will give better predictions.

11.101 a. $\hat{\beta}_1 = \dfrac{SS_{xy}}{SS_{xx}} = \dfrac{-88}{55} = -1.6$, $\hat{\beta}_0 = \bar{y} - \hat{\beta}_1 \bar{x} = 35 - (-1.6)(1.3) = 37.08$

The least squares line is $\hat{y} = 37.08 - 1.6x$.

b.

$\hat{y} = 37.08 - 1.6$

c. $SSE = SS_{yy} - \hat{\beta}_1 SS_{xy} = 198 - (-1.6)(-88) = 57.2$

d. $s^2 = \dfrac{SSE}{n-2} = \dfrac{57.2}{15-2} = 4.4$

e. For confidence coefficient .90, $\alpha = .10$ and $\alpha/2 = .10/2 = .05$. From Table III, Appendix D, with $df = n - 2 = 15 - 2 = 13$, $t_{.05} = 1.771$. The 90% confidence interval for β_1 is:

$$\hat{y} \pm t_{\alpha/2}\dfrac{s}{\sqrt{SS_{xx}}} \Rightarrow -1.6 \pm 1.771\dfrac{\sqrt{4.4}}{\sqrt{55}} \Rightarrow -1.6 \pm .50 \Rightarrow (-2.10, -1.10)$$

We are 90% confident the change in the mean value of y for each unit change in x is between -2.10 and -1.10.

f. For $x_p = 15$, $\hat{y} = 37.08 - 1.6(15) = 13.08$

The 90% confidence interval is:

$$\hat{y} \pm t_{\alpha/2}\, s\sqrt{\dfrac{1}{n} + \dfrac{(x_p - \bar{x})^2}{SS_{xx}}} \Rightarrow 13.08 \pm 1.771(\sqrt{4.4})\sqrt{\dfrac{1}{15} + \dfrac{(15 - 1.3)^2}{55}} \Rightarrow 13.08 \pm 6.93 \Rightarrow (6.15,\ 20.01)$$

g. The 90% prediction interval is:

$$\hat{y} \pm t_{\alpha/2}\, s\sqrt{1 + \dfrac{1}{n} + \dfrac{(x_p - \bar{x})^2}{SS_{xx}}} \Rightarrow 13.08 \pm 1.771(\sqrt{4.4})\sqrt{1 + \dfrac{1}{15} + \dfrac{(15 - 1.3)^2}{55}} \Rightarrow 13.08 \pm 7.86$$
$$\Rightarrow (5.22,\ 20.94)$$

11.103   a.   Using MINITAB, the scattergram of the data is:

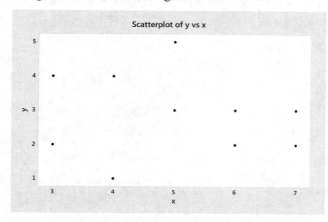

b.   Some preliminary calculations are:

$$\sum x = 50 \qquad \sum x^2 = 270 \qquad \sum xy = 143 \qquad \sum y = 29 \qquad \sum y^2 = 97$$

$$SS_{xy} = \sum xy - \frac{\sum x \sum y}{n} = 143 - \frac{50(29)}{10} = -2 \qquad SS_{xx} = \sum x^2 - \frac{\left(\sum x\right)^2}{n} = 270 - \frac{50^2}{10} = 20$$

$$SS_{yy} = \sum y^2 - \frac{\left(\sum y\right)^2}{n} = 97 - \frac{29^2}{10} = 12.9$$

$$r = \frac{SS_{xy}}{\sqrt{SS_{xx}SS_{yy}}} = \frac{-2}{\sqrt{20(12.9)}} = -.1245 \qquad r^2 = (-.1245)^2 = .0155$$

c.   Some preliminary calculations are:

$$\hat{\beta}_1 = \frac{SS_{xy}}{SS_{xx}} = \frac{-2}{20} = -.1 \qquad\qquad SSE = SS_{yy} - \hat{\beta}_1 SS_{xy} = 12.9 - (-.1)(-2) = 12.7$$

$$s^2 = \frac{SSE}{n-2} = \frac{12.7}{10-2} = 1.5875 \qquad s = \sqrt{1.5875} = 1.25996$$

To determine if x and y are linearly correlated, we test:

$$H_0 : \beta_1 = 0$$
$$H_a : \beta_1 \neq 0$$

The test statistic is $t = \dfrac{\hat{\beta}_1 - 0}{\dfrac{s}{\sqrt{SS_{xx}}}} = \dfrac{-.1 - 0}{\dfrac{1.25996}{\sqrt{20}}} = -.35$

The rejection requires $\alpha / 2 = .10 / 2 = .05$ in the each tail of the t-distribution with $df = n - 2 = 10 - 2 = 8$. From Table III, Appendix D, $t_{.05} = 1.86$. The rejection region is $t < -1.86$ or $t > 1.86$.

Since the observed value of the test statistic does not fall in the rejection region $(t = -.35 \not< -1.86)$, H_0 is not rejected. There is insufficient evidence to indicate that x and y are linearly correlated at $\alpha = .10$.

11.105   a.   The value of r is .70. Since this number is somewhat close to 1, there is a moderate positive linear relationship between self-knowledge skill level and goal-setting ability.

  b.   Since the p-value is so small $(p = 0.001)$, there is evidence to reject H_0. There is sufficient evidence to indicate a significant linear relationship between self-knowledge skill level and goal-setting ability for any value of $\alpha > .001$.

  c. $r^2 = .70^2 = .49$. 49% of the total sample variability around the sample mean goal-setting ability is explained by the linear relationship between self-knowledge skill level and goal-setting ability.

11.107   a.   Using MINITAB, the scattergram is:

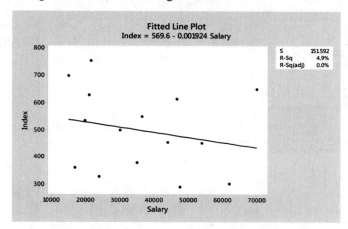

It appears as salary increases, the retaliation index decreases.

  b. $$\sum x = 544,100 \qquad \sum y = 7,497 \qquad \sum xy = 263,977,000 \qquad \sum x^2 = 23,876,290,000$$

$$\sum y^2 = 4,061,063 \qquad \bar{x} = \frac{\sum x}{n} = \frac{544,100}{15} = 36,273.333 \qquad \bar{y} = \frac{\sum y}{n} = \frac{7,497}{15} = 499.8$$

$$SS_{xy} = \sum xy - \frac{\left(\sum x\right)\left(\sum y\right)}{n} = 263,977,000 - \frac{(544,100)(7,497)}{15} = 263,977,000 - 271,941,180 = -7,964,180$$

$$SS_{xx} = \sum x^2 - \frac{\left(\sum x\right)^2}{n} = 23,876,290,000 - \frac{(544,100)^2}{15} = 23,876,290,000 - 19,736,320,670 = 4,139,969,330$$

$$\hat{\beta}_1 = \frac{SS_{xy}}{SS_{xx}} = \frac{-7,964,180}{4,139,969,330} = -.001923729 \approx -.00192$$

$$\hat{\beta}_0 = \bar{y} - \hat{\beta}_1\bar{x} = 499.8 - (-.001923729)(36,273.333) = 499.8 + 69.78007144$$
$$= 569.5800714 \approx 569.5801$$

The fitted regression line is $\hat{y} = 569.5801 - .00192x$.

c.   The least squares line supports the answer because the line has a negative slope.

d. $\hat{\beta}_0 = 569.58$ This has no meaning because $x = 0$ is not in the observed range.

e. $\hat{\beta}_1 = -.00192$ When the salary increases by \$1, the mean retaliation index is estimated to decrease
    by .00192. This is meaningful for the range of x from \$16,900 to \$70,000.

f.   Some preliminary calculations are:

$$SS_{yy} = \sum y^2 - \frac{\left(\sum y\right)^2}{n} = 4,061,063 - \frac{7,497^2}{15} = 314,062.4$$

$$SSE = SS_{yy} - \hat{\beta}_1 SS_{xy} = 314,062.4 - (-.001923729)(-7,964,180) = 298,741.476$$

$$s^2 = MSE = \frac{SSE}{n-2} = \frac{298,741.476}{15-2} = 22,980.11354 \qquad s = \sqrt{22,980.11354} = 151.591931$$

$$s_{\hat{\beta}_1} = \frac{s}{\sqrt{SS_{xx}}} = \frac{151.591931}{\sqrt{4,139,969,330}} = .002356$$

To determine if the model is adequate, we test:

$$H_0 : \beta_1 = 0$$
$$H_a : \beta_1 \neq 0$$

The test statistic is $t = \dfrac{\hat{\beta}_1}{s_{\hat{\beta}_1}} = \dfrac{-.00192}{.002356} = -.82$.

The rejection region requires $\alpha/2 = .05/2 = .025$ in each tail of the t-distribution with
$df = n - 2 = 15 - 2 = 13$. From Table III, Appendix D, $t_{.025} = 2.160$. The rejection region is
$t < -2.160$ or $t > 2.160$.

Since the observed value of the test statistic does not fall in the rejection region $(t = -.82 \not< -2.160)$,
H_0 is not rejected. There is insufficient evidence to indicate that the model is adequate at $\alpha = .05$.

11.109 a.   The straight-line model is $y = \beta_0 + \beta_1 x + \varepsilon$.

b.   The least squares line is $\hat{y} = -2,298.3676 + 11,598.884x$.

c.   Since 0 is not in the range of observed number of carats, $\hat{\beta}_0$ has no practical interpretation.

d.   The 95% confidence interval is $(11,146.0846,\ 12,051.6834)$. We are 95% confident that for each
    additional carat, the mean asking price is estimated to increase from between \$11,146.0846 and
    \$12,051.6834.

e. The estimated standard deviation is $s = RMSE = 1,117.5642$. Most of the observed values of asking price will fall within approximately $2s$ or $2(1,117.5642) = 2,235.1284$ dollars of their respective predicted values.

f. To determine if a positive linear relationship exits between asking price and size, we test:

$$H_0 : \beta_1 = 0$$
$$H_a : \beta_1 > 0$$

g. The p-value is $p < 0.0001$. Since the p-value is less than $\alpha\,(p < .0001 < .05)$, H_0 is rejected. There is sufficient evidence to indicate a positive linear relationship exits between asking price and size at $\alpha = .05$.

h. $r^2 = .8925$. 89.25% of the total sample variation in the asking prices around their sample mean is explained by the linear relationship between size and asking price.

i. $r = .9447$. Since this value is very close to 1, it indicates that there is a strong, positive linear relationship between size and asking price.

j. The prediction interval is $(1,297.6366,\ 5,704.5322)$. We are 95% confident that the true asking price will fall between $1,297.6366 and $5,704.5322 when the size is .5 carats.

k. The confidence interval is $(3,362.4670,\ 3,639.7018)$. We are 95% confident that the true mean asking price will fall between $3,362.4670 and $3,639.7018 when the size is .5 carats.

11.111 a. Using MINITAB, the scattergram is:

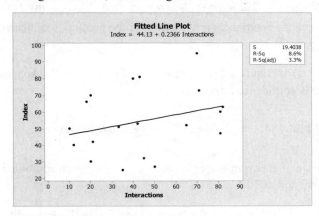

b. Using MINITAB, the regression analysis is:

Regression Analysis: Index versus Interactions
```
The regression equation is
Index = 44.1 + 0.237 Interactions

Predictor        Coef      SE Coef          T          P
Constant       44.130        9.362       4.71      0.000
Interact       0.2366       0.1865       1.27      0.222

S = 19.40        R-Sq = 8.6%        R-Sq(adj) = 3.3%
```

```
Analysis of Variance

Source            DF        SS        MS        F       P
Regression         1      606.0     606.0     1.61   0.222
Residual Error    17     6400.6     376.5
Total             18     7006.6
```

From the printout, the least squares line is $\hat{y} = 44.13 + .2366x$.

c.   From the printout, $s = 19.40$.

The standard deviation s represents the spread of the manager success index about the least squares line. Approximately 95% of the manager success indexes should lie within $2s = 2(19.40) = 38.8$ units of the least squares line.

d.   Refer to the scattergram in part **a**. The number of interactions with outsiders might contribute some information in the prediction of managerial success, but it does not look like a very strong relationship.

e.   To determine if the number of interactions contributes information for the prediction of managerial success, we test:

$$H_0 : \beta_1 = 0$$
$$H_a : \beta_1 \neq 0$$

The test statistic is $t = \dfrac{\hat{\beta}_1 - 0}{s_{\hat{\beta}_1}} = 1.27$ .and the p-value is $p = .222$.

Since the p-value is not less than $\alpha(p = .222 \not< .05)$, H_0 is not rejected. There is insufficient evidence to indicate the number of interactions contributes information for the prediction of managerial success at $\alpha = .05$.

f.   For confidence coefficient .95, $\alpha = .05$ and $\alpha / 2 = .05 / 2 = .025$. From Table III, Appendix D, with $df = 17$, $t_{.025} = 2.110$. The 95% confidence interval is:

$$\hat{\beta}_1 \pm t_{.025} s_{\hat{\beta}_1} \Rightarrow .2366 \pm 2.110(.1865) \Rightarrow .2366 \pm .3935 \Rightarrow (-.1569, .6301)$$

We are 95% confident the change in the mean manager success index for each additional interaction with outsiders is between $-.1569$ and $.6301$.

g.   For confidence coefficient .90, $\alpha = .10$ and $\alpha / 2 = .10/2 = .05$. From Table III, Appendix D, with $df = n - 2 = 19 - 2 = 17$, $t_{.05} = 1.740$.

When $x_p = 55$, $\hat{y} = 44.13 + .2366(55) = 57.143$

The prediction interval is:

$$\hat{y}\pm t_{\alpha/2}s\sqrt{1+\frac{1}{n}+\frac{\left(x_p-\bar{x}\right)^2}{SS_{xx}}} \Rightarrow 57.143\pm1.74(19.40)\sqrt{1+\frac{1}{19}+\frac{\left(55-44.1579\right)^2}{10,824.5263}}$$

$$\Rightarrow 57.143\pm34.811\Rightarrow\left(22.332,\ 91.954\right)$$

h.   The number of interactions with outsiders in the study went from 10 to 82. The value 110 is not within this interval. We do not know if the relationship between *x* and *y* is the same outside the observed range. Also, the farther x_p lies from $\bar{x}$ the larger will be the error of prediction. The prediction interval for a particular value of *y* will be very wide when $x_p = 110$.

i.   The prediction interval for a manager's success index will be narrowest when the number of contacts with people outside her work unit is $\bar{x} = 44.1579\ (44)$.

11.113   a.   A proposed model is $y=\beta_o+\beta_1 x+\varepsilon$.

b.   Some preliminary calculations are:

$$\sum x=1,292.7 \quad \sum y=3,781.1 \quad \sum xy=218,291.63 \quad \sum x^2=88,668.43 \quad \sum y^2=651,612.45$$

$$\bar{x}=\frac{\sum x}{n}=\frac{1,292.7}{22}=58.75909091 \qquad \bar{y}=\frac{\sum y}{n}=\frac{3,781.1}{22}=171.8681818$$

$$SS_{xy}=\sum xy-\frac{\left(\sum x\right)\left(\sum y\right)}{n}=218,291.63-\frac{1,292.7(3,781.1)}{22}$$
$$=218,291.63-222,173.9986=-3,882.3686$$

$$SS_{xx}=\sum x^2-\frac{\left(\sum x\right)^2}{n}=88,668.43-\frac{\left(1,292.7\right)^2}{22}=88,668.43-75,957.87682=12,710.55318$$

$$SS_{yy}=\sum y^2-\frac{\left(\sum y\right)^2}{n}=651,612.45-\frac{\left(3,781.1\right)^2}{22}=651,612.45-649,850.7823=1,761.6677$$

$$\hat{\beta}_1=\frac{SS_{xy}}{SS_{xx}}=\frac{-3,882.3686}{12,710.55318}=-0.305444503\approx-0.305$$

$$\hat{\beta}_o=\bar{y}-\hat{\beta}_1\bar{x}=171.8681818-\left(-0.305444503\right)(58.75909091)=189.8158231\approx189.816$$

The fitted regression line is: $\hat{y}=189.816-0.305x$

c.   Using MINITAB, a graph of the fitted regression line is:

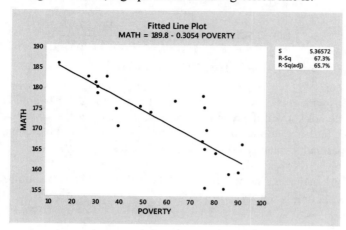

From the fitted regression line, the relationship between the two variables is negative.

d. $\hat{\beta}_o = 189.816$.   Since 0 is not in the range of observed values of the variable % Below Poverty, the y-intercept has no meaning.

$\hat{\beta}_1 = -0.305$.   For each one percent increase in the % Below Poverty, the mean value of FCAT-Math is estimated to decrease by 0.305.

e.   Some preliminary calculations are:
$$SSE = SS_{yy} - \hat{\beta}_1 SS_{xy} = 1,761.6677 - (-0.305444503)(-3,882.3686) = 575.8195525$$

$$s^2 = \frac{SSE}{n-2} = \frac{575.8195525}{22-2} = 28.79097763 \qquad s = \sqrt{28.79097763} = 5.3657$$

$$s_{\hat{\beta}_1} = \frac{s}{\sqrt{SS_{xx}}} = \frac{5.3657}{\sqrt{12,710.55318}} = .0476$$

To determine if math score and percentage below the poverty level are linearly related, we test:

$$H_0 : \beta_1 = 0$$
$$H_a : \beta_1 \neq 0$$

The test statistic is $t = \dfrac{\hat{\beta}_1 - 0}{s_{\hat{\beta}_1}} = \dfrac{-.3054 - 0}{.0476} = -6.42$.

The rejection region requires $\alpha / 2 = .05 / 2 = .025$ in each tail of the t-distribution. From Table III, Appendix D, $t_{.025} = 2.086$ with $df = n - 2 = 22 - 2 = 20$. The rejection region is $t < -2.086$ or $t > 2.086$.

Since the observed value of the test statistic falls in the rejection region $(t = -6.42 < -2.086)$, H_0 is rejected. There is sufficient evidence to indicate that math score and percentage below the poverty level are linearly related at $\alpha = .05$.

f.   A proposed model is $y = \beta_0 + \beta_1 x + \varepsilon$.

Some preliminary calculations are:

$$\sum x = 1{,}292.7 \qquad \sum y = 3{,}764.2 \qquad \sum xy = 217{,}738.81 \qquad \sum x^2 = 88{,}668.43 \qquad \sum y^2 = 645{,}221.16$$

$$\bar{x} = \frac{\sum x}{n} = \frac{1{,}292.7}{22} = 58.75909091 \qquad\qquad \bar{y} = \frac{\sum y}{n} = \frac{3{,}764.2}{22} = 171.1$$

$$SS_{xy} = \sum xy - \frac{(\sum x)(\sum y)}{n} = 217{,}738.81 - \frac{1{,}292.7(3{,}764.2)}{22}$$
$$= 217{,}738.81 - 221{,}180.97 = -3{,}442.16$$

$$SS_{xx} = \sum x^2 - \frac{(\sum x)^2}{n} = 88{,}668.43 - \frac{(1{,}292.7)^2}{22} = 88{,}668.43 - 75{,}957.87682 = 12{,}710.55318$$

$$SS_{yy} = \sum y^2 - \frac{(\sum y)^2}{n} = 645{,}221.16 - \frac{(3{,}764.2)^2}{22} = 645{,}221.16 - 644{,}054.62 = 1{,}166.54$$

$$\hat{\beta}_1 = \frac{SS_{xy}}{SS_{xx}} = \frac{-3{,}442.16}{12{,}710.55318} = -0.270811187 \approx -0.271$$

$$\hat{\beta}_0 = \bar{y} - \hat{\beta}_1\bar{x} = 171.1 - (-0.270811187)(58.75909091) = 187.0126192 \approx 187.013$$

The fitted regression line is: $\hat{y} = 187.013 - 0.271x$

Using MINITAB, a graph of the fitted regression line is:

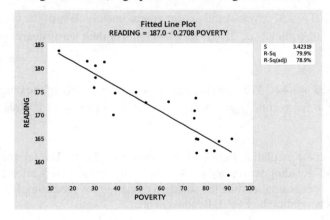

From the fitted regression line, the relationship between the two variables is negative.

$\hat{\beta}_0 = 187.013$.   Since 0 is not in the range of observed values of the variable % Below Poverty, the y-intercept has no meaning.

$\hat{\beta}_1 = -0.271$.   For each additional one percent increase in % Below Poverty, the mean value of FCAT-Reading is estimated to decrease by .271.

Some preliminary calculations are:

$$SSE = SS_{yy} - \hat{\beta_1}SS_{xy} = 1,166.54 - (-0.270811187)(-3,442.16) = 234.3645646$$

$$s^2 = \frac{SSE}{n-2} = \frac{234.3645646}{22-2} = 11.71822823 \qquad s = \sqrt{11.71822823} = 3.4232$$

$$s_{\hat{\beta_1}} = \frac{s}{\sqrt{SS_{xx}}} = \frac{3.4232}{\sqrt{12,710.55318}} = .0304$$

To determine if reading score and percentage below the poverty level are linearly related, we test:

$$H_0 : \beta_1 = 0$$
$$H_a : \beta_1 \neq 0$$

The test statistic is $t = \dfrac{\hat{\beta_1} - 0}{s_{\hat{\beta_1}}} = \dfrac{-.2708 - 0}{.0304} = -8.91$.

The rejection region requires $\alpha/2 = .05/2 = .025$ in each tail of the t-distribution. From Table III, Appendix D, $t_{.025} = 2.086$ with $df = n-2 = 22-2 = 20$. The rejection region is $t < -2.086$ or $t > 2.086$.

Since the observed value of the test statistic falls in the rejection region $(t = -8.91 < -2.086)$, H_0 is rejected. There is sufficient evidence to indicate that reading score and percentage below the poverty level are linearly related at $\alpha = .05$.

g.   From part e, $s = \sqrt{28.79097763} = 5.37$. We would expect approximately 95% of the observed values of y (FCAT-Math scores) to fall within $2s$ or $2(5.37) = 10.74$ units of their least squares predicted values.

h.   From part f, $s = \sqrt{11.71822823} = 3.42$. We would expect approximately 95% of the observed values of y (FCAT-Reading scores) to fall within $2s$ or $2(3.42) = 6.84$ units of their least squares predicted values.

i.   The sample standard deviation for predicting FCAT-Math scores is $s = 5.37$. The sample standard deviation for predicting FCAT-Reading scores is $s = 3.42$. Since the standard deviation for predicting FCAT-Reading scores is smaller than the standard deviation for predicting FCAT-Math scores, we can more accurately predict the FCAT-Reading scores.

11.115 a. Using MINITAB, the scattergram of the data is:

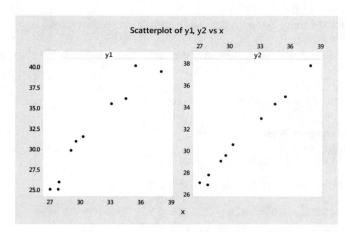

b. It appears that the weigh-in-motion reading after calibration adjustment is more highly correlated with the static weight of trucks than prior to calibration adjustment. The scattergram is closer to a straight line.

c. Some preliminary calculations are:

$$\sum x = 312.8 \qquad \sum x^2 = 9,911.42 \qquad \sum xy_1 = 10,201.41 \qquad \sum xy_2 = 9,859.84$$

$$\sum y_1 = 320.2 \qquad \sum y_1^2 = 10,543.68 \qquad \sum y_2 = 311.2 \qquad \sum y_2^2 = 9,809.52$$

$$SS_{xy_1} = \sum xy_1 - \frac{\sum x \sum y_1}{n} = 10,201.41 - \frac{312.8(320.2)}{10} = 185.554$$

$$SS_{xx} = \sum x^2 - \frac{\left(\sum x\right)^2}{n} = 9,911.42 - \frac{312.8^2}{10} = 127.036$$

$$SS_{y_1 y_1} = \sum y_1^2 - \frac{\left(\sum y_1\right)^2}{n} = 10,543.68 - \frac{320.2^2}{10} = 290.876$$

$$SS_{xy_2} = \sum xy_2 - \frac{\sum x \sum y_2}{n} = 9,859.84 - \frac{312.8(311.2)}{10} = 125.504$$

$$SS_{y_2 y_2} = \sum y_2^2 - \frac{\left(\sum y_2\right)^2}{n} = 9,809.52 - \frac{311.2^2}{10} = 124.976$$

$$r_1 = \frac{SS_{xy_1}}{\sqrt{SS_{xx} SS_{y_1 y_1}}} = \frac{185.554}{\sqrt{127.036(290.876)}} = .965 \qquad r_2 = \frac{SS_{xy_2}}{\sqrt{SS_{xx} SS_{y_2 y_2}}} = \frac{125.504}{\sqrt{127.036(124.976)}} = .996$$

$r_1 = .965$ implies the static weight of trucks and weigh-in-motion prior to calibration adjustment have a strong positive linear relationship.

$r_2 = .996$ implies the static weight of trucks and weigh-in-motion after calibration adjustment have a stronger positive linear relationship.

The closer r is to 1 indicates the more accurate the weigh-in-motion readings are.

d.   Yes. If the weigh-in-motion readings were all exactly the same distance below (or above) the actual readings, r would be 1.

11.117 a.   Using MINITAB, the results of the regression analysis are:

Regression Analysis: Managers versus UnitsSold
```
The regression equation is
Managers = 5.33 + 0.586 UnitsSold

Predictor         Coef      SE Coef          T        P
Constant         5.325        1.180       4.51    0.000
UnitsSol       0.58610      0.03818      15.35    0.000

S = 2.566        R-Sq = 92.9%      R-Sq(adj) = 92.5%

Analysis of Variance

Source           DF          SS         MS         F        P
Regression        1      1552.0     1552.0    235.63    0.000
Residual Error   18       118.6        6.6
Total            19      1670.5
```

To determine the usefulness of the model, we test:

$$H_0 : \beta_1 = 0$$
$$H_a : \beta_1 \neq 0$$

The test statistic is $t = \dfrac{\hat{\beta}_1 - 0}{s_{\hat{\beta}_1}} = 15.35$ and the p-value is $p = 0.000$.

Since the p-value is less than $\alpha (p = 0.000 < .05)$, H_0 is rejected. There is sufficient evidence to indicate the model is useful at $\alpha = .05$. Therefore, the monthly sales is useful in predicting the number of managers at $\alpha = .05$.

b.   For confidence coefficient .90, $\alpha = .10$ and $\alpha / 2 = .10 / 2 = .05$. From Table III, Appendix D, with $df = n - 2 = 20 - 2 = 18$, $t_{.05} = 1.734$.

For $x_p = 39$, $\bar{x} = \dfrac{\sum x}{n} = \dfrac{540}{20} = 27$, and $\hat{y} = 5.325 + .5861(39) = 28.1829$. Also, $SS_{xx} = 4,518$.

The 90% prediction interval is:

$$\hat{y} \pm t_{\alpha/2} s \sqrt{1 + \frac{1}{n} + \frac{\left(x_p - \bar{x}\right)^2}{SS_{xx}}} \Rightarrow 28.183 \pm 1.734(2.566) \sqrt{1 + \frac{1}{20} + \frac{(39 - 27)^2}{4,518}}$$
$$\Rightarrow 28.183 \pm 4.628 \Rightarrow (23.555, \ 32.811)$$

c.   We are 90% confident the actual number of managers needed when 39 units are sold is between 23.55 and 32.81.

11.119 Using MINITAB, the two regression analyses are:

Regression Analysis: IndCosts versus MachHours
```
The regression equation is
Ind.Costs = 301 + 10.3 MachHours

Predictor        Coef        StDev           T          P
Constant        301.0        229.8        1.31      0.219
MachHour       10.312        3.124        3.30      0.008

S = 170.5       R-Sq = 52.1%      R-Sq(adj) = 47.4%

Analysis of Variance

Source            DF          SS          MS          F          P
Regression         1      316874      316874      10.90      0.008
Residual Error    10      290824       29082
Total             11      607698
```

Regression Analysis: IndCosts versus DirectHour
```
The regression equation is
Ind.Costs = 745 + 7.72 DirectHour

Predictor        Coef        StDev           T          P
Constant        744.7        217.6        3.42      0.007
DirectHo        7.716        5.396        1.43      0.183

S = 224.6       R-Sq = 17.0%      R-Sq(adj) = 8.7%

Analysis of Variance

Source            DF          SS          MS          F          P
Regression         1      103187      103187       2.05      0.183
Residual Error    10      504511       50451
Total             11      607698
```

From these two cost functions, the model containing Machine-Hours should be used to predict Indirect Manufacturing Labor Costs. There is a significant linear relationship between Indirect Manufacturing Labor Costs and Machine-Hours $(t = 3.30,\ p = 0.008)$. There is not a significant linear relationship between Indirect Manufacturing Labor Costs and Direct Manufacturing Labor-Hours $(t = 1.43,\ p = 0.183)$. The r^2 for the first model is .521 while the r^2 for the second model is .170. In addition, the standard deviation for the first model is 170.5 while the standard deviation for the second model is 224.6. All of these lead to the better model as the model containing Machine-Hours as the independent variable.

Chapter 12
Multiple Regression and Model Building

12.1   a. $E(y) = \beta_0 + \beta_1 x_1 + \beta_2 x_2$

b. $E(y) = \beta_0 + \beta_1 x_1 + \beta_2 x_2 + \beta_3 x_3 + \beta_4 x_4$

c. $E(y) = \beta_0 + \beta_1 x_1 + \beta_2 x_2 + \beta_3 x_3 + \beta_4 x_4 + \beta_5 x_5$

12.3   a.   We are given $\hat{\beta}_2 = 2.7$, $s_{\hat{\beta}_2} = 1.86$, and $n = 30$.

$$H_0 : \beta_2 = 0$$
$$H_a : \beta_2 \neq 0$$

The test statistic is $t = \dfrac{\hat{\beta}_2 - 0}{s_{\hat{\beta}_2}} = \dfrac{2.7}{1.86} = 1.45$

The rejection region requires $\alpha / 2 = .05 / 2 = .025$ in each tail of the t distribution with $df = n - (k+1) = 30 - (3+1) = 26$. From Table III, Appendix D, $t_{.025} = 2.056$. The rejection region is $t < -2.056$ or $t > 2.056$.

Since the observed value of the test statistic does not fall in the rejection region $(t = 1.45 \not> 2.056)$, H_0 is not rejected. There is insufficient evidence to indicate $\beta_2 \neq 0$ at $\alpha = .05$.

b.   We are given $\hat{\beta}_3 = .93$, $s_{\hat{\beta}_3} = .29$, and $n = 30$.

$$H_0 : \beta_3 = 0$$
$$H_a : \beta_3 \neq 0$$

The test statistic is $t = \dfrac{\hat{\beta}_3 - 0}{s_{\hat{\beta}_3}} = \dfrac{.93}{.29} = 3.21$

The rejection region is the same as part **a**, $t < -2.056$ or $t > 2.056$.

Since the observed value of the test statistic falls in the rejection region $(t = 3.21 > 2.056)$, H_0 is rejected. There is sufficient evidence to indicate $\beta_3 \neq 0$ at $\alpha = .05$.

c. $\hat{\beta}_3$ has a smaller estimated standard error than $\hat{\beta}_2$. Therefore, the test statistic is larger for $\hat{\beta}_3$ even though $\hat{\beta}_3$ is smaller than $\hat{\beta}_2$.

12.5   The number of degrees of freedom available for estimating σ^2 is $n - (k+1)$ where k is the number of independent variables in the regression model. Each additional independent variable placed in the model causes a corresponding decrease in the degrees of freedom.

12.7   a.   Yes. Since $R^2 = .92$ is close to 1, this indicates the model provides a good fit. Without knowledge of the units of the dependent variable, the value of SSE cannot be used to determine how well the model fits.

     b. $H_0 : \beta_1 = \beta_2 = \cdots = \beta_5 = 0$

           H_a : At least one $\beta_i \neq 0$

The test statistic is $F = \dfrac{R^2 / k}{\left(1 - R^2\right) / \left[n - (k+1)\right]} = \dfrac{.92 / 5}{(1 - .92) / \left[30 - (5+1)\right]} = 55.2$

The rejection region requires $\alpha = .05$ in the upper tail of the F distribution with $v_1 = k = 5$ and $v_2 = n - (k + 1) = 30 - (5+1) = 24$. From Table VI, Appendix D, $F_{.05} = 2.62$. The rejection region is $F > 2.62$.

Since the observed value of the test statistic falls in the rejection region $(F = 55.2 > 2.62)$, H_0 is rejected. There is sufficient evidence to indicate the model is useful in predicting y at $\alpha = .05$.

12.9   a.   The first order model is $E(y) = \beta_0 + \beta_1 x_1 + \beta_2 x_2 + \beta_3 x_3 + \beta_4 x_4 + \beta_5 x_5 + \beta_6 x_6$.

     b. $\hat{\beta}_1$: For each unit increase in air quality, the mean satisfaction score is estimated to increase by .122.

           $\hat{\beta}_2$: For each unit increase in temperature, the mean satisfaction score is estimated to increase by .018.

           $\hat{\beta}_3$: For each unit increase in odor/aroma, the mean satisfaction score is estimated to increase by .124.

           $\hat{\beta}_4$: For each unit increase in music, the mean satisfaction score is estimated to increase by .119.

           $\hat{\beta}_5$: For each unit increase in noise/sound level, the mean satisfaction score is estimated to increase by .101.

           $\hat{\beta}_6$: For each unit increase in overall image, the mean satisfaction score is estimated to increase by .463.

     c.   We are 99% confident that mean satisfaction will increase between .350 and .576 units for each unit increase in overall image.

     d. $R_{adj}^2 = .501$. 50.1% of the simple variation in satisfaction scores is explained by the model including the 6 vairables, adjusted for the number of variables and the simple size.

     e.   Yes. The test statistic is $F = 71.42$. Using MINITAB with $v_1 = k = 6$ and $v_2 = n - (k+1) = 422 - (6+1) = 415$, the p-value is $p = P(F > 71.42) \approx 0$. Since the p-value is less than $(p = 0 < .01)$, H_0 is rejected. There is sufficient evidence to indicate the overall model is useful for predicting hotel image at $\alpha = .01$.

12.11   a.   To determine if the model is useful, we test:

$$H_0 : \beta_1 = \beta_2 = \beta_3 = \beta_4 = 0$$
$$H_a : \text{At least one } \beta_i \neq 0$$

From the problem, the test statistic is $F = 4.74$ and the p-value is $p < .01$. Since the p-value is less than $\alpha (p < .01 < .05)$, H_0 is rejected. There is sufficient evidence to indicate the model is useful for predicting accountant's Mach scores at $\alpha = .05$.

b. $R^2 = .13$. 13% of the total sample variation of the accountant's Mach scores around their means is explained by the model containing age, gender, education, and income.

c.   To determine if income is a useful predictor of Mach score, we test:

$$H_0 : \beta_4 = 0$$
$$H_a : \beta_4 \neq 0$$

From the printout, $t = 0.52$ and the p-value is $p > .10$. Since the p-value is not less than $\alpha (p > .10 \not< .05)$, H_0 is not rejected. There is insufficient evidence to indicate that income is a useful predictor of Mach score adjusted for age, gender, and education at $\alpha = .05$.

12.13   a.   To determine if the overall model is useful, we test:

$$H_0 : \beta_1 = \beta_2 = \beta_3 = 0$$
$$H_a : \text{At least one } \beta_i \neq 0$$

The p-value is $p = .049$. Since the p-value is less than $\alpha (p = .049 < .05)$, H_0 is rejected. There is sufficinet evidence to indicate the model is useful at $\alpha = .05$.

$R^2 = .075$. 7.5% of the simple variation of the percentages of silver in the alloy can be explained by the model.

b.   To determine if the overall model is useful, we test:

$$H_0 : \beta_1 = \beta_2 = \beta_3 = 0$$
$$H_a : \text{At least one } \beta_i \neq 0$$

The p-value is $p < .001$. Since the p-value is less than $\alpha (p < .001 < .05)$, H_0 is rejected. There is sufficinet evidence to indicate the model is useful at $\alpha = .05$.

$R^2 = .783$. 78.3% of the simple variation of the percentages of iron in the alloy can be explained by the model.

c.   Using MINITAB, the relationship between percentage of siver and proportion of aluminum scraps from cans could look something like:

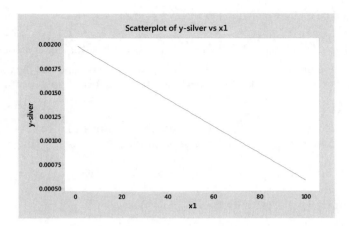

To determine if the relationship between percentage of silver and the proportion of aluminum scaps from cans is significant, we test:

$$H_0 : \beta_1 = 0$$
$$H_a : \beta_1 \neq 0$$

The p-value is $p = .015$. Since the p-value is less than $\alpha\left(p < .015 < .05 \right)$, H_0 is rejected. There is sufficinet evidence to indicate the relationship between percentage of silver and the proportion of aluminum scaps from cans is significant at $\alpha = .05$.

c.   Using MINITAB, the relationship between percentage of iron and proportion of aluminum scraps from cans could look something like:

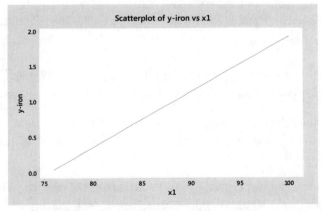

To determine if the relationship between percentage of iron and the proportion of aluminum scaps from cans is significant, we test:

$$H_0 : \beta_1 = 0$$
$$H_a : \beta_1 \neq 0$$

The p-value is $p < .001$. Since the p-value is less than $\alpha\left(p < .001 < .05 \right)$, H_0 is rejected. There is sufficinet evidence to indicate the relationship between percentage of iron and the proportion of aluminum scaps from cans is significant at $\alpha = .05$.

12.15   a.   The first order model would be $E(y) = \beta_0 + \beta_1 x_1 + \beta_2 x_2 + \beta_3 x_3 + \beta_4 x_4$.

   b.   Since the p-value is less than $\alpha(p = .005 < .01)$, H_0 is rejected. There is sufficient evidence to indicate that there is a negative linear relationship between change from routine and the number of years played golf, holding number of rounds of golf per year, total number of golf vacations, and average golf score constant.

   c.   The statement would be correct if the independent variables are not correlated. However, if the independent variables are correlated, then this interpretation would not necessarily hold.

   d.   To determine if the overall first-order regression model is adequate, we test:

$$H_0 : \beta_1 = \beta_2 = \beta_3 = \beta_4 = 0$$

   e.   For all dependent variables, the rejection region requires $\alpha = .01$ in the upper tail of the F-distribution with $v_1 = k = 4$ and $v_2 = n - (k+1) = 393 - (4+1) = 388$. From Table VIII, Appendix D, $F_{.01} \approx 3.32$. The rejection region is $F > 3.32$. Using MINITAB, $F_{.01,4,388} = 3.67$. The true rejection region is $F > 3.67$.

   f.   For **Thrill**: Since the observed value of the test statistic falls in the rejection region $(F = 5.56 > 3.67)$, H_0 is rejected. There is sufficient evidence to indicate at least one of the 4 independent variables is linearly related to Thrill at $\alpha = .01$.

   For **Change from Routine**: Since the observed value of the test statistic does not fall in the rejection region $(F = 3.02 \not> 3.67)$, H_0 is not rejected. There is insufficient evidence to indicate at least one of the 4 independent variables is linearly related to Change from Routine at $\alpha = .01$.

   For **Surprise**: Since the observed value of the test statistic does not fall in the rejection region $(F = 3.33 \not> 3.67)$, H_0 is not rejected. There is insufficient evidence to indicate at least one of the 4 independent variables is linearly related to Surprise at $\alpha = .01$.

   g.   For **Thrill**: Since the p-value is less than $\alpha(p < .001 < .01)$, H_0 is rejected. There is sufficient evidence to indicate that at least one of the independent variables is linearly related to Thrill at $\alpha = .01$.

   For **Change from Routine**: Since the p-value is not less than $\alpha(p = .018 \not< .01)$, H_0 is not rejected. There is insufficient evidence to indicate that at least one of the independent variables is linearly related to Change from Routine at $\alpha = .01$.

   For **Surprise**: Since the p-value is not less than $\alpha(p = .011 \not< .01)$, H_0 is not rejected. There is insufficient evidence to indicate that at least one of the independent variables is linearly related to Surprise at $\alpha = .01$.

   h.   For **Thrill**: $R^2 = .055$. 5.5% of the total variability around the mean thrill values can be explained by the model containing the 4 independent variables: x_1 = number of rounds of golf per year, x_2 = total number of golf vacations taken, x_3 = number of years played golf, and x_4 = average golf score.

   For **Change from Routine**: $R^2 = .030$. 3.0% of the total variability around the mean change from routine values can be explained by the model containing the 4 independent variables: x_1 = number of rounds of golf per year, x_2 = total number of golf vacations taken, x_3 = number of years played golf, and x_4 = average golf score.

For **Surprise**: $R^2 = .023$. 2.3% of the total variability around the mean surprise values can be explained by the model containing the 4 independent variables: x_1 = number of rounds of golf per year, x_2 = total number of golf vacations taken, x_3 = number of years played golf, and x_4 = average golf score.

12.17   a.   Using MINITAB, the results of fitting the first-order model are:

Regression Analysis: DESIRE versus GENDER, SELFESTM, BODYSAT, IMPREAL
```
The regression equation is
DESIRE = 14.0 - 2.19 GENDER - 0.0479 SELFESTM - 0.322 BODYSAT + 0.493 IMPREAL

Predictor        Coef  SE Coef       T      P
Constant      14.0107   0.7753   18.07  0.000
GENDER        -2.1865   0.6766   -3.23  0.001
SELFESTM     -0.04794  0.03669   -1.31  0.193
BODYSAT       -0.3223   0.1435   -2.25  0.026
IMPREAL        0.4931   0.1274    3.87  0.000

S = 2.25087   R-Sq = 49.8%    R-Sq(adj) = 48.5%

Analysis of Variance

Source           DF       SS      MS      F      P
Regression        4   827.83  206.96  40.85  0.000
Residual Error  165   835.95    5.07
Total           169  1663.79

Source     DF   Seq SS
GENDER      1   674.64
SELFESTM    1    57.66
BODYSAT     1    19.62
IMPREAL     1    75.91
```

The least squares prediction equation is $\hat{y} = 14.0107 - 2.1865x_1 - .04794x_2 - .3223x_3 + .4931x_4$

b. $\hat{\beta}_0 = 14.0107$. This has no meaning other than the y-intercept.

$\hat{\beta}_1 = -2.1865$. The mean value of desire to have cosmetic surgery is estimated to be 2.1865 units lower for males than females, holding all other variables constant.

$\hat{\beta}_2 = -0.04794$. For each unit increase in self-esteem, the mean value of desire to have cosmetic surgery is estimated to decrease by 0.04794 units, holding all other variables constant.

$\hat{\beta}_3 = -0.3223$. For each unit increase in body satisfaction, then mean value of desire to have cosmetic surgery is estimated to decrease by .3223 units, holding all other variables constant.

$\hat{\beta}_4 = 0.4931$. For each unit increase in impression of reality TV, the mean value of desire to have cosmetic surgery is estimated to increase by 0.4931 units, holding all other variables constant.

c.   To determine if the overall model is useful for predicting desire to have cosmetic surgery, we test:

$$H_0 : \beta_1 = \beta_2 = \beta_3 = \beta_4 = 0$$
$$H_a : \text{At least } 1\beta_i \neq 0$$

From the printout, the test statistic is $F = 40.85$ and the p-value is $p = 0.000$.

Since the p-value is less than $\alpha(p = 0.000 < .01)$, H_0 is rejected. There is sufficient evidence to indicate the overall model is useful for predicting desire to have cosmetic surgery at $\alpha = .01$.

d. R_a^2 is the preferred measure of model fit. From the printout, $R_a^2 = .485$. This indicates that 48.5% of the total sample variation in desire values is explained by the model containing gender, self-esteem, body satisfaction and impression of reality TV, adjusting for the sample size and the number of variables in the model.

e.   To determine if the desire to have cosmetic surgery decreases linearly as level of body satisfaction increases, we test:

$$H_0 : \beta_3 = 0$$
$$H_a : \beta_3 < 0$$

From the printout, the test statistic is $t = -2.25$ and the p-value is $p = .026 / 2 = .013$.

Since the p-value is less than $\alpha(p = 0.013 < .05)$, H_0 is rejected. There is sufficient evidence to indicate the desire to have cosmetic surgery decreases linearly as level of body satisfaction increases, holding all other variables constant at $\alpha = .05$.

f.   For confidence coefficient .95, $\alpha = .05$ and $\alpha / 2 = .05 / 2 = .025$. From Table III, Appendix D, with $df = n - (k + 1) = 170 - (4 + 1) = 165$, $t_{.025} \approx 1.98$. The 95% confidence interval is

$$\hat{\beta}_4 \pm t_{.025} s_{\hat{\beta}_4} \Rightarrow .4931 \pm 1.98(.1274) \Rightarrow .4931 \pm .2523 \Rightarrow (.2408, .7454)$$

We are 95% confident that the increase in mean desire for cosmetic surgery is between .2408 and .7454 for each unit increase in impression of reality TV, holding all other variables constant.

12.19   a.   The 1st-order model is $E(y) = \beta_0 + \beta_1 x_1 + \beta_2 x_2 + \beta_3 x_3 + \beta_4 x_4 + \beta_5 x_5$.

b.   Using MINITAB, the results are:

Regression Analysis: HEATRATE versus RPM, INLET-TEMP, ...
```
The regression equation is
HEATRATE = 13614 + 0.0888 RPM - 9.20 INLET-TEMP + 14.4 EXH-TEMP
               + 0.4 CPRATIO - 0.848 AIRFLOW

Predictor        Coef   SE Coef       T       P
Constant      13614.5     870.0   15.65   0.000
RPM           0.08879   0.01391    6.38   0.000
INLET-TEMP     -9.201     1.499   -6.14   0.000
EXH-TEMP       14.394     3.461    4.16   0.000
CPRATIO          0.35     29.56    0.01   0.991
AIRFLOW       -0.8480    0.4421   -1.92   0.060

S = 458.828   R-Sq = 92.4%   R-Sq(adj) = 91.7%

Analysis of Variance

Source           DF          SS        MS       F      P
Regression        5   155055273  31011055  147.30  0.000
Residual Error   61    12841935    210524
Total            66   167897208
```

```
Source        DF      Seq SS
RPM            1   119598530
INLET-TEMP     1    26893467
EXH-TEMP       1     7784225
CPRATIO        1        4623
AIRFLOW        1      774427
```

The least squares prediction equation is:

$$\hat{y} = 13,614.5 + 0.08879x_1 - 9.201x_2 + 14.394x_3 + 0.35x_4 - 0.848x_5$$

c. $\hat{\beta}_o = 13,614.5$. Since 0 is not within the range of all the independent variables, this value has no meaning.

$\hat{\beta}_1 = 0.08879$. For each unit increase in RPM, the mean heat rate is estimated to increase by .08879, holding all the other 4 variables constant.

$\hat{\beta}_2 = -9.201$. For each unit increase in inlet temperature, the mean heat rate is estimated to decrease by 9.201, holding all the other 4 variables constant.

$\hat{\beta}_3 = 14.394$. For each unit increase in exhaust temperature, the mean heat rate is estimated to increase by 14.394, holding all the other 4 variables constant.

$\hat{\beta}_4 = 0.35$. For each unit increase in cycle pressure ratio, the mean heat rate is estimated to increase by 0.35, holding all the other 4 variables constant.

$\hat{\beta}_5 = -0.8480$. For each unit increase in air flow rate, the mean heat rate is estimated to decrease by .848, holding all the other 4 variables constant.

d. From the printout, $s = 458.828$. We would expect to see most of the heat rate values within $2s = 2(458.828) = 917.656$ units of the least squares line.

e. To determine if at least one of the variables is useful in predicting the heat rate values, we test:

$$H_0 : \beta_1 = \beta_2 = \beta_3 = \beta_4 = \beta_5 = 0$$
$$H_a : \text{At least one } \beta_i \neq 0$$

The test statistic is $F = 147.30$ and the p-value is $p = .000$. Since the p-value is less than $\alpha(p = .000 < .01)$, H_0 is rejected. There is sufficient evidence to indicate at least one of the variables is useful in predicting the heat rate values at $\alpha = .01$.

f. $R_a^2 = \text{R-Sq}(\text{adj}) = .917$. 91.7% of the total sample variance of the heat rate values is explained by the model containing the 5 independent variables, adjusted for the number of variable and the sample size.

g. To determine if there is evidence to indicate heat rate is linearly related to inlet temperature, we test:

$$H_0 : \beta_2 = 0$$
$$H_a : \beta_2 \neq 0$$

The test statistic is $t = -6.14$ and the p-value is $p = .000$. Since the p-value is less than $\alpha\,(p = .000 < .01)$, H_0 is rejected. There is sufficient evidence to indicate heat rate is linearly related to inlet temperature, adjusted for the other 4 variables at $\alpha = .01$.

12.21   a.   Using MINITAB, the results are:

Regression Analysis: Diameter versus MassFlux, HeatFlux
```
Analysis of Variance

Source       DF   Adj SS   Adj MS   F-Value  P-Value
Regression    2  0.11914  0.05957     1.00    0.391
  MassFlux    1  0.10832  0.10832     1.82    0.198
  HeatFlux    1  0.01082  0.01082     0.18    0.676
Error        15  0.89350  0.05957
Total        17  1.01264
```

```
Model Summary

       S    R-sq  R-sq(adj)  R-sq(pred)
0.244063  11.77%      0.00%       0.00%
```

```
Coefficients

Term            Coef   SE Coef  T-Value  P-Value   VIF
Constant       1.088     0.184     5.92    0.000
MassFlux   -0.000234  0.000174    -1.35    0.198  1.00
HeatFlux      -0.080     0.188    -0.43    0.676  1.00
```

```
Regression Equation

Diameter = 1.088 - 0.000234 MassFlux - 0.080 HeatFlux
```

The fitted model is $\hat{y} = 1.088 - .000234x_1 - .080x_2$.

To determine if the overall model is adequate, we test:

$$H_0 : \beta_1 = \beta_2 = 0$$
$$H_a : \text{At least one } \beta_i \neq 0$$

The test statistic is $F = 1.00$ and the p-value is $p = .391$. Since the p-value is not small, H_0 is not rejected. There is insufficinet evidence to indicate the overall model is adequate for any $\alpha < .391$.

b.   Using MINITAB, the results are:

Regression Analysis: Density versus MassFlux, HeatFlux
```
Analysis of Variance

Source       DF       Adj SS       Adj MS  F-Value  P-Value
Regression    2  1.92985E+11  96492327113   121.31    0.000
  MassFlux    1   6614680108   6614680108     8.32    0.011
  HeatFlux    1  1.86370E+11  1.86370E+11   234.31    0.000
Error        15  11931156939    795410463
Total        17  2.04916E+11
```

```
Model Summary

     S      R-sq   R-sq(adj)   R-sq(pred)
28203.0   94.18%     93.40%       91.27%

Coefficients

Term         Coef   SE Coef   T-Value   P-Value   VIF
Constant    -1030     21237     -0.05     0.962
MassFlux    -57.9      20.1     -2.88     0.011    1.00
HeatFlux   332037     21692     15.31     0.000    1.00

Regression Equation

Density = -1030 - 57.9 MassFlux + 332037 HeatFlux
```

The fitted model is $\hat{y} = -1,030 - 57.9x_1 + 332,037x_2$.

To determine if the overall model is adequate, we test:

$$H_0 : \beta_1 = \beta_2 = 0$$
$$H_a : \text{At least one } \beta_i \neq 0$$

The test statistic is $F = 121.31$ and the p-value is $p = .000$. Since the p-value is so small, H_0 is rejected. There is sufficinet evidence to indicate the overall model is adequate for any reasonable value of α.

c.   The density is better predicted by mass flux and heat flux. The model predicting diameter is not adequate and should not be used, while the model predicting density is adequate.

12.23   a. $$H_0 : \beta_1 = 0$$
$$H_a : \beta_1 \neq 0$$

The test statistic is $t = \dfrac{\hat{\beta}_1 - 0}{s_{\hat{\beta}_1}} = \dfrac{.03}{.006} = 5.00$

Since no α was given, we will use $\alpha = .05$. The rejection region requires $\alpha/2 = .05/2 = .025$ in each tail of the t-distribution. From Table III, Appendix D, with $df = n - (k+1) = 29 - (5+1) = 23$, $t_{.025} = 2.069$. The rejection region is $t < -2.069$ or $t > 2.069$.

Since the observed value of the test statistic falls in the rejection region $(t = 5.00 > 2.069)$, H_0 is rejected. There is sufficient evidence to indicate that there is a linear relationship between vintage year and the logarithm of price, adjusting for all other variables at $\alpha = .05$.

$$H_0 : \beta_2 = 0$$
$$H_a : \beta_2 \neq 0$$

The test statistic is $t = \dfrac{\hat{\beta}_2 - 0}{s_{\hat{\beta}_2}} = \dfrac{.60}{.120} = 5.00$.

The rejection region is $t < -2.069$ or $t > 2.069$.

Since the observed value of the test statistic falls in the rejection region $(t = 5.00 > 2.069)$, H_0 is rejected. There is sufficient evidence to indicate that there is a linear relationship between average growing season temperature and the logarithm of price, adjusting for all other variables at $\alpha = .05$.

$$H_0 : \beta_3 = 0$$
$$H_a : \beta_3 \neq 0$$

The test statistic is $t = \dfrac{\hat{\beta}_3 - 0}{s_{\hat{\beta}_3}} = \dfrac{-.004}{.001} = -4.00$

The rejection region is $t < -2.069$ or $t > 2.069$.

Since the observed value of the test statistic falls in the rejection region $(t = -4.00 < -2.069)$, H_0 is rejected. There is sufficient evidence to indicate that there is a linear relationship between Sept./Aug. rainfall and the logarithm of price, adjusting for all other variables at $\alpha = .05$.

$$H_0 : \beta_4 = 0$$
$$H_a : \beta_4 \neq 0$$

The test statistic is $t = \dfrac{\hat{\beta}_4 - 0}{s_{\hat{\beta}_4}} = \dfrac{.0015}{.0005} = 3.00$

The rejection region is $t < -2.069$ or $t > 2.069$.

Since the observed value of the test statistic falls in the rejection region $(t = 3.00 > 2.069)$, H_0 is rejected. There is sufficient evidence to indicate that there is a linear relationship between rainfall in months preceding vintage and the logarithm of price, adjusting for all other variables at $\alpha = .05$.

$$H_0 : \beta_5 = 0$$
$$H_a : \beta_5 \neq 0$$

The test statistic is $t = \dfrac{\hat{\beta}_5 - 0}{s_{\hat{\beta}_5}} = \dfrac{.008}{.550} = .015$.

The rejection region is $t < -2.069$ or $t > 2.069$.

Since the observed value of the test statistic does not fall in the rejection region $(t = .015 \not> 2.069)$, H_0 is not rejected. There is insufficient evidence to indicate that there is a linear relationship between average September temperature and the logarithm of price, adjusting for all other variables at $\alpha = .05$.

b. $\hat{\beta}_1 = .03$, $e^{.03} - 1 = .030$

We estimate that the mean price will increase by 3.0% for each additional year increase in x_1, vintage year (with all other variables held constant).

$\hat{\beta}_2 = .60$, $e^{.60} - 1 = .822$

We estimate that the mean price will increase by 82.2% for each additional degree increase in x_2, average growing season temperatures in °C (with all other variables held constant).

$\hat{\beta_3} = -.004$, $e^{-.004} - 1 = -.004$

We estimate that the mean price will decrease by .4% for each additional centimeter increase in x_3, Sept./Aug. rainfall in cm, (with all other variables held constant).

$\hat{\beta_4} = .0015$, $e^{.0015} - 1 = .0015$

We estimate that the average mean price will increase by .15% for each additional centimeter increase in x_4, rainfall in months preceding vintage in cm (with all other variables held constant).

$\hat{\beta_5} = .008$, $e^{.008} - 1 = .008$

We estimate that the average mean price will increase by .8% for each additional degree increase in x_5, average Sept. temperature in °C (with all other variables held constant).

c. $R^2 = .85$. 85% of the sample variation in the logarithm of price values is explained by the model containing the 5 variables.

$s = .30$. Approximately 95% of the values of the logarithm of price will fall within $2s = 2(.30) = .60$ units of their predicted values.

This model appears to be a fairly good model. The standard deviation is fairly small and the R^2 valuie is fairly large. Four of the five independent variables are significant. A better model might be one that does not include x_5, the average September temperature because it was not statistically significant.

12.25 a. For $x_1 = 1$, $x_2 = 10$, $x_3 = 5$, and $x_4 = 2$, $\hat{y} = 3.58 + .01(1) - .06(10) - .01(5) + .42(2) = 3.78$

 b. For $x_1 = 0$, $x_2 = 8$, $x_3 = 10$, and $x_4 = 4$, $\hat{y} = 3.58 + .01(0) - .06(8) - .01(10) + .42(4) = 4.68$

12.27 a. The confidence interval is $(13.42, 14.31)$. We are 95% confident that the mean desire to have cosmetic surgery is between 13.42 and 14.31 for females with a self-esteem of 24, body satisfaction of 3 and impression of reality TV of 4.

The confidence interval is $(8.79, 10.89)$. We are 95% confident that the mean desire to have cosmetic surgery is between 8.79 and 10.89 for males with a self-esteem of 22, body satisfaction of 9 and impression of reality TV of 4.

12.29 a. The 95% prediction interval is $(11,599.6, 13,665.5)$. We are 95% confident that the actual heat rate will be between 11,599.6 and 13.665.5 when the RPM is 7,500, the inlet temperature is 1,000, the exhaust temperature is 525, the cycle pressure ratio is 13.5 and the air flow rate is 10.

 b. The 95% confidence interval is $(12,157.9, 13,107.1)$. We are 95% confident that the mean heat rate will be between 12,157.9 and 13,107.1 when the RPM is 7,500, the inlet temperature is 1,000, the exhaust temperature is 525, the cycle pressure ratio is 13.5 and the air flow rate is 10.

 c. Yes. The confidence interval for the mean will always be smaller than the prediction interval for the actual value. This is because there are 2 error terms involved in predicting an actual value and only one error term involved in estimating the mean. First, we have the error in locating the mean of the distribution. Once the mean is located, the actual value can still vary around the mean, thus, the second error. There is only one error term involved when estimating the mean, which is the error in locating the mean.

12.31   You would look up the number of walks (x_1), singles (x_2), doubles (x_3), triples (x_4), home runs (x_5), stolen bases (x_6), caught stealing (x_7), strikeouts (x_8), and outs (x_9) for your favorite team. Then use the following fitted regression line to predict the number of runs scored:

$$\hat{y} = 40 + .2538x_1 + .407x_2 + .841x_3 + 1.633x_4 + 1.092x_5 + .05x_6 - .044x_7 - .0911x_8 - .1218x_9$$

12.33   a.   The first-order model would be $E(y) = \beta_0 + \beta_1 x_1 + \beta_2 x_2 + \beta_3 x_3$.

   b.   Using MINITAB, the results are:

Regression Analysis: Project versus Intrapersonal, Stress, Mood
```
Analysis of Variance
```

Source	DF	Adj SS	Adj MS	F-Value	P-Value
Regression	3	70.29	23.429	2.66	0.077
Intrapersonal	1	44.25	44.251	5.03	0.037
Stress	1	34.19	34.186	3.89	0.063
Mood	1	10.48	10.482	1.19	0.289
Error	19	167.08	8.794		
Total	22	237.37			

```
Model Summary
```

S	R-sq	R-sq(adj)	R-sq(pred)
2.96544	29.61%	18.50%	3.79%

```
Coefficients
```

Term	Coef	SE Coef	T-Value	P-Value	VIF
Constant	86.90	3.20	27.17	0.000	
Intrapersonal	-0.2099	0.0936	-2.24	0.037	1.06
Stress	0.1515	0.0769	1.97	0.063	1.06
Mood	0.0733	0.0671	1.09	0.289	1.09

```
Regression Equation

Project = 86.90 - 0.2099 Intrapersonal + 0.1515 Stress + 0.0733 Mood
```

The fitted regression model is $\hat{y} = 86.90 - .2099x_1 + .1515x_2 + .0733x_3$.

   c.   To determine if the overall model is useful for predictin y, we test:

$$H_0 : \beta_1 = \beta_2 = \beta_3 = 0$$
$$H_a : \text{At least one } \beta_i \neq 0$$

The test statistic is $F = 2.66$ and the p-value is $p = .077$. Since the p-value is less than $\alpha(p = .077 < .10)$, H_0 is rejected. There is sufficinet evidence to indicate the overall model is useful for predicting y at $\alpha = .10$.

   d. $R^2_{adj} = .185$. 18.5% of the sample variation in the project scores is explained by the model containing the 3 variables, adjusted for the simple size and the number of parameters in the model.

$s = 2.96544$ and $2s = 2(2.96544) = 5.93$. Approximately 95% of the observed values of Project scores will fall within 5.93 units of their predicted values.

e. Using MINITAB, the resutls are:

Prediction for Project
```
Regression Equation

Project = 86.90 - 0.2099 Intrapersonal + 0.1515 Stress + 0.0733 Mood

Variable        Setting
Intrapersonal      20
Stress             30
Mood               25


   Fit     SE Fit        95% CI              95% PI
89.0837  0.892843  (87.2149, 90.9524)  (82.6017, 95.5656)
```

The 95% prediction interval is $(82.60, 95.57)$. We are 95% confident that the actual Project score will be between 82.60 and 95.57 when the range of interpersonal scores is 20, the range of management scores is 30, and the range of mood scores is 25.

12.35 a. The response surface is a twisted surface in three-dimensional space.

b. For $x_1 = 0$, $E(y) = 3 + 0 + 2x_2 - 0x_2 = 3 + 2x_2$
   For $x_1 = 1$, $E(y) = 3 + 1 + 2x_2 - 1x_2 = 4 + x_2$
   For $x_1 = 2$, $E(y) = 3 + 2 + 2x_2 - 2x_2 = 5$

The plot of the lines is

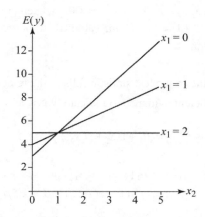

c. The lines are not parallel because interaction between x_1 and x_2 is present. Interaction between x_1 and x_2 means that the effect of x_2 on y depends on what level x_1 takes on.

d. For $x_1 = 0$, as x_2 increases from 0 to 5, $E(y)$ increases from 3 to 13.
   For $x_1 = 1$, as x_2 increases from 0 to 5, $E(y)$ increases from 4 to 9.
   For $x_1 = 2$, as x_2 increases from 0 to 5, $E(y) = 5$.

e. For $x_1 = 2$ and $x_2 = 4$, $E(y) = 5$. For $x_1 = 0$ and $x_2 = 5$, $E(y) = 13$.

Thus, $E(y)$ changes from 5 to 13.

12.37   a.   The prediction equation is $\hat{y} = -2.55 + 3.82x_1 + 2.63x_2 - 1.29x_1x_2$

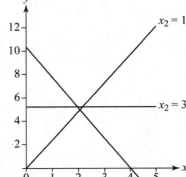

b.   For $x_2 = 10$, $\hat{y} = -2.55 + 3.82x_1 + 2.63(10) - 1.29x_1(10) = 23.75 - 9.08x_1$. The estimate of the slope of the line is -9.08.

c.   For $x_2 = 1$, $\hat{y} = -2.55 + 3.82x_1 + 2.63(1) - 1.29x_1(1) = .08 + 2.53x_1$
For $x_2 = 3$, $\hat{y} = -2.55 + 3.82x_1 + 2.63(3) - 1.29x_1(3) = 5.34 - .05x_1$
For $x_2 = 5$, $\hat{y} = -2.55 + 3.82x_1 + 2.63(5) - 1.29x_1(5) = 10.6 - 2.63x_1$

d.   If x_1 and x_2 interact, the effect of x_1 on $\hat{y}$ is different at different levels of x_2. When $x_2 = 1$, as x_1 increases, $\hat{y}$ also increases. When $x_2 = 5$, as x_1 increases, $\hat{y}$ decreases.

e.   The hypotheses are:

$$H_0 : \beta_3 = 0$$
$$H_a : \beta_3 \neq 0$$

f.   The test statistic is $t = \dfrac{\hat{\beta}_3}{s_{\hat{\beta}_3}} = \dfrac{-1.285}{.159} = -8.06$

The rejection region requires $\alpha/2 = .01/2 = .005$ in each tail of the t-distribution with $df = n - (k+1) = 15 - (3+1) = 11$. From Table III, Appendix D, $t_{.005} = 3.106$. The rejection region is $t < -3.106$ or $t > 3.106$.

Since the observed value of the test statistic falls in the rejection region $(t = -8.06 < -3.106)$, H_0 is rejected. There is sufficient evidence to indicate that x_1 and x_2 interact at $\alpha = .01$.

12.39   a.   The interaction model is $E(y) = \beta_0 + \beta_1 x_1 + \beta_2 x_2 + \beta_3 x_1 x_2$.

b.   For $x_2 = 2.5$, $E(y) = \beta_0 + \beta_1 x_1 + \beta_2(2.5) + \beta_3 x_1(2.5) = \beta_0 + 2.5\beta_2 + (\beta_1 + 2.5\beta_3)x_1$. The change in revenue for every 1-tweet increase in tweet rate is $(\beta_1 + 2.5\beta_3)$.

c.   For $x_2 = 5$, $E(y) = \beta_0 + \beta_1 x_1 + \beta_2(5) + \beta_3 x_1(5) = \beta_0 + 5\beta_2 + (\beta_1 + 5\beta_3)x_1$. The change in revenue for every 1-tweet increase in tweet rate is $(\beta_1 + 5\beta_3)$.

d.   For $x_1 = 100$, $E(y) = \beta_0 + \beta_1(100) + \beta_2 x_2 + \beta_3(100)x_2 = \beta_0 + 100\beta_1 + (\beta_2 + 100\beta_3)x_2$. The change in revenue for every 1-unit increase in PN-ratio is $(\beta_2 + 100\beta_3)$.

e.   To determine if tweet rate and PN-ratio interact, we test:

$$H_0 : \beta_3 = 0$$

12.41   a.   To determine if the overall model is adequate, we test:

$$H_0 : \beta_1 = \beta_2 = \beta_3 = 0$$
$$H_a : \text{At least one } \beta_i \neq 0$$

The test statistic is $F = 31.98$ and the p-value is $p < .001$. Since the p-value is less than $\alpha\left(p < .001 < .01\right)$, H_0 is rejected. There is sufficinet evidence to indicate the overall model is useful at $\alpha = .01$.

b.   To determine if the effect of perceived effect of experience on tilting$\left(x_1\right)$ on the rate of change of severity of tilting$\left(y\right)$ depends on póker experience$\left(x_2\right)$, we test:

$$H_0 : \beta_3 = 0$$
$$H_a : \beta_3 \neq 0$$

The test statistic is $t = -5.61$ andthe p-value is $p < .001$. Since the p-value is less than $\alpha\left(p < .001 < .01\right)$, H_0 is rejected. There is sufficinet evidence to indicate the effect of perceived effect of experience on tilting$\left(x_1\right)$ on the rate of change of severity of tilting$\left(y\right)$ depends on póker experience$\left(x_2\right)$ at $\alpha = .01$.

12.43   a.   The least squares prediction equation is $\hat{y} = 11.779 - 1.972x_1 + .585x_4 - .553x_1 x_4$.

b.   For $x_1 = 1$ and $x_4 = 5$, $\hat{y} = 11.779 - 1.972\left(1\right) + .585\left(5\right) - .553\left(1\right)\left(5\right) = 9.967$.

c.   To determine if the model is adequate, we test:

$$H_0 : \beta_1 = \beta_2 = \beta_3 = 0$$
$$H_a : \text{At least } 1 \beta_i \neq 0$$

The test statistic is $F = 45.086$ and the p-value is $p = .000$.

Since the p-value is less than $\alpha\left(p = .000 < .10\right)$, H_0 is rejected. There is sufficient evidence to indicate the model is adequate in predicting desire to have cosmetic surgery at $\alpha = .10$.

d. $R_a^2 = .439$. 43.9% of the sample variation in the desire to have cosmetic surgery around its mean is explained by the model containing gender, impression of reality TV and the interaction of the two variables.

e. $s = 2.350$. Most of the observed values of desire will fall within $2s = 2\left(2.350\right) = 4.70$ units of their predicted values.

f.   To determine if gender and impression of reality TV interact, we test:

$$H_0 : \beta_3 = 0$$
$$H_a : \beta_3 \neq 0$$

The test statistic is $t = -2.004$ and the p-value is $p = .047$.

Since the p-value is less than $\alpha (p = .047 < .10)$, H_0 is rejected. There is sufficient evidence to indicate gender and impression of reality TV interact to affect desire to have cosmetic surgery at $\alpha = .10$.

12.45   a.   The first-order model would be $E(y) = \beta_0 + \beta_1 x_1 + \beta_2 x_2 + \beta_3 x_3 + \beta_4 x_4$.

b.   The β-coefficient that measures the effect of flexibility on relationship quality independently of the other independent variables is β_1.

c.   The β-coefficient that measures the effect of reputation on relationship quality independently of the other independent variables is β_2.

The β-coefficient that measures the effect of empathy on relationship quality independently of the other independent variables is β_3.

The β-coefficient that measures the effect of task alignment on relationship quality independently of the other independent variables is β_4.

d.   The interaction model is $E(y) = \beta_0 + \beta_1 x_1 + \beta_2 x_2 + \beta_3 x_3 + \beta_4 x_4 + \beta_5 x_1 x_4 + \beta_6 x_2 x_4 + \beta_7 x_3 x_4$.

e.   The null hypothesis to determine if the effect of flexibility (x_1) on relationship quality (y) depends on task alignment (x_4) would be $H_0 : \beta_5 = 0$.

f.   The null hypothesis to determine if the effect of reputation (x_2) on relationship quality (y) depends on task alignment (x_4) would be $H_0 : \beta_6 = 0$.

The null hypothesis to determine if the effect of empathy (x_3) on relationship quality (y) depends on task alignment (x_4) would be $H_0 : \beta_7 = 0$.

g.   Yes. Since none of the interaction terms are significant, there is no evidence to indicate the impact of each $x (x_1, x_2, \text{ or } x_3)$ on y depends on x_4.

12.47   a.   Let x_1 = latitude, x_2 = longitude, and x_3 = depth. The model is

$$E(y) = \beta_0 + \beta_1 x_1 + \beta_2 x_2 + \beta_3 x_3 + \beta_4 x_1 x_3 + \beta_5 x_2 x_3.$$

b. Using MINITAB, the results are:

Regression Analysis: ARSENIC versus LATITUDE, LONGITUDE, ...
```
The regression equation is
ARSENIC = 10845 - 1280 LATITUDE + 217 LONGITUDE - 1549 DEPTH-FT - 11.0 Lat_d
          + 20.0 Long_d

327 cases used, 1 cases contain missing values

Predictor       Coef   SE Coef      T      P
Constant       10845     67720   0.16  0.873
LATITUDE       -1280      1053  -1.22  0.225
LONGITUDE      217.4     814.5   0.27  0.790
DEPTH-FT     -1549.2     985.6  -1.57  0.117
Lat_D         -11.00     11.86  -0.93  0.355
Long_D         19.98     11.20   1.78  0.076

S = 103.072    R-Sq = 13.7%    R-Sq(adj) = 12.4%

Analysis of Variance

Source           DF        SS       MS       F      P
Regression        5    542303   108461   10.21  0.000
Residual Error  321   3410258    10624
Total           326   3952562

Source        DF    Seq SS
LATITUDE       1    132448
LONGITUDE      1    320144
DEPTH-FT       1     53179
Lat_D          1      2756
Long_D         1     33777
```

The least squares model is: $\hat{y} = 10,845 - 1,280x_1 + 217.4x_2 - 1,549.2x_3 - 11.00x_1x_3 + 19.98x_2x_3$

c. To determine if latitude and depth interact to affect arsenic level, we test:

$$H_0 : \beta_4 = 0$$
$$H_a : \beta_4 \neq 0$$

From the printout, the test statistic is $F = -.93$ and the p-value is $p = .355$. Since the p-value is not less than $\alpha(p = .355 \not< .05)$, H_o is not rejected. There is insufficient evidence to indicate latitude and depth interact to affect arsenic level at $\alpha = .05$.

d. To determine if longitude and depth interact to affect arsenic level, we test:

$$H_0 : \beta_5 = 0$$
$$H_a : \beta_5 \neq 0$$

From the printout, the test statistic is $F = 1.78$ and the p-value is $p = .076$. Since the p-value is not less than $\alpha(p = .076 \not< .05)$, H_o is not rejected. There is insufficient evidence to indicate longitude and depth interact to affect arsenic level at $\alpha = .05$.

e. Because the interactions are not significant, this means that the effect of latitude on the arsenic levels does not depend on the depth and the effect of longitude on the arsenic levels does not depend on the depth.

12.49   a. $E(y) = \beta_0 + \beta_1 x + \beta_2 x^2$

b. $E(y) = \beta_0 + \beta_1 x_1 + \beta_2 x_2 + \beta_3 x_1 x_2 + \beta_4 x_1^2 + \beta_5 x_2^2$

c. $E(y) = \beta_0 + \beta_1 x_1 + \beta_2 x_2 + \beta_3 x_3 + \beta_4 x_1 x_2 + \beta_5 x_1 x_3 + \beta_6 x_2 x_3 + \beta_7 x_1^2 + \beta_8 x_2^2 + \beta_9 x_3^2$

12.51   a.   To determine if the model contributes information for predicting y, we test:

$$H_0 : \beta_1 = \beta_2 = 0$$
$$H_a : \text{At least one } \beta_i \neq 0$$

The test statistic is $F = \dfrac{R^2 / k}{(1 - R^2)/[n - (k+1)]} = \dfrac{.91/2}{(1-.91)/[20-(2+1)]} = 85.94$.

The rejection region requires $\alpha = .05$ in the upper tail of the F-distribution, with $v_1 = k = 2$, and $v_2 = n - (k+1) = 20 - (2+1) = 17$. From Table VI, Appendix D, $F_{.05} = 3.59$. The rejection region is $F > 3.59$.

Since the observed value of the test statistic falls in the rejection region $(F = 85.94 > 3.59)$, H_0 is rejected. There is sufficient evidence that the model contributes information for predicting y at $\alpha = .05$.

b.   To determine if upward curvature exists, we test:

$$H_0 : \beta_2 = 0$$
$$H_a : \beta_2 > 0$$

c.   To determine if downward curvature exists, we test:

$$H_0 : \beta_2 = 0$$
$$H_a : \beta_2 < 0$$

12.53   a.   To determine if at least one of the parameters is nonzero, we test:

$$H_0 : \beta_1 = \beta_2 = \beta_3 = \beta_4 = \beta_5 = 0$$
$$H_a : \text{At least one } \beta_i \neq 0$$

The test statistic is $F = 25.93$ and the p-value is $p = 0.000$. Since the p-value is less than $\alpha (p = 0.000 < .05)$, H_0 is rejected. There is sufficient evidence to indicate that at least one of the parameters β_1, β_2, β_3, β_4, and β_5 is nonzero at $\alpha = .05$.

b. $$H_0 : \beta_4 = 0$$
$$H_a : \beta_4 \neq 0$$

The test statistic is $t = -10.74$ and the p-value is $p = 0.000$. Since the p-value is less than $\alpha (p = 0.000 < .01)$, H_0 is rejected. There is sufficient evidence to indicate that $\beta_4 \neq 0$ at $\alpha = .01$.

c.
$$H_0 : \beta_5 = 0$$
$$H_a : \beta_5 \neq 0$$

The test statistic is $t = .60$ and the p-value is $p = .550$. Since the p-value is greater than $\alpha (p = .550 \not< .01)$, H_0 is not rejected. There is insufficient evidence to indicate that $\beta_5 \neq 0$ at $\alpha = .01$.

d.   A possible graph may look like:

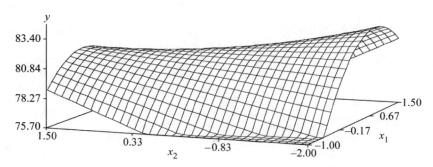

Notice that there is no curvature in the x_2 plane but there is curvature in the x_1 plane.

12.55   a. $\hat{\beta}_0 = 6.13$. Since 0 is not in the observed range (one cannot have the ball on the goal line), this has no meaning other than the y-intercept.

$\hat{\beta}_1 = .141$. Since the quadratic term is present in the model, this is no longet the slope of the line. It is simply a location parameter.

$\hat{\beta}_2 = -.0009$. Since this term is negative, it indicates that the shape of the relationship is mound-shaped, or concave downward. As the distance from the goal line increases, the predicted number of points scored will increase to some point and then start decreasing.

b. $R^2 = .226$. 22.6% of the sample variation in the number of points scored around their mean is explained by the quadratic relationship between the number of points scored and the number of yards from the opposing goal line.

c.   No. Even though the value of R^2 has increased, we do not know if the increase is statistically significant.

d.   To determine if the quadratic model is a better fit, we would test:

$$H_0 : \beta_2 = 0$$
$$H_a : \beta_2 \neq 0$$

12.57   Because the graph is curveved, we would hypothesize that the model should be $E(y) = \beta_0 + \beta_1 x + \beta_2 x^2$. Since the curve opens down, β_2 will be negative.

12.59   a.   The complete 2nd order model is $E(y) = \beta_0 + \beta_1 x_1 + \beta_2 x_2 + \beta_3 x_1 x_2 + \beta_4 x_1^2 + \beta_5 x_2^2$.

b. $R^2 = .14$. 14% of the total variation in the efficiency scores is explained by the complete 2nd order model containing level of CEO leadership and level of congruence between the CEO and the VP.

c.   If the β-coefficient for the x_2^2 term is negative, then as the value of the level of congruence increases, the efficiency will increase at a decreasing rate to some point and then the efficiency will decrease at an increasing rate, holding level of CEO leadership constant.

d.   Since the p-value is less than $\alpha\left(p = .02 < .05\right)$, H_0 is rejected. There is sufficient evidence to indicate that the level of CEO leadership and the level of congruence between the CEO and the VP interact to affect efficiency. This means that the effect of CEO leadership on efficiency depends on the level of congruence between the CEO and the VP.

12.61   a.   A first order model is $E\left(y\right) = \beta_0 + \beta_1 x$.

b.   A second order model is $E\left(y\right) = \beta_0 + \beta_1 x + \beta_2 x^2$.

c.   Using MINITAB, a scattergram of these data is:

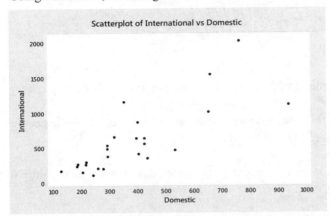

From the plot, it appears that the first-order model might fit the data better. There does not appear to be a curve to the relationship.

d.   Using MINITAB, the output is:

Polynomial Regression Analysis: International versus Domestic
```
The regression equation is
International = - 323.0 + 2.887 Domestic - 0.000989 Domestic^2

S = 293.541    R-Sq = 64.3%    R-Sq(adj) = 61.1%

Analysis of Variance

Source        DF        SS        MS        F        P
Regression     2   3420771   1710385    19.85    0.000
Error         22   1895665     86167
Total         24   5316436

Sequential Analysis of Variance

Source       DF        SS        F        P
Linear        1   3370161    39.83    0.000
Quadratic     1     50610     0.59    0.452
```

To investigate the usefulness of the model, we test:

$$H_0 : \beta_1 = \beta_2 = 0$$
$$H_a : \text{At least } 1 \beta_i \neq 0$$

The test statistic is $F = 19.85$ and the p-value is $p = .000$.

Since the p-value is less than $\alpha (p = .000 < .05)$, H_0 is rejected. There is sufficient evidence to indicate the model is useful for predicting foreign gross revenue at $\alpha = .05$.

To determine if a curvilinear relationship exists between foreign and domestic gross revenues, we test:

$$H_0 : \beta_2 = 0$$
$$H_a : \beta_2 \neq 0$$

The test statistic is $t = .59$ and the p-value is $p = .452$.

Since the p-value is not less than $\alpha (p = .452 \not< .05)$, H_0 is not rejected. There is insufficient evidence to indicate that a curvilinear relationship exists between foreign and domestic gross revenues at $\alpha = .05$.

  e. From the analysis in part **d**, the first-order model better explains the variation in foreign gross revenues. In part **d**, we concluded that the second-order term did not improve the model.

12.63 a. Using MINITAB, the scattergram of the data is:

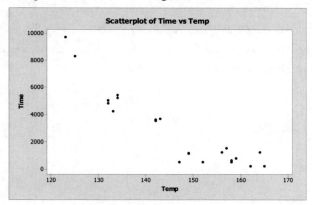

The relationship appears to be curvilinear. As temperature increases, the value of time tends to decrease but at a decreasing rate.

b.   Using MINITAB the results are:

Regression Analysis: Time versus Temp, Tempsq
```
The regression equation is
Time = 154243 - 1909 Temp + 5.93 Tempsq

Predictor      Coef   SE Coef       T      P
Constant     154243     21868    7.05  0.000
Temp        -1908.9     303.7   -6.29  0.000
Tempsq        5.929     1.048    5.66  0.000

S = 688.137    R-Sq = 94.2%    R-Sq(adj) = 93.5%

Analysis of Variance

Source            DF          SS        MS       F      P
Regression         2   144830280  72415140  152.93  0.000
Residual Error    19     8997107    473532
Total             21   153827386
Source    DF      Seq SS
Temp       1   129663987
Tempsq     1    15166293
```

The fitted regression line is $\hat{y} = 154{,}243 - 1{,}908.9x + 5.929x^2$.

c.   To determine if there is an upward curvature in the relationship between failure time and solder temperature, we test:

$$H_0 : \beta_2 = 0$$
$$H_a : \beta_2 > 0$$

From the printout, the test statistic is $t = 5.66$ and the p-value is $p = 0.000$. Since the p-value is less than $\alpha (p = 0.000 < .05)$, H_0 is rejected. There is sufficient evidence to indicate an upward curvature in the relationship between failure time and solder temperature at $\alpha = .05$.

12.65   a.   A scatterplot of the data is:

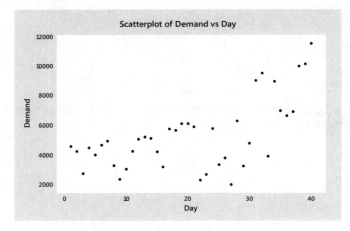

b.   From the plot, it looks like a second-order model would fit the data better than a first-order model. There is little evidence that a third-order model would fit the data better than a second-order model.

c.   Using MINITAB, the output for fitting a first-order model is:

Regression Analysis: Demand versus Day
```
The regression equation is
Demand = 2802 + 123 Day

Predictor     Coef   SE Coef     T      P
Constant    2802.4     604.7   4.63  0.000
Day         122.95     25.70   4.78  0.000

S = 1876.57    R-Sq = 37.6%    R-Sq(adj) = 35.9%

Analysis of Variance

Source            DF         SS         MS      F      P
Regression         1   80572885   80572885  22.88  0.000
Residual Error    38  133817026    3521501
Total             39  214389911
```

To see if there is a significant linear relationship between day and demand, we test:

$$H_0 : \beta_1 = 0$$
$$H_a : \beta_1 \neq 0$$

The test statistic is $t = 4.78$ and the p-value is $p = .000$. Since the p-value is less than $\alpha(p = .000 < .05)$, H_0 is rejected. There is sufficient evidence to indicate that there is a linear relationship between day and demand at $\alpha = .05$.

d.   Using MINITAB, the output for fitting a second-order model is:

Regression Analysis: Demand versus Day, Day-sq
```
The regression equation is
Demand = 4944 - 183 Day + 7.46 Day-sq

Predictor     Coef    SE Coef      T      P
Constant    4944.2      829.6   5.96  0.000
Day        -183.03      93.32  -1.96  0.057
Day-sq       7.463      2.207   3.38  0.002

S = 1662.23    R-Sq = 52.3%    R-Sq(adj) = 49.7%

Analysis of Variance

Source            DF         SS         MS      F      P
Regression         2  112158325   56079162  20.30  0.000
Residual Error    37  102231587    2763016
Total             39  214389911

Source    DF      Seq SS
Day        1    80572885
Day-sq     1    31585440
```

To see if there is a significant quadratic relationship between day and demand, we test:

$$H_0 : \beta_2 = 0$$
$$H_a : \beta_2 \neq 0$$

The test statistic is $t = 3.38$ and the p-value is $p = .002$. Since the p-value is less than $\alpha (p = .002 < .05)$, H_0 is rejected. There is sufficient evidence to indicate that there is a quadratic relationship between day and demand at $\alpha = .05$.

e. Since the quadratic term is significant in the second-order model in part **d**, the second order model is better.

12.67   The model is $E(y) = \beta_0 + \beta_1 x_1 + \beta_2 x_2$

where $x_1 = \begin{cases} 1 & \text{if the variable is at level 2} \\ 0 & \text{otherwise} \end{cases}$ $x_2 = \begin{cases} 1 & \text{if the variable is at level 3} \\ 0 & \text{otherwise} \end{cases}$

$\beta_0 = $ mean value of y when qualitative variable is at level 1.
$\beta_1 = $ difference in mean value of y between level 2 and level 1 of qualitative variable.
$\beta_2 = $ difference in mean value of y between level 3 and level 1 of qualitative variable.

12.69   a.   Level 1 implies $x_1 = x_2 = x_3 = 0$. $\hat{y} = 10.2 - 4(0) + 12(0) + 2(0) = 10.2$

Level 2 implies $x_1 = 1$ and $x_2 = x_3 = 0$. $\hat{y} = 10.2 - 4(1) + 12(0) + 2(0) = 6.2$

Level 3 implies $x_2 = 1$ and $x_1 = x_3 = 0$. $\hat{y} = 10.2 - 4(0) + 12(1) + 2(0) = 22.2$

Level 4 implies $x_3 = 1$ and $x_1 = x_2 = 0$. $\hat{y} = 10.2 - 4(0) + 12(0) + 2(1) = 12.2$

b.   The hypotheses are:

$$H_0 : \beta_1 = \beta_2 = \beta_3 = 0$$
$$H_a : \text{At least one } \beta_i \neq 0$$

12.71   a.   Let $x_1 = \begin{cases} 1 \text{ if grape-picking method is manual} \\ 0 \text{ otherwise} \end{cases}$ Let $x_2 = \begin{cases} 1 \text{ if soil type is clay} \\ 0 \text{ otherwise} \end{cases}$

Let $x_3 = \begin{cases} 1 \text{ if soil type is gravel} \\ 0 \text{ otherwise} \end{cases}$ Let $x_4 = \begin{cases} 1 \text{ if slope orientation is East} \\ 0 \text{ otherwise} \end{cases}$

Let $x_5 = \begin{cases} 1 \text{ if slope orientation is South} \\ 0 \text{ otherwise} \end{cases}$ Let $x_6 = \begin{cases} 1 \text{ if slope orientation is West} \\ 0 \text{ otherwise} \end{cases}$

Let $x_7 = \begin{cases} 1 \text{ if slope orientation is Southeast} \\ 0 \text{ otherwise} \end{cases}$

b.   The model is: $E(y) = \beta_0 + \beta_1 x_1$

$\beta_0 = $ mean wine quality for grape-picking method automated
$\beta_1 = $ difference in mean wine quality between grape-picking methods manual and automated

c.   The model is: $E(y) = \beta_0 + \beta_1 x_2 + \beta_2 x_3$

$\beta_0 = $ mean wine quality for soil type sand
$\beta_1 = $ difference in mean wine quality between soil types clay and sand
$\beta_2 = $ difference in mean wine quality between soil types gravel and sand

d. The model is: $E(y) = \beta_0 + \beta_1 x_4 + \beta_2 x_5 + \beta_3 x_6 + \beta_4 x_7$

β_0 = mean wine quality for slope orientation Southwest

β_1 = difference in mean wine quality between slope orientations East and Southwest

β_2 = difference in mean wine quality between slope orientations South and Southwest

β_3 = difference in mean wine quality between slope orientations West and Southwest

β_4 = difference in mean wine quality between slope orientations Southeast and Southwest

12.73 a. The model is $E(y) = \beta_0 + \beta_1 x_1 + \beta_2 x_2 + \beta_3 x_3$

where $x_1 = \begin{cases} 1 & \text{if dosage group A} \\ 0 & \text{otherwise} \end{cases}$ $x_2 = \begin{cases} 1 & \text{if dosage group B} \\ 0 & \text{otherwise} \end{cases}$ $x_3 = \begin{cases} 1 & \text{if dosage group C} \\ 0 & \text{otherwise} \end{cases}$

b. β_1 is the difference in the meanweight loss between AA groups A and D.

β_2 is the difference in the meanweight loss between AA groups B and D.

β_3 is the difference in the meanweight loss between AA groups C and D.

c. The mean weight loss is reduced in goats administered AA compared to goats not given any AA. Therefore, both $\beta_1 < 0$ and $\beta_2 < 0$.

12.75 a. Let $x_1 = \begin{cases} 1 & \text{if blonde Caucasian} \\ 0 & \text{otherwise} \end{cases}$ Let $x_2 = \begin{cases} 1 & \text{if brunette Caucasian} \\ 0 & \text{otherwise} \end{cases}$

b. The model would be: $E(y) = \beta_0 + \beta_1 x_1 + \beta_2 x_2$

c. The mean for a blonde Caucasian solicitor would be $E(y) = \beta_0 + \beta_1(1) + \beta_2(0) = \beta_0 + \beta_1$.

d. The difference in the mean level of contribution between a blode solicitor and a minority female solicitor is β_1.

e. If the theory is correct, then β_0 (mean for minority female solicitors) will be positive, β_1 will be positive (mean for female Caucasian solicitors is greator than the means of the other groups), and β_2 will be close to 0 (no difference in the means for minority female solicitors and brunette Caucasian solicitors).

f. Yes. The β-estimate for the dummy variable for blonde Caucasian solicitors should be positive and significantly different from 0. The β-estimate for the dummy variable for brunette Caucasian solicitors should be close to 0. In this case, it is not statistically different from 0.

12.77 a. Since there are four groups, we need 3 dummy variables.

Let $x_1 = \begin{cases} 1 & \text{if large/private} \\ 0 & \text{otherwise} \end{cases}$ Let $x_2 = \begin{cases} 1 & \text{if small/public} \\ 0 & \text{otherwise} \end{cases}$ Let $x_3 = \begin{cases} 1 & \text{if small/private} \\ 0 & \text{otherwise} \end{cases}$

b.   The model is $E(y) = \beta_0 + \beta_1 x_1 + \beta_2 x_2 + \beta_3 x_3$.

β_0 = mean likelihood of reporting sustainability policies for large/public firms.

β_1 = difference in mean likelihood of reporting sustainability policies between large/private firms and large/public firms.

β_2 = difference in mean likelihood of reporting sustainability policies between small/public firms and large/public firms.

β_3 = difference in mean likelihood of reporting sustainability policies between small/private firms and large/public firms.

c.   Since the p-value is very small $(p < .001)$, H_0 would be rejected for any reasonable value of α. There is sufficient evidence to indicate a difference in the mean likelihood of reporting sustainability policies among the 4 groups.

d.   Since there are 2 levels of each of the 2 variables, we need to create 2 dummy variables.

$$\text{Let } x_1 = \begin{cases} 1 & \text{if small} \\ 0 & \text{otherwise} \end{cases} \qquad \text{Let } x_2 = \begin{cases} 1 & \text{if private} \\ 0 & \text{otherwise} \end{cases}.$$

e.   The main effects model would be: $E(y) = \beta_0 + \beta_1 x_1 + \beta_2 x_2$.

f.   For large/public, $E(y) = \beta_0 + \beta_1(0) + \beta_2(0) = \beta_0$.

For large/private, $E(y) = \beta_0 + \beta_1(0) + \beta_2(1) = \beta_0 + \beta_2$.

For small/public, $E(y) = \beta_0 + \beta_1(1) + \beta_2(0) = \beta_0 + \beta_1$.

For small/private, $E(y) = \beta_0 + \beta_1(1) + \beta_2(1) = \beta_0 + \beta_1 + \beta_2$.

g.   For public firms, the difference between small and large firms is $(\beta_0 + \beta_1) - \beta_0 = \beta_1$.

For private firms, the difference between small and large firms is $(\beta_0 + \beta_1 + \beta_2) - (\beta_0 + \beta_2) = \beta_1$.

h.   The model is $E(y) = \beta_0 + \beta_1 x_1 + \beta_2 x_2 + \beta_3 x_1 x_2$.

i.   For large/public, $E(y) = \beta_0 + \beta_1(0) + \beta_2(0) + \beta_3(0)(0) = \beta_0$.

For large/private, $E(y) = \beta_0 + \beta_1(0) + \beta_2(1) + \beta_3(0)(1) = \beta_0 + \beta_2$.

For small/public, $E(y) = \beta_0 + \beta_1(1) + \beta_2(0) + \beta_3(1)(0) = \beta_0 + \beta_1$.

For small/private, $E(y) = \beta_0 + \beta_1(1) + \beta_2(1) + \beta_3(1)(1) = \beta_0 + \beta_1 + \beta_2 + \beta_3$.

j.   For public firms, the difference between small and large firms is $(\beta_0 + \beta_1) - \beta_0 = \beta_1$.

For private firms, the difference between small and large firms is
$(\beta_0 + \beta_1 + \beta_2 + \beta_3) - (\beta_0 + \beta_2) = \beta_1 + \beta_3$.

12.79   a.   The model is $E(y) = \beta_0 + \beta_1 x_1 + \beta_2 x_2 + \beta_3 x_3$

where $x_1 = \begin{cases} 1 & \text{if continuous verbal} \\ 0 & \text{otherwise} \end{cases}$ $x_2 = \begin{cases} 1 & \text{if late verbal} \\ 0 & \text{otherwise} \end{cases}$ $x_3 = \begin{cases} 1 & \text{if no verbal} \\ 0 & \text{otherwise} \end{cases}$

b.   From the printout, $\hat{\beta}_0 = 49.00$, $\hat{\beta}_1 = 34.30 - 49.00 = -14.7$, $\hat{\beta}_2 = 63.40 - 49.00 = 14.4$,
$\hat{\beta}_3 = 63.90 - 49.00 = 14.9$

c.   Using MINITAB, the results are:

Regression Analysis: y versus x1, x2, x3
```
Analysis of Variance

Source        DF  Adj SS  Adj MS   F-Value  P-Value
Regression     3    5922  1973.9      5.39    0.004
  x1           1    1080  1080.4      2.95    0.095
  x2           1    1037  1036.8      2.83    0.101
  x3           1    1110  1110.1      3.03    0.090
Error         36   13189   366.4
Total         39   19111


Model Summary

      S    R-sq  R-sq(adj)  R-sq(pred)
19.1409  30.99%     25.23%      14.80%


Coefficients

Term          Coef  SE Coef  T-Value  P-Value   VIF
Constant     49.00     6.05     8.10    0.000
x1          -14.70     8.56    -1.72    0.095  1.50
x2           14.40     8.56     1.68    0.101  1.50
x3           14.90     8.56     1.74    0.090  1.50


Regression Equation
y = 49.00 - 14.70 x1 + 14.40 x2 + 14.90 x3
```

From the output, the β estimates are: $\hat{\beta}_0 = 49.00$, $\hat{\beta}_1 = -14.7$, $\hat{\beta}_2 = 14.4$, $\hat{\beta}_3 = 14.9$.

d.   To determine if the the mean recall percentage differs for student-drivers in the four groups, we test:

$H_0 : \beta_1 = \beta_2 = \beta_3 = 0$
$H_a :$ At least $1\beta_i \neq 0$

The test statistic is $F = 5.39$ and the p-value is $p = .004$.

Since the p-value is less than $\alpha(p = .004 < .01)$, H_0 is rejected. There is sufficient evidence to indicate the mean recall percentage differs for student-drivers in the four groups at $\alpha = .01$.

12.81   a.   The model is $E(y) = \beta_0 + \beta_1 x_1 + \beta_2 x_2 + \beta_3 x_3$

where $x_1 = \begin{cases} 1 & \text{if banned/other} \\ 0 & \text{otherwise} \end{cases}$ $x_2 = \begin{cases} 1 & \text{if banned/no other} \\ 0 & \text{otherwise} \end{cases}$ $x_3 = \begin{cases} 1 & \text{if no ban/other} \\ 0 & \text{otherwise} \end{cases}$

b.   Using MINITAB, the results are:

Regression Analysis: MVL versus X1, X2, X3
```
Analysis of Variance

Source        DF   Adj SS   Adj MS   F-Value   P-Value
Regression     3  189.391   63.130    105.37    0.000
  X1           1  125.640  125.640    209.70    0.000
  X2           1  107.559  107.559    179.52    0.000
  X3           1    1.184    1.184      1.98    0.162
Error        173  103.651    0.599
Total        176  293.042
Model Summary

      S   R-sq   R-sq(adj)   R-sq(pred)
0.774039  64.63%    64.02%       63.09%

Coefficients

Term       Coef   SE Coef   T-Value   P-Value   VIF
Constant  6.376    0.104     61.09     0.000
X1        2.137    0.148     14.48     0.000    1.38
X2        2.171    0.162     13.40     0.000    1.33
X3        0.253    0.180      1.41     0.162    1.27

Regression Equation

MVL = 6.376 + 2.137 X1 + 2.171 X2 + 0.253 X3
```

The least squares prediction equation is $\hat{y} = 6.38 + 2.14x_1 + 2.17x_2 + .25x_3$.

c. $\hat{\beta}_0 = 6.38$ The mean MVL for the "no ban/no other" group is estimated to be 6.38.

$\hat{\beta}_1 = 2.14$ The difference in the mean MVL between the "banned/other" group and the "no ban/no other" group is estimated to be 2.14.

$\hat{\beta}_2 = 2.17$ The difference in the mean MVL between the "banned/no other" group and the "no ban/no other" group is estimated to be 2.17.

$\hat{\beta}_3 = .25$ The difference in the mean MVL between the "no ban/other" group and the "no ban/no other" group is estimated to be .25.

d.   To determine if there are differences in mean MVL vales among the four groups, we test:

$H_0 : \beta_1 = \beta_2 = \beta_3 = 0$
H_a : At least $1\beta_i \neq 0$

The test statistic is $F = 105.37$ and the p-value is $p = .000$.

Since the p-value is less than $\alpha (p = .000 < .05)$, H_0 is rejected. There is sufficient evidence to indicate there are differences in mean MVL vales among the four groups at $\alpha = .05$.

e.   The mean MVL value for the "banned/other" group is estimated to be $\hat{\beta}_1 + \hat{\beta}_0 = 2.14 + 6.38 = 8.52$.
The mean MVL value for the "banned/no other" group is estimated to be
$\hat{\beta}_2 + \hat{\beta}_0 = 2.17 + 6.38 = 8.55$.

The mean MVL value for the "no ban/other" group is estimated to be $\hat{\beta}_3 + \hat{\beta}_0 = .25 + 6.38 = 6.63$.

The mean MVL value for the "no ban/no other" group is estimated to be $\hat{\beta}_0 = 6.38$.

12.83   a.   The complete second-order model is $E(y) = \beta_0 + \beta_1 x_1 + \beta_2 x_1^2$.

b.   The new model is $E(y) = \beta_0 + \beta_1 x_1 + \beta_2 x_1^2 + \beta_3 x_2 + \beta_4 x_3$.

where $x_2 = \begin{cases} 1 \text{ if level 2} \\ 0 \text{ otherwise} \end{cases}$ $x_3 = \begin{cases} 1 \text{ if level 3} \\ 0 \text{ otherwise} \end{cases}$

c.   The model with the interaction terms is:

$$E(y) = \beta_0 + \beta_1 x_1 + \beta_2 x_1^2 + \beta_3 x_2 + \beta_4 x_3 + \beta_5 x_1 x_2 + \beta_6 x_1 x_3 + \beta_7 x_1^2 x_2 + \beta_8 x_1^2 x_3$$

d.   The response curves will have the same shape if none of the interaction terms are present or if
$\beta_5 = \beta_6 = \beta_7 = \beta_8 = 0$.

e.   The response curves will be parallel lines if the interaction terms as well as the second-order terms
are absent or if $\beta_2 = \beta_5 = \beta_6 = \beta_7 = \beta_8 = 0$.

f.   The response curves will be identical if no terms involving the qualitative variable are present or
$\beta_3 = \beta_4 = \beta_5 = \beta_6 = \beta_7 = \beta_8 = 0$

12.85   a.   For $x_2 = 0$ and $x_3 = 0$, $E(y) = \beta_0 + \beta_1 x_1 + \beta_2 x_1^2$

For $x_2 = 1$ and $x_3 = 0$,
$E(y) = \beta_0 + \beta_1 x_1 + \beta_2 x_1^2 + \beta_3 + \beta_5 x_1 + \beta_7 x_1^2 = (\beta_0 + \beta_3) + (\beta_1 + \beta_5) x_1 + (\beta_2 + \beta_7) x_1^2$

For $x_2 = 0$ and $x_3 = 1$,
$E(y) = \beta_0 + \beta_1 x_1 + \beta_2 x_1^2 + \beta_4 + \beta_6 x_1 + \beta_8 x_1^2 = (\beta_0 + \beta_4) + (\beta_1 + \beta_6) x_1 + (\beta_2 + \beta_8) x_1^2$

b.   Foe level 1, $\hat{y} = 48.8 - 3.4 x_1 + .07 x_1^2$

For level 2, $\hat{y} = 48.8 - 3.4 x_1 + .07 x_1^2 - 2.4(1) + 3.7 x_1 (1) - .02 x_1^2 (1) = 46.4 + 0.3 x_1 + .05 x_1^2$

For level 3, $\hat{y} = 48.8 - 3.4 x_1 + .07 x_1^2 - 7.5(1) + 2.7 x_1 (1) - .04 x_1^2 (1) = 41.3 - 0.7 x_1 + 0.03 x_1^2$

The plots of the lines are:

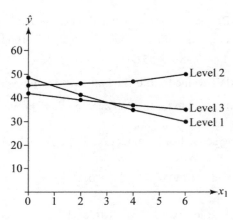

12.87   a.   For female students, the equation is $\hat{y} = 11.78 - 1.97(0) + .58x_4 - .55(0)x_4 = 11.78 + .58x_4$. Thus, for females for each 1-point increase in impression of reality TV show, the mean desire is estimated to increase by .58.

b.   For male students, the equation is $\hat{y} = 11.78 - 1.97(1) + .58x_4 - .55(1)x_4 = 9.81 + .03x_4$. Thus, for males for each 1-point increase in impression of reality TV show, the mean desire is estimated to increase by .03.

12.89   a.   When $x_2 = 0$, $E(y) = \beta_0 + \beta_1 x_1 + \beta_2 x_1^2 + \beta_3(0) + \beta_4 x_1(0) + \beta_5 x_1^2(0) = \beta_0 + \beta_1 x_1 + \beta_2 x_1^2$

b.   When $x_2 = 1$,
$$E(y) = \beta_0 + \beta_1 x_1 + \beta_2 x_1^2 + \beta_3(1) + \beta_4 x_1(1) + \beta_5 x_1^2(1) = (\beta_0 + \beta_3) + (\beta_1 + \beta_4)x_1 + (\beta_2 + \beta_5)x_1^2$$

c.   Answers will vary. Using MINITAB, a possible graph is:

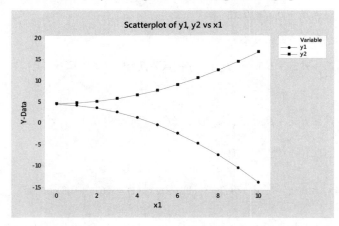

The graph of y_1 is an example of plotting the line when the team leader is not effective. This has a downward curvature. The graph of y_2 is an example of plotting the line when the team leader is effective. This has an upward curvature.

12.91   a.   Let $x_2 = \begin{cases} 1 \text{ if perceived organizational support is low} \\ 0 \text{ otherwise} \end{cases}$

$x_3 = \begin{cases} 1 \text{ if perceived organizational support is neutral} \\ 0 \text{ otherwise} \end{cases}$

b. The model would be $E(y) = \beta_0 + \beta_1 x_1 + \beta_2 x_2 + \beta_3 x_3$.

c. The model would be $E(y) = \beta_0 + \beta_1 x_1 + \beta_2 x_2 + \beta_3 x_3 + \beta_4 x_1 x_2 + \beta_5 x_1 x_3$.

d. If the effect of bullying on intention to leave is greater at the low level of POS than at the high level of POS, this indicates that POS and bullying interact. Thus, the model in part c supports these findings.

12.93 a. Let $x_1 = \begin{cases} 1 & \text{if channel catfish} \\ 0 & \text{otherwise} \end{cases}$ $x_2 = \begin{cases} 1 & \text{if largemouth bass} \\ 0 & \text{otherwise} \end{cases}$

b. Let x_3 = weight. The model would be: $E(y) = \beta_0 + \beta_1 x_1 + \beta_2 x_2 + \beta_3 x_3$

c. The model would be: $E(y) = \beta_0 + \beta_1 x_1 + \beta_2 x_2 + \beta_3 x_3 + \beta_4 x_1 x_3 + \beta_4 x_2 x_3$

d. From MINITAB, the output is:

Regression Analysis: DDT versus x1, x2, Weight
```
The regression equation is
DDT = 3.1 + 26.5 x1 - 4.1 x2 + 0.0037 Weight

Predictor         Coef      SE Coef          T         P
Constant          3.13        38.89       0.08     0.936
x1               26.51        21.52       1.23     0.220
x2               -4.09        37.91      -0.11     0.914
Weight         0.00371      0.02598       0.14     0.887

S = 98.57       R-Sq = 1.7%       R-Sq(adj) = 0.0%

Analysis of Variance

Source             DF           SS         MS         F         P
Regression          3        23652       7884      0.81     0.490
Residual Error    140      1360351       9717
Total             143      1384003

Source       DF    Seq SS
x1            1     23041
x2            1       414
Weight        1       198
```

The least squares prediction equation is: $\hat{y} = 3.13 + 26.51 x_1 - 4.09 x_2 + 0.00371 x_3$

e. $\hat{\beta}_3 = 0.00371$. For each additional gram of weight, the mean level of DDT is expected to increase by 0.00371 units, holding species constant.

f. From MINITAB, the output is:

Regression Analysis: DDT versus x1, x2, Weight, x1Weight, x2Weight
```
The regression equation is
DDT = 3.5 + 25.6 x1 - 3.5 x2 + 0.0034 Weight + 0.0008 x1Weight
            - 0.0013 x2Weight

Predictor         Coef      SE Coef          T         P
Constant          3.50        54.69       0.06     0.949
x1               25.59        67.52       0.38     0.705
x2               -3.47        84.70      -0.04     0.967
```

```
Weight           0.00344      0.03843      0.09    0.929
x1Weight         0.00082      0.05459      0.02    0.988
x2Weight        -0.00129      0.09987     -0.01    0.990

S = 99.29        R-Sq = 1.7%      R-Sq(adj) = 0.0%

Analysis of Variance

Source            DF          SS        MS        F       P
Regression         5       23657      4731      0.48    0.791
Residual Error   138     1360346      9858
Total            143     1384003

Source         DF      Seq SS
x1              1       23041
x2              1         414
Weight          1         198
x1Weight        1           4
x2Weight        1           2
```

The least squares prediction equation is:

$$\hat{y} = 3.50 + 25.59x_1 - 3.47x_2 + 0.00344x_3 + 0.00082x_1x_3 - .00129x_2x_3$$

g.   For channel catfish, $x_1 = 1$ and $x_2 = 0$. The least squares line is

$$\hat{y} = 3.50 + 25.59(1) - 3.47(0) + 0.00344x_3 + 0.00082(1)x_3 - .00129(0)x_3 = 29.09 + .00426x_3$$

The estimated slope is .00426.

12.95   a.   Let x_1 = sales volume

$$x_2 = \begin{cases} 1 \text{ if NW} \\ 0 \text{ if not} \end{cases} \qquad x_3 = \begin{cases} 1 \text{ if S} \\ 0 \text{ if not} \end{cases} \qquad x_4 = \begin{cases} 1 \text{ if W} \\ 0 \text{ if not} \end{cases}$$

The complete second order model for the sales price of a single-family home is:

$$E(y) = \beta_0 + \beta_1 x_1 + \beta_2 x_1^2 + \beta_3 x_2 + \beta_4 x_3 + \beta_5 x_4 + \beta_6 x_1 x_2 + \beta_7 x_1 x_3 + \beta_8 x_1 x_4 + \beta_9 x_1^2 x_2 + \beta_{10} x_1^2 x_3 + \beta_{11} x_1^2 x_4$$

b.   For the West, $x_2 = 0$, $x_3 = 0$, and $x_4 = 1$. The equation would be:

$$E(y) = \beta_0 + \beta_1 x_1 + \beta_2 x_1^2 + \beta_3(0) + \beta_4(0) + \beta_5(1) + \beta_6 x_1(0) + \beta_7 x_1(0) + \beta_8 x_1(1)$$
$$+ \beta_9 x_1^2(0) + \beta_{10} x_1^2(0) + \beta_{11} x_1^2(1)$$
$$= \beta_0 + \beta_1 x_1 + \beta_2 x_1^2 + \beta_5 + \beta_8 x_1 + \beta_{11} x_1^2 = (\beta_0 + \beta_5) + (\beta_1 + \beta_8)x_1 + (\beta_2 + \beta_{11})x_1^2$$

c.   For the Northwest, $x_2 = 1$, $x_3 = 0$, and $x_4 = 0$. The equation would be:

$$E(y) = \beta_0 + \beta_1 x_1 + \beta_2 x_1^2 + \beta_3(1) + \beta_4(0) + \beta_5(0) + \beta_6 x_1(1) + \beta_7 x_1(0) + \beta_8 x_1(0)$$
$$+ \beta_9 x_1^2(1) + \beta_{10} x_1^2(0) + \beta_{11} x_1^2(0)$$
$$= \beta_0 + \beta_1 x_1 + \beta_2 x_1^2 + \beta_3 + \beta_6 x_1 + \beta_9 x_1^2 = (\beta_0 + \beta_3) + (\beta_1 + \beta_6)x_1 + (\beta_2 + \beta_9)x_1^2$$

d. The parameters β_3, β_4, and β_5 allow for the y-intercepts of the 4 regions to be different. The parameters β_6, β_7, and β_8 allow for the peaks of the curves to be a different value of sales volume (x_1) for the four regions. The parameters β_9, β_{10}, and β_{11} allow for the shapes of the curves to be different for the four regions. Thus, all the parameters from β_3 through β_{11} allow for differences in mean sales prices among the four regions.

e. Using MINITAB, the printout is:

Regression Analysis: Price versus X1, X1SQ, ...

```
The regression equation is
Price = 1904740 - 70.4 X1 + 0.000721 X1SQ + 159661 X2 + 5291908 X3 + 3663319 X4
        + 22.2 X1X2 - 23.9 X1X3 - 37 X1X4 - 0.000421 X1SQX2 - 0.000404 X1SQX3
        - 0.000181 X1SQX4
```

Predictor	Coef	SE Coef	T	P
Constant	1904740	1984278	0.96	0.351
X1	-70.44	72.09	-0.98	0.343
X1SQ	0.0007211	0.0006515	1.11	0.285
X2	159661	2069265	0.08	0.939
X3	5291908	4812586	1.10	0.288
X4	3663319	4478880	0.82	0.425
X1X2	22.25	73.74	0.30	0.767
X1X3	-23.86	92.09	-0.26	0.799
X1X4	-37.2	103.0	-0.36	0.723
X1SQX2	-0.0004210	0.0006589	-0.64	0.532
X1SQX3	-0.0004044	0.0006777	-0.60	0.559
X1SQX4	-0.0001810	0.0007333	-0.25	0.808

```
S = 24365.8   R-Sq = 85.0%   R-Sq(adj) = 74.6%
```

Analysis of Variance

Source	DF	SS	MS	F	P
Regression	11	53633628997	4875784454	8.21	0.000
Residual Error	16	9499097458	593693591		
Total	27	63132726455			

Source	DF	Seq SS
X1	1	3591326
X1SQ	1	64275360
X2	1	11338642654
X3	1	10081000583
X4	1	241539024
X1X2	1	18258475317
X1X3	1	5579187440
X1X4	1	7566169810
X1SQX2	1	138146367
X1SQX3	1	326425228
X1SQX4	1	36175888

To determine if the model is useful for predicting sales price, we test:

$$H_0 : \beta_1 = \beta_2 = \cdots = \beta_{11} = 0$$
$$H_a : \text{At least one } \beta_i \neq 0$$

The test statistic is $F = \dfrac{MS(Model)}{MSE} = 8.21$ and the p-value is $p = .000$. Since the p-value is less than

$\alpha(p = .000 < .01)$, H_0 is rejected. There is sufficient evidence to indicate the model is useful in predicting sales price at $\alpha = .01$.

12.97   The models in parts **a** and **b** are nested:

The complete model is $E(y) = \beta_0 + \beta_1 x_1 + \beta_2 x_2$.
The reduced model is $E(y) = \beta_0 + \beta_1 x_1$.

The models in parts **a** and **d** are nested.

The complete model is $E(y) = \beta_0 + \beta_1 x_1 + \beta_2 x_2 + \beta_3 x_1 x_2$.
The reduced model is $E(y) = \beta_0 + \beta_1 x_1 + \beta_2 x_2$.

The models in parts **a** and **e** are nested.

The complete model is $E(y) = \beta_0 + \beta_1 x_1 + \beta_2 x_2 + \beta_3 x_1 x_2 + \beta_4 x_1^2 + \beta_5 x_2^2$.
The reduced model is $E(y) = \beta_0 + \beta_1 x_1 + \beta_2 x_2$.

The models in parts **b** and **c** are nested.

The complete model is $E(y) = \beta_0 + \beta_1 x_1 + \beta_2 x_1^2$.
The reduced model is $E(y) = \beta_0 + \beta_1 x_1$.

The models in parts **b** and **d** are nested.

The complete model is $E(y) = \beta_0 + \beta_1 x_1 + \beta_2 x_2 + \beta_3 x_1 x_2$.
The reduced model is $E(y) = \beta_0 + \beta_1 x_1$.

The models in parts **b** and **e** are nested.

The complete model is $E(y) = \beta_0 + \beta_1 x_1 + \beta_2 x_2 + \beta_3 x_1 x_2 + \beta_4 x_1^2 + \beta_5 x_2^2$
The reduced model is $E(y) = \beta_0 + \beta_1 x_1$.

The models in parts **c** and **e** are nested.

The complete model is $E(y) = \beta_0 + \beta_1 x_1 + \beta_2 x_2 + \beta_3 x_1 x_2 + \beta_4 x_1^2 + \beta_5 x_2^2$
The reduced model is $E(y) = \beta_0 + \beta_1 x_1 + \beta_2 x_1^2$

The models in parts **d** and **e** are nested.

The complete model is $E(y) = \beta_0 + \beta_1 x_1 + \beta_2 x_2 + \beta_3 x_1 x_2 + \beta_4 x_1^2 + \beta_5 x_2^2$
The reduced model is $E(y) = \beta_0 + \beta_1 x_1 + \beta_2 x_2 + \beta_3 x_1 x_2$

12.99   a.   Including β_0, there are five β parameters in the complete model and three in the reduced model.

   b.   The hypotheses are:

$$H_0 : \beta_3 = \beta_4 = 0$$
$$H_a : \text{At least one } \beta_i \neq 0, \; i = 3, 4$$

   c.   The test statistic is $F = \dfrac{(SSE_R - SSE_C)/(k-g)}{SSE_C/[n-(k+1)]} = \dfrac{(160.44 - 152.66)/(4-2)}{152.66/[20-(4+1)]} = \dfrac{3.89}{10.1773} = .38$

The rejection region requires $\alpha = .05$ in the upper tail of the F-distribution with $v_1 = k - g = 4 - 2 = 2$ and $v_2 = n - (k+1) = 20 - (4+1) = 15$. From Table VI, Appendix D, $F_{.05} = 3.68$. The rejection region is $F > 3.68$.

Since the observed value of the test statistic does not fall in the rejection region $(F = .38 \ngtr 3.68)$, H_0 is not rejected. There is insufficient evidence to indicate the complete model is better than the reduced model at $\alpha = .05$.

12.101   a.   To determine whether the quadratic terms in the model are statistically useful for predicting relative optimism, we test:

$$H_0 : \beta_4 = \beta_5 = 0$$
$$H_a : \text{At least one } \beta_i \neq 0$$

   b.   The complete model is $E(y) = \beta_0 + \beta_1 x_1 + \beta_2 x_2 + \beta_3 x_1 x_2 + \beta_4 x_2^2 + \beta_5 x_1 x_2^2$ and the reduced model is $E(y) = \beta_0 + \beta_1 x_1 + \beta_2 x_2 + \beta_3 x_1 x_2$.

   c.   To determine whether the interaction terms in the model are statistically useful for predicting relative optimism, we test:

$$H_0 : \beta_3 = \beta_5 = 0$$
$$H_a : \text{At least one } \beta_i \neq 0$$

   d.   The complete model is $E(y) = \beta_0 + \beta_1 x_1 + \beta_2 x_2 + \beta_3 x_1 x_2 + \beta_4 x_2^2 + \beta_5 x_1 x_2^2$ and the reduced model is $E(y) = \beta_0 + \beta_1 x_1 + \beta_2 x_2 + \beta_4 x_2^2$.

   e.   To determine whether the dummy variable terms in the model are statistically useful for predicting relative optimism, we test:

$$H_0 : \beta_1 = \beta_3 = \beta_5 = 0$$
$$H_a : \text{At least one } \beta_i \neq 0$$

   f.   The complete model is $E(y) = \beta_0 + \beta_1 x_1 + \beta_2 x_2 + \beta_3 x_1 x_2 + \beta_4 x_2^2 + \beta_5 x_1 x_2^2$ and the reduced model is $E(y) = \beta_0 + \beta_2 x_2 + \beta_4 x_2^2$.

12.103 a. Let x_1 = cycle speed and x_2 = cycle pressure ratio. A complete second order model is:

$$E(y) = \beta_0 + \beta_1 x_1 + \beta_2 x_2 + \beta_3 x_1^2 + \beta_4 x_2^2 + \beta_5 x_1 x_2$$

b. To determine whether the curvature terms in the complete 2nd –order model are useful for predicting heat rate, we test:

$$H_0 : \beta_3 = \beta_4 = 0$$
$$H_a : \text{At least one } \beta_i \neq 0$$

c. The complete model is $E(y) = \beta_0 + \beta_1 x_1 + \beta_2 x_2 + \beta_3 x_1^2 + \beta_4 x_2^2 + \beta_5 x_1 x_2$

The reduced model is $E(y) = \beta_0 + \beta_1 x_1 + \beta_2 x_2 + \beta_5 x_1 x_2$

d. From the printout the test statistic is $F = 9.35$

f. The rejection region requires $\alpha = .10$ in the upper tail of the F-distribution with $v_1 = k - g = 5 - 3 = 2$ and $v_2 = n - (k+1) = 67 - (5+1) = 61$. From Table V, Appendix D, $F_{.10} = 2.39$. The rejection region is $F > 2.39$.

The p-value is $p = .000$.

g. Since the observed value of the test statistic falls in the rejection region $(F = 9.35 > 2.39)$, H_0 is rejected. There is sufficient evidence to indicate at least one of the curvature terms in the complete 2nd –order model are useful for predicting heat rate at $\alpha = .10$.

12.105 a. The model would be: $E(y) = \beta_0 + \beta_1 x_1 + \beta_2 x_2 + \beta_3 x_3 + \beta_4 x_4 + \beta_5 x_1 x_4 + \beta_6 x_2 x_4 + \beta_7 x_3 x_4$

b. Using MINITAB, the results are:

Regression Analysis: DESIRE versus GENDER, SELFESTM, ...
```
The regression equation is
DESIRE = 13.1 - 1.89 GENDER - 0.091 SELFESTM + 0.135 BODYSAT + 0.746 IMPREAL
         - 0.065 G_I + 0.0098 SE_I - 0.112 BS_I

Predictor      Coef   SE Coef       T       P
Constant     13.092     2.013    6.50   0.000
GENDER       -1.890     2.074   -0.91   0.363
SELFESTM    -0.0908    0.1176   -0.77   0.441
BODYSAT      0.1350    0.4749    0.28   0.777
IMPREAL      0.7460    0.4918    1.52   0.131
G_I         -0.0647    0.5110   -0.13   0.899
SE_I        0.00977   0.02808    0.35   0.728
BS_I        -0.1121    0.1160   -0.97   0.335

S = 2.23593   R-Sq = 51.3%   R-Sq(adj) = 49.2%

Analysis of Variance

Source           DF       SS      MS       F       P
Regression        7   853.89  121.98   24.40   0.000
Residual Error  162   809.90    5.00
Total           169  1663.79

Source     DF   Seq SS
GENDER      1   674.64
SELFESTM    1    57.66
BODYSAT     1    19.62
IMPREAL     1    75.91
G_I         1    20.36
SE_I        1     1.03
BS_I        1     4.67
```

To determine the overall utility of the model, we test:

$$H_0 : \beta_1 = \beta_2 = \beta_3 = \beta_4 = \beta_5 = \beta_6 = \beta_7 = 0$$
$$H_a : \text{At least } 1 \beta_i \neq 0$$

The test statistic is $F = 24.40$ and the p-value is $p = .000$. Since the p-value is so small, H_0 will be rejected for any reasonable value of α. There is sufficient evidence to indicate the model is useful for predicting desire to have cosmetic surgery.

c.   To determine if impression of reality TV interacts with each of the other independent variables, the null hypothesis is:

$$H_0 : \beta_5 = \beta_6 = \beta_7 = 0$$

d.   The reduced model is $E(y) = \beta_0 + \beta_1 x_1 + \beta_2 x_2 + \beta_3 x_3 + \beta_4 x_4$. This model was fit in Exercise 12.17. From this exercise, $SSE_R = 835.95$.

The test statistic is $F = \dfrac{(SSE_R - SSE_C)/(k-g)}{SSE_C/[n-(k+1)]} = \dfrac{(835.95 - 809.90)/(7-4)}{809.90/[170-(7+1)]} = 1.74$.

Since no α was given, we will use $\alpha = .05$. The rejection region requires $\alpha = .05$ in the upper tail of the F-distribution with $v_1 = k - g = 7 - 4 = 3$ and $v_2 = n - (k+1) = 170 - (7+1) = 162$. From Table VI, Appendix D, $F_{.05} \approx 2.68$. The rejection region is $F > 2.68$.

Since the observed value of the test statistic does not fall in the rejection region $(F = 1.74 \not> 2.68)$, H_0 is not rejected. There is insufficient evidence to indicate impression of reality TV interacts with each of the other independent variables at $\alpha = .05$.

12.107   a.   If the theory is correct, then the sign of β_3 should be positive.

b.   A possible graph might look like:

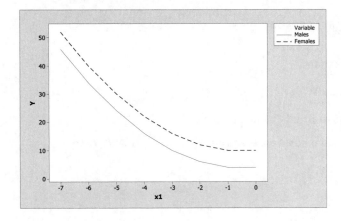

c.   The complete 2nd-order model is $E(y) = \beta_0 + \beta_1 x_1 + \beta_2 x_1^2 + \beta_3 x_2 + \beta_4 x_1 x_2 + \beta_5 x_1^2 x_2$.

d. A possible graph might look like:

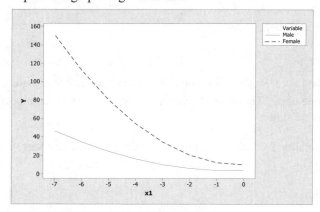

e. To compare the two models, we test:

$$H_0 : \beta_4 = \beta_5 = 0$$
$$H_a : \text{At least } 1 \beta_i \neq 0$$

f. Using MINITAB, the results of fitting the model in part a are:

Regression Analysis: Income versus Agree, Agree-sq, Gender
```
The regression equation is
Income = - 21657 + 37155 Agree - 7056 Agree-sq + 25482 Gender

Predictor      Coef   SE Coef       T       P
Constant     -21657     31780   -0.68   0.497
Agree         37155     19257    1.93   0.057
Agree-sq      -7056      2903   -2.43   0.017
Gender        25482      1552   16.42   0.000


S = 7737.36    R-Sq = 76.5%    R-Sq(adj) = 75.8%


Analysis of Variance

Source          DF           SS          MS        F       P
Regression       3  18708663846  6236221282   104.17   0.000
Residual Error  96   5747214158    59866814
Total           99  24455878004

Source     DF       Seq SS
Agree       1   1896882849
Agree-sq    1    663015651
Gender      1  16148765346
```

Using MINITAB, the results of fitting the model in part c are:

Regression Analysis: Income versus Agree, Agree-sq, Gender, G_A, G_A-sq
```
The regression equation is
Income = - 9847 + 27248 Agree - 5169 Agree-sq + 42549 Gender - 4765 G_A
         - 128 G_A-sq

Predictor      Coef   SE Coef       T       P
Constant      -9847     45303   -0.22   0.828
Agree         27248     28743    0.95   0.346
Agree-sq      -5169      4520   -1.14   0.256
Gender        42549     71654    0.59   0.554
G_A           -4765     43177   -0.11   0.912
G_A-sq         -128      6474   -0.02   0.984
```

```
S = 7751.27    R-Sq = 76.9%    R-Sq(adj) = 75.7%

Analysis of Variance

Source            DF          SS          MS       F      P
Regression         5    18808157832   3761631566  62.61  0.000
Residual Error    94     5647720172     60082129
Total             99    24455878004

Source      DF        Seq SS
Agree        1     1896882849
Agree-sq     1      663015651
Gender       1    16148765346
G_A          1       99470471
G_A-sq       1          23515
```

The test statistic is $F = \dfrac{(SSE_R - SSE_C)/(k-g)}{SSE_C/[n-(k+1)]} = \dfrac{(5,747,214,158 - 5,647,720,172)/(5-3)}{5,647,720,172/[100-(5+1)]} = .83$.

The rejection region requires $\alpha = .10$ in the upper tail of the F-distribution with $v_1 = k - g = 5 - 3 = 2$ and $v_2 = n - (k+1) = 100 - (5+1) = 94$. From Table V, Appendix D, $F_{.10} \approx 2.37$. The rejection region is $F > 2.37$.

Since the observed value of the test statistic does not fall in the rejection region $(F = .83 \ngtr 2.37)$, H_0 is not rejected. There is insufficient evidence to indicate the interaction terms improve the model at $\alpha = .10$.

12.109   a.   The model would be $E(y) = \beta_0 + \beta_1 x_1 + \beta_2 x_2 + \beta_3 x_3$.

b.   The model including the interaction terms is: $E(y) = \beta_0 + \beta_1 x_1 + \beta_2 x_2 + \beta_3 x_3 + \beta_4 x_1 x_2 + \beta_5 x_1 x_3$

c.   For AL, $x_2 = x_3 = 0$. The model would be:

$E(y) = \beta_0 + \beta_1 x_1 + \beta_2(0) + \beta_3(0) + \beta_4 x_1(0) + \beta_5 x_1(0) = \beta_0 + \beta_1 x_1$

The slope of the line is β_1.

For TDS-3A, $x_2 = 1$ and $x_3 = 0$. The model would be:

$E(y) = \beta_0 + \beta_1 x_1 + \beta_2(1) + \beta_3(0) + \beta_4 x_1(1) + \beta_5 x_1(0) = (\beta_0 + \beta_2) + (\beta_1 + \beta_4)x_1$

The slope of the line is $\beta_1 + \beta_4$.

For FE, $x_2 = 0$ and $x_3 = 1$. The model would be:

$E(y) = \beta_0 + \beta_1 x_1 + \beta_2(0) + \beta_3(1) + \beta_4 x_1(0) + \beta_5 x_1(1) = (\beta_0 + \beta_3) + (\beta_1 + \beta_5)x_1$

The slope of the line is $\beta_1 + \beta_5$.

d. To test for the presence of temperature-waste type interaction, we would fit the complete model listed in part **b** and the reduced model found in part **a**. The hypotheses would be:

$$H_0 : \beta_4 = \beta_5 = 0$$
$$H_a : \text{At least one } \beta_i \neq 0$$

The test statistic would be $F = \dfrac{(SSE_R - SSE_C)/(k-g)}{SSE_C/[n-(k+1)]}$ where $k = 5$, $q = 3$, SSE_R is the SSE for the reduced model, and SSE_c is the SSE for the complete model.

12.111 a. The best one-variable predictor of y is the one whose t statistic has the largest absolute value. The t statistics for each of the variables are:

Independent Variable	$t = \dfrac{\hat{\beta}_i}{s_{\hat{\beta}_i}}$
x_1	$t = 1.6 / .42 = 3.81$
x_2	$t = -.9 / .01 = -90$
x_3	$t = 3.4 / 1.14 = 2.98$
x_4	$t = 2.5 / 2.06 = 1.21$
x_5	$t = -4.4 / .73 = -6.03$
x_6	$t = .3 / .35 = .86$

The variable x_2 is the best one-variable predictor of y. The absolute value of the corresponding t score is 90. This is larger than any of the others.

b. Yes. In the stepwise procedure, the first variable entered is the one which has the largest absolute value of t, provided the absolute value of the t falls in the rejection region.

c. Once x_2 is entered, the next variable that is entered is the one that, in conjunction with x_2, has the largest absolute t value associated with it.

12.113 a. There would be five 1-variable models fit in step 1.

b. There would be four 2-variable models fit in step 2.

c. There would be three 3-variable models fit in step 3.

d. There would be two 4-variable models fit in step 4.

e. There would be a total of fourteen t-tests performed. For each individual t-test, $P(\text{Type I error}) = .05$.

$$P(\text{at least Type I error}) = 1 - P(0 \text{ Type I error}) = 1 - \binom{14}{0}(.05)^0(.95)^{14} = 1 - .49 = .51$$

12.115 a. In step 1, there were 11 one-variable models fit to the data. Thus, there were 11 t-tests run.

b. In step 2, there were 10 two-variable models fit to the data. Thus, there were 10 t-tests run.

c. The Global F p-value $= .001$. Since this p-value is so small, there is evidence that the final model is useful for predicting TME. $R^2 = .988$. 98.8% of the total sample variation of TME about its mean is explained by the model containing AMAP and NDF.

d. The stepwise procedure does not guarantee that the "best" model has been determined. It is possible that important variables were not located. In addition, 2nd order terms and interaction terms should be considered.

e. The complete 2nd order model would be:

$$E(y) = \beta_0 + \beta_1(AMAP) + \beta_2(NDF) + \beta_3(AMAP)^2 + \beta_4(NDF)^2 + \beta_5(AMAP)(NDF)$$

f. To determine if the terms in the model that allow for curvature are statistically significant, we test:

$$H_0 : \beta_3 = \beta_4 = \beta_5 = 0$$
$$H_a : \text{At least } 1 \beta_i \neq 0$$

We would compare the complete model (form part e) to the reduced model with just the main effects of AMAP and NDF using the test statistic $F = \dfrac{(SSE_R - SSE_C)/(k-g)}{SSE_C/[n-(k+1)]}$.

12.117 a. In step 1, all 1 variable models are fit. Thus, there are a total of 11 models fit.

b. In step 2, all two-variable models are fit, where 1 of the variables is the best one selected in step 1. Thus, a total of 10 two-variable models are fit.

c. In the 11th step, only one model is fit – the model containing all the independent variables.

d. The model would be $E(y) = \beta_0 + \beta_1 x_{11} + \beta_2 x_4 + \beta_3 x_2 + \beta_4 x_7 + \beta_5 x_{10} + \beta_6 x_1 + \beta_7 x_9 + \beta_8 x_3$.

e. 67.7% of the total sample variability of overall satisfaction is explained by the model containing the independent variables safety on bus, seat availability, dependability, travel time, convenience of route, safety at bus stops, hours of service, and frequency of service.

f. Using stepwise regression does not guarantee that the best model will be found. There may be better combinations of the independent variables that are never found, because of the order in which the independent variables are entered into the model. In addition, there are no squared or interaction terms included. There is a high probability of making at least one Type 1 error.

2.119 No, we would not suggest using stepwise regression because there are only two independent variables. In order to find the best model, several models could be tested. A first-order model could be fit with the two independent variables, artist death status and album sales. The interaction term between artist death status and album sales could then be added to the model. A second-order model could be fit with album sales and the square of album sales along with artist death status. Finally, the interaction terms between artist death status and album sales and between artist death status and the square of album sales could be added to the second-order model.

12.121 Yes. x_2 and x_4 are highly correlated (.93), as well as x_4 and x_5 (.86). When highly correlated independent variables are present in a regression model, the results can be confusing. The researcher may want to include only one of the variables.

12.123   a.   For a basic wooden casket $(x_2 = 1)$ and funeral home in a restricted state $(x_1 = 1)$,

$\hat{y} = 1,432 + 793(1) - 252(1) + 261(1)(1) = 2,234$.

b.   No, this would not be an outlier. The point $2,200 is less than one standard deviation from its predicted value.

c.   Yes. This data point is $z = \dfrac{2,500 - 2,200}{50} = 6$ standard deviations from its predicted value.

12.125   a.   The number of females in managerial positions is the dependent variable. The correlation between it and the independent variables does not imply multicollinearity.

b.   Again, the number of females in managerial positions is the dependent variable. The correlation between it and the independent variables does not imply multicollinearity.

c.   Since the absolute value of the correlation coefficient is .722, this would imply there is a moderate potential for multicollinearity.

d.   Since the absolute value of the correlation coefficient is .528, this would imply there is a moderate potential for multicollinearity.

12.127   Using MINITAB, the residual plots are:

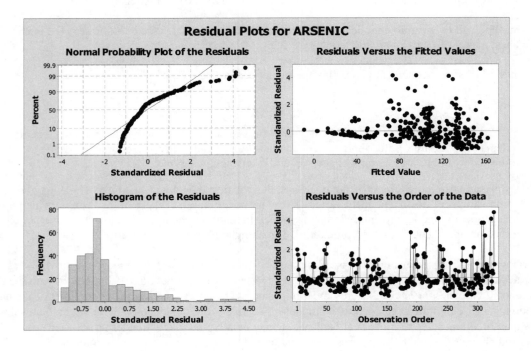

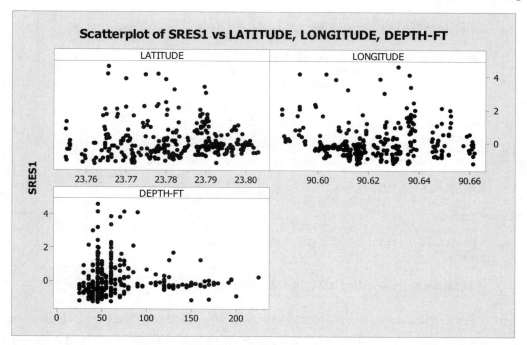

a. From the histogram of the standardized residuals, it appears that the mean of the residuals is close to 0. Thus, the assumption that the mean error is 0 appears to be met.

b. From the plot of the standardized residuals versus the fitted values, it appears that the spread of the residuals increases as the fitted values increase. Thus, it appears that the assumption of constant variance is violated.

c. From the plots of the standardized residuals versus the fitted values, it appears that there are some outliers. There are several observations with standardized residuals of 4 or more.

d. From the normal probability plot, the data do not form a straight line. Thus, it appears that the assumption of normal error terms is violated.

e. Using MINITAB, the correlations among the independent variables are:

Correlations: LATITUDE, LONGITUDE, DEPTH-FT

```
               LATITUDE   LONGITUDE
LONGITUDE         0.311
                  0.000

DEPTH-FT          0.151      -0.328
                  0.006       0.000

Cell Contents:  Pearson correlation
                P-Value
```

None of the pairwise correlations are large in absolute value, so there is no evidence of multicollinearity. In addition, the global test indicates that at least one of the independent variables is significant and each of the independent variables is statistically significant. This also indicates that multicollinearity does not exist.

12.129 a.   Using MINITAB, the results are:

Regression Analysis: Time versus Temp
```
The regression equation is
Time = 30856 - 192 Temp

Predictor       Coef   SE Coef        T       P
Constant       30856      2713    11.37   0.000
Temp         -191.57     18.49   -10.36   0.000

S = 1099.17    R-Sq = 84.3%    R-Sq(adj) = 83.5%

Analysis of Variance

Source            DF          SS          MS        F       P
Regression         1   129663987   129663987   107.32   0.000
Residual Error    20    24163399     1208170
Total             21   153827386
```

The fitted regression line is $\hat{y} = 30,856 - 191.57x$.

b.   For temperature $= 149$, $\hat{y} = 30,856 - 191.57(150) = 2,312.07$. There are 2 observations with a temperature of 149. The residuals for the microchips manufactured at a temperature of $149°$ C are $\hat{\varepsilon} = y - \hat{y} = 1,100 - 2,312.07 = -1,212.07$ and $\hat{\varepsilon} = y - \hat{y} = 1,150 - 2,312.07 = -1,162.07$.

c.   Using MINITAB, the plot of the residuals versus temperature is:

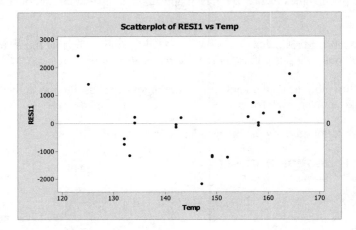

There appears to be a U-shaped trend to the data.

d.   Yes. Because there appears to be a U-shaped trend to the data, this indicates that there is a curvilinear relationship between temperature and time.

12.131   Using MINITAB, the results are:

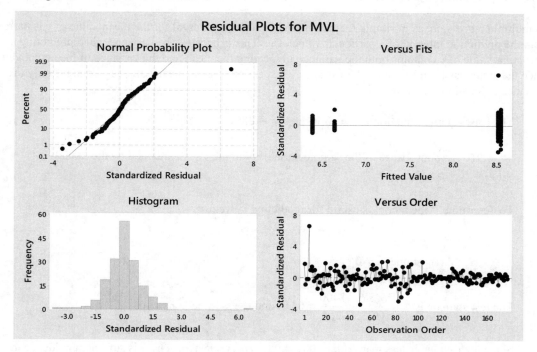

From the normal probability plot, the points do not fall on the straight line, indicating the residuals are not normal. The histogram of the standardized residuals is fairly mound-shaped except for the outlier to the right, again indicating that the data are not normal. The plot of the standardized residuals versus the fitted values indicates the variance is not constant. As the fitted value increases, the spread of the residuals increases. The assumptions for the model do not appear to be met.

12.133   Using MINITAB, the residual plots are:

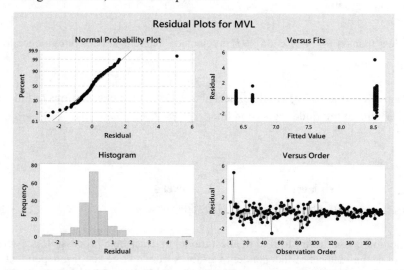

From the plot of the standardized residuals versus the fitted values, there is a slight increase in the spread of the residuals as the fitted values increase. There is some evidence of non-constant variance. All of the standardized residuals are less than 3 in absolute value, indicating there are no outliers. Looking at the normal probability plot and the histogram of the residuals, there is no evidence that the error terms are not normal. The data were not collected sequentially, so the plot of the residuals versus time is meaningless.

To correct the non-constant variance, one might transform the dependent variable.

12.135   In multiple regression, as in simple regression, the confidence interval for the mean value of y is narrower than the prediction interval of a particular value of y. This is because the variance when predicting a particular value of y contains both the variance in locating the mean and the variance of the actual values once the mean has been located. The variance when estimating the mean value is y contains only the variance in locating the mean.

12.137   a.   The least squares equation is $\hat{y} = 90.1 - 1.836x_1 + .285x_2$.

b. $R^2 = .916$. About 91.6% of the sample variability in the y's is explained by the model $E(y) = \beta_0 + \beta_1 x_1 + \beta_2 x_2$.

c.   To determine if the model is useful for predicting y, we test:

$$H_0 : \beta_1 = \beta_2 = 0$$
$$H_a : \text{At least one } \beta_i \neq 0$$

The test statistic is $F = \dfrac{MSR}{MSE} = \dfrac{7400}{114} = 64.91$ and the p-value is $p = .001$.

Since the p-value is less than $\alpha (p = .001 < .05)$, H_0 is rejected. There is sufficient evidence to indicate the model is useful for predicting y at $\alpha = .05$.

d.
$$H_0 : \beta_1 = 0$$
$$H_a : \beta_1 \neq 0$$

The test statistic is $t = \dfrac{\hat{\beta}_1}{s_{\hat{\beta}_1}} = \dfrac{-1.836}{.367} = -5.01$ and the p-value is $p = .001$.

Since the p-value is less than $\alpha (p = .001 < .05)$, H_0 is rejected. There is sufficient evidence to indicate β_1 is not 0 at $\alpha = .05$.

e.   The standard deviation is $s = 10.68$. We would expect about 95% of the observations to fall within $2s = 2(10.68) = 21.36$ units of the fitted regression line.

12.139 $E(y) = \beta_0 + \beta_1 x_1 + \beta_2 x_2 + \beta_3 x_3$

where $x_1 = \begin{cases} 1 & \text{if level 2} \\ 0 & \text{otherwise} \end{cases}$ $x_2 = \begin{cases} 1 & \text{if level 3} \\ 0 & \text{otherwise} \end{cases}$ $x_3 = \begin{cases} 1 & \text{if level 4} \\ 0 & \text{otherwise} \end{cases}$

12.141   The stepwise regression method is used to try to find the best model to describe a process. It is a screening procedure that tries to select a small subset of independent variables from a large set of independent variables that will adequately predict the dependent variable. This method is useful in that it can eliminate some unimportant independent variables from consideration.

12.143 Even though $SSE = 0$, we cannot estimate σ^2 because there are no degrees of freedom corresponding to error. With three data points, there are only two degrees of freedom available. The degrees of freedom corresponding to the model is $k = 2$ and the degrees of freedom corresponding to error is $df = n - (k+1) = 3 - (2+1) = 0$. Without an estimate for σ^2, no inferences can be made.

12.145 a. A confidence interval for the difference of two population means, $(\mu_1 - \mu_2)$, could be used. Since both sample sizes are over 30, the large sample confidence interval is used (with independent samples).

    b. Let $x = \begin{cases} 1 \text{ if public college} \\ 0 \text{ otherwise} \end{cases}$ The model is $E(y) = \beta_0 + \beta_1 x_1$.

    c. β_1 is the difference between the two population means. A point estimate for β_1 is $\hat{\beta}_1$. A confidence interval for β_1 could be used to estimate the difference in the two population means.

12.147 a. The type of juice extractor is qualitative. The size of the orange is quantitative.

    b. The model is $E(y) = \beta_0 + \beta_1 x_1 + \beta_2 x_2$ where $x_1 =$ diameter of orange and $x_2 = \begin{cases} 1 \text{ if Brand B} \\ 0 \text{ if not} \end{cases}$

    c. To allow the lines to differ, the interaction term is added: $E(y) = \beta_0 + \beta_1 x_1 + \beta_2 x_2 + \beta_3 x_1 x_2$

    d. For part **b**:

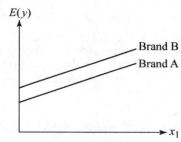

    For part **c**:

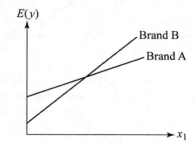

    e. To determine whether the model in part **c** provides more information for predicting yield than does the model in part **b**, we test:

$$H_0 : \beta_3 = 0$$
$$H_a : \beta_3 \neq 0$$

f.   The test statistic would be $F = \dfrac{\left(SSE_R - SSE_C\right)/(k-g)}{SSE_C \,/\left[n-(k+1)\right]}$.

To compute SSE_R: The model in part **b** is fit and SSE_R is the sum of squares for error.

To compute SSE_C: The model in part **c** is fit and SSE_C is the sum of squares for error.

$k - g = 3 - 2 = 1 =$ number of parameters in H_0

$n - (k+1) =$ degrees of freedom for error in the complete model

12.149   a.   A regression model incorporating interaction between x_1 and x_2 would be:

$$E(y) = \beta_o + \beta_1 x_1 + \beta_2 x_2 + \beta_3 x_1 x_2$$

b.   If the slope of the relationship between number of defects (y) and turntable speed (x_1) is steeper for lower values of cutting blade speed, then the interaction term must be negative. As the value of cutting speed increases, the steepness gets smaller, thus, the interaction term must get smaller. This implies $\beta_3 < 0$.

12.151   a. $\hat{\beta}_0 = -.0304$. Since $x_1 = 0$ and $x_2 = 0$ would not be in the observed range, this is simply the y-intercept.

$\hat{\beta}_1 = 2.006$. For each unit increase in the proportion of block with low-density residential areas, the mean population density is estimated to increase by 2.006, holding proportion of block with high-density residential areas constant. Since x_1 is a proportion, it is unlikely that it can increase by one unit. A better interpretation is: For each increase of .1 in the proportion of block with low-density residential areas, the mean population density is estimated to increase by .2006, holding proportion of block with high-density residential areas constant.

$\hat{\beta}_2 = 5.006$. For each unit increase in the proportion of block with high-density residential areas, the mean population density is estimated to increase by 5.006, holding proportion of block with low-density residential areas constant. Since x_2 is a proportion, it is unlikely that it can increase by one unit. A better interpretation is: For each increase of .1 in the proportion of block with high-density residential areas, the mean population density is estimated to increase by .5006, holding proportion of block with low-density residential areas constant.

b. $R^2 = .686$. 68.6% of the total sample variation of the population densities is explained by the linear relationship between population density and the independent variables proportion of block with low-density residential areas and the proportion of block with high-density residential areas.

c.   To determine if the overall model is adequate, we test:

$H_0 : \beta_1 = \beta_2 = 0$

$H_a :$ At least one $\beta_i \neq 0$

d.   The test statistic is $F = \dfrac{R^2 / k}{\left(1 - R^2\right)/\left[n-(k+1)\right]} = \dfrac{.686/2}{(1-.686)/\left[125-(2+1)\right]} = 133.27$.

e. The rejection region requires $\alpha = .01$ in the upper tail of the F-distribution with $v_1 = k = 2$ and $v_2 = n - (k+1) = 125 - (2+1) = 122$. From Table VIII, Appendix D, $F_{.01} \approx 4.79$. The rejection region is $F > 4.79$.

Since the observed value of the test statistic falls in the rejection region $(F = 133.27 > 4.79)$, H_0 is rejected. There is sufficient evidence to indicate the model is adequate at $\alpha = .01$.

12.153 a. To determine if the model is adequate, we test:

$$H_0 : \beta_1 = \beta_2 = \cdots = \beta_{12} = 0$$
$$H_a : \text{At least one } \beta_i \neq 0$$

The test statistic is $F = 26.9$.

Using MINITAB with $v_1 = k = 12$ and $v_2 = n - (k+1) = 148 - (12+1) = 135$,

Cumulative Distribution Function
```
F distribution with 12 DF in numerator and 135 DF in denominator

    x   P( X <= x )
26.9              1
```

The p-value associated with $F = 26.9$ is $p = 1 - 1 = 0$. Since the p-value is so small, H_0 is rejected. There is sufficient evidence to indicate the model is adequate for any reasonable value of α.

$R^2 = .705$. 70.5% of the total variation of the natural logarithm of card prices is explained by the model with the 12 variables in the model.

$R_a^2 = .681$. 68.1% of the total variation of the natural logarithm of card prices is explained by the model with the 12 variables in the model, adjusting for the sample size and the number of variables in the model.

Since these R^2 values are fairly large, it indicates that the model is pretty good.

b. To determine if race contributes to the price, we test:

$$H_0 : \beta_1 = 0$$
$$H_a : \beta_1 \neq 0$$

The test statistic is $t = -1.014$ and the p-value is $p = .312$. Since the p-value is so large, H_0 is not rejected. There is insufficient evidence to indicate race has an impact on the value of professional football player's rookie cards for any reasonable value of α, holding the other variables constant.

c. To determine if card vintage contributes to the price, we test:

$$H_0 : \beta_3 = 0$$
$$H_a : \beta_3 \neq 0$$

The test statistic is $t = -10.92$ and the p-value is $p = .000$. Since the p-value is so small, H_0 is rejected. There is sufficient evidence to indicate card vintage has an impact on the value of professional football player's rookie cards for any reasonable value of α, holding the other variables constant.

d. The first order model is:

$$E(y) = \beta_0 + \beta_1 x_3 + \beta_2 x_5 + \beta_3 x_6 + \beta_4 x_7 + \beta_5 x_8 + \beta_6 x_9 + \beta_7 x_{10} + \beta_8 x_{11} + \beta_9 x_{12}$$
$$+ \beta_{10} x_5 x_3 + \beta_{11} x_6 x_3 + \beta_{12} x_7 x_3 + \beta_{13} x_8 x_3 + \beta_{14} x_9 x_3 + \beta_{15} x_{10} x_3 + \beta_{16} x_{11} x_3 + \beta_{17} x_{12} x_3$$

12.155 a. In Step 1, all one-variable models are fit to the data. These models are of the form: $E(y) = \beta_0 + \beta_1 x_i$

Since there are 7 independent variables, 7 models are fit. (Note: There are actually only 6 independent variables. One of the qualitative variables has three levels and thus two dummy variables. Some statistical packages will allow one to bunch these two variables together so that they are either both in or both out. In this answer, we are assuming that each x_i stands by itself.)

b. In Step 2, all two-variable models are fit to the data, where the variable selected in Step 1, say x_1, is one of the variables. These models are of the form: $E(y) = \beta_0 + \beta_1 x_1 + \beta_2 x_i$

Since there are 6 independent variables remaining, 6 models are fit.

c. In Step 3, all three-variable models are fit to the data, where the variables selected in Step 2, say x_1 and x_2, are two of the variables. These models are of the form: $E(y) = \beta_0 + \beta_1 x_1 + \beta_2 x_2 + \beta_3 x_i$

Since there are 5 independent variables remaining, 5 models are fit.

d. The procedure stops adding independent variables when none of the remaining variables, when added to the model, have a p-value less than some predetermined value. This predetermined value is usually $\alpha = .05$.

e. Two major drawbacks to using the final stepwise model as the "best" model are:

(1) An extremely large number of single β parameter t-tests have been conducted. Thus, the probability is very high that one or more errors have been made in including or excluding variables.

(2) Often the variables selected to be included in a stepwise regression do not include the high-order terms. Consequently, we may have initially omitted several important terms from the model.

12.157 a. $\hat{\beta}_4 = .296$. The difference in the mean value of DTVA between when the operating earnings are negative and lower than last year and when the operating earnings are not negative and lower than last year is estimated to be .296, holding all other variables constant.

b. To determine if the mean DTVA for firms with negative earnings and earnings lower than last year exceed the mean DTVA of other firms, we test:

$$H_0 : \beta_4 = 0$$
$$H_a : \beta_4 > 0$$

The p-value for this test is $p = .001/2 = .0005$. Since the p-value is so small, we would reject H_0 for $\alpha = .05$. There is sufficient evidence to indicate the mean DTVA for firms with negative earnings and earnings lower than last year exceed the mean DTVA of other firms at $\alpha = .05$.

c. $R_a^2 = .280$.   28% of the variability in the DTVA scores is explained by the model containing the 5 independent variables, adjusted for the number of variables in the model and the sample size.

12.159   a.   Not necessarily. If Nickel was highly correlated with several other variables, then it might be better to keep Nickel and drop some of the other highly correlated variables.

b.   Using stepwise regression is a good start for selecting the best set of predictor variables. However, one should use caution when looking at the model selected using stepwise regression. Sometimes important variables are not selected to be entered into the model. Also, many *t*-tests have been run, thus inflating the Type I and Type II error rates. One must also consider using higher order terms in the model and interaction terms.

c.   No, further exploration should be used. One should consider using higher order terms for the variables (i.e. squared terms) and also interaction terms

12.161   a.   Using MINITAB, the scattergram is:

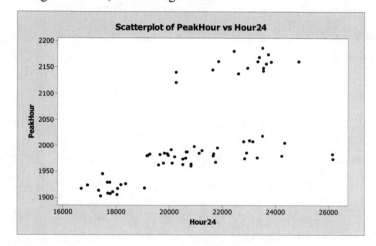

b.   Let $x_2 = \begin{cases} 1 \text{ if I-35W} \\ 0 \text{ if not} \end{cases}$

The complete second-order model would be $E(y) = \beta_0 + \beta_1 x_1 + \beta_2 x_1^2 + \beta_3 x_2 + \beta_4 x_1 x_2 + \beta_5 x_1^2 x_2$

c.   Using MINITAB, the printout is:

Regression Analysis: PeakHour versus x1, x1-sq, x2, x1x2, x1-sqx2
```
The regression equation is
PeakHour = 776 + 0.104 x1 - 0.000002 x1-sq + 232 x2 - 0.0091 x1x2
           + 0.000000 x1-sqx2

Predictor           Coef      SE Coef        T       P
Constant           776.4        144.5     5.37   0.000
x1               0.10418      0.01388     7.50   0.000
x1-sq        -0.00000223   0.00000033    -6.73   0.000
x2                   232         1094     0.21   0.833
x1x2            -0.00914      0.09829    -0.09   0.926
x1-sqx2       0.00000027   0.00000220     0.12   0.903

S = 15.5829    R-Sq = 97.2%    R-Sq(adj) = 97.0%
```

```
Analysis of Variance

Source              DF       SS       MS        F       P
Regression           5   555741   111148   457.73   0.000
Residual Error      66    16027      243
Total               71   571767

Source    DF   Seq SS
x1         1   254676
x1-sq      1    21495
x2         1   279383
x1x2       1      183
x1-sqx2    1        4
```

The fitted model is $\hat{y} = 776 + .104x_1 - .000002x_1^2 + 232x_2 - .0091x_1x_2 + .00000027x_1^2x_2$.

To determine if the curvilinear relationship is different at the two locations, we test:

$$H_0 : \beta_3 = \beta_4 = \beta_5 = 0$$
$$H_a : \text{At least one } \beta_i \neq 0$$

In order to test this hypothesis, we must fit the reduced model $E(y) = \beta_0 + \beta_1 x_1 + \beta_2 x_1^2$.

Using MINITAB, the printout from fitting the reduced model is:

Regression Analysis: PeakHour versus x1, x1-sq
```
The regression equation is
PeakHour = 197 + 0.149 x1 - 0.000003 x1-sq

Predictor           Coef      SE Coef       T       P
Constant           197.5        578.9    0.34   0.734
x1               0.14921      0.05551    2.69   0.009
x1-sq        -0.00000295   0.00000132   -2.24   0.028

S = 65.4523   R-Sq = 48.3%    R-Sq(adj) = 46.8%

Analysis of Variance

Source              DF       SS       MS        F       P
Regression           2   276171   138085   32.23   0.000
Residual Error      69   295597     4284
Total               71   571767

Source   DF   Seq SS
x1        1   254676
x1-sq     1    21495
```

The fitted regression line is $\hat{y} = 197 + .149x_1 - .000003x_1^2$.

To determine if the curvilinear relationship is different at the two locations, we test:

$$H_0 : \beta_3 = \beta_4 = \beta_5 = 0$$
$$H_a : \text{At least one } \beta_i \neq 0$$

The test statistic is $F = \dfrac{(SSE_R - SSE_C)/(k-g)}{SSE_C/[n-(k+1)]} = \dfrac{(295,597-16,027)/(5-2)}{16,027/[72-(5+1)]} = 383.76$.

Since no α was given we will use $\alpha = .05$. The rejection region requires $\alpha = .05$ in the upper tail of the F-distribution with $v_1 = k - g = 5 - 2 = 3$ and $v_2 = n - (k+1) = 72 - (5+1) = 66$. From Table VI, Appendix D, $F_{.05} \approx 2.76$. The rejection region is $F > 2.76$.

Since the observed value of the test statistic falls in the rejection region $(F = 383.76 > 2.76)$, H_0 is rejected. There is sufficient evidence to indicate the curvilinear relationship is different at the two locations at $\alpha = .05$.

d. Using MINITAB, the residual plots are:

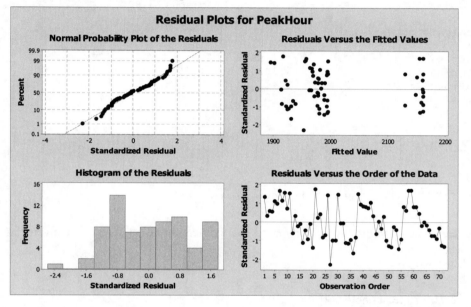

From the plot of the standardized residuals versus the fitted value, we notice that there is only one point more than 2 standard deviations from the mean and no points that are more than 3 standard deviations from the mean. Thus, there do not appear to be any outliers. There is no curve to the residuals, so we have the appropriate model. In addition, there is no cone shape to the plot, so it appears that there is no problem with constant variance.

The normal probability plot looks like a fairly straight line, so it appears that the assumption of normality is valid. Also, the histogram of the residuals is somewhat mound shaped.

12.163 a. The model is $E(y) = \beta_0 + \beta_1 x_1 + \beta_2 x_2 + \beta_3 x_3$ where y = market share

$$x_1 = \begin{cases} 1 \text{ if M} \\ 0 \text{ otherwise} \end{cases} \qquad x_2 = \begin{cases} 1 \text{ if H} \\ 0 \text{ otherwise} \end{cases} \qquad x_3 = \begin{cases} 1 \text{ if VH} \\ 0 \text{ otherwise} \end{cases}$$

We assume that the error terms (ε_i) or y's are normally distributed at each exposure level, with a common variance. Also, we assume the ε_i's have a mean of 0 and are independent.

b. No interaction terms were included because we have only one independent variable, exposure level. Even though we have 3 x_i's in the model, they are dummy variables and correspond to different levels of the one independent variable.

c. Using MINITAB, the output is:

Regression Analysis: y versus x1, x2, x3
```
The regression equation is
y = 10.2 + 0.683 x1 + 2.02 x2 + 0.500 x3

Predictor         Coef     SE Coef          T         P
Constant       10.2333      0.1084      94.41     0.000
x1              0.6833      0.1533       4.46     0.000
x2              2.0167      0.1533      13.16     0.000
x3              0.5000      0.1533       3.26     0.004
S = 0.265518      R-Sq = 90.4%      R-Sq(adj) = 89.0%

Analysis of Variance

Source             DF          SS          MS         F         P
Regression          3     13.3433      4.4478     63.09     0.000
Residual Error     20      1.4100      0.0705
Total              23     14.7533

Source        DF     Seq SS
x1             1     0.1089
x2             1    12.4844
x3             1     0.7500
```

The fitted model is $\hat{y} = 10.2 + .683x_1 + 2.02x_2 + .5x_3$.

d. To determine if the firm's expected market share differs for different levels of advertising exposure, we test:

$$H_0 : \beta_1 = \beta_2 = \beta_3 = 0$$
$$H_a : \text{At least one } \beta_i \neq 0$$

The test statistic is $F = 63.09$ and the p-value is $p = .000$. Since the p-value is less than $\alpha(p = .000 < .05)$, H_0 is rejected. There is sufficient evidence to indicate the firm's expected market share differs for different levels of advertising exposure at $\alpha = .05$.

12.165 a. $\hat{\beta}_0 = -105$ has no meaning because $x_3 = 0$ is not in the observable range. $\hat{\beta}_0$ is simply the y-intercept.

$\hat{\beta}_1 = 25$. The estimated difference in mean attendance between weekends and weekdays is 25, holding temperature and weather constant.

$\hat{\beta}_2 = 100$. The estimated difference in mean attendance between sunny and overcast days is 100, holding type of day (weekend or weekday) and temperature constant.

$\hat{\beta}_3 = 10$. The estimated change in mean attendance for each additional degree of temperature is 10, holding type of day (weekend or weekday) and weather (sunny or overcast) held constant.

b.   To determine if the model is useful for predicting daily attendance, we test:

$$H_0 : \beta_1 = \beta_2 = \beta_3 = 0$$
$$H_a : \text{At least one } \beta_i \neq 0$$

The test statistic is $F = \dfrac{R^2 / k}{\left(1 - R^2\right) / \left[n - \left(k + 1\right)\right]} = \dfrac{.65 / 3}{\left(1 - .65\right) / \left[30 - \left(3 + 1\right)\right]} = 16.10$.

The rejection region requires $\alpha = .05$ in the upper tail of the F-distribution with $v_1 = k = 3$ and $v_2 = n - \left(k + 1\right) = 30 - \left(3 + 1\right) = 26$. From Table VI, Appendix D, $F_{.05} = 2.98$. The rejection region is $F > 2.98$.

Since the observed value of the test statistic falls in the rejection region $\left(F = 16.10 > 2.98\right)$, H_0 is rejected. There is sufficient evidence to indicate the model is useful for predicting daily attendance at $\alpha = .05$.

c.   To determine if mean attendance increases on weekends, we test:

$$H_0 : \beta_1 = 0$$
$$H_a : \beta_1 > 0$$

The test statistic is $t = \dfrac{\hat{\beta}_1}{s_{\hat{\beta}_1}} = \dfrac{25 - 0}{10} = 2.5$.

The rejection region requires $\alpha = .10$ in the upper tail of the t-distribution with $df = n - \left(k + 1\right) = 30 - \left(3 + 1\right) = 26$. From Table III, Appendix D, $t_{.10} = 1.315$. The rejection region is $t > 1.315$.

Since the observed value of the test statistic falls in the rejection region $\left(t = 2.5 > 1.315\right)$, H_0 is rejected. There is sufficient evidence to indicate the mean attendance increases on weekends at $\alpha = .10$.

d.   Sunny $\Rightarrow x_2 = 1$, Weekday $\Rightarrow x_1 = 0$, Temperature $95° \Rightarrow x_3 = 95°$
$$\hat{y} = -105 + 25\left(0\right) + 100\left(1\right) + 10\left(95\right) = 945$$

e.   We are 90% confident that the actual attendance for sunny weekdays with a temperature of 95° is between 645 and 1245.

12.167   a. $E\left(y\right) = \beta_0 + \beta_1 x_1 + \beta_2 x_6 + \beta_3 x_7$

where $x_6 = \begin{cases} 1 \text{ if condition is good} \\ 0 \text{ otherwise} \end{cases}$ $x_7 = \begin{cases} 1 \text{ if condition is fair} \\ 0 \text{ otherwise} \end{cases}$

b.   The model specified in part **a** seems appropriate. The points for E, F, and G cluster around three parallel lines.

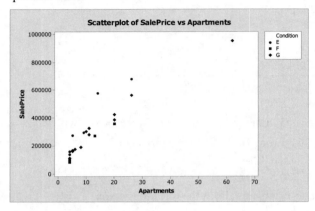

c.   Using MINITAB, the output is

Regression Analysis: SalePrice versus X1, X6, X7
```
The regression equation is
SalePrice = 188875 + 15617 X1 - 103046 X6 - 152487 X7

Predictor      Coef  SE Coef       T      P
Constant     188875    28588    6.61  0.000
X1            15617     1066   14.66  0.000
X6          -103046    31784   -3.24  0.004
X7          -152487    39157   -3.89  0.001

S = 64623.6   R-Sq = 91.8%   R-Sq(adj) = 90.7%

Analysis of Variance

Source           DF           SS          MS      F      P
Regression        3  9.86170E+11  3.28723E+11  78.71  0.000
Residual Error   21  87700442851   4176211564
Total            24  1.07387E+12

Source  DF      Seq SS
X1       1  9.15776E+11
X6       1    7061463149
X7       1   63332198206
```

The fitted model is $\hat{y} = 188,875 + 15,617x_1 - 103,046x_6 - 152,487x_7$

For excellent condition, $\hat{y} = 188,875 + 15,617x_1$
For good condition, $\hat{y} = 85,829 + 15,617x_1$
For fair condition, $\hat{y} = 36,388 + 15,617x_1$

d. Using MINITAB, the plot is:

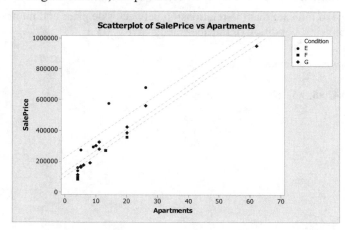

e. We must first fit a reduced model with just x_1, number of apartments. Using MINITAB, the output is:

Regression Analysis: SalePrice versus X1
```
The regression equation is
SalePrice = 101786 + 15525 X1


Predictor      Coef  SE Coef       T       P
Constant     101786    23291    4.37   0.000
X1            15525     1345   11.54   0.000


S = 82907.5    R-Sq = 85.3%    R-Sq(adj) = 84.6%


Analysis of Variance

Source          DF           SS           MS        F       P
Regression       1  9.15776E+11  9.15776E+11   133.23   0.000
Residual Error  23  1.58094E+11   6873656705
Total           24  1.07387E+12
```

The fitted model is $\hat{y} = 101,786 + 15,525x_1$.

To determine if the relationship between sale price and number of units differs depending on the physical condition of the apartments, we test:

$H_0 : \beta_2 = \beta_3 = 0$
$H_a :$ At least one $\beta_i \neq 0$

The test statistic is $F = \dfrac{\left(SSE_R - SSE_C\right)/\left(k-g\right)}{SSE_C /\left[n-\left(k+1\right)\right]} = \dfrac{\left(1.58094 \times 10^{11} - 87,700,442,851\right)/\left(3-1\right)}{87,700,442,851/\left[25-\left(3+1\right)\right]} = 8.43$

The rejection region requires $\alpha = .05$ in the upper tail of the F-distribution with $\nu_1 = k - g = 3 - 1 = 2$ and $\nu_2 = n - \left(k+1\right) = 25 - \left(3+1\right) = 21$. From Table VI, Appendix D, $F_{.05} = 3.47$. The rejection region is $F > 3.47$.

Since the observed value of the test statistic falls in the rejection region $(F = 8.43 > 3.47)$, H_0 is rejected. There is evidence to indicate that the relationship between sale price and number of units differs depending on the physical condition of the apartments at $\alpha = .05$.

f. Using MINITAB, the pairwise correlations are:

Correlations: x1, x2, x3, x4, x5, x6, x7

	x1	x2	x3	x4	x5	x6
x2	-0.014					
	0.946					
x3	0.800	-0.191				
	0.000	0.361				
x4	0.224	-0.363	0.167			
	0.281	0.075	0.425			
x5	0.878	0.027	0.673	0.089		
	0.000	0.898	0.000	0.671		
x6	0.175	-0.447	0.273	0.112	0.020	
	0.403	0.025	0.187	0.594	0.923	
x7	-0.128	0.392	-0.123	0.050	-0.238	-0.564
	0.541	0.053	0.557	0.814	0.252	0.003

When highly correlated independent variables are present in a regression model, the results are confusing. The researchers may only want to include one of the variables. This may be the case for the variables: x_1 and x_3, x_1 and x_5, x_3 and x_5

g. Using MINITAB, the residual plots are:

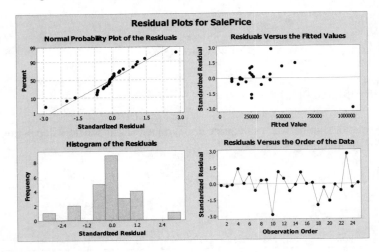

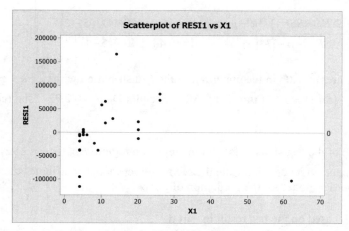

From the plots of the residuals versus the fitted values, there do not appear to be any outliers - no standardized residuals are larger than 3 in magnitude. In addition, there is no trend that would indicate non-constant variance (no funnel shape). There is a possible upside-down U shape that would indicate that the relationship between price and number of apartments might be curvilinear. In the histogram of the residuals, the plot is fairly mound-shaped, which would indicate the residuals are approximately normally distributed. Also, the normal probability plot looks to be a fairly straight line, indicating the residuals are approximately normal. In the plot of the residuals versus x_1, there is a possible upside-down U shape that would indicate that the variable number of apartments should be squared. Otherwise, all of the assumptions appear to be met.

12.169   a.   To determine whether the complete model contributes information for the prediction of y, we test:

$$H_0 : \beta_1 = \beta_2 = \beta_3 = \beta_4 = \beta_5 = 0$$
$$H_a : \text{At least one } \beta_i \neq 0$$

b. $MSR = \dfrac{SS(Model)}{k} = \dfrac{4,911.5}{5} = 982.3$ $MSE = \dfrac{SSE}{n-(k+1)} = \dfrac{1,830.44}{40-(5+1)} = 53.84$

The test statistic is $F = \dfrac{MSR}{MSE} = \dfrac{982.31}{53.84} = 18.24$.

The rejection region requires $\alpha = .05$ in the upper tail of the F-distribution with $v_1 = k = 5$ and $v_2 = n-(k+1) = 40-(5+1) = 34$. From Table VI, Appendix D, $F_{.05} \approx 2.53$. The rejection region is $F > 2.53$.

Since the observed value of the test statistic falls in the rejection region $(F = 18.24 > 2.53)$, H_0 is rejected. There is sufficient evidence to indicate that the complete model contributes information for the prediction of y at $\alpha = .05$.

c.   To determine whether a second-order model contributes more information than a first-order model for the prediction of y, we test:

$$H_0 : \beta_3 = \beta_4 = \beta_5 = 0$$
$$H_a : \text{At least one } \beta_i \neq 0$$

d.   The test statistic is $F = \dfrac{\left(SSE_R - SSE_C\right)/(k-g)}{SSE_C/\left[n-(k+1)\right]} = \dfrac{(3197.16 - 1830.44)/(5-2)}{1830.44/\left[40-(5+1)\right]} = 8.46$.

The rejection region requires $\alpha = .05$ in the upper tail of the F-distribution with $v_1 = k - g = 5 - 2 = 3$ and $v_2 = n - (k+1) = 40 - (5+1) = 34$. From Table VI, Appendix D, $F_{.05} \approx 2.92$. The rejection region is $F > 2.92$.

Since the observed value of the test statistic falls in the rejection region $\left(F = 8.46 > 2.92\right)$, H_0 is rejected. There is sufficient evidence to indicate the second-order model contributes more information than a first-order model for the prediction of y at $\alpha = .05$.

e.   The second-order model, based on the test result in part **d**.

12.171 a. $R^2 = .78$. 78% of the total sample variation in the price of a direct burial about its mean is explained by the model that contains type of state, type of casket, and the interaction of the two.

b.   To determine if the overall model is adequate, we test:

$$H_0 : \beta_1 = \beta_2 = \beta_3 = 0$$
$$H_a : \text{At least } 1 \, \beta_i \neq 0$$

The test statistic is $F = \dfrac{R^2/k}{\left(1-R^2\right)/\left[n-(k+1)\right]} = \dfrac{.78/3}{(1-.78)/\left[1,437-(3+1)\right]} = 1693.55$.

The rejection region requires $\alpha = .05$ in the upper tail of the F-distribution with $v_1 = k = 3$ and $v_2 = n - (k+1) = 1,437 - (3+1) = 1,433$. From Table VI, Appendix D, $F_{.05} \approx 2.60$. The rejection region is $F > 2.60$.

Since the observed value of the test statistic falls in the rejection region $\left(F = 8.96 > 2.60\right)$, H_0 is rejected. There is sufficient evidence to indicate the model is adequate for the prediction of sales price at $\alpha = .05$.

c.   For $x_1 = 1$ and $x_2 = 1$ (wooden casket in restrictive state),

$$\hat{y} = 1,432 + 793(1) - 252(1) + 261(1)(1) = 2,234 .$$

d.   For $x_1 = 1$ and $x_2 = 0$ (no casket in restrictive state), $\hat{y} = 1,432 + 793(1) - 252(0) + 261(1)(0) = 2,225$.

The difference would be $\$2,234 - \$2,225 = \$9$.

e.   For $x_1 = 0$ and $x_2 = 1$ (wooden casket in non-restrictive state),

$$\hat{y} = 1,432 + 793(0) - 252(1) + 261(0)(1) = 1,180 .$$

For $x_1 = 0$ and $x_2 = 0$ (no casket in non-restrictive state),

$$\hat{y} = 1,432 + 793(0) - 252(0) + 261(0)(0) = 1,432 .$$

The difference would be $\$1,180 - \$1,432 = -\$252$.

f. To determine if the difference between the mean price of a direct burial with a basic wooden casket and the mean of a burial with no casket depends on whether the funeral home is in a restrictive state, we test:

$$H_0 : \beta_3 = 0$$
$$H_a : \beta_3 \neq 0$$

The test statistic is $t = \dfrac{\hat{\beta}_3 - 0}{s_{\hat{\beta}_3}} = \dfrac{261 - 0}{109} = 2.39$.

The rejection region requires $\alpha / 2 = .05 / 2 = .025$ in each tail of the t-distribution with $df = n - (k+1) = 1,437 - (3+1) = 1,433$. From Table III, Appendix D, $t_{.025} = 1.96$. The rejection region is $t < -1.96$ or $t > 1.96$.

Since the observed value of the test statistic falls in the rejection region $(t = 2.39 > 1.96)$, H_0 is rejected. There is sufficient evidence to indicate the difference between the mean price of a direct burial with a basic wooden casket and the mean of a burial with no casket depends on whether the funeral home is in a restrictive state at $\alpha = .05$.

12.173 First, we will fit the simple linear regression model $E(y) = \beta_0 + \beta_1 x_1 + \beta_2 x_2$. Using MINITAB, the results are:

Regression Analysis: y versus x1, x2
```
The regression equation is
y = - 1.57 + 0.0257 x1 + 0.0336 x2

Predictor        Coef      SE Coef         T          P
Constant      -1.5705       0.4937     -3.18      0.003
x1           0.025732     0.004024      6.40      0.000
x2           0.033615     0.004928      6.82      0.000

S = 0.4023      R-Sq = 68.1%     R-Sq(adj) = 66.4%

Analysis of Variance

Source            DF           SS         MS         F        P
Regression         2      12.7859     6.3930     39.51    0.000
Residual Error    37       5.9876     0.1618
Total             39      18.7735

Source       DF      Seq SS
x1            1      5.2549
x2            1      7.5311
```

To determine if the model is useful in the prediction of y (GPA), we test:

$$H_0 : \beta_1 = \beta_2 = 0$$
$$H_a : \text{At least one } \beta_i \neq 0$$

The test statistic is $F = 39.51$ and the p-value is $p = .000$. Since the p-value is so small, H_0 is rejected for any reasonable value of α. There is sufficient evidence to indicate at least one of the variables Verbal score or Mathematics score is useful in predicting GPA.

To determine if Verbal score is useful in predicting GPA, controlling for Mathematics score, we test:

$$H_0 : \beta_1 = 0$$
$$H_a : \beta_1 \neq 0$$

The test statistic is $t = 6.40$ and the p-value is $p = .000$. Since the p-value is so small, H_0 is rejected for any reasonable value of α. There is sufficient evidence to indicate Verbal score is useful in predicting GPA, controlling for Mathematics score.

To determine if Mathematics score is useful in predicting GPA, controlling for Verbal score, we test:

$$H_0 : \beta_2 = 0$$
$$H_a : \beta_2 \neq 0$$

The test statistic is $t = 6.82$ and the p-value is $p = .000$. Since the p-value is so small, H_0 is rejected for any reasonable value of α. There is sufficient evidence to indicate Mathematics score is useful in predicting GPA, controlling for Verbal score.

Thus, both terms in the model are significant. The R-squared value is $R^2 = .681$.
This indicates that 68.1% of the sample variance of the GPA's is explained by the model.
Now, we need to check the residuals. From MINITAB, the plots are:

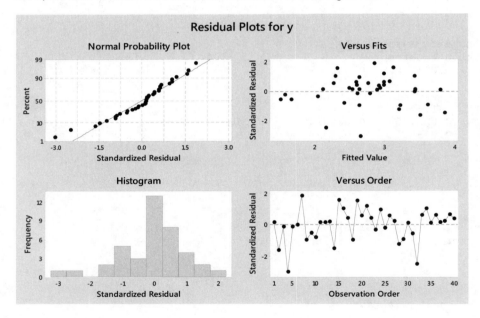

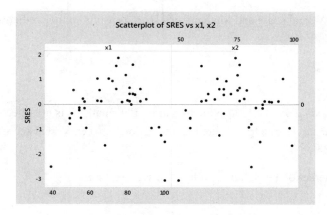

From the normal probability plot, it appears that the assumption of normality is valid. The points are very close to a straight line except for the first 2 points. The histogram of the residuals implies that the residuals are slightly skewed to the left. I would still consider the assumption to be valid. The plot of the residuals versus the fitted values indicates a random spread of the residuals between the two bands. This indicates that the assumption of equal variances is probably valid. The plot of the residuals versus x_1 indicates that the relationship between GPA and Verbal score may not be linear, but quadratic because the points form a somewhat upside down U shape. The plot of the residuals versus x_2 indicates that the relationship between GPA and Mathematics score may or may not be quadratic.

Since the plots indicate a possible 2nd order model and the R^2 value is not real large, we will fit a complete 2nd order model:

$$E(y) = \beta_0 + \beta_1 x_1 + \beta_2 x_2 + \beta_3 x_1^2 + \beta_2 x_2^2 + \beta_5 x_1 x_2$$

Using MINITAB, the results are:

Regression Analysis: y versus x1, x2, x1sq, x2sq, x1x2
```
      The regression equation is
y = - 9.92 + 0.167 x1 + 0.138 x2 - 0.00111 x1sq - 0.000843 x2sq + 0.000241 x1x2

Predictor          Coef     SE Coef       T       P
Constant         -9.917       1.354   -7.32   0.000
x1              0.16681     0.02124    7.85   0.000
x2              0.13760     0.02673    5.15   0.000
x1sq         -0.0011082   0.0001173   -9.45   0.000
x2sq         -0.0008433   0.0001594   -5.29   0.000
x1x2          0.0002411   0.0001440    1.67   0.103


S = 0.187142    R-Sq = 93.7%    R-Sq(adj) = 92.7%


Analysis of Variance

Source           DF        SS       MS        F       P
Regression        5   17.5827   3.5165   100.41   0.000
Residual Error   34    1.1908   0.0350
Total            39   18.7735


Source    DF   Seq SS
x1         1   5.2549
x2         1   7.5311
x1sq       1   3.6434
x2sq       1   1.0552
x1x2       1   0.0982
```

To determine if the interaction between Verbal score and Mathematics score is useful in the prediction of y (GPA), we test:

$$H_0 : \beta_5 = 0$$
$$H_a : \beta_5 \neq 0$$

The test statistic is $t = 1.67$ nd the p-value is $p = .103$. Since the p-value is not small, H_0 is not rejected for any value of $\alpha < .10$. There is insufficient evidence to indicate the interaction between Verbal score and Mathematics score is useful in predicting GPA.

Now, we will fit a model without the interaction term, but including the squared terms:

$$E(y) = \beta_0 + \beta_1 x_1 + \beta_2 x_2 + \beta_3 x_1^2 + \beta_2 x_2^2$$

Using MINITAB, the results are:

Regression Analysis: y versus x1, x2, x1sq, x2sq
```
The regression equation is
y = - 11.5 + 0.189 x1 + 0.159 x2 - 0.00114 x1sq - 0.000871 x2sq

Predictor         Coef     SE Coef        T       P
Constant       -11.458       1.019   -11.24   0.000
x1             0.18887     0.01709    11.05   0.000
x2             0.15874     0.02417     6.57   0.000
x1sq        -0.0011412   0.0001186    -9.62   0.000
x2sq        -0.0008705   0.0001626    -5.35   0.000

S = 0.191905    R-Sq = 93.1%    R-Sq(adj) = 92.3%

Analysis of Variance

Source              DF        SS       MS       F       P
Regression           4   17.4845   4.3711  118.69   0.000
Residual Error      35    1.2890   0.0368
Total               39   18.7735

Source   DF   Seq SS
x1        1   5.2549
x2        1   7.5311
x1sq      1   3.6434
x2sq      1   1.0552
```

To determine if the relationship between Verbal score and GPA is quadratic, controlling for Mathematics score, we test:

$$H_0 : \beta_3 = 0$$
$$H_a : \beta_3 \neq 0$$

The test statistic is $t = -9.62$ nd the p-value is $p = .000$. Since the p-value is so small, H_0 is rejected for any reasonable value of α. There is sufficient evidence to indicate the relationship between Verbal score and GPA is quadratic, controlling for Mathematics score.

To determine if the relationship between Verbal score and GPA is quadratic, controlling for Mathematics score, we test:

$$H_0 : \beta_4 = 0$$
$$H_a : \beta_4 \neq 0$$

The test statistic is $t = -5.35$ nd the p-value is $p = .000$. Since the p-value is so small, H_0 is rejected for any reasonable value of α. There is sufficient evidence to indicate the relationship between Mathematics score and GPA is quadratic, controlling for Verbal score.

Thus, both quadratic terms in the model are significant. The R-squared value is $R^2 = .913$. This indicates that 91.3% of the sample variance of the GPA's is explained by the model.

Now, we need to check the residuals. From MINITAB, the plots are:

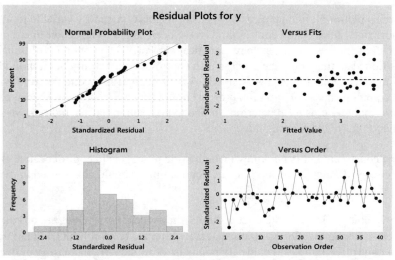

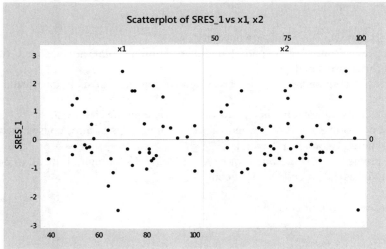

From the normal probability plot, it appears that the assumption of normality is valid. The points are very close to a straight line. The histogram of the residuals also implies that the residuals are approximately normal. The plot of the residuals versus the fitted values indicates a random spread of the residuals between the two bands. This indicates that the assumption of equal variances is probably valid. The plot of the residuals versus x_1 indicates a random spread of the residuals between the two bands. This indicates that the order of x_1 (2nd) is appropriate. The plot of the residuals versus x_2 indicates a random spread of the residuals between the two bands. This indicates that the order of x_2 (2nd) is appropriate.

The model appears to be pretty good. All terms in the model are significant, the residual analysis indicates the assumptions are met and the R-squared value is fairly close to 1. The fitted model is
$$\hat{y} = -11.5 + .189x_1 + .159x_2 - .0114x_1^2 - .00087x_2^2$$

Chapter 13
Methods for Quality Improvement: Statistical Process Control

13.1   A control chart is a time series plot of individual measurements or means of a quality variable to which a centerline and two other horizontal lines called control limits have been added. The center line represents the mean of the process when the process is in a state of statistical control. The upper control limit and the lower control limit are positioned so that when the process is in control the probability of an individual measurement or mean falling outside the limits is very small. A control chart is used to determine if a process is in control (only common causes of variation present) or not (both common and special causes of variation present). This information helps us to determine when to take action to find and remove special causes of variation and when to leave the process alone.

13.3   When a control chart is first constructed, it is not known whether the process is in control or not. If the process is found not to be in control, then the centerline and control limits should not be used to monitor the process in the future.

13.5   Even if all the points of an $\bar{x}$-chart fall within the control limits, the process may be out of control. Nonrandom patterns may exist among the plotted points that are within the control limits, but are very unlikely if the process is in control. Examples include six points in a row steadily increasing or decreasing and 14 points in a row alternating up and down.

13.7   Rule 1:   One point beyond Zone A: No points are beyond Zone A.
         Rule 2:   Nine points in a row in Zone C or beyond: No sequence of nine points are in Zone C (on one side of the centerline) or beyond.
         Rule 3:   Six points in a row steadily increasing or decreasing: No sequence of six points steadily increase or decrease.
         Rule 4:   Fourteen points in a row alternating up and down: This pattern does not exist.
         Rule 5:   Two out of three points in Zone A or beyond: There are no groups of three consecutive points that have two or more in Zone A or beyond.
         Rule 6:   Four out of five points in a row in Zone B or beyond: Points 18 through 21 are all in Zone B or beyond. This indicates the process is out of control.

         Thus, rule 6 indicates this process is out of control.

13.9   Using Table IX, Appendix D:

         a.   With $n = 3$, $A_2 = 1.023$

         b.   With $n = 10$, $A_2 = 0.308$

         c.   With $n = 22$, $A_2 = 0.167$

13.11   a.   For each sample, we compute $\bar{x}_1 = \dfrac{\sum x}{n}$ and R = range = largest measurement - smallest measurement. The results are listed in the table:

Sample No.	$\bar{x}_1$	R	Sample No.	$\bar{x}_2$	R
1	20.225	1.8	11	21.225	3.2
2	19.750	2.8	12	20.475	0.9
3	20.425	3.8	13	19.650	2.6
4	19.725	2.5	14	19.075	4.0
5	20.550	3.7	15	19.400	2.2
6	19.900	5.0	16	20.700	4.3
7	21.325	5.5	17	19.850	3.6
8	19.625	3.5	18	20.200	2.5
9	19.350	2.5	19	20.425	2.2
10	20.550	4.1	20	19.900	5.5

b. $\bar{\bar{x}} = \dfrac{\bar{x}_1 + \bar{x}_2 + \cdots \bar{x}_{20}}{k} = \dfrac{402.325}{20} = 20.11625$ $\bar{R} = \dfrac{R_1 + R_2 + \cdots R_{20}}{k} = \dfrac{66.2}{20} = 3.31$

c.   *Centerline* $= \bar{\bar{x}} = 20.116$

From Table IX, Appendix D, with $n = 4$, $A_2 = .729$.

Upper control limit $= \bar{\bar{x}} + A_2\bar{R} = 20.116 + .729(3.31) = 22.529$

Lower control limit $= \bar{\bar{x}} - A_2\bar{R} = 20.116 - .729(3.31) = 17.703$

d.   *Upper* A-B *boundary* $= \bar{\bar{x}} + \dfrac{2}{3}(A_2\bar{R}) = 20.116 + \dfrac{2}{3}(.729)(3.31) = 21.725$

Lower A-B *boundary* $= \bar{\bar{x}} - \dfrac{2}{3}(A_2\bar{R}) = 20.116 - \dfrac{2}{3}(.729)(3.31) = 18.507$

Upper B-C *boundary* $= \bar{\bar{x}} + \dfrac{1}{3}(A_2\bar{R}) = 20.116 + \dfrac{1}{3}(.729)(3.31) = 20.920$

Lower B-C *boundary* $= \bar{\bar{x}} - \dfrac{1}{3}(A_2\bar{R}) = 20.116 - \dfrac{1}{3}(.729)(3.31) = 19.312$

e.   The $\bar{x}$ -chart is:

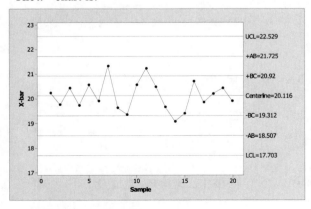

Rule 1:   One point beyond Zone A: No points are beyond Zone A.

Rule 2:   Nine points in a row in Zone C or beyond: No sequence of nine points are in Zone C (on one side of the centerline) or beyond.

Rule 3:   Six points in a row steadily increasing or decreasing: No sequence of six points steadily increase or decrease.

Rule 4:   Fourteen points in a row alternating up and down: This pattern does not exist.

Rule 5:   Two out of three points in Zone A or beyond: There are no groups of three consecutive points that have two or more in Zone A or beyond.

Rule 6:   Four out of five points in a row in Zone B or beyond: No sequence of five points has four or more in Zone B or beyond.

The process appears to be in control.

13.13   a.   From the prinout, $\bar{x} = 100.59$ and $s = .454$.

b.   The senterline would be $\bar{x} = 100.59$.
The upper control limit is $UCL = \bar{x} + 3(s) = 100.59 + 3(.454) = 101.952$.
The lower control limit is $LCL = \bar{x} - 3(s) = 100.59 - 3(.454) = 99.228$.

c.   Using MINITAB, the x-chart is

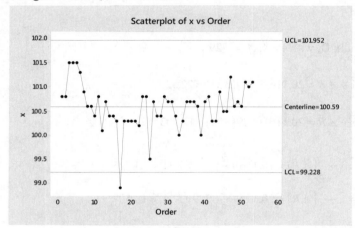

The process is not in control as there is an observation below the lower control limit.

13.15   a. $\bar{\bar{x}} = \dfrac{\bar{x}_1 + \bar{x}_2 + \cdots + \bar{x}_{20}}{k} = \dfrac{1,400}{20} = 70$

b. $\bar{R} = \dfrac{R_1 + R_2 + \cdots + R_{22}}{k} = \dfrac{650}{20} = 32.5$

c.   From Table IX, Appendix D, with $n = 10$, $A_2 = .308$.

Upper control limit $= \bar{\bar{x}} + A_2\bar{R} = 70 + .308(32.5) = 80.01$
Lower control limit $= \bar{\bar{x}} - A_2\bar{R} = 70 - .308(32.5) = 59.99$

d.   *Upper* A–B *boundary* $= \bar{\bar{x}} + \dfrac{2}{3}\left(A_2\bar{R}\right) = 70 + \dfrac{2}{3}(.308)(32.5) = 76.67$

Lower A–B *boundary* $= \overline{\overline{x}} + \dfrac{2}{3}\left(A_2\overline{R}\right) = 70 - \dfrac{2}{3}(.308)(32.5) = 63.33$

Upper B–C *boundary* $= \overline{\overline{x}} + \dfrac{1}{3}\left(A_2\overline{R}\right) = 70 + \dfrac{1}{3}(.308)(32.5) = 73.34$

Lower B–C *boundary* $= \overline{\overline{x}} + \dfrac{1}{3}\left(A_2\overline{R}\right) = 70 - \dfrac{1}{3}(.308)(32.5) = 66.66$

The $\overline{x}$-chart is:

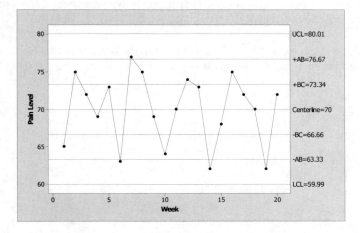

Rule 1:   One point beyond Zone A: No points are beyond Zone A.
Rule 2:   Nine points in a row in Zone C or beyond: No sequence of nine points are in Zone C (on one side of the centerline) or beyond.
Rule 3:   Six points in a row steadily increasing or decreasing: No sequence of six points steadily increase or decrease.
Rule 4:   Fourteen points in a row alternating up and down: This pattern does not exist.
Rule 5:   Two out of three points in Zone A or beyond: There are no groups of three consecutive points that have two or more in Zone A or beyond.
Rule 6:   Four out of five points in a row in Zone B or beyond: No sequence of five points has four or more in Zone B or beyond.

The process appears to be in control.

e.   The $\overline{x}$-chart with the additional points is:

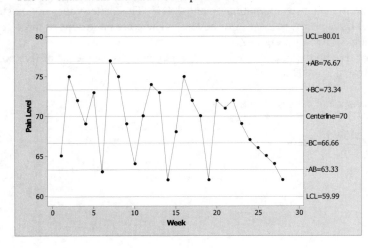

f.   Rule 1:   One point beyond Zone A: No points are beyond Zone A.

Rule 2:   Nine points in a row in Zone C or beyond: No sequence of nine points are in Zone C (on one side of the centerline) or beyond.

Rule 3:   Six points in a row steadily increasing or decreasing: There are six points steadily decreasing. This indicates the process is out of control.

Rule 4:   Fourteen points in a row alternating up and down: This pattern does not exist.

Rule 5:   Two out of three points in Zone A or beyond: There are no groups of three consecutive points that have two or more in Zone A or beyond.

Rule 6:   Four out of five points in a row in Zone B or beyond: No sequence of five points has four or more in Zone B or beyond.

Rule 3 indicates the process is out of control. There is a shift in the pain level of the patients following the intervention because the new observations are steadily decreasing.

13.17   a. $\bar{\bar{x}} = \dfrac{\bar{x}_1 + \bar{x}_2 + \cdots + \bar{x}_{10}}{k} = \dfrac{151}{10} = 15.1$

b.   The $\bar{x}$ -chart is:

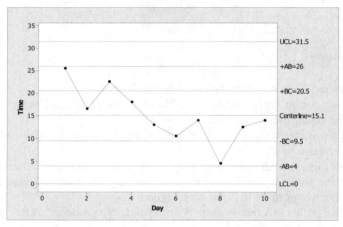

c.   Rule 1:   One point beyond Zone A: No points are beyond Zone A.

Rule 2:   Nine points in a row in Zone C or beyond: No sequence of nine points are in Zone C (on one side of the centerline) or beyond.

Rule 3:   Six points in a row steadily increasing or decreasing: This pattern does not exist.

Rule 4:   Fourteen points in a row alternating up and down: This pattern does not exist.

Rule 5:   Two out of three points in Zone A or beyond: There are no groups of three consecutive points that have two or more in Zone A or beyond.

Rule 6:   Four out of five points in a row in Zone B or beyond: No sequence of five points has four or more in Zone B or beyond.

There is no evidence of special causes of variation.

d. $\bar{\bar{x}} = \dfrac{\bar{x}_1 + \bar{x}_2 + \cdots + \bar{x}_{14}}{k} = \dfrac{152.5}{14} = 10.9$.

The $\bar{x}$-chart is:

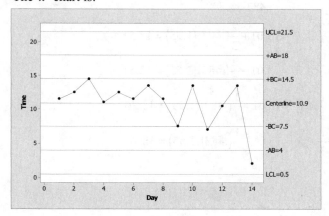

Rule 1:   One point beyond Zone A: No points are beyond Zone A.

Rule 2:   Nine points in a row in Zone C or beyond: No sequence of nine points are in Zone C (on one side of the centerline) or beyond.

Rule 3:   Six points in a row steadily increasing or decreasing: This pattern does not exist.

Rule 4:   Fourteen points in a row alternating up and down: This pattern does not exist.

Rule 5:   Two out of three points in Zone A or beyond: There are no groups of three consecutive points that have two or more in Zone A or beyond.

Rule 6:   Four out of five points in a row in Zone B or beyond: No sequence of five points has four or more in Zone B or beyond.

There is no evidence of special causes of variation.

e.   The side-by-side $\bar{x}$-charts are:

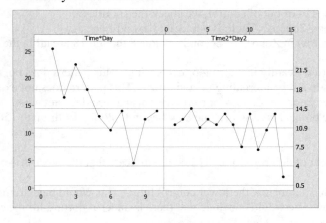

It appears that a process shift has occurred. All of the points after the implementation are below the centerline of the points before the implementation.

13.19   a.   From the problem, we are given $LCL = 12.3$ and $UCL = 13.8$. We are given the sample means for the 30 observations, but not the Ranges. Thus, we will have to compute $\bar{R}$ from the UCL and UCL. We can also compute $\bar{\bar{x}}$ from the UCL and LCL. From Table IX, Appendix D, with $n = 6$, $A_2 = .483$.

$$\bar{\bar{x}} = \frac{UCL + LCL}{2} = \frac{13.76 + 12.26}{2} = 13.01$$

$$UCL = \overline{\overline{x}} + A_2\overline{R} \Rightarrow \overline{R} = \frac{UCL - \overline{\overline{x}}}{A_2} = \frac{13.76 - 13.01}{.483} = 1.55$$

$$\text{Upper A-B } boundary = \overline{\overline{x}} + \frac{2}{3}A_2\overline{R} = 13.01 + \frac{2}{3}(.483)(1.55) = 13.51$$

$$\text{Lower A-B } boundary = \overline{\overline{x}} - \frac{2}{3}A_2\overline{R} = 13.01 - \frac{2}{3}(.483)(1.55) = 12.51$$

$$\text{Upper B-C } boundary = \overline{\overline{x}} + \frac{1}{3}A_2\overline{R} = 13.01 + \frac{1}{3}(.483)(1.55) = 13.26$$

$$\text{Lower B-C } boundary = \overline{\overline{x}} - \frac{1}{3}A_2\overline{R} = 13.01 - \frac{1}{3}(.483)(1.55) = 12.76$$

The $\overline{x}$-chart is:

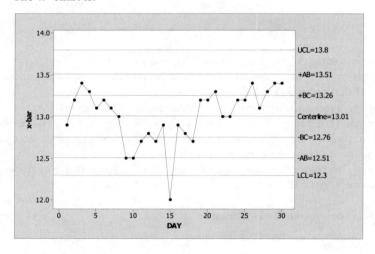

b.   To determine if the process is in or out of control, we check the six rules:

Rule 1:   One point beyond Zone A: There is one point beyond Zone A.

Rule 2:   Nine points in a row in Zone C or beyond: Points 8 though 18 are all in the lower Zone C or below

Rule 3:   Six points in a row steadily increasing or decreasing: This pattern does not exist.

Rule 4:   Fourteen points in a row alternating up and down: This pattern does not exist.

Rule 5:   Two out of three points in Zone A or beyond: This pattern does not exist.

Rule 6:   Four out of five points in a row in Zone B or beyond: Points 11 through 156 satisfy this rule.

This process appears to be out of control. Rules 1, 2, and 6 indicate that the process is out of control.

c.   Nine of these ten observations fall below the lower control limit. This would be extremely unusual if there was no under-reporting. We would conclude that there is under-reporting for the emissions data for this 10-day period.

13.21 a. The sample means and ranges are:

Sample	$\bar{x}$	Range	Sample	$\bar{x}$	Range	Sample	$\bar{x}$	Range
1	99.743	0.12	15	100.543	0.24	28	100.597	0.37
2	99.447	1.53	16	100.503	1.19	29	100.180	1.77
3	100.040	0.29	17	100.087	1.14	30	99.940	0.47
4	100.353	1.68	18	99.383	0.20	31	100.653	0.77
5	99.287	0.38	19	100.457	0.86	32	99.473	0.65
6	99.507	0.79	20	100.863	0.97	33	99.877	0.99
7	99.707	0.28	21	99.713	0.65	34	100.503	0.39
8	99.717	0.83	22	100.050	0.69	35	100.053	0.76
9	100.537	1.26	23	100.283	1.24	36	99.783	1.23
10	100.097	0.39	24	99.910	0.75	37	100.367	1.69
11	99.633	0.92	25	100.510	1.62	38	100.503	0.70
12	100.883	1.05	26	99.723	0.79	39	100.270	0.69
13	100.843	1.01	27	99.327	0.23	40	99.377	0.18
14	100.507	0.50						

$$\bar{\bar{x}} = \frac{\bar{x}_1 + \bar{x}_2 + \dots + \bar{x}_{40}}{k} = \frac{4,003.229}{40} = 100.081 \qquad \bar{R} = \frac{R_1 + R_2 + \dots + R_{40}}{40} = \frac{32.26}{40} = .8065$$

Centerline $= \bar{\bar{x}} = 100.081$

From Table IX, Appendix D, with $n = 3$, $A_2 = 1.023$.

Upper control limit $= \bar{\bar{x}} + A_2\bar{R} = 100.081 + 1.023(.8065) = 100.906$

Lower control limit $= \bar{\bar{x}} - A_2\bar{R} = 100.081 - 1.023(.8065) = 99.256$

Upper A-B *boundary* $= \bar{\bar{x}} + \frac{2}{3}A_2\bar{R} = 100.081 + \frac{2}{3}(1.023)(.8065) = 100.631$

Lower A-B *boundary* $= \bar{\bar{x}} - \frac{2}{3}A_2\bar{R} = 100.081 - \frac{2}{3}(1.023)(.8065) = 99.531$

Upper B-C *boundary* $= \bar{\bar{x}} + \frac{1}{3}A_2\bar{R} = 100.081 + \frac{1}{3}(1.023)(.8065) = 100.356$

Lower B-C *boundary* $= \bar{\bar{x}} - \frac{1}{3}A_2\bar{R} = 100.081 - \frac{1}{3}(1.023)(.8065) = 99.806$

The $\bar{x}$-chart is:

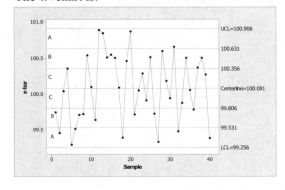

Using Rule 1, there are no points beyond Zone A. Therefore, the process appears to be in control.

b.   The sample means and ranges for the rounded data are:

Sample	$\bar{x}$	Range	Sample	$\bar{x}$	Range	Sample	$\bar{x}$	Range
1	100.000	0	15	100.667	1	28	100.333	1
2	99.333	1	16	100.667	1	29	100.000	2
3	100.000	0	17	100.333	1	30	100.000	0
4	100.333	2	18	99.000	0	31	100.667	1
5	99.000	0	19	100.667	1	32	99.667	1
6	99.667	1	20	101.333	1	33	99.667	1
7	100.000	0	21	99.667	1	34	100.333	1
8	99.667	1	22	100.000	0	35	100.000	0
9	100.667	1	23	100.333	1	36	99.667	1
10	100.000	0	24	100.000	0	37	100.333	1
11	99.667	1	25	100.667	1	38	100.333	1
12	101.333	1	26	99.667	1	39	100.333	1
13	101.333	1	27	99.000	0	40	99.000	0
14	100.333	1						

$$\bar{\bar{x}} = \frac{\bar{x}_1 + \bar{x}_2 + ... + \bar{x}_{40}}{k} = \frac{4,003.667}{40} = 100.092 \qquad \bar{R} = \frac{R_1 + R_2 + ... + R_{40}}{40} = \frac{30}{40} = .75$$

$Centerline = \bar{\bar{x}} = 100.092$

From Table IX, Appendix D, with $n = 3$, $A_2 = 1.023$.

$Upper\ control\ limit = \bar{\bar{x}} + A_2\bar{R} = 100.092 + 1.023(.75) = 100.859$

$Lower\ control\ limit = \bar{\bar{x}} - A_2\bar{R} = 100.092 - 1.023(.75) = 99.325$

$Upper\ A\text{-}B\ boundary = \bar{\bar{x}} + \frac{2}{3}A_2\bar{R} = 100.092 + \frac{2}{3}(1.023)(.75) = 100.604$

$Lower\ A\text{-}B\ boundary = \bar{\bar{x}} - \frac{2}{3}A_2\bar{R} = 100.092 - \frac{2}{3}(1.023)(.75) = 99.581$

$Upper\ B\text{-}C\ boundary = \bar{\bar{x}} + \frac{1}{3}A_2\bar{R} = 100.092 + \frac{1}{3}(1.023)(.75) = 100.348$

$Lower\ B\text{-}C\ boundary = \bar{\bar{x}} - \frac{1}{3}A_2\bar{R} = 100.02 - \frac{1}{3}(1.023)(.75) = 99.836$

The $\bar{x}$ -chart is:

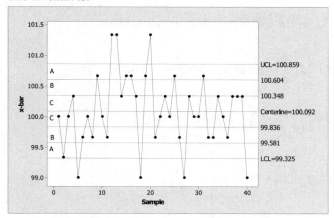

Using Rule 1, there are seven points beyond Zone A. This process appears to be out of control. When the data are rounded, the process is obviously out of control.

13.23 The *R*-chart is designed to monitor the variation of the process.

13.25 Using Table IX, Appendix D:

a. With $n = 4$, $D_3 = 0.000$ and $D_4 = 2.282$

b. With $n = 12$, $D_3 = 0.283$ and $D_4 = 1.717$

c. With $n = 24$, $D_3 = 0.451$ and $D_4 = 1.548$

13.27 a. From Exercise 13.11, the *R* values are:

Sample No.	R	Sample No.	R
1	1.8	11	3.2
2	2.8	12	0.9
3	3.8	13	2.6
4	2.5	14	4.0
5	3.7	15	2.2
6	5.0	16	4.3
7	5.5	17	3.6
8	3.5	18	2.5
9	2.5	19	2.2
10	4.1	20	5.5

$$\bar{R} = \frac{R_1 + R_2 + \cdots R_{20}}{k} = \frac{66.2}{20} = 3.31$$

Centerline $= \bar{R} = 3.31$

From Table IX, Appendix D, with $n = 4$, $D_4 = 2.282$, and $D_3 = 0$.

Upper control limit $= \bar{R}D_4 = 3.31(2.282) = 7.553$

Since $D_3 = 0$, the lower control limit is negative and is not included on the chart.

b.   From Table IX, Appendix D, with $n = 4$, $d_2 = 2.059$, and $d_3 = .880$.

$$Upper\ A\text{–}B\ boundary = \bar{R} + 2d_3\frac{\bar{R}}{d_2} = 3.31 + 2(.880)\frac{3.31}{2.059} = 6.139$$

$$Lower\ A\text{–}B\ boundary = \bar{R} - 2d_3\frac{\bar{R}}{d_2} = 3.31 - 2(.880)\frac{3.31}{2.059} = 0.481$$

$$Upper\ B\text{–}C\ boundary = \bar{R} + d_3\frac{\bar{R}}{d_2} = 3.31 + (.880)\frac{3.31}{2.059} = 4.725$$

$$Lower\ B\text{–}C\ boundary = \bar{R} - d_3\frac{\bar{R}}{d_2} = 3.31 - (.880)\frac{3.31}{2.059} = 1.895$$

c.   The R-chart is:

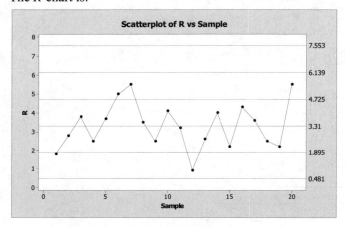

To determine if the process is in or out of control, we check the four rules:

Rule 1:   One point beyond Zone A: No points are beyond Zone A.
Rule 2:   Nine points in a row in Zone C or beyond: No sequence of nine points are in Zone C (on one side of the centerline) or beyond.
Rule 3:   Six points in a row steadily increasing or decreasing: No sequence of six points steadily increase or decrease.
Rule 4:   Fourteen points in a row alternating up and down: This pattern does not exist.

The process appears to be in control.

13.29   a.   The rational subgroups used to construct the R-chart are the 40 samples of size $n = 5$.

b.   No, the process is not in control. There are two observations outside the control limits. Since the process is out of control, the special causes of variation need to be identified andeliminated.

13.31   a. $\bar{R} = \dfrac{R_1 + R_2 + \cdots R_{20}}{k} = \dfrac{650}{20} = 32.5$.

b. $Centerline = \bar{R} = 32.5$

From Table IX, Appendix D, with $n = 10$, $D_4 = 1.777$, and $D_3 = .223$.

$Upper\ control\ limit = \bar{R}D_4 = 32.5(1.777) = 57.753$

$Lower\ control\ limit = \bar{R}D_3 = 32.5(.223) = 7.248$

c.   From Table IX, Appendix D, with $n = 10$, $d_2 = 3.078$, and $d_3 = .797$.

$$Upper\ \text{A–B}\ boundary = \bar{R} + 2d_3\frac{\bar{R}}{d_2} = 32.5 + 2(.797)\frac{32.5}{3.078} = 49.331$$

$$Lower\ \text{A–B}\ boundary = \bar{R} - 2d_3\frac{\bar{R}}{d_2} = 32.5 - 2(.797)\frac{32.5}{3.078} = 15.669$$

$$Upper\ \text{B–C}\ boundary = \bar{R} + d_3\frac{\bar{R}}{d_2} = 32.5 + (.797)\frac{32.5}{3.078} = 40.915$$

$$Lower\ \text{B–C}\ boundary = \bar{R} - d_3\frac{\bar{R}}{d_2} = 32.5 - (.797)\frac{32.5}{3.078} = 24.085$$

The *R*-chart is:

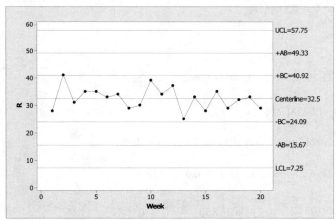

The process appears to be in control. All of the observations are very close to the centerline and none of the patterns appear in the chart.

d.   The *R*-chart with the addional points is:

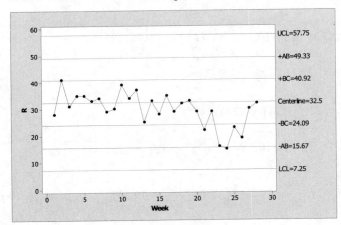

e.   To determine if the process is in or out of control, we check the four rules:

Rule 1:   One point beyond Zone A: No points are beyond Zone A.
Rule 2:   Nine points in a row in Zone C or beyond: There are nine points in Zone C (on one side of the centerline) or beyond. The last 9 points fit this pattern.
Rule 3:   Six points in a row steadily increasing or decreasing: No sequence of six points steadily increase or decrease.
Rule 4:   Fourteen points in a row alternating up and down: This pattern does not exist.

Because of Rule 2, it appears that the process variation is not in control.

13.33   a. $\bar{R} = \dfrac{R_1 + R_2 + ... + R_{16}}{16} = \dfrac{.3800}{16} = .0238$

$Centerline = \bar{R} = .0238$

From Table IX, Appendix D, with $n = 2$, $D_3 = 0.000$ and $D_4 = 3.267$.

$Upper\ control\ limit = \bar{R}D_4 = .0238(3.267) = .0778$

Since $D_3 = 0$, the lower control limit is negative and not included.

From Table IX, Appendix D, with $n = 2$, $d_2 = 1.128$ and $d_3 = .853$.

$Upper$ A-B $boundary = \bar{R} + 2d_3 \dfrac{\bar{R}}{d_2} = .0238 + 2(.853)\dfrac{.0238}{1.128} = .0598$

$Lower$ A-B $boundary = \bar{R} - 2d_3 \dfrac{\bar{R}}{d_2} = .0238 - 2(.853)\dfrac{.0238}{1.128} = -.0122$ or 0 (cannot be negative)

$Upper$ B-C $boundary = \bar{R} + d_3 \dfrac{\bar{R}}{d_2} = .0238 + (.853)\dfrac{.0238}{1.128} = .0418$

$Lower$ B-C $boundary = \bar{R} - d_3 \dfrac{\bar{R}}{d_2} = .0238 - (.853)\dfrac{.0238}{1.128} = .0058$

The *R*-chart is:

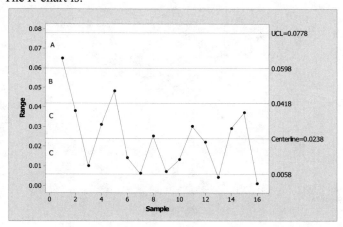

To determine if the process is in or out of control, we check the four rules:

Rule 1:   One point beyond Zone A: No points are beyond Zone A.
Rule 2:   Nine points in a row in Zone C or beyond: This pattern doe not exist.
Rule 3:   Six points in a row steadily increasing or decreasing: This pattern doe not exist.
Rule 4:   Fourteen points in a row alternating up and down: This pattern doe not exist.

The process appears to be in control.

b. $\overline{\overline{x}} = \dfrac{\overline{x}_1 + \overline{x}_2 + \ldots + \overline{x}_{16}}{k} = \dfrac{3.5430}{16} = .2214$

$Centerline = \overline{\overline{x}} = .2214$

From Table IX, Appendix D, with $n = 2$, $A_2 = 1.880$.

$Upper\ control\ limit = \overline{\overline{x}} + A_2 \overline{R} = .2214 + 1.880(.0238) = .2661$

$Lower\ control\ limit = \overline{\overline{x}} - A_2 \overline{R} = .2214 - 1.880(.0238) = .1767$

$Upper\ \text{A-B}\ boundary = \overline{\overline{x}} + \dfrac{2}{3} A_2 \overline{R} = .2214 + \dfrac{2}{3}(1.880)(.0238) = .2512$

$Lower\ \text{A-B}\ boundar\ y = \overline{\overline{x}} - \dfrac{2}{3} A_2 \overline{R} = .2214 - \dfrac{2}{3}(1.880)(.0238) = .1916$

$Upper\ \text{B-C}\ boundary = \overline{\overline{x}} + \dfrac{1}{3} A_2 \overline{R} = .2214 + \dfrac{1}{3}(1.880)(.0238) = .2363$

$Lower\ \text{B-C}\ boundary = \overline{\overline{x}} - \dfrac{1}{3} A_2 \overline{R} = .2214 - \dfrac{1}{3}(1.880)(.0238) = .2065$

The $\bar{x}$-chart is:

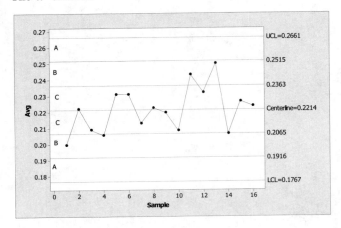

To determine if the process is in or out of control, we check the six rules:

Rule 1:   One point beyond Zone A: There are no points beyond Zone A.
Rule 2:   Nine points in a row in Zone C or beyond: This pattern does not exist.
Rule 3:   Six points in a row steadily increasing or decreasing: This pattern does not exist.
Rule 4:   Fourteen points in a row alternating up and down: This pattern does not exist.
Rule 5:   Two out of three points in Zone A or beyond: This pattern does not exist.
Rule 6:   Four out of five points in a row in Zone B or beyond: This pattern does not exist.

This process appears to be in control.

c.   Based on the R-chart and the $\bar{x}$-chart, the process appears to be in control. An estimate of the true average thickness of the expensive layer would be $\bar{\bar{x}} = .2214$.

13.35   a.   The values of R for the samples are:

Sample	R	Sample	R	Sample	R	Sample	R
1	0.12	11	0.92	21	0.65	31	0.77
2	1.53	12	1.05	22	0.69	32	0.65
3	0.29	13	1.01	23	1.24	33	0.99
4	1.68	14	0.5	24	0.75	34	0.39
5	0.38	15	0.24	25	1.62	35	0.76
6	0.79	16	1.19	26	0.79	36	1.23
7	0.28	17	1.14	27	0.23	37	1.69
8	0.83	18	0.2	28	0.37	38	0.7
9	1.26	19	0.86	29	1.77	39	0.69
10	0.39	20	0.97	30	0.47	40	0.18

$$Centerline = \bar{R} = \frac{R_1 + R_2 + \cdots R_{40}}{k} = \frac{32.26}{40} = .8065 .$$

From Table IX, Appendix D, with $n = 3$, $D_4 = 2.574$, and $D_3 = 0$.

$$Upper\ control\ limit = \bar{R}D_4 = .8065(2.574) = 2.076$$

Since $D_3 = 0$, the lower control limit is negative and is not included on the chart.

From Table IX, Appendix D, with $n = 3$, $d_2 = 1.693$, and $d_3 = .888$.

$$Upper\ A\text{–}B\ boundary = \overline{\overline{R}} + 2d_3\frac{\overline{R}}{d_2} = .8065 + 2(.888)\frac{.8065}{1.693} = 1.653$$

$$Lower\ A\text{–}B\ boundary = \overline{\overline{R}} - 2d_3\frac{\overline{R}}{d_2} = .8065 - 2(.888)\frac{.8065}{1.693} = -.040$$

$$Upper\ B\text{–}C\ boundary = \overline{\overline{R}} + d_3\frac{\overline{R}}{d_2} = .8065 + (.888)\frac{.8065}{1.693} = 1.23$$

$$Lower\ B\text{–}C\ boundary = \overline{\overline{R}} - d_3\frac{\overline{R}}{d_2} = .8065 - (.888)\frac{.8065}{1.693} = .383$$

The *R*-chart is:

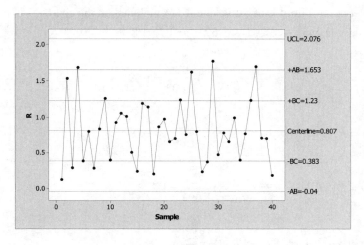

To determine if the process is in or out of control, we check the four rules:

Rule 1: One point beyond Zone A: No points are beyond Zone A.
Rule 2: Nine points in a row in Zone C or beyond: No sequence of nine points are in Zone C (on one side of the centerline) or beyond.
Rule 3: Six points in a row steadily increasing or decreasing: No sequence of six points steadily increase or decrease.
Rule 4: Fourteen points in a row alternating up and down: This pattern does not exist.

It appears that the process variation is in control.

b. The values of *R* for the rounded data are:

Sample	R	Sample	R	Sample	R	Sample	R
1	0	11	1	21	1	31	1
2	2	12	1	22	1	32	1
3	0	13	1	23	1	33	1
4	2	14	1	24	1	34	0

5	0	15	0	25	2	35	1
6	1	16	1	26	1	36	1
7	0	17	1	27	0	37	2
8	1	18	0	28	0	38	1
9	1	19	1	29	2	39	1
10	0	20	1	30	0	40	0

$$Centerline = \bar{R} = \frac{R_1 + R_2 + \cdots R_{40}}{k} = \frac{33}{40} = .825 \,.$$

From Table IX, Appendix D, with $n = 3$, $D_4 = 2.574$, and $D_3 = 0$.

$$Upper\ control\ limit = \bar{R}D_4 = .825(2.574) = 2.124$$

Since $D_3 = 0$, the lower control limit is negative and is not included on the chart.
From Table IX, Appendix D, with $n = 3$, $d_2 = 1.693$, and $d_3 = .888$.

$$Upper\ A\text{–}B\ boundary = \bar{R} + 2d_3\ \frac{\bar{R}}{d_2} = .825 + 2(.888)\frac{.825}{1.693} = 1.69$$

$$Lower\ A\text{–}B\ boundary = \bar{R} - 2d_3\ \frac{\bar{R}}{d_2} = .825 - 2(.888)\frac{.825}{1.693} = -.04$$

$$Upper\ B\text{–}C\ boundary = \bar{R} + d_3\ \frac{\bar{R}}{d_2} = .825 + (.888)\frac{.825}{1.693} = 1.258$$

$$Lower\ B\text{–}C\ boundary = \bar{R} - d_3\ \frac{\bar{R}}{d_2} = .825 - (.888)\frac{.825}{1.693} = .392$$

The R-chart for the rounded data is:

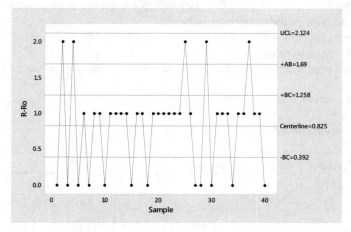

To determine if the process is in or out of control, we check the four rules:

Rule 1: One point beyond Zone A: No points are beyond Zone A.

Rule 2: Nine points in a row in Zone C or beyond: No sequence of nine points are in Zone C (on one side of the centerline) or beyond.

Rule 3: Six points in a row steadily increasing or decreasing: No sequence of six points steadily increase or decrease.

Rule 4: Fourteen points in a row alternating up and down: This pattern does not exist.

It appears that the process variation is in control. There are very few different values for R, once the data have been rounded off.

13.37   From Exercise 13.22, $\bar{R} = \dfrac{R_1 + R_2 + \cdots R_{25}}{k} = \dfrac{4.67}{25} = .1868$

Centerline $= \bar{R} = .1868$

From Table IX, Appendix D, with $n = 4$, $D_4 = 2.282$ and $D_3 = 0$.

Upper control limit $= \bar{R}D_4 = .1868(2.282) = .4263$

Since $D_3 = 0$, the lower control limit is negative and is not included on the chart.

From Table IX, Appendix D, with $n = 4$, $d_2 = 2.059$, and $d_3 = .880$.

$$\text{\textit{Upper A–B boundary}} = \bar{R} + 2d_3 \frac{\bar{R}}{d_2} = .1868 + 2(.880)\frac{.1868}{2.059} = .346$$

$$\text{\textit{Lower A–B boundary}} = \bar{R} - 2d_3 \frac{\bar{R}}{d_2} = .1868 - 2(.880)\frac{.1868}{2.059} = .027$$

$$\text{\textit{Upper B–C boundary}} = \bar{R} + d_3 \frac{\bar{R}}{d_2} = .1868 + (.880)\frac{.1868}{2.059} = .267$$

$$\text{\textit{Lower B–C boundary}} = \bar{R} - d_3 \frac{\bar{R}}{d_2} = .1868 - (.880)\frac{.1868}{2.059} = .107$$

The *R*-chart is:

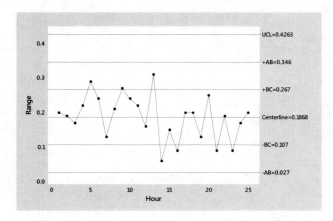

To determine if the process is in or out of control, we check the four rules:

Rule 1: One point beyond Zone A: No points are beyond Zone A.

Rule 2: Nine points in a row in Zone C or beyond: No sequence of nine points are in Zone C (on one side of the centerline) or beyond.

Rule 3:   Six points in a row steadily increasing or decreasing: No sequence of six points steadily increase or decrease.

Rule 4:   Fourteen points in a row alternating up and down: This pattern does not exist.

The process appears to be in control.

13.39   The *p*-chart is designed to monitor the proportion of defective units produced by a process.

13.41   The sample size is determined as follows: $n > \dfrac{9(1-p_0)}{p_0} = \dfrac{9(1-.08)}{.08} = 103.5 \approx 104$

13.43   a.   We must first calculate $\bar{p}$. To do this, it is necessary to find the total number of defectives in all the samples. To find the number of defectives per sample, we multiple the proportion by the sample size, 150. The number of defectives per sample are shown in the table:

Sample No.	p	No. Defectives	Sample No.	p	No. Defectives
1	.03	4.5	11	.07	10.5
2	.05	7.5	12	.04	6.0
3	.10	15.0	13	.06	9.0
4	.02	3.0	14	.05	7.5
5	.08	12.0	15	.07	10.5
6	.09	13.5	16	.06	9.0
7	.08	12.0	17	.07	10.5
8	.05	7.5	18	.02	3.0
9	.07	10.5	19	.05	7.5
10	.06	9.0	20	.03	4.5

Note: There cannot be a fraction of a defective. The proportions presented in the exercise have been rounded off. I have used the fractions to minimize the roundoff error.

To get the total number of defectives, sum the number of defectives for all 20 samples. The sum is 172.5. To get the total number of units sampled, multiply the sample size by the number of samples: $150(20) = 3000$.

$$\bar{p} = \frac{\text{Total defective in all samples}}{\text{Total units sampled}} = \frac{172.5}{3000} = .0575$$

$Centerline = \bar{p} = .0575$

$Upper\ control\ limit = \bar{p} + 3\sqrt{\dfrac{\bar{p}(1-\bar{p})}{n}} = .0575 + 3\sqrt{\dfrac{.0575(.9425)}{150}} = .1145$

$Lower\ control\ limit = \bar{p} - 3\sqrt{\dfrac{\bar{p}(1-\bar{p})}{n}} = .0575 - 3\sqrt{\dfrac{.0575(.9425)}{150}} = .0005$

b. $Upper\ \text{A–B}\ boundary = \bar{p} + 2\sqrt{\dfrac{\bar{p}(1-\bar{p})}{n}} = .0575 + 2\sqrt{\dfrac{.0575(.9425)}{150}} = .0955$

$$Lower \text{ A-B } boundary = \overline{p} - 2\sqrt{\frac{\overline{p}(1-\overline{p})}{n}} = .0575 - 2\sqrt{\frac{.0575(.9425)}{150}} = .0195$$

$$Upper \text{ B-C } boundary = \overline{p} + \sqrt{\frac{\overline{p}(1-\overline{p})}{n}} = .0575 + \sqrt{\frac{.0575(.9425)}{150}} = .0765$$

$$Lower \text{ B-C } boundary = \overline{p} - \sqrt{\frac{\overline{p}(1-\overline{p})}{n}} = .0575 - \sqrt{\frac{.0575(.9425)}{150}} = .0385$$

c.   The *p*-chart is:

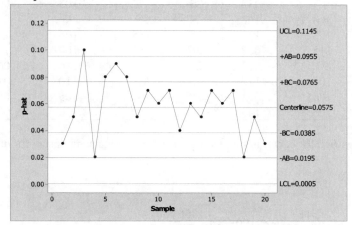

d.   To determine if the process is in or out of control, we check the four rules:

Rule 1:   One point beyond Zone A: No points are beyond Zone A.

Rule 2:   Nine points in a row in Zone C or beyond: No sequence of nine points are in Zone C (on one side of the centerline) or beyond.

Rule 3:   Six points in a row steadily increasing or decreasing: No sequence of six points steadily increase or decrease.

Rule 4:   Fourteen points in a row alternating up and down: Points 7 through 20 alternate up and down. This indicates the process is out of control.

Rule 4 indicates that the process is out of control.

e.   Since the process is out of control, the centerline and control limits should not be used to monitor future process output. The centerline and control limits are intended to represent the behavior of the process when it is under control.

13.45   a.   The attribute of interest is post-operative complications.

b.   The rational subgroups are the months.

c. $$\overline{p} = \frac{\text{Total defective in all samples}}{\text{Total units sampled}} = \frac{294}{2939} = .100$$

d.   The proportions are found by dividing the number of complications each month by the number of procedures each month. The proportions are:

Month	Complications	Procedures	Prop.	Month	Complications	Procedures	Prop.
1	14	105	.133	16	13	110	.118
2	12	97	.124	17	7	97	.072
3	10	115	.087	18	10	105	.095
4	12	100	.120	19	8	71	.113
5	9	95	.095	20	5	48	.104
6	7	111	.063	21	12	95	.126
7	9	68	.132	22	9	110	.082
8	11	47	.234	23	7	103	.068
9	9	83	.108	24	9	95	.095
10	12	108	.111	25	15	105	.143
11	10	115	.087	26	12	100	.120
12	7	94	.074	27	8	116	.069
13	12	107	.112	25	2	110	.018
14	9	99	.091	29	9	105	.086
15	15	105	.143	30	10	120	.083

e.   Since the sample sizes varied for each sample, we will use the average sample size for n:

$$n = \frac{2939}{30} \approx 98$$

$$Upper\ control\ limit = \bar{p} + 3\sqrt{\frac{\bar{p}(1-\bar{p})}{n}} = .100 + 3\sqrt{\frac{.100(.900)}{98}} = .191$$

$$Lower\ control\ limit = \bar{p} - 3\sqrt{\frac{\bar{p}(1-\bar{p})}{n}} = .100 - 3\sqrt{\frac{.100(.900)}{98}} = .009$$

$$Upper\ A\text{–}B\ boundary = \bar{p} + 2\sqrt{\frac{\bar{p}(1-\bar{p})}{n}} = .100 + 2\sqrt{\frac{.100(.900)}{98}} = .161$$

$$Lower\ A\text{–}B\ boundary = \bar{p} - 2\sqrt{\frac{\bar{p}(1-\bar{p})}{n}} = .100 - 2\sqrt{\frac{.100(.900)}{98}} = .039$$

$$Upper\ B\text{–}C\ boundary = \bar{p} + \sqrt{\frac{\bar{p}(1-\bar{p})}{n}} = .100 + \sqrt{\frac{.100(.900)}{98}} = .130$$

$$Lower\ B\text{–}C\ boundary = \bar{p} - \sqrt{\frac{\bar{p}(1-\bar{p})}{n}} = .100 - \sqrt{\frac{.100(.900)}{98}} = .070$$

f. The *p*-chart for the data is:

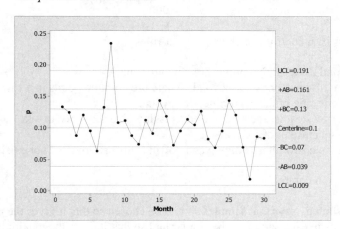

g. To determine if the process is in or out of control, we check the four rules:

Rule 1: One point beyond Zone A: One point is beyond Zone A.

Rule 2: Nine points in a row in Zone C or beyond: No sequence of nine points are in Zone C (on one side of the centerline) or beyond.

Rule 3: Six points in a row steadily increasing or decreasing: No sequence of six points steadily increase or decrease.

Rule 4: Fourteen points in a row alternating up and down: This pattern does not exist.

Rule 1 is violated. The process appears to be out of control.

13.47 a. Yes. The minimum sample size necessary so the lower control limit is not negative is $n > \dfrac{9(1-p_0)}{p_0}$.

From the data, $p_0 \approx .01$. Thus, $n > \dfrac{9(1-.01)}{.01} = 891$. Our sample size was 1000.

b. *Upper control limit* $= \bar{p} + 3\sqrt{\dfrac{\bar{p}(1-\bar{p})}{n}} = .0105 + 3\sqrt{\dfrac{.0105(.9895)}{1000}} = .0202$

Lower control limit $= \bar{p} - 3\sqrt{\dfrac{\bar{p}(1-\bar{p})}{n}} = .0105 - 3\sqrt{\dfrac{.0105(.9895)}{1000}} = .0008$

c. To determine if special causes are present, we must complete the *p*-chart.

Upper $\mathrm{A} - \mathrm{B}$ *boundary* $= \bar{p} + 2\sqrt{\dfrac{\bar{p}(1-\bar{p})}{n}} = .0105 + 2\sqrt{\dfrac{.0105(.9895)}{1000}} = .0169$

Lower $\mathrm{A} - \mathrm{B}$ *boundary* $= \bar{p} - 2\sqrt{\dfrac{\bar{p}(1-\bar{p})}{n}} = .0105 - 2\sqrt{\dfrac{.0105(.9895)}{1000}} = .0041$

Upper $\mathrm{B} - \mathrm{C}$ *boundary* $= \bar{p} + \sqrt{\dfrac{\bar{p}(1-\bar{p})}{n}} = .0105 + \sqrt{\dfrac{.0105(.9895)}{1000}} = .0137$

$$Lower\ B-C\ boundary = \overline{p} - \sqrt{\frac{\overline{p}(1-\overline{p})}{n}} = .0105 - \sqrt{\frac{.0105(.9895)}{1000}} = .0073$$

To determine if the process is in control, we check the four rules.

Rule 1:   One point beyond Zone A: No points are beyond Zone A.
Rule 2:   Nine points in a row in Zone C or beyond: There are not nine points in a row in Zone C (on one side of the centerline) or beyond.
Rule 3:   Six points in a row steadily increasing or decreasing: No sequence of six points steadily increase or decrease.
Rule 4:   Fourteen points in a row alternating up and down: This pattern does not exist.

It appears that the process is in control.

    d.   The rational subgrouping strategy says that samples should be chosen so that it gives the maximum chance for the measurements in each sample to be similar and so that it gives the maximum chance for the samples to differ. By selecting 1000 consecutive chips each time, this gives the maximum chance for the measurements in the sample to be similar. By selecting the samples every other day, there is a relatively large chance that the samples differ.

13.49   a.   To compute the proportion of defectives in each sample, divide the number of defectives by the number in the sample, 100:

$$\hat{p} = \frac{No.\ of\ defectives}{No.\ in\ sample}$$

The sample proportions are listed in the table:

Sample No.	$\hat{p}$	Sample No.	$\hat{p}$
1	.02	16	.03
2	.04	17	.02
3	.13	18	.07
4	.04	19	.03
5	.01	20	.02
6	.01	21	.03
7	.10	22	.07
8	.11	23	.04
9	.09	24	.03
10	.00	25	.02
11	.03	26	.02
12	.04	27	.00
13	.02	28	.03
14	.08	29	.01
15	.02	30	.04

To get the total number of defectives, sum the number of defectives for all 30 samples. The sum is 120. To get the total number of units sampled, multiply the sample size by the number of samples: $100(30) = 3000$.

$$\overline{p} = \frac{Total\ defective\ in\ all\ samples}{Total\ units\ sampled} = \frac{120}{3000} = .04$$

The centerline is $= \bar{p} = .04$

$$Upper\ control\ limit = \bar{p} + 3\sqrt{\frac{\bar{p}(1-\bar{p})}{n}} = .04 + 3\sqrt{\frac{.04(1-.04)}{100}} = .099$$

$$Lower\ control\ limit = \bar{p} - 3\sqrt{\frac{\bar{p}(1-\bar{p})}{n}} = .04 - 3\sqrt{\frac{.04(1-.04)}{100}} = -.019\ or\ 0\ \ (cannot\ be\ negative)$$

$$Upper\ A\text{–}B\ boundary = \bar{p} + 2\sqrt{\frac{\bar{p}(1-\bar{p})}{n}} = .04 + 2\sqrt{\frac{.04(1-.04)}{100}} = .079$$

$$Lower\ A\text{–}B\ boundary = \bar{p} - 2\sqrt{\frac{\bar{p}(1-\bar{p})}{n}} = .04 - 2\sqrt{\frac{.04(1-.04)}{100}} = .001$$

$$Upper\ B\text{–}C\ boundary = \bar{p} + \sqrt{\frac{\bar{p}(1-\bar{p})}{n}} = .04 + \sqrt{\frac{.04(1-.04)}{100}} = .060$$

$$Lower\ B\text{–}C\ boundary = \bar{p} - \sqrt{\frac{\bar{p}(1-\bar{p})}{n}} = .04 - \sqrt{\frac{.04(1-.04)}{100}} = .020$$

The *p*-chart is:

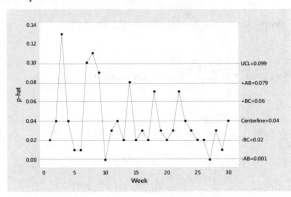

b.   To determine if the process is in or out of control, we check the four rules for the *p*-chart.

Rule 1:   One point beyond Zone A: There are 3 points beyond Zone A—points 3, 7, and 8.

Rule 2:   Nine points in a row in Zone C or beyond: No sequence of nine points are in Zone C (on one side of the centerline) or beyond.

Rule 3:   Six points in a row steadily increasing or decreasing: This pattern is not present.

Rule 4:   Fourteen points in a row alternating up and down: This pattern does not exist.

The process does not appear to be in control. Rule 1 indicates that the process is out of control.

c.   No. Since the process is not in control, then these control limits are meaningless.

13.51   To compute the proportion of leaky pumps in each sample, divide the number of leaky pumps by the number in the sample, 500:

$$\hat{p} = \frac{No.\ leaky\ pumps}{No.\ in\ sample}$$

The sample proportions are listed in the table:

Week	$\hat{p}$	Week	$\hat{p}$
1	0.72	8	.056
2	.056	9	.062
3	.048	10	.052
4	.052	11	.068
5	.040	12	.052
6	.112	13	.064
7	.052		

To get the total number of leaky pumps, sum the number of leaky pumps for all 13 samples. The sum is 393. To get the total number of pumps sampled, multiply the sample size by the number of samples: $500(13) = 6,500$.

$$\overline{p} = \frac{\text{Total leaky pumps in all samples}}{\text{Total pumps sampled}} = \frac{393}{6500} = .060$$

The *Centerline* is $\overline{p} = .060$

$$Upper\ control\ limit = \overline{p} + 3\sqrt{\frac{\overline{p}(1-\overline{p})}{n}} = .060 + 3\sqrt{\frac{.06(1-.06)}{500}} = .060 + .032 = .092$$

$$Lower\ control\ limit = \overline{p} - 3\sqrt{\frac{\overline{p}(1-\overline{p})}{n}} = .060 - 3\sqrt{\frac{.06(1-.06)}{500}} = .060 - .032 = .028$$

$$Upper\ A\text{-}B\ boundary = \overline{p} + 2\sqrt{\frac{\overline{p}(1-\overline{p})}{n}} = .060 + 2\sqrt{\frac{.06(1-.06)}{500}} = .060 + .021 = .081$$

$$Lower\ A\text{-}B\ boundary = \overline{p} - 2\sqrt{\frac{\overline{p}(1-\overline{p})}{n}} = .060 - 2\sqrt{\frac{.06(1-.06)}{500}} = .060 - .021 = .039$$

$$Upper\ B\text{-}C\ boundary = \overline{p} + \sqrt{\frac{\overline{p}(1-\overline{p})}{n}} = .060 + \sqrt{\frac{.06(1-.06)}{500}} = .060 + .011 = .071$$

$$Lower\ B\text{-}C\ boundary = \overline{p} - \sqrt{\frac{\overline{p}(1-\overline{p})}{n}} = .060 - \sqrt{\frac{.06(1-.06)}{500}} = .060 - .011 = .049$$

The *p*-chart is:

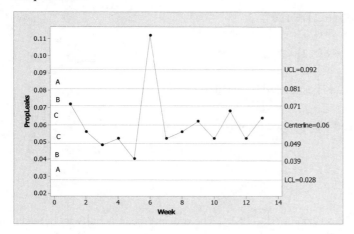

To determine if the process is in or out of control, we check the four rules:

Rule 1:   One point beyond Zone A: One point lies beyond Zone A.
Rule 2:   Nine points in a row in Zone C or beyond: This pattern doe not exist.
Rule 3:   Six points in a row steadily increasing or decreasing: This pattern doe not exist.
Rule 4:   Fourteen points in a row alternating up and down: This pattern doe not exist.

The process appears to be out of control because Rule 1 is not followed. One observation is beyond Zone A. It appears that the process is not stable.

13.53   A capability analysis is a methodology used to help determine when common cause variation is unacceptably high. If a process is not in statistical control, then both common causes and special causes of variation exist. It would not be possible to determine if the common cause variation is too high because it could not be separated from special cause variation.

13.55   One way to assess the capability of a process is to construct a frequency distribution or stem-and-leaf display for a large sample of individual measurements from the process. Then, the specification limits and the target value for the output variable are added to the graph. This is called a capability analysis diagram. A second way to assess the capability of a process is to quantify capability. The most direct way to quantify capability is to count the number of items that fall outside the specification limits in the capability analysis diagram and report the percentage of such items in the sample. Also, one can construct a capability index. This is the ratio of the difference in the specification spread and the difference in the process spread. This measure is called C_P. If C_P is less than 1, then the process is not capable.

13.57   a. $C_p = 1.00$. For this value, the specification spread is equal to the process spread. This indicates that the process is capable. Approximately 2.7 units per 1,000 will be unacceptable.

         b. $C_p = 1.33$. For this value, the specification spread is greater than the process spread. This indicates that the process is capable. Approximately 63 units per 1,000,000 will be unacceptable.

         c. $C_p = 0.50$. For this value, the specification spread is less than the process spread. This indicates that the process is not capable.

         d. $C_p = 2.00$. For this value, the specification spread is greater than the process spread. This indicates that the process is capable. Approximately 2 units per billion will be unacceptable.

13.59   The process spread is 6σ.

   a.   For $\sigma = 21$, the process spread is $6(21) = 126$.

   b.   For $\sigma = 5.2$, the process spread is $6(5.2) = 31.2$.

   c.   For $s = 110.06$, the process spread is estimated by $6(110.06) = 660.36$

   d.   For $s = .0024$, the process spread is estimated by $6(.0024) = .0144$

13.61   We know that $C_p = \dfrac{USL - LSL}{6\sigma}$

   Thus, if $C_p = 2$, then $2 = \dfrac{USL - LSL}{6\sigma} \Rightarrow 12\sigma = USL - LSL$. The process mean is halfway between the USL and the LSL. Since the specification spread covers 12σ, then the USL must be $12\sigma/2 = 6\sigma$ from the process mean.

13.63   The capability index is $C_p = \dfrac{USL - LSL}{6\sigma} = \dfrac{.7 - .1}{6(.265)} = \dfrac{.6}{1.59} = .377$.

   Since the capability index is less than 1, the process is not capable. The process spread is wider than the specification spread.

13.65   a.   A capability diagram is (LSL = 35 is off the chart.):

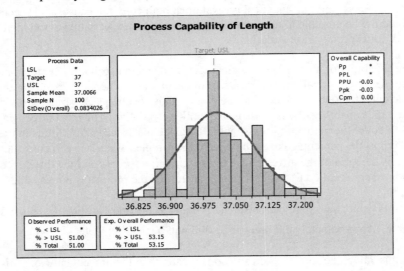

   b.   Fifty-one percent of the observations are above the upper specification limit.

   c.   From the sample, $\bar{x} = 37.007$ and $s = .0834$.

   $$C_p = \dfrac{USL - LSL}{6s} \approx \dfrac{37 - 35}{6(.0834)} = \dfrac{2}{.5004} = 3.9968$$

   d.   Since the C_P value is greater than 1, the process is capable.

13.67   Using MINITAB, the capability analysis diagram is:

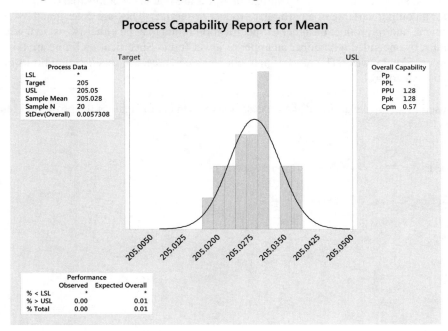

From the sample. $\bar{x} = 205.028$ and $s = .0057308$.

$$C_P = \frac{\text{USL - LSL}}{6\sigma} \approx \frac{205.05 - 204.05}{6(.0057308)} = \frac{1}{.03438} = 29.08$$

Since the C_P value is greater than 1, the process is capable.

From the chart, we know that none of the 20 obervations fall outside the specification limits. This is also an indication that the process is capable.

13.69   The quality of a good or service is indicated by the extent to which it satisfies the needs and preferences of its users. Its eight dimensions are: performance, features, reliability, conformance, durability, serviceability, aesthetics, and other perceptions that influence judgments of quality.

13.71   A system is a collection or arrangement of interacting components that has an on-going purpose or mission. A system receives inputs from its environment, transforms those inputs to outputs, and delivers those outputs to its environment.

13.73   Yes. Even though the output may all fall within the specification limits, the process may still be out of control.

13.75   Solution will vary. See Section 13.7 for Guided Solutions.

13.77   If a process is in control and remains in control, its future will be like its past. It is predictable in that its output will stay within certain limits. If a process is out of control, there is no way of knowing what the future pattern of output from the process may look like.

13.79   Control limits are a function of the natural variability of the process. The position of the limits is a function of the size of the process standard deviation. Specification limits are boundary points that define the acceptable values for an output variable of a particular product or service. They are determined by customers, management, and/or product designers. Specification limits may be either two-sided, with upper and lower limits, or one-sided with either an upper or lower limit. Specification limits are not dependent on the process in any way. The process may not be able to meet the specification limits even when it is under statistical control.

13.81   The C_P statistic is used to assess capability if the process is stable (in control) and if the process is centered on the target value.

13.83   a.   The centerline is $\bar{x} = \dfrac{\sum x}{n} = \dfrac{96}{15} = 6.4$. The time series plot is:

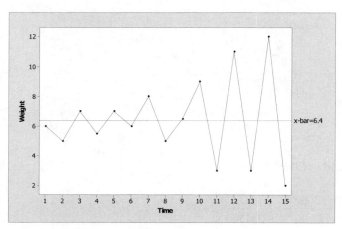

   b.   The type of variation best described by the pattern in this plot is increasing variance. The spread of the measurements increases with the passing of time.

13.85   To determine if the process is in or out of control, we check the six rules:

   Rule 1:   One point beyond Zone A: No points are beyond Zone A.
   Rule 2:   Nine points in a row in Zone C or beyond: Points 8 through 16 are in Zone C (on one side of the centerline) or beyond. This indicates the process is out of control.
   Rule 3:   Six points in a row steadily increasing or decreasing: No sequence of six points steadily increase or decrease.
   Rule 4:   Fourteen points in a row alternating up and down: This pattern does not exist.
   Rule 5:   Two out of three points in Zone A or beyond: No group of three consecutive points have two or more in Zone A or beyond.
   Rule 6:   Four out of five points in a row in Zone B or beyond: No sequence of five points has four or more in Zone B or beyond.

   Rule 2 indicates that the process is out of control. A special cause of variation appears to be present.

13.87   a.   For each sample, we compute the mean and range:

Sample	$\bar{x}$	R	Sample	$\bar{x}$	R
1	54.00	0.4	9	55.30	2.3
2	54.24	1.4	10	54.68	3.4
3	54.54	2.8	11	54.46	5.3
4	52.82	1.3	12	54.02	3.7
5	52.52	1.7	13	55.14	4.4
6	54.12	1.4	14	54.78	3.2
7	54.36	3.7	15	54.28	0.9
8	54.18	5.6	16	54.74	2.6

$$Centerline = \bar{R} = \frac{R_1 + R_2 + \cdots + R_{16}}{k} = \frac{44.1}{16} = 2.75625$$

From Table IX, Appendix D, with $n = 5$, $D_4 = 2.114$, and $D_3 = 0$.

$$Upper\ control\ limit = \bar{R}D_4 = 2.75625(2.114) = 5.827$$

Since $D_3 = 0$, the lower control limit is negative and is not included on the chart.

From Table IX, Appendix D, with $n = 5$, $d_2 = 2.326$, and $d_3 = .864$.

$$Upper\ A\text{–}B\ boundary = \bar{R} + 2d_3 \frac{\bar{R}}{d_2} = 2.75625 + 2(.864)\frac{2.75625}{2.326} = 4.804$$

$$Lower\ A\text{–}B\ boundary = \bar{R} - 2d_3 \frac{\bar{R}}{d_2} = 2.75625 - 2(.864)\frac{2.75625}{2.326} = .709$$

$$Upper\ B\text{–}C\ boundary = \bar{R} + d_3 \frac{\bar{R}}{d_2} = 2.75625 + (.864)\frac{2.75625}{2.326} = 3.780$$

$$Lower\ B\text{–}C\ boundary = \bar{R} - d_3 \frac{\bar{R}}{d_2} = 2.75625 - (.864)\frac{2.75625}{2.326} = 1.732$$

The *R*-chart is:

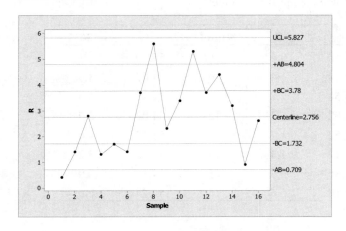

b. $$Centerline = \overline{\overline{x}} = \frac{\overline{x}_1 + \overline{x}_2 + \cdots + \overline{x}_{16}}{k} = \frac{868.18}{16} = 54.26125$$

From Table IX, Appendix D, with $n = 5$, $A_2 = .577$

$$Upper\ control\ limit = \overline{\overline{x}} + A_2\overline{R} = 54.26125 + .577(2.75625) = 55.8516$$

$$Lower\ control\ limit = \overline{\overline{x}} - A_2\overline{R} = 54.26125 - .577(2.75625) = 52.6709$$

$$Upper\ \text{A} - \text{B}\ boundary = \overline{\overline{x}} + \frac{2}{3}\left(A_2\overline{R}\right) = 54.26125 + \frac{2}{3}(.577)(2.75625) = 55.3215$$

$$Lower\ \text{A} - \text{B}\ boundary = \overline{\overline{x}} - \frac{2}{3}\left(A_2\overline{R}\right) = 54.26125 - \frac{2}{3}(.577)(2.75625) = 53.2010$$

$$Upper\ \text{B} - \text{C}\ boundary = \overline{\overline{x}} + \frac{1}{3}\left(A_2\overline{R}\right) = 54.26125 + \frac{1}{3}(.577)(2.75625) = 54.7914$$

$$Lower\ \text{B} - \text{C}\ boundary = \overline{\overline{x}} - \frac{1}{3}\left(A_2\overline{R}\right) = 54.26125 - \frac{1}{3}(.577)(2.75625) = 53.7311$$

The $\overline{x}$-chart is:

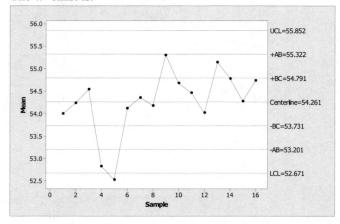

c.   For the *R*-chart: To determine if the process is in or out of control, we check the four rules:

Rule 1:   One point beyond Zone A: No points are beyond Zone A.
Rule 2:   Nine points in a row in Zone C or beyond: No sequence of nine points are in Zone C (on one side of the centerline) or beyond.
Rule 3:   Six points in a row steadily increasing or decreasing: No sequence of six points steadily increase or decrease.
Rule 4:   Fourteen points in a row alternating up and down: This pattern does not exist.

This process appears to be in control.

For the $\bar{x}$ -chart: To determine if the process is in or out of control, we check the six rules:

Rule 1:   One point beyond Zone A: One point is beyond Zone A.
Rule 2:   Nine points in a row in Zone C or beyond: No sequence of nine points are in Zone C (on one side of the centerline) or beyond.
Rule 3:   Six points in a row steadily increasing or decreasing: No sequence of six points steadily increase or decrease.
Rule 4:   Fourteen points in a row alternating up and down: This pattern does not exist.
Rule 5:   Two out of three points in Zone A or beyond: There are two sets of three consecutive points (data points 3, 4, and 5 and data points 4, 5, and 6) that have two points in Zone A or beyond.
Rule 6:   Four out of five points in a row in Zone B or beyond: No sequence of five points has four or more in Zone B or beyond.

Special causes of variation appear to be present. The process appears to be out of control. Rules 1 and 5 indicate the process is out of control.

d.   Since the process is out of control, these control limits should not be used to monitor future process outputs.

13.89   a.   For each sample, we compute $\bar{x} = \dfrac{\sum x}{n}$ and R = range = largest measurement - smallest measurement.

The results are listed in the table:

Sample No.	$\bar{x}$	R	Sample No.	$\bar{x}$	R
1	4.36	7.1	11	3.32	4.8
2	5.10	7.7	12	4.02	4.8
3	4.52	5.0	13	5.24	7.8
4	3.42	5.8	14	3.58	3.9
5	2.62	6.2	15	3.48	5.5
6	3.94	3.9	16	5.00	3.0
7	2.34	5.3	17	3.68	6.2
8	3.26	3.2	18	2.68	3.9
9	4.06	8.0	19	3.66	4.4
10	4.96	7.1	20	4.10	5.5

$$\bar{\bar{x}} = \frac{\bar{x}_1 + \bar{x}_2 + \cdots + \bar{x}_{20}}{k} = \frac{77.34}{20} = 3.867 \qquad \bar{R} = \frac{R_1 + R_2 + \cdots + R_{20}}{k} = \frac{109.1}{20} = 5.455$$

First, we construct an R-chart.

$$Centerline = \bar{R} = 5.455$$

From Table IX, Appendix D, with $n = 5, D_3 = 0.000,$ and $D_4 = 2.114$.

$$Upper\ control\ limit = \bar{R}D_4 = 5.455(2.114) = 11.532$$

Since $D_3 = 0$, the lower control limit is negative and is not included on the chart.

$$Upper\ A\text{–}B\ boundary = \bar{R} + 2d_3\frac{\bar{R}}{d_2} = 5.455 + 2(.864)\frac{(5.455)}{2.326} = 9.508$$

$$Lower\ A\text{–}B\ boundary = \bar{R} - 2d_3\frac{\bar{R}}{d_2} = 5.455 - 2(.864)\frac{(5.455)}{2.326} = 1.402$$

$$Upper\ B\text{–}C\ boundary = \bar{R} + d_3\frac{\bar{R}}{d_2} = 5.455 + (.864)\frac{(5.455)}{2.326} = 7.481$$

$$Lower\ B\text{–}C\ boundary = \bar{R} - d_3\frac{\bar{R}}{d_2} = 5.455 - (.864)\frac{(5.455)}{2.326} = 3.429$$

The R-chart is:

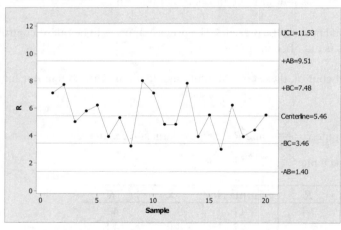

b.   To determine if the process is in or out of control, we check the four rules:

Rule 1:   One point beyond Zone A: No points are beyond Zone A.
Rule 2:   Nine points in a row in Zone C or beyond: No sequence of nine points are in Zone C (on one side of the centerline) or beyond.
Rule 3:   Six points in a row steadily increasing or decreasing: No sequence of six points steadily increase or decrease.
Rule 4:   Fourteen points in a row alternating up and down: This pattern does not exist.

The process appears to be in control. Since the process variation is in control, it is appropriate to construct the $\bar{x}$-chart.

c.   In order for the $\bar{x}$-chart to be valid, the process variation must be in control. The R-chart checks to see if the process variation is in control. For more details, see the answer to Exercise 13.24.

d. To construct an $\bar{x}$-chart, we first calculate the following:

$$\bar{\bar{x}} = \frac{\bar{x}_1 + \bar{x}_2 + \cdots + \bar{x}_{20}}{k} = \frac{77.24}{20} = 3.867 \qquad \bar{R} = \frac{R_1 + R_2 + \cdots + R_{20}}{k} = \frac{109.1}{20} = 5.4557$$

Centerline $= \bar{\bar{x}} = 3.867$

From Table IX, Appendix D, with $n = 5$, $A_2 = .577$.

Upper control limit $= \bar{\bar{x}} + A_2\bar{R} = 3.867 + .577(5.455) = 7.015$

Lower control limit $= \bar{\bar{x}} - A_2\bar{R} = 3.867 - .577(5.455) = .719$

Upper A–B boundary $= \bar{\bar{x}} + \frac{2}{3}(A_2\bar{R}) = 3.867 + \frac{2}{3}(.577)(5.455) = 5.965$

Lower A–B boundary $= \bar{\bar{x}} - \frac{2}{3}(A_2\bar{R}) = 3.867 - \frac{2}{3}(.577)(5.455) = 1.769$

Upper B–C boundary $= \bar{\bar{x}} + \frac{1}{3}(A_2\bar{R}) = 3.867 + \frac{2}{3}(.577)(5.455) = 4.916$

Lower B–C boundary $= \bar{\bar{x}} - \frac{1}{3}(A_2\bar{R}) = 3.867 - \frac{2}{3}(.577)(5.455) = 2.818$

The $\bar{x}$-chart is:

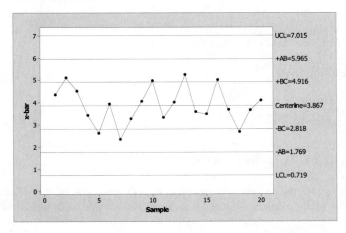

e. To determine if the process is in or out of control, we check the six rules:

Rule 1: One point beyond Zone A: No points are beyond Zone A.

Rule 2: Nine points in a row in Zone C or beyond: No sequence of nine points are in Zone C (on one side of the centerline) or beyond.

Rule 3: Six points in a row steadily increasing or decreasing: No sequence of six points steadily increases or decreases.

Rule 4: Fourteen points in a row alternating up and down: This pattern does not exist.

Rule 5: Two out of three points in Zone A or beyond: There are no groups of three consecutive points that have two or more in Zone A or beyond.

Rule 6:   Four out of five points in a row in Zone B or beyond: No sequence of five points has four or more in Zone B or beyond.

The process appears to be in control.

f.   Since both the R-chart and the $\bar{x}$-chart are in control, these control limits should be used to monitor future process output.

g.   A capability analysis diagram is:

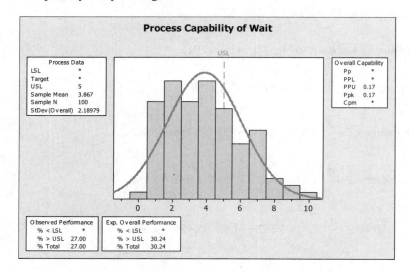

h.   For an upper specification limit of 5, there are 27 observations above this limit. Thus, $(27/100)\times100\% = 27\%$ of the observations are unacceptable. It does not appear that the process is capable.

i.   It is appropriate to estimate C_P because the process is in control.

From the sample, $\bar{x} = 3.867$ and $s = 2.190$

$$C_p = \frac{USL - LSL}{6s} \approx \frac{5-0}{6(2.19)} = \frac{5}{13.14} = .381$$

Since the C_P value is less than 1, the process is not capable.

j.   There is no lower specification limit because management has no time limit below which is unacceptable. The variable being measured is time customers wait in line. The actual lower limit would be 0.

13.91 a. The capability analysis diagram is:

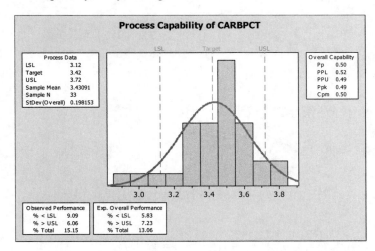

b. Two observations are above the upper specification limit and three observations are below the lower specification limit. Thus, the proportion of measurements that fall outside the specifications is $5/33 = .1515$.

c. From the sample, $\bar{x} = 3.43$ and $s = .1982$.

$$C_p = \frac{\text{USL} - \text{LSL}}{6\sigma} = \frac{3.72 - 3.12}{6(.1982)} = \frac{.6}{1.1892} = .505$$

Since the C_p value is less than 1, the process is not capable.

13.93 First, we must compute the range for each sample. The range $= R =$ largest measurement $-$ smallest measurement. The results are listed in the table:

Sample No.	R	Sample No.	R	Sample No.	R	Sample No.	R
1	2.0	19	4.8	37	10.2	55	2.2
2	2.1	20	5.4	38	5.5	56	3.6
3	1.8	21	5.5	39	4.7	57	2.6
4	1.6	22	3.8	40	4.7	58	2.0
5	3.1	23	3.6	41	3.6	59	1.5
6	3.1	24	2.5	42	3.0	60	6.0
7	4.2	25	4.6	43	2.2	61	5.7
8	3.6	26	3.0	44	3.3	62	5.6
9	4.6	27	3.4	45	3.2	63	2.3
10	2.6	28	2.3	46	0.8	64	2.3
11	3.5	29	2.2	47	4.2	65	2.6
12	5.3	30	3.3	48	5.6	66	3.8
13	5.5	31	3.6	49	4.0	67	2.8
14	5.6	32	4.2	50	4.9	68	2.2
15	4.6	33	2.4	51	3.8	69	4.2
16	3.0	34	4.5	52	4.6	70	2.6
17	4.6	35	5.6	53	7.1	71	1.0
18	4.5	36	4.9	54	4.6	72	1.9

$$\bar{\bar{x}} = \frac{\bar{x}_1 + \bar{x}_2 + \cdots + \bar{x}_{72}}{k} = \frac{3537.3}{72} = 49.129 \qquad \bar{R} = \frac{R_1 + R_1 + \cdots + R_{72}}{k} = \frac{268.8}{72} = 3.733$$

Centerline $= \bar{\bar{x}} = 49.129$

From Table IX, Appendix D, with $n = 6$, $A_2 = .483$.

Upper control limit $= \bar{\bar{x}} + A_2\bar{R} = 49.129 + .483(3.733) = 50.932$

Lower control limit $= \bar{\bar{x}} - A_2\bar{R} = 49.129 - .483(3.733) = 47.326$

Upper A–B *boundary* $= \bar{\bar{x}} + \frac{2}{3}\left(A_2\bar{R}\right) = 49.129 + \frac{2}{3}(.483)(3.733) = 50.331$

Lower A–B *boundary* $= \bar{\bar{x}} - \frac{2}{3}\left(A_2\bar{R}\right) = 49.129 - \frac{2}{3}(.483)(3.733) = 47.927$

Upper B–C *boundary* $= \bar{\bar{x}} + \frac{1}{3}\left(A_2\bar{R}\right) = 49.129 + \frac{1}{3}(.483)(3.733) = 49.730$

Lower B–C *boundary* $= \bar{\bar{x}} - \frac{1}{3}\left(A_2\bar{R}\right) = 49.129 - \frac{1}{3}(.483)(3.733) = 48.528$

The $\bar{x}$-chart is:

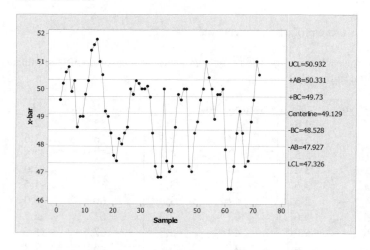

To determine if the process is in or out of control, we check the six rules:

Rule 1:   One point beyond Zone A: There are a total of 17 points beyond Zone A.
Rule 2:   Nine points in a row in Zone C or beyond: No sequence of nine points are in Zone C (on one side of the centerline) or beyond.
Rule 3:   Six points in a row steadily increasing or decreasing: There is one sequence of seven points that are steadily increasing—Points 15 through 21.
Rule 4:   Fourteen points in a row alternating up and down: This pattern does not exist.
Rule 5:   Two out of three points in Zone A or beyond: There are four groups of at least three points in Zone A or beyond—Points 12–16, Points 35–37, Points 39–41, and Points 60–63.

Rule 6:   Four out of five points in a row in Zone B or beyond: There are several groups of points that satisfy this rule.

The process appears to be out of control. Rules 1, 3, 5, and 6 indicate that the process is out of control.

No. The problem does not give the times of the shifts. However, suppose we let the first shift be from 6:00 A.M. to 2:00 P.M., the second shift be from 2:00 P.M. to 10:00 P.M., and the third shift be from 10:00 P.M. to 6:00 A.M. If this is the case, the major problems are during the second shift.

Chapter 14
Time Series: Descriptive Analyses, Models, and Forecasting

14.1   To calculate a simple index number, first obtain the prices or quantities over a time period and select a base year. For each time period, the index number is the number at that time period divided by the value at the base period multiplied by 100.

14.3   A Laspeyres index uses the purchase quantity at the base period as the weights for all other time periods. A Paasche index uses the purchase quantity at each time period as the weight for that time period. The weights at the specified time period are also used with the base period to find the index.

14.5   a.   To find Laspeyres index, we use the quantities for the base period as the weights. We multiply the quantity for quarter 1 times the prices for quarters 1 and 4 for each product (A, B, or C). We then sum the products for both time periods. Finally, we divide the sum for quarter 4 by the sum for quarter 1. The sum of the products for quarter 1 is
$100(3.25) + 20(1.75) + 50(8.00) = 325 + 35 + 400 = 760$. The sum of the products for quarter 4 is
$100(4.25) + 20(1.00) + 50(10.50) = 425 + 20 + 525 = 970$. Laspeyres index is $(970 / 760) \times 100 = 127.63$.

       b.   To find Paasche index, we use the quantities for all time periods as weights. We multiple the quantity for each quarter and each product by the corresponding price. We then sum these products for the base period quarter 2 and the quarter for which we want to compute Paasche's index (quarter 4). The sum for quarter 2 is $300(3.50) + 100(1.25) + 20(9.35) = 1050 + 125 + 107 = 1362$. The sum of the products for quarter 4 is $300(4.25) + 100(1.00) + 20(10.50) = 1275 + 100 + 210 = 1585$. Paasche's index is
$(1585 / 1362) \times 100 = 116.37$.

14.7   a.   To find the simple index, divide each value by the value for the base year and multiply by 100. The index numbers are:

Year	Simple Index (Base Year = 2004)	Simple Index (Base Year = 2010)
2004	$(5.83/5.83) \times 100 = 100.00$	$(5.83/10.13) \times 100 = 57.55$
2005	$(6.29/5.83) \times 100 = 107.89$	$(6.29/10.13) \times 100 = 62.09$
2006	$(7.10/5.83) \times 100 = 121.78$	$(7.10/10.13) \times 100 = 70.09$
2007	$(7.98/5.83) \times 100 = 136.88$	$(7.98/10.13) \times 100 = 78.78$
2008	$(8.49/5.83) \times 100 = 145.63$	$(8.49/10.13) \times 100 = 83.81$
2009	$(9.07/5.83) \times 100 = 155.57$	$(9.07/10.13) \times 100 = 89.54$
2010	$(10.13/5.83) \times 100 = 173.76$	$(10.13/10.13) \times 100 = 100.00$
2011	$(11.46/5.83) \times 100 = 196.57$	$(11.46/10.13) \times 100 = 113.13$
2012	$(13.24/5.83) \times 100 = 227.10$	$(13.24/10.13) \times 100 = 130.70$
2013	$(15.51/5.83) \times 100 = 266.04$	$(15.51/10.13) \times 100 = 153.11$
2014	$(22.16/5.83) \times 100 = 380.10$	$(22.16/10.13) \times 100 = 218.76$
2015	$(24.52/5.83) \times 100 = 420.58$	$(24.52/10.13) \times 100 = 242.05$

The index value for 2015 is 420.58 when the base is 2004. Thus, the craft beer production for 2015 increased by $420.58 - 100 = 320.58\%$ over craft beer production in 2004.

b.   This is a quantity index.

c.   The values of the simple index using 2010 as the base are listed in the table in part a. Using MINITAB, the graph of the indeces is:

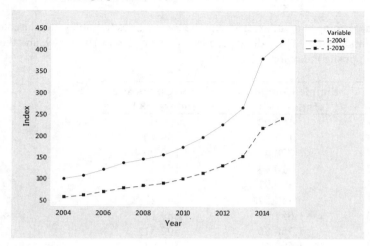

Both indieces increase over tmie. Both increase at an increasing rate.

14.9   a.   To compute the simple index, divide each spot price value by the 1997 value, 2.49 and then multiply by 100.

Year	Simple Index		Year	Simple Index	
1997	$(2.49/2.49) \times 100 =$	100.00	2007	$(6.97/2.49) \times 100 =$	279.92
1998	$(2.09/2.49) \times 100 =$	83.94	2008	$(8.86/2.49) \times 100 =$	355.82
1999	$(2.27/2.49) \times 100 =$	91.16	2009	$(3.94/2.49) \times 100 =$	158.23
2000	$(4.31/2.49) \times 100 =$	173.09	2010	$(4.37/2.49) \times 100 =$	175.50
2001	$(3.96/2.49) \times 100 =$	159.04	2011	$(4.00/2.49) \times 100 =$	160.64
2002	$(3.38/2.49) \times 100 =$	135.74	2012	$(2.75/2.49) \times 100 =$	110.44
2003	$(5.47/2.49) \times 100 =$	219.68	2013	$(3.73/2.49) \times 100 =$	149.80
2004	$(5.89/2.49) \times 100 =$	236.55	2014	$(4.37/2.49) \times 100 =$	175.50
2005	$(8.69/2.49) \times 100 =$	349.00	2015	$(2.62/2.49) \times 100 =$	105.22
2006	$(6.73/2.49) \times 100 =$	270.28			

The plot of the simple index is:

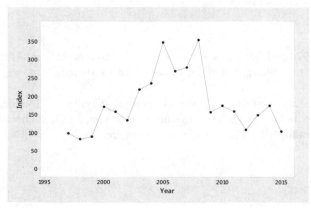

b.   The gas price of natural gas basically increased from 1995 to 2005, remained fairly high from 2005 to 2008, and thenbasically decreased to 2015.

c.   This is a price index because the values used were the spot prices of natural gas.

14.11   a.   To compute the simple composite index, first sum the three values (durables, nondurables, and services) for every time period. Then, divide each sum by the sum in 1970, 649, and then multiply by 100. The simple composite index for 1970 is:

Year	Sum	Simple Composite Index-1970	Simple Composite Index-1980
1970	649	100.00	36.98
1975	1,025	157.94	58.40
1980	1,755	270.42	100.00
1985	2,667	410.94	151.97
1990	3,835	590.91	218.52
1995	4,988	768.57	284.22
2000	6,830	1,052.39	389.17
2005	8,819	1,358.86	502.51
2010	10,348	1,594.45	589.63
2015	12,276	1,891.53	699.49

b.   To update the 1970 index to the 1980 index, divide the 1970 index values by the 1970 index value for 1980, 270.42, and then multiply by 100. The 1980 simple composite index is also listed in the table in part **a**.

c.   The graph of the two indices is:

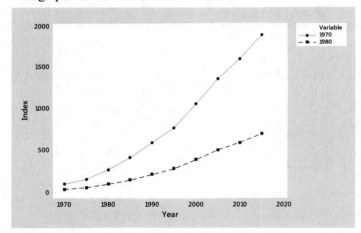

Changing the base year from 1970 to 1980 flattens out the graph. Also, the spread of the values for the 1980 index is much smaller than the spread of the values in the 1970 index.

14.13   a.   To compute the simple index for the men data, divide each men value by the 2007 value, 766, and then multiply by 100. To compute the simple index for the women data, divide each women value by the 2007 value, 614, and then multiply by 100.   The two indices are:

Year	Men Index		Women Index	
2007	$(766/766) \times 100=$	100.00	$(614/614) \times 100=$	100.00
2008	$(798/766) \times 100=$	104.18	$(638/614) \times 100=$	103.91
2009	$(819/766) \times 100=$	106.92	$(657/614) \times 100=$	107.00
2010	$(824/766) \times 100=$	107.57	$(670/614) \times 100=$	109.12
2011	$(831/766) \times 100=$	108.49	$(683/614) \times 100=$	111.24
2012	$(854/766) \times 100=$	111.49	$(691/614) \times 100=$	112.54
2013	$(861/766) \times 100=$	112.40	$(706/614) \times 100=$	114.98
2014	$(870/766) \times 100=$	113.58	$(719/614) \times 100=$	117.10
2015	$(894/766) \times 100=$	116.71	$(726/614) \times 100=$	118.24

b.   The graph of the two indices is:

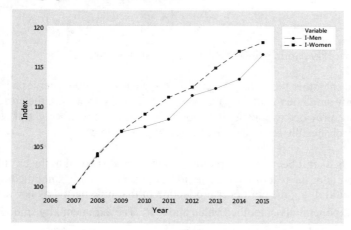

The wekly earnings for women increased at a faster rate than the weekly earnings for men.

c.   To compute the simple composite index, first sum the two values (men and women) for every time period. Then, divide each sum by the sum in 2007 (1,380) and then multiply by 100. The simple composite index is:

Year	Sum	Simple Composite Index	
2007	1,380	$(1,380/1,380) \times 100=$	100.00
2008	1,436	$(1,436/1,380) \times 100=$	104.06
2009	1,476	$(1,476/1,380) \times 100=$	106.96
2010	1,494	$(1,494/1,380) \times 100=$	108.26
2011	1,514	$(1,514/1,380) \times 100=$	109.71
2012	1,545	$(1,545/1,380) \times 100=$	111.96
2013	1,567	$(1,567/1,380) \times 100=$	113.55
2014	1,589	$(1,589/1,380) \times 100=$	115.14
2015	1,620	$(1,620/1,380) \times 100=$	117.39

d.   The graph of the index is:

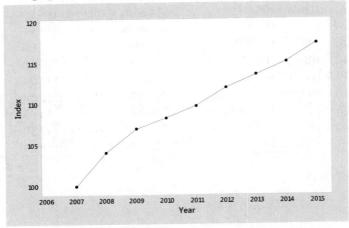

From 2007 to 2015, the weekly earnings increased at a fairly steady rate.

14.15   The smaller the value of w, the smoother the series. With $w = .2$, the current value receives a weight of .2 while the previous exponentially smoothed value receives a weight of .8. With $w = .8$, the current value receives a weight of .8 while the previous exponentially smoothed value receives a weight of .2. The smaller the value of w, the less chance the series can be affected by large jumps.

14.17   a.   The exponentially smoothed craft beer production for the first period is equal to the craft beer production for that period. For the rest of the time periods, the exponentially smoothed craft beer production is found by multiplying the craft beer production of that time period by $w = .2$ and adding to that $(1-.2)$ times the exponentially smoothed value above it. The exponentially smoothed value for the second period is $.2(6.29)+(1-.2)(5.83)=5.922$.

The rest of the values are shown in the following table.

Year	Craft Beer Production	Exponentially Smoothed Production $w = .2$	Exponentially Smoothed Production $w = .8$
2004	5.83	5.830	5.830
2005	6.29	5.922	6.198
2006	7.10	6.158	6.920
2007	7.98	6.522	7.768
2008	8.49	6.916	8.346
2009	9.07	7.347	8.925
2010	10.13	7.903	9.889
2011	11.46	8.615	11.146
2012	13.24	9.540	12.821
2013	15.51	10.734	14.972
2014	22.16	13.019	20.722
2015	24.52	15.319	23.760

b.   The exponentially smoothed craft beer production for the first period is equal to the craft beer production for that period. For the rest of the time periods, the exponentially smoothed craft beer production is found by multiplying $w = .8$ times the beer production of that time period and adding to that $(1-.8)$ times the value of the exponentially smoothed beer production figure of the previous time period. The exponentially smoothed beer production for the second time period is $.8(194)+(1-.8)(188)=192.8$. The rest of the values are shown in the table in part **a**.

c.   The plot of the two series is:

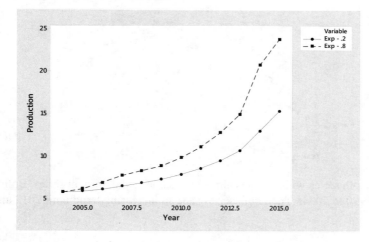

Because the craft beer production is steadily increasing, the exponentially smoothed series with $w=.8$ better represents the actual craft beer production than the series with $w=.2$. Thus, the series with $w=.8$ best portrays the long-term trend.

14.19   a.   The exponentially smoothed gold price for the first period is equal to the gold price for that period. For the rest of the time periods, the exponentially smoothed gold price is found by multiplying the price for the time period by $w=.8$ and adding to that $(1-.8)$ times the exponentially smoothed value from the previous time period. The exponentially smoothed value for the second time period is $.8(362)+(1-.8)(384)=366.40$. The rest of the values are shown in the table.

Year	Price	Exponentially Smoothed $w=.8$	Year	Price	Exponentially Smoothed $w=.8$
1990	384	384.00	2003	363	350.91
1991	362	366.40	2004	410	398.18
1992	344	348.48	2005	445	435.64
1993	360	357.70	2006	603	569.53
1994	384	378.74	2007	695	669.91
1995	384	382.95	2008	872	831.58
1996	388	386.99	2009	972	943.92
1997	331	342.20	2010	1,225	1,168.78
1998	294	303.64	2011	1,572	1,491.36
1999	279	283.93	2012	1,669	1,633.47
2000	279	279.99	2013	1,411	1,455.49
2001	271	272.80	2014	1,267	1,304.70
2002	310	302.56	2015	1,160	1,188.94

b.   The plot of the two series is:

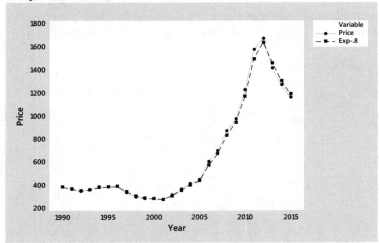

The exponentially smooth series with $w = .8$ is almost the same as the original series. Both series are fairly constant from 1990 to 2004. Then both series start an increasing trend until 2012 and then start a decreasing trend.

14.21   a.   The exponentially smoothed imports for the first period is equal to the imports that period. For the rest of the time periods, the exponentially smoothed imports is found by multiplying $w = .1$ times the imports for that time period and adding to that $(1-.1)$ times the value of the exponentially smoothed imports figure of the previous time period. The exponentially smoothed imports for the second time period is $.1(1,541) + (1-.1)(1,544) = 1,543.70$. The rest of the values are shown in the table.

The same procedure is followed for $w = .9$. The exponentially smoothed imports/exports for the second time period is $.9(1,541) + (1-.9)(1,544) = 1,541.30$. The rest of the values are shown in the table.

Year	t	Imports	Exponentially Smoothed $w = .1$	Exponentially Smoothed $w = .9$
1995	1	1,544	1,544.00	1,544.00
1996	2	1,541	1,543.70	1,541.30
1997	3	1,668	1,556.13	1,655.33
1998	4	1,790	1,579.52	1,776.53
1999	5	1,808	1,602.37	1,804.85
2000	6	1,904	1,632.53	1,894.09
2001	7	2,018	1,671.08	2,005.61
2002	8	1,681	1,672.07	1,713.46
2003	9	1,884	1,693.26	1,866.95
2004	10	2,086	1,732.54	2,064.09
2005	11	2,039	1,763.18	2,041.51
2006	12	2,014	1,788.26	2,016.75
2007	13	2,183	1,827.74	2,166.38
2008	14	2,179	1,862.86	2,177.74
2009	15	1,743	1,850.88	1,786.47
2010	16	1,791	1,844.89	1,790.55
2011	17	1,663	1,826.70	1,675.75

2012	18	1,563	1,800.33	1,574.28
2013	19	1,358	1,756.10	1,379.63
2014	20	1,181	1,698.59	1,200.86
2015	21	1,058	1,634.53	1,072.29

b.   The plot of the three series is:

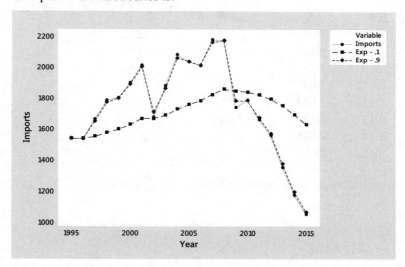

The exponentially smoothed series with $w = .9$ looks more like the original series. The closer w is to 1 the closer the exponentially smoothed curve looks like the original.

14.23   If w is small (near 0), one will obtain a smooth, slowly changing series of forecasts. If w is large (near 1), one will obtain more rapidly changing forecasts that depend mostly on the current values of the series.

14.25   a.   We first compute the exponentially smoothed values $E_1, E_2, \ldots, E_t$ for years 2004 – 2013.

$E_1 = Y_1 = 5.83$

For $w = .3$, $E_2 = wY_2 + (1-w)E_1 = .3(6.29) + (1-.3)(5.83) = 5.968$
$E_3 = wY_3 + (1-w)E_2 = .3(7.10) + (1-.3)(5.968) = 6.308$

The rest of the values appear in the table.

For $w = .7$, $E_2 = wY_2 + (1-w)E_1 = .7(6.29) + (1-.7)(5.83) = 6.152$
$E_3 = wY_3 + (1-w)E_2 = .7(7.10) + (1-.7)(6.152) = 6.816$

The rest of the values appear in the table.

Year	Beer	Exponentially Smoothed $w = .3$	Exponentially Smoothed $w = .7$
2004	5.83	5.830	5.830
2005	6.29	5.968	6.152
2006	7.10	6.308	6.816
2007	7.98	6.809	7.631
2008	8.49	7.314	8.232
2009	9.07	7.840	8.819
2010	10.13	8.527	9.737
2011	11.46	9.407	10.943
2012	13.24	10.557	12.551
2013	15.51	12.043	14.622
2014	22.16		
2015	24.52		

To forecast using exponentially smoothed values, we use the following:

For $w = .3$:

$$F_{2014} = F_{t+1} = E_t = 12.043$$
$$F_{2015} = F_{t+2} = F_{t+1} = 12.043$$

For $w = .7$:

$$F_{2014} = F_{t+1} = E_t = 14.622$$
$$F_{2015} = F_{t+2} = F_{t+1} = 14.622$$

b. We first compute the Holt-Winters values for the years 2004-2013.

With $w = .7$ and $v = .3$,

$$E_2 = Y_2 = 6.29$$
$$E_3 = wY_3 + (1-w)(E_2 + T_2) = .7(7.10) + (1-.7)(6.29 + .46) = 6.995$$

$$T_2 = Y_2 - Y_1 = 6.29 - 5.83 = .46$$
$$T_3 = v(E_3 - E_2) + (1-v)T_2 = .3(6.995 - 6.290) + (1-.3)(.46) = .534$$

The rest of the E_t's and T_t's appear in the table that follows.

With $w = .3$ and $v = .7$,

$$E_2 = Y_2 = 6.29$$
$$E_3 = wY_3 + (1-w)(E_2 + T_2) = .3(7.10) + (1-.3)(6.29 + .46) = 6.855$$

$$T_2 = Y_2 - Y_1 = 6.29 - 5.83 = .46$$
$$T_3 = v(E_3 - E_2) + (1-v)T_2 = .7(6.855 - 6.290) + (1-.7)(.46) = .534$$

The rest of the E_t's and T_t's appear in the table that follows.

		Holt-Winters		Holt-Winters	
		E_t	T_t	E_t	T_t
Year	Beer	$w = .7$	$v = .3$	$w = .3$	$v = .7$
2004	5.83				
2005	6.29	6.290	0.460	6.290	0.460
2006	7.10	6.995	0.534	6.855	0.534
2007	7.98	7.845	0.628	7.566	0.658
2008	8.49	8.485	0.632	8.304	0.714
2009	9.07	9.084	0.622	9.033	0.725
2010	10.13	10.003	0.711	9.869	0.803
2011	11.46	11.236	0.868	10.909	0.968
2012	13.24	12.899	1.106	12.286	1.255
2013	15.51	15.059	1.422	14.131	1.668
2014	22.16				
2015	24.52				

To forecast using the Holt-Winters Model:

For $w = .7$ and $v = .3$,

$$F_{2014} = F_{t+1} = E_t + T_t = 15.059 + 1.422 = 16.481$$
$$F_{2015} = F_{t+2} = E_t + 2T_t = 15.059 + 2(1.422) = 17.903$$

For $w = .3$ and $v = .7$,

$$F_{2014} = F_{t+1} = E_t + T_t = 14.131 + 1.668 = 15.799$$
$$F_{2015} = F_{t+2} = E_t + 2T_t = 14.131 + 2(1.668) = 17.468$$

14.27   a.   Using MINITAB, the time series plot is:

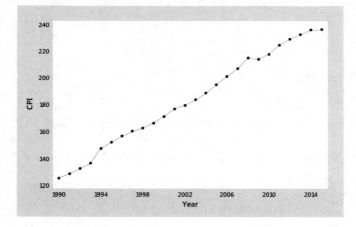

There appears to be an increasing trend in CPI over time.

   b.   To compute the exponentially smoothed values, we follow these steps:

$$E_1 = Y_1 = 125.8$$

$$E_2 = wY_2 + (1-w)E_1 = .4(129.1) + (1-.4)(125.8) = 127.12$$
$$E_3 = wY_3 + (1-w)E_2 = .4(132.8) + (1-.4)(127.12) = 129.39$$

The rest of the values are computed in a similar manner and are listed in the table:

Year	CPI	Exponentially Smoothed $w = .4$	Year	CPI	Exponentially Smoothed $w = .4$
1990	125.8	125.80	2003	184.0	177.97
1991	129.1	127.12	2004	188.9	182.34
1992	132.8	129.39	2005	195.3	187.53
1993	136.8	132.36	2006	201.6	193.16
1994	147.8	138.53	2007	207.3	198.81
1995	152.4	144.08	2008	215.3	205.41
1996	156.9	149.21	2009	214.5	209.04
1997	160.5	153.72	2010	218.1	212.67
1998	163.0	157.43	2011	224.9	217.56
1999	166.6	161.10	2012	229.6	222.38
2000	171.5	165.26	2013	233.0	226.63
2001	177.1	170.00	2014	236.7	230.66
2002	179.9	173.96	2015	237.0	233.19

Using MINITAB, the plot is:

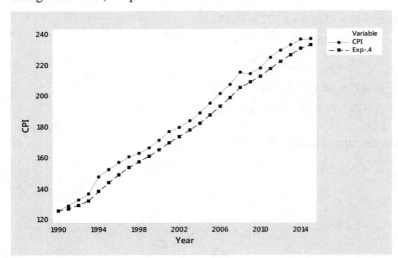

To forecast using exponentially smoothed values, we use the following: $F_{2016} = F_{t+1} = E_t = 233.19$

c.   We first compute the Holt-Winters values for the years 1990-2010. With $w = .4$ and $v = .5$,

$$E_2 = Y_2 = 129.1$$
$$E_3 = wY_3 + (1-w)(E_2 + T_2) = .4(132.8) + (1-.4)(129.1 + 3.3) = 132.56$$

$$T_2 = Y_2 - Y_1 = 129.1 - 125.8 = 3.3$$
$$T_3 = v(E_3 - E_2) + (1-v)T_2 = .5(132.56 - 129.1) + (1-.5)(3.3) = 3.38$$

The rest of the E_t's and T_t's appear in the table that follows.

| | | Holt-Winters | |
| | | E_t | T_t |
Year	CPI	$w = .4$	$v = .5$
1990	125.8		
1991	129.1	129.10	3.30
1992	132.8	132.56	3.38
1993	136.8	136.28	3.55
1994	147.8	143.02	5.14
1995	152.4	149.86	5.99
1996	156.9	156.27	6.20
1997	160.5	161.68	5.81
1998	163.0	165.69	4.91
1999	166.6	169.00	4.11
2000	171.5	172.47	3.79
2001	177.1	176.59	3.96
2002	179.9	180.29	3.83
2003	184.0	184.07	3.80
2004	188.9	188.28	4.01
2005	195.3	193.50	4.61
2006	201.6	199.50	5.31
2007	207.3	205.81	5.81
2008	215.3	213.09	6.54
2009	214.5	217.58	5.52
2010	218.1	221.10	4.52
2011	224.9	225.33	4.37
2012	229.6	229.66	4.35
2013	233.0	233.61	4.15
2014	236.7	237.34	3.94
2015	237.0	239.56	3.08

To forecast using the Holt-Winters Model:

For $w = .4$ and $v = .5$, $\quad F_{2016} = F_{t+1} = E_t + T_t = 239.56 + 3.08 = 242.64$

14.29   a.   To compute the exponentially smoothed values, we follow these steps:

$$E_t = Y_1 = 1,322.7$$

For $w = .7$,

$$E_2 = wY_2 + (1-w)E_1 = .7(1,280.0) + (1-.7)(1,322.7) = 1,292.8$$
$$E_3 = wY_3 + (1-w)E_2 = .7(1,164.7) + (1-.7)(1,292.8) = 1,203.1$$

The rest of the values are computed in a similar manner and are listed in the table:

Year	Quarter	S&P 500	Exponentially Smoothed $w = .7$	Exponentially Smoothed $w = .3$
2008	1	1,322.7	1,322.7	1,322.7
	2	1,280.0	1,292.8	1,309.9
	3	1,164.7	1,203.1	1,266.3
	4	903.3	993.2	1,157.4
2009	1	797.9	856.5	1,049.6
	2	919.3	900.5	1,010.5
	3	1,057.1	1,010.1	1,024.5
	4	1,115.1	1,083.6	1,051.7
2010	1	1,169.4	1,143.7	1,087.0
	2	1,030.7	1,064.6	1,070.1
	3	1,141.2	1,118.2	1,091.4
	4	1,257.6	1,215.8	1,141.3
2011	1	1,325.8	1,292.8	1,196.6
	2	1,320.6	1,312.3	1,233.8
	3	1,131.4	1,185.7	1,203.1
	4	1,257.6	1,236.0	1,219.4
2012	1	1,348.8	1,315.0	1,258.3
	2	1,349.7	1,339.3	1,285.7
	3	1,400.9	1,382.4	1,320.3
	4	1,418.1	1,407.4	1,349.6
2013	1	1,514.0	1,482.0	1,398.9
	2	1,609.5	1,571.3	1,462.1
	3	1,674.9	1,643.8	1,525.9
	4	1,768.7	1,731.2	1,598.8
2014	1	1,834.9	1,803.8	1,669.6
	2	1,900.4	1,871.4	1,738.8
	3	1,975.9	1,944.6	1,810.0
	4	2,009.3	1,989.9	1,869.8
2015	1	2,063.7		
	2	2,101.8		
	3	2,027.2		
	4	2,052.3		

The forecasts using the exponentially smoothed values with $w = .7$ are:

$$F_{2015,1} = F_{t+1} = E_t = 1,989.9$$
$$F_{2015,2} = F_{t+2} = F_{t+1} = 1,989.9$$
$$F_{2015,3} = F_{t+3} = F_{t+1} = 1,989.9$$
$$F_{2015,4} = F_{t+4} = F_{t+1} = 1,989.9$$

b.   To compute the exponentially smoothed values, we follow these steps:

$$E_t = Y_1 = 1,322.7$$

For $w = .3$,

$$E_2 = wY_2 + (1-w)E_1 = .3(1,280.0) + (1-.3)(1,322.7) = 1,309.9$$
$$E_3 = wY_3 + (1-w)E_2 = .3(1,164.7) + (1-.3)(1,309.9) = 1,266.3$$

The rest of the values are computed in a similar manner and are listed in the table above.

The forecasts using the exponentially smoothed values with $w = .3$ are:

$$F_{2015,1} = F_{t+1} = E_t = 1,869.8$$
$$F_{2015,2} = F_{t+2} = F_{t+1} = 1,869.8$$
$$F_{2015,3} = F_{t+3} = F_{t+1} = 1,869.8$$
$$F_{2015,4} = F_{t+4} = F_{t+1} = 1,869.8$$

14.31   a.   We first compute the exponentially smoothed values $E_1, E_2, \ldots, E_t$ for 2009 through 2014.

$$E_1 = Y_1 = 858.70$$

For $w = .5$,

$$E_2 = wY_2 + (1-w)E_1 = .5(943.2) + (1-.5)(858.7) = 900.95$$
$$E_3 = wY_3 + (1-w)E_2 = .5(924.3) + (1-.5)(900.95) = 912.63$$

The rest of the values are found in the table:

		Gold	Exponentially Smoothed	Holt-Winters E_t	T_t
Year	Month	Price	$w=.5$	$w=.5$	$v=.5$
2009	Jan	858.7	858.70		
	Feb	943.2	900.95	943.20	84.50
	Mar	924.3	912.63	976.00	58.65
	Apr	890.2	901.41	962.43	22.54
	May	928.6	915.01	956.78	8.45
	Jun	945.7	930.35	955.46	3.56
	Jul	934.2	932.28	946.61	-2.64
	Aug	949.4	940.84	946.69	-1.29
	Sep	996.6	968.72	971.00	11.51
	Oct	1,043.2	1,005.96	1,012.86	26.69
	Nov	1,127.0	1,066.48	1,083.27	48.55
	Dec	1,134.7	1,100.59	1,133.26	49.27
2010	Jan	1,118.0	1,109.29	1,150.27	33.14
	Feb	1,095.4	1,102.35	1,139.40	11.14
	Mar	1,113.3	1,107.82	1,131.92	1.83
	Apr	1,148.7	1,128.26	1,141.22	5.57
	May	1,205.4	1,166.83	1,176.09	20.22
	Jun	1,232.9	1,199.87	1,214.61	29.37
	Jul	1,193.0	1,196.43	1,218.49	16.62
	Aug	1,215.8	1,206.12	1,225.45	11.80
	Sep	1,271.1	1,238.61	1,254.17	20.26
	Oct	1,342.0	1,290.30	1,308.22	37.15
	Nov	1,369.9	1,330.10	1,357.63	43.28

	Dec	1,390.6	1,360.35	1,395.76	40.70
2011	Jan	1,356.4	1,358.38	1,396.43	20.69
	Feb	1,372.7	1,365.54	1,394.91	9.58
	Mar	1,424.0	1,394.77	1,414.25	14.46
	Apr	1,473.8	1,434.28	1,451.25	25.73
	May	1,560.4	1,497.34	1,518.69	46.59
	Jun	1,528.7	1,513.02	1,546.99	37.44
	Jul	1,572.8	1,542.91	1,578.62	34.53
	Aug	1,755.8	1,649.36	1,684.47	70.20
	Sep	1,771.9	1,710.63	1,763.29	74.50
	Oct	1,665.2	1,687.91	1,751.49	31.36
	Nov	1,739.0	1,713.46	1,760.93	20.39
	Dec	1,652.3	1,682.88	1,716.81	-11.86
2012	Jan	1652.2	1,667.54	1,678.57	-25.05
	Feb	1742.1	1,704.82	1,697.81	-2.90
	Mar	1673.8	1,689.31	1,684.35	-8.18
	Apr	1649.7	1,669.50	1,662.94	-14.80
	May	1591.2	1,630.35	1,619.67	-29.03
	Jun	1598.8	1,614.58	1,594.72	-26.99
	Jul	1589.9	1,602.24	1,578.81	-21.45
	Aug	1630.3	1,616.27	1,593.83	-3.21
	Sep	1744.8	1,680.53	1,667.71	35.33
	Oct	1746.6	1,713.57	1,724.82	46.22
	Nov	1721.6	1,717.58	1,746.32	33.86
	Dec	1684.8	1,701.19	1,732.49	10.02
2013	Jan	1652.2	1,676.70	1,697.35	-12.56
	Feb	1742.1	1,709.40	1,713.45	1.77
	Mar	1673.8	1,691.60	1,694.51	-8.59
	Apr	1649.7	1,670.65	1,667.81	-17.64
	May	1591.2	1,630.92	1,620.68	-32.38
	Jun	1598.8	1,614.86	1,593.55	-29.76
	Jul	1589.9	1,602.38	1,576.85	-23.23
	Aug	1630.3	1,616.34	1,591.96	-4.06
	Sep	1744.8	1,680.57	1,666.35	35.17
	Oct	1746.6	1,713.59	1,724.06	46.44
	Nov	1721.6	1,717.59	1,746.05	34.21
	Dec	1684.8	1,701.20	1,732.53	10.35
2014	Jan	1652.2	1,676.70	1,697.54	-12.32
	Feb	1742.1	1,709.40	1,713.66	1.90
	Mar	1673.8	1,691.60	1,694.68	-8.54
	Apr	1649.7	1,670.65	1,667.92	-17.65
	May	1591.2	1,630.92	1,620.73	-32.42
	Jun	1598.8	1,614.86	1,593.56	-29.80
	Jul	1589.9	1,602.38	1,576.83	-23.26
	Aug	1630.3	1,616.34	1,591.93	-4.08
	Sep	1744.8	1,680.57	1,666.33	35.16
	Oct	1746.6	1,713.59	1,724.04	46.44
	Nov	1721.6	1,717.59	1,746.04	34.22

	Dec	1684.8	1,701.20	1,732.53	10.35
2015	Jan	1652.2	1,676.70	1,697.54	-12.32
	Feb	1742.1	1,709.40	1,713.66	1.90
	Mar	1673.8	1,691.60	1,694.68	-8.54
	Apr	1649.7	1,670.65	1,667.92	-17.65
	May	1591.2	1,630.92	1,620.74	-32.42
	Jun	1598.8	1,614.86	1,593.56	-29.80
	Jul	1589.9	1,602.38	1,576.83	-23.26
	Aug	1630.3	1,616.34	1,591.93	-4.08
	Sep	1744.8	1,680.57	1,666.33	35.16
	Oct	1746.6	1,713.59	1,724.04	46.44
	Nov	1721.6	1,717.59	1,746.04	34.22
	Dec	1684.8	1,701.20	1,732.53	10.35

To forecast the monthly prices for 2015 using the data through December 2014:

$$F_{t+1} = E_t \qquad F_{t+1} = F_{t+i} = E_t \text{ for } i = 2, 3, \dots$$
$$F_{t+1} = E_{\text{Dec},2014} = 1,701.20$$

Year	Month	Forecast
2015	Jan	1,701.20
	Feb	1,701.20
	Mar	1,701.20
	Apr	1,701.20
	May	1,701.20
	Jun	1,701.20
	Jul	1,701.20
	Aug	1,701.20
	Sep	1,701.20
	Oct	1,701.20
	Nov	1,701.20
	Dec	1,701.20

b.   To compute the one-step-ahead forecasts for 2015, we use $F_{t+1} = E_t$, where E_t is recomputed each time period (month). The forecasts are obtained from the table in part **a**.

Year	Month	Forecast
2015	Jan	1,701.20
	Feb	1,676.70
	Mar	1,709.40
	Apr	1,691.60
	May	1,670.65
	Jun	1,630.92
	Jul	1,614.86
	Aug	1,602.38
	Sep	1,616.34
	Oct	1,680.57
	Nov	1,713.59
	Dec	1,717.59

c.   First, we compute the Holt-Winters values for the years 2009-2014.

With $w = .5$ and $v = .5$,

$$E_2 = Y_2 = 943.2$$
$$E_3 = wY_3 + (1-w)(E_2 + T_2) = .5(924.3) + (1-.5)(943.2 + 84.5) = 976.0$$

$$T_2 = Y_2 - Y_1 = 943.2 - 858.7 = 84.5$$
$$T_3 = v(E_3 - E_2) + (1-v)T_2 = .5(976.00 - 943.20) + (1-.5)(84.5) = 58.65$$

The rest of the E_t's and T_t's appear in the table in part a.

To forecast the monthly prices for 2015 using the data through December 2014:

$$F_{t+1} = E_t + T_t = 1,732.53 + 10.35 = 1,742.88$$
$$F_{t+2} = E_t + 2T_t = 1,732.53 + 2(10.35) = 1,753.23$$
$$F_{t+n} = E_t + nT_t$$

The rest of the forecasts appear in the table:

Year	Month	Forecast
2015	Jan	1,742.88
	Feb	1,753.23
	Mar	1,763.59
	Apr	1,773.94
	May	1,784.29
	Jun	1,794.64
	Jul	1,804.99
	Aug	1,815.35
	Sep	1,825.70
	Oct	1,836.05
	Nov	1,846.40
	Dec	1,856.76

To compute the one-step-ahead forecasts for 2015, we use $F_{t+1} = E_t + T_t$ where E_t and T_t are recomputed each time period. The forecasts are obtained from the table in part **a**.

$$F_{Jan,2015} = E_{Dec, 2014} + T_{Dec, 2014} = 1,732.53 + 10.35 = 1,742.88$$
$$F_{Feb,2015} = E_{Jan, 2015} + T_{Jan, 2015} = 1,697.54 - 12.32 = 1,685.22$$

The rest of the values appear in the table:

Year	Month	Forecast
2015	Jan	1,742.88
	Feb	1,685.22
	Mar	1,715.56
	Apr	1,686.14
	May	1,650.27
	Jun	1,588.32
	Jul	1,563.76
	Aug	1,553.57
	Sep	1,587.85
	Oct	1,701.48
	Nov	1,770.48
	Dec	1,780.26

14.33   a.   From Exercise 14.25b, the Holt-Winters forecasts for 2014-2015 using $w = .3$ and $v = .7$ are:

$$F_{2014} = 16.481$$
$$F_{2015} = 17.903$$

The errors are the differences between the actual values and the predicted values. Thus, the errors are:

$$Y_{2014} - F_{2014} = 22.16 - 16.481 = 5.679$$
$$Y_{2015} - F_{2015} = 24.52 - 17.903 = 6.617$$

b.   From Exercise 14.25b, the Holt-Winters forecasts for 2014-2015 using $w = .7$ and $v = .3$ are:

$$F_{2014} = 15.799$$
$$F_{2015} = 17.468$$

The errors are:

$$Y_{2014} - F_{2014} = 22.16 - 15.799 = 6.361$$
$$Y_{2015} - F_{2015} = 24.52 - 17.468 = 7.052$$

c.   For the Holt-Winters forecasts with $w = .3$ and $v = .7$,

$$\text{MAD} = \frac{\sum_{t=11}^{12} |Y_t - F_t|}{m} = \frac{|22.16 - 16.481| + |24.52 - 17.903|}{2} = \frac{12.296}{2} = 6.148$$

$$\text{MAPE} = \left[\frac{\sum_{t=11}^{12} \left| \frac{(Y_t - F_t)}{Y_t} \right|}{m} \right] 100$$

$$= \left[\frac{\left| \frac{22.16 - 16.481}{22.16} \right| + \left| \frac{24.52 - 17.903}{24.52} \right|}{2} \right] 100 = \left[\frac{.52613}{2} \right] 100 = 26.307$$

$$\text{RMSE} = \sqrt{\frac{\sum_{t=11}^{12}(Y_t - F_t)^2}{m}} = \sqrt{\frac{(22.16 - 16.481)^2 + (24.52 - 17.903)^2}{2}}$$

$$= \sqrt{\frac{76.03573}{2}} = 6.166$$

d.   For the Holt-Winters forecasts with $w = .7$ and $v = .3$,

$$\text{MAD} = \frac{\sum_{t=11}^{12}|Y_t - F_t|}{m} = \frac{|22.16 - 15.799| + |24.52 - 17.468|}{2} = \frac{13.413}{2} = 6.707$$

$$\text{MAPE} = \left[\frac{\sum_{t=11}^{12}\left|\frac{(Y_t - F_t)}{Y_t}\right|}{m} \right] 100$$

$$= \left[\frac{\frac{|22.16 - 15.799|}{22.16} + \frac{|24.52 - 17.468|}{24.52}}{2} \right] 100 = \left[\frac{.57465}{2} \right] 100 = 28.733$$

$$\text{RMSE} = \sqrt{\frac{\sum_{t=11}^{12}(Y_t - F_t)^2}{m}} = \sqrt{\frac{(22.16 - 15.799)^2 + (24.52 - 17.468)^2}{2}}$$

$$= \sqrt{\frac{90.193025}{2}} = 6.715$$

e.   Two of the three measures of forecast accuracy for the Holt-Winters forecast with $w = .3$ and $v = .7$ are smaller than the corresponding values for the Holt-Winters forecast with $w = .7$ and $v = .3$. We recommend using the Holt-Winters forecast with $w = .3$ and $v = .7$.

14.35   a.   From Exercise 14.30, the forecasts for the 4 quarters of 2015 using the Holt-Winters forecasts with $w = .3$ and $v = .5$ are:

$$F_{2015,1} = 2,114.54$$
$$F_{2015,2} = 2,177.67$$
$$F_{2015,3} = 2,240.80$$
$$F_{2015,4} = 2,303.93$$

$$\text{MAD} = \frac{\sum_{t=29}^{32}|Y_t - F_t|}{m}$$

$$= \frac{|2,063.7 - 2,114.54| + |2,101.8 - 2,177.67| + |2,027.2 - 2,240.80| + |2,052.3 - 2,303.93|}{4}$$

$$= \frac{591.94}{4} = 147.985$$

$$\text{MAPE} = \left[\frac{\sum_{t=29}^{32} \left| \frac{(Y_t - F_t)}{Y_t} \right|}{m} \right] 100$$

$$= \left[\frac{\left| \frac{2,063.7 - 2,114.54}{2,063.7} \right| + \left| \frac{2,101.8 - 2,177.67}{2,101.8} \right| + \left| \frac{2,027.2 - 2,240.80}{2,027.2} \right| + \left| \frac{2,052.3 - 2,303.93}{2,052.3} \right|}{4} \right] 100$$

$$= \left[\frac{0.288709}{4} \right] 100 = 7.218$$

$$\text{RMSE} = \sqrt{\frac{\sum_{t=29}^{32} (Y_t - F_t)^2}{m}}$$

$$= \sqrt{\frac{(2,063.7 - 2,114.54)^2 + (2,101.8 - 2,177.67)^2 + (2,027.2 - 2,240.80)^2 + (2,052.3 - 2,303.93)^2}{4}}$$

$$= \sqrt{\frac{117,283.6}{4}} = 171.234$$

b. From Exercise 14.30, the forecasts for the 4 quarters of 2011 using the Holt-Winters forecasts with $w = .7$ and $v = .5$ are:

$$F_{2015,1} = 2,078.58$$
$$F_{2015,2} = 2,136.35$$
$$F_{2015,3} = 2,194.12$$
$$F_{2015,4} = 2,251.89$$

$$\text{MAD} = \frac{\sum_{t=29}^{32} |Y_t - F_t|}{m}$$

$$= \frac{|2,063.7 - 2,078.58| + |2,101.8 - 2,136.357| + |2,027.2 - 2,194.12| + |2,052.3 - 2,251.89|}{4}$$

$$= \frac{415.94}{4} = 103.985$$

$$\text{MAPE} = \left[\frac{\displaystyle\sum_{t=29}^{32}\left|\frac{(Y_t - F_t)}{Y_t}\right|}{m}\right]100$$

$$= \left[\frac{\left|\dfrac{2,063.7 - 2,078.58}{2,063.7}\right| + \left|\dfrac{2,101.8 - 2,136.35}{2,101.8}\right| + \left|\dfrac{2,027.2 - 2,194.120}{2,027.2}\right| + \left|\dfrac{2,052.3 - 2,251.89}{2,052.3}\right|}{4}\right]100$$

$$= \left[\frac{0.203241}{4}\right]100 = 5.081$$

$$\text{RMSE} = \sqrt{\frac{\displaystyle\sum_{t=29}^{32}(Y_t - F_t)^2}{m}}$$

$$= \sqrt{\frac{(2,063.7 - 2,078.58)^2 + (2,101.8 - 2,136.35)^2 + (2,027.2 - 2,194.12)^2 + (2,052.3 - 2,251.89)^2}{4}}$$

$$= \sqrt{\frac{69,113.57}{4}} = 131.4473$$

c. For all three measures of error, the Holt-Winters series with $w = .7$ and $v = .5$ is smaller than the Holt-Winters series with $w = .3$ and $v = .5$. Thus, the more accurate series would be the Holt-Winters series with $w = .7$ and $v = .5$.

14.37 a. To compute the exponentially smoothed values, we follow these steps:

$$E_1 = Y_1 = 60,267$$
$$E_2 = wY_2 + (1 - w)E_1 = .8(61,605) + (1 - .8)(60,267) = 61,337.4$$
$$E_3 = wY_3 + (1 - w)E_2 = .8(62,686) + (1 - .8)(61,337.4) = 62,416.3$$

The rest of the values are computed in a similar manner and are listed in the table:

| | | Exponentially Smoothed | Holt-Winters | |
| | | | Et | Tt |
Year	Enroll	w = .8	w = .8	v = .7
1990	60,267	60,267.0		
1991	61,605	61,337.4	61,605.0	1,338.0
1992	62,686	62,416.3	62,737.4	1,194.1
1993	63,241	63,076.1	63,379.1	807.4
1994	63,986	63,804.0	64,026.1	695.1
1995	64,764	64,572.0	64,755.4	719.1
1996	65,743	65,508.8	65,689.3	869.4
1997	66,470	66,277.8	66,487.7	819.7
1998	66,983	66,842.0	67,047.9	638.0
1999	67,667	67,502.0	67,670.8	627.4
2000	68,146	68,017.2	68,176.4	542.2
2001	69,936	69,552.2	69,692.5	1,223.9

2002	71,215	70,882.4	71,155.3	1,391.1
2003	71,442	71,330.1	71,662.9	772.6
2004	71,688	71,616.4	71,837.5	354.0
2005	72,075	71,983.3	72,098.3	288.8
2006	73,318	73,051.1	73,131.8	810.1
2007	73,685	73,558.2	73,736.4	666.2
2008	74,079	73,974.8	74,143.7	485.0
2009	77,288	76,625.4	76,756.1	1,974.2
2010	78,519	78,140.3	78,561.3	1,855.8
2011	79,043	78,862.5	79,317.8	1,086.3
2012	78,426			
2013	77,772			
2014	77,214			

The forecasts for 2012-2014 using the exponential smoothing series with $w = .8$ are:

$$F_{2012} = F_{t+1} = E_t = 78,862.5$$
$$F_{2013} = F_{t+2} = F_{t+1} = 78,862.5$$
$$F_{2014} = F_{t+3} = F_{t+1} = 78,862.5$$

b. To compute the Holt-Winters values with $w = .8$ and $v = .7$:

$$E_2 = Y_2 = 61,605$$
$$E_3 = wY_3 + (1-w)(E_2 + T_2) = .8(62,686) + (1-.8)(61,605 + 1,338) = 62,737.4$$

$$T_2 = Y_2 - Y_1 = 61,605 - 60,267 = 1,338$$
$$T_3 = v(E_3 - E_2) + (1-v)T_2 = .7(62,737.4 - 61,605) + (1-.7)(1,338) = 1,194.1$$

The rest of the E_t's and T_t's appear in the table in part a,

The forecasts for 2012-2014 using the Holt-Winters series with $w = .8$ and $v = .7$ are:

$$F_{2012} = F_{t+1} = E_t + T_t = 79,317.8 + 1,086.3 = 80,404.1$$
$$F_{2013} = F_{t+2} = E_t + 2T_t = 79,317.8 + 2(1,086.3) = 81,490.4$$
$$F_{2014} = F_{t+3} = E_t + 3T_t = 79,317.8 + 3(1,086.3) = 82,576.7$$

c. For the exponential smoothing forecasts with $w = .8$:

$$\text{MAD} = \frac{\sum_{t=23}^{25} |Y_t - F_t|}{m}$$

$$= \frac{|77,426 - 78,862.5| + |77,772 - 78,862.5| + |77,214 - 78,862.5|}{3} = \frac{3,175.5}{3} = 1,058.5$$

$$\text{MAPE} = \left[\frac{\sum_{t=23}^{25} \frac{|(Y_t - F_t)|}{Y_t}}{m} \right] 100$$

$$= \left[\frac{\left| \frac{78,426 - 78,862.5}{78,426} \right| + \left| \frac{77,772 - 78,862.5}{77,772} \right| + \left| \frac{77,214 - 78,862.5}{77,214} \right|}{3} \right] 100$$

$$= \left[\frac{.040937}{3} \right] 100 = 1.3646$$

$$\text{RMSE} = \sqrt{\frac{\sum_{t=23}^{25} (Y_t - F_t)^2}{m}}$$

$$= \sqrt{\frac{(78,426 - 78,862.5)^2 + (77,772 - 78,862.5)^2 + (77,214 - 78,862.5)^2}{3}}$$

$$= \sqrt{\frac{4,097,274.75}{3}} = 1,168.6566$$

For the Holt-Winters forecasts with $w = .8$ and $v = .7$:

$$\text{MAD} = \frac{\sum_{t=23}^{25} |Y_t - F_t|}{m}$$

$$= \frac{|77,426 - 80,404.1| + |77,772 - 81,490.4| + |77,214 - 82,576.7|}{3} = \frac{11,059.2}{3} = 3,686.4$$

$$\text{MAPE} = \left[\frac{\sum_{t=23}^{25} \frac{|(Y_t - F_t)|}{Y_t}}{m} \right] 100$$

$$= \left[\frac{\left| \frac{78,426 - 80,404.1}{78,426} \right| + \left| \frac{77,772 - 81,409.4}{77,772} \right| + \left| \frac{77,214 - 82,576.7}{77,214} \right|}{3} \right] 100$$

$$= \left[\frac{.142486}{3} \right] 100 = 4.7496$$

$$RMSE = \sqrt{\frac{\sum_{t=23}^{25}(Y_t - F_t)^2}{m}}$$

$$= \sqrt{\frac{(78,426-80,404.1)^2 + (77,772-81,490.4)^2 + (77,214-82,576.7)^2}{3}}$$

$$= \sqrt{\frac{46,497,929.5}{3}} = 3,936.9163$$

For all three measures of forecast errors, the exponential smoothing forecasts have smaller errors than the Holt-Winters forecasts. Thus, the exponential smoothing forecasts are better.

14.39   a.   Let $x_1 = \begin{cases} 1 \text{ if quarter 1} \\ 0 \text{ otherwise} \end{cases}$ $x_2 = \begin{cases} 1 \text{ if quarter 2} \\ 0 \text{ otherwise} \end{cases}$ $x_3 = \begin{cases} 1 \text{ if quarter 3} \\ 0 \text{ otherwise} \end{cases}$

$t = \text{time} = 1, 2, \ldots, 40$

The model is $E(Y_t) = \beta_0 + \beta_1 t + \beta_2 x_1 + \beta_3 x_2 + \beta_4 x_3$

   b.   Using MINITAB, the output is:

Regression Analysis: Y versus T, X1, X2, X3
```
The regression equation is
Y = 11.5 + 0.510 T - 3.95 X1 - 2.09 X2 - 4.52 X3

Predictor        Coef       SE Coef          T          P
Constant       11.4933       0.2420       47.49      0.000
T             0.509848     0.007607       67.02      0.000
X1             -3.9505       0.2483      -15.91      0.000
X2             -2.0903       0.2477       -8.44      0.000
X3             -4.5202       0.2473      -18.28      0.000

S = 0.5528      R-Sq = 99.3%      R-Sq(adj) = 99.2%

Analysis of Variance

Source             DF           SS          MS          F        P
Regression          4      1558.79      389.70    1275.44    0.000
Residual Error     35        10.69        0.31
Total              39      1569.48

Source        DF      Seq SS
T              1     1433.96
X1             1       22.56
X2             1        0.21
X3             1      102.06
```

The fitted model is $\hat{Y}_t = 11.4933 + .5098t - 3.9505x_1 - 2.0903x_2 - 4.5202x_3$.

To determine if the model is adequate, we test:

$H_0 : \beta_1 = \beta_2 = \beta_3 = \beta_4 = 0$
$H_a :$ At least one $\beta_i \neq 0$

The test statistic is $F = 1,275.44$.

The rejection region requires $\alpha = .05$ in the upper tail of the F-distribution with $v_1 = k = 4$ and $v_2 = n - (k+1) = 40 - (4+1) = 35$. From Table VI, Appendix D, $F_{.05} \approx 2.69$. The rejection region is $F > 2.69$.

Since the observed value of the test statistic falls in the rejection region $(F = 1,275.44 > 2.69)$, H_0 is rejected. There is sufficient evidence to indicate the model is useful at $\alpha = .05$.

c.   From MINITAB, the predicted values and prediction intervals are:

Predicted Values for New Observations
```
New Obs      Fit      SE Fit         95.0% CI             95.0% PI
1         28.4467     0.2420    ( 27.9554, 28.9379)  ( 27.2217, 29.6716)
```

Values of Predictors for New Observations

```
New Obs           T        X1        X2        X3
1              41.0      1.00  0.000000  0.000000
```

Predicted Values for New Observations
```
New Obs      Fit      SE Fit         95.0% CI             95.0% PI
2         30.8167     0.2420    ( 30.3254, 31.3079)  ( 29.5917, 32.0416)
```

Values of Predictors for New Observations

```
New Obs           T        X1        X2        X3
2              42.0  0.000000      1.00  0.000000
```

Predicted Values for New Observations
```
New Obs      Fit      SE Fit         95.0% CI             95.0% PI
3         28.8967     0.2420    ( 28.4054, 29.3879)  ( 27.6717, 30.1216)
```

Values of Predictors for New Observations

```
New Obs           T        X1        X2        X3
3              43.0  0.000000  0.000000      1.00
```

Predicted Values for New Observations
```
New Obs      Fit      SE Fit         95.0% CI             95.0% PI
4         33.9267     0.2420    ( 33.4354, 34.4179)  ( 32.7017, 35.1516)
```

Values of Predictors for New Observations

```
New Obs           T        X1        X2        X3
4              44.0  0.000000  0.000000  0.000000
```

From the above output, the predicted values and 95% prediction intervals are:

For year $= 11$, quarter $= 1$, $\hat{Y}_{41} = 28.4467$ and the 95% PI is $(27.22, 29.67)$

For year $= 11$, quarter $= 2$, $\hat{Y}_{42} = 30.8167$ and the 95% PI is $(29.59, 32.04)$

For year $= 11$, quarter $= 3$, $\hat{Y}_{43} = 28.8967$ and the 95% PI is $(27.67, 30.12)$

For year $= 11$, quarter $= 4$, $\hat{Y}_{44} = 33.9267$ and the 95% PI is $(32.70, 35.15)$

14.41   a.   Using MINITAB, the results are:

Regression Analysis: Interest versus t
```
Analysis of Variance

Source       DF  Adj SS   Adj MS  F-Value  P-Value
Regression    1   72.75  72.7476   145.07    0.000
  t           1   72.75  72.7476   145.07    0.000
Error        24   12.03   0.5014
Total        25   84.78
```

```
Model Summary

       S    R-sq  R-sq(adj)  R-sq(pred)
0.708131  85.81%     85.21%      82.61%
```

```
Coefficients

Term       Coef  SE Coef  T-Value  P-Value   VIF
Constant  9.372    0.270    34.72    0.000
t        -0.2230   0.0185   -12.04    0.000  1.00
```

```
Regression Equation

Interest = 9.372 - 0.2230 t
```

Prediction for Interest
```
Regression Equation

Interest = 9.372 - 0.2230 t
```

```
Variable  Setting
t              26
```

```
    Fit    SE Fit        95% CI                 95% PI
3.57295  0.285963  (2.98275, 4.16315)  (1.99677, 5.14914)
```

The fitted model is: $\hat{Y}_t = 9.372 - .2230t$

   b.   For 2016, $t = 26$. The forecast for the average interest rate in 2016 is $\hat{Y}_t = 9.372 - .2230(26) = 3.573$.

From the printout, the 95% prediction interval is $(1.997, 5.149)$.

14.43   a.   The regression model would be: $E(Y_t) = \beta_0 + \beta_1 X_t$

   b.   First, create dummy variables:

$$m_1 = \begin{cases} 1 \text{ if January} \\ 0 \text{ if not} \end{cases}, \quad m_2 = \begin{cases} 1 \text{ if February} \\ 0 \text{ if not} \end{cases}, \ldots, m_{11} = \begin{cases} 1 \text{ if November} \\ 0 \text{ if not} \end{cases}$$

The new model is: $E(Y_t) = \beta_0 + \beta_1 X_t + \beta_2 m_1 + \beta_3 m_2 + \cdots + \beta_{12} m_{11}$

    c. To determine if mean gasoline consumption varies from month to month, we test:

$$H_0 : \beta_2 = \beta_3 = \cdots = \beta_{12} = 0$$

    d. Let $t = 0$ for time January, 2002. Then for January, 2017, $t = 180$. The forecast would be

$$\hat{Y}_{180} = \hat{\beta}_0 + \hat{\beta}_1 (180) + \hat{\beta}_2$$

14.45   a. Using $t = 1$ for 1985, the results using MINITAB are:

Regression Analysis: Policies versus t
```
Analysis of Variance

Source        DF   Adj SS   Adj MS   F-Value   P-Value
Regression     1    28047  28047.0     44.99     0.000
Error         28    17454    623.4
Total         29    45501
```

```
Model Summary

      S     R-sq   R-sq(adj)   R-sq(pred)
24.9674   61.64%      60.27%       55.87%
```

```
Coefficients

Term         Coef   SE Coef   T-Value   P-Value    VIF
Constant   409.19      9.35     43.77     0.000
t          -3.533     0.527     -6.71     0.000   1.00
```

```
Regression Equation

Policies = 409.19 - 3.533 t
```

Prediction for Policies
```
Regression Equation

Variable   Setting
t               31
```

```
    Fit    SE Fit          95% CI                   95% PI
299.678   9.34960   (280.526, 318.830)   (245.067, 354.290)
```

Prediction for Policies
```
Regression Equation

Variable   Setting
t               32
```

```
    Fit    SE Fit          95% CI                   95% PI
296.146   9.81278   (276.045, 316.246)   (241.194, 351.097)
```

The fitted model is: $\hat{Y}_t = 409.19 - 3.533t$

    b. From the printout, the forecasted values for 2015 and 2016 ($t = 31$ and $t = 32$) are:

          2015: 299.678
          2016: 296.146

c.   From the printout, the 95% prediction intervals for 2015 and 2016 are:

$$2015:\ (245.067,\ 354.290)$$

$$2016:\ (241.194,\ 351.097)$$

14.47   a.   The regression model for liquidity risk at quarter t as a linear function of DELR in the previous quarter is: $E(Y_t) = \beta_0 + \beta_1 X_{1,t-1}$.

b.   The new model is: $E(Y_t) = \beta_0 + \beta_1 X_{1,t-1} + \beta_2 X_{2,t-1} + \beta_3 X_{3,t-1} + \beta_4 X_{4,t-1}$.

c.   The new model is: $E(Y_t) = \beta_0 + \beta_1 X_{1,t-1} + \beta_2 Q_1 + \beta_3 Q_2 + \beta_4 Q_3$

where $Q_1 = \begin{cases} 1 & \text{if Quarter 1} \\ 0 & \text{if not} \end{cases}$ $Q_2 = \begin{cases} 1 & \text{if Quarter 2} \\ 0 & \text{if not} \end{cases}$ $Q_3 = \begin{cases} 1 & \text{if Quarter 3} \\ 0 & \text{if not} \end{cases}$

14.49   a.   For $\alpha = .05$, the rejection region is $d < d_{L,\alpha} = d_{L,.05} = 1.10$. The value of $d_{L,.05}$ is found in Table X, Appendix D, with $k = 2$, $n = 20$, and $\alpha = .05$. Also, $d_{U,.05} = 1.54$.

Since the test statistic falls between $d_{L,.05}$ and $d_{U,.05}$ $(1.10 \leq 1.10 \leq 1.54)$, no decision can be made.

b.   For $\alpha = .01$, the rejection region is $d < d_{L,\alpha} = d_{L,.01} = .86$. The value of $d_{L,.01}$ is found in Table XI, Appendix D, with $k = 2$, $n = 20$, and $\alpha = .01$. Also, $d_{U,.01} = 1.27$.

Since the test statistic falls between $d_{L,.01}$ and $d_{U,.01}$ $(.86 \leq 1.10 \leq 1.27)$, no decision can be made.

c.   For $\alpha = .05$, the rejection region is $d < d_{L,\alpha} = d_{L,.05} = 1.44$. The value of $d_{L,.05}$ is found in Table X, Appendix D, with $k = 5$, $n = 65$, and $\alpha = .05$.

Since the test statistic falls in the rejection region $(d = .95 < 1.44)$, H_0 is rejected. There is sufficient evidence to indicate positive first-order autocorrelation at $\alpha = .05$.

d.   For $\alpha = .01$, the rejection region is $d < d_{L,\alpha} = d_{L,.01} = 1.15$. The value of $d_{L,.01}$ is found in Table XI, Appendix D, with $k = 1$, $n = 31$, and $\alpha = .01$. Also, $d_{U,.01} = 1.27$.

Since the test statistic does not fall in the rejection region $(d = 1.35 \not< 1.15)$, and the test statistic is above $d_{U,.01}$ $(d = 1.35 > 1.27)$ H_0 is not rejected.

14.51   a.   To determine if positive first-order autocorrelation exists, we test:

H_0: No autocorrelation
H_a: Positive autocorrelation exists

b.   The p-value is $p < .0001$. Since the p-value is so small, H_0 is rejected. There is sufficient evidence to indicate that positive autocorrelation exists for any reasonable value of α. The researchers should not proceed.

14.53   To determine if positive autocorrelation is present, we test:

H_0: No first-order autocorrelation
H_a: Positive first-order autocorrelation of residuals

The test statistics is $d = 1.77$.

For $\alpha = .05$, the rejection region is $d < d_{L,\alpha} = d_{L,.05} = .93$. The value $d_{L,.05}$ is found in Table X, Appendix D, with $k = 5$, $n = 24$, and $\alpha = .05$.

Since the observed value of the test statistic does not fall in the rejection region $(d = 1.77 \not< .93)$, H_0 is not rejected. There is insufficient evidence to indicate the time series residuals are positively autocorrelated at $\alpha = .05$.

14.55   a.   Using MINITAB, the plot of the residuals against t is:

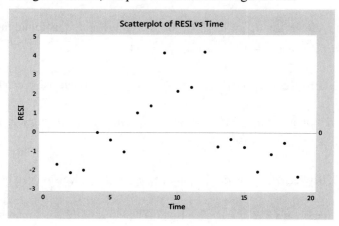

There is not a random scattering of the residuals. The first 6 residuals are negative, the next 6 are positive, and the last 7 are negative. This does not appear to be a random scattering. The plot suggests the possibility of autocorrelation.

b.   Using MINITAB, the output is:

Regression Analysis: Price versus Time
Analysis of Variance

Source	DF	Adj SS	Adj MS	F-Value	P-Value
Regression	1	1.016	1.016	0.23	0.634
Error	17	73.586	4.329		
Total	18	74.601			

Model Summary

S	R-sq	R-sq(adj)	R-sq(pred)
2.08052	1.36%	0.00%	0.00%

Coefficients

Term	Coef	SE Coef	T-Value	P-Value	VIF
Constant	4.151	0.994	4.18	0.001	
Time	0.0422	0.0871	0.48	0.634	1.00

```
Regression Equation

Price = 4.151 + 0.0422 Time

Durbin-Watson Statistic =  0.750323
```

To determine if positive autocorrelation is present, we test:

H_0: No first-order autocorrelation
H_a: Positive first-order autocorrelation of residuals

The test statistics is $d = 0.750323$.

For $\alpha = .05$, the rejection region is $d < d_{L,\alpha} = d_{L,.05} = 1.18$. The value $d_{L,.05}$ is found in Table X, Appendix D, with $k = 1$, $n = 19$, and $\alpha = .05$.

Since the observed value of the test statistic falls in the rejection region $(d = 0.750323 < 1.18)$, H_0 is rejected. There is sufficient evidence to indicate the time series residuals are positively autocorrelated at $\alpha = .05$.

c.   Since the error terms are dependent, the validity of the test for the model adequacy appears to be questionable.

14.57 a.   For Bank 1, $R^2 = .914$. 91.4% of the sample variation of the deposit shares of Bank 1 is explained by the model containing expenditures on promotion-related activities, expenditures on service-related activities, and expenditures on distribution-related activities.

For Bank 2, $R^2 = .721$. 72.1% of the sample variation of the deposit shares of Bank 2 is explained by the model containing expenditures on promotion-related activities, expenditures on service-related activities, and expenditures on distribution-related activities.

For Bank 3, $R^2 = .926$. 92.6% of the sample variation of the deposit shares of Bank 3 is explained by the model containing expenditures on promotion-related activities, expenditures on service-related activities, and expenditures on distribution-related activities.

For Bank 4, $R^2 = .827$. 82.7% of the sample variation of the deposit shares of Bank 4 is explained by the model containing expenditures on promotion-related activities, expenditures on service-related activities, and expenditures on distribution-related activities.

For Bank 5, $R^2 = .270$. 27.0% of the sample variation of the deposit shares of Bank 5 is explained by the model containing expenditures on promotion-related activities, expenditures on service-related activities, and expenditures on distribution-related activities.

For Bank 6, $R^2 = .616$. 61.6% of the sample variation of the deposit shares of Bank 6 is explained by the model containing expenditures on promotion-related activities, expenditures on service-related activities, and expenditures on distribution-related activities.

For Bank 7, $R^2 = .962$. 96.2% of the sample variation of the deposit shares of Bank 7 is explained by the model containing expenditures on promotion-related activities, expenditures on service-related activities, and expenditures on distribution-related activities.

For Bank 8, $R^2 = .495$. 49.5% of the sample variation of the deposit shares of Bank 8 is explained by the model containing expenditures on promotion-related activities, expenditures on service-related activities, and expenditures on distribution-related activities.

For Bank 9, $R^2 = .500$. 50.0% of the sample variation of the deposit shares of Bank 9 is explained by the model containing expenditures on promotion-related activities, expenditures on service-related activities, and expenditures on distribution-related activities.

b.   For all banks, to determine if the model is adequate, we test:

$$H_0 : \beta_1 = \beta_2 = \beta_3 = 0$$
$$H_a : \text{At least one } \beta_i \neq 0$$

For Bank 1, the p-value is $p = 0.000$. Since the p-value is less than $\alpha = .01$, H_0 is rejected. There is sufficient evidence to indicate the model is adequate at $\alpha = .01$.

For Bank 2, the p-value is $p = 0.004$. Since the p-value is less than $\alpha = .01$, H_0 is rejected. There is sufficient evidence to indicate the model is adequate at $\alpha = .01$.

For Bank 3, the p-value is $p = 0.000$. Since the p-value is less than $\alpha = .01$, H_0 is rejected. There is sufficient evidence to indicate the model is adequate at $\alpha = .01$.

For Bank 4, the p-value is $p = 0.000$. Since the p-value is less than $\alpha = .01$, H_0 is rejected. There is sufficient evidence to indicate the model is adequate at $\alpha = .01$.

For Bank 5, the p-value is $p = 0.155$. Since the p-value is not less than $\alpha = .01$, H_0 is not rejected. There is insufficient evidence to indicate the model is adequate at $\alpha = .01$.

For Bank 6, the p-value is $p = 0.012$. Since the p-value is not less than $\alpha = .01$, H_0 is not rejected. There is insufficient evidence to indicate the model is adequate at $\alpha = .01$.

For Bank 7, the p-value is $p = 0.000$. Since the p-value is less than $\alpha = .01$, H_0 is rejected. There is sufficient evidence to indicate the model is adequate at $\alpha = .01$.

For Bank 8, the p-value is $p = 0.014$. Since the p-value is not less than $\alpha = .01$, H_0 is not rejected. There is insufficient evidence to indicate the model is adequate at $\alpha = .01$.

For Bank 9, the p-value is $p = 0.011$. Since the p-value is not less than $\alpha = .01$, H_0 is not rejected. There is insufficient evidence to indicate the model is adequate at $\alpha = .01$.

c.   To determine if positive autocorrelation is present, we test:

H_0: No positive first-order autocorrelation
H_a: Positive first-order autocorrelation of residuals

The test statistics is d.

For $\alpha = .01$, the rejection region is $d < d_{L,\alpha} = d_{L,.01} = .77$. The value $d_{L,.01}$ is found in Table XI, Appendix D, with $k = 3$, $n = 20$, and $\alpha = .01$. Also, $d_{U,.01} = 1.41$.

For Bank 1, $d = 1.3$. Since the observed value of the test statistic does not fall in the rejection region $(d = 1.3 \nless .77)$ and is not greater thn $d_{U,.01} (d = 1.3 \ngtr 1.41)$, no decision can be made at $\alpha = .01$.

For Bank 2, $d = 3.4$. Since the observed value of the test statistic does not fall in the rejection region $(d = 3.4 \not< .77)$ and is greater than $d_{U,.01} (d = 3.4 > 1.41)$, H_0 is not rejected. There is insufficient evidence to indicate the time series residuals are positively autocorrelated at $\alpha = .01$.

For Bank 3, $d = 2.7$. Since the observed value of the test statistic does not fall in the rejection region $(d = 2.7 \not< .77)$ and is greater than $d_{U,.01} (d = 2.7 > 1.41)$, H_0 is not rejected. There is insufficient evidence to indicate the time series residuals are positively autocorrelated at $\alpha = .01$.

For Bank 4, $d = 1.9$. Since the observed value of the test statistic does not fall in the rejection region $(d = 1.9 \not< .77)$ and is greater than $d_{U,.01} (d = 1.9 > 1.41)$, H_0 is not rejected. There is insufficient evidence to indicate the time series residuals are positively autocorrelated at $\alpha = .01$.

For Bank 5, $d = .85$. Since the observed value of the test statistic does not fall in the rejection region $(d = .85 \not< .77)$ and is not greater thn $d_{U,.01} (d = .85 \not> 1.41)$, no decision can be made at $\alpha = .01$.

For Bank 6, $d = 1.8$. Since the observed value of the test statistic does not fall in the rejection region $(d = 1.8 \not< .77)$ and is greater than $d_{U,.01} (d = 1.8 > 1.41)$, H_0 is not rejected. There is insufficient evidence to indicate the time series residuals are positively autocorrelated at $\alpha = .01$.

For Bank 7, $d = 2.5$. Since the observed value of the test statistic does not fall in the rejection region $(d = 2.5 \not< .77)$ and is greater than $d_{U,.01} (d = 2.5 > 1.41)$, H_0 is not rejected. There is insufficient evidence to indicate the time series residuals are positively autocorrelated at $\alpha = .01$.

For Bank 8, $d = 2.3$. Since the observed value of the test statistic does not fall in the rejection region $(d = 2.3 \not< .77)$ and is greater than $d_{U,.01} (d = 2.3 > 1.41)$, H_0 is not rejected. There is insufficient evidence to indicate the time series residuals are positively autocorrelated at $\alpha = .01$.

For Bank 9, $d = 1.1$. Since the observed value of the test statistic does not fall in the rejection region $(d = 1.1 \not< .77)$ and is not greater thn $d_{U,.01} (d = 1.1 \not> 1.41)$, no decision can be made at $\alpha = .01$.

14.59 a. Compute the exponentially smoothed values $E_1, E_2, \ldots, E_t$ for years 2000 to 2011:

$$E_1 = Y_1 = 140.9$$

For $w = .5$, $E_2 = wY_2 + (1-w)E_1 = .5(142.9) + (1-.5)140.9 = 141.9$
$$E_3 = wY_3 + (1-w)E_2 = .5(144.9) + (1-.5)(141.9) = 143.4$$

The rest of the values appear in the table.

Year	Fully Permanent	Exponentially Smoothed $w=.5$	Year	Fully Permanent	Exponentially Smoothed $w=.5$
2000	140.9	140.9	2008	157.4	155.4
2001	142.9	141.9	2009	159.2	157.3
2002	144.9	143.4	2010	161.1	159.2
2003	147.0	145.2	2011	163.1	161.1
2004	149.0	147.1	2012	163.3	162.2
2005	151.1	149.1	2013	165.3	163.8
2006	153.3	151.2	2014	167.3	165.5
2007	155.4	153.3	2015	169.4	167.5

b. Using MINITAB, the plot of the workers and the exponentially smoothed values is:

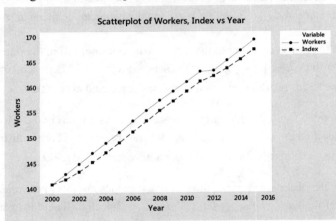

c. To forecast using the exponentially smoothed values, we use the following:

For $w = .5$:

$$F_{2016} = F_{t+1} = E_t = 167.5$$
$$F_{2017} = F_{t+2} = F_{t+1} = 167.5$$

The drawback to these forecasts is that all the forecasts for future values are the same.

14.61   a.   Using MINITAB, the output is:

Regression Analysis: Daily Visits versus t
```
The regression equation is
Daily Visits = 38.2 + 7.32 t

Predictor        Coef      SE Coef          T          P
Constant       38.171        4.420       8.64      0.000
t              7.3192       0.7123      10.27      0.000


S = 6.470        R-Sq = 93.0%      R-Sq(adj) = 92.1%


Analysis of Variance

Source            DF          SS         MS          F          P
Regression         1      4419.5     4419.5     105.57      0.000
Residual Error     8       334.9       41.9
Total              9      4754.4
```

Predicted Values for New Observations

New Obs	Fit	SE Fit	95.0% CI	95.0% PI
1	118.68	4.42	(108.49, 128.87)	(100.61, 136.75)

Values of Predictors for New Observations

New Obs	t
1	11.0

Predicted Values for New Observations

New Obs	Fit	SE Fit	95.0% CI	95.0% PI
2	126.00	5.06	(114.33, 137.67)	(107.06, 144.94)

Values of Predictors for New Observations

New Obs	t
2	12.0

Predicted Values for New Observations

New Obs	Fit	SE Fit	95.0% CI	95.0% PI
3	133.32	5.72	(120.13, 146.51)	(113.40, 153.24)

Values of Predictors for New Observations

New Obs	t
3	13.0

The fitted regression line is: $\hat{Y}_t = 38.171 + 7.319t$

The forecasts for the next 3 years are:

$$\hat{Y}_{11} = 38.171 + 7.319(11) = 118.68$$
$$\hat{Y}_{12} = 38.171 + 7.319(12) = 126.00$$
$$\hat{Y}_{13} = 38.171 + 7.319(13) = 133.32$$

b. From the printout, the 95% prediction intervals for the 3 years are:

Year 11: (100.61, 136.75)
Year 12: (107.06, 144.94)
Year 13: (113.40, 153.24)

c. There are basically two problems with using simple linear regression for predicting time series data. First, we must predict values of the time series for values of time outside the observed range. We observe data for time periods 1, 2, ..., t and use the regression model to predict values of the time series for $t + 1$, $t + 2$, ... The second problem is that simple linear regression does not allow for any cyclical effects such as seasonal trends.

d. We could use an exponentially smoothed series to forecast patient visits or we could use a Holt-Winters series to forecast patient visits.

14.63 a. We first calculate the exponentially smoothed values for 1995–2015.

$$E_1 = Y_1 = 41.05$$
$$E_2 = .8Y_2 + (1-.8)E_1 = .8(50.75) + .2(41.05) = 48.81$$
$$E_3 = .8Y_3 + (1-.8)E_2 = .8(65.50) + .2(48.81) = 62.16$$

The rest of the values appear in the table.

Year	Closing Price	Exponentially Smoothed $w = .8$	Holt-Winters Et $w=.8$	Tt $v=.5$
1995	41.05	41.05		
1996	50.75	48.81	50.75	9.70
1997	65.50	62.16	64.49	11.72
1998	49.00	51.63	54.44	0.84
1999	36.31	39.37	40.10	-6.75
2000	48.44	46.63	45.42	-0.72
2001	55.75	53.93	53.54	3.70
2002	40.00	42.79	43.45	-3.20
2003	46.60	45.84	45.33	-0.66
2004	46.65	46.49	46.25	0.13
2005	39.43	40.84	40.82	-2.65
2006	48.71	47.14	46.60	1.57
2007	56.15	54.35	54.55	4.76
2008	53.37	53.57	54.56	2.38
2009	53.99	53.91	54.58	1.20
2010	47.91	49.11	49.48	-1.95
2011	56.23	54.81	54.49	1.53
2012	65.50	63.36	63.60	5.32
2013	38.33	43.34	44.45	-6.92
2014	45.02	44.68	43.52	-3.92
2015	44.91	44.86	43.85	-1.80

The forecasts for 2016 and 2017 are:

$$F_{2016} = F_{t+1} = E_t = 44.86$$
$$F_{2017} = F_{t+2} = E_t = 44.86$$

The expected gain is $F_{2017} - Y_{2015} = 44.86 - 44.91 = -.05$. Since this number is negative, it is actually a loss.

b. We first calculate the Holt-Winters values for 1995-2015.

For $w = .8$ and $v = .5$,

$$E_2 = Y_2 = 50.75$$
$$E_3 = .8Y_3 + (1-.8)(E_2 + T_2) = .8(65.50) + .2(50.75 + 9.70) = 64.49$$

$$T_2 = Y_2 - Y_1 = 50.75 - 41.05 = 9.70$$
$$T_3 = .5(E_3 - E_2) + (1-.5)(T_2) = .5(64.49 - 50.75) + .5(9.70) = 11.72$$

The rest of the values appear in the table in part **a**.

The forecasts for 2016 and 2017 are:

$$F_{2016} = F_{t+1} = E_t + T_t = 43.85 + (-1.80) = 42.05$$
$$F_{2017} = F_{t+2} = E_t + 2T_t = 43.85 + 2(-1.80) = 40.25$$

The expected gain is $F_{2017} - Y_{2015} = 40.25 - 44.91 = -4.66$.

c. Generally, we have more confidence in the Holt-Winters forecasts because the forecasts can change each year. Using the exponentially smoothed forecasts, the forecasts are the same for each additional year.

14.65 a. To find the simple index for "Other Plans", divide each value by 6.0 (the value for the base year) and then multiply by 100. To find the simple index for "DC Plans", divide each value by 3.0 (the value for the base year) and then multiply by 100. To find the simple index for "IRAs", divide each value by 2.6 (the value for the base year) and then multiply by 100. The indeces are found in the following table.

Year	Other Plans	DC plans (includes 401K)	IRAs
1995	65.0	56.7	50.0
2000	100.0	100.0	100.0
2002	90.0	86.7	96.2
2005	123.3	123.3	130.8
2007	145.0	153.3	180.8
2008	116.7	120.0	142.3
2010	140.0	160.0	192.3
2012	148.3	176.7	226.9
2013	166.7	210.0	269.2
2014	173.3	226.7	284.6

b. Using MINITAB, the plot of the indecies is:

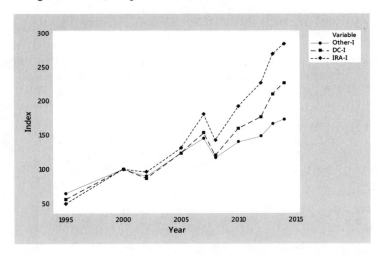

c. Based on the retirement assets in 2000, the retirement assests for IRAs increased the most (184.6%), the retirement assests for DC plans increased the next most (126.7%), and the retirement assests for other plans increased the least (73.3%).

14.67   a.   Using MINITAB, the results from fitting the model $E(Y_t) = \beta_0 + \beta_1 t$ starting with $t = 0$ are:

Regression Analysis: GDP versus t
Analysis of Variance

Source	DF	Adj SS	Adj MS	F-Value	P-Value
Regression	1	15349815	15349815	3268.90	0.000
Error	18	84523	4696		
Total	19	15434337			

Model Summary

S	R-sq	R-sq(adj)	R-sq(pred)
68.5253	99.45%	99.42%	99.35%

Coefficients

Term	Coef	SE Coef	T-Value	P-Value	VIF
Constant	15283.0	29.5	517.53	0.000	
t	151.93	2.66	57.17	0.000	1.00

Regression Equation

GDP = 15283.0 + 151.93 t

Durbin-Watson Statistic = 1.26496

Prediction for GDP
Regression Equation

GDP = 15283.0 + 151.93 t

Variable	Setting
t	20

Fit	SE Fit	95% CI	95% PI
18321.5	31.8321	(18254.7, 18388.4)	(18162.8, 18480.3)

Variable	Setting
t	21

Fit	SE Fit	95% CI	95% PI
18473.5	34.1853	(18401.6, 18545.3)	(18312.6, 18634.4)

Variable	Setting
t	22

Fit	SE Fit	95% CI	95% PI
18625.4	36.5801	(18548.5, 18702.2)	(18462.2, 18788.6)

Variable	Setting
t	23

Fit	SE Fit	95% CI	95% PI	
18777.3	39.0089	(18695.4, 18859.3)	(18611.7, 18943.0)	X

The fitted regression line is: $\hat{Y}_t = 15,283.0 + 151.93t$.

From the printout, the 2016 quarterly GDP forecasts are:

Year	Quarter	Forecast	95% Lower Limit	95% Upper Limit
2016	Q1	18,321.5	18,162.8	18,480.3
	Q2	18,473.5	18,312.6	18,634.4
	Q3	18,625.4	18,462.2	18,788.6
	Q4	18,777.3	18,611.7	18,943.0

b.   The following model is fit: $E(Y_t) = \beta_0 + \beta_1 t + \beta_2 Q_1 + \beta_3 Q_2 + \beta_4 Q_3$

where $Q_1 = \begin{cases} 1 \text{ if quarter 1} \\ 0 \text{ otherwise} \end{cases}$ $Q_2 = \begin{cases} 1 \text{ if quarter 2} \\ 0 \text{ otherwise} \end{cases}$ $Q_3 = \begin{cases} 1 \text{ if quarter 3} \\ 0 \text{ otherwise} \end{cases}$

The MINITAB printout is:

Regression Analysis: GDP versus t, Q1, Q2, Q3
```
Analysis of Variance

Source       DF     Adj SS    Adj MS   F-Value   P-Value
Regression    4   15361950   3840487    795.82     0.000
Error        15      72387      4826
Total        19   15434337


Model Summary

       S    R-sq   R-sq(adj)   R-sq(pred)
 69.4682  99.53%      99.41%       99.22%


Coefficients

Term          Coef   SE Coef   T-Value   P-Value    VIF
Constant   15300.2      43.3    353.10     0.000
t           151.27      2.75     55.09     0.000   1.04
Q1           -53.0      44.7     -1.19     0.254   1.55
Q2            -3.0      44.3     -0.07     0.947   1.52
Q3            12.1      44.0      0.27     0.788   1.51


Regression Equation

GDP = 15300.2 + 151.27 t - 53.0 Q1 - 3.0 Q2 + 12.1 Q3


Durbin-Watson Statistic =   1.12241
```

Prediction for GDP
```
Regression Equation

GDP = 15300.2 + 151.27 t - 53.0 Q1 - 3.0 Q2 + 12.1 Q3


Variable   Setting
t               20
Q1               1
Q2               0
Q3               0


    Fit    SE Fit         95% CI               95% PI
18272.6   45.2877   (18176.1, 18369.1)   (18095.9, 18449.4)
```

```
Variable  Setting
t             21
Q1             0
Q2             1
Q3             0
```

```
    Fit   SE Fit        95% CI               95% PI
18474.0  45.2877  (18377.4, 18570.5)  (18297.2, 18650.7)
```

```
Variable  Setting
t             22
Q1             0
Q2             0
Q3             1
```

```
    Fit   SE Fit        95% CI               95% PI
18640.3  45.2877  (18543.7, 18736.8)  (18463.5, 18817.0)
```

```
Variable  Setting
t             23
Q1             0
Q2             0
Q3             0
```

```
    Fit   SE Fit        95% CI               95% PI
18779.5  45.2877  (18682.9, 18876.0)  (18602.7, 18956.2)
```

The fitted regression line is: $\hat{Y}_t = 15{,}300.2 + 151.27t - 53.0Q_1 - 3.0Q_2 + 12.1Q_3$

To determine whether the data indicate a significant seasonal component, we test:

$H_0 : \beta_2 = \beta_3 = \beta_4 = 0$

H_a : At least one $\beta_i \neq 0$

The test statistic is

$$F = \frac{(SSE_R - SSE_C)/(k-g)}{SSE_C/[n-(k+1)]} = \frac{(84{,}523 - 72{,}387)/(4-1)}{72{,}387/[20-(4+1)]} = \frac{4{,}045.33333}{4{,}825.8} = .838$$

Since no α is given, we will use $\alpha = .05$. The rejection region requires $\alpha = .05$ in the upper tail of the F-distribution with $v_1 = k - g = 4 - 1 = 3$ and $v_2 = n - (k+1) = 20 - (4+1) = 15$. From Table VI, Appendix D, $F_{.05} = 3.29$. The rejection region is $F > 3.29$.

Since the observed value of the test statistic does not fall in the rejection region $(F = .838 \not> 3.29)$, H_0 is not rejected. There is insufficient evidence to indicate a seasonal component at $\alpha = .05$. This supports the assertion that the data have been seasonally adjusted.

c.   From the printout, the 2016 quarterly forecasts are:

Year	Quarter	Forecast	95% Lower Limit	95% Upper Limit
2016	Q1	18,272.6	18,095.9	18,449.4
	Q2	18,474.0	18,297.2	18,650.7
	Q3	18,640.3	18,463.5	18,817.0
	Q4	18,779.5	18,602.7	18,956.2

d. To determine if the time series residuals are autocorrelated, we test:

H_0: No first-order autocorrelation of residuals
H_a: Positive or negative first-order autocorrelation of residuals

The test statistic is $d = 1.12241$.

For $\alpha = .10$, the rejection region is $d < d_{L,\alpha/2} = d_{L,.05} = .90$ or $(4-d) < d_{L,.05} = .90$. The value of $d_{L,.05}$ is found in Table X, Appendix D, with $k = 4$ and $n = 20$. Also, $d_{U,.05} = 1.83$

Since the observed value of the test statistic does not fall in the rejection region $(d = 1.12241 \nless .90)$, H_0 is not rejected. Also, the observed value of the test statistic is not greater than the upper bound $(d = 1.12241 \ngtr 1.83)$. Thus, there is not enough evidence to make a decision about whether the time series residuals are autocorrelated at $\alpha = .10$. More information is needed.

14.69 a. Using MINITAB, the results from fitting the model $E(Y_t) = \beta_0 + \beta_1 t$ starting with $t = 0$ are:

Regression Analysis: Revolving versus t
```
Analysis of Variance

Source        DF  Adj SS  Adj MS  F-Value  P-Value
Regression     1  351475  351475    65.79    0.000
Error         19  101505    5342
Total         20  452980
```

```
Model Summary

      S    R-sq  R-sq(adj)  R-sq(pred)
73.0916  77.59%     76.41%      72.69%
```

```
Coefficients

Term       Coef  SE Coef  T-Value  P-Value   VIF
Constant  550.1     30.8    17.86    0.000
t         21.36     2.63     8.11    0.000  1.00
```

```
Regression Equation

Revolving = 550.1 + 21.36 t
```

```
Durbin-Watson Statistic =  0.297292
```

Prediction for Revolving
```
Regression Equation

Revolving = 550.1 + 21.36 t
```

```
Variable  Setting
t              21
```

```
    Fit   SE Fit          95% CI                 95% PI
998.776  33.0744  (929.551, 1068.00)  (830.860, 1166.69)
```

```
Variable  Setting
t              22
```

```
    Fit   SE Fit          95% CI                 95% PI
1020.14  35.4047  (946.038, 1094.24)  (850.156, 1190.13)
```

The fitted regression line is: $\hat{Y}_t = 550.1 + 21.36t$

For the years 2016 and 2017, $t = 21$ and 22. From the printout, the predicted values and 95% prediction intervals for 2016 and 2017 are:

Year	Forecast	95% Lower Limit	95% Upper Limit
2016	998.78	830.86	1,166.69
2017	1,020.14	850.16	1,190.13

b. To compute the Holt-Winters values for the years 1995-2015:

With $w = .7$ and $v = .7$,

$$E_2 = Y_2 = 508$$
$$E_3 = wY_3 + (1-w)(E_2 + T_2) = .7(538) + (1-.7)(508+64) = 548.20$$

$$T_2 = Y_2 - Y_1 = 508 - 444 = 64$$
$$T_3 = v(E_3 - E_2) + (1-v)T_2 = .7(548.20 - 508.00) + (1-.7)(64) = 47.34$$

The rest of the values appear in the table:

		Holt-Winters	
		Et	Tt
Year	Revolving	$w = .7$	$v = .7$
1995	444		
1996	508	508.00	64.00
1997	538	548.20	47.34
1998	579	583.96	39.24
1999	609	613.26	32.28
2000	683	671.76	50.64
2001	716	717.92	47.50
2002	749	753.93	39.46
2003	771	777.71	28.49
2004	800	801.86	25.45
2005	825	825.69	24.32
2006	875	867.50	36.56
2007	942	930.62	55.15
2008	958	966.33	41.54
2009	866	908.56	-27.98
2010	801	824.88	-66.97
2011	841	816.07	-26.26
2012	846	829.14	1.27
2013	858	849.73	14.79
2014	892	883.75	28.26
2015	938	930.20	40.99

Using the Holt-Winters series, the forecasts for 2016 and 2017 are:

$$F_{2016} = F_{t+1} = E_t + T_t = 930.20 + 40.99 = 971.19$$
$$F_{2017} = F_{t+2} = E_t + 2T_t = 930.20 + 2(40.99) = 1{,}012.18$$

These values are smaller than the forecasts using simple linear regression.

14.71   a.   To compute the exponentially smoothed values $E_1, E_2, \ldots, E_t$ for months January through September:

$$E_1 = Y_1 = 153.31$$

For $w = .5$, $E_2 = wY_2 + (1-w)E_1 = .5(161.94) + (1-.5)(153.31) = 157.63$
 $E_3 = wY_3 + (1-w)E_2 = .5(160.50) + (1-.5)(157.63) = 159.06$

The rest of the values appear in the table.

Month	IBM	Exponentially Smoothed $w = .5$
JAN	153.31	153.31
FEB	161.94	157.63
MAR	160.50	159.06
APR	171.29	165.18
MAY	169.65	167.41
JUN	162.66	165.04
JUL	161.99	163.51
AUG	147.89	155.70
SEP	144.97	150.34
OCT	140.08	
NOV	139.42	
DEC	137.62	

The forecasts for October through December 2015 are:

$$F_{2015,\text{Oct}} = F_{t+1} = E_t = 150.34$$
$$F_{2015,\text{Nov}} = F_{t+2} = F_{t+1} = 150.34$$
$$F_{2015,\text{Dec}} = F_{t+3} = F_{t+1} = 150.34$$

The forecast errors are the differences between the actual values and the forecasted values. The forecast errors are:

Month	Y_{t+i}	F_{t+i}	Difference
Oct	140.08	150.34	-10.26
Nov	139.42	150.34	-10.92
Dec	137.62	150.34	-12.72

b.   Using MINITAB, the output is:

Regression Analysis: IBM versus Time
```
Analysis of Variance

Source        DF   Adj SS   Adj MS   F-Value   P-Value
Regression     1   109.8    109.78     1.42     0.272
Error          7   539.4     77.06
Total          8   649.2

Model Summary

       S     R-sq   R-sq(adj)   R-sq(pred)
 8.77842   16.91%       5.04%        0.00%
Coefficients

Term        Coef   SE Coef   T-Value   P-Value   VIF
Constant  166.12      6.38     26.05     0.000
Time       -1.35      1.13     -1.19     0.272   1.00

Regression Equation

IBM = 166.12 - 1.35 Time

Durbin-Watson Statistic =   0.823812
```

Prediction for IBM
```
Regression Equation

IBM = 166.12 - 1.35 Time

Variable   Setting
Time            10

    Fit    SE Fit         95% CI               95% PI
152.592   6.37738   (137.512, 167.672)   (126.935, 178.249)


Variable   Setting
Time            11

    Fit    SE Fit         95% CI               95% PI
151.240   7.40262   (133.735, 168.744)   (124.087, 178.393)   X


Variable   Setting
Time            12

    Fit    SE Fit         95% CI               95% PI
149.887   8.45548   (129.893, 169.881)   (121.066, 178.708)   X
```

The least squares fitted model is: $\hat{Y}_t = 166.12 - 1.35t$

$\hat{\beta}_0 = 162.68$.   The estimated stock price for IBM in December 2014 is 166.12.

$\hat{\beta}_1 = -1.35$.   The estimated decrease in the value of stock for IBM for each additional month is 1.35.

c.   The approximate precision is $\pm 2s$ or $\pm 2(8.77842)$ or ± 17.56.

d.   The forecasts and prediction intervals are found at the bottom of the printout in part **b**.

Month	IBM	Forecast	95% Lower Limit	95% Upper Limit
Oct	140.08	152.59	126.94	178.25
Nov	139.42	151.24	124.09	178.39
Dec	137.62	149.89	121.07	178.71

The precision for October is approximately $\dfrac{178.25 - 126.94}{2} = 25.66$.

The precision for November is approximately $\dfrac{178.39 - 124.09}{2} = 27.15$.

The precision for December is approximately $\dfrac{178.71 - 121.07}{2} = 28.82$

These are somewhat close to the 17.56 from part **c**.

e.   The MAD, MAPE, and RMSE for the smoothed series are:

$$\text{MAD} = \frac{\sum_{t=10}^{12} |Y_t - F_t|}{m} = \frac{|140.08 - 150.34| + |139.42 - 150.34| + |137.62 - 150.34|}{3} = \frac{33.9}{3} = 11.3$$

$$\text{MAPE} = \left[\frac{\sum_{t=10}^{12} \frac{|(Y_t - F_t)|}{Y_t}}{m} \right] 100 = \left[\frac{\frac{|140.08 - 150.34|}{140.08} + \frac{|139.42 - 150.34|}{139.42} + \frac{|137.62 - 150.34|}{137.62}}{3} \right] 100$$

$$= \left[\frac{.243997}{3} \right] 100 = 8.133$$

$$\text{RMSE} = \sqrt{\frac{\sum_{t=10}^{12} (Y_t - F_t)^2}{m}} = \sqrt{\frac{(140.08 - 150.34)^2 + (139.42 - 150.34)^2 + (137.62 - 150.34)^2}{3}}$$

$$= \sqrt{\frac{386.3124}{3}} = 11.348$$

The MAD, MAPE, and RMSE for the regression model are:

$$\text{MAD} = \frac{\sum_{t=10}^{12} |Y_t - F_t|}{m} = \frac{|140.08 - 152.59| + |139.42 - 151.24| + |137.62 - 149.89|}{3} = \frac{36.6}{3} = 12.2$$

$$\text{MAPE} = \left[\frac{\sum\limits_{t=10}^{12}\frac{|(Y_t - F_t)|}{Y_t}}{m}\right]100 = \left[\frac{\left|\frac{140.08-152.59}{140.08}\right| + \left|\frac{139.42-151.24}{139.42}\right| + \left|\frac{137.62-149.89}{137.62}\right|}{3}\right]100$$

$$= \left[\frac{.263244}{3}\right]100 = 8.775$$

$$\text{RMSE} = \sqrt{\frac{\sum\limits_{t=10}^{12}(Y_t - F_t)^2}{m}} = \sqrt{\frac{(140.08-152.59)^2 + (139.42-151.24)^2 + (137.62-149.89)^2}{3}}$$

$$= \sqrt{\frac{446.7654}{3}} = 12.203$$

The values of MAD, MAPE, and RMSE for the exponentially smoothed model are all smaller than their corresponding values for the regression model.

f.   We have to assume that the error terms are independent.

g.   To determine if positive autocorrelation is present, we test:

H_0: No first-order autocorrelation of residuals
H_a: Positive first-order autocorrelation of residuals

From the printout, the test statistic is $d = .823812$.

The critical value for $k = 1$ and $n = 9$ cannot be found in Table X, Appendix D. Using a table online, $d_{L,.05} = .824$ and $d_{U,.05} = 1.320$. The rejection region is $d < .824$.

Since the observed value of the test statistic falls in the rejection region $(d = .823812 < .824)$, H_0 is rejected. There is sufficient evidence to indicate the time series residuals are positively autocorrelated at $\alpha = .05$. Since there is evidence of positive autocorrelation, the validity of the regression model is questionable.

Chapter 15
Nonparametric Statistics

15.1   The sign test is preferred to the *t*-test when the population from which the sample is selected is not normal.

15.3   a. $P(x \geq 7) = 1 - P(x \leq 6) = 1 - .965 = .035$

      b. $P(x \geq 5) = 1 - P(x \leq 4) = 1 - .637 = .363$

      c. $P(x \geq 8) = 1 - P(x \leq 7) = 1 - .996 = .004$

      d. $P(x \geq 10) = 1 - P(x \leq 9) = 1 - .849 = .151$

$$\mu = np = 15(.5) = 7.5 \text{ and } \sigma = \sqrt{npq} = \sqrt{15(.5)(.5)} = 1.9365$$

$$P(x \geq 10) \approx P\left(z \geq \frac{(10 - .5) - 7.5}{1.9365} \right) = P(z \geq 1.03) = .5 - .3485 = .1515 \quad \text{(Using Table II, Appendix D)}$$

      e. $P(x \geq 15) = 1 - P(x \leq 14) = 1 - .788 = .212$

$$\mu = np = 25(.5) = 12.5 \text{ and } \sigma = \sqrt{npq} = \sqrt{25(.5)(.5)} = 2.5$$

$$P(x \geq 15) \approx P\left(z \geq \frac{(15 - .5) - 12.5}{2.5} \right) = P(z \geq .80) = .5 - .2881 = .2119 \quad \text{(Using Table II, Appendix D)}$$

15.5   To determine if the median is greater than 75, we test:

$$H_0 : \eta = 75$$
$$H_a : \eta > 75$$

The test statistic is $S =$ number of measurements greater than 75 = 17.

The *p*-value $= P(x \geq 17)$ where x is a binomial random variable with $n = 25$ and $p = .5$. From Table I,

$$p - \text{value} = P(x \geq 17) = 1 - P(x \leq 16) = 1 - .946 = .054$$

Since the *p*-value is less than $\alpha(p = .054 < .10)$, H_0 is rejected. There is sufficient evidence to indicate the median is greater than 75 at $\alpha = .10$.

We must assume the sample was randomly selected from a continuous probability distribution.

Note: Since $n \geq 10$, we could use the large-sample approximation.

15.7   a.   To determine if the median income of graduates of the MBA program is more than $125,000, we test:

$$H_0 : \eta = 125,000$$
$$H_a : \eta > 125,000$$

b.   The test statistic is $S =$ {Number of observations greater than 125,000} = 9.

The p-value $= P(x \geq 9)$ where x is a binomial random variable with $n = 15$ and $p = .5$. From Table I,

$$p - \text{value} = P(x \geq 9) = 1 - P(x \leq 8) = 1 - .696 = .304$$

Since the p-value is not less than $\alpha (p = .304 \not< .05)$, H_0 is not rejected. There is insufficient evidence to indicate the median income of graduates of the MBA program is more than $125,000 at $\alpha = .05$.

c.   We must assume only that the sample is selected randomly from a continuous probability distribution.

15.9   To determine if half of all stocks with suspended short-sales have a positive return rate, we test:

$$H_0 : \eta = 0$$
$$H_a : \eta \neq 0$$

$S_1 =$ {Number of measurements < 0} = 11.
$S_2 =$ {Number of measurements > 0} = 6.

The test statistic S is the larger of S_1 and S_2. Thus, $S = 11$.

The p-value $= 2P(x \geq 11)$ where x is a binomial random variable with $n = 17$ and $p = .5$. Using MINITAB,

$$p - \text{value} = 2P(x \geq 11) = 2(1 - P(x \leq 10)) = 2(1 - .834) = .332$$

Since the p-value is not less than $\alpha (p = .332 \not< .05)$, H_0 is not rejected. There is insufficient evidence to indicate half of all stocks with suspended short-sales have a positive return rate at $\alpha = .05$.

15.11   To determine if the median ratio of repair to replacement cost differs from 7.0, we test:

$$H_0 : \eta = 7$$
$$H_a : \eta \neq 7$$

$S_1 =$ {Number of measurements > 7} = 11.
$S_2 =$ {Number of measurements < 7} = 2.

The test statistic S is the larger of S_1 and S_2. Thus, $S = 11$.

The p-value $= 2P(x \geq 11)$ where x is a binomial random variable with $n = 13$ and $p = .5$.

$$p - \text{value} = 2P(x \geq 11) = 2(1 - P(x \leq 10)) = 2(1 - .989) = .022$$

Since the p-value is less than $\alpha (p = .022 < .10)$, H_0 is rejected. There is sufficient evidence to indicate the median ratio of repair to replacement cost differs from 7 at $\alpha = .10$.

15.13 To determine if the median radon exposure is less than 6,000, we test:

$$H_0 : \eta = 6,000$$
$$H_a : \eta < 6,000$$

The test statistic is $S =$ number of measurements less than $6,000 = 9$.

The p-value $= P(x \geq 9)$ where x is a binomial random variable with $n = 12$ and $p = .5$. Using MINITAB,

$$p - \text{value} = P(x \geq 9) = 1 - P(x \leq 8) = 1 - .927 = .073$$

Since the p-value is less than $\alpha(p = .073 < .10)$, H_0 is rejected. There is sufficient evidence to indicate the median radon exposure is less than 6,000 at $\alpha = .10$.

No, the tombs should not be closed.

15.15 To determine if the distribution of A is shifted to the left of distribution B, we test:

H_0: The two sampled populations have identical distributions
H_a: The probability distribution for population A is shifted to the left of population B.

The test statistic is $z = \dfrac{T_1 - \dfrac{n_1(n_1 + n_2 + 1)}{2}}{\sqrt{\dfrac{n_1 n_2(n_1 + n_2 + 1)}{12}}} = \dfrac{173 - \dfrac{15(15 + 15 + 1)}{2}}{\sqrt{\dfrac{15(15)(15 + 15 + 1)}{12}}} = -2.47$

The rejection region requires $\alpha = .05$ in the lower tail of the z-distribution. From Table II, Appendix D, $z_{.05} = 1.645$. The rejection region is $z < -1.645$.

Since the observed value of the test statistic falls in the rejection region $(z = -2.47 < -1.645)$, H_0 is rejected. There is sufficient evidence to indicate the distribution of A is shifted to the left of distribution B at $\alpha = .05$.

15.17 a. The hypotheses are:

H_0: Two sampled populations have identical distributions
H_a: The probability distribution for population B is shifted to the right of that for population B

b. First, we rank all the data:

A				B	
Observation	Rank	Observation	Rank	Observation	Rank
37	8	33	3.5	65	13
40	9	35	6.5	35	6.5
33	3.5	28	1	47	11
29	2	34	5	52	12
42	10				
			$T_A = 48.5$		$T_B = 42.5$

The test statistic is $T_B = 42.5$ because $n_B < n_A$.

The rejection region is $T_B \geq 39$ from Table XII, Appendix D, with $n_A = 9$, $n_B = 4$, and $\alpha = .05$ ..

Since the observed value of the test statistic falls in the rejection region $(T_B = 42.5 \geq 39)$, H_0 is rejected. There is sufficient evidence to indicate the distribution for population B is shifted to the right of the distribution for population A at $\alpha = .05$.

15.19   a.   To determine if the median responses for the two groups of students differ, we test:

H_0: The two sampled populations have identical probability distributions
H_a: The probability distribution for non-texting group is shifted to the right or left of that for texting group

b.   Since the p-value is so small $(p = .004)$, H_0 is rejected. There is sufficient evidence to indicate the median responses for the two groups of students differ for any reasonable value of α. Since the sample median for the students in the texting group is greater than the sample median of the non-texting group, the students in the texting group have more of a preference for face-to-face meetings with their professor.

15.21   a.   The ranks of the data are:

Old Design	Rank	New Design	Rank
210	9	216	16.5
212	13.5	217	18.5
211	11	162	4
211	11	137	1
190	7	219	20
213	15	216	16.5
212	13.5	179	6
211	11	153	3
164	5	152	2
209	8	217	18.5
	$T_1 = 104$		$T_2 = 106$

b.   The sum of the ranks is $T_1 = 104$.

c.   The sum of the ranks is $T_2 = 106$.

d.   Since $n_1 = n_2 = 10$, either T_1 or T_2 can be used. We will pick $T_1 = 104$.

e.   To determine if the distributions of bursting strengths differ for the two designs, we test:

H_0: The two sampled populations have identical probability distributions
H_a: The probability distribution of the new design is located to the right or left of that for the old design.

The test statistic is $T_1 = 104$.

The null hypothesis will be rejected if $T_1 \leq T_L$ or $T_1 \geq T_U$ where T_L and T_U correspond to $\alpha = .05$ (two-tailed) and $n_1 = n_2 = 10$. From Table XII, Appendix D, $T_L = 79$ and $T_U = 131$.

Reject H_0 if $T_1 \leq 79$ or $T_1 \geq 131$.

Since $T_1 = 104 \nleq 79$ and $T_1 = 104 \ngeq 131$, H_0 is not rejected. There is insufficient evidence to indicate the distributions of bursting strengths differ for the two designs at $\alpha = .05$.

15.23   a.   The Wilcoxon Rank Sum Test would be appropriate for analyzing these data.

   b.   To determine if the low-handicapped golfers have a higher X-factor than high-handicapped golfers, we test:

   H_0: The probability distributions of the X-factors for low-handicapped and high handicapped golfers are identical
   H_a: The probability distribution of the X-factors for low-handicapped golfers is shifted to the right of that for high-handicapped golfers

   c.   The rejection region is $T_2 \leq 41$, from Table XII, Appendix D, with $n_1 = 8$, $n_2 = 7$, and $\alpha = .05$.

   d.   Since the *p*-value is not less than $\alpha \left(p = .487 \nless .05 \right)$, H_0 is not rejected. There is insufficient evidence to indicate that low-handicapped golfers have a higher X-factor than high-handicapped golfers at $\alpha = .05$.

15.25   Some preliminary calculations:

Commercial Suppliers	Rank	Government Employees	Rank
30	15.5	15	8
10	6	30	15.5
9	4	30	15.5
10	6	25	12
5	2	6	3
10	6	3	1
		20	9.5
		25	12
		30	15.5
		20	9.5
		25	12
$T_1 = 39.5$		$T_2 = 113.5$	

To determine if commercial suppliers of the DoD have less experience than government employees, we test:

   H_0: The two sampled populations have identical probability distributions
   H_a: The probability distribution for commercial suppliers of the DoD is shifted to the left of that for government employees

The test statistic is $T_1 = 39.5$ since the sample from the commercial supplies has the smallest number of observations.

Using MINITAB, the results are:

Mann-Whitney Test and CI: Com, Gov
```
        N  Median
Com     6   10.00
Gov    11   25.00


Point estimate for η1 - η2 is -11.00
96.1 Percent CI for η1 - η2 is (-20.00,4.00)
W = 39.5
Test of η1 = η2 vs η1 < η2 is significant at 0.0797
The test is significant at 0.0773 (adjusted for ties)
```

The p-value is $p = .0797$

Since the p-value is not less than $\alpha (p = .0797 \not< .05)$, H_0 is not rejected. There is insufficient evidence to indicate commercial suppliers of the DoD have less experience than government employees at $\alpha = .05$.

The nonparametric test may be more appropriate because the distributions of the years of experience for the two groups are probably not normal.

15.27   a.   Using MINITAB, the histrograms of the data are:

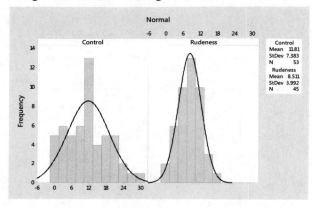

As you can see from the above graphs, the distribution for the control group is skewed to the right while the distribution for the Rudeness group is fairly normal.

b.　We first rank the data:

Control Group				Rudeness Condition			
Score	Rank	Score	Rank	Score	Rank	Score	Rank
1	5.5	9	42	4	17	7	30.5
24	96	12	66.5	11	58.5	11	58.5
5	22	18	85.5	18	85.5	4	17
16	81.5	5	22	11	58.5	13	73
21	93.5	21	93.5	9	42	5	22
7	30.5	30	98	6	25.5	4	17
20	91	15	78	5	22	7	30.5
1	5.5	4	17	11	58.5	8	36
9	42	2	9	9	42	3	12.5
20	91	12	66.5	12	66.5	8	36
19	88	11	58.5	7	30.5	15	78
10	50	10	50	5	22	9	42
23	95	13	73	7	30.5	16	81.5
16	81.5	11	58.5	3	12.5	10	50
0	2	3	12.5	11	58.5	0	2
4	17	6	25.5	1	5.5	7	30.5
9	42	10	50	9	42	15	78
13	73	13	73	11	58.5	13	73
17	84	16	81.5	10	50	9	42
13	73	12	66.5	7	30.5	2	9
0	2	28	97	8	36	13	73
2	9	19	88	9	42	10	50
12	66.5	12	66.5	10	50		
11	58.5	20	91				
7	30.5	3	12.5				
1	5.5	11	58.5				
19	88						
		$T_1 = 2,964.5$				$T_2 = 1,886.5$	

To determine if the distribution of the rudeness condition is shifted to the left of that for the control group, we test:

H_0: The distributions of the two sampled populations are identical
H_a: The distribution of the rudeness group scores is shifted to the left of that for the control group

The test statistic is $z = \dfrac{T_1 - \dfrac{n_1(n_1 + n_2 + 1)}{2}}{\sqrt{\dfrac{n_1 n_2(n_1 + n_2 + 1)}{12}}} = \dfrac{2,964.5 - \dfrac{53(53 + 45 + 1)}{2}}{\sqrt{\dfrac{53(45)(53 + 45 + 1)}{12}}} = 2.43$

The rejection region requires $\alpha = .01$ in the upper tail of the z-distribution. From Table II, Appendix D, $z_{.01} = 2.33$. The rejection region is $z > 2.33$.

Since the observed value of the test statistic falls in the rejection region $(z = 2.43 > 2.33)$, H_0 is rejected. There is sufficient evidence to indicate the distribution of the rudeness condition scores is shifted to the left of that for the control group at $\alpha = .01$.

c.　Since the sample sizes for both groups were over 30, the Central Limit Theorem applies. Thus, the parametric 2-sample test in Exercise 8.21 is appropriate.

15.29   a.   The test statistic is the smaller of T_- or T_+.

The rejection region is $T \leq 152$, from Table XIII, Appendix D, with $n = 30$, $\alpha = .10$, and two-tailed.

b.   The test statistic is T_-.

The rejection region is $T_- \leq 60$, from Table XIII, Appendix D, with $n = 20$, $\alpha = .05$, and one-tailed.

c.   The test statistic is T_+.

The rejection region is $T_+ \leq 0$, from Table XIII, Appendix D, with $n = 8$, $\alpha = .005$, and one-tailed.

15.31   a.   The hypotheses are:

H_0:   The two sampled populations have identical probability distributions
H_a: The probability distributions for population A is shifted to the right of that for population B

b.   Some preliminary calculations are:

| Treatment | | Difference | Rank of Absolute |
A	B	A - B	Difference
54	45	9	5
60	45	15	10
98	87	11	7
43	31	12	9
82	71	11	7
77	75	2	2.5
74	63	11	7
29	30	−1	1
63	59	4	4
80	82	−2	2.5
			$T_- = 3.5$

The test statistic is $T_- = 3.5$.

The rejection region is $T_- \leq 8$, from Table XIII, Appendix D, with $n = 10$ and $\alpha = .025$.

Since the observed value of the test statistic falls in the rejection region $(T_- = 3.5 \leq 8)$, H_0 is rejected. There is sufficient evidence to indicate the responses for A tend to be larger than those for B at $\alpha = .025$.

15.33   a.   In order for the confidence interval to be valid, the distribution of the differences must be normal. This may not be the case.

b.   For this paired comparison, the appropriate nonparametric test is the Wilcoxon Signed Rank Test. To determine if there is a difference in the true THM means between the original holes and their twin holes, we test:
H_0: The distributions of the the THM values for the original holes and their twins are identical
H_a: The distribution of the THM values for the the original holes is shfted to the right or left of that for the twin holes.

c & d. The differences and the ranks are in the following table:

Location	1st Hole	2nd Hole	Diff $1^{st} - 2^{nd}$	Rank of Absolute Difference
1	5.5	5.7	-0.2	3.5
2	11.0	11.2	-0.2	3.5
3	5.9	6.0	-0.1	1.5
4	8.2	5.6	2.6	15
5	10.0	9.3	0.7	6
6	7.9	7.0	0.9	7
7	10.1	8.4	1.7	13.5
8	7.4	9.0	-1.6	12
9	7.0	6.0	1.0	8
10	9.2	8.1	1.1	9
11	8.3	10.0	-1.7	13.5
12	8.6	8.1	0.5	5
13	10.5	10.4	0.1	1.5
14	5.5	7.0	-1.5	11
15	10.0	11.2	-1.2	10
				$T_- = 55$

e. $T_- = 3.5 + 3.5 + 1.5 + 12 + 13.5 + 11 + 10 = 55$ and $T_+ = 15 + 6 + 7 + 13.5 + 8 + 9 + 5 + 1.5 = 65$

f. The test statistic is the smaller of T_- and T_+ which is $T_- = 55$.

The rejection region is $T_- \leq 25$, from Table XIII, Appendix D, with $n = 15$ and $\alpha = .05$.

Since the observed value of the test statistic does not fall in the rejection region $(T_- = 55 \not\leq 25)$, H_0 is not rejected. There is insufficient evidence to indicate that there is a difference in the true THM means between the original holes and their twin holes at $\alpha = .05$.

15.35 a. The test statistic is $z = \dfrac{T_- - \dfrac{n(n+1)}{4}}{\sqrt{\dfrac{n(n+1)(2n+1)}{24}}} = \dfrac{11.50 - \dfrac{31(31+1)}{4}}{\sqrt{\dfrac{31(31+1)(2(31)+1)}{24}}} = -4.63$.

b. To determine if handling a museum object has a positive impact on a sick patient's well-being, we test:

H_0: The distributions of patients' heath statuses before and after handling museum pieces are identical

H_a: The distribution of patients' heath statuses after handling museaum pieces is shifted to the right of the distribution before handling museum pieces

The test statistic is $z = -4.63$. From the printout, the two-tailed p-value is $p = .000$. The one-tailed p-value is $p = .000 / 2 = .000$.

Since the p-value is less than $\alpha (p = .000 < .01)$, H_0 is rejected. There is sufficient evidence to indicate handling a museum object has a positive impact on a sick patient's well-being at $\alpha = .01$.

15.37   To determine if the photo-red enforcement program is effective in reducing red-light-running crash incidents at intersections, we test:

H_0: The two sampled populations have identical probability distributions
H_a: The probability distribution after the camera installation is shifted to the left of that before the camera installation

From the printout, the test statistic is $T = 79$ and the p-value is $p = .011$. Since the p-value is so small, H_0 is rejected. There is sufficient evidence to indicate the photo-red enforcement program is effective in reducing red-light-running crash incidents at intersections for any value of α greater than .011.

15.39

Operator	Before Policy	After Policy	Difference	Rank of Absolute Difference
1	10	5	5	5.5
2	3	0	3	4
3	16	7	9	8
4	11	4	7	7
5	8	6	2	2.5
6	2	4	−2	2.5
7	1	2	−1	1
8	14	3	11	9
9	5	5	0	(eliminated)
10	6	1	5	5.5
				$T_- = 3.5$
				$T_+ = 41.5$

To determine if the distributions of the number of complaints differs for the two time periods, we test:

H_0: The distributions of the number of complaints for the two years are the same
H_a: The distribution of the number of complaints after the policy change is shifted to the right or left of the distribution before the policy change.

The test statistic is $T_- = 3.5$.

Since no α is given we will use $\alpha = .05$. The null hypothesis will be rejected if $T_- \leq T_o$ where T_o corresponds to $\alpha = .05$ (two-tailed) and $n = 9$. From Table XIII, Appendix D, $T_o = 6$.

Reject H_0 if $T_- \leq 6$.

Since the observed value of the test statistic falls in the rejection region $\left(T_- = 3.5 \leq 6\right)$, H_0 is rejected.

There is sufficient evidence to indicate the distributions of the complaints are different for the two years at $\alpha = .05$.

15.41   Some preliminary calculations are:

Month	East-West	North-South	Difference	Rank of Absolute Difference
February	8,658	8,921	-263	2
April	7,930	8,317	-387	5
July	5,120	5,274	-154	1
September	6,862	7,148	-286	3
October	8,608	8,936	-328	4

$$T_- = 15$$
$$T_+ = 0$$

To determine if the distribution of monthly solar energy levels for north-south oriented highways is shifted above the corresponding distribution for east-west oriented highways, we test:

H_0: The distributions of monthly solar energy levels for the two types of highways are the same
H_a: The distribution of monthly solar energy levels for north-south oriented highways is shifted above the corresponding distribution for east-west oriented highways

The test statistic is $T_+ = 0$.

The null hypothesis will be rejected if $T_+ \le T_o$ where T_o corresponds to $\alpha = .05$ (one-tailed) and $n = 5$. From Table XIII, Appendix D, $T_o = 1$.

Reject H_0 if $T_- \le 6$.

Since the observed value of the test statistic falls in the rejection region $(T_+ = 0 \le 1)$, H_0 is rejected. There is sufficient evidence to indicate the distribution of monthly solar energy levels for north-south oriented highways is shifted above the corresponding distribution for east-west oriented highways at $\alpha = .05$.

15.43   The χ^2 distribution provides an appropriate characterization of the sampling distribution of H if the p sample sizes exceed 5.

15.45   a.   A completely randomized design was used.

b.   The hypotheses are:

H_0: The three probability distributions are identical
H_a: At least two of the three probability distributions differ in location

c.   The rejection region requires $\alpha = .01$ in the upper tail of the χ^2 distribution with $df = k - 1 = 3 - 1 = 2$. From Table IV, Appendix D, $\chi^2_{.01} = 9.21034$. The rejection region is $H > 9.21034$.

d.   Some preliminary calculations are:

I		II		III	
Observation	**Rank**	**Observation**	**Rank**	**Observation**	**Rank**
66	13	19	2	75	14.5
23	3	31	6	96	19
55	10	16	1	102	21
88	18	29	4	75	14.5
58	11	30	5	98	20
62	12	33	7	78	16
79	17	40	8		
49	9				
$R_A = 93$		$R_B = 33$		$R_C = 105$	

$$\bar{R}_A = \frac{R_A}{8} = \frac{93}{8} = 11.625 \quad \bar{R}_B = \frac{R_B}{7} = \frac{33}{7} = 4.714 \quad \bar{R}_C = \frac{R_C}{6} = \frac{105}{6} = 17.5 \quad \bar{R} = \frac{n+1}{2} = \frac{21+1}{2} = 11$$

The test statistic is:

$$H = \frac{12}{n(n+1)} \sum n_j (\bar{R}_j - \bar{R})^2$$

$$= \frac{12}{21(22)} \left[8(11.625 - 11)^2 + 7(4.714 - 11)^2 + 6(17.5 - 11)^2 \right] = 13.85$$

Since the observed value of the test statistic falls in the rejection region $(H = 13.85 > 9.21034)$, H_0 is rejected. There is sufficient evidence to indicate at least two of the three probability distributions differ in location at $\alpha = .01$.

15.47   a.   To determine if the number of collisions over a 3-year period differ among the 5 road patterns, we test:

H_0: The five probability distributions are identical
H_a: At least two of the five probability distributions differ in location

b. $\bar{R}_A = \dfrac{R_A}{30} = \dfrac{3,398}{30} = 113.267 \qquad \bar{R}_B = \dfrac{R_B}{30} = \dfrac{2,249.5}{30} = 74.983 \qquad \bar{R}_C = \dfrac{R_C}{30} = \dfrac{3,144}{30} = 104.8$

$\bar{R}_D = \dfrac{R_D}{30} = \dfrac{1,288.5}{30} = 42.95 \qquad \bar{R}_E = \dfrac{R_E}{30} = \dfrac{1,245}{30} = 41.5$

$\bar{R} = \dfrac{n+1}{2} = \dfrac{150+1}{2} = 75.5$

The test statistic is:

$$H = \frac{12}{n(n+1)} \sum n_j (\bar{R}_j - \bar{R})^2$$

$$= \frac{12}{150(151)} \left[\begin{array}{l} 30(113.267 - 75.5)^2 + 30(74.983 - 75.5)^2 + 30(104.8 - 75.5)^2 \\ + 30(42.95 - 75.5)^2 + 30(41.5 - 75.5)^2 \end{array} \right] = 71.53$$

c.   The rejection region requires $\alpha = .05$ in the upper tail of the χ^2 distribution with $df = k - 1 = 5 - 1 = 4$. From Table IV, Appendix D, $\chi^2_{.05} = 9.48773$. The rejection region is $H > 9.48773$.

Since the observed value of the test statistic falls in the rejection region $(H = 71.53 > 9.48773)$, H_0 is rejected. There is sufficient evidence to indicate that the probability distributions number of collisions of at least two of the raod patterns differ in location at $\alpha = .05$.

15.49   To determine if there are differences in the distributions of recall percentages for student-drivers in the four groups, we test:

H_0: The four probability distributions are identical
H_a: At least two of the four probability distributions differ in location

The test statistic is $H = 12.846$ and the p-value is $p = .005$. Since the p-value is less than $\alpha (p = .005 < .01)$, H_0 is rrejected. There is sufficient evidence to indicate there are differences in the distributions of recall percentages for student-drivers in the four groups at $\alpha = .01$.

15.51   a.   The F-test would be appropriate if:

1.   All k populations sampled from are normal.
2.   The variances of the k populations are equal.
3.   The k samples are independent.

   b.   The variances for the three populations are probably not the same and the populations are probably not normal.
   c.   To determine whether the salary distributions differ among the three cities, we test:

H_0: The three probability distributions are identical
H_a: At least two of the three probability distributions differ in location

Some preliminary calculations are:

Atlanta	Rank	Los Angeles	Rank	Washington,D.C.	Rank
39,600	1	47,400	3	48,000	4
89,900	19	140,000	21	86,900	17
66,700	11	68,000	12	58,000	7
43,900	2	48,700	5	82,600	15
82,200	14	74,400	13	83,200	16
88,600	18	102,000	20	61,800	8
64,800	9	54,500	6	65,000	10
	$R_1 = 74$		$R_2 = 80$		$R_3 = 77$

$$\bar{R}_1 = \frac{R_1}{n_1} = \frac{74}{7} = 10.571 \qquad\qquad \bar{R}_2 = \frac{R_2}{n_2} = \frac{80}{7} = 11.429$$

$$\bar{R}_3 = \frac{R_3}{n_3} = \frac{77}{7} = 11 \qquad\qquad \bar{R} = \frac{n+1}{2} = \frac{21+1}{2} = 11$$

The test statistic is

$$H = \frac{12}{n(n+1)} \sum n_j \left(\bar{R}_j - \bar{R}\right)^2 = \frac{12}{21(21+1)} \left[7(10.571-11)^2 + 7(11.429-11)^2 + 7(11-11)^2 \right] = 0.07$$

The rejection region requires $\alpha = .05$ in the upper tail of the χ^2 distribution with $df = k - 1 = 3 - 1 = 2$. From Table IV, Appendix D, $\chi^2_{.05} = 5.99147$. The rejection region is $H > 5.99147$.

Since the observed value of the test statistic does not fall in the rejection region $(H = .07 \not> 5.99147)$, H_0 is not rejected. There is insufficient evidence to indicate the salary distributions differ among the three cities at $\alpha = .05$.

d.   We must assume we have independent random samples, sample sizes greater than or equal to 5 from each population, and that all populations are continuous.

15.53   Some preliminary calculations:

Honey Dosage				DM Dosage				No Dosage			
Change	Rank	Change	Rank	Change	Rank	Change	Rank	Change	Rank	Change	Rank
12	88	12	88	4	12	6	24.5	5	18.5	5	18.5
11	78.5	8	47	6	24.5	8	47	8	47	11	78.5
15	102	12	88	9	59	12	88	6	24.5	9	59
11	78.5	9	59	4	12	12	88	1	3	5	18.5
10	70.5	11	78.5	7	35	4	12	0	1	6	24.5
13	96.5	15	102	7	35	12	88	8	47	8	47
10	70.5	10	70.5	7	35	13	96.5	12	88	8	47
4	12	15	102	9	59	7	35	8	47	6	24.5
15	102	9	59	12	88	10	70.5	7	35	7	35
16	105	13	96.5	10	70.5	13	96.5	7	35	10	70.5
9	59	8	47	11	78.5	9	59	1	3	9	59
14	99	12	88	6	24.5	4	12	6	24.5	4	12
10	70.5	10	70.5	3	6	4	12	7	35	8	47
6	24.5	8	47	4	12	10	70.5	7	35	7	35
10	70.5	9	59	9	59	15	102	12	88	3	6
8	47	5	18.5	12	88	9	59	7	35	1	3
11	78.5	12	88	7	35			9	59	4	12
12	88							7	35	3	6
								9	59		
				$R_1 = 2,549$				$R_2 = 1,693.5$				$R_3 = 1,322.5$

$$\bar{R}_1 = \frac{R_1}{n_1} = \frac{2549}{35} = 72.829 \qquad \bar{R}_2 = \frac{R_2}{n_2} = \frac{1693.5}{33} = 51.318$$

$$\bar{R}_3 = \frac{R_3}{n_3} = \frac{1322.5}{37} = 35.743 \qquad \bar{R} = \frac{n+1}{2} = \frac{105+1}{2} = 53$$

To determine if the distributions of improvement scores for the three groups differ in location, we test:

H_0: The three probability distributions are identical
H_a: At least two of the three improvement distributions differ in location

The test statistic is

$$H = \frac{12}{n(n+1)} \sum n_j \left(\bar{R}_j - \bar{R} \right)^2$$

$$= \frac{12}{105(105+1)} \left[35(72.829 - 53)^2 + 33(51.318 - 53)^2 + 37(35.743 - 53)^2 \right] = 26.82$$

The rejection region requires $\alpha = .01$ in the upper tail of the χ^2 distribution with $df = k - 1 = 3 - 1 = 2$. From Table IV, Appendix D, $\chi^2_{.01} = 9.21034$. The rejection region is $H > 9.21034$.

Since the observed value of the test statistic falls in the rejection region $(H = 26.82 > 9.21034)$, H_0 is rejected. There is sufficient evidence to indicate the distributions of improvement scores for the three groups differ in location at $\alpha = .01$.

15.55   a.   The hypotheses are:

H_0:   The probability distributions for three treatments are identical
H_a: At least two of the probability distributions differ in location

b.   The rejection region requires $\alpha = .10$ in the upper tail of the χ^2 distribution with $df = k - 1 = 3 - 1 = 2$. From Table IV, Appendix D, $\chi^2_{.10} = 4.60517$. The rejection region is $F_r > 4.60517$.

c.   Some preliminary calculations are:

Block	A	Rank	B	Rank	C	Rank
1	9	1	11	2	18	3
2	13	2	13	2	13	2
3	11	1	12	2.5	12	2.5
4	10	1	15	2	16	3
5	9	2	8	1	10	3
6	14	2	12	1	16	3
7	10	1	12	2	15	3
		$R_A = 10$		$R_B = 12.5$		$R_C = 19.5$

$$\bar{R}_A = \frac{R_A}{b} = \frac{10}{7} = 1.429 \qquad \bar{R}_B = \frac{R_B}{b} = \frac{12.5}{7} = 1.786 \qquad \bar{R}_C = \frac{R_C}{b} = \frac{19.5}{7} = 2.786$$

$$\bar{R} = \frac{1}{2}(k+1) = \frac{1}{2}(3+1) = 2$$

The test statistic is

$$F_r = \frac{12b}{k(k+1)}\sum(\bar{R}_j - \bar{R})^2 = \frac{12(7)}{3(3+1)}\left[(1.429-2)^2 + (1.786-2)^2 + (2.786-2)^2\right] = 6.93$$

Since the observed value of the test statistic falls in the rejection region $(F_r = 6.93 > 4.60517)$, H_0 is rejected. There is sufficient evidence to indicate the effectiveness of the three different treatments differ at $\alpha = .10$.

15.57   a.   The data are not independent. Each subject had measurements for each of the 4 time segments. Thus, the data are blocked. It would realistic to assume that the data might not be normally distributed, so the use of a nonparametric test would be appropriate. Thus, the Friedman test would be appropriate.

b.   The test statistic is $F_r = 14.37$ and the p-value is $p = .002$.

c.   Since the p-value is less than $\alpha (p = .002 < .01)$, H_0 is rejected. There is sufficient evidence to indicate the distribution of walking times differ for the four time segments at $\alpha = .01$.

15.59   a.   From the printout, the rank sums are 23 (before), 32 (after 2 months), and 35 (after 2 days).

b. $\bar{R}_1 = \dfrac{R_1}{b} = \dfrac{23}{15} = 1.533$ $\bar{R}_2 = \dfrac{R_2}{b} = \dfrac{32}{15} = 2.133$ $\bar{R}_3 = \dfrac{R_3}{b} = \dfrac{35}{15} = 2.333$

$\bar{R} = \dfrac{1}{2}(k+1) = \dfrac{1}{2}(3+1) = 2$

$F_r = \dfrac{12b}{k(k+1)}\sum(\bar{R}_j - \bar{R})^2 = \dfrac{12(15)}{3(3+1)}\left[(1.533-2)^2 + (2.133-2)^2 + (2.333-2)^2\right] = 5.2$

c.   From the printout, the test statistic is $F_r = 5.20$ and the p-value is $p = .074$.

d.   To determine if the distributions of the competence levels differ in location among the 3 time periods, we test:

H_0: The probability distributions of the three sampled populations are the same
H_a: At least two of the distributions of the competence levels differ in location

The test statistic is $F_r = 5.20$ and the p-value is $p = .074$. Since the p-value is not small, we would not reject H_0 for any values of $\alpha < .074$. There is insufficient evidence to indicate the distributions of the competence levels differ in location among the 3 time periods for $\alpha < .074$.

If we use $\alpha = .10$, then we would reject H_0.

15.61   Using MINITAB, the results of analyzing the data using Friedman's test are:

Friedman Test: Score versus Item blocked by Review
```
S = 29.11   DF = 10   P = 0.001
S = 31.39   DF = 10   P = 0.001 (adjusted for ties)

                    Sum
             Est    of
Item  N   Median  Ranks
 1    5    3.500   40.0
 2    5    2.500   28.5
 3    5    3.864   46.5
 4    5    3.591   40.0
 5    5    2.455   23.0
 6    5    3.591   41.0
 7    5    3.500   37.0
 8    5    3.227   32.0
 9    5    2.636   23.5
10    5    1.091    9.5
11    5    1.045    9.0

Grand median = 2.818
```

To determine if the distributions of the 11 item scores are different, we test:

H_0: The distributions of the 11 item scores are identical
H_a: At least two of the distributions of the item scores differ in location

From the printout, the test statistic is $F_r = 29.11$ and the p-value is $p = .001$. Since the p-value is so small, H_0 is rejected for any reasonable value of α. There is sufficient evidence to indicate that the distributions of the 11 item scores differ in location at any reasonable value of α.

15.63   Some preliminary calculations are:

Student	Rank Live Plant	Rank Plant Photo	Rank No Plant
1	1	2	3
2	2	3	1
3	3	2	1
4	1	2	3
5	2	3	1
6	3	2	1
7	2	1	3
8	1	3	2
9	2	1	3
10	2	1	3
	$R_1 = 19$	$R_2 = 20$	$R_3 = 21$

$$\bar{R}_1 = \frac{R_1}{n_1} = \frac{19}{10} = 1.9 \quad \bar{R}_2 = \frac{R_2}{n_2} = \frac{20}{10} = 2 \quad \bar{R}_3 = \frac{R_3}{n_3} = \frac{21}{10} = 2.1 \quad \bar{R} = \frac{k+1}{2} = \frac{3+1}{2} = 2$$

To determine if the students' finger temperatures depend on the experimental conditions, we test:

H_0: The probability distributions of finger temperatures are the same for the three conditions

H_a: At least two probability distributions of finger temperatures differ in location

The test statistic is $F_r = \frac{12b}{k(k+1)} \sum (\bar{R}_j - \bar{R})^2 = \frac{12(10)}{3(3+1)} \left[(1.9-2)^2 + (2-2)^2 + (2.1-2)^2 \right] = 0.2$

Since no α was given, we will use $\alpha = .05$. The rejection region requires $\alpha = .05$ in the upper tail of the χ^2 distribution with $df = k-1 = 3-1 = 2$. From Table IV, Appendix D, $\chi^2_{.05} = 5.99147$. The rejection region is $F_r > 5.99147$.

Since the observed value of the test statistic does not fall in the rejection region $(F_r = 0.2 \not> 5.99147)$, H_0 is not rejected. There is insufficient evidence to indicate that the students' finger temperatures depend on the experimental conditions at $\alpha = .05$.

Because the value of the test statistic is so small, H_0 would not be rejected for any reasonable value of α.

15.65   Some preliminary calculations are:

Subject	Rank Standard	Rank Supervent	Rank Ecopack
1	1	2	3
2	1	3	2
3	1.5	1.5	3
4	2	1	3
5	2	1	3
6	1	2	3
7	2	3	1
8	1	2	3
9	1	2	3
10	1	3	2
	$R_1 = 13.5$	$R_2 = 20.5$	$R_3 = 26$

$$\bar{R}_1 = \frac{R_1}{n_1} = \frac{13.5}{10} = 1.35 \quad \bar{R}_2 = \frac{R_2}{n_2} = \frac{20.5}{10} = 2.05 \quad \bar{R}_3 = \frac{R_3}{n_3} = \frac{26}{10} = 2.6 \quad \bar{R} = \frac{k+1}{2} = \frac{3+1}{2} = 2$$

To determine if the distributions of job suitability scores differ for the three candidates, we test:

H_0: The probability distributions of job suitability scores are the same for the three candidates
H_a: At least two probability distributions of job suitability scores differ in location

The test statistic is $F_r = \dfrac{12b}{k(k+1)}\sum\left(\bar{R}_j - \bar{R}\right)^2 = \dfrac{12(10)}{3(3+1)}\left[(1.35-2)^2 + (2.05-2)^2 + (2.6-2)^2\right] = 7.85$

The rejection region requires $\alpha = .01$ in the upper tail of the χ^2 distribution with $df = k-1 = 3-1 = 2$. From Table IV, Appendix D, $\chi^2_{.01} = 9.21034$. The rejection region is $F_r > 9.21034$.

Since the observed value of the test statistic does not fall in the rejection region $\left(F_r = 7.85 \not> 9.21034\right)$, H_0 is not rejected. There is insufficient evidence to indicate the distributions of job suitability scores differ for the three candidates at $\alpha = .01$.

15.67   a.   From Table XIV with $n = 10$, $r_{s,\alpha/2} = r_{s,.025} = .648$. The rejection region is $r_s < -.648$ or $r_s > .648$.

b.   From Table XIV with $n = 20$, $r_{s,\alpha} = r_{s,.025} = .450$. The rejection region is $r_s > .450$.

c.   From Table XIV with $n = 30$, $r_{s,\alpha} = r_{s,.01} = .432$. The rejection region is $r_s < -.432$.

15.69   Since there are no ties, we will use the shortcut formula.

a.   Some preliminary calculations are:

x Rank (u_i)	y Rank (v_i)	$d_i = u_i - v_i$	d_i^2
3	2	1	1
5	4	1	1
2	5	−3	9
1	1	0	0
4	3	1	1
			Total = 12

$$r_s = 1 - \frac{6\sum d_i^2}{n(n^2-1)} = 1 - \frac{6(12)}{5(5^2-1)} = 1 - .6 = .4$$

b.

x Rank (u_i)	y Rank (v_i)	$d_i = u_i - v_i$	d_i^2
2	3	−1	1
3	4	−1	1
4	2	2	4
5	1	4	16
1	5	−4	16
			Total = 38

$$r_s = 1 - \frac{6\sum d_i^2}{n(n^2-1)} = 1 - \frac{6(38)}{5(5^2-1)} = 1 - 1.9 = -.9$$

c.

x Rank (u_i)	y Rank (v_i)	$d_i = u_i - v_i$	d_i^2
1	2	-1	1
4	1	3	9
2	3	-1	1
3	4	-1	1
			Total = 12

$$r_s = 1 - \frac{6 \sum d_i^2}{n(n^2 - 1)} = 1 - \frac{6(12)}{4(4^2 - 1)} = 1 - 1.2 = -.2$$

d.

x Rank (u_i)	y Rank (v_i)	$d_i = u_i - v_i$	d_i^2
2	1	1	1
5	3	2	4
4	5	-1	1
3	2	1	1
1	4	-3	9
			Total = 16

$$r_s = 1 - \frac{6 \sum d_i^2}{n(n^2 - 1)} = 1 - \frac{6(16)}{5(5^2 - 1)} = 1 - .8 = .2$$

15.71   a.   Some preliminary calculations:

x	Rank, u	y	Rank, v	u^2	v^2	uv
28.582	2	3	2	4	4	4
24.374	1	1	1	1	1	1
31.666	3	10	5	9	25	15
40.530	6	14	6	36	36	36
38.808	5	7	4	25	16	20
33.309	4	4	3	16	9	12
	$\sum u = 21$		$\sum v = 21$	$\sum u^2 = 91$	$\sum v^2 = 91$	$\sum uv = 88$

$$SS_{uv} = \sum uv - \frac{\left(\sum u\right)\left(\sum v\right)}{n} = 88 - \frac{21(21)}{6} = 14.5 \qquad SS_{uu} = \sum u^2 - \frac{\left(\sum u\right)^2}{n} = 91 - \frac{(21)^2}{6} = 17.5$$

$$SS_{vv} = \sum v^2 - \frac{\left(\sum v\right)^2}{n} = 91 - \frac{(21)^2}{6} = 17.5 \qquad r_s = \frac{SS_{uv}}{\sqrt{SS_{uu} SS_{vv}}} = \frac{14.5}{\sqrt{(17.5)(17.5)}} = .8286 \; .$$

b. To determine if there is positive rank correlation between total US births and the number of software millionaire birthdays, we test:

$$H_0 : \rho_s = 0$$
$$H_a : \rho_s > 0$$

The test statistic is $r_s = .8286$.

Reject H_0 if $r_s > r_{s,\alpha}$ where $\alpha = .05$ and $n = 6$:

Reject H_0 if $r_s > .829$ (from Table XIV, Appendix D).

Since the observed value of the test statistic does not fall in the rejection region $\left(r_s = .8286 \not> .829\right)$, H_0 is not rejected. There is insufficient evidence to indicate total US births and the number of software millionaire birthdays are positively rank correlated at $\alpha = .05$.

c. Some preliminary calculations:

x	Rank, u	y	Rank, v	u^2	v^2	uv
2	2.5	3	2	6.25	4	5
2	2.5	1	1	6.25	1	2.5
23	5	10	5	25	25	25
38	6	14	6	36	36	36
9	4	7	4	16	16	16
0	1	4	3	1	9	3
	$\sum u = 21$		$\sum v = 21$	$\sum u^2 = 90.5$	$\sum v^2 = 91$	$\sum uv = 87.5$

$$SS_{uv} = \sum uv - \frac{\left(\sum u\right)\left(\sum v\right)}{n} = 87.5 - \frac{21(21)}{6} = 14 \qquad SS_{uu} = \sum u^2 - \frac{\left(\sum u\right)^2}{n} = 90.5 - \frac{(21)^2}{6} = 17$$

$$SS_{vv} = \sum v^2 - \frac{\left(\sum v\right)^2}{n} = 91 - \frac{(21)^2}{6} = 17.5 \qquad r_s = \frac{SS_{uv}}{\sqrt{SS_{uu}SS_{vv}}} = \frac{14}{\sqrt{(17)(17.5)}} = .8117.$$

d. To determine if there is positive rank correlation between the number of software millionaire birthdays and the number of CEO birthdays, we test:

$$H_0 : \rho_s = 0$$
$$H_a : \rho_s > 0$$

The test statistic is $r_s = .8117$.

Reject H_0 if $r_s > r_{s,\alpha}$ where $\alpha = .05$ and $n = 6$.

Reject H_0 if $r_s > .829$ (from Table XIV, Appendix D).

Since the observed value of the test statistic does not fall in the rejection region $\left(r_s = .8117 \not> .829\right)$, H_0 is not rejected. There is insufficient evidence to indicate the number of software millionaire birthdays and the number of CEO birthdays are positively rank correlated at $\alpha = .05$.

15.73   a.   **Navigability**: $r_s = .179$. Since this value is close to 0, there is a very weak positive rank correlation between the ranks of organizational internet use and the ranks of navigability.

Transactions: $r_s = .334$. Since this value is relatively close to 0, there is a weak positive rank correlation between the ranks of organizational internet use and the ranks of transactions.

Locatability: $r_s = .590$. Since this value is about half way between 0 and 1, there is a moderate positive rank correlation between the ranks of organizational internet use and the ranks of locatability.

Information Richness: $r_s = -.115$. Since this value is close to 0, there is a very weak negative rank correlation between the ranks of organizational internet use and the ranks of information richness.

Number of files: $r_s = .114$. Since this value is close to 0, there is a very weak positive rank correlation between the ranks of organizational internet use and the ranks of number of files.

b.   For each indicator, we will test:

$$H_0 : \rho_s = 0$$
$$H_a : \rho_s > 0$$

Navigability: p-value $= p = .148$. Since the p-value is greater than $\alpha = .10$, H_0 is not rejected. There is insufficient evidence to indicate a positive rank correlation between organizational internet use and navigability.

Transactions: p-value $= p = .023$. Since the p-value is less than $\alpha = .10$, H_0 is rejected. There is sufficient evidence to indicate a positive rank correlation between organizational internet use and transactions.

Locatability: p-value $= p = .000$. Since the p-value is less than $\alpha = .10$, H_0 is rejected. There is sufficient evidence to indicate a positive rank correlation between organizational internet use and locatability.

Information Richness: p-value $= p = .252$. Since the p-value is greater than $\alpha = .10$, H_0 is not rejected. There is insufficient evidence to indicate a positive rank correlation between organizational internet use and information richness.

Number of files: p-value $= p = .255$. Since the p-value is greater than $\alpha = .10$, H_0 is not rejected. There is insufficient evidence to indicate a positive rank correlation between organizational internet use and number of files.

15.75 Some preliminary calculations are:

Punish	Rank, u	Payoff	Rank, v	u^2	v^2	uv
0	1	0.50	13	1	169	13
1	2	0.20	9	4	81	18
2	3	0.30	11.5	9	132.25	34.5
3	4	0.25	10	16	100	40
4	5	0.00	6	25	36	30
5	6	0.30	11.5	36	132.25	69
6	7	0.10	7	49	49	49
8	8	-0.20	3.5	64	12.25	28
10	9	0.15	8	81	64	72
12	10	-0.30	1	100	1	10
14	11	-0.10	5	121	25	55
16	12	-0.20	3.5	144	12.25	42
17	13	-0.25	2	169	4	26
	$\sum u = 91$		$\sum v = 91$	$\sum u^2 = 819$	$\sum v^2 = 818$	$\sum uv = 486.5$

$$\text{SS}_{uv} = \sum uv - \frac{\left(\sum u\right)\left(\sum v\right)}{n} = 486.5 - \frac{91(91)}{13} = -150.5$$

$$\text{SS}_{uu} = \sum u^2 - \frac{\left(\sum u\right)^2}{n} = 819 - \frac{(91)^2}{13} = 182 \qquad \text{SS}_{vv} = \sum v^2 - \frac{\left(\sum v\right)^2}{n} = 818 - \frac{(91)^2}{13} = 181$$

$$r_s = \frac{\text{SS}_{uv}}{\sqrt{\text{SS}_{uu}\text{SS}_{vv}}} = \frac{-150.5}{\sqrt{(182)(181)}} = -.829$$

To determine if "punishers tend to have lower payoffs", we test:

$$H_0 : \rho_s = 0$$
$$H_a : \rho_s < 0$$

The test statistic is $r_s = -.829$

Since no α was given, we will use $\alpha = .05$.

Reject H_0 if $r_s < -r_{s,\alpha}$ where $\alpha = .05$ and $n = 13$.

Reject H_0 if $r_s < -.475$ (from Table XIV, Appendix D)

Since the observed value of the test statistic falls in the rejection region $\left(r_s = -.829 < -.475\right)$, H_0 is rejected. There is sufficient evidence to indicate "punishers tend to have lower payoffs" at $\alpha = .05$.

15.77 Some preliminary calculations are:

Year	R-Year	Cost	R-Cost	d	d²
1974	1	40	9	-8	64
1975	2	28	5	-3	9
1977	3	13	1	2	4
1978	4.5	26	4	0.5	0.25
1978	4.5	30	7	-2.5	6.25
1979	6	16	2	4	16
1981	7	20	3	4	16
1987	8	29	6	2	4
1989	9	31	8	1	1
1998	10	55	10	0	0
2005	11	105	12	-1	1
2012	12	80	11	1	1

$$\sum d_i^2 = 122.5$$

$$r_s = 1 - \frac{6\sum d_i^2}{n(n^2-1)} = 1 - \frac{6(122.5)}{12(12^2-1)} = 1 - .428 = .572$$

There is a positive linear relationship between the ranks of the year and the ranks of the estimates annual cost. As the year increases, the cost tends to increase.

15.79 Some preliminary calculations are:

2014	R-2014	2015	R-2015	d	d²
66.1	1	75.0	1	0	0
67.9	2	79.7	16	-14	196
69.2	3	80.0	17	-14	196
69.6	4	78.8	13	-9	81
69.7	5	75.2	3	2	4
70.6	6	75.1	2	4	16
71.5	7	81.5	18.5	-11.5	132.25
72.4	8	78.4	12	-4	16
72.6	9.5	84.1	20	-10.5	110.25
72.6	9.5	76.3	8	1.5	2.25
73.0	11	75.5	4	7	49
73.7	12.5	75.9	7	5.5	30.25
73.7	12.5	75.6	5.5	7	49
75.0	14.5	76.6	10	4.5	20.25
75.0	14.5	77.3	11	3.5	12.25
75.1	16	81.5	18.5	-2.5	6.25
77.2	17.5	75.6	5.5	12	144
77.2	17.5	79.3	15	2.5	6.25
77.3	19.5	79.2	14	5.5	30.25
77.3	19.5	76.4	9	10.5	110.25

$$\sum d_i^2 = 1,211.5$$

$$r_s = 1 - \frac{6\sum d_i^2}{n(n^2-1)} = 1 - \frac{6(1,211.5)}{20(20^2-1)} = 1 - .911 = .089$$

To determine if there is evidence of a positive rank correlation between global scores of firms in 2014 and 2015, we test:

$$H_0 : \rho_s = 0$$
$$H_a : \rho_s > 0$$

The test statistic is $r_s = .089$.

Reject H_0 if $r_s > r_{s,\alpha}$ where $\alpha = .01$ and $n = 20$:

Reject H_0 if $r_s > .534$ (from Table XIV, Appendix D).

Since the observed value of the test statistic does not fall in the rejection region $(r_s = .089 \not> .534)$, H_0 is not rejected. There is insufficient evidence to indicate a positive rank correlation between global scores of firms in 2014 and 2015 at $\alpha = .01$.

15.81   a.   Some preliminary calculations are:

Pair	x	Rank, u	y	Rank, v	u^2	v^2	uv
1	19	5	12	5	25	25	25
2	27	7	19	8	49	64	56
3	15	2	7	1	4	1	2
4	35	9	25	9	81	81	81
5	13	1	11	4	1	16	4
6	29	8	10	2.5	64	6.25	20
7	16	3.5	16	6	12.25	36	21
8	22	6	10	2.5	36	6.25	15
9	16	3.5	18	7	12.25	49	24.5
		$\sum u_i = 45$		$\sum v_i = 45$	$\sum u_i^2 = 284.5$	$\sum v_i^2 = 284.5$	$\sum u_i v_i = 248.5$

$$SS_{uv} = \sum u_i v_i - \frac{\sum u_i v_i}{n} = 248.5 - \frac{45(45)}{9} = 23.5$$

$$SS_{uu} = \sum u_i^2 - \frac{\left(\sum u_i\right)^2}{n} = 284.5 - \frac{(45)^2}{9} = 59.5 \qquad SS_{vv} = \sum v_i^2 - \frac{\left(\sum v_i\right)^2}{n} = 284.5 - \frac{(45)^2}{9} = 59.5$$

To determine if the Spearman rank correlation differs from 0, we test:

$$H_0 : \rho_s = 0$$
$$H_a : \rho_s \neq 0$$

The test statistic is $r_s = \dfrac{SS_{uv}}{\sqrt{SS_{uv} SS_{vv}}} = \dfrac{23.5}{\sqrt{(59.5)(59.5)}} = .39$

Reject H_0 if $r_s < -r_{s,\alpha/2}$ or $r_s > r_{s,\alpha/2}$ where $\alpha / 2 = .025$ and $n = 9$:

Reject H_0 if $r_s < -.683$ or $r_s > .683$ (from Table XIV, Appendix D)

Since the observed value of the test statistic does not fall in the rejection region $\left(r_s = .39 \not> .683\right)$, H_0 is not rejected. There is insufficient evidence to indicate that Spearman's rank correlation between x and y is significantly different from 0 at $\alpha = .05$.

b.   Use the Wilcoxon signed rank test. Some preliminary calculations are:

Pair	x	y	Difference	Rank of Absolute Difference
1	19	12	7	3
2	27	19	8	4.5
3	15	7	8	4.5
4	35	25	10	6
5	13	11	2	1.5
6	29	10	19	8
7	16	16	0	(eliminated)
8	22	10	12	7
9	16	18	-2	1.5
				$T_- = 1.5$

To determine if the probability distribution of x is shifted to the right of that for y, we test:

H_0:   The probability distributions are identical for the two variables
H_a: The probability distribution of x is shifted to the right of the probability distribution of y

The test statistic is $T = T_- = 1.5$.

Reject H_0 if $T \le T_0$ where T_0 is based on $\alpha = .05$ and $n = 8$ (one-tailed):

Reject H_0 if $T \le 6$ (from Table XIII, Appendix D).

Since the observed value of the test statistic falls in the rejection region $\left(T = 1.5 \le 6\right)$, H_0 is rejected. There is sufficient evidence to conclude that the probability distribution of x is shifted to the right of that for y at $\alpha = .05$.

15.83   Some preliminary calculations are:

Block	1	Rank	2	Rank	3	Rank	4	Rank	5	Rank
1	75	4	65	1	74	3	80	5	69	2
2	77	3	69	1	78	4	80	5	72	2
3	70	4	63	1.5	69	3	75	5	63	1.5
4	80	3.5	69	1	80	3.5	86	5	77	2
		$R_1 = 14.5$		$R_2 = 4.5$		$R_3 = 13.5$		$R_4 = 20$		$R_5 = 7.5$

$$\bar{R}_1 = \frac{R_1}{b} = \frac{14.5}{4} = 3.625 \quad \bar{R}_2 = \frac{R_2}{b} = \frac{4.5}{4} = 1.125 \quad \bar{R}_3 = \frac{R_3}{b} = \frac{13.5}{4} = 3.375 \quad \bar{R}_4 = \frac{R_4}{b} = \frac{20}{4} = 5$$

$$\bar{R}_5 = \frac{R_5}{b} = \frac{7.5}{4} = 1.875 \quad \bar{R} = \frac{k+1}{2} = \frac{5+1}{2} = 3$$

To determine whether at least two of the treatment probability distributions differ in location, use Friedman F_r test.

H_0:   The five treatments have identical probability distributions
H_a: At least two of the populations have probability distributions differ in location

The test statistic is

$$F_r = \frac{12b}{k(k+1)}\sum\left(\bar{R}_j - \bar{R}\right)^2 = \frac{12(4)}{5(5+1)}\left[(3.625-3)^2 + (1.125-3)^2 + (3.375-3)^2 + (5-3)^2 + (1.875-3)^2\right] = 14.9$$

The rejection region requires $\alpha = .05$ in the upper tail of the χ^2 distribution with $df = k-1 = 5-1 = 4$. From Table IV, Appendix D, $\chi^2_{.05} = 9.48773$. The rejection region is $F_r > 9.48773$.

Since the observed value of the test statistic falls in the rejection region $\left(F_r = 14.9 > 9.48773\right)$, H_0 is rejected. There is sufficient evidence to indicate that at least two of the treatment means differ in location at $\alpha = .05$.

15.85   a.   To determine if the distribution of the recalls for those receiving audiovisual presentation differs from that of the recalls of those receiving only the visual presentation, we test:

H_0: The two sampled distributions are identical
H_a: The distribution of recalls for those receiving audiovisual presentation is shifted to the right or left of that for those receiving only visual presentation

b.   First, we rank all of the data:

Audiovisual Group				Video Only Group			
Recall	Rank	Recall	Rank	Recall	Rank	Recall	Rank
0	1.5	1	5	6	34.5	6	34.5
4	24	2	12	3	19	2	12
6	34.5	6	34.5	6	34.5	3	19
6	34.5	1	5	2	12	1	5
1	5	3	19	2	12	3	19
2	12	0	1.5	4	24	2	12
2	12	2	12	7	40	5	28
6	34.5	5	28	6	34.5	2	12
6	34.5	4	24	1	5	4	24
4	24	5	28	3	19	6	34.5
		$T_1 = 385.5$				$T_2 = 434.5$	

The test statistic is $z = \dfrac{T_1 - \dfrac{n_1(n_1+n_2+1)}{2}}{\sqrt{\dfrac{n_1 n_2(n_1+n_2+1)}{12}}} = \dfrac{385.5 - \dfrac{20(20+20+1)}{2}}{\sqrt{\dfrac{20(20)(20+20+1)}{12}}} = -.66$

c.   The rejection region requires $\alpha/2 = .10/2 = .05$ in each tail of the z-distribution. From Table II, Appendix D, $z_{.05} = 1.645$. The rejection region is $z < -1.645$ or $z > 1.645$.

d.   Since the observed value of the test statistic does not fall in the rejection region $(z = -.66 \not< -1.645)$, H_0 is not rejected. There is insufficient evidence to indicate the distribution of the recalls for those receiving audiovisual presentation differs from that of the recalls of those receiving only the visual presentation at $\alpha = .10$. This supports the researchers' theory.

15.87   a.   To calculate the median, we first arrange the data in order from the smallest to the largest:

22, 28, 32, 33, 39, 41, 43, 43, 45, 47, 50, 54, 54, 59, 62

Since n is odd, the median is the middle number, which is 43.

b. To determine if the median age of the terminated workers exceeds the entire company's median age, we test:

$$H_0 : \eta = 37$$
$$H_a : \eta > 37$$

c. The test statistic is S = number of measurements greater than $37 = 11$.

The p-value $= P(x \geq 11)$ where x is a binomial random variable with $n = 15$ and $p = .5$. From Table I, Appendix D, $p - \text{value} = P(x \geq 11) = 1 - P(x \leq 10) = 1 - .941 = .059$.

Since no α value was given, we will use $\alpha = .05$. Since the p-value is greater than $\alpha (p = .059 > .05)$, H_0 is not rejected. There is insufficient evidence to indicate that the median age of the terminated workers exceeds the entire company's median age at $\alpha = .05$.

(Note: If $\alpha = .10$ was used, the conclusion would be to reject H_0.)

d. Since the conclusion using $\alpha = .10$ is to reject H_0 and conclude that there is sufficient evidence to indicate that the median age of the terminated workers exceeds the entire company's median age, we would advise the company to reevaluate its planned RIF. With the proposed sample, there is evidence that the company is discriminating with respect to age.

15.89 a. Some preliminary calculations are:

Brand	Expert 1	Expert 2	Difference d_1	d_i^2
A	6	5	1	1
B	5	6	−1	1
C	1	2	−1	1
D	3	1	2	4
E	2	4	−2	4
F	4	3	1	1
				$\sum d_i^2 = 12$

$$r_s = 1 - \frac{6\sum d_i^2}{n(n^2 - 1)} = 1 - \frac{6(12)}{6(6^2 - 1)} = 1 - .343 = .657$$

b. To determine if there is a positive correlation in the rankings of the two experts, we test:

$$H_0 : \rho_s = 0$$
$$H_a : \rho_s > 0$$

The test statistic is $r_s = .657$.

Reject H_0 if $r_s > r_{s,\alpha}$ where $\alpha = .05$ and $n = 6$. From Table XIV, Appendix D, $r_{s,.01} = .829$
Reject H_0 if $r_s > .829$.

Since the observed value of the test statistic does not fall in the rejection region $(r_s = .657 \not> .829)$, H_0 is not rejected. There is insufficient evidence to indicate a positive correlation in the rankings of the two experts at $\alpha = .05$.

5.91   a.   Since only 70 of the 80 customers responded to the question, only the 70 will be included.

To determine if the median amount spent on hamburgers at lunch at McDonald's is less than $2.25, we test:

$$H_0 : \eta = 2.25$$
$$H_a : \eta < 2.25$$

S = number of measurements less than 2.25 = 20.

The test statistic is $z = \dfrac{(S - .5) - .5n}{.5\sqrt{n}} = \dfrac{(20 - .5) - .5(70)}{.5\sqrt{70}} = -3.71$

Since no α was given in the exercise, we will use $\alpha = .05$. The rejection region requires $\alpha = .05$ in the upper tail of the z-distribution. From Table II, Appendix D, $z_{.05} = 1.645$. The rejection region is $z > 1.645$.

Since the observed value of the test statistic does not fall in the rejection region $(z = -3.71 \not> 1.645)$, H_0 is not rejected. There is insufficient evidence to indicate that the median amount spent on hamburgers at lunch at McDonald's is less than $2.25 at $\alpha = .05$.

b.   No. The survey was done in Boston only. The eating habits of those living in Boston are probably not representative of all Americans.

c.   We must assume that the sample is randomly selected from a continuous probability distribution.

15.93   a.   Some preliminary calculations are:

Circuit	Standard Method	Huffman-coding Method	Difference S-H	Rank of Absolute Differences
1	0.80	0.78	0.02	2
2	0.80	0.80	0.00	(eliminated)
3	0.83	0.86	-0.03	3
4	0.53	0.53	0.00	(eliminated)
5	0.50	0.51	-0.01	1
6	0.96	0.68	0.28	8
7	0.99	0.82	0.17	5
8	0.98	0.72	0.26	7
9	0.81	0.45	0.36	9
10	0.95	0.79	0.16	4
11	0.99	0.77	0.22	6
				$T_- = 4$

To determine if the Huffman-coding method yields a smaller mean compression ratio, we test:
H_0: The two sampled populations have identical probability distributions.
H_a: The probability distribution of the Standard Method is shifted to the right of that for the Huffman-coding Method.

The test statistic is $T_- = 4$.

The rejection region is $T_- \leq 8$, from Table XIII, Appendix D, with $n = 9$ and $\alpha = .05$ (one-tailed).

Since the observed value of the test statistic falls in the rejection region $\left(T_- = 4 \le 8\right)$, H_0 is rejected. There is sufficient evidence to indicate the Huffman-coding method yields a smaller mean compression ratio at $\alpha = .05$

b. In Exercise 8.110, we concluded that the Huffman-coding method yields a smaller mean compression ratio than the standard method which is the same as the conclusion above.

15.95 a. Using MINITAB, histograms of the two data sets are:

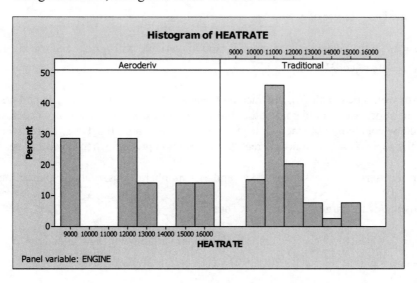

From the histograms, the data for each group do not look like they are mound-shaped. The variance of the aeroderivative engines is greater than that of the traditional engines. Thus, the assumptions of normal distributions and equal variances necessary for the *t*-test are probably not met.

b. Using MINITAB, the results are:

Mann-Whitney Test and CI: Trad, Aero
```
        N   Median
Trad   39   11183
Aero    7   12414

Point estimate for η1 - η2 is -1125
95.3 Percent CI for η1 - η2 is (-2358,1448)
W = 885.0
Test of η1 = η2 vs η1 ≠ η2 is significant at 0.3431
The test is significant at 0.3431 (adjusted for ties)
```

To determine if the distributions of the heat rates for traditional and aeroderivative engines differ, we test:

H_0: The distributions of the heat rates for the two types of engines are identical
H_a: The distribution of the heat rates traditional engines is shifted to the right or left of that for aeroderivative engines

The test statistic is $T = 885$ and the *p*-value is $p = .3431$. Since this *p*-value is not small, H_0 is not rejected. There is no evidence to indicate that the heat rate distribution of the traditional turbine engines is shifted to the right or left of that for the aeroderivative turbine engines for any reasonable value of α.

15.97   a.   To determine if the median level differs from the target, we test:

$$H_0 : \eta = .75$$
$$H_a : \eta \neq .75$$

b. S_1 = number of observations less than .75 and S_2 = number of observations greater than .75.

The test statistic is S = larger of S_1 and S_2.

The p-value = $2P(x \geq S)$ where x is a binomial random variable with $n = 25$ and $p = .5$. If the p-value is less than $\alpha = .10$, reject H_0.

c.   A Type I error would be concluding the median level is not .75 when it is. If a Type I error were committed, the supervisor would correct the fluoridation process when it was not necessary. A Type II error would be concluding the median level is .75 when it is not. If a Type II error were committed, the supervisor would not correct the fluoridation process when it was necessary.

d. S_1 = number of observations less than .75 = 7 and S_2 = number of observations greater than .75 = 18.

The test statistic S is the larger of S_1 and S_2. Thus, $S = 18$.

The p-value = $2P(x \geq 18)$ where x is a binomial random variable with $n = 25$ and $p = .5$. From Table I, p-value = $2P(x \geq 18) = 2(1 - P(x \leq 17)) = 2(1 - .978) = 2(.022) = .044$

Since the p-value = $.044 < \alpha = .10$, H_0 is rejected. There is sufficient evidence to indicate the median level of fluoridation differs from the target of .75 at $\alpha = .10$.

e.   A distribution heavily skewed to the right might look something like the following:

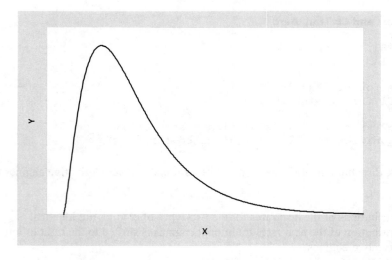

One assumption necessary for the t-test is that the distribution from which the sample is drawn is normal. A distribution which is heavily skewed in one direction is not normal. Thus, the sign test would be preferred.

15.99   Since the data are already ranked, it is clear that:

$$R_1 = 19 \qquad R_2 = 21.5 \qquad R_3 = 27.5 \qquad R_4 = 32$$

$$\bar{R}_1 = \frac{R_1}{n_1} = \frac{19}{10} = 1.9 \qquad \bar{R}_2 = \frac{R_2}{n_2} = \frac{21.5}{10} = 2.15 \qquad \bar{R}_3 = \frac{R_3}{n_3} = \frac{27.5}{10} = 2.75 \qquad \bar{R}_4 = \frac{R_4}{n_4} = \frac{32}{10} = 3.2$$

$$\bar{R} = \frac{k+1}{2} = \frac{4+1}{2} = 2.5$$

To determine if the probability distributions of ratings differ for at least two of the items, we test:

H_0: The probability distributions of responses are identical for the four aspects
H_a: At least two of the probability distributions differ in location

The test statistic is

$$F_r = \frac{12b}{k(k+1)} \sum \left(\bar{R}_j - \bar{R}\right)^2 = \frac{12(10)}{4(4+1)} \left[(1.9-2.5)^2 + (2.15-2.5)^2 + (2.75-2.5)^2 + (3.2-2.5)^2\right] = 6.21$$

The rejection region requires $\alpha = .05$ in the upper tail of the χ^2 distribution with $df = k-1 = 4-1 = 3$. From Table IV, Appendix D, $\chi^2_{.05} = 7.81473$. The rejection region is $F_r > 7.81473$.

Since the observed value of the test statistic does not fall in the rejection region $\left(F_r = 6.21 \not> 7.81473\right)$, H_0 is not rejected. There is insufficient evidence to conclude that at least two of the probability distributions of ratings differ at $\alpha = .05$.

15.101 **Method I and Method II:** $r_s = .189$. Since this value is close to 0, there is a very weak positive rank correlation between the ranks of Method I and the ranks of Method II.

Method I and Method III: $r_s = .592$. Since this value is about half way between 0 and 1, there is a moderate positive rank correlation between the ranks of Method I and the ranks of Method III.

Method I and Method IV: $r_s = .340$. Since this value is fairly close to 0, there is a weak positive rank correlation between the ranks of Method I and the ranks of Method IV.

Method II and Method III: $r_s = .205$. Since this value is close to 0, there is a very weak positive rank correlation between the ranks of Method II and the ranks of Method III.

Method II and Method IV: $r_s = .324$. Since this value is fairly close to 0, there is a weak positive rank correlation between the ranks of Method II and the ranks of Method IV.

Method III and Method IV: $r_s = .314$. Since this value is fairly close to 0, there is a weak positive rank correlation between the ranks of Method III and the ranks of Method IV.

NOTES

NOTES

NOTES

NOTES

NOTES

S0-AIO-197

The Tiger Wore Spikes

An informal biography of
Ty Cobb

The Tiger
Wore Spikes

by John McCallum

A. S. Barnes and Company   •   New York

Published on the same day in the Dominion of Canada
by THE COPP CLARK COMPANY, LTD., TORONTO

Library of Congress Catalog Card Number: 56-5563

DEDICATION

To the keepers of the records of
the Baseball Hall of Fame whose
dedication and devotion share a
vital role in keeping alive the
spirit of the game's immortals.

Foreword

by Ernest J. Lanigan
Baseball Hall of Fame's Official Historian

Putting my memories of Tyrus Raymond Cobb into the Foreword of a book about his spectacular baseball career is as natural as breathing. I have been writing about the Georgia Peach for so long, now, I feel as though I practically invented him.

Tyrus Raymond, come to think of it, was only two years old when I got my first baseball writing job. That was with the Sporting News, in 1888. I was made baseball editor of the old New York Press in 1907, the season Cobb won his first of nine straight American League batting championships. Four years later I became secretary of the Eastern League. During the World War I years, I put in tours of duty with the Cleveland Leader, Boston Record, and Boston American. I've been the Hall of Fame's Historian since 1946. All told, I have been associated with baseball in one capacity or another for 68 years—which should qualify me to say a few well-chosen words about the main subject of this book.

I suppose I knew Tyrus as well as any man writing baseball

in the old days, and I feel elated that he still numbers me among his closest friends in the sporting world. To me, he will always be far and away the greatest ballplayer who ever lived. He was truly all competitor, in every meaning of the word.

I recall that when he first started on his 24-year march as the master of them all, folks commented on his extreme nervousness. He was always kicking at the bags strapped onto the bases. It was years before it dawned on anybody that he was kicking the bags a few inches closer to where he might be if he needed to reach them.

In his early seasons Cobb never thought anything of himself or his records, if the Tigers could win a ball game. The team came first. He'd sacrifice himself every time to get that extra run across the plate. If there was a runner on third and Tyrus was on first, he'd go down to second, even to be thrown out. But the shortstop or second baseman who went over to tag him found himself all tangled up as though in a rassling match, so that there was no chance to throw to the plate.

After Cobb hung up his spikes for good, I must admit that the game was never quite the same for me. I never see a runner rounding second anymore, hesitating and dancing back to the bag like a scared bird whose Maw is trying to push him out of the nest, without recalling what Tyrus would have done in the same situation. It was really something to see the way Cobb worked those bases. Tom Sheehan pitched for the Yankees when he was young, and he told me that Tyrus would make a grab at a base with his right hand and when the fielder started to tag his arm, Cobb would suddenly lash out with his other paw and tag the base.

Tyrus came clattering up the pike from Dixie in an era of giants, and by dint of his persistency, driving ambition, he fought his way, literally fought, to the top of the heap to stand alone, unbeatable and untouched. Pop Anson, who played against the cream of the Old Guard and saw the best

viii

of the Cobb Era, admitted to me one time that there was no question about it—Cobb was the king of them all. Charley Comiskey, for 30 years the most prominent owner in baseball, told me the same thing.

Well, when you study the records, an almost irrefutable case can be made out in Cobb's behalf, as the most superior ballplayer of all time. And I know a little bit about the significance of baseball figures. I invented such columns in the official record book as "Runs Batted In," "Times Thrown Out Stealing," and had John Heydler add first and middle names in the averages. I spent three years figuring out Cobb's lifetime batting average against individual big-league pitchers, published for the first time in this book.

Life itself, or Fate or Circumstance, made Tyrus one of the most dramatic, exciting and courageous athletes ever to stride across the great American sport scene. He was a hero drawn from our national life, for like the early pioneers who battled their way West, he had to conquer life's many handicaps, overcome emotional conflict, to scale the heights. Sure, Tyrus made enemies, lots of them, along the way, but even his detractors had to admire him and all that he stood for.

I was happy to assist the author in every way, to fill him in on certain phases of Cobb's background, for any book on the playing career of Tyrus is a valuable contribution to baseball history. The younger generation, especially, will enjoy meeting the immortal Georgia Peach for the first time here.

The author has depicted Cobb as the great talent he was via the most microscopic of methods. Tyrus is excellently analyzed, psychologically and spiritually, and fans will learn just why Tyrus must be rated above all others. His theories on training, batting, running, fielding and team psychology are told expertly in a neat package of the best on diamond philosophy.

Tyrus has shied away from publicity in more recent years, but historians will be writing about him for as long as the game of baseball is played. No study will cover his tremendous career more excitingly or comprehensively than it is covered here.

One aspect of Cobb's career was not touched upon, however—his acting career! Perhaps it was just as well. He played the role of Billie Bolton in a stage comedy called "The College Widow," and as I told Ward Morehouse, the drama critic and a native Georgian, it was probably the worst production I ever saw in my 83 years. In those days Tyrus needed the money and would do anything.

Tyrus Raymond has never been a great one to talk about his personal life, but he will gab for hours about baseball to anyone. In 1936, I remember, he journeyed all the way from Menlo Park, California, to Cooperstown for the formal dedication of the Hall of Fame. He brought his son, Howell, then 17, and daughter, Beverly, then 19, along with him. Incidentally, his other daughter, Shirly, now the proprietor of a thriving book store in California, confesses that she knew very little of her father's baseball career—until, one day, she started pasting up his scrapbook!

Anyway, Tyrus was the man of the hour at that Hall of Fame dedication. Old opponents and fellow H of F tenants rushed to greet him. There was moisture in his eyes as he embraced Connie Mack. Cobb always has been a sentimental man, though the public seldom sees this side of his personality. Tyrus must have signed a thousand autographs that day. As Larry Lajoie signed his name for an admirer, he pointed to Cobb and said, "Now, son, go over there and get the champ."

One of Cobb's biggest complaints down through the years is that the boys in the press coop have all too often made him look like a villain, frequently misquoting him and failing to get *his* side of the many controversial issues identified with his name. Well, the author here is not guilty of that. John McCallum spent many hours in the summer of 1955 at Cobb's home, and Tyrus filled him in on many of the facts. The author also talked to many of Cobb's contemporaries—men like Larry Lajoie, Cy Young, Ed Walsh, Honus Wagner and Mickey Cochrane—to compare notes and thus get an honest, fair study of the old Detroit star.

In 1914, Tyrus wrote a book titled "Busting 'Em," sort of a semi-autobiography. He was only 28 years old then, still a long way from the end of the line. There since have been two other tomes written about him, neither of which could compare with this latest one. Tyrus has been saying for years that one of these days he is going to sit down and write another book, clearing the record.

"When you get my age (69)," he told a gathering at Cooperstown last summer, "you get on the square. You tell the facts. You tell the way it really happened."

Well, until he *does* get around to writing that book—though he admits the very thought of tackling such a monumental project tires him out—John McCallum's portrait of the greatest baseball player that ever lived greatly covers the subject, and then some. I'm sure you will agree after you have read—

"The Tiger Wore Spikes."

Contents

The Tiger Wore Spikes

Part I

The Gaslight Era

1890-1906

Preface

The Gay Nineties and those years on the early edge of the Twentieth Century had their own special blend of color and charm. A sort of Victorian composure gripped the nation, but the Union was showing flutters of emerging from its cocoon. Historians gently refer to the period as the "good old days"— the age of the tiny-waisted Gibson girl, hoop skirts, bustles. The handle-bar mustache, slick-parted hair, high-buttoned jacket and tall stiff collar. Days when a free lunch went with a beer, when Dad rode Mom on a bicycle built for two—and two could live as cheaply as one without both working.

Despite this cloak of conservativeness, however, America's pulse beat was speeding up. Out at Wounded Knee Creek, South Dakota, the Seventh Cavalry was bringing to a close gory-pitched battles between redskins and whites by kicking hell out of 200 Indians in the Army's revenge for the massacre of Custer. The first major industrial strike in U.S. history shut down the Carnegie Steel empire. Benjamin Harrison was finishing his term as President. Grover Cleveland, William McKinley and Teddy Roosevelt were warming up in the bullpen.

They called it the Gay Nineties, but a tourist's view of the

5

times would indicate that there were also many not-so-gay moments.

Between the years 1889 and 1906, Johnstown, Pennsylvania, suffered a disastrous flood, Chicago a horrible fire, and San Francisco a devastating earthquake. While the populace from the shattered areas recovered from these holocausts, the rest of the country plunged on. The Duryea, a 4-h.p. automobile, one of the first, made its appearance. Edison built his Kinetographic Theatre, the initial movie studio. Vaudeville boomed. Buffalo Bill Cody, western hero of the day, toured the theatre circuit. Joseph Jefferson III enthralled audiences with his characterization of Rip Van Winkle. Millions flocked to the Chicago World's Fair of 1893.

But there was trouble abroad. The U.S. had to send relief corps to the Far East to suppress the bloody Boxer Rebellion in China. The *Maine*, American battleship, was blown up in Havana Harbor, killing 260 men, and igniting the Spanish-American fracas. Teddy Roosevelt led a charge of his Rough Riders up San Juan Hill, Cuba; later he won the Nobel Peace Prize for settling the war between Russian and Japanese troops, in 1905. Leon Czolgosz, a young anarchist, shocked the world by assassinating President McKinley, September 6, 1901, at Buffalo's Pan-American Exposition—and Teddy Roosevelt peeled off his spurs and took over the Chief Executive's chair.

The Wright brothers, on December 17, 1903, made the first successful airplane flight, at Kitty Hawk, North Carolina. John D. Rockefeller struck oil, amassed a fortune of more than 300 million at the turn of the century. Edison's movie of "The Great Train Robbery" was the first film to tell a story.

John L. Sullivan went around shouting, "I can lick any guy in the house!" And most of the time the Boston Strong Boy was right. Jim Corbett knocked him out in twenty-one rounds in New Orleans, September 7, 1892, the first heavyweight championship match in which the combatants wore gloves.

The diversity among pugilists added tremendous spice and drama to the sport—the flamboyant John L., the clever Gentleman Jim, the sullen Jim Jeffries, the shuffling Bob Fitzsimmons, the intemperate Stanley Ketchel.

Harvard men dominated the national tennis picture. The game was beginning to change from patty-pat to hard-socking play. Terms like "passing shot," "twist service," "drop shot," and "lob" were used more commonly. The original Davis Cup team, three Harvards, startled the world in 1900 by crushing a trio of British, 5 to 0.

Walter J. Travis was the demon of golf, winning the U.S. Amateur and the British Amateur, the first American to bring the latter title to this country.

Sports had advanced tremendously since the Civil War, but we were only emerging from swaddling clothes. Basketball was just eight years old in 1900; most speed swimmers used the side stroke; track athletes won Olympic titles in times that schoolboys would scoff at today; and horse racing was about to see a reform wave which would close every track except those in Kentucky and Maryland.

Football, still dominated by Yale, Harvard and Princeton, was a push-and-pull business based on power and brawn. Old Back Number, Pudge Heffelfinger, was leading the way at New Haven, an active playing career that was to last for half a century.

Baseball in the Nineties was still creaking along on legs as unsteady as a new-born colt's. Fans rode to the ball parks in horse-drawn buses. John J. McGraw was then a five-foot-six, 121-pound third baseman, the brain and sparkplug of the championship Baltimore Orioles, considered by some to be the greatest ball club of all time. These were the early days, when a ball park was a rough, uncultivated lot, a grandstand was a jumble of rickety slats, and a club payroll looked like the wage list of a logging camp.

John J. McGraw and others were playing exhibition con-

7

tests in Havana, Cuba, and touring with ball clubs through the south and middle west when baseball was in its infancy, making a bid to become our national game.

In those days, the game had only one umpire.

The feats of the old Orioles have become legend. Their skill, their flaming courage, their team spirit, has never been surpassed. McGraw played third base on the 1894 championship Oriole team. Hugh Jennings was at short, Brouthers at first, Reitz at second. In the outfield were Steve Brodie, Joe Kelly, and the "hit-'em-where-they-ain't" guy, Wee Willie Keeler.

In 1902, John McGraw was to cuss out Ban Johnson, president of the year-old, upstart American League, and jump as manager to the Giants, taking along with him Iron Man McGinnity, Roger Bresnahan, Dan McGann and Jack Cronin from the Orioles. John J. was destined to take the Giants from the cellar in 1902 to second in 1903. In '04, he was to bring the Giants their first modern pennant.

There was also to come a day in '02 when Bones Ely of the Pirates complained of a sore finger and refused to play shortstop. Manager Fred Clarke turned to a top-heavy, clumsy-looking giant and said, "All right, you play in Ely's place."

"Hell, I'm no shortstop," the giant said. "I've never played it in the majors." The giant was to become the greatest shortstop in the history of man. His name?—Honus Wagner.

Baseball fans, in '03, would witness their first World Series on record. Deacon Phillippe, pitching for Pittsburgh, was to defeat the Red Sox three times in the first four games. And two Fall classics later, the big right arm of the magnificent Christy Mathewson, rising and falling, was to fashion one of baseball's all-time individual Series performances, pitching three shutouts against the Athletics to hang up a record that still stands.

Baseball was getting a New Look. Ban Johnson organized the American League on the basis that "honesty and gentlemanliness" was its slogan, and that umpires were inviolate, sacrosanct, and must not be kicked, punched, mobbed or spat upon, as was the good old custom of the National League.

A French-Canadian hack driver—Larry Lajoie by name— was the sensation of the new league. As far as the box office was concerned, he was responsible for pulling the AL through its infancy. Larry was such an idol that the crowds followed him down the streets, and kids worshipped him. When he indorsed a certain brand of chewing tobacco half the kids of the nation got sick giving the foul weed a trial in the hope it would make them sluggers, too.

Other et ceteras who helped to pack the hatbox-sized parks in those dear old golden days were Connie Mack, Eddie Plank, Cap Anson, Billy Sunday, Charley Comiskey, Old Hoss Radbourn and Clark Griffith . . . Big Ed Delahanty, King Kelly and Dan Brouthers . . . Louie Sockalexis, Iron Man McGinnity, Turkey Mike Donlin, Rajah Bresnahan, Jimmy Collins and Happy Jack Chesbro.

America had yet to get its first real glimpse of the young man who was to eventually become the champ of them all—

Tyrus Raymond Cobb.

The Early Years

On the morning of December 18, 1886, in the tiny southern community of Narrows, in Bank County, Georgia, near the Carolina border, Tyrus Raymond Cobb first saw the light of day. He came equipped with the standard apparatus, big appetite and strong lungs. History is not clear on the subject, but it is doubtful that his parents imagined the tyke would some day grow up and meet and talk to presidents, travel the whole world, make a fortune, become a fabulous, international figure. Professor Cobb's only ambition, the chief hope he carried in his heart for his son, was that he might eventually become a student of medicine, perhaps graduate and hang out the shingle of the M.D.

Not even in his dizziest day dream, or his wildest flight of fancy, could the strait-laced professor have foreseen in those early years that the toddler would, in the end, be judged by experts as the greatest competitor, the most dominating figure the game of baseball ever knew. His son, a professional ballplayer? How ridiculous! Yet this was the way it was to be for the child born to Scotch-English parents 69 years ago in an obscure southern hamlet.

Professor Cobb, you understand, had nothing particular

against athletes. It was simply that he strongly felt that the mind should be developed as well as the body. You can better understand his cultural viewpoint when you learn that Ty's father was one of the south's leading educators, a superintendent of schools, a gentleman of tremendous prominence who became a senator in the state legislature of Georgia. He was an honored man of deep principles, a devout disciple of the Ten Commandments . . . the king and master of his household in every way.

Mrs. Cobb, who was only in her early teens when she married, was a quiet, charming lady who knew her station and duty in life. That station was the home, the duty to raise three children—another son and daughter followed Ty—and look after them.

The Cobbs were decent, sober, highly respected folk who brought up their three children in the strict, old-fashioned way. Glimpses of Ty in those short-pants years may be culled from casual conversation with him, or by talking to antiques still alive and kicking who remember his boyhood in Royston, Georgia, where the Cobbs moved when Ty was about six. They were a proud family, proud of their forbears, a lot of whom were buried back in the coves and hollows of the Appalachians and the Blue Ridges of Western North Carolina.

The Cobb antecedents never had a chance at an education, but they saw to it that somehow the mud wasn't too deep on the roads to get their children, Ty's father among them, out to college.

The Cobbs were Baptists, and young Ty and his brother and sister were marched off regularly to Sunday School.

In the early years of his development, Ty was small for his age. The other kids in Royston would have ganged up and chased him if he had let them. They would have called him yellow, with that refined cruelty of bigger boys, thrown stones at him, chased him away from their games, wouldn't have let him play with them—if he hadn't stood right up to them.

At first this was the normal trial of any kid who was under-sized and had not yet found himself. Eventually, Ty gained some sort of tolerance when he showed them he was a battler on the ball diamond. That was his meat, baseball. He was all baseball, living and eating it all the time.

Ty's best pal in early life was little Joe Cunningham, who lived next door to the Cobbs. When Ty's family first moved to Royston, Ty and Joe didn't get along. Joe thought Ty was the cockiest li'l ol' boy he ever saw. Ty had a similar opinion of Joe. They had their fights, like small boys will have, but after awhile they ironed out their differences and became pals.

Ty was only a splinter of bone and a shred of muscle about the size of a sack of popcorn when he and Joe began playing baseball. In one respect, Royston, Georgia, was just like Puy-allup, Washington, or Ottumwa, Iowa, are today. That is, Ty and Joe and all of the kids in Royston played baseball. Well, most of the boys played baseball. Ty's brother, Paul, was one of the few who didn't. He showed little interest in athletics until graduation from high school, when, suddenly, he began playing baseball. Perhaps this is skipping ahead in the story too fast, but by the time Paul enrolled at Georgia Tech he was six-foot tall and weighed 168. From 1907 to 1916 he played for no less than a dozen minor league clubs. Along the way he hit .310 for Lincoln of the Western League in 1910, .306 for the same team in 1911. In 1913, he played for Ogden, Utah, of the Union Association, batted .333, added a .331 performance at Ogden the following season, when the St. Louis Browns bought him. Strangely, and for reasons never known, Paul refused to report to the American Leaguers, a transgression which infuriated brother Ty. This is all in pass-ing because few people even knew that Ty had a brother, let alone one who played baseball well enough to get a call from the majors.

But to return to Ty's boyhood again, Joe Cunningham's father made water wheels and coffins in an old shed, and Joe and Ty would cut ash timber and make their own baseball bats with Mr. Cunningham's tools. Ty, quick to take charge, made Joe pitch to him until Joe thought his arm would drop off. When Joe pleaded for mercy, Tyrus coaxed other kids to pitch to him. As an extra inducement, he'd pay them a couple of pennies for their service. If there was a secret to batting, Tyrus wanted to find out what it was. Even as a kid, you see, he was as shrewd in baseball matters as you can possibly get. He knew how to threaten and bargain. You have to admire the way he was as a youngster, with nerve a mile long, an alert and lively brain, and the ability to use both. These qualities stayed with him all his life and made him a great competitor.

If it is true that a champion must be born with competitive fire, then it was the boys of Ty's community who fanned the flames. They flaunted their achievements on the battle field, and took their defeats with all the graciousness of enraged bulldogs, rising to awesome heights of foaming fury. They hated like sin to lose. Tyrus let his older companions set the laws, and he lived up to them. If they wanted a winner, then he'd be a winner. By golly, he'd be first—at anything! You name it—checkers, marbles, foot racing, tight-rope walking, baseball—Tyrus Raymond Cobb would take you on.

Tight-rope walking you say? Particularly tight-rope walking. Tyrus would string a line between two houses. "There," he'd say, "I defy any of you to walk it." One by one they'd try it, and one by one they'd end up in a heap on the ground. Then Tyrus would walk the length of the rope. He had practiced until he was the champion.

Later, many years later, Joe Cunningham, reading in the papers about the phantom mercury sweeping across the major league baseball horizon, was to think about his boyhood pal and reflect: "You knew Tyrus had something nobody else had right away. He was the champ. He just seemed to *think*

14

quicker and run faster. He was always driving and pushing. He went with a girl whose daddy didn't approve of him because he played baseball. Ballplayers were looked on as roughnecks then. I always figured Tyrus drove himself so hard to prove to everybody that ballplayers were okay."

The story of Cobb is the story of a quarter-century of baseball. At twelve, he was a skinny sandlot shortstop in Royston. At seventeen, flushed up from the semi-professionals, he was signed by Augusta, released, caught on with Anniston, Alabama, and got his first large helping of professional baseball. At eighteen, he was slamming base hits and stealing bases in the big leagues for Detroit. And for twenty-four of the most stormy, action-packed years any ballplayer has lived through —filling the books with hitting, base stealing and endurance records— he kept it up.

Baseball seems almost like a new game when you talk to Cobb, when you see him today at a gathering swapping yarns with a big leaguer, when you realize that he started playing what the kids called Town Ball. It wasn't exactly like sandlot baseball as we know it today. The rules, among other things, were different. In Town Ball, for example, a base runner was out if a fielder hit him with the ball while the runner was fleeing between the sacks. Tyrus practiced diligently dodging those throws when he was on base. This gave him a shiftiness, a stop-and-go quickness, he would use one day in the big leagues to upset defenses.

Town Ball also gets credit for teaching Tyrus how to place his hits, another device that was to drive big league fielders crazy. Town Ball rules allowed a team to use as many players in the lineup as it wanted. Also, if a batter smacked a home run he could go back to the plate and take another turn. As long as he homered each time, he could stay up there and bat all day.

One afternoon, Tyrus accompanied his cousin to a nearby

15

community and challenged the whole school team to a friendly game of Town Ball.

The captain of the school team laughed.

"You wouldn't have a chance," he chortled smugly. "There are only two of you. You guys must be kidding."

Ty and his cousin weren't kidding. They meant it.

"What's the matter, 'fraid we'll beat you?" challenged Tyrus. "Just the two of us against your whole team. We'll take our chances."

"Okay, wise guys!" said the captain, burning.

Tyrus and his cousin insisted that they bat first. They knew that if the school team ever got to the plate the game would develop into a rout. Without fielders, the visitors would never get 'em out.

Cobb batted first. Seeing that he hit left-handed, the defense shaded toward the right, leaving a hole down the left field line. Ty met the first pitch in front of the plate, driving the ball into the hole. He says he can still see the left fielder, his shirttail flying in the wind, chasing the ball. It was a home run. Ty batted again, and this time the outfield moved to the left. Cobb crossed them up again by hitting to right field. The defense became so rattled it didn't know where to play Cobb after that. Ty and his cousin stayed at the plate batting all afternoon. Ty's cousin later became an insurance company executive in Chicago, and when the Tigers were in town to play the White Sox Ty would drop in on him. Invariably the subject of that game back in Georgia came up, and thinking about it, they would get to laughing until tears came to their eyes.

Little did Ty realize that the tricks he learned playing Town Ball eventually would carry him to the heights in professional baseball. His style—batting, running, fielding and bunting—varied imperceptibly from his boyhood days to the big leagues. He practiced place-hitting so tirelessly, for example, that by the time Detroit beckoned he had become pretty adroit at calling his shots, angling the ball at will over first and third bases.

Years later, while Ty was taking his cuts during batting practice in New York, some of the Yankees sat on the bench trying to bait him.

"Let's see you hit one down the right field foul line," taunted one of them. Cobb promptly obliged. "Now knock one inside third," he shouted, a bit chastened. Again Cobb obeyed instructions. "Pretty lucky," he cried. "Bet you can't raise a foul back of the catcher." Cobb did that, too. Then giving him a snarl, Cobb yelled, "Duck your head, fresh guy! I'm going to foul the next one into your dugout." The whole mob ducked as Cobb kept his promise.

"You win," the wise guy said. "Cobb, I believe you could place your hits on a handkerchief spread in the outfield."

Despite the fact that his family was pretty well off, Ty's father wanted him to know the value of honest toil. When Ty wasn't at school he was working in the fields alongside his brother Paul, behind a plow. Ty was on the smallish side, short and lean, and his father felt that rigorous labor was just the thing to build him up and strengthen his bones and harden his muscles. But when he wasn't in school, or out in the cornfields, he was playing shortstop for the Royston town team. This sometimes led to conflict. Often Ty found himself on the day of an important game groping behind the plow. It took a carload of ingenuity on the part of the team captain to get the star hitter off the hook. He would collar a Negro lad and the two of them would march over and talk to Professor Cobb.

"Mr. Cobb," he'd plead, "Tyrus is our best hitter. We can't start the game till he arrives."

"But who's going to replace my boy in the cornfield?" Professor Cobb would ask, a twinkle in his eye.

"Mose here," the captain would say. "He'll do Tyrus' work." The team always sent along a Negro boy to take Ty's place.

"In that case," there was a pause, then, "he may go."

17

Professor Cobb always let his son go, but not before the boy had done some sweating. Looking back, Ty realizes it was good discipline. It taught him to respect the judgment of his superiors.

When Ty was fourteen or fifteen years old he got his first glimpse of a real, genuine big league team. There was a young sports writer named Grantland Rice covering the Atlanta beat and Ty fell in the habit of reading his baseball stories. Cleveland trained at Atlanta and according to Sportswriter Rice they were really something to see. Ty pestered his parents to let him go. They finally consented.

Arriving in Atlanta, Ty caught a trolley car and went out to old Piedmont Park where the Indians practiced. Fear gripped the boy as he stood outside the gate. He didn't know whether or not he would even be allowed inside the park. There was no one guarding the gate so he sneaked in. Not wanting to attract any attention, and doubtful if he would be allowed to sit in the grandstand, he went to the left field bleachers, out of sight. Ty sat there, like on a cloud, watching the big leaguers throw and bat baseballs.

Suddenly, as if out of nowhere, a guy in a Cleveland uniform stood at the bleacher railing. There was a smile on his face and he appeared friendly.

"Hi, kid," he said, grinning up at young Cobb.

Ty didn't answer, too scared to open his mouth, so the ballplayer said, "My name's Bill Bradley. What's yours?"

"M-m-my n-n-name's Cobb—Tyrus Cobb." Ty alway was addressed as Tyrus in those days. Not until he climbed to the majors did Damon Runyon or Ring Lardner or one of the New York writers shorten it to "Ty." Ty says he thinks he was the first "Tyrus" in the United States, though folks have since named their youngsters after him.

Anyway, Bill Bradley, a highly understanding man, could see that Cobb was nervous and frightened, sitting out there in the left field bleachers at old Piedmont Park, miles from home, and seeing all of those great ballplayers—real big leaguers—working out for the first time.

Ty was carrying a little camera with him and, spotting it, Bill Bradley said, "Want to take a picture of me?"

For the first time that day Ty relaxed.

"Sure," he beamed, getting up and moving down to the railing. Bradley struck a batting pose and Ty took his picture. Then he said, "Want me to bring a couple of the other players over so you can take their pictures, too?"

Exultation swept through Ty and all he could do was nod.

Bill Bradley called the whole club over, and, one by one, Ty snapped their pictures. He saved those photos—still has them somewhere—and from then on Bill Bradley was Ty's hero. Ty never saw Bill Bradley again until 1928, just before Ty retired from baseball. Ty told him about that day at Atlanta. Bradley thought Ty was joking. He didn't believe Cobb was the same person. Funny, isn't it, how the world goes?

Actually, when Cobb started out, professional baseball was farthest from his mind. His real ambition was to be a surgeon, and he harbored dreams of going to the University of Georgia. He began playing amateur team ball when he was about twelve, and kept on for three or four years. He was crazy about baseball and football. Some of the neighboring towns used to ask some of the Royston boys to play with them and, when Ty got older, they asked him, too. They paid a little money, but Ty never took any, because he wanted to go to the university and play baseball and football. He didn't want to ruin his amateur status.

Finally a friend of Ty's who played on the same team went to the Southern League for a tryout. Ty watched the papers for news of his pal's progress, and in that way he began to read the news of the big leagues and became interested in the pros. At the end of the season his friend returned and fired Ty, who was now about sixteen, with tales of his team and the league.

19

"You oughta try it, too," the friend said. These were the fearless outpourings of a young man of conviction and of dedication.

When spring came along Ty, with frenzied zeal and a sort of sublime assurance in his cause, sat down and wrote letters to two teams in the old South Atlantic League. He received a reply from the Augusta team, telling him he could have a trial if he paid his own way. That obstacle out of the way, Ty knew he would still have to get around his father, who was dead set against his son becoming a professional ballplayer. First, however, Ty packed his bag—a telescope—and then he went to his father. Professor Cobb didn't like the idea at all, but at three in the morning he gave in.

Cobb bought a ticket to Augusta. Arriving in town, he sought Con Strouthers, the manager. Strouthers eyed the kid keenly.

"The season starts next week, kid," he said. "Show me you can play ball and I might be able to use you. One of my regular outfielders played outlaw ball and is under suspension. He has to wait till his case is fixed up."

The youth's face was suddenly like the risen sun. This was more than he had hoped for—a chance to be in the starting lineup on opening day.

Luck was with Cobb. Strouthers was awed by the lad's unquenchable zest and confidence and decided to find out what Ty could do under fire.

"You're starting in center field," he told Ty on the eve of the bell ringer.

Wild, incoherent joy filled Cobb. Here was his chance. He would not wait for opportunities to speak. He would make them.

Ty's bat fortunately was red-hot. He took charge immediately. In the first game he hit a booming home run and doubled. He added a single the next day. Now they would have to keep him, Ty thought. For a rookie—and even a veteran—he was doing all right. Ty was peeling off his flannels in the dressing room when Manager Strouthers collared him.

"Kid," the pilot said, "soon as you dress come into my office."

Oh, boy, Cobb thought, they were going to sign him to a regular contract. This was it.

But a deadly coldness met Ty when he entered Strouthers' inner sanctum. He could sense something was wrong. The manager got right to the point.

"The suspension on our regular center fielder has been lifted," Strouthers announced abruptly. "He arrives tomorrow. You're no longer needed around here."

Ty felt his Adam's apple choking him. He surveyed Strouthers with angry eyes. He didn't quite understand.

"B-b-but . . ." Ty started to protest.

"That'll be all, kid," Strouthers interrupted, waving to the door. "You're a free agent. You can do business with any club you want."

Inside, Ty's chest started to rumble like a volcano. Lava began to boil and splash and bubble in the deep caverns and the smell of brimstone emanated from his nostrils, but he didn't erupt. He pivoted and walked out the door without another word.

At first Ty didn't know what to do. Then an idea hit him like a flying bottle in a barroom. He would call home. His father would tell him what to do.

Professor Cobb answered the phone.

"Father," Ty said, "this is Tyrus. I've just been cut loose from Augusta."

Professor Cobb was strangely non-committal. Ty was sure he would ask him to come home. The professor hadn't wanted him to play ball anyhow. Instead the elder Cobb inquired, "Well, son, what are you going to do now?"

Ty analyzed his emotions. He hadn't anticipated this. "There's still Anniston, Alabama, of the Southeastern League," Ty said. "They've offered me a tryout."

There was another pause.

"Going to accept it?" Professor Cobb asked.

"I don't know," Ty said.

"Take it," his father commanded, "and don't come home until you've made good. Show them you are not a failure!"

That was the turning point of Ty's career. He went to Anniston and practically overnight was leading the league in batting. Word of his meteoric start got back to Augusta, and soon the fans, taunted by the memory of the bad shake Cobb had received there, were demanding his recall.

"Get the kid back—or else!" Strouthers was told. Ty immediately got a call from the Augusta manager. This time his voice bubbled like carbonated water.

"Ty," he said vibrantly, "I hear you're goin' great down there. How'd you like to play for me again?"

This was Cobb's opportunity to avenge Strouthers' earlier treatment of him, and he said curtly, "Sorry, Strouthers, but I'll never play for you again—at Augusta or anywhere else."

The young man, pinpoints of anger flaring in his eyes, hung up. He meant that. He never wanted to see Strouthers again.

Well, it wasn't long before Augusta fired Strouthers and replaced him with wise old George Leidy. Leidy was a smart baseball man, a disciple of human psychology, and a gentle soul with a heart as big as the national debt. He phoned Cobb and offered him a contract.

Cobb's feelings were beyond resurrection.

"I told Strouthers I want nothing more to do with Augusta as long as he's connected with the club," Ty said. But he was batting .370 for Anniston by this time and figured he had earned a promotion, so he heard out Leidy before hanging up.

"Listen," Leidy said, "Strouthers is gone. He's no longer associated with us."

Ty whooped fit to bust a lung.

22

"In that case I'll catch the next train," Ty said, his voice high-pitched with sudden excitement.

Naturally, Ty polished himself up as he went along, but while with Augusta in 1904 and 1905 he was the same daring and explosive combatant who later was to hold or tie ninety-three major league records.

"Cobb was a real farmer boy in those days," said Bill Croke, who owned the Augusta franchise. "I remember our opening game in Savannah in 1905 . . . 3300 paid admissions, a real big crowd for that era. We beat Savannah, 2 to 1, and their only run was scored on a hit past Ty in center field. I recall the run because Ty was eating popcorn when the ball was hit. Ty was a hot-headed youngster and liked his own way from the outset. He'd fight for it. On the road I had to feed the rest of the team before Cobb and Nap Rucker got into the dining room. If I hadn't the others would have gone hungry."

Cobb says that in a way it was that sack of popcorn that started him thinking seriously about professional baseball. He learned from that embarrassing experience that baseball is worth a player's full-time attention—and all the practice he can get—if he is going to play it at all. Ty was only seventeen years old and playing mostly for the laughs, without any real thought of someday going to the big league. He liked to run the bases and take his turn at bat, but he couldn't be bothered with the finer points of the game.

Manager Leidy didn't say anything to Ty when he got trapped with his hands full of popcorn, but after the game George took Cobb for a streetcar ride. He opened the boy's eyes to what baseball should mean. He wasn't mad, he said, just disappointed.

"Son," Leidy said, "baseball is a great game. It offers you unlimited opportunities. Eating popcorn in the outfield is okay if you think the game is just a joke. But suppose you are too ambitious for that kind of horseplay? Now suppose you

23

keep your eye on the ball? Suppose you study? Suppose you practice, and learn to make the most of what nature has given you? You can go to towns that'll make Augusta look like a crossroads. You can be famous. You can make a fortune. Every boy in America would idolize you. Your name would even go down in the history books."

His clear gaze studied the boy.

"Well, how about it, son?" he said.

The past events flowed over young Cobb like drowning waters. Slowly, calculatingly he digested the manager's words. Before he could reply, Leidy continued, "Listen, I'll be glad to help you. I know some big-time tricks like the hit-and-run. I can teach you to bunt. And I have some ideas about getting the jump on the ball in the outfield, provided, of course, that you don't concentrate all your attention on popcorn."

That broke the tension, and they both laughed. That night Ty promised himself, "Tyrus, you're going to be a big leaguer even if it kills you." He never again thought of anything else while he was on the diamond. Leidy turned him loose on the bases, and worked with him zealously in the mornings. The veteran threw the ball to Cobb with an arm that had long since gone dead and painful, while Ty tried to bunt it into his sweater. Leidy taught him how to poke a hit-and-run ball through the yawning gap the infielders left while covering second base. He taught the kid how to lure the third baseman in for a bunt, then slash the ball past him. Suddenly baseball was far more than simply a game of hit, run, throw and catch. It was now a highly scientific challenge to Cobb, a game as fascinating as chess.

You couldn't stop Cobb with a horsewhip after that. He never lost a chance to study the game. Ty recollects a strapping pitcher named Happy Harry Hale who came from Happy Hollow, Tennessee. Grantland Rice was writing glowing stories about the giant, and on the day he was to make his debut with Atlanta, Cobb got permission to travel down and

24

study him. Happy Hale was six-feet-six. He was long-legged, split clear to his chest, and he had, among other items, a smoldering fastball.

Happy Hale was absolutely unbeatable for four innings, well on his way to a no-hitter. Then the visitors got wise. They started bunting. Happy Hale had never seen a bunt before. He looked silly trying to field the dropshots. When the third straight batter laid down a perfect bunt on him, Happy Hale stumbled in, arms and legs flying, made a desperate stab at the ball, and spiked his own hand.

That was the end of Unhappy Harry Hale's abbreviated pitching career—and the beginning of Tyrus Raymond Cobb's bunting career. He had learned something new about baseball, a lethal weapon that he was to use in the years to come which would make Humpty Dumpties of infields.

Returning to Augusta on the train after the game, Cobb fell into conversation with a large fat boy from Milledgeville, Georgia.

"What's your name?" Ty asked.

"Babe Hardy."

"Mine's Cobb," Ty said. "Tyrus Raymond Cobb."

"What do you do?" the fat boy asked.

"I play baseball for Augusta," Ty said.

"Oh, are you the bat boy?" he inquired.

"Bat boy!" roared Ty indignantly. "You come to the game tomorrow and I'll show you what I am."

"I'll be there," the fat boy said.

Cobb had a pretty fair day, at that, a home run, triple, two doubles, a single, and a couple of stolen bases.

As for Babe Hardy, you might have heard of him. He later became famous in the movies as a member of the comedy team—Laurel and Hardy!

"The Big Leagues
Are Calling"

The doubts of Ty's father in the beginning, the challenges he was meeting daily along the stony path to the major leagues, now were serving only to spur Ty on to the searing years that lay stretched out in front of him.

Despite the fact that he hit only .237 in his first season at Augusta, Cobb came back in 1905 and told his mates in no uncertain terms that he didn't intend to spend the rest of his life in the bush leagues. By now the game was as serious as life and taxes to him, and he had become an aggressive, driving player, possessed of a fierce will to win at all costs. He was so wrapped up in it that if he cut his finger he'd have bled batting, fielding and pitching statistics.

That season another stripling named George (Nap) Rucker joined Augusta from Atlanta and he and Cobb were assigned the same room. Nap was a left-handed pitcher of considerable promise. He and Ty were the only youngsters in a crowd of oldtimers. In a mutual stand against the veterans' hazing and practical jokes, Ty and Nap became warm friends. Incidentally, when Nap pitched on the sandlots of Alpharetta,

Georgia, a couple of years before, an ice cream peddler sold a confection called "Napoleon." The homespun Georgian with the Cracker drawl went for Napoleons a mile a minute. When his teamates would see the peddler, they'd shout, "There's your Napoleon, Rucker." Thus the famous nickname. Brooklyn fans later cut it to "Nap."

Anyhow, Cobb demonstrated to his new roomie in 1905 the strongest determination any athlete was ever born with. Nap got his first sample of Ty's unflagging ambition when the outfielder talked him into pitching batting practice every morning before the rest of the team came out.

"I've heard that left-handed batters have trouble hitting southpaw pitching," Cobb told Rucker. "I ain't gonna let that stop me. Throw anything you want to. Just don't pitch so close I'll start pulling away from the plate."

After Rucker had thrown as many balls as they thought his arm would stand, Cobb would have the pitcher knock him fly balls. At first Ty had trouble judging balls, but Nap hit them to him until he could almost snag them with his eyes closed. Ty's hitting improved tremendously, too, until by the middle of the campaign they thought they would have to call out the fire department to keep him from burning up the league.

"One day," backtracked Rucker, "the Columbia, South Carolina, team came to town with a former big leaguer named Elliott. He was credited with having invented the hook slide. Ty was waiting at the gate when Columbia arrived and grabbed Elliott by the sleeve. I doubt if anybody else could have done it, but in ten minutes Cobb had talked the guy into coming down to second base for a demonstration. Ty stood right over the base as Elliott came in with a slide that seems ordinary now, but was brand new to us then. Ty backed over toward first and hollered, 'I want to try that!' And here he came, a blurred streak that exploded in a cloud of dust, with spikes flashing out front and high up in the air. As he slid even with the bag his left toe hooked it and he came to a stop.

"Elliott threw both hands above his head and started backing away, an expression of amazement on his face. Ty bounced to his feet like a jack-in-the-box and went after him, yelling, 'Hey, what's the matter? What'd I do wrong?'

"'Matter?' Elliott said. 'Nothing's the matter. There's not a man alive can do that the way you did—and on the first time, too! From now on, boy, you be the teacher. I'll study under you.'

"Ty didn't have to practice his sliding much. He was perfect the first time he did it, and in all his life he never let his spikes touch the dirt when he slid. A lot of other base runners have dug their spikes in the ground and got broken ankles and legs.

"How he did it, I can't tell you, unless he just lifted himself down there with that ingrown determination of his. He seemed to be on his way by the time his bat hit the ball, and he was halfway to first before another man could start moving. When infielders saw they couldn't throw him out they started moving in from their regular positions, five feet at first, then ten, and finally fifteen. This gave Ty a better chance to hit between them, and he started swinging harder in our morning batting practice. He aimed at left field, which gave him more time to beat out weak hits. Ty wasn't especially fast. I never was known as a speed merchant, and I outran him every time we raced, and that was pretty often. But I will stand up with the shortstops and agree that no man on earth could move from the plate to first base as fast.

"Base running, the way he did it, was a science, a highly specialized art, and it had a breathtaking effect on the other side. When Ty got on base you knew he'd steal the next base or bust. The pitcher, to keep him from it, would hurry his delivery and maybe miss the plate, or still worse, serve up a fat pitch right where the batter wanted it. Or the catcher

28

might throw before he got set, and chuck one to the outfield while Cobb streaked for home. If everybody played just right Ty would beat the throw, and if they started making errors he'd get them so rattled that they couldn't put out the next three or four batters, either.

"While he practiced hitting and chasing fly balls every morning, and played like a big leaguer every afternoon, Ty was equally determined that those hairy-eared teammates of ours should never put anything over on us. We had a lot of battles with the bunch, and we never lost a decision."

There was one fight that neither Nap nor Ty talk about. It involved a couple of guys named Rucker and Cobb. Knowing of Ty's got-to-be-first-in-everything spirit, you can better appreciate the story.

Affable, gentle, slow-going Nap got along fine with Cobb until one afternoon he was shelled from the mound and retired to his hotel room early. Ballplayers dressed in their hotels in those days, and it was the custom of Nap and Ty to tub themselves in their room after every game. There never had been any problem because Cobb always got home ahead of Nap and therefore was first into the tub. But this time Nap got there first.

Ty paced the room like a caged lion when he arrived, while Nap bathed. As Nap stepped from the tub, Ty rushed him. Nap, despite the unexpectedness of the onslaught, managed to hold off his enraged roommate.

"Have you gone crazy, a-fussin' and a-fightin' like this?" demanded Rucker. "Just because I happened to be in the bath first today! And for the first time, too!"

"You don't understand, Nap," pleaded Cobb, "I've got to be first—all the time."

That was the young man's credo, and he was first nearly all of the time, too.

Cobb was a man of action. Almost from the start he planned and plotted means of reaching the major leagues. Playing ball in the minors was no business for him. He realized immediately that if the outside baseball world ever was to hear of Ty Cobb he would have to expose his guile. He decided to play a trick on Grantland Rice, an artifice that was to stand up for more than 40 years.

Granny was writing sports for the *Atlanta Journal,* a paper Ty's parents subscribed to. They did not get the Augusta paper. Ty knew that if his father was going to keep up with his progress he would have to read it in the papers, in this case the *Atlanta Journal.* One morning Granny received a telegram:

"Tyrus Raymond Cobb, the dashing young star from Royston, is burning up the Southern League. He is a terrific hitter and faster than a deer. At the age of 17 he is undoubtedly a phenom."

Rice tore up the wire and returned to the business of writing sports for his paper. Later that afternoon, however, he answered the wire.

"After this," he telegraphed the sender, "the mails are fast enough for Cobb."

Still the wires kept flooding Granny's desk; ditto letters and postcards, and all about "this boy Cobb."

"Keep your eye on Tyrus Cobb," was the general theme of the missives. "He's one of the finest hitting prospects I've ever seen."

And, "Watch Cobb of Augusta. He is a real sensation."

Or, "Have you seen Tyrus Cobb play ball yet? He is the swiftest base runner I have seen in baseball."

Good, tasty, meaty messages. These and dozens like them were signed "Brown," "Smith," "White," "Jones" and so forth. By golly, Granny simply had to go and see the dauntless young Mr. Cobb for himself. He could ignore the issue no longer. But first he sat down and wrote a column announcing to the world that a "new wonder has arrived." Then he sped to Augusta to see his "discovery" in the flesh. Ty stood five-feet-eleven, weighed about 155, and was hard as nails. Granny visited Cobb in the dugout before the game.

"My name's Grantland Rice," he said. "I write baseball for the *Atlanta Journal*. I've been hearing a lot about you."

"I've heard about you, too," Ty said. "I've been following your columns in the *Journal*."

That was their first meeting, the beginning of a cherished friendship. At a baseball banquet many years later, Granny and Ty were placed side by side on the dais. When it came Cobb's turn to speak, he stood and told the story about all those wires, letters and postcards that Rice had received.

"And now," he added, turning and addressing his remarks directly at Granny beside him, "I've a confession to make. Granny, I sent you those wires and letters and postcards. I signed names like Smith and Jones and Brown to them to make you think I was a whiz. I had to do something to get attention. The big leagues may never have heard of Ty Cobb if it hadn't been for all those letters."

Granny suppressed a grin.

He said, "It's taken you a few years to get around to telling me."

Then they all laughed.

Al Simmons took a leaf from the Cobb book of tricks on his way to the majors. When Al was a schoolboy in Milwaukee he played for a semi-professional team. In addition to holding down a regular job in the outfield, he was also a sort of press agent for the team. Simmons was the one selected to drop in at the local paper on his way home after the game and tell a vivid story of the gripping contest to a third-string cub reporter who wrote a baseball column called "Diamond Dust."

Al's square name was Szymanski, not Simmons, and he used to hitch up a chair and tell the cub reporter very stirring tales of his team's performance, not omitting to mention the heroic batting and superb fielding of Al Szymanski. In the language of all the columns called "Diamond Dust," Szymanski was a "tower of strength." Sometimes Al Szymanski asked himself if he wasn't over-rating the Szymanski boy, but the obvious reply was that the kid really was a sensation. "I'm no knocker," he would tell himself.

Al's last name didn't remain Szymanski for long because the reporter who wrote "Diamond Dust" and the printers who set up the stuff in the little flyspeck type which some papers used for the column were strong agents for the Americanization of different European names. Subsequently Aloysius Harry Szymanski became Al Simmons.

The cub who ran the "Diamond Dust" department and the printers may have given Al Simmons his baseball name, but he himself exploited it. Al wrote to Connie Mack in the spring of 1922, enclosing a peck of laudatory "Diamond Dust," and offered to hop right over and solve one-third of Mr. Mack's outfield problem for him. Two years later he was an A's regular.

Self-confidence, such as Cobb and Simmons showed, is the hallmark of a champion.

Bill Croke testifies that Augusta knew it had an outstanding player in Cobb and so did Detroit. Bill Armour, the Tiger manager, saw Ty the season before he bought him. Augusta and Detroit shared the same training site in 1904 and got a tremendous kick out of watching Ty perform. Unorthodox was the only word they could find to describe him. Frank Navin, part owner of the Tigers, was in camp to get the lowdown on some of his rookies. George Leidy told Navin about Cobb.

"He's like a wild colt," Leidy said. "He needs some polishing, but as soon as he gets used to a bridle you are going to see the world's greatest ballplayer."

Navin listened, said nothing, but it was evident from the look in his eyes that he was not greatly impressed.

Detroit, in lieu of rent for the use of the Augusta ball park, offered to loan the Georgians a player for the season. In return, Augusta agreed to give the Tigers first crack at their manpower when the season was over. Detroit promised to pay $750 for the player they chose.

Pitcher Eddie Cicotte was optioned to Augusta. He weighed a trifling 135. Navin didn't like small pitchers. He wanted them on the general order of Paul Bunyan.

In 1905, Andy Roth replaced Leidy as manager and he took an immediate dislike to Cobb. They never got along. Roth decided to get rid of Ty. He arranged to sell the blatant gamecock to Charleston for the munificent fee of twenty-five dollars! When Owner Croke heard about it, he broke Charley Paddock's best time in calling that one off. Croke liked Ty. He had been paying the boy $90 a month in the spring, raised him to $125 when Ty got along so well. Croke feared that Cobb would be drafted for $350 and, according to the Detroit agreement, the Tigers would pay more than twice that figure for the Augusta player they selected.

"I had a perfectly good reason for selling Cobb to Detroit for $750—which was a good price in those days, by the way," Croke explained later. "Augusta previously had been in the Southern Association. The Sally League was new. Few major league clubs paid any attention to it, and the Southern Association, of higher classification, could at the time draft Cobb from us for $350."

As it was, Frank Navin favored Clyde Engle. Bill Byron, who umpired in the Sally League and later graduated to the National League, told the Tiger executive he was making a mistake. Byron told Bill Armour to "hold out for Cobb." George Leidy, who had stayed on with Augusta as an outfielder and continued to work with Cobb, told Armour the same thing. So Armour held out for Cobb. Navin demanded Engle. Navin finally gave in. A week after the Tigers bought Ty, four major league clubs claimed him in the draft.

Tyrus Raymond Cobb was on his way.

Part II

The Cobbian Age

1905-1912

Preface

The tall, thin bewhiskered fellow in the striped pants and stovepipe lid rolled up his sleeves, flexed his muscles, and began to make the furnaces in his factories burn with energy in the years encompassing 1905–12. The Machine Age was here.

Aviation achievements mounted. Wilbur Wright flew seventy-seven miles in a little more than two hours, establishing the world's duration-distance record. Henri Fabre of France piloted the first seaplane, and a fellow countryman, George Chavez, became the first fly-boy to wing his way over the top of the Swiss Alps. The Wrights collected twenty-five grand in '09 for a plane—and the U.S. Air Force was on its way. But skeptical editorials continued to ask, "Is Flying Worth While?" And the obvious answer was: "Flying may never be worth much commercially, or even for military purposes, but its poetic value is immense." Count Zeppelin made aerial navigation history by steering a balloon over a prescribed 900-mile course in the amazing time of 25 m.p.h. The Count's airborne voyage ended rather abruptly, however —he, er, collided with a pear tree!

Henry Ford revolutionized the automotive industry by introducing his Model-T. Mass production of the horseless flivvers got under way in '08, was in full swing on the assembly line four years later. Vogue kept pace with the changing times. Ladies wore enormous wide-brimmed hats, flaring, gored skirts, and put color on their cheeks.

Progress. De Forest invented the radio telephone. Pioneers closed in on the last frontier. Arizona, in 1912, became the forty-eighth state to be admitted to the Union. Jes' like Topsy, the corps of college graduates grew. A total of 37,000 diplomas had been issued by 1910. Expansion.

There was a honey of a race for the presidency. William H. Taft beat another William—Bryant—and inaugurated a series of "firsts." Taft was the first president to set foot on foreign soil, the first to have a government car, first to play golf, and the first Chief Executive to toss out the first ball opening the major league baseball season.

Sports had found a rabid friend.

Well, what about sports? For one thing, there wasn't anything mamby-pamby about them. Nothing played to the tune of hearts and flowers. Games weren't contests played for the sweet joy of sport by Sunday School book characters. No, sir. They were fierce, fire-eating, deadly serious battles performed as professions and businesses by a bunch of tough-fibered, thrill-hungry combatants.

Pudge Heffelfinger, a veritable Paul Bunyan with a varsity Y on his chest, long since removed from the Yale grid, was touring the country, still playing football. They couldn't get Old Back Number out of there. The fabled Percy Haughton became Harvard's first paid football coach. Michigan and Minnesota brawled over the "Little Brown Jug." Backs started using the forward pass as a means of attack.

Road racing zoomed in popularity, topped by the New York-to-Paris extravaganza in '08. Indianapolis Speedway joined the act in '11, opening its doors to the death wagons for the first Memorial Day production. Ray Harroun averaged 74.59 m.p.h. in his Marmon Wasp to win it. The stocks and hot-rods were a long way off yet.

The summer of 1907 was to produce a big moment in the life and times of an Atlantan going on six—Bobby Jones got his first golf club, a discarded cleek, cut down to his size. In 1911 Johnny McDermott was to be the first American to bag the U.S. Open. Johnny Hayes won the Fourth Olympiad's marathon in London (in '08), a victory which wound up in one of the most celebrated rhubarbs in the history of the Games. The dazzling Jim Thorpe was becoming known as the All-American Boy via his all-around excellence at Carlisle.

Boxing boomed. Tex Rickard began his career as the country's all-time champ of the promoters by staging a lightweight championship match between the Old Master, Joe Gans, and the Durable Dane, Battling Nelson, at Goldfield, Nevada, September 3, 1906. Abe Attell ruled the featherweights, Jimmy Walsh the bantams, Mike Sullivan the welters, Billy Papke and Stanley Ketchel, the Michigan Assassin, the middleweights, Philadelphia Jack O'Brien the light-heavies, and a big, burly boilermaker, Jim Jeffries, the heavies. Pugilism never had had it so good.

Big Jeff's fight with Jack Johnson at Reno, Nevada, remains a subject they still talk about. Few sporting events ever attracted more attention. The whole world stopped what it was doing to await the outcome. The date was July 4, 1910. Li'l Arthur, he of the teeth-flashing smile and the tooth-smashing left uppercut, knocked Jeffries out in the fifteenth round to become the first Negro to win the heavyweight championship. Race riots broke out, but there was joy rampant in the black belts, notwithstanding.

Dentists and oculists who happened along the Negro settlements had a splendid opportunity to study their trades. The thoroughfares in those places were illuminated by thousands of eyes, contrasting vividly with the ebony skin of their

39

owners, like pearl buttons on a black cassock. They had backed their dusky compatriot well, wagering every penny they could beg or borrow. Barbers had hocked their razors, and it wasn't only the barbers who did the hocking, either! And so, laden with the gold and silver pieces of their winnings, which caused them to clank like knights in armor as they moved about, they cavorted among the gay places and celebrated the victory of Jack Johnson, their hero.

Ballplayers were as hard as Li'l Arthur's jaw during this period, a strange, hard-bitten and ambitious crew. They were mostly up from small towns and hamlets and by no means very eager to go back. They trained at nothing but that one idea and fought to hang on to it with their last breath. They were lean and hungry, and they played the game for keeps. They studied, practiced, lived baseball every second, except when they were sleeping, and often dreamed about it at night. They came up the hard route, fighting through the alfalfa leagues, literally fighting, and undergoing the horrible hazing of the greenhand whose older colleagues were going to make him a man or, by golly, smash his spirit doing it.

Christy Mathewson continued to be the Giants' principal fire-fighter, and fans were now beginning to call him Big Six, which was the number of New York City's main fire engine house. In '08, Matty bagged 37 games, walked only 42 in 416 innings! Connie Mack cracked, "It's a pleasure to watch him pitch—when he isn't pitching against you." That same season, Fred Merkle committed his lamentable "bonehead" play against the Cubs by failing to touch second base, an unfortunate incident that was to prompt him to remark bitterly many years later:

"Folks won't let me forget it. When I die I guess they'll put on my tombstone—'Here lies Bonehead Merkle.'"

Things changed fast in the coming of the "The Cobbian Age." Women began to go to ball parks. Players had to stop cussing.

40

But the year 1905 was to bring the biggest change in the personal life of Ty Cobb. It produced a freakish tragedy that has haunted him all these years. On August 9th of that year, only three weeks before Ty reported to the Detroit Tigers, death snuffed out his father's life like a candle. Professor Cobb died of bullet wounds in a gun accident.

The Royston newspaper said of Professor Cobb:

"Mr. Cobb had been prominent in political and educational affairs both in the county and state. He was senator for the 31st senatorial district in 1901 and 1902 and was county school commissioner of Franklin county at the time of his death.

"Mr. Cobb came to Georgia from North Carolina about 20 years ago and began teaching in Banks county. Later he graduated with honors from the North Georgia Agricultural College. He married the daughter of Captain Caleb Chitwood, of Banks county. Three children were born to them. They are Tyrus, the oldest, now a member of the Augusta team of the South Atlantic League; Paul, about 16, and Florence, 11.

"Soon after his marriage, Mr. Cobb began teaching in this section of the state and was principal of the high schools at Lavonia, Harmony Grove, Carnesville and Royston, in the order named.

"In 1900, he was elected by a large majority as senator from the 31st senatorial district, which position he filled with distinction. At the close of his term he was prominently spoken of as a candidate for state school commissioner on account of interest he had taken in educational matters as a member of the general assembly. He decided, however, not to make the race and was elected county school commissioner of Franklin county, which place he held at the time of his death. There has been much advancement in educational matters in this county since his election, largely due to his efforts and influence. Mr. Cobb, about 43, had lately entered the news-

41

paper field as editor of the Royston Record and was rapidly making a success in this line.

"Mr. Cobb was recognized by all who knew him as a gentleman of honor and integrity. He stood high in Masonic circles, and was a prominent member of the Baptist church."

Ty's most powerful reaction to this tragedy was to drive himself all the harder, to carry out the promise he had made to his father—not to return home until he had become a success in professional baseball.

Early Days in Detroit

Sitting on the Detroit bench before the game Cobb watched the Tiger veterans warm up. The date was August 29, 1905, a day he still talks about. He had arrived in town only the evening before and here he was, at last, wearing a big league uniform. He had finally made it. Perhaps it was still a boyhood dream; certainly he would wake up any second now and discover himself back in Georgia. But Royston and Anniston and Augusta seemed like faraway places now, belonging to another country and another century. Thinking about it, a flutter of excitement stirred the muscles of the rookie southerner's stomach.

"Hey, Cobb!" It was the master's voice, Bill Armour. "Look alive! Get out there and warm up, you're starting today."

"Yes, sir," responded Cobb, hopping off the bench in one fluid motion. The Detroit manager had taken him by surprise. Amazement must have shown in his eyes, for Armour quickly explained that Dick Cooley, the regular centerfielder, was sick.

"I'm batting you fifth, right behind Sam Crawford," Armour said. "I know this is your first day, but don't let that worry

43

you. Just go out there and play the way you have always played. You'll do okay."

The Tiger manager could not have been more prophetic.

Detroit was opposing New York and the great Jack Chesbro was pitching for the Highlanders. Ty was nervous at first; the crowds and the playing conditions were strange to him. The infielders, for instance, looked miles away, and the outfield fences were so far away it seemed hopeless to try to reach them even with a cannon.

In the very first inning the Tigers got two runners on, and here came the eighteen-year-old Cobb's turn to bat. A sudden outraged tumult smote Ty as he walked to the plate. Was Armour crazy, letting an untried greenpea bat in a crucial situation like this! Ty gave the stands a scalding look. He'd show 'em.

Cobb dug in, braced himself for the pitch.

"Stee-rike one!"

Chesbro had slipped one past him. Ty tapped the plate with his bat a couple of times, then set himself once more. Again, "Stee-rike two!"

"Com' on," shouted Armour, "get a good piece of it."

Ty nervously knocked the dirt loose from his spikes. Only takes one to hit it, he told himself. He sure would like to get ahold of one and drive those two runners home. Chesbro pumped, here came his arm around, here—

Wham! Cobb connected. It was a clean double. Ty moved around the base paths as if the ground beneath him was hot. The Tigers went on to win, 5 to 3. Young Cobb wasn't wasting any time taking command.

After watching the aggressive, fiery, clear-eyed bundle of nerve, nerves, and sinews for six or seven games, Hugh Fullerton, hoary baseball encyclopedia of the day, made a wager that Cobb wouldn't last two years, and he predicted the young man would break a leg or be indicted by killing a second baseman and go out of the business.

44

Cobb played in forty-one games in 1905, and batted .240. He could hear Augusta calling, but the Tigers brought him back in '06 for another chance.

Ty had one of the toughest starts any rookie ever faced when he reported to Detroit for his first full season in the American League. It was the sort of start that would have broken the heart and spirit of an ordinary competitor. Ty, of course, was not ordinary.

At the start Ty was eager to be on good terms with his teammates, but early differences quickly developed between Ty and a certain clique of Detroit veterans. They resented the brash youngster trying to reduce one of the regulars to the status of spectator, and, banding together, refused to eat with him and goaded him into fist fights.

Probably Ty's greatest handicap was that he was super-sensitive, shy, quick to take hurt and slow to recover therefrom. The older men were aware of this nature and made Ty's life unbearable. But Cobb stuck to his guns, squaring his shoulders and fighting back at them with his chin up and his determination blazing. He demonstrated in those early days he had all of the ingredients that go to make up what we select as a hero, among other things, the capacity for uncomplaining suffering, the guts to absorb mental, as well as physical, punishment, and never to let the rest of the world suspect that he was taking it. As to what Ty thought, he never told anybody.

The clique had driven Ty off by himself, had converted him from a keen, cheerful youth into a lone wolf who felt that the rest of the world was against him, but it had failed to stop him. Baseball had suddenly become his bread and butter, and by his unswerving persistency, his gnawing ambition, tenacity and iron will power, he was set on establishing himself as a major leaguer.

It was perhaps at this stage of Ty's career that he learned a basic fact about human relations: to wit, life is not the work of a master dramatist. The hero does not simply snap his fingers and—p-s-s-t-t—a path is cleared for him. He has to make his own path. Life, pure and simple, is hard work and sweat and self-sacrifice.

Cobb promised himself that he would pay the price for greatness. He worked and he sweated and he sacrificed . . . and, yes, he fought . . . to land himself a place on the Tigers. Few men would have endured the hell he did to achieve perfection. There were gory mix-ups, both in the southern training camp and later back north, with Charley Schmidt, the burly catcher. There were brawls with the players from other teams. And there were hassles with the fans.

Years later, as he looked back upon these early, stormy days, Ty was to admit to himself that he surely made a fool of himself. "I thought all the oldtimers were against me," he was to confess, "and trying to keep me out of a job, so I came up a-fightin'." Ty was determined the vets wouldn't keep him from making good, and because he battled them he got a reputation as a headstrong scrapper. After that he had to keep fighting, whether he wanted to or not, or be called yellow. Ty was years finding out that most of the fellows would have helped a kid who showed anything and that all the fighting was useless.

Ty thought perhaps he had lost his one-man battle for a varsity job when Davey Jones started the 1906 season in centerfield for Detroit. Jones shortly injured his leg, however, and Cobb went back to center.

"Tyrus," he said to himself, "you're back out here again and no one's going to take the job away from you this time."

Cobb finished the season with a .320 batting average, fifth in the American League, the first of twenty-three straight years he was to hit .300 or more.

The question of Cobb's courage as a ballplayer never was better illustrated than in 1906. He was spiked and bounced around innumerable times, but nobody spoke or wrote about it because the kid never considered a husky bruise or a slashed leg important enough to mention.

Grantland Rice saw Cobb in one series where each leg was a mass of raw flesh and where he had a temperature around 103. "The doctor had ordered him to bed for a four-day rest," Granny said. "That afternoon he made three hits and stole three bases, sliding to second or third upon sore-battered flesh."

Hugh Fullerton told of going to see Ty in a New York hotel. Ty was in bed, a bruise on his hip which would have sent anyone else to a hospital, an electric heater spread over the injury to draw out the inflammation. That day he got out of bed and led the Tigers to victory over the Yankees. Above all, Cobb was game.

Another time that season Ty was suffering from tonsillitis as the Tigers reached New York. Cobb had a high fever. He should have been under a doctor's care. He played. The following morning he dragged himself to a surgeon, who found his tonsils in terrible condition, and advised treatment before they were removed.

"Take 'em out now," Cobb ordered.

The surgeon protested, advised reducing the inflammation and a week in bed. Cobb was obdurate. When the surgeon wanted to give him an anaesthetic, he refused, saying it would make him sick. The tonsils were in such condition that the surgeon was forced to remove them in sections. Every fifteen minutes Cobb would demand a rest, lie on a sofa, then return to the chair.

Weak from pain, fever, and loss of blood, he returned to the hotel. He was unable to eat, but he dressed and went to the ball park. He played seven innings, and refused to leave the game until it was won.

There was a rule on the Detroit club of those wild days never to let the other team know you were hurt. No matter how badly a player might be injured, he was supposed to smile. Once, after a game with Philadelphia, Cobb returned to the hotel with a gash four inches long chopped along his shinbone. No one except those on the bench knew he had been touched.

Cobb told Frank Graham that he guessed he hated that certain clique of Tiger veterans as much as they hated him. Later he said he was grateful for what they did for him by driving him off by himself. He ate alone, roomed alone, and walked alone. What else could he do between dinner and bedtime? There were no movies or, if there were, he had no recollection of them. He couldn't go to a vaudeville show every night and he didn't want to hang out in pool parlors, bowling alleys, or saloons. He wasn't as much of a reader in those days as he is now. So he would walk the streets for a couple of hours, which helped to keep his legs in shape, and, walking or sitting in his room or lying in bed before he went to sleep, he had plenty of time to think. And what else was he to think about but baseball—how to hit pitchers, how to play for hitters, and how to run the bases?

One night while sitting in the lobby of a hotel in Chicago after dinner Cobb fretted and thought about Doc White, the White Sox southpaw who was giving him so much trouble. Doc was hard for Ty to hit, fanning him frequently with a drop. White's drop was a beauty, and Ty was breaking his back trying to hit it. Cobb was beginning to fear that the southpaw would drive him out of the league. All of a sudden Ty had Doc figured out. He could picture him out there on the pitching mound, as plain as day. Ty saw what Doc was doing and how he did it. Ty sprang from his chair like he'd been sitting on a burr and shouted to no one in particular, "I've got it!"

"Got what?" asked Wild Bill Donovan, who was parked next to Cobb studying a list of newspaper pitching averages.

"A way to hit Doc White's drop," Ty blurted.

48

Here's Cobb as he looked to enemy pitchers in his first season at Detroit.

Cobb, a deadly-serious combatant, was so sincerely a bad loser that he became a terrific winner.

The Detroit outfield composed of, left, Bob Veach, Cobb and Sam Crawford was one of the game's greatest.

Considered the greatest action picture ever shot on the diamond, Cobb slashes into third base under Jimmy Austin in 1909.

Infielders gave Cobb plenty of room when he hit the dirt, spikes aglimmer.

At his peak, the man who stole 892 bases in 24 seasons had no peer as a base runner. Here is a cameraman's view, in sequence, of how Cobb did it.

Popular with the kids, Cobb shows his famous grip to a group of handicapped boys. He kept his hands a few inches apart on the bat, explained it gave him more control.

Though he is best remembered as the phantom mercury sweeping the base paths, Cobb was one of the most spectacular outfielders of his time.

"Swell," Donovan muttered indifferently, and went on with his pitching statistics.

Cobb could hardly wait his turn at bat the next time Doc White pitched against Detroit. He was anxious to test his new theory. Before, he had stood up front in the batter's box, and Doc's drop broke just as it reached the plate. There was no way for Ty to check his swing. He saw that if he moved to the rear of the batter's box, he would get the drop *after* it broke and have a chance to gauge it.

Doc went to work on Ty with the drop. Ty let the first one go by to see how it looked from his new position in the box. It looked fat and juicy. Doc wasted the next pitch. With the count 1-1, Doc came back with the drop. Sock! Cobb smashed the ball on a line across second base. Doc never struck Ty out again.

"I was sorry to see him leave the league," Ty said. "He had become a soft spot for me. All that was necessary was to hold my swing until his drop broke."

Ty Cobb used his head for more than just to keep his ears apart.

Every time there's talk of Ty and his fights on the ball field the subject of his battle with Buck Herzog, Giant infielder, is recalled. The Tigers and Giants returned north together on a barnstorming series one spring. The series opened in Dallas on a Saturday and Ty was late getting to the ball park. The Giants took this tardiness as a cue to ride Cobb unmercifully, accusing him of delaying his entrance to take bows, et cetera. And they kept it up during the game.

On Ty's first trip to the plate, Jeff Tesreau hit him on the shoulder with an inside pitch. Cobb thought it was deliberate. He stared at the Giant bench defiantly as he moved down to first base, vowing he would get every last buck of 'em, Tesreau in particular.

Herzog, from second base, dared Cobb to steal. Sparks

49

bounced around in Ty's eyes like a sponge, and Cobb went roaring down on the first pitch with the throttle wide open. Catcher Lew McCarty had expected this and called for a pitch-out. His throw to second beat Ty to the bag, but it didn't stop the Georgia Express. Cobb ripped into Herzog like a ten-ton truck coming out of a blind alley, shaking up Buck's bridgework. Buck crashed to the ground, but came up swinging.

Other players joined in and umpires and the police had their hands full, not merely halting a fight, but preventing a riot. Both Buck and Ty were banished, of course.

That night in the lobby of the Oriental Hotel, McGraw's path crossed that of Cobb. John J. promptly lit into Cobb. Ty, realizing that two decades separated them in age, kept his temper, coldly insulting Mac in return and driving him to the verge of apoplexy.

Later, through pre-arrangement, Herzog went to Cobb's room. Heinie Zimmerman, the Giant third baseman, went with him. A couple of Detroit players were also in the room. Herzog and Cobb stripped to the waist and tore at each other. Buck dropped Ty with his first punch, but it was also his last. Cobb sailed back and pounded him savagely. Only his teammates kept him from killing Herzog.

Still playing in Dallas the next afternoon, which was a Sunday, fans poured into the park hoping to see another fist fight. Cobb, however, refused to play, just as he had threatened when he was thrown out of the game for fighting the day before—and Herzog was so badly bruised and lame he couldn't play.

Ty never did play again in the series, leaving the Tigers to finish his training with another team. When the Giants and Tigers split up at Kansas City, the Giants, it is reported, sent a postcard to Cobb:

"It's safe to rejoin your club now. We've left."

All the Giants had signed it. Thus, they had the last word

50

with Cobb. And in the only safe way to have the last word with him—via Uncle Sam's mail!

After his series of spats with the Giants, word soon got around the American League not to get Cobb mad.

"Ty likes a funny story," said Fielder Jones, the St. Louis Browns manager. "Now the Tigers are coming to town and I want you guys to think of some good yarns to tell him before the game. Keep him in good humor."

The New Deal

Life went on for the Tigers in 1907. Arms wore out, legs slowed down, old faces were replaced by new ones. Bill Armour received his pink slip and colorful Hugh Jennings came in as manager. A New Look was underway in Tigertown. In the next three years it was to produce pennants instead of penance.

The "New Deal" which Jennings brought with him to Detroit was that he started the players to *thinking* baseball. This had considerable to do with the Tigers winning the championship in 1907 from the Athletics in a driving finish. For the Tigers then began to improvise plays that jolted their opponents, and in this improvisation Cobb led all their counsels.

Night after night as Cobb sat alone, he began to figure out plays that might be tried the next day or later on. He began to make a more careful study of the pitchers he was facing, what they had and how they used it.

It was during one of these evenings of contemplation that he decided to run wild just often enough to keep his opponents guessing. He decided that the most effective method of attack was to break down the enemy's mental balance and force them into hurried throws. Ty was a quick starter and he had the speed to back up his plan, but his wild base-running had an ulterior motive. It was about this time that certain rival pitchers had been told to "dust off" Cobb at the plate, using the bean ball to do the dusting. Cobb had to find a way to break this up. He found it. Being an expert bunter, when the pitcher started throwing at Cobb's head the Georgian would wait for the right moment and then drop a bunt down the first base line. Naturally the pitcher would have to cover the play. Ty's retaliation along the base line was quite effective. The resultant collision usually made the pitcher more careful of his control.

Manager Hugh Jennings was one of the original holler guys. You always knew when he was in the ball park. He could be heard. He was perhaps the most colorful manager in baseball history. Jennings was scoffed at as a manager in some quarters, yet he led Detroit to three straight pennants, 1907–08–09. With Jennings whistling and EE-yahing! in the third base coach's box—arms spread, right leg hoisted high—and Cobb on the bases driving the opposition daffy, all was confusion.

Nowadays they still use the hit-and-run, but somehow the play has lost something. The lively ball doesn't give the boys a chance to do much but whale away at it. The way they work the hit-and-run now reminds graybeards of what big Claude Rossman, the demon first-base slugger who followed Ty in the batting order, thought it was.

Cobb was on first base and Jennings signaled to Rossman for the hit-and-run. Rossman nodded. Instead of pushing the ball through any hole in the infield, however, he dug his spikes into the ground, swung from his heels, and promptly lost the ball over the outfield fence. Home run.

The crowd's roar of delight rose to almost a physical pressure, but Jennings was smoldering. Rossman had not obeyed orders.

"Didn't I give you the hit-and-run?" he bawled irritably.

"Sure," said the surprised Rossman, "and didn't I hit it?"

Jennings was temporarily stopped, and then, puzzled, he asked, "What do you think the hit-and-run is?"

"Why," said Rossman, "you hit the ball and everybody runs like hell."

Still Cobb gives Claude Rossman the credit for some of the best plays he pulled. "Ross was the best sacrifice hitter I ever saw," Ty said. "Tall, long-armed, easy-going, he also had a lot of stuff between the ears. I roomed with Claude my first couple of years in Detroit. In the old days, before the invention of the batting practice cage, hitters had to go chase the ball if the batting-practice pitcher threw wild. Rossman saw no reason to wear himself out walking back and forth to the backstop, so he developed the trick of reaching across with his bat, held in those long arms, and stopping anything that came within a city block of the plate. He got so good at this that pitchers couldn't get the ball past him in games. Frequently he did it with one hand. It took the pressure off me. On the bunt play I knew he wouldn't leave me stranded, even when the other side knew we were going to use it. I had tons of confidence in him, knowing I could count on him getting at least a piece of the ball. That's why I always pointed for third when leading off first base. I knew Rossman would protect me."

On the Tigers' last trip to New York in 1907, when they had to win fourteen out of sixteen to grab the pennant, Cobb opened the series by walking. Rossman sacrificed. The bunt was cleanly handled, slick as a whistle, and Claude was out. But Ty was on third base, with Hal Chase, the Highlanders' great first baseman, holding the ball—and by the time he shot it to George Moriarty, New York third sacker, Ty was past the plate dusting himself off.

The water cooler which both teams used was situated just outside the New York dressing room. After the game Ty walked over to get himself a drink. Inside the Highlander quarters Manager Clark Griffith bawled out Chase and Moriarty. Cobb listened.

"But how was I to know what that southern madman was going to do?" shouted Chase.

"He won't do it again," promised Moriarty, "we'll be watching for that so-and-so."

Cobb's hot southern blood boiled. That evening he hunted up Rossman. "Every time I get on first tomorrow you bunt," Ty said. Rossman agreed.

And so the very next afternoon, with all the Highlanders watching and waiting for Cobb to pull his trick, with Chase laying for him—Ty did it again. The defense was overanxious. In the seventh inning, on another perfectly timed sacrifice bunt, Ty slid into third. Moriarty was so piping mad about it he threw the ball on the ground and caught it on the bounce. But too late! Cobb was over the plate again.

"That's what makes baseball the great scientific game that it is," Ty said. "A man loves to know he has fooled the opposition."

Cobb won his first American League batting title in 1907. He also led the league in total hits (212), stolen bases (49) and runs batted in (116). He batted .350. And he was only twenty years old. Coincidentally, the only other twenty-year-old ever to win a major league batting championship was another Tiger—Al Kaline, in 1955.

Little had Ty realized what was in store for him early in 1907, for Manager Jennings had ignored him in spring training and Ty began to worry about his status with the ball club. His spirits zoomed sky-high following a quote he read in the paper, however. Jennings had told a reporter:

"Young Cobb has the makings of the greatest ballplayer that ever lived. That's what he will be in the next three years."

Still Jennings never said anything to Cobb personally— until one day he asked the boy to come into his office.

"Perhaps," he said, "you are thinking that I have overlooked you. Actually I've watched you very closely. I've come to the conclusion that there's very little I can teach you. Anything I might tell you will simply cramp your style and hurt you. So you set the pace. Play as you please. I will back you all the way."

Cobb became a law unto himself.

Ty played in more than 4000 games during his career, but the one he picks as the most exciting, the one which gave him the greatest satisfaction, was played against the Athletics in Philadelphia on September 30, 1907, when he was still a kid of twenty.

Only percentage points separated Detroit and Philadelphia as the frontrunners were scheduled to play a doubleheader, closing their series for the year. It was the sort of pairing movie script writers dream about. Detroit led the race by a couple of points, having won 87 and lost 56 games, while the A's had won 83 and lost 55. To win both games meant the lead for the Mack team and probably the championship. The largest crowd ever assembled in the Athletic park— more than 40,000—was gathered. The crowd spilled onto the field, and when the first game started the symptoms of trouble were in the air. Cobb was hooted, jeered, and insulted at every turn.

Jennings had chosen Wild Bill Donovan, who later was to die a tragic death in the wreck of a train, as his pitcher. The Athletics hammered Donovan hard from the start, and as their lead increased the crowd grew ribald and confident.

Detroit drove Jimmy Dygert off the slab in less than two innings and then the great Rube Waddell ascended the mound, struck out six of the first eight batters who faced him, and set the immense throng wild. The score was 7 to 1 in favor of the Athletics when the seventh inning started. With victory in their grasp, the Athletics went into panic and, while Oldring and Nichols erred, Sam Crawford followed with a double and before the track meet had stopped the Tigers had four

56

more runs and were fighting hard. Donovan had been slammed for fourteen hits in seven innings, but as his team rallied behind him, he steadied and grew stronger, although in their seventh the A's made another run. In the eighth inning, little Charlie O'Leary doubled and scored on Davey Jones' hit, but still the Tigers lacked two runs of a tie.

The ninth came with the situation desperate for Detroit. After hope seemed dead, Crawford drove out a double and, in the crisis of the year, Cobb came up and smashed a long home run into the seats. The score was tied, the great crowd moaning with disappointment. Cobb was giving one of the most superb exhibitions of his career.

Ty doubled in the eleventh inning and raced home on Rossman's single. The game seemed to be won. But the Athletics fought back. In their half of the frame Nichols doubled, a wild pitch put him on third, and he scored on Davis' long fly after Seybold had been purposely passed. The bases were filled when Jimmy Collins ended it, and the fans plunged again into sickening silence.

Detroit fought right back, filling the bases in the twelfth, but little Topsy Hartsel went back almost to the flag pole and dragged down Crawford's long drive to end the threat. Hartsel doubled in the twelfth, only to be caught off second by a quick throw which dashed Philadelphia's hopes. The crowd, edging closer to the field and growing more and more tense with each pitch, broke bounds in the fourteenth inning. Davis hit a fly to center field, and Crawford, jogging back to the edge of the crowd, was in the act of catching the ball when the fans broke loose, rushed him, and knocked the ball out of his hands.

In an instant there was a wild riot. The entire Detroit team rushed from the field and the bench and charged Silk O'-Loughlin and Tommy Connolly, the umpires, calling their attention to the interference rule. Rossman, over-excited, lost his head and swung at Coach Monte Cross, who slugged back. Police sped to the scene. In a minute a giant of a battle was going on. When at last the police led Rossman away, O'Loughlin allowed the catch and the struggle resumed.

Donovan seemed to grow stronger and swifter, and Detroit, keeping up the pressure, threatened to score in each round. Schaefer singled in the fifteenth, Crawford sacrificed him to second, but Eddie Plank, who had succeeded Waddell after Cobb's home run tied the score in the ninth, walked Cobb purposely. Then he retired the next two batters and saved the day.

Cobb made a heroic effort to win the game unaided in the seventeenth. He singled sharply, stole second with a delayed dash, and when the throw got past Murphy, Philadelphia second baseman, he tore for third, slid a twister under the baseman, and was safe. He was racing for the plate, trying to steal home, when the batter flied out.

Darkness was falling when the inning ended. They had been fighting nearly four hours and, instead of two games and a decision of the championship, the one game ended in a tie.

The Tigers, with but a few games remaining on the schedule, clung hungrily to their lead to the end and won their first of three straight pennants under Hugh Jennings.

Ty Meets "The Train"

Ty Cobb is not an "oldtimer" today. He is still young at heart, for time is measured by heart-beats, not by gray hairs and a bald spot. Suddenly he is back on the diamond again! Walter Johnson is pitching. Cobb at bat. It is the first meeting between the two. "Whang!"

Cobb, now sixty-nine years old, was telling the story as if it had happened yesterday, although it actually occurred forty-nine years ago, when life was hell on earth for any rival showing up in the same vicinity as either Cobb or Johnson. He told it with warmth, his alert, clear eyes enjoying each remembered detail.

"I'd been in the American League only a couple of years when Walter came out of the west to join the Senators," Ty said. "This was in 1907, I think, and though he finished with a 5-9 record that year, word of his blazing speed soon got around. Nobody believed the tales at first. But Walter quickly convinced us it wasn't just rumor."

Upon hearing about the amazing twenty-year-old's smoke ball, Ty began asking questions of those who had batted against him. Was this kid Johnson really as good as they said?

"He's got a fast ball you can't even see," Cobb was told. "It looks like bird shot whistling across the plate."

Still Cobb couldn't believe it, yet the replies never wavered: "That Washington pitcher's got a fast ball that's fast and faster. He doesn't need a curve ball or change-up. The only change-up he has is to throw the ball faster. He doesn't mess around out there; he simply looks down for the signal, rears back, and whooshes the ball past ya'."

Cobb's love of facing all challenges was akin to a passion, and he was anxious to bat against the Weiser, Idaho, youngster. He eyed the papers keenly, getting all the information he could about Johnson. Then one morning the Senators arrived in Detroit. Johnson would start. The fans flocked to the ball park to see for themselves if he was real, or just the figment of a sport writer's imagination. If anybody could hit him, Cobb, the people's choice, could.

Before the game Ty sat on the bench watching Johnson warm up. Walter limbered up very deliberately, like a mechanic sharpening his tools. Goodness gracious, sakes alive! He was fast, all right. This guy was no ordinary pitcher. Ty frowned ferociously, as though he were faced with slaying lions in the arena.

Now here was where Cobb's study of Johnson paid off. He knew that Walter was fearful of killing a man with that blinding fast ball, that once when he beaned a batter he had to retire for the day, so upset was he by the incident. Walter never threw at a batter. Fortunately he was not normally wild, though, ironically, he holds the American League record for wild pitches over a season and for an inning. He was charged with twenty-one wild pitches in 1910, and four years later he had his big inning, throwing four wild pitches. Cobb knew, too, that Johnson was a kindly, gentle soul. He wouldn't hurt a fly, what's more a rival batter.

"Tyrus," Cobb told himself, "you can take liberties with this fellow. Take advantage of his warm nature and crowd the plate. He won't hit you. He will pitch wide. Then after he gets himself in a hole, step back to your normal position in the box. He'll have to come in with the pitch or walk you."

The wisdom of nearly three seasons in the big league behind Cobb was paying off. He assessed the plan quickly, challenging it for faults. It seemed sound enough.

In the bottom of the first inning Cobb walked to the plate with his strategy all set. He planted his feet close to the plate, hunched over so that his knees and arms covered the strike zone, and Walter was forced to throw to the outside. Cobb knew the easy-going Johnson was too ethical to throw at his head, which other pitchers would have done to keep him honest, and he walked.

Cobb came to bat again, a couple of innings later. Mischief sparkled in his eyes. He had not forgotten how Happy Harry Hale had been driven out of baseball by bunts that day in Atlanta. Johnson looked pretty clumsy fielding his position, so Cobb dropped a bunt down the third base line on the first pitch. Johnson was caught flat-footed. Immediately the whole Detroit batting order was doing likewise. They bunted poor Walter to death, beating him, 3 to 2.

"Things were different the next time Walter pitched against us," Ty grinned. "My first time up I bunted again. Johnson bolted off the mound like a shot, fielded the ball expertly, and I was out. Just as simple as that. That's the last time we tried to bunt on him. I later learned that after we beat him the first time, Walter went back and practiced fielding bunts for hours. In my estimation he has to be put down as the greatest pitcher of all time. He had no peer. It wasn't long after he came to Washington that some of our batters, arriving in Walter's vicinity, were reporting on the sick list. Seems a sudden and mysterious epidemic had broken out among the men, with about half of them requesting the afternoon off. The thought of facing Walter's fast one had upset their digestions. About the only way you could beat Walter was to outwit him. There was no mystery about what he was going to throw. Everybody in the park knew what was coming. But that didn't do the batter any good. You can't hit what you can't see. By studying him carefully, I knew when he *wasn't* going to throw his famous fast ball. He'd shake his head, the tip-off that the batter had better get set for his dinky curve. Most batters looked for the curve—if they were lucky."

One time Billy Evans called a second strike on Ray Chapman, the Cleveland shortstop, in a game pitched by Johnson. Chapman started for the dugout.

"You have another strike coming, Ray," said Umpire Evans.

"Never mind, Billy," replied Chapman, "I don't want it."

Some years ago Cobb and Johnson took the long train ride together from Cooperstown to New York, following the annual Baseball Hall of Fame celebration. They got to discussing the old days.

"Shucks," Cobb said, "I wasn't much of a hitter when I broke in."

"That's when I should have known you," Walter said.

"I never hit much against you, Walter," Ty said.

"Not at first, I will admit," Johnson said, "but once you caught on to me you never let go. I can't complain, though. I wasn't the only pitcher you abused."

For the record, Ty hit .335 against Johnson.

"Walter," he said, "I never abused you or anybody else. I just figured a way to get a base hit off you once in a while. But, as I was saying, I wasn't much of a hitter when I was a kid. For one reason, I played with boys older and bigger and stronger than I was, and I had to use their bats and they were too heavy for me. I had to learn to swing them and I finally did. People have asked me many times where I got that unusual grip I used, with my hands about six inches apart. Well, I will tell you."

Cobb looked to the far end of the club car, forming an analogy in his mind.

62

"Look," he said finally, "if you had a long pole and you wanted to touch that end of the car with it, how do you think you could manage it best? By holding it away down on the end with both hands? Or by putting one hand down here and the other up here to give you better leverage? Well, that's what I did with a bat. Then I could get it around on a ball. Once I was able to do that, I might have been a good hitter right away. But I wasn't."

As Cobb said, he was undersized when he joined the Royston town team, much smaller than his playmates, and since they only had one or two bats, Ty had to get used to swinging a stick too thick and too heavy for his size. He gripped it with his hands spread wide apart to give him balance and control. That was the origin of his unique batting grip. He never changed it. He carried the things he learned as a boy all the way to the major league.

Ty often wonders what the modern batters would have done against the old trick pitching he broke in against, like the spitball and the other freaks. Jack Chesbro was the first real spitball specialist. The Highlanders' great righthander wet the ball with slippery elm. He gripped it with his first two fingers. His thumb applied the spin, just the opposite of what happens in an ordinary delivery. Chesbro's overhand pitch came up to the plate like a regular fast ball—then suddenly dove under the bat. His sidearm fast ball, instead of breaking inward, developed into an outshoot. In 1904, he won forty-one games.

Ed Walsh was another master of the spitter. Fortunately, Cobb knew when it was coming. Walsh tipped him off unconsciously.

"I discovered that when he brought his hands together in front of his mouth at the top of his windup," Ty explained, "he'd hesitate ever so slightly and rub the ball against his mouth like this. Every pitch wasn't the spitter, of course, but I always knew when it was coming because he'd have to open his mouth to spit on the ball—and that jiggled the bill of his cap. I kept my eye on that cap."

The spitball never bothered Ty after that. He got so he could even hit it on the dry side!

Eddie Cicotte, who played with Cobb at Augusta, was perhaps the oddest pitcher of all. Later he kicked around the big leagues for a long time, with only a minimum of success, and then—p-s-s-t-t—he suddenly popped up with the strangest pitch Cobb ever saw. It floated up to the plate like a snake on a hot griddle and batters broke their backs trying to swat it. Talk about frustration. Ty always liked a high fast ball and Cicotte peppered him with them. Ty had it measured and took a good healthy poke at it, but he couldn't connect. He kept cutting under it. Cicotte never imparted his secret formula to anybody, not even his catcher, and Ty still is trying to solve the riddle. Cobb's theory is that Cicotte created a way of reversing the spitball idea by wetting the ball under his thumb, or some other part of his hand, to give him an extra amount of spin from his first two fingers. It didn't dip and swoop like a spitball sinker; rather it skipped a little. Whatever his secret, nobody ever succeeded in imitating Cicotte and he became a star of stars.

The emery ball was another baffler. It drove batters frantic. Russell Ford invented it, discovered it quite by accident while twirling in the minors.

"Ford was warming up one day and he threw a wild pitch," Cobb recalled. "It slammed into the grandstand, striking a cement pillar. The ball was returned to Ford and he threw it again. This time it sailed off in a dipsydoodle flight, the dawgonnest thing you ever saw. Ford and his catcher couldn't believe it. They examined the ball, discussed the pitch, and tried to come up with an answer. They finally realized that the cover of the ball had been scuffed when it hit the cement, making a little wing stick out like an unpredictable rudder."

When the old Highlanders graduated Ford to the majors,

he insisted on bringing his own catcher, Ed Sweeney, who was only a .240 hitter. Sweeney was below big league calibre, but Ford wouldn't come without him. They practiced their chicanery tirelessly. Ford's pet pitch was far more than a curve. It bobbed around like a cork on a wind-tossed sea. Batters couldn't figure it out. They watched him, studied him, but it was a waste of time. Eddie Collins got inquisitive.

"Why does Ford always carry his glove back to the dugout in his pocket instead of throwing it on the ground between innings?" asked the classy second baseman. Further investigation by Collins revealed that the glove had a hole at the base of one finger. Ford concealed a patch of emery paper underneath for the purpose of "working" on the ball.

Once the secret was out the parade soon followed. Other pitchers got ideas. They scuffed the ball with all sorts of crude instruments, everything ranging from belt buckles to a piece of nutmeg grater stuck in the shirt pocket. When these primitive methods were exposed, the burden was passed along to the catcher. Then the first baseman took over the job. No matter how hard the umpire watched, the defense never stopped trying.

The late, great Cy Young, winner of 511 games in the majors, a record, always insisted the hurlers of his era had all the best of it. The modern pitcher, he said, doesn't enjoy anywhere near the advantages of his day.

"The strike zone was wider, fences longer, ball deader, and we always pitched a *dark* ball," Denton Tecumseh Young admitted. "We never threw the ball until we added something to it first, a little tobacco juice and dirt to blacken and liven it up. Nowadays they don't let you get away with that stuff."

Time marches on. Whereas if three or four balls were used up during a game in the old days the owners demanded that the auditor make an investigation, from five to six dozen break out of their boxes now. Under today's rules, as soon as a ball gets a spot on it, out it goes. Even if it is only a little rust off the screen, or it gets a tiny bit soiled from the mud, the umpires toss it back to the ball boy. Not so in the olden days. Ask one of the genuine antiques to tell you about Clark Griffith, shifting around out there on the mound and tapping away at the ball with his spikes. It was a common sight for the pitcher to get on his bony knees, not to pray but to rub the ball on the grass and gravel to give it wings.

Tommy Bridges, a cool little operator, once broke off a sharp curve that looked as if it dropped off the end of a table. Mickey Cochrane was working behind the plate and he rolled the ball back to his Detroit battery mate. After the game, Spike Briggs, Jr., the Tiger owner now, collared Cochrane in the dressing room.

"Why'd you roll the ball back to Tommy on the ground instead of throwing it to him like you're supposed to?" Briggs asked.

The burly Detroit catcher wrinkled his face owlishly.

"Well," he replied, "I had to do something to try and get the chewing gum off the ball."

That's all out now. Balls are as smooth as billiards. The pitcher gets few, if any, breaks—except in his arm and heart. With little chance to doctor the horsehide, except with a little resin, he's under a constant baptism of fire.

Oldtimers, on the other hand, found many ways to tamper with the ball. The home team furnished the balls. There was no rule, such as now, that the arbiters had to break them out of factory-sealed boxes.

"A lot of the boys did fairly well with the help of BB shot, meticulously poked under one seam and flattened with a wooden mallet," Cobb said. "The local pitcher, knowing where the weight was located, spun the ball just right and found that the BB gave his sinker something extra. The visiting pitcher, unsuspecting, scratched his head and wondered why so many of his pitches were horribly missing the target. But the BB secret was solved in time, and the pitchers had

66

to try new inventions, such as weighting the baseball seams with paraffin. This gave the ball the same effect as the BB trick. It could be done right on the field by simply carrying a bit of transparent paraffin on a pant leg. Dose the pant leg with talcum powder and you had the shine ball."

Back in the halcyon days, when the world was younger and every park fence had knotholes, pitching was an art.

Now it's an adventure into the valley of the shadow.

Deep in this vein, Joe McCarthy sat talking to Tris Speaker last summer at the annual Oldtimers Game in Yankee Stadium. Lefty Gomez sat nearby telling funny stories, and McCarthy said to Speaker, "They know Lefty now as a very funny man who sells sporting goods. I wish they knew him as I did. He was not only a great pitcher, but the hardest time I had with him was to keep him from pitching out of turn. The day after he pitched, he would drive me crazy on the bench. If the pitcher we had in there was in trouble, Lefty would look at me and wink and nod toward the bullpen, or he'd walk up and down the dugout until I had to tell him to go to the clubhouse or go some place where I couldn't see him. I hear they don't have pitchers around like that any more, Tris."

And Tris said, "I'm sorry to say, Joe, that's what I hear, too."

The Home Run Baker Incident

One of Cobb's most sterling performances was the second game of the World Series between Detroit and Pittsburgh in 1909—a series which, in spite of the marvelous work of Ty, the Tigers lost by bad judgment in attack.

Cobb was a whirlwind—hitting, running, jockeying, and fighting for the victory; and, after making one of the greatest catches of his life of a low line drive, followed by a snap throw to third that stopped the Pirates, he climaxed the performance by stealing home on a desperate twisting slide around the catcher.

Ty was a bundle of nerves. Germany Schaefer said he kept his eyes glued to Cobb, paying slight attention to the game. Ty moved incessantly, jumping into position, shifting, moving, poising ready to sprint as each ball was pitched, starting on a dead run when the ball was hit, hustling every second of the game. He must have covered as much ground as all the others combined.

Cobb said he gained the greatest respect for Honus Wagner, his foremost contemporary rival of the National League, during that 1909 classic. Wagner was playing shortstop for the Bucs, and the first time Cobb got on base he cupped his hands and shouted, "Hey, Krauthead, I'm coming down on the next pitch!" Ol' Hans said nothing, but when Ty got there Hans had the ball. He slapped it into Ty's mouth and split his lip. The wound required three stitches.

Later, Wagner said, "I like Ty. He's a fighter and he knows it's a fella's duty to protect himself. Lots of 'em have trouble with him, but I don't."

Cobb ran the bases hard and he carries dozens of spike scars, all the way from his ankles to his thighs. But those who knew Ty best think the worst hurt he ever suffered was being accused of deliberately injuring Frank Baker at Detroit in August of 1909. Home Run Baker was one of those stationary third basemen, heavy, with big legs, who used to anchor one leg in front of the base and block off runners. Every runner jockeying around second used to yell at Baker to look out, they were coming, in an effort to scare that big piano leg off the base line.

Cobb gives you his version of the infamous incident:

"Even now, kids whose parents weren't even alive when the play occurred, will walk up to me and say, 'Oh, you're the guy who spiked Home Run Baker.' I have always liked children, doing my share in Little League and Boy Scout work, and I want them to know once and for all what really happened in Detroit forty-seven years ago.

"If I were guilty of dirty play I'd be willing to take my medicine. The facts are these, however. Study a photograph of the play in question, and one is available, and you will see that Baker was clearly on the baseline. He's on the attack, his arms extended to tag me. I am pulling away, but trying to reach the bag. You will particularly note that my foot has passed by his right forearm, and the force of the so-called 'spiking' hasn't even moved his arm from its position.

"Those who covered the game will have you believe that I knocked Baker's arm clear behind his back, that he was sprawled flat on the ground and smeared with blood. Why, study the records and you'll find that Baker didn't lose an inning of play, and went on playing, I am certain, in every game for the remainder of the season.

"Frankly I didn't even know Baker was hurt in the slightest way. No one gathered around him. There was no scene. Actually I took a bigger chance than Frank did. I tried to avoid touching him, and risked breaking a leg to do it.

"The incident would have been forgotten immediately if Horace Fogel, a Philadelphia baseball writer, hadn't gotten his facts wrong in the story he sent back to his paper. Shortly after, the Philadelphia fans were up in arms against me. I received numerous letters warning me to stay out of town, that I'd get a cracked skull the next time we played there. One letter writer said he would shoot me.

" 'If you come to Philadelphia you will be shot by a man standing atop a building outside the right field fence,' the letter said. 'We know you are yellow because you showed it when you spiked Baker. Now let's see if you've guts enough to come here for the next series. If you do, you are done.'

"I figured the writer was bluffing. He was trying to frighten me so that I would stay out of the lineup and weaken the team. I'll admit I was a bit scared on that visit and kept my eye out behind me if I had occasion to walk in a deserted side street. But shucks! a ballplayer is always getting threatening letters.

"My wife didn't want me to play, but I had to. Newspapers printed the letter. I was on the spot. Folks would have said I was yellow if I sat out the series. I didn't want them saying things like that. I'd rather have taken a chance of being shot. I wasn't trying to pose as a hero, don't think that. I freely admit I was scared. I spent several uncomfortable moments shaking in my boots out there in the field.

"In the second game, when I was just beginning to get used to the idea that some crackpot might be crazy enough to use

70

me for target practice, a nerve-screeching 'bang!' exploded behind the right field fence. I must have jumped eight feet. Sam Crawford was playing in right field, and he yelled at me, 'What's wrong, Ty?'

"It was a second before I could get my voice. 'W-w-what . . . what was that?' I cried.

"Sam began to laugh.

" 'What's so funny about being shot at?' I shouted.

" 'No one's shooting at you, Ty,' he said. 'Some guy blew an automobile tire out in the street.' "

Cobb received exactly thirteen letters vowing to kill or maim him, but nothing ever did happen.

"I am now sixty-nine years old," Ty said. "I still resent the charge of brutal and intentional spiking. Historians will have you believe that I'd have cut down my own grandmother if she got in my way. Perhaps I was pretty rough out there, but nobody can honestly say I was dirty. Aggressive, yes, but not dirty. I took the stand that the baselines belonged to the base runner and it was up to the tagger to protect himself. I never deliberately cut a fellow except to protect myself. Never in my twenty-four years in the American League was I accused by a ballplayer of purposely spiking him. Moreover, I can honestly say that I never felt I was spiked deliberately.

"Only twice did I bring my spikes into play against rivals. One was against the Cleveland catcher, Harry Bemis. I didn't like the way he blocked the plate on me or the names he called me while doing it. I might have stood for one or the other but not for both. So the next time I set out to let him have it. It so happens that I missed him, but that ended the dirty name-calling and roughhousing."

Cobb also fixed Hub Leonard's wagon. The Red Sox pitcher had the annoying habit of throwing bean balls at Ty, his way of trying to tone down the broiling Tiger star. Cobb never did fancy the thought of a pitcher deliberately risking his life and limb, and decided to put a stop to this show of foolishness. It was time to use his dissuaders. Before he was finished Leonard would look like a pincushion.

One afternoon the Tigers were playing the Red Sox, and Leonard was up to his old tricks again. His first pitch barely missed Ty's head, but his second missile was more successful, hitting Cobb on the back of the neck. Ty checked his extravagant temper before it erupted, and strolled down to first base in stormy silence. Black clouds mounted inside him. He would get Leonard the next time around.

A couple of innings later Cobb stepped into the batter's box again, as self-assured as a newly-elected senator. He looked out at Leonard with an expression as cold as a snowman's. Leonard didn't catch its meaning. Too bad. Ty went after the first pitch, deliberately dragging a bunt down the first baseline. The first baseman bolted in, scooped up the ball crablike, and threw to Leonard, who in the meantime rushed over and covered the bag. Cobb was out. But that didn't foil his plan. He ignored the bag and slid into Leonard, spikes shining, dumping the pitcher heels over head, his stockings cut to shreds. That ended the bean balling!

Cobb admits that the oldtimers were rougher than the more moderns, but he also feels that today's "polite" game has produced the most bruising single play he has seen. He means the football scrimmage commonly tolerated nowadays when a base runner hurtles into second base in an attempt to break up a double play by banging into the pivot man and sending him crashing to the ground. That isn't baseball as Cobb and his contemporaries played it, and Ty is astonished that the infielders of today put up with it. An infielder subjected to that kind of hostility in his day would have blandly made his throw to first in the exact direction of the runner's face. Or he would have come down with gleaming spikes planted none too gently in the runner's ribs. No runner would have tried it twice. Cobb says he often thinks that today's players, with their awkward sliding and those blocks at second base, actually do more damage than the ancients did for all their fierce tactics.

But Chuck Dressen lamented that one of the things wrong with today's game is that the players are still too *courteous* toward their rivals.

"What is it?" he demanded of his players in a club meeting. "Is knighthood back in flower or something? Or are they your lodge brothers? You take a thing like picking up the opposing catcher's mask. Sure, it's not important, but there's something behind it. You pick up the mask, wipe it on your clean uniforms, and hand it back on a tray to the catcher. I'm expecting any day one of you will go sliding into a base and a guy from the other team will borrow the ump's whiskbroom to brush you off."

Times change. The young men of today are far more considerate of the enemy than their predecessors were . . . when, for instance, dusting off the hitters was an accepted part of a pitcher's tactics. The only time a hitter really worried was when they didn't dust him off. It made him think he was through!

Deep in this vein, Casey Stengel, whom Cobb rates as one of the all-time great managers, was asked to enlarge upon the kind of team he expected to have at Brooklyn in 1934.

"It will be a fighting team," Casey said, "but at the same time it will be a very polite team. Whenever one of my pitchers hits a .400 hitter in the head with the ball he must apologize. He must walk up to the man and say:

" 'My dear fellow, I am awfully sorry. Please view this regrettable incident as an accident.'

"If my men are not courteous to the men they hit, I will have no part of them. I am constitutionally opposed to low, vulgar tactics."

Before the Dodgers took the field against the Giants in an exhibition game that spring, Stengel delivered a locker room lecture.

"I don't want any handshaking out there this afternoon," he said. "If any of you guys have friends on the other side, wait till next October to become sociable. I don't want any talking either. If you feel you must say something, be sure to say it with a snarl. A ball game ain't a junior prom. Get what I mean?"

One of the rookies didn't. He wanted details.

"What's a junior prom?" he asked.

"You don't know what a junior prom is?" thundered Casey. "A junior prom's a prom that ain't old enough to be a senior prom!"

One spring Abe Pollock, having refereed prize fights, thought he would combine refereeing with baseball umpiring. He started in the bush leagues and didn't finish the first season, giving you some smattering as to the hammering around the men in blue received in the old days, too.

"I stood for everything," Abe mourned. "They stepped on my feet with spikes, kicked me on the shins, and bumped me. One day in Fort Wayne the crowd was after me. I didn't mind what they said or did, how many pop bottles they threw, or anything. But, in the middle of the game, a man walked down the aisle carrying a bull terrier on a shawl strap, dropped it over the front of the stand, and yelled, 'Sic him!'

"That's when I quit."

A Lesson in Psychology

Ty was never willing to believe that anyone could beat him or that any odds were too overwhelming to master. In 1911, for example, Detroit, then out of the pennant race, was playing at Chicago early in September. After the game Cobb and Ring Lardner dined together. Ring had a copy of the latest batting averages.

"How do we stand?" Ty asked.

"Jackson and Speaker are over .400 and you're .383," Ring said.

"That means," Cobb said, in a voice that seemed to vibrate with energy and self-assurance, like an atom bomb biding its time, "it's time for me to get busy and make my move. Just watch me close that gap."

In the next twenty-one times at bat, under the heaviest sort of pressure down the stretch, Ty got eighteen hits. He breezed on to win his fifth straight batting championship.

"There's a story behind that particular title," Ty said. "I practically went out and stole it from Jackson by waging a simple war of nerves against him. I never could have beaten the Cleveland outfielder if I'd waited for nature to take its course. I had to think of something."

75

The answer came to Cobb one night while lying in bed in his hotel room. Out of the dark came an idea, full-blown and shining with purpose. The Tigers were going to Cleveland for a crowded six-game-in-four-days series. Jackson and Cobb were both southerners and always had been friendly. Ty knew Joe would come over to greet him before the first game. He also knew that Jackson was a nice, simple, gullible fellow. Once a pitcher deliberately threw two straight balls at Joe's head. Jackson turned to the catcher and quietly remarked, "Boy, this guy's wild today." Then with the courage of innocence he whomped the next pitch to the fence. That was Joe Jackson!

Cobb waited back in the clubhouse before the first game until Jackson finished batting practice. Ty arranged for one of the clubhouse boys to tip him off when Joe was through. He wanted to be sure to bump into him when he walked out. Sure enough, Jackson spotted Cobb immediately and ambled over, grinning like the Cheshire cat.

"Hello, Ty," he said, amiably.

Cobb's eyes narrowed, and he scowled, "Get away from me!" Jackson's grin slowly faded from his face. He gasped. It was plain to see that he was puzzled and hurt.

"What's eatin' you?" he said mournfully. "What are you mad about? I ain't done nothin' to you."

"Stay away from me," Ty said, glowering at Jackson. Cobb pivoted and walked away.

For every inning during the game Cobb arranged to pass near Jackson on the way to the outfield when the teams changed sides. At first Joe kept asking, "What's wrong, Ty? What did I do to you?" Cobb, a great actor, looked as though anger was teetering on his tongue, and, swallowing it, he kept silent. Finally Jackson stopped speaking altogether. He couldn't figure it out.

Jackson brooded so much he went hitless the first three games while Cobb fattened his average. His mind was on only one thing: getting base hits. Jackson's mind was on a lot of things. In the remainder of the series Cobb passed him in the averages. To keep his stratagem alive, Cobb had to think of a new angle. He had to keep Jackson upset for the rest of the season.

After the final game of the Cleveland series, Ty ran over to Joe, slapped him cordially on the back, and pumped his hand enthusiastically.

"Joe, old boy!" he beamed, "it's been great seeing you. How's everything? How are things back home?"

An appraising glance told Cobb that Jackson was befuddled by this abrupt change of attitude. Joe stared at Ty, his mouth open. He was clearly stifled. Ty surely was laying down a nifty smoke screen and sneaking up for a surprise attack. The rascal! Then Joe knew he had been hoaxed—and there's nothing so frustrating as knowing you've been taken. His hitting continued to nosedive and Ty beat him out for the crown, .420 to .408.

That's one for the book, batting .408 and still finishing only second!

Some years later, Grantland Rice and Cobb were driving north from Augusta, where they had watched the Masters Golf Tournament. This was in the spring of 1947, and as they hit Greenville, South Carolina, Ty said, "Grant, I've got an old friend in this town. Let's look him up."

"Who's that?" Granny said.

"Joe Jackson," Ty said.

They asked a policeman where Joe Jackson might be found. He directed them to a small liquor store down the street. They had no trouble finding it, and went in. Joe was behind the counter. Ty looked him squarely in the eye, and said, "How's business?"

"Fine, sir," Jackson said, turning to the wall to rearrange a shelf.

"You ol' gaffer," Ty said, "don't you remember me?"

Jackson wheeled around.

"Cripes, yes!" he said. "Sure, I know you. I just didn't think you knew me after all these years. I didn't want to embarrass you or nuthin'."

Jackson, you'll recall, was involved in the Black Sox scandal of 1919.

It was a pleasant visit, three of the greatest fanning about the good old days. Joe died four years later, in December of 1951. And Granny, God rest his soul, followed on July 13, 1954.

"Jackson was the only really great hitter who got away with a careless, free-swinging style," Cobb said. "He just busted them and hoped for the best. A born hitter, Joe had a marvelous eye and enormous natural strength. Men like Eddie Collins, Home Run Baker and myself were developed batters and had to be scientific in our work. I shudder to think how many points Jackson would have added to his average had he played percentage baseball. He lost a lot of hits because he didn't study the game more scientifically. Joe couldn't tell anyone else how to bat. He didn't know himself how he hit, or when he was going to hit, or where to hit. He just did what came naturally."

Jackson was born in Greenville, South Carolina, not far from Ty's birthplace. He was a cotton millworker. Joe began playing baseball only as a sideline, but built up such a prodigious reputation as a batter that Connie Mack sent for him.

Mr. Mack was sold on Jackson immediately and, learning that Joe had neglected his education, offered to put shoes on him and send him to school.

Joe joined the Athletics in 1908, but he wasn't happy. Oppressed and homesick, he longed for the smell of the cotton mills and leisure of the south. Mr. Mack wasn't playing him regularly. Jackson was itching to bat. Restlessness nagged him ceaselessly and he threatened to pack his bags and return to Greenville.

"Be patient, son," Mr. Mack urged. "This is where you belong. Don't throw it away."

78

" 'Tain't no good for me," wailed Joe. "I want to play—every day!"

"But first you must get big league habits," Mr. Mack said. Jackson agreed to stay.

Then about a week later the A's went to Washington for a series against the Nats. During the second or third game Mr. Mack suddenly realized that his malcontent wasn't sitting in his customary place on the bench. This roused Mr. Mack to lively interest and, cocking an inquiring eyebrow to the spot, he asked, "Where's Mr. Jackson? Sick?" Nobody seemed to know.

Mr. Mack scoured the locker room, he scoured the hotel . . . the whole town. No Joe. He went back to his ball-players and canvassed them. No one had seen him—oh, wait, one of the players said now that he thought of it he did see Joe near Union Station the night before.

"He said he was going to buy a newspaper," the player added. Jackson hadn't been buying a paper, however. He had been buying a one-way train ticket back to Greenville. Joe's geography was normally rusty, but not so poor he couldn't figure out that Washington was the closest American League point to home. Logically that was the place to jump the club.

Mr. Mack broke Man o' War's fastest time in getting to the nearest Western Union office. "Join the team in Philadelphia immediately if you don't want to be suspended," he wired Jackson.

"Don't want to stay in the big league," Jackson wired back, collect. "Am tired of it."

Mr. Mack was persistent. He did some beautiful broken field running coaxing the wayward outfielder back into the fold.

"And you can bring your wife along, too," Mr. Mack said, cinching the deal.

Life among the Athletics was a scene of high, friendly

spirits for the following weeks. The problem of Joe Jackson appeared to be solved at last. Then, as suddenly as the first time, the slugging Carolinian turned up missing from the roll call again one morning. The Missing Persons Bureau reported that a man filling Jackson's description was below the Mason-Dixon Line punching the whey out of South Atlantic League pitching. It was Joe all right. He won the Sally League batting championship and Cleveland grabbed him faster than a Mississippi River cardsharp's hand after Mr. Mack formally announced he was relinquishing all claim to the shoeless one.

"Jackson was one of the greatest hitters of all time," Cobb said, "but I have always said he would have been even greater if he'd stuck with Mr. Mack. Mr. Mack had the knack of developing hitters and getting the most out of a man's potentialities. He would have taught Jackson some batting science."

It curdles one's blood to think about it.

The season before Cobb beat out Jackson for the batting title, the whole St. Louis Browns lineup conspired to help Nap Lajoie lift the crown from Ty. There were just a couple of games left on the 1910 schedule—in fact, as Ty recalls, Detroit had already finished the season—and Cleveland was playing the Browns two games to end the campaign.

Cobb and Lajoie had battled neck and neck for the batting title right down to the wire. Cleveland was in fifth place, St. Louis a cool eighth, and there was nothing at stake in the doubleheader save the batting championship in which the Browns were supposed to have only an academic interest. But before the first game began the Browns agreed among themselves to help Lajoie make base hits. The Indian second baseman evidently was aware of the conspiracy, for he kept bunting the ball safely, largely because the Browns made puny effort to field it.

Reporters scented something wrong before the outrageous hoax had proceeded far. But Harry Harper, a St. Louis pitcher, made it unanimous by sending word to Jim Crusinberry in the press box that Jim, as official scorer, should credit them all hits and give Lajoie the batting honors of the year. Lajoie was scored eight hits in the two games.

The ugly plot caused a scandal. No money was involved. It was an out-and-out plot of those who liked Lajoie and had it in for Cobb.

Hugh Fullerton, who worshipped Cobb, saw him a day or two later and was indignant. Cobb laughed.

"It doesn't make any difference," Ty shrugged. "Larry is a good fellow. I've had the title often. And, besides, the hits I made helped Detroit win ball games. I'm satisfied."

On the face of the unofficial figures, Lajoie led the league. But the official final averages were not yet out. Fullerton discovered that he had been the official scorer in one game between Chicago and Detroit in which Cobb had beaten out a questionable hit. After some argument, the boys in the press coop had agreed to score it an error—but the official score hadn't gone through. Since they were trying to cheat, Hugh salved his conscience and scored that play a hit for Ty.

Final official figures: Cobb .385, Lajoie .384.

Fair enough.

Part III

At the Peak

1912-1919

Preface

Time marches on. The next half-dozen years were to find the powers that peopled the world in a constant state of flux and disorder. Britain was warning Bulgaria, accusing Germany of attempting to disrupt the Balkans and enslave the states that played the Kaiser's game. A former football coach —Woodrow Wilson—was in the White House and snarling at German submarine warfare. Congress was to be asked for $400 millions to begin national defense, and raise the Army to 120,000 men.

Pancho Villa, tough bandit chief, was to rate headlines with his hit-and-run raids on the Rio Grande. The civil war in Mexico was to produce the first aerial battle in aviation history. The Bolsheviks were to revolt in Russia.

Despite the smog of gloom hanging over their heads, the deep thinkers continued to move ahead. Henry Ford had more than a half-million Model-T's on the roads, was paying employees a minimum wage of five dollars a day. Gasoline was now being perfected on a broad commercial scale. An American astronomer, Percival Lowell, was trying to convince scientists that the planet Pluto actually existed—they told him to get a new pair of glasses. After a decade in the construction of it, the Panama Canal was to be formally opened to commerce.

The "feminism" movement was sweeping the U.S., crying for women's suffrage. Lillian Russell was the sweetheart of musical comedy, Enrico Caruso the apple of every opera lover's eye, and William Gillette was playing return engagements of Sherlock Holmes.

Americans, craving for stimulation and excitement to replace the terrible nervous pitch which the international situation was causing, turned to sports to release their pent-up emotions. In 1914, a hungry, scowling, restless fist-fighter from out of the jungle camps of the Golden West was to begin campaigning professionally as "Kid Blackie." The world was to come to know him later as William Harrison Dempsey—the most spectacular tiger ever to hold the heavyweight championship.

Cowboy Jess Willard, six-foot-six, 250 pounds, was to knock out Li'l Arthur Jack Johnson in twenty-six rounds in Havana, April 5, 1915, and win the heavyweight title, then lose it to Tiger Man Dempsey four years later in Toledo. Other leading lights to skip across the pugilistic stage during the period would be Jack Dillon, Battling Levinsky, Willie Ritchie, Freddy Welsh, Johnny Kilbane, Kid Williams, Ted Kid Lewis, Jack Britton and Jimmy Wilde.

This was the era when organized baseball was to go through the shadow of death. The impending war in Europe wasn't the only threat. Suspicion and skepticism regarding the honesty of professional baseball was growing daily in proportion to the attendance and to the salaries paid the players. Many fans were beginning to believe that the whole fabric of major league baseball was rotten and that games were being "fixed" regularly. The scandals of the Chicago Black Sox, of Hal Chase, Lee Magee, and Jimmy O'Connell, in 1919 was to feed this contention.

86

After Hugh Fullerton, Sr., exposed the Black Sox in 1919, Mike Donlin, one of the famed writer's closest friends, threatened to punch him on the nose and admonished that he ought to have sense enough to know baseball could not be framed. Most of the reporters who were connected intimately with the game believed that to be true, and found it hard to think anything else, even after Chase demonstrated that he could throw games and cause all the blame to fall on others.

But there were happier moments, too. The Boston Braves, in 1914, were to make Manager George Stallings a "Miracle Man," coming from dead last on July 8 and roaring like the Super Chief Express through the second half of the campaign to top the Giants' bid for a fourth consecutive pennant and win by ten and one-half games. Then, to the astonishment of all, they crushed the supposedly invincible Athletics four straight in the World Series. During that incredible stretch drive, the Braves' pitching triumvirate—Dick Rudolph, Bill James and Lefty Tyler—won forty-nine games and lost only ten for a percentage of .831! Rudolph won 20 out of 23, James 19 out of 20, and Tyler 10 out of 16. The Braves were to turn out to be only one-year wonders—but never to be forgotten.

The following year another Boston team, this time the Red Sox, was to win the World Series, beating the Phillies four games to one. Woodrow Wilson attended, the first President to see a World Series. On the Boston team was an outfielder named Tris Speaker, a small but durable shortstop named Everett Scott, and a new pitcher up from Baltimore only the year before called Babe Ruth. He was later to go down in history as the vaunted Sultan of Swat, but of all his records he was to be proudest of having pitched twenty-nine and two-thirds scoreless innings for the Bosox in the World Series, against the Dodgers in 1916 and the Cubs in '18.

Grover Cleveland Alexander was the magic name over in the National League in 1915, winner of thirty-one games. Walter Johnson was burning them over the plate for the

Senators, his pendulum arm propelling the ball like a sling-shot. They had nicknamed him the Big Train, and in 1913 he had an earned-run figure of 1.15. On the Fourth of July, 1915, a former University of Michigan star athlete named George Sisler was to pitch for the St. Louis Browns, and win his game, 3 to 1. The same year the Federal League, an "out-law" circuit which sprung up in 1914, was to fold after fruit-lessly attempting to recruit the big stars from the National and American wheels with bonus promises.

The Yankees' harassing Murderer's Row was still ten years away at this time, but Greater New York had its heroes none-theless. Snodgrass and Burns and Fletcher and Merkle and Hans Lobert and Chief Myers and Larry Doyle and Rube Marquard and Jeff Tesreau and Christy Mathewson were McGraw's stalwarts on the Giants. The Dodgers had Zack Wheat and Jake Daubert.

These were some of the famous names of the day, and the heroes of a twelve-year-old janitor's kid in cast-off clothing who attended P.S. 132 in Manhattan—Henry Louis Gehrig. The world was to hear of him some day, too.

The fathers of Georgia, by now, weren't telling their youngsters legitimate bedtime stories anymore. They were telling them tales about Ty Cobb—Dixie's greatest invention since the cotton gin. Boys and girls in every community in the south were learning about the amazing Peach before they could even read. They were being told how, in 1911, the gal-loping Georgian set a new modern high batting mark of .420, a record, incidentally, which was to be broken thirteen years later, in 1924, by one of his most ardent admirers, Rogers Hornsby, who clouted an unbelievable .424. They were hear-ing of his startling speed on the base paths, of the 46 bases he stole in 1907 to top the American League, 76 in 1909, and 83 in 1911.

But Cobb was to prove between the years 1912 and 1919 that he was only getting a running start. Come 1915 and he would win his ninth consecutive batting crown (.370) and steal ninety-six bases, another record performance. Tris Speaker would come along in 1916 and break Cobb's string by hitting .386, as against Cobb's .371, but the determined Tiger would bounce back in '17 and bunch together a string of three more batting championships. He practically went with the lease.

And, finally, there was to come a day when Tris Speaker would be asked to compare Cobb and Ruth. This would be many years later, and Speaker, because of his own marvelous skills on offense and defense, was the logical choice to make such a comparison. He had a clearer view of them than most ballplayers did because he was on the same level with Cobb and Ruth through all the years he battled them.

"When Ty and I were both young and going good," Speaker was to say, "the writers were kind enough to say to me that I was the closest thing to him. Now, let's not be immodest about this. I was good and I knew it. I had to know it. It says so in the book. But, good as I was, I was never close to Cobb and neither was Ruth or anybody else. Babe was a truly great ballplayer but, in my opinion, Cobb was even greater. Ruth could knock your brains out, but Cobb would drive you crazy."

Yes, during the next six years Ty Cobb was to reach full flower. He would become a living legend.

Here, now, is how he dreamed, planned and plotted to keep that legend alive.

The Phantom Mercury

No game in the world was as tidy and dramatically neat as baseball a la Cobb at his peak—with cause and effect, crime and punishment, motive and result so cleanly defined. It was as full of surprises as a mystery play. The plot and its ending may have been perfectly apparent up to the last inning and the last man at bat, and then with stunning suddenness change entirely and go on to a new ending as Cobb circled the bases on a puny hit by the batter.

When Detroit was a run behind in a late inning, and Cobb was the first man up, you could get a price that the Tigers would tie the score. The ball was "hot" when he was on base. Ty upset infields as he upset batteries—scoring from first on singles, going from first to third on sacrifice bunts, scoring from second on infield outs and sacrifice flies, stealing, making delayed steals, purposely getting himself trapped between bases. If a base runner today took the chances Cobb did, they'd look at him as though he was as cracked up as a Sunday driver. But Cobb got away with it. His unbelievable base-running stratagems stupefied the fielders into insensibility, and they often reacted as if in a drugged lethargy, unable to muster sufficient mental energy to stop him.

Pretty was the personal duel between Cobb and the opposing battery. Every inch of ground Cobb could chisel by increasing his lead off first brought him that much closer to victory. The contest developed into a battle of highly-tuned science between pitcher and runner. Those seemingly endless throws that the pitcher made over to first to hold Cobb close to the bag were not made for exercise or to annoy the customers, but to reduce those inches. Those inches otherwise would have been translated into hundredths of a second around second base and spelled the difference between safe and out. Cobb needed little encouragement to go all the way. One pause, one tiny mistake, and he was off with the speed of a bullet.

Runs depended upon those infinitesimal measurements.

Probably the greatest action picture ever made on the ball field—certainly it is the most famous—shows Cobb booming into third base at the finish of a swirling hook slide. For sweeping movement, intensity of effort and zest of adventure, the effect has not been matched by any inspired brush.

Joe Williams said that for twenty-one years he wondered what unnamed master of the graflex pinned this flash of baseball drama to the gelatin surface of an Eastman plate. Then one day, in 1930, he got to fanning with Charlie Conlon. Charlie was a veteran proof reader on the old *New York Telegram* whose hobby was photography.

"Would you like to see the original plate of that picture?" Conlon asked the *Telegram* sports editor. And then the story came out. It was Conlon who took it. "And the odd thing about it," he told Williams, "is that I didn't know I had snapped the play at all."

The Yankees were playing Detroit. In those days New York was called the Highlanders and they played their games at the old Hilltop grounds. It was late in the summer of 1909 and the Tigers were in the thick of a pennant scramble. Cobb was running wild on the bases. He stole seventy-six bases that season, practically doubling his highest total up to then. Conlon had a buddy on the old Highlanders, Jimmy Austin, who played third base. Conlon spent most of his time in the vicinity of third base chatting with Austin and casually shooting pictures, pictures which he would bring to his home, develop at night, and file away in his collection.

Well, on this particular day and in this particular game Cobb had worked his way down to second base. One was out and the following hitter was trying to bunt. Austin moved in to be in position to field the ball, and as he was standing there waiting for the batter to swing, a sharp, gasping short-spaced shout arose from the stands. Cobb was off for third. Sensing this, and knowing that he had no time to turn, Austin backed into the bag, and as he did Cobb threw himself into the dirt, spikes first.

Conlon's first thought was that his pal Jimmy was going to be cut down by the desperate Georgian. He stood there motionless with his box in his hands. He saw a blur of arms and legs through a screen of flying dirt. It was a bright day and to his death Conlon said he had never forgotten Cobb's lips grimly parted and the sun glinting off his clenched teeth.

"Jimmy never got his hands on the throw the catcher made to head off the runner," Conlon told Williams. "He was knocked over and fell forward on his face. But in a moment I realized he wasn't hurt, and I was relieved because Jimmy and I were very close friends. Then I began to wonder if by any chance I had snapped the play. I couldn't remember that I had, but I decided to play safe and change the plates anyway. It was fortunate that I did for that night when I developed my stuff there was the whole thing plain as day."

A curious circumstance in connection with this photo which they call the most memorable picture ever made on the diamond—and a circumstance which modern editors will find hard to comprehend—is that the picture wasn't printed. Not that season at any rate. It made its first appearance in a baseball guide published in the winter. The answer is that in 1909 not a great deal of art was used in the sport pages and baseball did not enjoy the extensive ballyhoo that it commands now.

Better than a volume of words that picture of Conlon's, showing Cobb crashing into third like an India-rubber idjit on a spree, tells you the story of Cobb the base runner. Like they speak of the Elizabethan era, or the Renaissance, or the glory that was Greece and the grandeur that was Rome, it is well for historians to speak of the Cobbian age. Before his time, the base runner was the natural prey of the team in the field. He was a hunted creature with nine men trying to put the slug on him. In this sense he was on the defensive. It was his job to see that he didn't get caught.

Cobb changed all that. When he reached first base, the whole infield was on the defensive, in blind terror of what he might do to make them look very silly indeed. Pitcher, catcher and infielders spent so much time worrying about what he was going to do to them that the batter looked like the forerunner of the Forgotten Man. With Ty on the bags, it was much easier for the batters following him to get hits. The pitcher had something else on his mind.

"Make 'em throw it!" was always Cobb's theory. He knew that if the boys tossed it around long enough in their nervousness they would bobble it and he—and his teammates— would be home free. They used to call Ty a lucky stiff. That would make his eyes burn like live coals and make him more furious than usual. "I create my own luck," he'd retort, which was just what he did. His spirit was contagious, giving the other Tigers daring ideas. For instance, with Davey Jones, the Tigers' astute little lead-off man, on third base one time and Germany Schaefer on first, the sign was given for the double

94

steal. Germany was an uncanny base runner, a master at timing. Like Cobb, he always stole second on the *pitcher* and not on the *catcher*. He was usually on his way before the ball left the pitcher's hand. This particular game he was all the way down to second as the ball whizzed across the plate. Detroit was playing Cleveland. Jones stood anchored on third, taking no chances of being tagged. That tickled Germany. "We'll try it again," he yelled down at Davey—and he dashed all the way back to first base. Such an unorthodox thing so upset Cleveland's rookie pitcher that when Germany started for second again, he held the ball too long and Davey sprinted across the plate with the winning run. Thus not once but often Germany Schaefer stole first base in order to win games. All the rest of the season, incidentally, Schaefer argued with the official scorer that he was entitled to three stolen bases when the play worked—second, first, and then second again.

Cobb owns the game's greatest lifetime batting average, but he confessed that he got almost as much satisfaction out of stealing bases as he did out of adding to his base-hit collection.

"I guess it dates back to my boyhood days," Ty said. "The old *Police Gazette* used to run coupon ads which a kid could cut out and for twenty-five cents mail in for those pamphlets telling how to play games. I wrote in for every baseball booklet they advertised, showing how to pitch, catch, play the infield and the outfield. They also had one on track and, just for good measure, I mailed in for that one, too. Even then, you can see, I wanted to know all I could about foot-speed, quick starts, and stopping on a dime."

The day that Ty's booklet on track fundamentals arrived was a big moment in his life. He read it thoroughly from cover to cover, then dashed over to a vacant lot next to his home and practiced the lessons for hours. Ty, by his own admission, never had much natural speed, but he studied the science passionately. The booklet instructed him to pump the knees high, and he pumped his knees high. It told him to break into a fast start, and he broke into a fast start. Ahh, progress. He'd pour over the pamphlet, digesting each word carefully, then, stuffing it into his pocket, begin his workout: a slow jog for ten steps, break into a sprint, slow down, and then start over again. He spent hours running in a straight line at top speed with his head turned over his right shoulder. He didn't know it at the time, but here was an exercise that he was going to use daily in the American League so that he could watch what the outfielders were doing with the ball.

Cobb never stopped working at this phase of the sport. Even after rising to stardom he'd stay on the field till after dark, alone, running short wind sprints between the bases. He concentrated on cutting sharply around the bags, touching them properly, zig-zagging back and forth, the way football halfbacks practice dodging tacklers. He even practiced limping. He would go onto the field at the start of the game, limping as though he had a Charley horse. He would keep on limping and complaining—within earshot of the opposition—about how his leg hurt him. Then, suddenly and at the strategic moment, the pain would conveniently disappear and he'd be running through the astonished defense faster than a secret through a women's bridge party.

Cobb discovered that it was a big help to stumble deliberately at first base and come up apparently lame, or to seem to be hurt by his slide. He knew that if he was a good enough actor the pitcher and catcher would relax, let their guards down, and then it was no trick at all to steal second base.

In the twilight of his career, Ty got to figuring there would come a day when he could stumble at third base and sort of limp down the baseline toward the plate, gingerly rubbing his leg and looking as if he meant to call time and get out the trainer. Sooner or later, he thought, he would be able to limp close enough so that a sudden burst of speed would score him. But that was one ruse he never got a chance to try.

"In my estimation," Ty said with studied casualness, "players who don't know how to run the bases are a drag on the team. Even if they get on base it generally takes a couple of solid blows to score them. Think how much more valuable they'd be if they could run. I used to pick out the bad base runners in the league and lay for them. They never got wise to one play I had. If a man was on first and a fly was lifted my way, I made it appear that the ball was going over my head. The runner got careless and broke for second. Then I made my move, catching the ball and whipping it back to first base to double up the runner. I know it sounds like a deceptively simple trick, but you'd be amazed how often it worked."

Cobb found that the secret to being a good base runner was to hit the dirt with the feeling that you liked the sensation. He was always covered with blisters and scrapes on his thighs the early part of the season, but as the months wore on his body became hardened to the bouncing around. Few players wear them anymore, but Ty never was without his sliding pads. They were an important part of his equipment, and added years to his active career.

Apropos to this, in July of 1955, on the eve of the annual Baseball Hall of Fame celebration at Cooperstown, Ty and the author were invited to a dinner party at the summer home of Dr. Blalock, the famous Johns Hopkins "Blue baby" surgeon. Dr. Blalock, a fellow Georgian, leases a summer place at Cooperstown, and he is a Cobb fan extraordinary. Many prominent names of medicine were present, but Ty Cobb was the thing. He was the one the gathering wanted to hear. Ty, in rare form, entertained them for hours with colorful stories about his baseball career. It was the son of Dr. Blalock who posed an interesting question.

"Why, for heaven's sake," he asked, "isn't there more of your equipment in the Baseball Museum? You can imagine my disappointment the first time I visited there and found only a pair of your baseball stockings and sliding pads. How come?"

"That's an interesting question," Ty smiled. "I am a sentimental man and used to save my gear. I kept it stored in the guest house on my place at Augusta years ago. One day I discovered that my sons had taken some of the stuff to outfit the whole neighborhood. Well, I didn't say much about it because I was happy to see them play ball. But when I was elected to the Hall of Fame in 1936, the Museum people wanted some souvenirs. I went to my trunk to see what I could dig up for them. There was nothing left—except a pair of sliding pads and stockings. The kids had cleaned me out. Which is why you'll see only pads and stockings hanging in the locker marked 'Ty Cobb' at Cooperstown."

As great as he was in all other departments, Cobb is best remembered as a phantom mercury sweeping the base paths. He stole a total of 892! Everett Scott, who played shortstop for both the Red Sox and Yankees, said the greatest thrill he ever got out of baseball was watching Cobb streak from first to second.

"He always reminded me of a great thoroughbred coming down the home stretch," Scott said.

Pitchers disposed of Babe Ruth and other renowned hitters simply by walking them. Babe got so many free passes to first base he moaned that he felt like the president of a railroad. But they didn't walk Cobb if they could help it. He was even more dangerous once on base.

Cobb gave catchers hallucinations. It was virtually mandatory for them to throw a base ahead of him to head him off.

Lou Criger of the Red Sox aroused Cobb's antagonism one day with an interview he gave reporters. The burly backstop boasted he would show up the phantom mercury.

"Listen, smart guy," growled Cobb before the game, "I'm

gonna get on base and then steal third and maybe even home on ya'! You said you can stop me. Let's see ya' prove it!"

His first time up, Cobb walked and promptly stole second and third. Before the afternoon was over, the snorting Georgian racked up five thefts.

On three different occasions during his career, he stole all the way from first to home.

"Cobb," muttered Catcher Ray Schalk, "would have stolen my mask if it hadn't been strapped on."

The Athletics were scheduled to play the Tigers one day and before the game Connie Mack called his players together for a skull session.

"Now, Wally," he said, turning to Wally Schang, his spunky catcher, "suppose Cobb was on second and you knew he was going to steal third. What would you do?"

Schang evaluated the question for a flicker of a second, then blurted, "Why, Mr. Mack, I'd fake a throw to third, hold the ball, and tag the son o' gun as he slid into the plate."

Cobb often did things that appeared utterly foolish to the untutored eye. But he had a reason for every move he made. Many times he went from the plate all the way to second merely on a single. He figured it out this way: He knew precisely how long it took him to run two bases. There was seldom any variation, not more than a half step. And on a hit to center, right or left center, he figured that any one of six things could happen: The fielder may fumble the ball, as it takes a bad bounce. It may slip from his grasp as he goes to throw it. He may make a bad throw. He may make a perfect throw that may take a bad bounce. He may make a perfect throw that the second baseman may drop. The baseman may make a perfect catch of a perfect throw and the runner may still evade him.

"As manufacturers look ahead in their work," Ty reasoned, "there is no reason why ballplayers shouldn't. At least that was my theory when I was active. A manufacturer doesn't wait until the last minute to order his raw material. If he did, his factory would have to close down. I figured the same idea could be applied to baseball. It didn't seem possible at first, but I finally got it started.

"When Detroit was ahead, say 7 to 1, and the game was near the end, I'd do what I called 'establishing a threat.' Now, you understand that the game doesn't mean anything. What I mean is, with a six run lead and our pitcher going good, one out, more or less, isn't going to harm us. So I could afford to be thrown out. Very well. Now remember that on a hit to the outfield you usually get about half-way to second, if you run fast and turn first at top speed. All right. You still return to first before the ball, because the outfielder throws to second and you beat the ball as it's relayed to first. Now here's the point. The fielders are on the defensive. The runner isn't. He's the attacker. If he is speedy, all that hinders him from moving on toward his objective is stumbling over the bag or on the base lines. But the runner has those six chances to get to second.

"I put this theory to work. Sure, I got thrown out in a one-sided contest when we were, as I said, six or so runs in front. But the damage was done. I had established a threat in the minds of the fielders. They had seen me dash for second and almost make it.

"Now a few weeks later in a close game, where one run was needed, I'd hit the ball and again attempt to stretch it into a double. The fielder would tighten up on the play. He'd get tense trying to hurry the ball to second ahead of me. Often he'd rush so that one of the six possible mischances would happen and I'd be safe. But the play wasn't made then and there. It had been made, really, weeks before when I tried for second and was thrown out."

Cobb never missed a trick. He developed base running to its keenest degree of science. By watching the baseman's

100

eyes, for example, Cobb always made up his mind on which side of the bag to slide. He never decided this until he got a look at those eyes and, once his decision was made, he never changed it.

"More base runners have been injured because they changed their minds at the last moment trying to decide which side of the base to hit," Cobb said. "This is mighty dangerous. The runner is liable to sprain an ankle, probably break a leg. By sticking to my original decision, I never got worse than some sliding gooseberries or a minor spike wound."

Ty said he used to get a lot of credit he didn't deserve. He'd get an extra base on a bobble or a wild throw and— well, everybody was very kind to him.

"That Cobb!" they would say. "What a hair-trigger mind he has! He's got only a split second in which to think, but he always knows what to do. And that speed of his!"

"Actually, it wasn't split-second thinking most of the time," Ty said. "It only looked that way. What I did at the moment was what I had planned weeks before. I said to myself that if this happened, this is what I would do. Speed? Sure, I could run. I suppose I could run the hundred yards in ten seconds or thereabouts at my peak. But there were a lot faster guys in the league.

"Two stars of my day, Eddie Collins and Clyde Milan, each stole in one season more bases than the entire ball club of fourteen of the sixteen major league teams in 1951. Isn't that a travesty? Sure, you have men today who would be great base stealers—if they applied themselves by studying the pitcher and catcher closer and get a lead off first base, which you seldom see anymore. I looked faster than I was because I got the jump."

Cobb once told Mickey Cochrane that when he got the jump on the pitcher, even the greatest of catchers didn't have a ghost of a chance to throw him out, no matter how strong and accurate his arm. He told Cochrane he could have been slower and still, in most cases, Cochrane himself couldn't have stopped him with a cannon.

Years later, Mickey confirmed this.

"Ty was a pippin," Black Mike said. "He was so swift he could advertise his intentions and then make good his boasts. I was catching for the Athletics against Detroit one time. Stepping into the batter's box, Ty nodded casually to me and said, 'The hit and run is on. I'm hitting the first pitch.'

"I thought he was joking, but signaled for a pitchout to be on the safe side. Ty reached clear across the plate and slapped the ball into center field. I was speechless. I took off my mask, stepped in front of the plate, and bowed deeply to Cobb, who was smiling on first base.

" 'Ty,' I shouted, 'you're not even human. I wouldn't have believed it if I hadn't just seen it.'

"It is small wonder the public came to think of him not as a man but as some superior being from another planet. Ty was my boyhood idol. I admired his competitive spirit, and tried to pattern myself after him. It was practically impossible to stop Ty from scoring. All he needed was four inches of the platter and you were a dead duck.

"Cobb was right when he said I didn't have a chance of nabbing him when he got a jump on the pitcher. Too many catchers have been blamed for a runner stealing. Remember the 1931 World Series? Remember how Pepper Martin ran wild against the A's? He stole five bases, and I was blamed for them all. Tell me, how could I have thrown him out? I couldn't have stopped him with a shotgun. Once, just once during the entire Series, one of our pitchers threw to first base to hold a runner on."

"Bases aren't stolen on a catcher," somebody piped up. "They're swiped on a pitcher."

"You know it and I know it," Cochrane lamented, "but that's not enough. The fans don't know it. They'll always remember me as the catcher Pepper Martin ran wild on."

Talking to Martin later about the '31 Series, the Wild Horse of the Osage said, "Oh, everybody knows I didn't steal on Cochrane. I was stealing on Lefty Grove and George Earnshaw. What sort of tricks or signs did I watch the pitcher for to tell me when it was safe to steal? I've read about guys who could watch the way the pitcher held his mouth or something and know if he was going to pitch or try to pick 'em off. Not me. To me the pitcher was just a sort of silhouette, kind of foggy, and I'd look at him and something about him would give me a signal: 'Go!' I never knew what it was. I ran by instinct."

Catchers in Cobb's day practiced getting the ball out of their gloves fast and snapping their arms into throwing position. All the while they were warming up, they sprang into position after each pitch. Most of them, and particularly Billy Sullivan of the White Sox, had uncanny speed. Ty never could quite get down to second on Sullivan until he applied psychology.

One day while taking his turn at bat, Cobb turned to Sullivan and said, "If I get down to first, I'm going to steal on you on the very first pitch."

Sullivan only grunted.

Cobb did get on base, but Billy didn't pay any attention to him. Billy imagined Cobb was only bluffing. On the first pitch Cobb stole second, catching the astonished Sullivan flat-footed.

Ty's voice was filled with authority when he came to bat a couple of innings later.

"Billy," he said, "I did it once and I'll do it again. If I get on base, watch me on the first pitch."

Again Cobb got on base. Sullivan wasn't taking any chances this time. He called for a pitchout. Ty stood as still as a mummy, until the count reached two balls and no strikes on the batter. Now the next pitch had to be over. Cobb went

103

down on that one and caught Sullivan napping again. He never had much trouble running on the Chisox catcher after that.

Psychology was also at the bottom of the play that gave Ty one of his greatest moments on the base paths. The victim this time was Hal Chase, the great New York first baseman who had a slingshot for a throwing arm and could shoot the ball across the infield like a bullet. The incident happened when Chase was young, when he was without a peer, and writers were referring to him as "poetry in motion" in almost every paragraph. That's why Cobb always has been proud to say that one day he tricked the great New York first baseman. Here was the setup:

If a runner was on second base and a ball was hit to the infield and the throw was to first, the runner on second had to watch out when he got to third, because if he rounded the bag by just this much Chase fired the ball over and the startled runner was dead before he could get back. Cobb knew this and practiced on Chase. He'd round the bag, and dive back, always just ahead of the ball. This cat-and-mouse game went on for a good part of the season. What Cobb was waiting for was the exact moment when he had Chase used to it.

The day finally arrived. Ty was on second and the ball was hit to the second baseman. Ty ran to third and rounded the bag. Chase, having taken the throw from the second baseman to make the putout, threw over to third. The third baseman swung around to tag Cobb as Ty slid back—but Ty wasn't sliding back. By that time, he was scoring. The third baseman was so petrified he didn't even bother to throw home.

Here again Ty showed that his genius was strategy, to pull the unexpected, to outwit the opposition. He never wanted any infield, pitcher or catcher, to have a moment's rest. He wanted them so badly scared they'd still be frightened the next day. One of his tricks was, with another runner on third

104

and him on second, to come home on a fly ball, following so closely after the runner on third that the catcher was what you might call bewildered.

Cobb was on first one afternoon, playing against the Athletics, and Rossman hit a low line drive over third base. Socks Seybold played it like an infielder. Ty had rounded second with the sweep of a seagull diving for his dinner, and was on his way to third. Home Run Baker, the A's third baseman, stood with his back to the plate waiting for the throw from Socks to put the ball on Cobb. Baker knew Cobb was coming—the phantom mercury was always coming.

As the ball shot into Baker's mitt, he swung around to his right to tag Ty. No target. Ty figured that that was just what Baker was going to do and he came into third sprinting, his body on an angle of 45 degrees. His toe touched the sack with the grace of a Nijinski—and he was headed for home, without even a change of pace. As always on a close play, Cobb threw himself far away from the plate and swept his hand over it, a swell target for a catcher to tag indeed! Ty was so safe that the catcher didn't even squawk.

Billy Evans was umpiring behind the plate and he was gasping at the daring of it.

"Ty," he said, "that looked like sure suicide."

"Suicide nothing!" snorted Cobb. "Didn't Baker have to uncross his legs, turn around—and then throw?"

All of which was very true. Home Run Baker looked like a pretzel trying to tag a guy who wasn't even there. That one play demonstrated four parts of the Cobb personality: his lightninglike thought processes, his power of concentration, his sublime courage, and his ruthless will to win.

Cobb's grandeur and his glory was on the bases. In 1915—after ten years of play—he stole ninety-six bases, the all-time high. Now to illustrate the significance of that production, the entire Detroit team of 1937 stole only eighty-nine bases. Philadelphia led the American League that season with ninety-five. And the champion Yankees, the whole gang of 'em, stole only sixty.

A great deal of the battle of wits was centered around the steal, an important play in the Cobbian Era when a single run still meant something. Pitchers were awfully cute with a man on first base. Their tricks weren't restricted by anything like today's balk rule. They could be murder on the base runner. Nick Altrock of the White Sox once caught three men off first in a single inning!

But, alas, the old science has changed. Today all good managers will ask you, why take chances on smart baseball just to get one run? What good is one run in a game nowadays? The idea now is to get a whole flock of them in one round. The players watch for the "explosion" inning when a pitcher weakens and he is pounced on by the heavy artillery—like hungry wolves ganging up on a weary rabbit.

Cobb argues that many of today's base runners don't know how to slide. He points out that nearly half of them make the elementary time-killing error of running right over the top of the bag and going wide on the turns. The old boys could slide from any direction and they cut the corners like a razor, pushing their left foot against the inside of the bag for a quick turn. Cobb feels there isn't enough stress put on base running anymore. "Why," he said, "few teams even have sliding pits at training camp."

When Cobb broke into professional baseball he was unable to slide. He dug a pit in one corner of the outfield and practiced sliding morning and night, day after day, until he became the best and was able to slide automatically.

Ty started out as a head-first slider but was cured of this dangerous habit his second day in the big leagues. He tried to steal second and went in head-first against Kid Elberfeld, the tough little rooster who played shortstop for the Highlanders. The Kid politely but firmly brought his knee down on the back of Ty's neck and Ty's forehead went grinding into the dirt, leaving most of the skin behind. Ty never tried it again.

The next time Cobb met Elberfeld at second he slid feet first, caught the Kid by surprise and knocked him kicking. The Kid could take it as well as dish it out and he patted Cobb on the back and said, "Now, *that's* the way to play, sonny boy." Cobb had been accepted into the lodge.

Base running is a dangerous branch of baseball, for the runner as well as the baseman, and, contrary to the stories that have been written about him, Cobb denies he made a practice of sliding in high with his spikes.

"How could I?" he said. "I used a fallaway or a hook slide. I couldn't go in high with my spikes shining as everybody says."

Ty sighed deeply.

"I suppose," he said, "if they ever made a movie of my career they'd want the opening sequence showing me crashing into third cutting some guy's leg off."

Cobb may or may not have been the first one to attempt the double steal, but certainly he perfected it. Sometimes the infielders anticipated it and set out to upset his strategy. The shortstop would move in about ten yards in front of second base to take a short throw from the catcher, in case the Detroit runner on third started for the plate. If the latter broke, then the shortstop grabbed the catcher's throw and whipped the ball back to the plate. If not, he let the ball sail through to the second baseman, who was covering the base, and slap the ball on the runner tearing down from first.

If Cobb was the runner on first, and he knew that his mate on third was only stalling, with no intention whatever of trying to score, he'd yell at the shortstop, "Take it! Take it!"

The shortstop was invariably watching the flight of the ball and couldn't see what the runner on third was doing. What's more, he didn't recognize Cobb's voice. He'd cut off the throw —and Cobb was in free standing up.

If, on the other hand, the runner on third started for the plate, then Cobb shouted, "Let it go! Let it go!" The shortstop frequently ducked, allowing the catcher's throw to sail through, and Cobb wheeled around and dashed back to first. One run, still no outs. The defense was shattered. They were so rattled by this time that Cobb could run almost at will.

Cobb said he found it easier to steal third base than second. "The reason I didn't do it more often is because the gain didn't warrant the risk involved," he said. "When I was on second I was able to take a wider lead because the pitcher had to turn way around to watch the base. If he wanted to get me, he had to whirl and throw without looking. He took his signal from the catcher on this play. He had to depend upon his shortstop or second baseman to cover. The pitcher didn't have a good target to fire at. His keystoners were on the run. Often the throw was poor and a mixup followed.

"I found little advantage in stealing third, however, and generally stayed put. A clean hit could score me from second just as easy. But if I was on my way to a base-stealing record, I occasionally went for that extra base.

"I had a philosophy about stealing second and third: 'Tyrus,' I told myself, 'you steal second for the *team*—and third for *yourself.*'"

On plays at third base, Cobb soon learned to watch the baseman's eyes. If the throw was coming from right field, he could line his body up with it as he approached the bag and try to let it hit him. If he was lucky enough to have it carom off one side of his body, often he made it all the way home. Even it the ball didn't hit him, at least he got in the third baseman's line of vision. The third baseman would just stand there wondering where the ball was coming from, and

108

as often as not dropped it after he finally spied it. Then, while crashing in, Cobb merely kicked the ball away. Remember Eddy Stanky kicking the ball out of Phil Rizzuto's hand in the 1951 World Series? That was nothing. Cobb often booted the ball all the way into the dugout—accidentally, of course—and romped on home to score.

In 1913, Casey Stengel was a rookie with Brooklyn. The Dodgers were training at Macon, Georgia, and Cobb, who was a Detroit holdout at the time, came over and worked out with the team.

"Ty," inquired Casey, "what's your secret to stretching outfield singles into doubles?"

Casey knew he couldn't run like Cobb, but he knew it wasn't Ty's quickness alone which enabled him to stretch hits. If there was an angle to it, Stengel wanted to find out what it was.

"On any ball hit to the outfield," Ty told him, "I always round first base at full speed. If the ball is hit to the outfielder's gloved hand side, I never break stride but keep going because that means the outfielder will have to turn around to throw."

That sounded good to Casey, but he knew there was more to it than that. Here is what made Cobb truly great:

"If the ball was hit to the outfielder's bare hand," Casey said, "Ty made the turn at full speed anyway and watched the second baseman and shortstop. If he saw either one of them move out toward the outfield to take the throw, that meant the throw was short, and he kept going to second. I tried it and it worked sometimes for me. I didn't have Cobb's gift of quickness, but I caught a couple of guys napping with his tricks."

Cobb's automobile driving habits back in those days around the First World War, incidentally, were about the same as his methods on the bases—very reckless indeed! He was something of a racing car fanatic, you know. He had only two speeds—fast and faster. When he had the wheel, it was every man for himself. John Wheeler once told about a visit he made to Ty's Augusta home in 1914.

The first couple of days that the Bell Syndicate executive was there, Ty was busy at the Georgia-Carolina State Fair. Ty, being a celebrity, was paid fifty dollars a day to start the automobile races. The races were quite an event in the south, and local sports backed their favorite cars heavily. "Doped" machines had been imported from various surrounding areas in the hope of lugging off some of the prize money. "Doped" is the term applied by those amateur mechanics in overalls who got grease on their hands in stripping down their cars until they looked undressed beside the conventional racing buggies. Certain devices were also applied to increase the speed, such as boring out the piston rods and removing all impediments. So it was apparent that Cobb's job was an important one in seeing that each delicately prepared automobile got a square shake. All beefs came to Ty, and he had to smooth over many disputes. None questioned his word. In fact, certain of the entrants appeared to dream up arguments so that they might have a legitimate excuse for talking to the great Detroit ballplayer.

"That's Ty Cobb," whispered one driver to his mechanic after he had held a lengthy conversation with Ty. The driver was from Charleston, South Carolina, incidentally, and his car looked like a crab, its wheels being spread so far apart. But the theory made sense, since it eventually roared home with most of the money. It could stick fast on the sharp turns of the half mile course and not sling out from the rail.

"They've doped that car for this track," explained Cobb to Wheeler, quick to catch the vernacular of any sport. "It's all spread out and will win sure. Get your money on it."

Through Cobb's influence, Wheeler was appointed a judge. On the first day one of the drivers blew a shoe on a sharp turn, ripping down about a hundred yards of fence. He landed

110

on his head, and they had to carry him off to the hospital. Cobb, in no time, took personal charge of the wreck until everything had been straightened out.

One of the events on the program was called "A Perfect Gentlemen's Race." Every mongrel-bred car in Augusta, most of them of doubtful age, entered. Cobb started them off and then, fired by the spirit of competition, grabbed hold of Wheeler and hopped into his own car and raced after the field, slinging it recklessly around the curves and sounding the alarm for everybody to clear the way.

For a time folks were sure baseball would lose a great star and literature a leading light.

Who won?

"Why, Ty did, of course," John Wheeler said.

"It wasn't his nature to lose—at anything."

One evening, many years later, Cobb talked about his enthusiasm for steering wheels, and what brought about an abrupt end to his howling across the landscape at 100 miles an hour.

"I never competed at Indianapolis or in any of the big events," Ty said. "Mostly raced just for my own amusement. But it was exciting, and fun. One day I accompanied a friend, a star driver of the day, on a trial run. We hit about 105 miles per hour and I said to myself, 'This is great. Look at us rip along.' Afterward I started to think seriously about entering the big ones myself.

"A few days later I saw in the papers that my friend had been killed. His car skidded into a bellyroll, did a couple of flip-flops, and whanged into a tree during a race. I was shocked, and couldn't believe it. I reminded myself: 'Why, only a couple of days ago I was riding alongside him, now he's dead.' That experience finished me. I never raced again."

111

Ty's Training Tips

Those who watched the Georgia Peach for so many years streak from first to third on an ordinary single and slide into bases at breakneck speed, could not understand how he kept from getting seriously hurt. Cobb's endurance smashed baseball precedent.

The secret to this $64,000 question is that Ty kept in rigid training and was always in A-1 shape. He became a slave to the rules of conditioning, taking it out on himself and being cruel about it. Baseball actually is a science and Ty studied it from that angle. If there was any truth in the scientific angle, it could, with study, application, and practice, be made to serve his purpose. He always knew what he wanted and how to play the game to get it. He knew that without condition and perfect training he could not carry out the maneuvers demanded by the science for survival and victory. He also was aware that he must always be in shape to withstand punishment, as the ballplayer has not been born who can go the full route, carry any kind of attack, and not have to take considerable busting around.

No athlete in history subjected his legs to a strain as severe

112

Until he hurt it, Cobb had a strong, accurate throwing arm. One afternoon while playing right field, he threw out three runners at first base in one game.

Shown with Captain Travis Jackson, left, and John J. McGraw of the Giants.
Cobb feuded furiously with the New York Nationals, but became a good friend
of McGraw's in the twilight of his career.

After he had led the American League in hitting for two straight years, Cobb was still making $4500 a season. He held out all winter to get raised to $9000 before signing, in 1909.

In 1914, Cobb turned author, wrote a book titled "Busting 'Em," and spent a lot of time with his family at his home in Augusta, Georgia. He is with his first wife and two of his five children.

Ty passed his off-seasons relaxing in the south. Here he takes movies of his son, Howell, and a nephew, John Paul Cobb, Jr.

Cobb always has loved to hunt and shoot. While cleaning his shotgun in 1914, he gets expert advice from one of his sons and hunting dog.

Ty was no novice nimrod, as witness the results of one big game expedition he took with his first wife.

Another of Ty's off-season recreations was training dogs for field trial competition. Here he discusses his prize dogs with the late O. B. Keeler, famous Georgia golf writer, before the start of the 1925 Georgia field trials at Waynesboro.

And a duck hunter, too!

Ty and his brother, Paul, get together for an early-day pose. Paul was a fine ballplayer, too.

When the U. S. went to war, Cobb went along, and rose to Army captain in World War I.

Will Rogers demonstrates a rope trick to Ty Cobb, Jr., while Ty, Sr., looks on. This was in 1921, shortly after Cobb was appointed Detroit manager.

Durability? In 1922, 18 years after he broke into the majors, player-manager
Cobb batted an incredible .401!

As Detroit manager, Cobb, right, was always in there battling to the hilt for his players.

Intellectually, Ty always has had a hunger for good books. Here Senator Harris and Representative McLeod present the Detroit manager with a prize collection before a game in Washington.

In 1924, during an exhibition game at Atlanta, Manager Cobb announced it would be his last season in baseball. He went on to play four more years.

Ty signed with Connie Mack in 1927. Though 40 years old, the old Georgia Peach was a tremendous aid in the Athletics' reconstruction program.

Still a threat at 40, Cobb batted .357 for the A's in 1927, and .323 his next and final season.

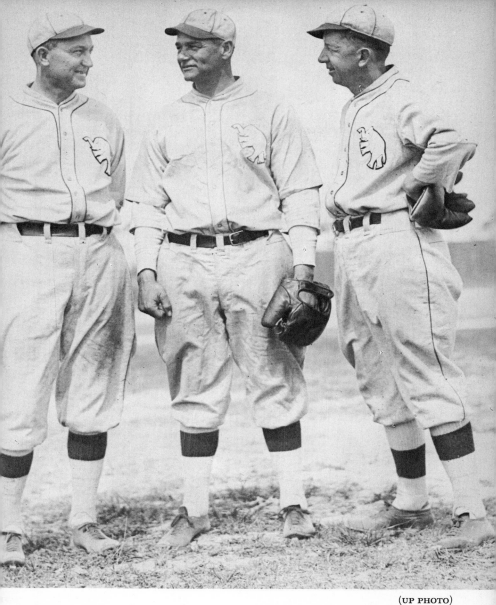

The A's of 1927-28 were composed of seven men who later were elected to the Hall of Fame, among them Cobb, left, and Eddie Collins, right. Zach Wheat is pictured with them.

Cobb and Tris Speaker, two-thirds of Philadelphia's 1927-28 "Hall of Fame" outfield. Al Simmons filled the other slot.

and long sustained as Cobb. Continuous starting and stopping puts terrific stress on the tendons and sinews, but Ty's superior legs stood the test of time. He was still a star at forty!

"I recall one spring, I'm sure it was 1911, the year after I'd left Nashville to come to New York, that Cobb was a holdout," Granny Rice said one time. "He'd been with Detroit five years—a veteran. The stories drifting back from spring camp questioned Cobb's fitness, when and if he decided to report. I didn't hold much stock in them. Cobb never had to work into condition . . . he was always in condition. Knowing he was ready, he merely didn't care to report so soon. He got his raise and reported one week before the season opened. That was the season Cobb rapped out 248 base hits for an average of .420, while stealing 83 bases. His legs must have been the most remarkable pair ever known to man—even Paavo Nurmi."

Hugh Fullerton, Sr., went to see Cobb one season to talk with him about keeping in physical condition and to ask him whether he thought drinking alcoholic beverages was injurious to ballplayers. Cobb told the sports writer that, under certain circumstances, drinking was the best possible thing for an athlete—but never as an habitual beverage. He did not mean that getting drunk or drinking heavily helps condition. He never advocated heavy drinking or hard drinks. But Cobb drank and the great majority of his contemporaries drank. Cobb drank *champagne*. He liked champagne. But the difference between Ty Cobb's drinking and that of many others long since gone was that Ty drank, as he did everything else, with a purpose. If he was going stale, was beginning to slow up, he hoisted a glass or two of champagne which took the edge off his condition and he was in better shape than before.

"Practically all ballplayers I've known have drunk," Fullerton said. "In fact, the list of teetotalers would be smaller than the number of .300 hitters. And most of them were great ballplayers, too. Those who drank beer, ale, and such beverages with a view to preventing staleness, being strong, were able to throw off the bad effects quickly and showed no evil results but, on the contrary, were benefited.

"Johnny Evers, high strung, nervous, drank very little. When he was getting near the breaking point of nerves and in too fine condition, Frank Chance told him to load up on beer—and after a day or two Evers was good for another month. Mathewson drank little and judiciously. Grover Alexander took a swallow whenever he felt like it. Hans Wagner never tasted hard liquor, but liked beer. You can run through the list. The fellows who used liquor carefully lasted a long time. Those who abused it went out of baseball."

Men like Fullerton considered Cobb the greatest student of condition and of physical form that baseball has developed —and he learned it by himself.

"I didn't know anything," said Ty to Fullerton. "Every kid is the same. I reached the stage where kids commence to flex their muscles and compare arms, and if any boy had a bigger muscle than I did I started to work to develop one just as big.

"When I got into baseball I didn't know anything about condition and had to find out from my own experience, and often wonder now that I didn't make more mistakes. I used to eat lunch, go out to the park, start playing, get all warmed up and then get sick. I figured that if my stomach rebelled against that, then eating before a game was not the right thing to do. So I cut down on the lunch and never since then have I eaten more than two meals a day.

"That is the way I had to learn—by experience. It was years later before I realized that I had done nearly the right thing, without knowing it, and that I was lucky.

"Take drinking, for instance. Now no manager with any sense, and no ballplayer with any sense, will say drinking makes a good man, and I don't want to be quoted as defending drinking. At the same time there never was anything better

114

for a baseball player than beer, ale, porter or burgundy when he's in danger of going stale.

"I never defended drinking for beverage purposes. In the old days I saw too many ballplayers drink and eat their way out of the business to have any delusions about the effect of drinking for drinking's sake or for what they call good fellowship. Nor would I speak a word for hard drinks. But good beer and ale were fine for ballplayers, taken in moderation, when they were going stale, and staleness is the most dangerous thing baseball players have to contend with.

"A ballplayer has to keep just below *the pink* of condition all the time and hold that condition for seven months. It is hard work. We go stale, get too *fine*—and slump in the work. There was nothing like beer or ale to take the edge off and put a fellow back in shape—if used properly. Mighty few used it right. The general idea was to make the condition plea an excuse to take too much.

"The best way to get in condition is to keep in condition. I never permit myself to get out of shape, or get fat. In winter I hunt, walk, and play golf—and forget baseball as much as possible. There's something that wears out ballplayers almost as much as playing. A player, especially when he gets so almost everyone knows him, has to talk, eat, and sleep baseball. There's no escape and it wears one out. If a ballplayer's friends really want to help the team, as of course they do, they'll come around with some other interesting subject to talk about and help the player forget his work for half an hour instead of coming around to talk baseball, which he has heard all day long.

"Forgetting the game and plenty of sleep will keep a man in shape. I get at least eight hours' sleep and lie down for half an hour, or an hour, even more, as often as possible during the day, resting and relaxing. More ballplayers tire themselves out standing around hotel lobbies and lounging about hotels than are wrecked on ball fields.

115

"I do not much believe in hard and fast rules of training. Each one must work out his own, but the general principles are the same with everyone."

So saying, Cobb, who had been lying in bed as he talked to Fullerton, removed an electric heating pad from a bruise the size of a pie pan on his hip, tested his injured left leg to see whether or not it would fall off, and started to the park—where he made four hits!

Cobb, as he told Fullerton, hunted and fished and played golf during the off-season to keep trim. He used to tramp twenty and thirty miles a day through the swamplands and fields of Georgia, or go up to Canada and plow through the snow. He wore heavy boots or tacked lead weights on the instep of his shoes to strengthen his legs. He was in shape all the time. There was no fat on him. He was ready to play the full nine the day spring training started.

Cobb was always studying new methods to improve his stamina and efficiency. He got to figuring one training season how he might increase his speed. He took an old pair of baseball shoes to a shoemaker, and had him punch lead slugs into the soles. Ty wore the clodhoppers all spring. They toughened up his legs.

A young sports reporter was attached to the Detroit training camp that spring. He wrote for one of the papers back in Detroit. Anxious to impress his editors, the youngster noticed that Cobb wasn't as quick as usual. He was evidently over the hill, slowing up. Ty was also getting drubbed in intra-squad foot-races by the rookies. That *was* news! Sure enough, the next bundle of Detroit papers to arrive in camp carried this headline:

"Ty Cobb Going Back."

The young reporter's dispatch went on to relate the terrifying revelation that Cobb's speed was gone and, from all appearances, the sage and yellow of his career was practically at hand. The handwriting was on the wall.

116

Ty only smiled when Manager Hugh Jennings showed him the story. "Guess it's time for me to show that kid reporter a thing or two," Ty said.

En route north to open the regular season, the Tigers stopped off in Indianapolis to play the American Association club an exhibition game.

"Get out my regular shoes," commanded Cobb to the Detroit trainer. The standard spikes felt like feathers now, compared to the weighted ones he had been wearing all spring. That afternoon he stole three bases.

"Well, son, what d'ya think now?" Ty said, collaring the young correspondent after the game. "D'ya still believe I'm slowing up?"

The young reporter blinked.

"How did you do it?" he asked, scratching his head. "I never saw such a change. You weren't the same at all."

Ty told him the story, explaining about his experiment.

"Now," he said, "you have a *real* yarn to send back to your paper."

The Cobb of the summer and the Cobb of the winter were strange contrasts. Temperamentally, he was nervous, and he often admitted that the strain of the championship race got him down. Then he hated to have fans "buzzing" him all the time. He was obliged to keep dodging them whenever he was in a hotel.

But in the winter he relaxed.

He liked Augusta because they didn't pay much attention to celebrities there.

"I don't believe," he said once, "that if Abraham Lincoln were suddenly to appear on the main street of Augusta, at noon, that any one of the merchants would stop a sale to go out and give him the once over. I get a fine chance to rest here, and you can't pry me away from this town in the winter."

Cobb became a great star, better at baseball than any man ever has been, through years of painful, determined, serious

117

struggle with nobody else but himself. If this doesn't come through in all of the endless millions of words written about him, it is because he deliberately covered it up. He evidently felt that it is what a man does that is important, not what he goes through to do it.

Talking to Cobb, there is the suggestion that the biggest battle he faced was buried deeply inside him, more raw and challenging than any two-legged opponent—the ability with brain and heart, to control and master himself and his emotions. The road to the top was rugged. Along the way Ty experienced the full range of human feelings: tragedy and joy, hope and despair, hurt and vengeance, all with varying degrees of reality and maturity. Hence the importance of forming good training and living habits.

Boyhood training had much to do with his rigid program, besides the sound soul and spirit of the youth, but the early habits of Ty's life were also tremendously responsible. His clean living did not grow out of a smugness and prudery. The answer might be found in his stubborn, pushing ambition. He wanted something. He knew he would have to choose the most sensible and efficient route to getting it. Since control of his body was an important factor in his desire to be the best, he took care of it in an intelligent manner. He never made a parade of his virtues. He merely lived the only way he knew how to live.

Even in those early days Cobb realized that the better ball-player he became, the harder the game would be. It was every day. He walked up to the plate four times an afternoon. The pressure was constant. It was amazing that a nervous system as delicately balanced as Ty's didn't crack under the emotional burden. The pressure never stopped from the spring through the summer and on into the beginning of fall.

Cobb had to pay an exorbitant fee for greatness—he had to give up himself.

"The strain was terrible," Ty told me. "And to make it worse, I was a born tension guy. I'm still that way. Wish I could be different, but I can't."

In view of this admission, it is all the more remarkable that instead of burning up prematurely he held pace in fast company longer than any other star.

A ballplayer's life was a lot simpler during the Cobbian Era, which is perhaps one reason why Ty and some of the other stars didn't crack under the pressure. Unlike today, they weren't troubled by a lot of distractions, such as making television appearances, after-dinner speeches, radio commercials, testimonials, et al. Willie Mays of the Giants, in 1954, was hitting homers in the afternoon, and receiving $1000 a rattle at night endorsing cigarettes on TV, for example.

But the Old Guard took it much easier. When the daily fireworks were over, Ty and his mates usually returned to the clubhouse, where they took their time changing from their uniforms to their street clothes. They cooled off slowly and discussed among themselves what had happened in the game. If Detroit won, there wasn't much to talk about. Winning teaches little. You learn from your mistakes. When the Tigers lost they could always put their fingers on the mistakes: the outfielder who threw to the wrong base, the runner or batter who missed a hit-and-run signal, the runner who went too wide at second base, the runner who failed to get the jump on the pitcher, the batter who fell for a sucker pitch, the pitcher who mistakenly threw a "fat" one to the batter.

These post-mortems began in the clubhouse, and continued all the way back to the hotel and on into the night. After supper they would go outside and sit in chairs. There were no movies to go to. There was hardly anything to do at all, except hold a nightly postgraduate course in the finer points of baseball. The team veterans dominated the conversation. They were the experts, the teachers. The rookies, awed by their elders, just listened. Sometimes their ears burned. But they learned a lot, and when the meeting of the minds was finished, Ty and his teammates went to bed to rest up for the next day's game.

"All that has changed now," Ty said. "You can go around to a hotel where a visiting team is staying and sometimes never even see a ballplayer unless you want to sit waiting in the lobby from five o'clock till past midnight. The big salaries today have made businessmen of the boys. Now they file into the clubhouse, take a quick shower, dress hurriedly and beat it for some television appearance or something. They don't see their teammates until the next day. In the dear old golden days the boys weren't thinking of the dough. They were only thinking of winning."

A couple of seasons before Joe DiMaggio retired, Ty asked the great outfielder, who was sitting in front of his locker, what he usually did right after a game.

"What else?" DiMaggio said, looking at Cobb a little surprised. "I take a shower, get dressed, and go back to my hotel."

Ty looked at Joe in a sort of anguished amazement.

"Just like that," Ty said. "You take a shower, you dress, and then you go down to the hotel."

Joe laughed.

"Sure, Ty," he said. "Then I have dinner."

"You should have said that in the first place," Ty said. "In other words, you run into the shower, run out, get dressed, run down to the hotel and have dinner. Is that about it?"

"Yes," DiMaggio said. "There's nothing to do around here after the game and I'm hungry. What's wrong with that?"

"Just this," Ty said, with a gusty, mortified sigh. "A ballplayer is on the field only so many hours. He spends most of his time away from the field. Those are the hours in which he stays healthy—or doesn't. Don't get me wrong. I'm not preaching. I'm only telling you. Joe, because you play ball every day, you don't realize the strain it puts on your nervous system. But it's there. It's in your head and in your stomach. If you don't check it, it can take years off your life as a big league player. All the things I'm telling you I had to learn the hard way, such as what to do after a game.

"When you come into the clubhouse after playing, you're all sweated up. Sit down—in your uniform. Sit down and smoke a cigarette if you want to. Have a cup of coffee if that's what you want. Let the other fellows run into the shower. Let them take as long as they please. No matter how long they take—and they won't take long—there will always be plenty of soap and water left. Then you take your shower. Afterward, sit down or lie down and cool out. Then get dressed and go down to your hotel. But don't go to the dining room. Go to your own room. Read the papers or listen to the radio or look out the window for an hour or so. By that time, your stomach is ready for food. Keep doing this and you won't suffer from colds or nervous indigestion."

Ty always has had a special place in his heart for DiMaggio. "He was a great ballplayer," Cobb said. "He could run, hit, throw and field, and if it hadn't been for injuries there is no telling where he would be today in everybody's all-time baseball lineup. But how can you put DiMaggio or any other modern outfielder alongside Tris Speaker, Joe Jackson, or The Babe? Look at the records."

Cobb feels that if DiMaggio had kept moderately active during the off-season by fishing and hunting or working out in the gym at least once a week, he wouldn't have been troubled by bad knees or a sore heel. Ty's reasoning is that Joe would have been in shape for spring training, the time of year when he frequently hurt himself. Joe, instead, lounged around, let himself get hog fat, and when he showed up in camp in March he had to train extra hard. His muscles and bones were not in shape yet. They were susceptible to injury. Ty agrees with most that DiMaggio was perhaps the greatest natural ballplayer who ever lived. He had everything, speed, grace, agility, a good eye, long and strong arm muscles.

"But Joe will never know how great he might have been,"

Cobb said. "He'll never know how many more years he might have played—if he'd kept himself in shape during the winter months. What a ballplayer does during the winter is more important than what he does in spring training. Nowadays ballplayers seem to be just part-time athletes. This is contrary to all laws of nature. A couple of years ago when the Yankees were winning everything in sight, their key players were doing things in the wintertime that made my flesh crawl. DiMag was sitting around as usual. Rizzuto was working for a men's clothing store. Yogi Berra was a greeter at a St. Louis restaurant. No athlete, if he wants to be great, has any right spending nearly half the year in an armchair or a white collar job. He should go work in a warehouse or deliver himself some ice if he needs extra dough."

Ty always has been fond of hunting, and is still an excellent shot. In the old days he was not promiscuous about picking his hunting companions for he hated to return empty-handed, and counted his success by the number of birds he bagged. His two regular hunting cronies in Augusta were Dr. E. M. Wilder, who was an authority on dogs and could sketch off hand the family trees of all the famous bird dogs without once looking at his notes, and Tom Pilcher, a big, whole-souled fellow who owned a great kennel of setters. Ty, himself, had a Gordon setter, "Hoke" by name, and he was as proud of that dog as he was of his imposing batting average.

There was a special preserve about seventy miles from Augusta where Ty liked very much to hunt and which was equipped with a house that had adequate sleeping quarters for only three extra persons. There was also just one mule and side bar buggy that was necessary to the greatest success of the huntsmen. Cobb and his two companions had written the keeper of the preserve that they would visit him on a certain date, and two rival nimrods, as luck would have it, had selected the date Cobb had chosen. Ty was furious.

"I'll tell you what I'll do," he said to Dr. Wilder. "If those two fellows insist on coming down when they know we are going we'll just follow them and scare up all the birds. I don't care if we don't get one. They knew we had planned to make the trip that week."

"If they don't look out I'll miss a bird and bury a little fine shot into one of them," declared one member of the Cobb crowd. "Remember when they went the same time we did last year, and they took the best beds and didn't do any of the work after you let 'em ride down in your car?"

Those close to the story never did hear how the expedition came out, but as they did not read of any hunting casualties in the paper they assumed that an amicable settlement was made.

Ty was a much better shot at live birds than at trap shoots. One year he entered a trapshooting contest at the State Fair. Like everything else, he entered it impulsively, and with a borrowed gun, too. Some of the best marksmen in the south were competing. Ty was terribly disappointed because he could not break as many birds as the top-notchers. Yet never once did he try to alibi himself out of his performance, despite the fact he was unfamiliar with the borrowed gun he was using.

"I don't know how to bust these," he finally conceded. "You shoot straight at a live bird. You've got to get a little under these."

When he was younger, and livelier, Ty would sit in a big easy chair, smoke rings curling around his lean head and bronzed features, and dream of the big game he was going to hunt some day in Africa. He was going to do that for years, but he never got closer to the jungles with a gun than Canada. But he dreamed on. Plans were changed and rechanged. Bears, mountain lions, and moose fell before his crack shooting on preparatory trips. He wanted those elephants, crocodiles and rhinos, but something else always came up to postpone the expedition. Still he didn't do badly. His Lake Tahoe lodge is covered with animals he has killed, bear skins, tanned deer hides, and mounted wild mountain goat heads. He prided himself on being able to take young fellows out and "walk 'em down." He went after birds on horseback, hunted fox at night, and dropped deer with his rifle from a moving speed boat.

Another of Cobb's off-season recreations was golf. He liked to play golf. The weather in Augusta is warm enough to play year round, and right after retirement it soon became *his* game. He attacked it with the same fervor and zest that made him the greatest ballplayer of all time. Soon he was shooting in the low 80's—and he was a lefthander, too! One of his favorite tricks was to have caddies bounce a ball to him and hit it while it was in motion. He liked to kid the caddies, and he did not play the game according to Harry Vardon, for he talked profusely, a cardinal sin in golf. Ty said his main trouble was trying to kill the ball on every long shot and so he pressed. He hit wonderful slices.

Ty was playing one afternoon with Bobby Jones over a course in North Carolina. They were off their respective games. Both were slightly peeved. Coming up to the eighteenth tee Cobb decided to drive right-handed and Bobby swung from the left side. They put four balls in a creek in front of the green. Solemnly they shook hands and went home.

John Wheeler, the oldtime author, told of the time he played a few holes with Ty in Augusta.

"The first time I've touched a club in five years," he announced as the match started.

"That's what they all say," grinned Cobb, "like the pool player who has not had a cue in his hand since women quit wearing bustles."

Cobb was having one of his bad days, and at the end of the first nine they were all even.

"Let's play two more," Ty suggested, refusing to settle for a tie. Wheeler agreed, and Cobb won both. Then he was satisfied.

124

Ty's first wife used to say that she could tell from his footsteps when he hit the front porch whether or not he had a good day on the golf course. The stronger the opposition the better he played. And he couldn't bear to lose—at anything.

There was a time when Cobb played golf in the summer, too. But he believed it hurt his batting during the season. He finally cut it out after he had played eighteen holes in Detroit one morning and then struck out three times the same afternoon in a doubleheader against Boston. He put his clubs in the closet that night and left them there until the season closed.

Golf, incidentally, was the one thing that got Christy Mathewson in constant trouble with John J. McGraw. Matty was one of the best golfers in the major leagues. He shot in the middle 70's consistently. John J. didn't think baseball and golf were compatible. On road trips, however, Matty, the apple of John J.'s eye, took a big trunk along. Tucked in the bottom were his golf clubs. McGraw was always searching for them.

In Pittsburgh one morning, a day after Matty had beaten the Pirates, he shouldered his golf clubs and told Larry Doyle, his roommate, "I'm going to get in a little game. If McGraw asks for me, say I went shopping."

That very afternoon the Giants' starting pitcher was shelled off the mound and McGraw waved Mathewson to the bullpen to warm up. Matty went in the next inning and the Pirates, led by Honus Wagner, teed off on Matty as though they owned him. Coming out of the ball park after the game a friend of McGraw's stopped the martinet of the Polo Grounds.

"Say, McGraw," he said, "I saw Matty on the golf course this morning. He sure shoots a whale of a game."

McGraw blew his top. That night he slapped a hundred dollar fine on his ace pitcher and chewed him out for an hour.

"I want to know right now!" McGraw shouted. "Which

is it going to be, baseball or golf? You've got to make a choice." Matty said nothing, paid the fine—and went right on playing golf!

"Some players today play golf between games," Ty said, "but most managers frown on the practice. It is a ballplayer's duty to give all he has to his team, and he can't very well do it if he exhausts himself on the fairways and putting greens. I gave up golf when I finally realized that I was being paid well to win ball games. It was my duty to the fans, my team-mates, the game—myself—to try and win."

Grantland Rice once told of the time he arranged a friendly foursome at Pebble Beach, California, with Ty, Hal Sims, the bridge expert, and Mysterious Montague, the trick shot artist. It was a four-ball match, with Cobb and Granny playing Sims and Montague, the strongest fellow Granny ever knew.

"Sims was in good form," Rice said, "and when he was going good there was no better, or worse, needler. Before the match started Sims looked at Ty and said, 'Ty, I've always admired you. As a ballplayer you were in a world apart. But tell me this if you will. Why did you have to spike so many men?' Ty has always resented the insinuation that he was a dirty base runner. He was blazing, but managed to contain himself.

"Well," Granny continued, "we teed off. Cobb, normally a pretty fair player, was still writhing and lunged at the ball as if to kill it. We lost the first seven holes. Sims, as happy as he was tremendous, was playing well. Montague, of course, could spot us all ten strokes each and murder us, but awaiting the explosion, his mind wasn't on the game. I, meanwhile, was trying to soothe my partner. It was like throwing water on burning oil.

"On the eighth tee, Cobb pushed his drive almost out of bounds and hit a provisional. Both balls, however, had landed in a bunker, so naturally Ty played his ball first. He came out all right and managed a bogie five. Sims was keeping the card.

" 'What did you have, Ty?' Sims asked.

126

" 'A five,' Ty said.

" 'A five?' questioned Sims.

"Cobb exploded. Grabbing Sims' arm in his vise-like grip, he snarled, 'Listen, no one questions my word or score!'

"Montague bolted between the two. Holding each at arm's length, Monty advised both to act their age or he'd bash their heads together. Hal was visibly upset by Cobb's charge. Cobb, however, settled down and from that moment shot fine golf coming in. Sims couldn't hit a shot."

When fellow Georgian Bobby Jones was at his majestic height and the toast of the golfing world, Cobb was among the legions of Jones worshippers. Now Tyrus was as unlike the Emperor of Golf as any athlete, or man, could be. Once he took it upon himself to accompany the Atlanta hotshot around the links during a tournament in Augusta. Ty was eager to offer advice and moral support. Bobby accepted the company of his celebrated fan with grace. On the last three holes of the final round, Jones needed only three pars to get home in sixty-six and finish eighteen strokes ahead.

After finishing the sixteenth, the fast-playing Jones saw that he had caught up with the match just ahead of him. He sat down for a moment to rest. Cobb began to kick up a storm.

"Get up, get up!" he shouted, rushing over to Jones. "Move around, keep warm!"

Slightly bewildered, Jones got up and moved around to satisfy his excited compatriot.

"Move faster, don't get cold!" urged Cobb.

Ty's behavior must have upset Bobby, because he blew sky-high on the last three holes, taking a 6-5-6. He still won by thirteen strokes, but after the match, in the locker room, Cobb was still fuming.

"You should've moved around faster," he moaned. "You should've done what I told you to do!"

Jones shook his head. With a sly, sad grin he said, "I suppose you're right, Ty. I'll remember to move around faster next time."

Even in golf, as in baseball, Cobb retained the spirit of a sophomore college football player—always bearing down.

During his career, Ty said, he discovered tea to be soothing to his nerves. He made it a practice to drink a cup of hot tea, the best tea money could buy, after each game.

"Very relaxing," he said. "A doctor friend told me about it. He said not to mix sugar and milk in it because, due to a chemical reaction, this combination soured the stomach. I always drank my tea with one or the other, but not with both. I'd lay on my bed with my feet propped up above my head on a pillow and slowly sip the tea. It settled my nerves, and rested me up for the next day's work."

Babe Ruth was a physical freak. He defied all the laws of accepted conditioning. He was a slender kid when he first came up, but he blew up until he looked like a balloon on toothpicks. Ty said he never saw a person with such a devouring appetite. Had Babe been sawed in two on any given playing day, half of Stevens' concessions would have been found inside

"The Babe used to order five or six club sandwiches—smoking a huge stogie with each—and sit in bed at night and finish them all before going to sleep," Cobb said.

"I saw him do it.

"The man was simply unbelievable.

"I'd like to have read a daily log on Babe's activities. No other man could have done what he did and lasted so long.

"What a guy. What a ballplayer.

"His kind will never pass this way again."

Trouble in the Grandstand

One of the favorite legends surrounding Ty is about the after-noon in 1912 when he leaped into the stand at the old New York park and told a fan off—not too gently, either—who had been tormenting him wickedly with inflammatory language.

The row actually was the last straw of a verbal battle that had been building up for an explosion all season.

The fellow had been baiting Ty on previous appearances in New York, but Ty discounted this abuse at first as over-exuberance and home town partiality. On the day of the skirmish, however, the railbird cut loose at Ty with 16-inch guns. Each time Ty passed the stand where the heckler sat, he unloaded. Ty did his best to control his temper, but it began to rise to pressure-cooker proportions. Ty's teammates heard some of the things the guy was calling him and they began to bristle, too.

In the fourth inning Sam Crawford turned to Ty on the bench and said, "I wouldn't let him get away with that stuff."

And the rest of the Tigers coaxed, "We're all behind you if you go after him."

"Maybe he'll lay off," Ty deliberated. "Let's wait and see."

129

Cobb purposely didn't return to the bench when Detroit batted in the next inning because he wouldn't be hitting in that frame and he wanted to give the heckler a chance to simmer down. Ty hung around the outfield and avoided getting within earshot of the fellow.

The following inning he was on deck to bat and on the way to the bench he had to pass the left field bleachers, where the "foghorn" was sitting. This was the man's chance and he heaped a particularly vile volley on Cobb, making folks sitting around him blink. His booming voice filled the park. That was enough. All the king's horses couldn't have held Cobb back. Ty always has had a trigger-quick temper and, in his earlier days, it got him in a lot of trouble, but he has exercised great control over it in later years, realizing that it was a handicap and dangerous to him. But when this heckler gave him the works an old flash of temper seized him. No force could have kept him out of the stand even if he had known that every fan in it was armed with guns, and there was not a chance of him coming back alive. It was not necessarily raw courage that sent him up there. It was simply blind fury.

The details are all vague and hazy to Cobb today, but he recalls starting for the front of the stand, vaulting it, and plowing headlong up through the crowd until he spotted the culprit. Obviously the man never suspected that a ballplayer would dare raise a paw. He turned white when he saw the angry Cobb charging over the railing. The rest is quite blank, but Ty recalls crashing down over the bleacher seats again, while the crowd gaped open-mouthed at him. Everybody in the park was standing, straining, trying to see what was happening. Below, standing in belligerent attitudes directly in front of the bleachers, and ready to jump in and give Ty support in case anyone tried to lay a hand on him, were Sam Crawford and the rest of the Detroit squad. No one in the ball park moved a muscle.

130

It has been written that Ty beat up his antagonist but, oddly, he says that he has no recollection of pushing the guy around at all.

The umpire, of course, was waiting to give Cobb the heave as soon as he returned to the field. According to the league rules he had to put Ty out of the game, but he acted pretty apologetically about it. The rest of the Tigers went back to the bench and laid aside the bats they'd been lugging, still muttering to themselves.

"I knew Ty was going to do it," Jennings said. "Did you see that look in his eye? I knew there was no chance of stopping him. When he gets that look nothing can stop him."

Jennings knew Cobb well.

The upshot of the incident is that Ban Johnson, president of the American League, suspended Ty.

The Tigers were quick to go to Ty's defense and they raised cane. They argued that he had received a raw deal.

"No ballplayer," they cried, "should be made to take the abuse Cobb took."

But the edict stuck. Apparently President Johnson felt that the Yankees of 1912 had so few customers that they couldn't spare any for the purpose of assault. The Tigers fumed. They went on strike when they were told they would have to play the Athletics at Shibe Park without their great outfielder. Manager Jennings frantically rallied what players he could gather and put a team on the field. The A's laid it on thick, plastering the Tigers, 24 to 2.

Cobb now showed where he stood with the players. Ty urged them to return to the lineup and they consented. The upshot of it was that his suspension was lifted and he was fined fifty dollars. Ironically, his teammates who went to bat for him were each fined $100 apiece.

Following the Shibe Park incident, however, there were threats around the league to give Ty the works—physically and verbally—on Detroit's next trip through the east. In

Philadelphia, as a matter of fact, the mayor and public safety commissioner rushed practically a whole regiment of police to Shibe Park to prevent an attack on Ty, and a possible riot. But none of these precautions cooled him off. He was determined to give the east, especially Philadelphia, a batting show they'd never forget.

Through the first seven games of that eastern swing—in Boston and New York—Ty put together fourteen hits in twenty-eight times at bat. But he was saving the big show for Philadelphia, where Detroit had three straight double-headers on the program.

Boston and Philadelphia were battling for the pennant, and Ty told the Red Sox just before he left: "Don't worry, I'm going down there and polish off the A's for you."

That was pretty tall talk, even for Ty Cobb, but he was mad and had special reason to carry out the threat. He knew also that he was going to need some luck.

Arriving in Philly, Ty phoned his old friend, Stoney McLinn, who, incidentally, doubled as Ty's ghost writer in those days. Stoney was then sports editor of the old *Philadelphia Press*.

"Hello, Stoneyard," Ty said. "Stoney, I'm going to do a job of hitting against your A's these next three days, the likes of which has never been seen." He rapped on wood as he spoke. "I'm going to get more hits than anybody has before in a six-game series. Better be out there. You people really have me boiling."

Stoney wished him luck.

Well, there it was. Ty's head certainly was on the chopping block. But he still was burning from what had happened at Shibe Park following his suspension. He knew the only way to even the score was by a batting spree—and against the pitchers on what Connie Mack had many times said was his greatest team, including Eddie Plank, Chief Bender and Herb Pennock. And Mr. Cobb was calling his shots on them!

"Don't you think you're biting off more than you can chew?" Stoney asked Ty. "You're saying you are going to clobber the greatest pitchers in baseball as if you own them —not for one game, but for six in a row!"

On July 17, 1912, Mr. Mack assigned the great Plank and a rookie named Hardin Barry as the A's pitchers in the first game. Ty promptly got four hits in six times up. Chief Bender worked the second game. Ty got three more hits in five times at bat, a total of seven hits for the afternoon.

The following afternoon Carroll Brown, a high right-hander, and Herb Pennock, the great southpaw, divided the pitching chores for the Athletics—and Ty went five for five. He got two for three in the nightcap—seven for eight that day! That brought him up to the final doubleheader. Plank and Pennock were on the mound again. Ty got four more hits in the two games, bringing his total to 18 hits in 28 times at bat, a .643 average! Included were four doubles, a triple and a pair of home runs.

Ty told the author he considers that the greatest series he ever played.

It gave him plenty of personal satisfaction to know that he had knocked Philadelphia out of the pennant—the Red Sox went on to win it—after he had advertised his intentions so boldly.

He admits that it was mostly luck, sure, the way all his shots dropped in safely for base hits, but it was an experience he will never forget.

Cobb played some of his best baseball against the Athletics. He liked opposition from the crowd—it made him work harder—and the Philadelphians always rode him hard, probably because of the trouble he had there from time to time.

Probably no ballplayer of Ty's era had more experience with crowds than he did. He discovered that the most abusive and vociferous addicts were the mildest and most tranquil off the field. Cobb made it a habit to study crowds and their habits. He generally found, for example, that the fan who invariably screeched at him was a waiter or a bell hop or an elevator boy or some sort of servant who had no chance to assert himself except when he went to a ball game. Ty made allowances for these fans. He says he didn't mind having them yell at him. He played his best ball surrounded by a bunch of wild, excitable spectators.

Ty has always felt, and rightly so, that the crowd makes the ball game—today as well as in his day. How much pepper, how much spirit, and how much alert baseball do you suppose a player would show if no one came out to the games? Fans see the best baseball when the stands are bulging. A crowd and its rooting has a terrific effect on the players.

The crowd definitely helps to make the game. Although the yammering seldom bothered Ty, there was occasionally a guy in the bleachers with the lungs of a bull moose whose heckling got his goat—like that joker in New York. He remembers an incident when Detroit was playing in Cleveland. Ivy Olson, the Cleveland third baseman, pushed Ty off the bag after Ty had slid safely in on a steal. The umpire called Ty out. Being extra careful not to spike Olson, Ty had avoided the baseman, sliding around him with a hook slide. Ty had had his toe on the bag, but Olson shoved it off.

"Well," Ty said, "if that's the way you want to play, I guess I'll have to bang in a little differently the next time I get down this way."

Ty doubled his next time up and although the Tigers had a comfortable lead and it was no stage to steal, he made up his mind to break for third on the first ball. He'd show Olson he wasn't bluffing. Ty got a good jump on the ball and slid into third with his spikes aglimmer. He arrived just as Olson caught the ball and he kicked the ball out of his mitt and toward the left field bleachers. Then he bounced up and scored easily. The crowd yelled bloody murder for Cobb's scalp, figuring he tried to cut Olson down. Ivy, however, took the treatment in stride.

"Ty," he said, "I guess we'll call the bet off."

"Sure," Ty said.

One deep-voiced gink in the crowd wouldn't let up on Ty, however. His voice reminded Ty of a granddaddy bullfrog. He'd croak at Ty every time there was a lull.

"Dirty work! Dirty work, Cobb!" he'd yell. "I'll get you after the game! Look out for me at the players' gate!"

His constant hammering made Ty's temperature boil. Finally Ty turned and shouted something back at him, and he bawled at Ty again. Ty couldn't make him out in the sea of faces, but he was positive the guy must have been as big as a mountain, and hard as nails. As Ty passed through the players' gate with a couple of teammates after the game, a familiar fog-horn voice caught and held him.

"Hello, Ty, how are you?" The deep, rumbling voice was gentle and friendly now, and Ty searched for its owner. You could have whomped him over with a feather when his eyes finally rested on the man. He reminded Ty of a tugboat with an ocean liner's whistle. The "big guy" wasn't five feet tall!

Turning to a teammate, Ty said, "And he was the guy who was going to eat me up after the game."

It is strange that few fans will ever attack a ballplayer when he is in street clothes, whereas they often go after him when he is in his war togs. Frequently Ty had wild bleacherites threaten him with bodily harm after the game because of some play or kick, or perhaps they figured he had roughed up one of their pin-ups, only to find them waiting meek as lambs at the players' gate when he walked out in his street clothes after the game. Instead of attacking him, they'd holler cordially, "Hi, Ty! Nice game."

Many a time, however, when he first broke into the American League, he had to leave the field under police protection.

Few fans ever heard about it but Ty remembers the time the Athletics were mobbed in New York after the first game of the 1913 World Series. The ruckus started not at the ball park but over on Seventh Avenue as the string of taxicabs carrying the Philadelphia players was weaving its way down the line from the Polo Grounds to the hotel. Visiting teams in those days dressed at their hotels and had to travel to and from the ball park in cabs. The home club changed clothes at the field, the same as they do nowadays.

Eddie Collins and Eddie Murphy were riding down Seventh Avenue minding their own business when a bottle crashed through their cab window, showering glass all over them. The Athletics had just won the game and the Giant fans were sore about it. Murphy was cut behind the ear, and Collins flopped down on the floor of the cab while tomatoes, stones, bottles and other missiles whistled over his head. There were cops on the street corners, but they only stood back and laughed. They were Giant fans, too!

Murphy and Collins never took the Seventh Avenue route again. After that, they ordered the cab driver to go up Riverside Drive to 155th Street. The looks of the residents along that route were not so sinister.

Those were the days.

Part IV

The Golden Era

1918-1929

Preface

The post World War I years were to become a spiralling, dizzy, mad, whirling planet of play—a wonderful, chaotic universe of clashing temperaments and human emotions the likes of which mankind had never before known. Dynasties were to fall, nations collapse, politics change, dictators begin to rumble, countries torn apart by revolution. There were to come distant wars, but here in America the trend was toward fun, fanfare and frolic.

What a world! What a country! What a people!

Show biz boomed. Charlie Chaplin starred in "The Kid," one of his most memorable performances. Al Jolson starred in "The Jazz Singer," moviedom's first talkie, starting the fantastic Hollywood revolution. Women swooned at the sight of Rudolph Valentino, the screen's first Latin lover. The dance marathon dazzled the nation, and radio became a fact. Charleston dance contests packed 'em in.

The auto came of age when painted traffic lanes began to appear on streets and highways, and it was every pedestrian for himself—as growing auto accidents inspired the invention of safety bumpers.

General Billy Mitchell, first to destroy a ship from a plane, was court-martialed for insubordination. Air mail flights began from New York to San Francisco. Admiral Richard E. Byrd navigated the first flight over the North Pole. A lanky, thin-faced young man named Lindbergh thrilled the world as he flew his monoplane, "Spirit of St. Louis," from New York to Paris, nonstop, a monumental achievement in aviation annals.

In keeping with the crazy, turbulent Twenties, sports were to enjoy an abrupt and radical change. President Warren G. Harding played golf on the White House lawn, and Calvin Coolidge brought his fishing pole along when he started his two-term stretch in Washington. The Union was suddenly becoming sports-mad. Professional athletes no longer were regarded merely as crude, muscular muggs flushed up from the tall and uncut. Now they were being canonized one cut below sainthood.

Photographers were to have a field day: Cobb slashing into third, his spikes aglimmer; The Babe standing at the plate on his thin, matchstick ankles, slowly waving his bludgeon like a cobra poised to strike; Big Bill Tilden banging his unreturnable cannon-ball service across the net; Bobby Jones, waving to cheering thousands—after winning the golf titles of Britain—as he received a ticker-tape reception down Broadway, an event previously reserved solely for visiting royalty and transatlantic aviators; the death wagons roaring around the Indianapolis speedway track at 125 miles per; Paavo Nurmi dog-trotting around and around a track in a steady, devastating assault upon Time.

Tex Rickard, the fabulous former faro dealer from Texas, via Nome, was to promote the first million-dollar fist-fight on record, a strange brawl between Jack Dempsey and Georges Carpentier, of France, in Jersey City. And high water mark for this manner of squandering money was to be reached later when Dempsey fought Tunney for the second time in Chicago.

Tennis, heretofore gone relatively unnoticed, would ride the wave, too, suddenly finding itself catapulted into a position of some prominence and power as magic names like Big Bill Tilden, Little Bill Johnston, Helen Wills, Vinnie Richards and Suzanna Lenglen streaked across the turf and clay courts. The public was becoming aware that a good show was going on inside, and they "laid" it on the line.

Red Grange and Knute Rockne were to become the best-remembered football names of the Golden Age, closely followed by such prodigious coaches as Pop Warner, Gil Dobie, Alonzo Stagg, Fielding Yost, and gleaming players like the famous Four Horsemen of Notre Dame, Bronko Nagurski, Chris Cagle, Benny Friedman and Ernie Nevers.

Jack Kelly of Philadelphia was to bring back to U.S. shores its first Olympic Games sculling championship and entrench himself as the greatest oarsman in the nation's history.

There was to come during this incredible era the superb Earl Sande, matchless money-making jockey, Man o' War, thoroughbred of the first half-century, Tommy Hitchcock, incomparable polo-player, Glenna Collette, best of the women's golf field, and Walter Hagen and Gene Sarazen and Tommy Armour, hotshot golfers, and Gertrude Ederle, who swam the English Channel in the face of the most awesome handicaps an athlete has endured.

It was truly the Golden Era of Sport.

Baseball, too, was on the crest of uncorking its greatest binge. It all started when the genial brewmaster of New York, Jake Ruppert, opened his checkbook and bought out the stars of Boston from a theatrical entrepreneur—and along came a round, carefree southpaw pitcher out of the deck named George Herman Ruth. He had been working as a pitcher—and what a pitcher!—and as a substitute outfielder up through 1918. His batting average was barely .300 and his home-run output was scant. But he had been studying Joe Jackson's method of hitting a ball and he copied this, with a few changes and interpolations of his own.

The Babe began to get control of the home run swing by 1919, although his strikeout record at bat was still above normal. He batted .300 in 1918, .322 in 1919 and .376 in 1920. Now he was no longer merely a fine left-handed pitcher —he was the greatest slugger baseball ever was to know.

The Cobbian Era was fading like spent fog.

The Ruthian Attack was the thing.

They built the Yankee Stadium for the Babe to hit home runs in. On the road he was becoming an even greater drawing attraction than P. T. Barnum's blood-sweating elephants. His picture was beginning to appear in more places than Edward, Prince of Wales, and he was well on his way to receiving a salary larger than the President's.

Had Abner Doubleday suddenly popped up on the scene, he wouldn't have recognized his century-old recipe. Now it was becoming the broadax instead of the rapier, heavy artillery instead of a fencing match, power instead of skill, flash instead of finesse.

The moguls had to have something to take the place of Cobbian baseball to keep those turnstiles clicking. A new act! The game was moving into the circle of Business—Big Business. So they invented the livelier ball to make the hits, the Great Bambino's socks, more atavistic to the gawkers. Now, instead of Larry Lajoie being a sensation because he hit thirteen homers in one season, or Sam Crawford being a national idol because he whanged seven apples out of the orchard in 1908 against Cobb's nine in 1909—the boys were beginning to kiss the pill over the fence 20, 30, 40, 50, 60 times a season.

Come 1927 and the Babe would establish the all-time record of sixty.

The fans loved him.

Gunpowder was destroying the feudal system, and power batting was destroying the science of baseball. Where was the hit-and-run, the dragged bunt, and delayed steal, the squeeze? Where was the fielding pitcher, like Nick Altrock, who got three putouts and eight assists in that first World Series game against the Cubs, in 1906? Where was the battle of wits, the breath-taking, heart-stopping duels between the masters as Willie Keeler at bat and a Jimmy Collins playing third?

Except for Cobb and a handful of other antiques who had been weaned on the grand old science, they were gone. All gone.

June 1, 1925, was destined to become a memorable date in baseball annals. Lou Gehrig replaced Wallie Pipp in the New York lineup. Thereafter for fourteen consecutive years and 2130 consecutive games, Columbia Lou was to be heralded as Mr. First Base.

The upcoming glamor years of 1926–7–8, shortly before the roof was to cave in upon the American financial structure, brought to baseball the Yankees' fabulous Murderer's Row, headed by a sharp, dried-up, mite of a man named Miller Huggins. Hug was all wisdom and common sense and baseball brains. He had dream pitchers, Pennock, Hoyt, Moore and Pipgras. There were Earl Combs, Mark Koenig, Jumpin' Joe Dugan and Poosh-'em-up Tony Lazzeri. All this plus that heart-breaking, ball-bustin' one-two punch—George Herman Ruth and Henry Louis Gehrig. A mad, wild, goofy collection of baseball ivory, but how they could play ball.

Starting in 1921, the Giants were to win four straight pennants bringing John McGraw's grand total to ten National League pennants and three World Championships. The Giants and Yankees squared off in the '21 World Series, prompting a reporter to ask John J. if the Babe had him worried. "Why should I worry about Ruth?" McGraw grunted. "My pitchers have been throwing to a better hitter all summer." He meant Rogers Hornsby. The Rajah led the N.L. in batting seven years, six of those in succession. Twice, in 1922 and 1925, he was to top the National and American Leagues in homers, hitting forty-two and thirty-nine. And he had the Babe to beat out! He was to lead the Cardinals to a smashing four-game-to-three victory over the Yankees in the '26 World Series. Between 1919 and 1931, the unstoppable slugger hit over .300 every season, nine times .360 or better!

November of 1926 was to find Cobb leaving the Tigers just as he had found them his first full session in the American League—in sixth place. He was then almost forty years old, a tired, battle-scarred middle-aged man who, during twenty-two turbulent years, had proven beyond a shadow of a doubt that he was the greatest ballplayer the game of baseball has ever known.

Durability? Listen. In 1922, eighteen years after he broke into the majors, Cobb batted .401.

The Georgia Peach was to prove in the final years of his career that he was good to the last step.

The Generalissimo

In 1921, Frank Navin, owner of the Tigers, gave Cobb what many consider the meanest break of his baseball career. Navin made him a manager. Navin almost forced him to become the Detroit generalissimo. As brilliant a teacher as he was, it was as a manager that misfortune and trouble, in large red letters, moved in on Ty so often.

While he was player-manager of the Tigers, Cobb never had trouble in the open. Of course, there was an undercurrent of unrest, much as with any other team, but for the most part matters were always ironed out after a certain amount of grumbling. Hugh Jennings, after fourteen years at the helm, had dropped the first thirteen games in 1920, and, faced with open bolshevism, he got so far in the cellar that he pulled into seventh place only two weeks before the curtain dropped. Consequently Cobb inherited a badly demoralized club.

The fact that he was a player-manager made the row all the harder to hoe. Ty could not be on the field and the bench at the same moment. He knew that the ruler who sat on the bench, hotbed of team bolshevism, had an advantage. One or two misfortunes started the warmers to second-guessing, and with Ty on the field he had no way to control the sessions of bellyaching in the dugout. They grew disgruntled, rebellious, hard to handle. Ty knew if he hadn't had to get out in the field and at bat he could have curbed the second-guessing of the soreheads before it got serious enough to hurt the team.

Even so Ty continued to terrorize enemy pitchers with his broiling bat. No outside trouble ever affected his amazing concentration in a ball game. He might have been in physical agony and in deep mental trouble. Hostile crowds might have opened the Anvil Chorus on top of his head when he came onto the diamond, demonstrations that always cut him deeply. But when the starting gate opened this was all forgotten. He was out for the win.

Ty was asked one time by a reporter what he considered was the worst psychological factor that affects a ball club.

"Second-guessing," he said. "In almost every play in baseball an act of deliberate judgment occurs. I am a manager. I have a one-run lead. I want to increase it. I have two men on the bases. My pitcher, a weak hitter, is coming to bat. I want to get the two runners in. The pitcher has been going good, but I take him out and put in a pinch hitter. The pinch hitter comes through, say, but the second pitcher I put in isn't going good that day and they knock him all over the park. Then I sit down and mourn that I didn't keep my first pitcher going. That self-recrimination hurts my spirit. It is second-guessing.

"Or the pitcher's judgment goes wrong, and he asks himself the rest of the game: 'Why didn't I do the other thing?' Or the third baseman second-guesses his play on a bunt. But it is when they begin to second-guess each other that trouble begins. The right fielder explains to the pitcher where he made the mistake. The catcher second-guesses the manager. The second-guess in baseball is the greatest enemy of mankind."

Despite the lack of rapport between the Tigers, Cobb developed the greatest hitting team in American League history. That first season under his leadership Detroit compiled a .316 team batting average. Only shortstop Emory Rigney fell below the coveted .300 circle! That's a lot of stick work.

Perhaps Cobb's best achievement as a tutor was the job he did on Harry Heilmann. Heilmann hit .309 in 1920. Cobb knew he could do better.

"Harry," Ty said, studying Heilmann one morning during batting practice, "I think you'll get a freer swing if you move your hands away from your body."

Heilmann shifted his hands, obeying orders. The manager was right. He did get more zip.

"Another thing," Ty added, after a while, "let's try changing your stance slightly."

Heilmann stood farther back in the box. Pitchers couldn't hold the slugging outfielder after that. Cobb had found the answer. Heilmann went on to win four American League batting championships, wound up with a .342 lifetime average. He bloodied everything during Cobb's reign as manager; in successive years, from 1921 to 1926, when Ty resigned, Heilmann hit .394, .356, .403, .346, and .393. Harry, said Ty, was one of the two best right-handed hitters he saw during his twenty-four years in the major leagues.

Charlie Gehringer was another of Cobb's Tiger favorites. The Silent Knight reported to Detroit in 1924.

"I soon knew that here was a kid with plenty of natural ability," Cobb recalled, "but he was minus polish. I tried him out in a couple of games and his fielding was fine. When he trapped those grounders it sounded like a catcher's mitt, smack in the pocket every time. I was apprehensive, however,

147

about making a regular out of him right away. The wolves in the bleachers would have scalded me. Charlie wasn't ready for big league pitching yet. He needed seasoning. One of the things I did before farming him out for a while was to adjust his batting stance by moving his feet closer together and bringing his elbows slightly higher.

"Gehringer was a truly great competitor. I'd rank him right up there next to Eddie Collins as the greatest second baseman of all time, then Rogers Hornsby and Larry Lajoie. Among the current second basemen I like Red Schoendienst. Red reminds me a lot of Gehringer—quiet, methodical, a real battler.

"Gehringer was truly a man of few words. He'd say 'hello' at the start of spring training and 'goodby' at the end of the season. That was about all."

Charlie Gehringer let his bat do all of the noise-making for him.

Hub Leonard, who joined the Tigers in 1919, was one of the Cobb aginners. They never got along. Hub was a type that could not stand "riding" from a manager, and Ty, when fighting to win, rode with whip and spur. The fellows who understood him paid little attention to him, but a sensitive soul had no business around any team when Cobb was managing it.

Once an easy-going Detroit player was asked how he was getting along with Ty.

"Well," he replied, "half the time I'm trying to keep from busting him on the nose, and the other half I'm taking off my cap to him as the greatest of them all."

In Fred Haney's mind there was never any doubt as to who was baseball's most brilliant teacher. Cobb was a man apart. Haney, who played under Cobb for five seasons, vividly recalls one particular game in Cleveland. He remembers it because he was out of the lineup that afternoon and

148

Jim Bagby pitched for the Indians against Detroit. Cleveland had a rookie catcher working, giving the Tribe's regular receiver, Steve O'Neill, a day off. Haney figured that a star like Bagby wasn't going to let a greenpea tell him how to pitch. He figured the veteran hurler wouldn't take signs *from* the catcher. He'd be giving signs *to* the catcher. Haney watched closely for three innings. Then he walked over to Manager Cobb.

"Ty," Haney said, "I've stolen the Cleveland signs. I can call every pitch."

"Swell," Cobb said, "go out on the coaching line and tip off our batters."

Detroit won the game and Haney was happy because he helped the Tigers win and he wasn't even in the game. A few days later Detroit traveled to Chicago. Haney doesn't remember who the pitcher was, but he does recollect that the catcher was Ray Schalk, a trigger-quick operative. Cobb turned to Haney at the end of the third inning and said, "Steal any signs yet?"

"No," Haney said. "I can't get one. They're hiding them too cleverly."

"Son," Ty said, "I guess you're just not alert enough. The next pitch will be a fast ball. Now a curve. Now a . . ."

Cobb went on to call seventeen straight pitches correctly. Haney just sat there in hypnotized amazement.

"No wonder you're a .400 hitter," Haney said. "You know every pitch that's coming."

"It's not as simple as all that," Ty said. "The tip-off came to me not from intercepting any signals but from something I've learned about human nature. There's always a tendency in this business for a man to get too mechanical. Ray Schalk was a great catcher, but he's gettin' old now and he has let himself fall into a set pattern. I have studied him for so long that I even know how he thinks. I merely kept pace with his mental processes and that's why I was able to call those pitches correctly. I was thinking along the same lines as Schalk was."

Alarmists predicted that Cobb's skill as a ballplayer would fade rapidly once he was handed the burden of club management. The critics began to look like genuine prophets when the Tigers dropped into a horrible slump. Illness and injury robbed Ty of his best players. But in the midst of all this, Cobb fought back like an enraged bulldog. He personally took charge, clawing, battling, hustling, taking Detroit from sixth place in '21 to second in '23. In one spree he put together five homers in two games to halt a Detroit losing streak.

Cobb was again pacing the American League in almost every department of attack in '25, until another leg injury and siege of flu slowed him down. He nevertheless finished the season batting .378.

Even as a manager, Cobb never took it for granted that he was beyond mistakes. When his batting started to slip somewhat in 1924, he got one of his men to sit on the bench during batting practice and point out any faults.

"It is very easy to get into certain faults unconsciously," Ty said. "You may be hitting up or down. You may be getting your body in too soon. The main point is to check these faults before they develop into habits. A fault isn't hard to cure. A habit is another problem. Correct your mistakes before they turn into habits that will be much harder to correct."

Good managers always have been scarce. It is not an easy job. The man bossing a big league team is generally busier than a one-armed paperhanger with the flying hives.

Cobb learned that the secret of managing was all in sizing up the hired hands and properly coaching them. He also learned that all great leaders have one quality in common: They stick to their men through adversity and are prepared to take the blame if a man tries to obey instructions and slips up. Real managers don't alibi.

"Most fans who have followed the game still think of me as an umpire baiter," Ty said one night. "It may be true that I was a little rough on the boys when I first came up, but I soon stopped the nonsense. If I occasionally rode an umpire, it was because I wanted my men to see I was out there fighting to win. If one of my players got in a row with the ump, I had to back him up. If I didn't, the boy would lose spirit. He'd feel I wasn't supporting him. I couldn't have him thinking that. I'd tear after the umpire and go through the motions of arguing, battling for my man. I'd push the player away, then turn to the ump and say, 'I know you were right, Bill, but let's make this look good anyhow.' The wolves thought I was giving the ump hell and cheered me.

"Most umpires are fine fellows and I got along with them swell. Billy Evans was one of my favorites. He used to tell the story of how I put one over on him during a game in Detroit. This was in 1909 and Detroit had cinched the pennant. The game had no bearing on league standings. The game dragged along for an hour and a half. Only six innings had been played. Standing in the outfield I got to thinking about the terrific fishing in Michigan. We had no game scheduled for the next afternoon and I was anxious to break away from the ball park early and go up to Oxford and see how the fish were biting. The way the game was moving I'd never make it. I knew the only solution was to get thrown out of the game. I began to gripe and beef about every decision and create a scene. Evans would have normally sent me to the showers, but he was in a particularly gay mood and refused to get sore.

"In the seventh inning I barked at him over a called strike. I tossed my cap on the ground, threw my bat into the air and in general blew my stack—an unpardonable sin. No umpire likes to be embarrassed in front of a crowd.

"Evans just stared at me calmly.

"'What's wrong, Ty, that last one split the heart of the

151

plate,' he said evenly. 'What are you trying to show me up for?'

"I spread my hands apart and growled, 'That one was at least a foot off the plate!'

"That did it.

" 'Beat it!' blurted Billy. 'You're through for the day!'

"Without saying another word I scooted off to the clubhouse. Schaefer, our first base coach, who was evesdropping, walked over to Evans and said, 'That Cobb's a hot one. He wanted out of the game. He'd made plans to go fishing and wanted to leave early.'

"Billy fumed.

" 'Come back here,' he shouted after me. 'You're back in the game!'

"By then I was zooming across second base and gave a good demonstration of a deaf man. I didn't want to hear him. I kept right on going.

"P. S. The fishing was great."

The next time Evans umpired a Detroit game he wasted no time collaring young Cobb.

"Ty," he asked, "got any early dates today? Cancel them if you have. You couldn't blow yourself out of today's game with a truck load of nitroglycerine."

Ty grinned sheepishly.

"No appointments today," he said. "I'll play till midnight if you want, but much obliged for letting me off early the last time."

Cobb says there is one rule he would insist upon if he were still engaged in managing. That's a good fielding team.

"Fielding is mostly a matter of practice and almost any player can learn to do it," Ty said. "Any time you see a poor fielder you are looking at a man who just hasn't bothered to learn. In the olden days Rogers Hornsby was an example. He was the greatest right-hand hitter of all time, but you can't put him on the all-star team because his shortstop and first baseman used to have to go over to catch pop flies for him. Hornsby could not go back on fly balls."

Opposite cases were Hank Greenberg and Lou Gehrig. Greenberg was moved from his normal first base position to the outfield late in his career so the Tigers could put Rudy York's power in the lineup. Hank trotted out to the field mornings and on days off to shag fly balls and play them off the fences. He became a first-rater even though he started late.

Gehrig was as green as the hills of Scotland when he reported to the Yankees off the Columbia campus. George Sisler, a Hall of Fame first baseman himself, was coaching the Yankees and he liked the way Lou pelted the ball. But around first base! Columbia Lou couldn't have caught a bear in a phone booth. He was that awkward.

"I heard that Lou considered me his idol and I went to work on him," Sisler said. "So did Manager Miller Huggins. In the beginning, Lou would make one horrible play a game. Then he got so he'd make one a week, and then maybe one a month. In the end he was trying to keep it down to one a season."

There are almost as many managerial styles as there are candidates for the jobs. Some pilots are very liberal. Cobb made a gallant attempt to give his players plenty of freedom. One of the first things he did after Navin handed him the job was to call his men together in the locker room.

"There'll be few rules on this team," he announced. "You will be on the honor system. I'm not going to police you. If you get out of line I will soon know it. I will know it by the way you play the next day."

One evening following a game in New York the Tigers had to catch a sleeper for Boston. Cobb stood on the platform at Grand Central, leisurely taking his own sweet time about stepping aboard. Suddenly here came two of his men straggling down the ramp. Ty could tell they had been drinking, in this particular case only beer, as he found out later.

But they'd had even too much of that. Cobb didn't want them to see him. He ducked behind a pillar, waiting until they got on the train. He gave them plenty of time to get into bed before getting aboard himself. Why the cat and mouse game? Why didn't he come right out in the open and say here I am and I've caught you red-handed?

"Because," he explained, telling me the story, "I didn't want any of the team to get the idea I was *policing* them. Both of the boys who'd been drinking, incidentally, had miserable days at the plate the next day."

John J. McGraw used to assign detectives to keep check on Casey Stengel and some of the other Giant unreliables. One sleuth would tail Stengel and Irish Meusel, who were constant companions and madcaps. One night they spotted the detective. The following evening Stengel went one way and Meusel another. McGraw received a prompt report. He grabbed Casey the next morning.

"Why didn't you go out with Meusel last night, like you usually do?" demanded McGraw.

"Listen," Casey said, indignantly, "if you want me followed you will have to give me a detective of my own. I ain't gonna save this club no more dough doubling up!"

Casey went to the barber shop before reporting to the Polo Grounds one morning. That afternoon, during the game, he got in a fist-fight and was thrown out of the game.

"You've been drinking!" roared McGraw. "You're suspended for ten days."

Stengel protested. He had not been drinking. What John J. smelled was not on Casey's breath but was on his hair. Furthermore, it was not whiskey. It was perfumed hair oil.

"Get out of my sight!" thundered McGraw. "If there's one thing I can't stand it's a liar."

Those who played for John McGraw agree that he was an absolute czar, a stickler for obedience, but he never roasted a man over the coals if the player tried to obey instructions.

154

"Do what I tell you to and if things go wrong I'll take the blame," he said.

He did, too.

Another of those who played for Cobb was Rip Collins. Talking off the cuff one time, he said, "There's an impression that Cobb was not a good manager. It is true he never won a pennant. But now that I'm no longer with the club, I want to say that if Connie Mack had managed the Tigers, with John McGraw for his coach and Joe McCarthy for his bat boy, he wouldn't have done any better than Ty.

"I was one of the anti-Cobb men when he was manager. I will admit it. No one on the team was more critical of him, or as outspoken. I gave him a bad time. But I've had plenty of time to cool off. Now that I think of it, Cobb was a brilliant manager in many ways. He knew more baseball than anybody I ever saw. Chain lightning was no faster than his mind. He was always a fighter and he made us into a fightin' ball club. That's what the public wanted. He was as full of tricks as a coyote is full of fleas. They weren't parlor tricks, either. Ty was out to win ball games. He'd take all the law allowed and as much more as he could get away with. He never gave any favors, and he never asked for any. Surely those are strong points in his favor.

"Ty was a great coach. I doubt if his equal ever lived. He simply didn't have the horses. His pitching staff was bad, and his infield poor. Defensively, the Tigers were like a worn-out sieve. But how they could hit and score runs! Cobb coached them and made 'em hustle. Not even the Yankees had a more dangerous attack."

One of Cobb's most unusual managerial adventures occurred in 1928. He got $15,000 and all expenses to take a group of All-Stars to Japan for a series of exhibitions and clinical work.

"Talk about enthusiasm," Ty said. "I was whisked out to a huge stadium, shaped like our football arenas, where perhaps 50,000 or 60,000 fans were waiting. And I mean fans.

They had an interpreter for me, and school was in session. I lectured on baseball fundamentals, how to bat, throw, field, slide, etcetera, and the interpreter would interpret it for them. The fans and players alike had cameras and notebooks and they recorded everything I said and demonstrated.

"I picked out one of their players, a slim little sliver of a guy weighing, I'd guess, about 140 pounds. He belonged to one of their professional teams, and I went to work showing him how to bat for the benefit of the audience. I told him—via the interpreter—to shorten up his stance, among other things.

"That first clinical session lasted for an hour and a half and then I went back to my hotel. I lounged around until early afternoon, then returned to the stadium to play a game against the Japanese All-Stars. The fans were still there, where I'd left them. They hadn't budged an inch. Out on the field the Japanese ballplayers continued to work at the things I told them earlier in the day—this despite the fact they had to go nine innings against us that afternoon.

"That was a game to talk about. The Japs played only according to a set pattern. You could call the shots. That is, we were able to anticipate every move they made. We beat them by doing the unexpected, tricks like the drag bunt, hit-and-run, and swinging at the 3-and-0 pitch. This was not the way they played baseball; it confused and frustrated them to death. I was happy to see the slim little fellow, the one whose stance I altered, connect for a pair of hits, however. They're good students, learn fast.

"I hit about .600 on the tour, and even pitched a couple of times. I went one full game on the mound, relieved in two others, four and five innings apiece, a total of eighteen frames. I gave up one run. I wasn't much of a pitcher, but had a pretty fair knuckle ball, a curve, change-up, and a fast ball."

Monkeying around the mound was one of the reasons Cobb

hurt his arm. He had a powerful whip, and evidently thought it couldn't be damaged. He loved to pitch, and kept fooling around pitching in practice. Then one day something snapped in his arm, and it was never the same after that. He could still throw, but his ground covering was handicapped, forcing him to shift closer to the infield.

But here he was now talking about a game on an afternoon in Japan. Cobb on the mound. U. S. All-Stars versus the Japanese All-Stars.

"It was like teasing children with a piece of candy," he chuckled. "The second I did anything unorthodox the batter went blank. I tried a quick pitch on one of 'em and you should have heard the cackling on their bench and up in the stands. He went limp as rags, resembling a bloke who'd seen a ghost. They were dead ducks after that. If I threw a fast ball when they figured a curve, they were lost. No sense of strategy or psychology. It was all a blank wall. I beat 'em by pitching backwards. They had only one system. Mess it up and they were gone.

"Same situation on defense. Their pitchers had only one style. When the count was 1-and-0, you could expect a curve; 2-and-0, a curve, and so forth. We were able to call every pitch in advance. We rolled up football scores on them."

Ty Cobb showed 'em why baseball is our national sport.

The Battle of Minds

Baseball, to Cobb, was like an insect impaled on a pin. He was the scientist, intensely studying the intricacies of the game through a magnifying glass, painstakingly dissecting the various parts and classifying them.

In the Roaring Twenties, after Ty became manager of the Tigers, a reporter asked him to enlarge upon the sort of ballplayer he preferred.

"H'm'm," Ty said, after long reflection, "the *thinking* athlete is the fellow I want on my side. His kind is scarce. He's got nerve and courage and can be expected to pull the unexpected. He crosses up the enemy. He wins games for you."

That description could very well have been used to define Cobb's baseball character, for no athlete had more nerve and courage than the Georgia Peach. Ty, as it developed, needed that nerve, and that courage. Rival pitchers saw that Cobb was inclined to hug the plate when he first came up, and they tried to drive him out of the league by aiming at his head. The catchers joined the plot.

Each time the pitcher's missile barely missed Cobb's head,

the catcher jostled, "Better be alive, kid, he beaned one poor slob last week, an' the poor bum's still in the hospital."

Ty, as young as he was, knew dynamite when he saw it. He knew that his future in the big leagues was at stake. If he stepped back, or showed any sign of weakness, he'd be marked yellow. His distress was very real, but the knowledge of what the opposition was attempting to do only triggered his determination. He refused to budge an inch.

"I don't want anybody callin' me yellow," he told himself. "Let 'em throw at me."

Thereafter when a pitcher aimed at Ty he crowded the plate even more than before. He also hurled a deadly verbal volley back to the mound.

"You so-and-so," he'd yammer. "You're wild enough to play in the bush leagues. Those bean balls don't scare me. Throw another. Com'on, I wanta base on balls."

This show of boldness by a rookie flabbergasted the pitcher. Cobb's approach was highly irregular. Other batters would have been frightened to death, but Cobb was maddeningly complacent and visibly unruffled. Rival pitchers felt they could have cheerfully throttled him. He was putting them on the defensive, instead of vice versa. He wouldn't be bullied.

Cobb had a two-front war on his hands. Pitchers were attacking him from the front, the catchers from the rear. Backstops like Nig Clarke made baseball an adventure into higher science for Cobb. Clarke admittedly bothered Cobb a lot.

Detroit was battling Cleveland one afternoon, Cobb at bat. Clarke, behind the plate, signaled his pitcher, then reached down and grabbed a handful of dirt as if rubbing the sweat off his hands. The pitcher wheeled into his motion, brought the ball around. As the ball whizzed toward the plate Clarke tossed the dirt on Ty's feet. Distracted, Cobb hesitated just long enough to ruin his swing.

159

Cobb has always been a keen student of advanced baseball science, was always trying to invent new ways to confuse the enemy and add a hit or two to his string. Some of his neatest stratagems came to him in his sleep and, rousing himself, he'd jump out of bed and write them down so he wouldn't forget them.

Detroit had trouble every time they invaded New York to play the Highlanders. The hosts were whomping the visitors' mound corps severely, particularly Wild Bill Donovan, the old reliable. Wild Bill swore the Highlanders were stealing Tiger signals. One day he tried an experiment. Wee Willie Keeler was at bat, and the Detroit catcher signaled for a fast ball. Donovan had other ideas. He threw a curve, crossing everybody up, including his catcher. Keeler leaned in for the fast ball and took the curve flat in the pit of the breadbasket. That proved Donovan's theory. The Tigers sent their trainer running to center field. There, in a cubby hole in the fence, he uncovered the spy, who was equipped with binoculars. Detroit chased him out of there fast.

Signal-swiping was old hat even by the time Cobb arrived on the major league scene. The Philadelphia Phillies were guilty of planting a buzzer in the coach's box at third base. The Philadelphia coach kept his toe on the apparatus and waited nonchalantly for one buzz to forecast a fast ball and two buzzes a curve. This ingenious spy system was quite accidently discovered one day when a visiting third baseman happened to catch the sound and promptly ripped the whole works right out of the ground, wires and all.

Cobb only smiles when he thinks about it.

"Not that I approve of this signal-stealing," he said. "In fact, I personally preferred not to know what the pitcher was planning, but it does show to what extent the oldtimers went to win games."

And just about anything went—if you could get away with it. When George Stallings managed Rochester, he put

160

a spy in an apartment house beyond the centerfield fence for all home games. The spotter signaled the batter with the window shade.

Pittsburgh used the third hand on the scoreboard clock to signal their hitters: a curve if the hand moved, a fast ball if it didn't.

Eddie Collins told of the movable eyes on an Indian head painted on Cleveland's outfield fence. When the eyes rolled left—a curve. When they rolled right—a fast ball.

Red Ruffing said he was bending over one afternoon to cup a little dirt in his hands while batting against Cleveland. The old Yankee pitcher glanced sideways at Frankie Pytlak, the Tribe catcher, and found himself happily looking at the sign Pytlak was sending out to the mound. Red told the other Yankees about it. You never saw so many players scooping up dirt in all your life.

Cobb testifies that the oldtimers never complained much about stealing signals. It was simply a matter of not going into court with clean hands. There was a fellow in Detroit who used to sit in center field with a pair of glasses strong enough to bring out the color of the batter's eyes. He conveniently sat near an advertisement on the fence: "The Detroit News, Best Newspaper In The West." If you watched the B in the ad closely, you could see tiny slots open and close. If the slot was open in the top half of the B, the Tiger spotter had picked off the fast ball signal. Detroit batters knew the curve was on its way if the slot in the bottom of the B opened. It was hard to say if the advertisement fattened circulation, but it did a whale of a job for Tiger batting averages.

Baseball, to be sure, was an endless battle of minds in the "good old days."

One evening at a restaurant in New York, Cobb learned from a friend that Babe Ruth and Herb Pennock had been in the place only a few hours earlier. They had hoisted quite

161

a few beers. This came as comforting news to Ty because Detroit was in second place and fighting New York for the pennant.

"You guys ought to have it easy tomorrow," the informer said. "Ruth and Pennock will be in no shape to play."

Ty walked out of the restaurant in a kind of utopian dream, thinking how the Tigers would maul the Yankees without Babe and Pennock at their best.

"So what happened?" grinned Ty, as he told the story. "Pennock shut us out with three hits and Babe muscled a couple out of the park. They murdered us. Babe and Herb were only playing possum the night before. I'll never forget that.

"Speaking of the Babe, we used to take great delight in ribbing him. He could take it as well as dish it out. On a close play at second base, one day in 1925, he was called safe. An argument followed. I ran in from the outfield. Babe just stood on the bag saying nothing, looking like a juvenile delinquent who'd just put one over on his baby sitter. I glared at our shortshop and snorted, 'Do you smell something sour around here?' Taking his cue, the shortstop said he sure did. Sniffing loudly, he said, 'There *is* a funny odor in the air all right.' While we bantered back and forth like this, the shortstop stood next to Babe, and held the ball. The idea, of course, was to make Babe blow his stack and maybe step off the bag and rush us. He jawed back at us a blue streak, but not once did he take his foot off the base. He didn't fall for it."

Infielders used all sorts of tricks to catch base runners napping. Cobb recollects how Bill Coughlin, an infielder with an incredible gift for gab, literally *talked* runners off the base as easy as he put on his pants. First he'd start up a friendly conversation with the runner.

"We had some poker game last night," he'd begin. "There

was one pot I won which looked like my salary check. A pair of aces, and a little nerve, did it . . ."

Before the runner realized it he was so interested in the details that he unconsciously slipped his foot off the bag. Coughlin pounced on him with the ball and the duped runner was out. Rubbing salt in the wound, Bill generally added, "Come around again and listen to more of my stories."

"One afternoon the Yankees thought they'd have some fun with Ruth," Ty said. "Earlier he had come in and jerked Lou Gehrig off one of our pitchers. A general argument followed. I rushed in from the outfield, grabbed the first man I could reach, and pulled him away from the milling. Seeing it was Ruth, I said, 'Oh, sorry, I thought you were our pitcher.' In the New York dressing room after the game the Yankees started baiting Babe. They told him I'd shoved him around and kicked him. There'd been so much milling around, so many punches thrown—so many faces—Babe still wasn't quite certain who'd done what to whom. Everything was a blur.

" 'You gonna take that from Cobb?' Babe's teammates shouted.

" 'No, by gum!' roared Babe, and he bolted out of the locker room. Shoving his way into the Detroit quarters, he walked right up to me. Before he could open his mouth I growled, 'What are you doing in here? Get out before I throw you out!' Startled, Babe turned around and marched right back out of there, just as nice as you please. He didn't want to fight anyhow.

"What a colorful guy, the Babe. What a ballplayer. He gave me more laughs—and thrills—than anyone else in the game.

"Dizzy Dean was another of baseball's master psychologists, though I don't know yet whether or not he was aware of it. The Tigers and the Cardinals were all square going into the seventh and deciding game of the 1934 World

163

Series. Diz walked into the Detroit dressing room and interrupted a pre-game strategy session.

" 'You guys must be tryin' to figure out how to beat us,' he drawled. 'Well, forget it. *I'm* pitchin'! I'm gonna win. An' maybe you'd like to know *how* I'm gonna pitch to you fellas. Listen.'

"Diz then ran down the Detroit batting lineup, promising each man he would throw the batter's juiciest pitch. The Tigers, of course, took this as just another Dean gag and paid no attention to him. They were so surprised when he lived up to his words that they froze at the plate like wooden Indians. Diz had 'em in his hip pocket. That was one of the slickest bits of baseball psychology I ever saw."

They broke the mold and threw away the pieces when Dizzy Dean was born. An individualist, he just had to be himself. He didn't know how to be any other way. What's more, he saw no reason to reform. Diz always said that a reformer was nothing but a guy who never had any fun himself and was sore about it.

Cobb began to sense a change in baseball in 1924. The old game was being replaced by a newer edition. Power was replacing speed and skill. Base running was all but dead. They had all but stopped stealing. Now they were waiting for the long ball to drive them across.

Watching Babe Ruth rocket batting-practice pitches into the Yankee Stadium bleachers before a game with Detroit one day, Cobb thought to himself, "I guess more folks would rather see Babe hit one over the fence than see me steal second." Cobb felt bad about it because it wasn't the game he liked to see or play. The old game was one of skill—skill and speed. And quick thinking. This game was all power.

"But there'll never be another power-man like Babe," Cobb thought, as Ruth sent another drive screaming into the bleachers. "Just watch the ball next year. They'll start juicing it up like a tennis ball because Ruth has made the home run popular. But they'll ruin more sluggers than they will make. A lot of these kids, in place of learning the true science of hitting or base running, are trying to knock every pitch over the fence. Some of 'em will make good with the big blast, but most of 'em won't."

Cobb's friends frequently tell him that he is hopelessly out of date. They argue that today's fan would be bored to death by one of those oldtime 1 to 0 pitchers' battles. Cobb doesn't think so.

"Sure," Cobb says, "the rabbit ball brought a new kind of excitement to the game—for a while. The home run, when it still had a scarcity value, was a tremendous thrill. I used to like to sock a few out of the park myself. After the lively ball was adopted I announced one day in St. Louis that I would be shooting for the fences in a series against the Browns. I hit three homers the first day, two the second."

Ty Cobb could hit 'em a mile, too.

Back for Mr. Mack

In 1926, the glittering names in sport were Tilden, Jones, Dempsey, Hagen, Grange and Ruth. And the big, shocking splash on the November sport pages was:

"Cobb, Greatest Of 'Em All, Quits!"

Editorials in newspapers and magazines filled whole pages across the country. It was pretty well established that the Georgia Peach would have to retire some day, but still it was hard to believe now that it had finally happened.

Some literary observers didn't believe it.

"Retirements of famous baseball players are like the farewell tours of opera singers in that there is rarely a guaranty that either will be permanent," the *New York Sun* remarked in an editorial. "Doddering and senile as this baseball Methuselah of 40 is, there is still a wallop or two in his bat. It may be that before Tyrus can settle down to enjoy the million or more of dollars he has accumulated by thrift and speed on the bases there will be demands for his baseball experience that he will not be able to resist."

The *New York Evening Post* refused to take Cobb's announced retirement seriously, too:

"Ty says he has definitely given up the game, altho there will be many who will find it hard to believe that anyone who has loved baseball so fiercely as Ty Cobb can divorce himself from it altogether."

The *New York World* believed Cobb meant what he said, and its editorial read more like an obituary than a news story:

"With Cobb in the game, there was never any telling what might happen: whether he was at bat, on base, or in the field, the fantastic, impossible twist was an easy possibility, and we sat there like children eagerly waiting for the wonder man to perform his miracle. Also, under the swift decisiveness that marked his coups there was infectious, diabolical humor. Cobb, charging home when he was expected to stop at third, seemed to derive such unholy joy at the havoc he caused; and when the catcher had muffed the ball and the trick had succeeded, we, too, crowed with glee to behold mind triumphant over matter. The charm of Ruth lies in his eye and arm. The charm of Cobb lay in his head. His eye and arm, heaven knows, were such as most; but when in addition to directing these against the ball, he directed them against men, then we saw more than a game—we saw drama. He was a Br'er Fox of the diamond, and Br'er Fox, wherever we see him, is a never-failing source of enchantment."

167

Well, there it was. The great Ty Cobb had come to the end of the line. Or so he said.

"I have swung my last bat in the big leagues," he repeated. "And, of course, I will never walk to the plate in the minors."

"But you've still got lots of baseball in you," insisted one reporter. "You finished the season batting .339, which isn't exactly bad."

Cobb sighed wistfully.

"I am tired," he said. "I can't take chances any more. That's it. I can't take chances. A ballplayer who can't take chances ought to quit."

Yes, that must have been it. But what chances he took, and how he filled the air with red, white and blue sparks of electricity when he took them.

"Another thing," Cobb told reporters on the morning of his retirement, "I haven't had much time with my family. The life of a ballplayer is hard, and you are away on the roads a lot. I want to settle down and live with my folks for a while. That's another good reason for my resignation as Detroit manager. I don't want to be one of those guys who fade, or have to be pushed out. I want to quit while I am still one of those up among the best. The game's gettin' harder for me every year, and I'm getting older. Ballplayers should get out before they break. I have known good players who were the idols of the fans who finished their careers playing out the string and died broke and broken-hearted. My legs are still good, boys, my eyes are as good as ever, but I am not feeling any too good. I love the game. I have lived the game, but I know when to stop."

Cobb packed his bags and prepared to return to Augusta and Home Sweet Home. Millionaire Cobb, the first man in the history of baseball who accumulated a million without being connected with the ownership of a ball club. Down in quiet, pretty Augusta he would live the life of a small banker, a Georgia squire. His home was on a fine street. It was one of the best in town. His family was respected. His son, Tyrus, Jr., was headed for college—for Ty always envied those with college educations.

Ty was in tears as he made his farewell. His decision wasn't an overnight impulse. He had thought a lot about it for almost a year. He had played on three Tiger pennant winners, but had not been able to mastermind a championship drive himself. And, by his own admission, he was slipping. He finished the 1926 campaign managing from a seat on the bench, confessing that for the first time in two decades another player had crowded him out of the starting lineup.

The flesh quails and the ardor dulls.

All middle-aged American gentlemen who read in their newspapers that Cobb had retired must have heaved more or less involuntary sighs of regret. It was not that Ty was so very middle-aged himself—to repeat, he was only a couple of weeks short of forty—but it was because this reminder of the passage of time was so blunt that the retirement of the famed Georgia Peach seemed especially lamentable.

Cobb's resignation marked the sixth managerial change to be made in the major leagues since the close of the 1926 playing season. Five other managers who resigned or were deposed were Bill McKechnie of the Pirates, Arthur Fletcher of the Phillies, Lee Fohl of the Red Sox, George Sisler of the Browns, and Rogers Hornsby of the Cardinals.

It was open season on big league managers.

Cobb's successor in the management of the Tigers was George Moriarty, former Yankee and Detroit infielder and American League umpire.

For the first time in twenty-two years Cobb was out of a baseball job. Returning south, he told his Augusta neighbors he had no plans for the present except some shooting and a little golf. He was going to be a man of leisure. Later, he confided, he might look around for a ball team to buy, if the price was right. But as an active player he was definitely through.

Well, he did shoot, and he did play golf. Folks were just beginning to take his retirement seriously when, one morning, Dave Driscoll of the Brooklyn Dodger front office showed up in Ty's living room. Seems the Tigers had played an exhibition game at Ebbets Field the previous summer and the Dodger management had been so impressed with the way Cobb hustled—and made his players hustle—would he be willing to talk business with them?

Driscoll got right to the point.

"Listen, Ty," he said, "Robbie's (Wilbert Robinson) contract is just about ready to expire and we want you for the job."

"But why me?" Ty said. "I've always been an American Leaguer. It would be committing treason if I jumped to the National League now."

Driscoll was adamant.

"You're the first manager who ever came to Brooklyn to play an exhibition game and really went all out to give our fans their money's worth. You hustled, you left your regular stars in there, and you had them hustling, too. We know you will make the Dodgers hustle also."

Hustle! Cobb was the original Mr. Hustle himself. He never let up for a minute, never gave his body a rest from trying. He was out there every second of the game playing as hard as he could, no matter how many runs he was ahead. He didn't know what it meant to take it easy and loaf along. He was always working.

Lou Gehrig was the hustlingest player Ty ever saw, and he admired him for it. When he first saw the lumbering first baseman break into the Yankee lineup, as a rookie, Cobb went and told him just that.

While Driscoll was waiting for Cobb's answer, one of the

170

strangest coincidences occurred. The Cobb phone rang. It was Connie Mack phoning from Fort Myers, Florida.

"Tyrus," Mr. Mack began, "I have been reading in the papers that you are retiring, that you won't be back to play next season. Right?"

There was a slight pause.

"Yes, that's true, Mr. Mack. I'm pretty tired."

"Well," Mr. Mack said, "I want you to reconsider. I know you are a free agent now and I need you in Philadelphia. I know you've got a couple of seasons of good ball left in you and with you in the lineup there's a very strong chance we can win another pennant. Well, how about it?"

Cobb rubbed his chin reflectively. He would like to help out Mr. Mack. But then there was the promise he had made to himself: a family needs a father around the house. He needed more time to think about it.

"I will let you know my decision in a few days, Mr. Mack," Ty concluded, but before hanging up the receiver he knew what his answer was going to be.

Returning to Driscoll, Ty announced, "I'm sorry but I can't accept your generous offer."

"Is that final?" Driscoll asked.

"Yes," nodded Ty. "Mr. Mack needs me. I have to be loyal to the American League."

On the morning of February 9, 1927, Philadelphia headlines screamed: "Cobb Signs With Athletics For 1927 Season at Price Reported to Be $60,000."

A stillness as profound as a desert midnight exploded into pandemonium the previous evening when the great Georgian uttered the words that allied his fire and fury under the banner of the Athletics for the 1927 championship campaign. The setting was the Crystal Room at the Hotel Adelphia, jammed to stifling fullness with an overflow crowd attending the twenty-third annual dinner of the Philadelphia Sport Writers' Association. Ty was the guest of honor. It wasn't until he stood

171

up and made his speech that Philadelphians knew he had finally decided to cast his future fortunes with the army of the White Elephants of Tioga.

Cobb had arrived in Philadelphia at 3:20 that afternoon, and he refused to make any statement of his plans for the following spring. Mr. Mack was noncommittal, said he could only guess what Cobb's answer would be.

So when Ty rose to address the banquet a sudden hush of expectancy floated across the room. Then, with his own words —"I've decided to play for Mr. Mack"—the lid blew off, and the stillness of the desert became a wild, screeching bedlam. An ancient enemy had become their own.

What a study of contrasts. People who for twenty-two years had booed him and fought him and even threatened him with bodily violence stood on their chairs and cheered for a solid five minutes.

"Attaboy, Ty!"

"Yo, ho, Cobb!"

"Hooray for the champ!"

Cobb in Philadelphia always had been an inciter to noise, but never, through all the years when he stormed across the baseball stage as the game's No. 1 villain, did the city of Philadelphia produce as much uproar per capita as they did that night in the Adelphia's Crystal Room.

"The Cobb personality sheathed in a White Elephant uniform!" gloated one Philadelphia writer the next morning. "What a sight that will be at Shibe Park and in seven other American League battlegrounds this year! Whoopie!"

Mr. Mack rubbed his hands together like he was washing them with soap as he watched Cobb sign his contract, calling for in the neighborhood of $60,000—$25,000 for signing, $25,000 salary and a $10,000 bonus at the end of the season.

Cobb was worth every penny of it to Mr. Mack. The turnstiles in the Philadelphia owner-manager's head whirred audibly.

"In 1914," he said, "we won our fourth pennant in five seasons with one of our greatest teams. We were in first place and Detroit in sixth, but the Tigers drew three times as many fans as we did. What's the answer? You'll find it in center-field."

Folks never were late when Cobb was in town. He batted third in the lineup. If they were late they missed seeing him bat the first time around.

The Philadelphia kids especially adored the gigantic Georgian, even when he was wearing the Detroit colors. He was just as big a hero in Philadelphia as he was in the Motor City, contrary to what adults wanted to make of it. The kids hung around the outside of the ball yards waiting for some-one to knock a ball over the fence. After the game they'd wait around to see their idols come out. And until the advent of The Babe, Cobb was the greatest of these. He was wor-shipped by the juniors more than any other ballplayer. That proved itself by the fact that his picture, one of a series issued with a certain cigarette brand, was worth ten of the others. Christy Mathewson was worth five of the others, Nap Rucker, three, and so on.

That the Athletics finished second to the Yankees in the 1927 pennant drive was not Cobb's fault. He appeared in 134 games, drove in 93 runs, ninth best RBI production of his career, and had a .357 BA. He was still the most feared base runner in the game, swiping twenty-two bases. Why, the old man was just getting warmed up!

To illustrate how vaunted his reputation was as a base run-ner even in the twilight of his career, they tell the story about a rookie outfielder. The Georgian rammed a line shot out toward the youngster. Cobb turned first base as the rookie picked up the ball. Without a sign of hesitation, the green hand rifled the ball to home plate. Ty Cobb wasn't going to outmaneuver him!

Cobb was no longer a young ballplayer when he came back

to play for the Athletics in 1928. He was forty-one years old and his bones were beginning to ache and creak. But Mr. Mack paid him $35,000 because he needed him to complete the job of overhauling the Yankees. It was up to Ty to get around as best he could.

He got around. He hit .323 in 95 games, but his stolen base production dropped to five. Years before there had been afternoons when he stole that total in one game. No doubt about it now, Ty wasn't the athlete he once had been.

One afternoon Ty and Granny Rice sat talking in the Philadelphia dugout.

"Grant," Ty said, "speed is a great asset, but it's greater when it's combined with quickness—and there's a big difference. I'm about as fast as ever, once I get in motion. But my reflexes are fading. I'm starting much slower. I don't get the jump any more. I can see the ball as good as ever, but I don't get that quick start from the plate like I used to. If I could, I'd be a .350 hitter right to the end."

The 1928 Athletics, come to think about it, fill seven niches at Cooperstown—eight, if you want to include Manager Connie Mack. The seven players are Jimmy Foxx, Ty Cobb, Mickey Cochrane, Tris Speaker, Eddie Collins, Lefty Grove, and Al Simmons. It is a remarkable record, as Frank Graham points out, which no other club even remotely approaches, in the sense that these men were in action together at the same time.

The Athletics were rising swiftly in 1928 to the peak they gained when they won the pennant in 1929 and held for the next two years. Their rehabilitation had begun as far back as 1922, after they'd finished last seven times in a row, and only a great and courageous club such as the Yankees could hold them off in 1928.

The A's broke fast in 1928 and took the lead. The Yankees quickly snatched it from them and drew away until, in July,

174

they were seventeen games in front once more and riding easily. Then, almost overnight, they were riddled with injuries. Herb Pennock's arm was so lame that it was quite useless—and he was the Yanks' best pitcher. Tony Lazzeri's right shoulder bothered him so much that he was in and out of the lineup. Babe Ruth had a bad leg. Earle Combs was so wound in tape that he looked like a mummy. There scarcely was an able-bodied man in the squad.

As they hobbled through one defeat after another and Miller Huggins almost went out of his mind at the prospect of blowing the pennant that, only a short time before, had seemed so secure, the A's put on a terrific finish. On September 8, they lunged past the Yankees into first place.

Their lead, however, was short-lived. The Yankees, joined in a battle to the finish, forgot their aches and pains and, one day later, a Sunday at Yankee Stadium, they won both ends of a doubleheader as George Pipgras pitched a shutout in the first game and Bob Meusel hit a home run with the bases bulging in the second. Monday was an open date, but on Tuesday they hurled the A's back again as the Babe hit a big one in the clutch.

There was no holding the Yankees after that. They clinched the pennant in Detroit days later and then throttled the Cardinals in four straight to win the World Series.

The Yankees' back-breaking effort in 1928, however, took more out of the World Champions than they could afford. They were off in front again as 1929 came on, but the A's soon overhauled them and weren't headed again.

Cobb and Speaker had just about run out of time in 1928, and the third member of the only Hall of Fame outfield, Al Simmons, must have felt it was sheer hard work to be out there with the two over-aged glamor boys. Cobb still could hit, but as he told Granny Rice he'd lost his quickness. Speaker could neither hit nor run any more. And Simmons, in full

175

vigor of his 25 years, not only had to patrol left field but chase the long drives that got away from Speaker and Cobb in left or right center.

"If this keeps up," he growled one day, "by the end of the season I'll be an old man myself."

Ty retired for real at the end of the season.

Many of Cobb's intimate associates urged him to play one more season to round out twenty-five years in the big leagues, a nice, easy mark to remember.

Ty shook his head wistfully.

"Once it might have been an irresistible appeal," he told them. "But, in a baseball sense, I am too old, too weary of the constant strain. My ambition is gone. I'm through. That's final."

Later he told the whole story of how it felt to sit in the stands and watch others do the work he performed so incredibly for so many years.

"Why did I stick around baseball so long?" he asked. "It would puzzle me to answer that. I threatened to quit a number of times during my last ten years, and I meant it, too. But somehow I never could definitely turn my back on the grand old game. It was in my bones. You cannot eat baseball and sleep baseball and study baseball year after year and then stop just like that. It's in the blood stream. You crave it. You can't get along without it.

"I knew I could quit anytime, but I didn't do it. I was led on, not only by my sincere love for the game, but also by the driving ambition to establish records that will stand for all time—to pile up more hits and more runs and all the rest of it. I won't deny, too, that I hoped to get in one more World Series. That particular phase of my career has been a disappointment. My World Series experience came early, when I simply wasn't ripe to do my best work.

"I was fortunate to get an early start in life, to get going at full speed, and to exceed my wildest dreams in the record

176

Ty liked big and fast cars, used to drive in races.

Cobb and fellow Georgian Bobby Jones chat during the Masters' Invitation Golf Tournament at Augusta in 1941. Ty was one of the Emperor of Golf's most rabid supporters.

Three of the stars of the 1909 World Series meet 24 years later. George Gibson, left, caught in that Series for the Pirates, and Honus Wagner played shortstop.

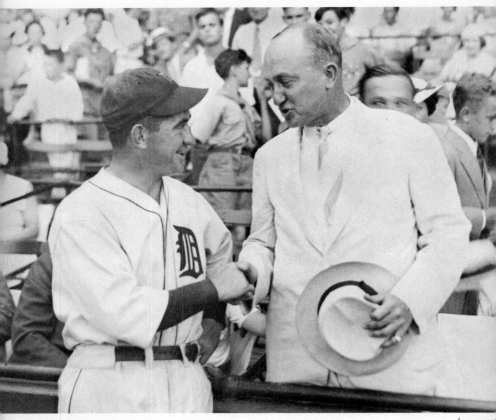

(AP PHO

Ty returns to Detroit, finds an old stable mate, Mickey Cochrane, holding down his old job as Tiger manager.

Time has mellowed Ty. He took up golf seriously after leaving baseball, swings southpaw, has been in the low 70s.

Babe Ruth and Ty clown for photographers before teeing off in a special USO golf match in 1941. The Babe won.

A southpaw, Ty hit 'em long and straight, drives one a mile at the Newton, Mass., Commonwealth Country Club.

Old pals meet again at the Polo Grounds. The Babe managed the East, Ty the West, in the Esquire All-America Boys' Game, 1945.

Cobb made many public appearances during World War II for fund drives, such as this one in Seattle in 1944.

There was a hot time in the old town (New York) as Ty, Charley Dressen, center, and Rogers Hornsby helped the National League celebrate its 75th anniversary in 1951.

On the ball. Ty was one of the speakers at the annual Hall of Fame ceremonies, Cooperstown, New York, in 1953 when Dizzy Dean and Al Simmons were formally inducted into the Hall.

When a congressional sub-committee held hearings in Washington as to whether organized baseball was violating anti-monopoly laws, Ty was the lead-off witness.

So that young men and women may go to college, Ty organized the "Ty Cobb Educational Foundation" in 1953. These are the three medallions he presented to trustees of the foundation.

It has been 28 years since Ty retired, but he still averages a dozen letters a day from fans. Cobb today is 69, retired and wealthy. Here he relaxes at his winter home in California.

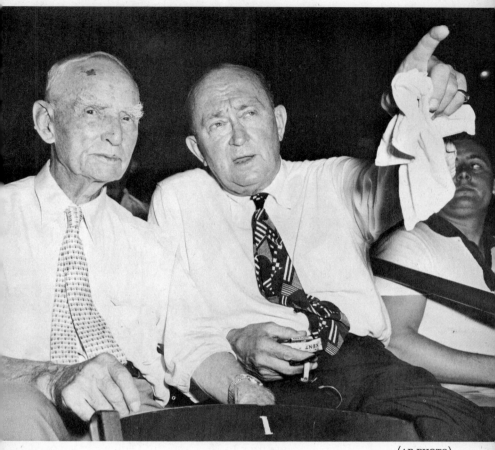

Old rivals chat for the last time. Not long after this photo was taken in 1955 Clark Griffith, left, died. Both Ty and the president of the Senators were on hand for the 48th anniversary of Walter Johnson's big league debut.

On July 30, 1955, Ty came back to New York for Oldtimers Day, paid his respects to Casey Stengel. Cobb says the Yankee manager is one of the best pilots in baseball history.

department. I never imagined I could possibly play so long. I might have broken a leg, let alone a neck, early in my career. Some severe sickness might have crippled me. But there's something I might say on that point. I played a lot of ball games when I had no business in there. I slid bases many times on black and blue legs and sides, and never gave the matter a thought. Perhaps it was fortunate I was born with that vying, burning spirit. When a ballplayer humors himself, he's likely to get hurt. And when he plays the game to the hilt, the way I did, he's apt to escape serious injury.

"Now old age is creeping up on me and that reckless, slave driving spirit has lost its appeal. As I grow older, I grow more irritable. In the end the strain of the game was making me nervous and fidgety. People pestered me a good deal. I couldn't sit down and talk fifteen minutes to a friend without being interrupted. There was a time when those things weren't worth mentioning. But they became unpleasant realities. I knew what the trouble was. I was thoroughly tired and needed a rest.

"If I had my career to live over I know I'd do some things differently. But it's idle conversation to speculate on that now. I suppose I'll leave a lot of enemies behind me. That's because I told the truth. If I knew a guy had no guts, I said so. I didn't expect him to love me for saying it. Possibly I've been too blunt and open in my remarks. I might have got along easier if I'd used more tact and diplomacy. But such things are foreign to me. I don't take to them naturally."

Part V

The Passing Show

1929-1956

Preface

The Honeymoon was over.

On the morning of October 29, 1929, America woke up suffering from a whopping headache. It had been a gay party while the money lasted. But now panic was running rampant on Wall Street. Within a couple of hours more than sixteen million shares were traded and averages nosedived nearly forty points. What a mess. Unemployment zoomed. Apple vendors and breadlines appeared on streets in every city in the country.

Oh, what a hangover.

But the country carried on. During the next couple of years John Dillinger would become Public Enemy No. 1, and an investigation into New York City politics would smoke Jimmy Walker, the playboy, out of the mayor's chair. The Al Capone mob was running things in Chicago, and illegal sitdown strikes were becoming a new bargaining weapon of labor.

In sports, college football was heading for Big Business. During Prohibition it struggled along, but with the coming of repeal and the legalization of betting on the horses in most states of the Union, the colleges were going to be able to say farewell and good riddance to poverty and strife. The kids in moleskins, fired up by stories of Rockne, the Four Horsemen, Grange and Nagurski, were to come into their own. Universities were to toss their football teams into the public entertainment markets to pick up their share of the swag. The day of high-pressured recruitment was not far off.

Elsewhere there was to be written a lot of explanations after the 1932 Olympic Games about the Japanese secret of swimming that enabled fourteen-year old schoolboys to carry off most of the Olympic prizes in competition against grown men and mature athletes from the U.S. and other countries.

America, which had the balance of power in tennis in the heyday of Tilden, Richards and Johnston, was to lose it to France's Borotra, Cochet and Lacoste.

The Opera Ballila, Italy's youth movement, and the Hitler Jugend, along with other Fascist states, were planting the seeds to train their upcoming generation to break America's stranglehold on track and field events.

Max Baer, Jack Sharkey and Max Schmeling slugged heavyweights around the prize ring. Baer brought a flash of color to pugilism, but he never came anywhere near living up to his tremendous potential and he faded out quicker than a three dollar gingham dress in a cloudburst. Jack Sharkey had everything but consistency, and he was in and out of the kingdom like the thread in a loom. Schmeling was good, sometimes, and he at least had a knockout right hand, but he was a plodding, methodical workman who didn't often stir up frenzied excitement. That was it. Excitement. The boxing world wouldn't taste it until the advent of the Brown Bomber —Joe Louis.

With the deadly accuracy of "Calamity Jane," his famous putter, Bobby Jones nailed down all the big golf championships of the world in one spectacular year—1930.

Baseball, meanwhile, jammed 'em in—depression period or no depression period. Somehow Gus Fan managed to scrape up four-bits for a bleacher seat. Miller Huggins died in 1929, and Joe McCarthy succeeded him.

Time passed.

On June 3, 1932, John Joseph McGraw left the Giants for the last time just as he had found them thirty years before— in last place. The cemetery gates were indeed closing in on the Old Guard. That same day Lou Gehrig astonishingly hit four home runs in one game at Philadelphia, the first player of the modern era to accomplish the feat.

The scene was changing at Yankee Stadium. Murderer's Row gave way to the Bronx Bombers, and during the transition, from 1929-30-31, Connie Mack took squatter's rights on the American League pennant. In '32, the Yanks won the championship again. The lineup now read . . Combs, Sewell, Ruth, Gehrig, Lazzeri, Dickey, Chapman and Crosetti. Gehrig led the A.L. winners to four straight over the Cubs in the World Series as the Babe's power began to wane a trifle. Since the Yankees got the habit in 1921, they were by this time getting in a rut, just pennant after pennant, championship after championship, season after season—21 times in 34 years!

Come 1935 and Columbia Lou would have the Yankees all to himself. The Great Man was gone. Wear and tear and time had tapped the Babe.

The Golden Era of Sport had come to an end—buried in the limbo of beautiful dreams.

Life Goes On

Life went on for Ty Cobb. A new life had come to him now in full measure. His struggles, as it were, had ended with his retirement from baseball's active roll call. He had fame, money, lots of money despite the disturbance down on Wall Street, a wife and five children.

Now he could feed his cultural tastes, reawaken his interests in good books, the theatre, travel, et cetera. To what is at best an abnormal life—that of a famous baseball figure—his retirement brought as much normalcy as possible.

In 1929, the Cobbs packed off to Europe. Shortly before departure the Cincinnati franchise was plunked down on the market and the banks that had loaned the Reds $425,000 asked Ty to put in a bid. He didn't want the club, but he made a bargain-counter offer of $275,000. Then he went to Europe. It was a good thing he did. Otherwise he might have gone ahead and purchased control of the team. A few weeks later the market crashed. Ty heaved a sigh of relief. He had come just this far from getting saddled with a ball club through the depression period, and losing gosh knows how much dough.

Ty was out of baseball, but the old competitive bonfires inside him still blazed. He hunted, fished, played golf, trained his hunting dogs. He even took to playing polo.

Cobb had been watching a polo match at Aiken, South Carolina. Something about the speed and fury of men on horseback galloping down each other's throats appealed to Ty. In no time he was in the saddle and riding bloody murder. One of the first things he wanted to do, after he got the hang of it, was to change the polo rules. Instead of three men to a side he wanted to play it one against one! Nobody wanted any part of him—including the ponies.

"That Mistah Cobb's a madman on a horse," muttered an old Negro groom. "He don't ride over you. He rides *through* you!"

Ty thought that perhaps a change would be good for his family upon returning from abroad. The summer at Augusta in 1930 had been a sizzler, more than Ty could stand. He had missed the south's summertime heat when he was playing ball, so the weather down there had made little difference to him. But after the summer of '30—whew! The Cobbs ran fans in rooms for fifty-three straight nights. Ty decided right then and there on a change of climate. He remembered a pleasant visit he once had made to Northern California. The moderate climate appealed to him immensely. So did improved educational facilities. The south's school system was feeling the pangs of the depression. Teachers were being paid off in script. With five growing children to look after, Ty wanted them to get the best education. In 1931, the Cobbs moved to Menlo Park, located just a mashie shot from San Francisco. He's been there ever since.

Now he was a long ways from the big leagues, far from the roar of the crowd, but not forgotten. Sincere tributes and appreciations of the man who gave so much of himself to the national game continued to appear in the columns and the sport pages. Wherever baseball was discussed, in the home, at the neighborhood pub, in the bleachers, the name Ty Cobb inevitably popped up in the discussion.

"Why, I remember the time Cobb . . ."

"Remember the day Cobb . . ."

"Cobb was on first, see . . ."

Ty Cobb, a yardstick of comparison. Oh, the memories, memories, memories . . . remember . . . remember . . . recount . . .

Cobb at bat. Catcher signals for a sizzler on the outside of the plate, loaded with spin. Cobb crouches, tightens the grip on his bat. The pitcher winds up. Now he is in a knot. Now he uncoils. Now he pitches—oops, slipped! Down the groove, all stitches showing. Cobb swings. Wham! Wood meets horsehide. Cobb runs. Cobb rounds first like Citation. Cobb slides into second in a swirling screen of dust. Two bagger on an ordinary base hit.

Look at the pitcher. Is he miserable. That (censored) Cobb! Always hustling. All the pitcher can do is stand there with his hands on his hips, feeling his ears burn and his eyebrows twitch, cussing under his breath at the grinning runner on second base.

One of the greatest of all spectator sights from the point of view of sustained suspense and nerve-crunching anticipation was Cobb hunched over the plate waiting for the ball to leave the pitcher's hand. The drama that was packed into the activity centered around home plate seemed tremendously magnified when fans considered what might be termed the ballistics and forces under which Cobb and the pitcher dueled.

The distance between the rubber and home plate was sixty and one-half feet. It took the ball about three-and-four-tenths of a second to make the trip from mound to plate. Not much time for a bloke to make up his mind whether to swing or let the ball go by. Cobb's bat was only about three feet long, and

187

his arms extended it another foot or so. Actually the ball was in position where Cobb could get a whack at it for only three feet of the journey. This brought the time element in which the ball remained in a position where Cobb could reach it with his bludgeon to something around two one-hundreths of a second. That was cutting it pretty thin. And still Cobb's lifetime batting average for twenty-four seasons in the majors was .367!

In view of the nice, even rows of awesome batting statistics trailing after Cobb's name in the record book, it is most difficult to conceive that he even knew what a "batting slump" was. Cobb in a slump? Absurd. But there he was—Cobb talking about the days when he couldn't buy a base hit.

"Sure, I had 'em," he was saying. "But I also had a remedy. I simply tried to hit the ball back to the pitcher. Ballplayers worry when they begin to slump, as I did. What bothers them is that they know they are the ones who are at fault. They know it can't be the pitchers, because some of the pitchers who have been their cousins for a long time are getting them out. Striking them out, or making them pop up, or hitting the ball into the dirt. It is their fault, and instead of thinking the thing out, they fight themselves. Every time they go up there, they try to powder the ball. When they don't, they get to a spot where they ask the other fellows on the club what it is they are doing wrong at the plate. They always get answers, of course. The trouble is, the answers are all different.

"One player says he is standing too far back. Another says he is standing too close. One says he has his feet too close together, and another says his feet are too far apart. One says he shouldn't try to outguess the pitcher and another says he should because he is hitting at too many bad balls and he should wait and make the pitcher come in with what he wants. Nobody ever tells the poor hitter how he should let the pitcher know what he wants or what to do if he has two strikes on him and the pitch he doesn't want is over the plate.

"Perhaps I was lucky. When I was a kid with the Tigers and in a batting slump, I couldn't ask the other players what I was doing wrong. We weren't speaking, for one thing. If I had asked them, they would have given me the wrong answer. I had to figure it out for myself, and this is what I figured:

"I could hit those pitchers—but now I wasn't hitting them. They didn't have any more stuff than they had the last time I saw them. My eyesight still was good, thank God, so that I still could see the ball as well as ever. I was standing at the plate as I always had. I held the bat the way I always had. The reason I couldn't hit the ball was because my stroke was off. I was hitting just under the ball, or just over it. The solution? Meet the ball right in the middle. And, seriously, that's what I did. I hit the ball back to the pitcher. That's all. That's all I tried to do. Just flatten out my stroke, so that when the pitcher threw to me, I could hit it back to him. After a day or so, I was hitting it where he couldn't reach it. Sounds very simple, and it is. I have been telling it to ballplayers for years and they don't believe me. But it is, so help me."

Cobb admits he really doesn't know what causes a batting slump. "It's entirely unconscious," he said. "Sometimes psychological, sometimes mechanical. A man may unconsciously change his style at the plate. He doesn't know he's doing it. And unless he asks somebody to watch him, he won't know what's wrong. Another reason is that a man may lift the ball out of the park for a homer and he changes his style to wallop every ball for a homer, instead of just meeting the ball. That ruins him.

"You know in batting you don't follow the ball till it hits the bat. Your eye sees the ball maybe six feet in front of you, telegraphs to your brain, which directs your wrists, and you either miss or hit it. You can see the curve break, but it's too late then, for your arms are already moving to hit the ball. The roar of the people in the stands doesn't make any difference. If you concentrate, you hear nothing. All you think is, 'I'm going to hit the ball; I'm going to hit it. I *can* hit it.'"

Cobb received a note from Cy Perkins, veteran catcher of seventeen major league campaigns, in 1955, which pretty well illustrates the tremendous respect oldtimers had for the Georgia Peach.

"Ty," wrote Perkins, "you knew more about hitting than anyone else. Why, the only season I hit .300 in the big leagues was when you moved me closer to the plate (.307, in 1925). I had a lifetime BA of around .270, but it would have been at least fifteen points higher if you'd been my regular batting instructor. Clark Griffith once said that you couldn't hit to left field. Ty, that made me laugh. You could hit to left any time you made up your mind to."

"While there are plenty of pitching coaches around baseball today," broke in Cobb, "I can't understand why they don't put more batting coaches on the pay rolls. There's a definite need for them."

Occasionally, a big league star, in the throes of a batting slump, will write to Cobb, hitting him up for advice. Does Ty have a solution? Ty writes back, offering a suggestion here and giving a tip there; then he sits back and patiently waits. Eight or nine days later, after the player has had time to experiment with Cobb's suggestions, Ty begins to scan the boxscores in the newspapers, keeping an eagle eye on the batter's daily progress.

"Over the years it is heart-warming to know that I have been able to help a number of hitters," Ty said. "Sometimes it is only a little suggestion.

"Once I met Ted Williams before a game in New York. A mutual friend introduced us.

"'Ted,' he said, 'this is Ty Cobb.'

"Ted's eyes seemed to light up, and he said warmly, 'Hello, Ty, I've been wanting to ask you a question for a long time.'

"'That so?' I said.

190

" 'Yes,' he said, 'how do you hit to left field?'

"I told him it was only a guess, but I explained to him how I would hit to left if I were Ted Williams. He seemed very delighted and appreciative.

"I don't know why or how, but the next day one of the papers ran a two-column box saying, in effect, that Williams thumbed his nose at the lesson I gave him. Ted was quoted as saying, 'Oh, Cobb! What does he know about it?' The facts, pure and simple, are that Ted said absolutely nothing. He was very attentive, which is the mark of all great students of the game. It astonished me that a paper would print such an erroneous story. I know it hurt Ted's feelings. I've always admired him and I know he wouldn't say anything to put me in a bad light."

Cobb's unorthodox batting style always has been a hot topic of debate. He batted with his feet close together and used a shifting grip. His right hand was placed about three inches from the knob of the bat, his left hand about three inches above his right. This sliding grip enabled him to swing from the end of the bat, choke up and hit to the opposite field or bunt. He was between the swinger and choke hitter, but definitely nearer the choke. All these points he polished up meticulously. His grip served to keep the defense in a constant state of flux. They had to guess what was coming next.

Cobb was one of the few stars to use the sliding grip. Babe Ruth's home runs caused the place-hitter to all but disappear from the scene. Yet when Cobb met up with Hans Wagner in the 1909 World Series, they discovered with amazement that they both gripped the bat the same way. Both stalwarts, coincidentally, led their respective leagues in batting that year. Only once since then, when Philadelphia's Al Simmons and Chick Hafey of the Cardinals teed off in 1931, have two champion batters of the rival circuits met in the Autumnal classic.

Harry Salsinger, *Detroit News* sports editor who practically went with the Briggs Stadium lease, remembers Cobb as a skinny kid. He was light and lacked the power and weight of king ball busters like Nap Lajoie and Sam Crawford. But, like everything else, Ty found a way to overcome that handicap, too. He began carrying three bats to the plate while awaiting in the on-deck circle. He swung them like a roman candle, kept swinging them until he reached the plate. Then he quickly discarded two of the sticks. Now the one in his grip felt three times as light. Cobb was the first batter to carry three bats to the plate. Nearly all batters do it today.

If you were to ask Cobb what one must do to make the batsman more feared than the pitcher, his answer would run something like this:

"To be a great hitter, a ballplayer must have a comfortable stance. My idea of a comfortable stance is both feet about six inches apart with the weight equally distributed. Such a style enables a batter to shift without being handicapped. According to the style ball pitched, he can step into the ball or pull back before taking his cut. This is a very necessary feature with most of the modern pitchers using a change of pace, which is virtually unhittable, if a batter takes a stance that is suited only for fast ball pitching.

"Keeping the arms away from the body is as necessary as a proper stance. Holding the arms close to the body makes the batter almost helpless against any ball that is pitched on the inside. It also makes it difficult to get any power back of the swing. The batter is practically forced to hit the ball with the handle of the bat, if at all. With the hands held away from the body, the batter is in a position to bring the hands and arms back and get plenty of power back of the swing, regardless what the pitch might be.

"The grip of the bat, like the stance and the position of the arms, should be comfortable. The grip is largely a matter of opinion. What suits one player is often poison to another. I have always favored spreading the hands a bit. I found it

192

much easier to control the desire to swing, as well as the actual swinging of the bat, with a spread grip, rather than holding the bat at the extreme end of the handle. With the lively ball in use, plus the wild desire to make home runs, the grip featuring holding the bat at the extreme end is much more popular than in the old days.

"It is very important, of course, that the batter conform his swing to the style of pitching he's facing. No batter can pull the unexpected to any great extent against a good pitcher. It's very difficult to bunt or try to place your hits against a pitcher with a world of stuff. The smartest thing to do is to hit straightaway, through the pitcher's box.

"Form naturally plays a definite part in any sport and baseball is no exception to the rule. Watch carefully the great golfers in action and you'll notice a similarity in style. Stance, grip, position of the head and the follow-through of the swing will be almost identical. True, there are exceptions to every rule. There are certain star golfers who do everything in an unorthodox manner. They're greatly in the minority, however.

"It is much the same in baseball. There are certain fixed fundamentals that are considered best. A majority of the players adhere to them. Yet, I believe, there are more exceptions to the set rules in baseball than golf, since the game offers more opportunities for an expression of individuality.

"Lastly, you must have confidence in your ability. Every great batter works on the theory that the pitcher is more afraid of him than he is of the pitcher. Proper stance, correct grip, perfect follow-through and implicit confidence are the chief ingredients in becoming a great hitter. There you have my formula. Try it out."

If there's one thing Cobb has against Casey Stengel's managerial theories, it is the Yankee chief's two-platoon system—his left-handed batters who only play against right-hand pitchers and his right-handed batters who only hit against southpaws.

"That's strictly hokum," Cobb said. "Any left-handed batter can learn to hit southpaws, but only by looking at them from the batter's box, not by sitting on the bench. When I first came up I was driven crazy by left-handers, but I loved them by the time I retired. If they'd been using the platoon system in those days I'd probably been benched every time a left-hander warmed up.

"The only difference to left-hand pitching is that the curve breaks away from you, rather than inward. What I did, after I wised up, was to stand as far back in the batter's box as I could. I got an extra split second to watch the ball that way and a chance to smack it after it broke. I also concentrated on hitting it in the direction it was breaking. In other words, poke it to left field instead of pulling it to right.

"All the managers now work themselves into a lather over the percentage of batting right-handed against southpaws and vice versa. Make a note of how many times you see a manager lift a .280 hitter and bring in a pinch hitter who has been averaging only .240—but is supposed to be magic because he swings from the other side of the plate. It's the stupidest move in modern baseball. The good hitter will do better against any kind of pitching than the poorer hitter. Besides he's been playing all day. He's been looking at the pitching. He's all warmed up. The pinch hitter, who comes off the bench cold and has seen no pitching all day except what was lobbed up to him in batting practice, has two strikes on him before he ever reaches the plate.

"Put the best team you can find on the field and then go all the way with it. Every time you see one of these modern box scores, where fifteen men played for one side and eighteen for the other, you can be sure a couple of managers have gone haywire."

What Cobb misses is the science, the skill, the strategy, the daring, the finesse of the old game when eighteen hired hands would battle from morn to dewy eve for one lone run.

194

How they gloried in the old Chicago White Sox of 1906! The Hitless Wonders! One run, just one li'l ol' teeny run, was all they ever needed, and the game was theirs. Defense was high art, and strategy a gift from the Olympian gods. The good old days of the hit-and-run, the dragged bunt, the delayed steal, the squeeze . . . the battle of wits, the breath-taking, heart-halting duels between Cobb at bat and Jimmy Collins playing third.

Ty can't understand why rival American League managers let Stengel two-platoon them to death.

"All you have to do is announce a right-hand pitcher and let him warm up," Cobb said. "This prompts Casey to put all his left-hand hitters into the starting lineup. You have your right-hander pitch to just one man and then bring in your sleeper, a left-hander who has been warming up out of sight under the stands. Now Stengel has to do one of two things. He's got to go along with his left-hand hitters, who aren't supposed to be worth a hoot against your left-hand pitcher. Or he has to yank them out and they're through for the day, even if badly needed later in the game. Bucky Harris pulled this trick against John McGraw in the 1924 World Series, but everybody seems to have forgotten."

Another stratagem that seems foolish to Cobb is the number of times managers make a batter take a pitch instead of swinging. They almost always flash the "take" signal when the count is 2-0 or 3-1, even with a good hitter at bat and a weak one coming up. So he misses a chance at the fattest pitch of all. Cobb reasons that a batter never should deliberately get himself into a position where he has only one strike left.

"It's too tough a mental hazard," Ty said. "I always figured a 3-2 count was rougher on the batter than the pitcher. If I were still managing today, I'd quit wasting time on all these crazy stratagems and do one thing that's terribly neglected: train the tailend of my batting order as bunters and hit-and-run experts. I wouldn't let them, least of all the pitchers, try

195

to reach the fences. They'd spend all their time in spring training learning to lay down bunts, and to poke the ball first toward left field and then toward right. I learned how to bunt by putting a sweater down on the infield and trying to stop the ball on it. If more .250 hitters, swinging for the fences and never quite reaching them, would tune up their bunting, they'd become .280 and .290 hitters. Give me this little edge in the batting averages, and some smart base running, and I could worry any other team in the league. All these things can be learned. As we used to say, 'Give 'em the *teach!*' "

Ballplayers had a lot to think about in the old days, such as trouble with their bats. Moisture would get into the wood, especially during the damp spring weather, and then they'd crack. That amounted to a tragedy, since the clubowners worked on slimmer budgets and were less generous about buying new ones. The players spent much time honing their favorite war clubs with neat's-foot oil or tobacco juice to keep the dampness out. Cobb's favorite prescription was a chewing tobacco called Nerve navy-cut, the juiciest kind he ever found, rubbed in by the hour with a piece of bone. The bone Cobb used, the hollowed-out thigh of a steer, was still anchored to a table in the Tiger clubhouse the last time he visited there.

Once, in Detroit, a fan introduced himself and told Cobb he had an idea for treating bats. He worked in a plant that made hammer handles, and they had some kind of machinery for treating the wood with oil under pressure. Cobb didn't think much of the idea but gave the man some old culls that he never planned to use anyway. When the plant worker brought them back they were so heavy with oil Ty could hardly swing them. But he hung them next to the furnace all winter. The excess oil drained out and the bats turned out to be the finest Cobb ever had. Unfortunately the plant worker must have died or moved away. Cobb never saw him again.

Cobb's favorite bat was a Louisville Slugger that was never revised in any way, except in weight, throughout his entire career. It was thirty-four and one-half inches long—a length easy to handle—had a medium small barrel with slight taper to medium large handle, then flared out slightly to a medium shallow knob. His bats weighed forty ounces right down to the last couple of seasons, when he started using thirty-five and thirty-six ounce clubs.

"I was very particular about my bats," Ty said. "They were specially made for me. The Hillerich & Bradsby people always assigned their best lathe man to make 'em for me. One time, when they sent me a check for seventy-five dollars because I permitted them to use my name on one of their models, in the interest of friendship, I returned it to them—and I needed the money in those days, too.

"I told Hillerich & Bradsby that I wanted my bats made out of a special kind of wood. No green stuff. When this wood arrived in their plant, they'd order, 'Put it aside—that's for Ty Cobb's bats.'

"One season I ran out of bats. I phoned Hillerich & Bradsby.

" 'You've got to do something,' I pleaded. 'I have nothing to bat with and I'm going after another batting championship.'

"Well, the lathe man who used to turn 'em out for me and by now had been kicked upstairs into an important executive post, slipped on his work clothes and went down into the machine shop and personally made me a dozen of the slickest bats you ever saw.

"I was caught in a similar pinch a year or so later. My supply of bats was exhausted and the factory discovered they had no more of my kind of required wood left. But that didn't stop Hillerich & Bradsby. They were just organizing a trophy room in the company office, stocking it with autographed balls and bats and whatnot—keepsakes that belonged to old-time greats. When told of my emergency, they went to their trophy case, bundled up an armload of the bats that had come from the oldtimers and were of the same wood as mine —and cut them down into bats my size."

Tailor-made war clubs for a tailor-made batting champion.

A Word About the
More Moderns

One night in 1935, seven years after Ty Cobb left baseball, Grantland Rice and Ty got together in the Detroit Athletic Club. Nig Clarke, the old Cleveland catcher, dropped by. Soon the three of them were back among their memories and going at high speed.

"Remember, Nig," said Granny, "that trick you had of tagging a runner out fast and then immediately tossing your catcher's mitt away, signifying the third out?"

Nig chuckled.

"I've a confession," Nig said. "Actually I missed many a runner who was called out." And nudging Cobb playfully, he said, "I missed you at least ten times at the plate, Ty—times when you were called out."

Immediately blood rushed to Cobb's face and he pounced on Clarke like an eagle on its prey.

"You cost me ten runs," he roared, shaking Nig violently. "Runs I earned!"

It was all Granny could do to pull Ty off the old catcher and calm him down.

198

Clarke left.

Ty was still burning a half hour later. Once again he demonstrated that he was so sincerely a bad loser that he became a terrific winner.

In his more mellow moments Ty, when asked which pitchers were hardest for him to hit, has said "they were all tough."

"One afternoon I'd get to a star like Ed Walsh," he related, "and then a game or two later some rinky-dink lefthander, one I never paid much attention to before, would stand out there and make me look like a plug nickel. I was lucky with stars like Eddie Plank and Walter Johnson and Lefty Grove—and study their records—and so it went.

"Look at the records of the pitchers of my era—their earned run averages, won-lost performances, their longevity, total games pitched per season, and you must admit it would be pretty difficult to get a modern pitcher on your all-time team. The old guard composed the swiftest era of pitchers the game has known. Those were the days of the dead ball, and lower down you had lesser pitchers using all of the tricks: shine ball, emery, knuckle, spitter, and the parafin ball.

"Still some of the oldtimers hit .400 against all this. Despite the lively ball and shortening of the fences by artificial and temporary obstruction, what do the boys hit today? They go out and celebrate if they drive in 100 runs. Yogi Berra was voted the most valuable player in the American League in 1951. He hit less than .300 (.294). The Yankee catcher was also up in the proper notch in the batting order to drive in runs—and on a pennant winner, too—yet banged in only eighty-eight runs. I don't understand it.

"In 1952, I by-lined a couple of articles for *Life Magazine*. They stirred up considerable national controversy. Let me say right here in defense, however, that parts of my interview were distorted. My contract with the magazine read that I was supposed to get to see the final draft of the manuscript.

I was to be allowed to blue pencil anything I didn't agree with. I never did see the final copy.

"But much of what was written in that series still goes. I analyzed the modern players, comparing them to the stars of my day. I pointed out, among other things, their utter disregard for conditioning. I told how some of today's batters apparently refuse to hit to all fields, using Ted Williams as a Grade-A illustration. The Boston slugger since has vastly improved in this department, but at the time the *Life* series was written he still refused to hit to left field, hence the birth of the 'Williams Shift,' inaugurated by Lou Boudreau in 1946.

"I wrote that both Williams and Joe DiMaggio possessed great natural ability, also that Phil Rizzuto and Stan Musial were the type of ballplayers who would have been great in any era. With the exception of the peerless Hans Wagner, there never has been a finer shortstop than Rizzuto. He is my kind of athlete—always thinking, always beating you. Phil is typical of the shortstops you find on so many championship teams. You remember him for the games he saves rather than for the ones he wins. Phil is getting old, but at his peak how many times did you see him bail a Yankee pitcher out of a jam with an impossible stop which started the desperately needed double play? You can't count them. Phil began to slip in 1954. His years began to show. It may have been something more than a coincidence that '54 was the season the Yankees lost the pennant.

"I did not say there were no other modern players who would not have been stars in my day. If you got that impression from reading the *Life* series, I'm sorry. There have been many who doubtlessly could have given us the business. Lack of space did not permit me to name them all.

"There has been no greater catcher than Roy Campanella, for example, few better or as superior as Pee Wee Reese at shortstop and Red Schoendienst at second base. I could name more, too, such as Don Mueller, whose hitting has always impressed me, and Willie Mays.

"I have always felt that Ted Williams has *great* hitting ability. But it is too bad he didn't break in back there with the oldsters. They would have taught him to hit to all fields —or else. With their measures of discipline, Ted would go down as one of the truly all-time stars.

"Ted's an example of the modern players' attitude. When he first graduated from the Pacific Coast League to the Red Sox, he really hustled. He hit .406 in his third season, 1941. He was *trying* to make good then. Came fame and fortune and evidently he began to relax somewhat, as figures seem to indicate that he wasn't up soaring where the eagles should be.

"Williams' stretch in Korea quite naturally brought him back somewhat apprehensive about resuming his career in a flourish. The advancing years also worried him. So what did he do? He started to hustle like he never hustled before. He made an enormous comeback which, to me, proves that ballplayers with the potential, but lacking the natural desire, will never know how great they could have been.

"As custodians of baseball to keep the real game alive and up to the standards it should be, what are today's players doing? Very little. They have the ability but not the true reverence for our national sport. They aren't putting out.

"Take today's baseball offense. Imagine three outstanding stars—Ted Williams, Joe DiMaggio and Ralph Kiner—and all three stealing a total of just three bases one year. Now tell me there aren't many games in a season, in the eighth or ninth innings or overtime, when a sacrifice isn't the wisest and most valuable play. Or the squeeze play. Yet you seldom see those tactics used anymore. It isn't right to let baseball deteriorate this way.

"Young batters now stand at the plate and practice for their own enjoyment and amusement, swinging from their heels for the bleachers. No wonder the fine and attractive plays are being ignored. They are all trying to emulate the great Ruth. But there was only one Babe. Yes, and he would hit to opposite field, too, and bunt and beat them out—yes, and steal, too.

"Following the *Life* series, news interviews were published quoting big league managers to the effect that I was an old fogey living in the past. What the public doesn't know is that those same managers later sat down and wrote me personal letters, blistering the modern players and telling me how right I was all the while."

End of interview.

The Clock Ticks On . . .

The good things of baseball are gone all too soon. Cobb slashing into third, Ruth's booming swing, the graceless, bowlegged Wagner fielding a ball—all vanished. Now the clock ticks on, and the life and times of Tyrus Raymond Cobb daily unfold. But only Ty knows the complete story, for only he lived through it.

As to what Ty knows—he grows reticent. To all intents and purposes, he goes about his private life calmly and with chin up. He has overcome many obstacles through life, self-doubt in his youth, a constant battle with his emotions, loneliness in his relationship with other ballplayers. He has taken a life that might have been very ordinary, and by dint of persistency, gnawing ambition, and raw courage has made something immortal out of it.

In 1936, eight years after his retirement, Ty won the distinction as the game's all-time immortal. In the very first Hall of Fame election, on February 2, he outscored greats like Ruth and Wagner and Mathewson and Johnson. They became the Big Five, the only ones to receive the required majority of votes to be enshrined. Of the 226 ballots cast by players and writers, Cobb collected 222. Ruth and Wagner were next with 215. Nap Lajoie, Tris Speaker, Cy Young and Rogers Hornsby didn't make it.

Ty was a man apart.

After the election, Connie Mack spoke to the press. "Cobb could do more to upset a pitcher and a whole team than any other player I ever saw," Mr. Mack said. "He could upset a crowd, too. Our crowds in Philadelphia were often very hostile to him, but it didn't deter nor discourage him. Talk about nerve. I know that deep down the fans admired him tremendously, as we all did, and it was great to hear the big ovation our fans gave him when he walked onto the field in a Philadelphia uniform for the first time. It was absolutely wonderful having him with us those two seasons. He did a lot to help us develop our championship club of 1929, particularly Al Simmons' hitting."

Mr. Mack and Cobb were something of a mutual admiration society. Upon hearing the ancient leader's words of praise, Ty said the only regret, the only thing left incomplete, was that he didn't get to play sooner for Connie.

"What fineness there was in that man," Ty said. "And as a manager he never made a mistake that I could see in the two years that I played for him. Sure, he waved me out or in. I asked him to when I first joined the A's. Sometimes I thought he was wrong, but, darnit, he was always right."

Some years ago Grantland Rice kidded Ty as to whether he or Ruth was the greatest ballplayer that ever lived.

"Why pick on Ruth or me?" Cobb said. "Why not turn to Connie Mack? Mr. Mack has done more for baseball and sportsmanship in general than any two men who ever lived. He is the ablest man and the squarest shooter I've ever known —and more than sixty working years couldn't knock him down."

Speaking of the greatest of the greats, no story of Ty

Cobb would be complete without asking him to name an all-time All-Star team.

And here's the only selection where you will not find Mr. C in the outfield:

Pitchers: Walter Johnson, Grover Cleveland Alexander, Christy Mathewson, Ed Walsh and Eddie Plank.
Catchers: Micky Cochrane and Bill Dickey.
First base: George Sisler.
Second base: Eddie Collins.
Third base: Buck Weaver.
Shortstop: Honus Wagner.
Outfield: Babe Ruth, Tris Speaker and Joe Jackson.

Through the years just about everyone with whom Cobb has come in contact has seen him in a different light. Some, such as Mickey Cochrane and Ernie Lanigan, worship him. Hendrik Van Loon admitted once that a sliding demonstration by Ty in his living room was as uplifting a show as the best Russian ballet he ever saw. It is never wise to speak disparagingly of Cobb *anywhere,* because the odds are that there will be within earshot some burly character who has been the recipient of Ty's spiritual or monetary benevolence. Others, who just haven't happened to bump into the finer side of the man, blanch at the mention of his name. Some take a neutral stand. Pro-, anti-, or neutral, everyone respects him.

It has been twenty-eight years since Cobb played his last game of baseball in the big leagues. Yet his name looms as large today as it did in the good old glory days. His record is certain to ring down through the ages—not written in sand, but carved in rock.

The Cobb of old, in many ways, has not changed greatly. He's still hanging in there driving the opposition daffy. Now you take the way he foiled a pesky burglar in the winter of

1954. The intruder broke into Ty's summer cottage at Lake Tahoe, Nevada, stealing valuable hunting and fishing equipment. As soon as Ty returned to his winter home at Menlo Park, California, the thief again went to work. These larcenous activities would have to stop. But how? An idea came to Ty just before locking up the cottage for the year.

"Get me a bed sheet," Ty told his wife.

"What for?" she asked.

"You'll see. Get it."

Ty took the bedspread and hung it on the clothesline. Then he scribbled the following note on a piece of paper and pinned it to the sheet:

"Joe, be back in a half-hour—Ty."

The burglarizing mysteriously stopped.

The Ty Cobb of today seldom has any halfway emotions toward any man. He either likes you a great deal, or dislikes you heartily. He can be extremely friendly with those he personally likes, treating them in cordial and lavish fashion. Those he doesn't like, he avoids. He seems to some of the sporting crowd to be a hard man to get to know. To those who know him best he has always appeared to be a sentimentalist, a humanitarian, one who sought virtues in man which were not there, one who was bitterly disappointed when he discovered that even idols have clay feet.

A couple of years ago Cobb gave $400,000 or thereabouts to endow a hospital, a fine medical plant, in Royston in the name of his beloved father and mother. Later he organized a foundation—The Ty Cobb Educational Foundation—which now yearly provides some needy boys and girls an opportunity to go to college. He doesn't talk much about these donations, prefers to stay in the background.

"I don't deserve any credit," he said modestly, when pressed on the subject. "Just thinking that maybe some rawboned boy out of the hills, or some girl hungry for educa-

206

tion, will get one of these scholarships and go to town with it—that's the most pleasure I know. I didn't go to college. I missed that. I missed something in life. I now want to make it possible for others to go. If we get one good, live one and he comes through for us—just one—then it's all worthwhile. It's the least I can do for my native state."

As hard and cold as this man may pretend to be to some people, many others have a deep affection and respect for him. His moods are quick changing. Generally he is friendly and cordial and his enthusiasms are tremendous. His outside interests continue to be of the field and stream variety. That's one side of him. On the other, he is an avid newspaper and magazine reader, a lover of good books, and he has a lively and comprehensive interest in current affairs, with emphasis on finance, domestic and foreign politics, and the general health of the nation's business.

Ty's summer lodge sits hidden among tall pines on the side of a hill overlooking beauteous Lake Tahoe—like a scene in a Technicolor movie. The snowy peaks and catwalk ridges of the Sierra Mountains accentuate its rugged beauty. Like a sleepy child, darkness was crawling into the lap of the lake one evening last summer as Ty and the author sat chatting in front of his huge fireplace. Though the days were warm, the nights were crisp in the Nevada mountain country, and a fire crackled in the hearth. Outside, the western peaks seemed like a giant magnet, pulling the orange ball of sun to its breast, causing magic colors to fade to pale blue. The silent pines were darkly outlined against the clear sky, and the crickets started a symphony of drowsy evening song.

There is something fascinating about sunsets. Each one is different. Each is magic. Each makes a breath-taking climax to the bustle and hustle of the day. The whole world seems to sink to rest.

Sitting there across from Ty, with only the light of the

flaming cedar logs in the fireplace to brighten the room, the author was entranced by the peace and quiet, thinking of Thomas Wolfe's words—"a stone, a leaf, a door . . . the lost lane-end into Heaven." In settings as this, one often gets closest to the soul of man, when his interpretation of the true meaning of the Ten Commandments is revealed. A cathedral hush settled over us, and then Ty said softly, "I have traveled the globe, run the gamut of emotion, have seen a lot of amazing sights in my lifetime, but here"—he nodded toward the lake outside—"to be here seems the place I am happiest."

Ty fell to silence again. The far-off, forlorn quaver of a bullfrog echoed his sentiments.

The Cobb sitting there must have been in sharp contrast to the Cobb that once upon a time spent his off-season months in Augusta. No one in the sleepy southern town appeared to be in a hurry except Ty. Southerners drawl when they talk. The Ty of those days snapped out and bit off his words. They drag their feet. It was almost necessary to run to maintain the ordinary Cobb pace.

The magnolia city was famous for two things: the wintertime home of Ty Cobb and the place formerly selected by William Howard Taft to tear gaping holes out of the face of the earth while he pursued the game of golf in the winter. After Mr. Taft took up the job of filling the chair of a college professor, however, Augusta leaned heavily on the Ty Cobb end for its reputation. They never have thought so highly of college professors down there as they do of Presidents, and even a President was liable to pass unnoticed on the street when Ty was around.

Ty's whole life has been dramatic. So when you sit across from him in the twilight of evening for the first time, just fanning, your feeling is one of mild surprise. Outwardly he appears rather solemn, dignified, on guard, almost suspicious, but once you get to know him better a subdued ray of humor breaks through the smog of reserve surrounding him. He can, and does, laugh often. Soon you feel the warmth of the inner man, of the tremendous range of his knowledge and the tight-knit quality of his thinking. He is an able conversationalist, rarely fumbles for a word, and is a forceful proponent of his ideas.

John Wheeler once called him a born reporter, one who would have been a star in the newspaper business if he had adopted that line of work instead of baseball. Ty can absorb information rapidly and set down his impressions easily and graphically. He is an intellectual blotter.

Although his life has been far from plain, Cobb seemingly prefers the plainer things today. The public sees little of him any more, though occasionally he will come out of seclusion to attend the annual Hall of Fame ceremony at Cooperstown, or address a banquet, or accept a guest shot on a television program. While the author was visiting him in Nevada last June he was preparing a speech to deliver to a convention of doctors at Reno. His topic: The Need For Improved Medical Facilities In Rural Areas. Last December he traveled all the way from California to Trenton, New Jersey, to grace the inauguration of 500 new Shriner members into the "Tyrus Raymond Cobb Class." It was a rare honor for Ty, a Shriner for nearly half a century.

Ty works at his obligation of being a baseball immortal, autographing pictures of himself for fans young and old, answering mail and stale questions about his great moments on the baseball diamond, a scholarly man playing out the full nine. This, then, is the haven in which the erstwhile storm-driven ship is resting.

His reading habits cover a wide range and include ancient history, politics, religion, sports, philosophy and medicine. History books especially intrigue him. The author recalled reading that when Ty lived in Augusta, his magnificent, beautifully furnished home was liberally scattered with pictures and statues of Napoleon. Was this in any way a pose with Ty as it was with many?

"No," he said, "I've always been a great admirer of that guy. Napoleon was a big leaguer all right."

The Cobb home library is lavishly stocked with books on the famous French General.

One afternoon Ty took the author to Virginia City, sort of a tourist's view of the old West. Frances, his second wife, went along. She drove. Frances and Ty were married in 1949. He and his first wife were divorced after a marriage that lasted for nearly thirty-nine years. Ty doesn't talk about it, nor does a reporter press the question. Nor does he talk much about his children, Shirley, Beverly, Herchel and Howell. Ty, Jr., a fine young doctor, died of cancer a couple of years ago. None of the Cobb boys showed much interest in baseball!

It was about a forty-four mile drive from Lake Tahoe to Virginia City. Ty settled himself back in the seat, reading the *Wall Street Journal*. He's been a big stockholder for years. It used to be a familiar sight to see him leave his stock broker's office for the ball park. He was hitting around .385 at the time and taking the American League apart like a Swiss watch. His interest in the stock ticker did absolutely nothing to him, except make him immensely rich and financially independent for the rest of his life. Just how much wealth he has compiled he won't say, but you get a fair idea when you know that his interests in Coca-Cola alone total more than 12,000 shares. He has also helped to make his sons and daughters financially healthy, turning over to them valuable stocks and advising them on sensible investment matters.

Ty glanced up from his paper, and said, "I always have tried to keep my finances to myself. I feel it is nobody's business how much I was paid for playing ball, or how much I have made in the stock market. Folks think I made it all

210

in Coca-Cola. Well, I was doing well on Wall Street before the soft drink became a household word, particularly in automotive stocks. In fact, my friends practically had to force me to take 300 shares of Coke back around the time of the first World War. Developed into one of the smartest buys I ever made."

"Tyrus," his wife interrupted, "what's Coke selling for today?"

"Lessee," Ty said, turning his attention back to the *Journal*. He ran his finger down the rows and rows of flyspeck columns.

"Mmmm, here it is . . . selling at 144. And with the hot weather still ahead, it should climb to 180 or more. Yes, sir, a good, solid stock."

Then turning to the author, he added, "Coke's an example of a good depression-proof stock. Even paid dividends to shareholders during the crash. The automotive industry is another sound investment . . . and steel . . . and public utilities. I tell folks not to speculate. You should know what you're buying, then stay with it. Don't buy today and pull out tomorrow. Smart thing for a young man to do is to sign up with one of these college extension courses. He should learn all he can about stocks and investments before he spends his money."

Ty never mentioned it, but Jimmy Powers, *New York Daily News* sports editor, once quoted him as saying he made more than $300,000 in baseball, ranging from $1800 he collected his first full season at Detroit, to $50,000 he received when the Tigers made him player-manager.

"When Joe DiMaggio first went from San Francisco to the Yankees," continued Ty, "he was very easy-going about his salary demands. Joe and I have always been good friends, closer than you know, and I took him aside one day and told him how important it was that the Yankees pay him what he was worth. Remember the battle he had with Ed Barrow one season? Well, I told Joe to hold out for more money. It wasn't too long before his income jumped from $16,600 to something like $32,500. I tried to show him by all this that a ballplayer's career is limited. It can be cut short by injury. He must get the big dough while he can."

A month and a half after that ride to Virginia City, Ty made a date with the author to drive him to Cooperstown for the annual Baseball Hall of Fame program. I picked him up at the Ambassador Hotel, where he always stays when he comes to New York, and we started cross-town to get to Riverside Drive. At 58th Street and Sixth Avenue, we stopped for a street signal. A shiny black Cadillac convertible floated up and halted beside us. Two men and a woman sat in the front seat. A dark-complexioned fellow, suit coat off and in shirt sleeves, sat on the right and nonchalantly looked our way as he waited for the light to turn green. Then he saw Ty. His mouth fell open.

"W-w-why . . . hey, Ty!" he cried, leaping out of the car.

Ty, who had been staring straight ahead, snapped his head around, startled to hear his name spoken right there in the middle of the street in a city of eight million.

"Wal dawgone!" drawled Ty. Talk about miracles. "Joe!"

And Ty Cobb and Joe DiMaggio held reunion.

"Congratulations, Joe," beamed Ty, meaning DiMag's selection to the Hall of Fame.

Joe grinned.

"It's been a long climb, Ty," he said, "but I finally made it. Feels great to be in there with a champ like you."

Strange that the first man elected to the Hall of Fame should bump into the latest addition this way—and both on their way to Cooperstown, too!

The loud honking of automobile horns jolted DiMaggio back to the realization that he was standing in the middle of the street, holding up traffic. He shook Ty's hand vigorously.

212

"See ya', Ty."

"See ya', Joe."

It was indeed a small world.

It has been a long, eventful ride, this life of Ty Cobb's. And all along the journey he has kept these words of his father's buried deep in his heart:

"Son, always be on the side of right. When you're faced with problems, try to solve those problems as if you were kneeling in front of God. Sometimes your decisions will be unpopular, but you have nothing to fear if, deep inside you, you know that you are on His side."

Those were the words by which Ty Cobb lived and played baseball.

He's lived his own life, in his own way.

He will stand on his record.

Appendix

Baseball's Most Fascinating Figures

COBB'S BEST YEARS

In	Record	Year
Batting	.420	1911
Games	156	1915
At bats	625	1924
Runs	147	1911
Hits	248	1911
Doubles	47	1911
Triples	24	1911
Home Runs	12	1921–1925
Sacrifices	27	1922
Steals	96	1915
Runs batted in	144	1911
Passes	118	1915
Slugging	.621	1911
°Whiffs	2	1926

° Fewest

TY COBB'S RECORD

Height 6' ¾". Weight 175. Batted left, threw right.

Year	Club	League	G	AB	R	H	HR	SB	RBI	BA
1904	Augusta	So. Atl.	37	135	14	32	1	4	—	.237
1904	Anniston	S.E.	22	—	—	—	0	6	—	.370
1905	Augusta	So. Atl.	104	411	60	134	0	40	—	.326
1905	Detroit	American	41	150	19	36	1	2	—	.240
1906	Detroit	American	97	350	44	112	1	23	—	.320
1907	Detroit	American	150	605	97	°212	5	°49	°116	°.350
1908	Detroit	American	150	581	88	°188	4	39	°101	°.324
1909	Detroit	American	156	573	°116	°216	°9	°76	°115	°.377
1910	Detroit	American	140	509	°106	196	8	65	88	°.385
1911	Detroit	American	146	591	♯147	°248	8	°83	♯144	°.420
1912	Detroit	American	140	553	119	♯227	7	61	90	°.410
1913	Detroit	American	122	428	70	167	4	52	65	°.390
1914	Detroit	American	97	345	69	127	2	35	57	°.368
1915	Detroit	American	156	563	°144	°208	3	°96	95	°.369
1916	Detroit	American	145	542	113	201	5	°68	67	.371
1917	Detroit	American	152	588	107	°225	7	°55	108	°.383
1918	Detroit	American	111	421	83	161	3	34	64	°.382
1919	Detroit	American	124	497	92	♯191	1	28	69	°.384
1920	Detroit	American	112	428	86	143	2	14	63	.334
1921	Detroit	American	128	507	124	197	12	22	101	.389
1922	Detroit	American	137	526	99	211	4	9	99	.401
1923	Detroit	American	145	556	103	189	6	9	88	.340
1924	Detroit	American	155	625	115	211	4	23	74	.338
1925	Detroit	American	121	415	97	157	12	13	102	.378
1926	Detroit	American	79	233	48	79	4	9	62	.339
1927	Phil.	American	134	490	104	175	5	22	93	.357
1928	Phil.	American	95	353	54	144	1	5	40	.323
Major League Totals:			3033	11,429	2244	4191	118	892	1901	.367

WORLD SERIES RECORD

Year	Club	League	G	AB	R	H	HR	SB	RBI	BA
1907	Detroit	American	5	20	1	4	0	0	0	.200
1908	Detroit	American	5	19	3	7	0	2	3	.368
1909	Detroit	American	7	26	3	6	0	2	5	.231
Totals:			17	65	7	17	0	4	8	.262

° Led League
Tied for lead
Managed Detroit Tigers, December 1920 to November 1926
Elected to Hall of Fame, 1936

OTHER OUTSTANDING COBB RECORDS

Led the American League outfielders in 1924 in percentage, made most putouts in 1911 and assists in 1908. Had 30 assists in 1907. Tied league record for highest percentage for 100 or more games, season—.420 (1911); played 3033 games in 24 years; most times at bat, league—11,429; most runs scored, league—2244; most stolen bases, league—892; most base hits, league—4191; most times five hits in one game, season—4 (May 7, July 7, second game, July 12 and July 17, 1922); six base hits in six times at bat—May 5, 1925; set major league record with most total bases, league—5863; tied league record with Lou Gehrig for most total bases, game—16, May 5, 1925; made most one-base hits, league—3052; most three-base hits, league—297; hit three home runs, game—May 5, 1925. Received Chalmers Award (automobile) for leading American League batters, 1910.

COBB VS.

RED SOX PITCHERS GOING ROUTE AGAINST HIM

Pitchers	Games	At Bats	Hits	2B	3B	HR	Pct.
Arellanes, Frank	1	6	1	0	0	0	.167
Burchell, Fred	3	11	1	1	0	0	.091
Bedient, Hugh	2	8	2	1	0	0	.250
Bush, Joe	5	20	2	0	0	0	.100
Barry, Ed	1	4	3	0	1	0	.750
Cicotte, Ed	5	20	7	0	1	1	.350
Collins, Ray	21	76	23	2	3	1	.303
Collins, Warren	3	7	2	1	0	0	.286
Dinneen, William	3	8	3	1	0	0	.375
Ehmke, Howard	8	26	7	2	1	0	.269
Foster, George	8	26	5	0	0	0	.192
Ferguson, Aleck	4	12	6	1	0	0	.500
Fullerton, Curt	3	12	7	1	1	1	.583
Fuhr, Oscar	2	7	1	1	0	0	.143
Gregg, Vean	3	10	6	1	1	0	.600
Gibson, Norwood	1	4	0	0	0	0	.000
Glaze, Ralph	1	4	2	0	0	0	.500

Pitchers	Games	At Bats	Hits	2B	3B	HR	Pct.
Harriss, Bryan	1	4	2	0	0	0	.500
Hall, Charles	2	8	4	2	0	0	.500
Hoyt, Waite	3	13	1	0	1	0	.077
Harper, Harry	2	8	2	0	0	0	.250
Harris, Joe	3	12	4	0	0	0	.333
Jones, Sam	9	32	9	3	0	0	.281
Karr, Ben	1	4	1	0	0	0	.250
Karger, Ed	8	30	9	4	0	0	.300
Leonard, Hubert	10	32	12	1	2	1	.375
Lundgren, Delmar	1	5	3	1	0	0	.600
Morgan, Harry	2	8	1	0	0	0	.125
Musser, Paul	1	3	2	0	0	0	.667
MacFayden, Dan	1	4	0	0	0	0	.000
Morris, Edward	2	8	2	2	0	0	.250
Mosely, Earl	3	11	4	0	1	0	.364
Myers, Elmer	5	20	6	3	1	0	.300
Mays, Carl	13	41	14	0	0	1	.341
O'Brien, Thos.	5	19	8	1	0	0	.421
Pennock, Herb	7	27	10	3	0	0	.370
Pape, Larry	1	4	1	0	0	0	.250
Piercy, Wm.	3	10	3	0	0	0	.300
Quinn, John	7	32	11	1	1	0	.344
Ruth, George	13	46	15	0	0	0	.326
Ruffing, Chas.	4	13	3	0	0	0	.231
Russell, Allan	3	13	3	0	1	0	.231
Steele, Elmer	2	8	2	0	0	0	.250
Shore, Ernest	7	28	11	3	1	0	.393
Thomas, Alphonse	1	5	2	1	0	0	.400
Tannehill, Jesse	4	15	4	0	0	0	.267
Wiltse, Harold	5	20	8	2	0	0	.400
Wingfield, Fred	5	15	6	0	1	0	.400
Winter, George	5	21	10	1	1	1	.476
Welzer, Tony	1	4	2	0	0	0	.500
Wood, Joseph	14	56	21	8	2	0	.375
Young, Denton	12	47	18	4	3	0	.383
Zahniser, Paul	2	8	1	0	0	0	.125
Total	242	895	293	52	23	7	.329
Detroit	228	838	272	46	23	7	.325
Philadelphia	14	57	21	6	0	0	.368

COBB VS. WHITE SOX

Pitchers	Games	At Bats	Hits	2B	3B	HR	Pct.
Altrock, Nick	7	30	7	1	0	0	.233
Adkins, Grady	1	1	0	0	0	0	.000
Burns, Bill	2	10	0	0	0	0	.000
Benz, Joe	2	8	2	0	0	0	.250
Blankenship, Ted	6	21	5	1	0	0	.238

Pitchers	Games	At Bats	Hits	2B	3B	HR	Pct.
Connally, George	3	11	3	0	0	1	.273
Cicotte, Edward	22	79	27	5	2	0	.342
Danforth, Dave	4	17	6	3	0	0	.353
Faber, Urban	31	112	29	6	1	1	.259
Hodge, Clarence	1	4	0	0	0	0	.000
Kerr, Dick	8	33	9	0	1	0	.273
Leverette, Gorham	3	9	5	1	0	0	.556
Lange, Frank	2	8	5	1	0	0	.625
Lyons, Ted	15	55	18	3	0	0	.327
Owen, Frank	3	11	3	1	0	0	.273
Olmstead, Fred	2	6	4	1	0	0	.667
Patterson, Roy	2	9	1	0	0	0	.111
Robertson, Charles	5	18	5	0	2	1	.278
Russell, Ewell	9	28	6	0	0	0	.214
Shellenback, Frank	1	3	0	0	0	0	.000
Scott, Jim	8	25	10	1	0	0	.400
Smith, Frank	18	66	17	3	0	0	.258
Thurston, Hollis	6	25	12	1	0	0	.480
Thomas, Alphonse	4	17	8	1	0	0	.471
Wilkinson, Roy	2	6	3	0	0	0	.500
Wolfgang, Mel	3	11	8	1	2	0	.727
Williams, Claude	10	40	11	1	0	0	.275
Walsh, Ed	22	88	27	6	0	0	.307
White, Guy	26	94	26	4	0	0	.278
Young, Irving	1	4	1	1	0	0	.250
Totals	229	849	258	42	8	3	.304
Detroit	213	793	237	39	8	2	.299
Philadelphia	166	56	21	3	0	1	.375

COBB VS. CLEVELAND

Pitchers	Games	At Bats	Hits	2B	3B	HR	Pct.
Baskette, Jim	1	3	0	0	0	0	.000
Buckeye, Garland	5	16	4	0	1	0	.250
Berger, Charles	1	3	2	0	0	0	.667
Bernhard, Bill	4	16	5	0	0	0	.311
Blanding, Fred	6	25	12	2	1	0	.480
Bagby, Jim	19	70	22	6	1	0	.314
Coumbe, Fred	3	10	1	0	0	0	.100
Chech, Charles	3	11	2	0	0	0	.181
Cullop, Nick	1	3	3	1	0	0	1.000
Caldwell, Ray	3	12	3	0	0	0	.250
Coveleskie, Stanley	20	77	21	3	1	0	.272
Dillinger, Harley	1	3	0	0	0	0	.000
Edwards, James	3	12	1	0	0	0	.083
Eels, Harry	2	5	3	0	1	0	.600
Falkenberg, Fred	4	15	4	0	0	0	.267
Gregg, Vean	8	30	10	1	1	1	.333

Pitchers	Games	At Bats	Hits	2B	3B	HR	Pct.
Hudlin, Willis	2	7	0	0	0	0	.000
Hagerman, Rip	3	11	4	3	0	0	.364
Hess, Otto	9	33	10	1	0	0	.303
Joss, Adrian	20	73	17	2	0	1	.233
Karr, Ben	1	5	2	1	0	0	.400
Krapp, Gene	2	6	2	1	0	0	.332
Klepfer, Ed	2	8	2	0	0	0	.250
Kahler, George	7	25	7	2	0	0	.280
Liebhardt, Glenn	6	21	5	1	0	0	.238
Lattimore, Bill	1	6	3	0	0	0	.500
Lowdermilk, Grover	1	1	1	0	0	0	1.000
Link, Fred	1	4	2	0	0	0	.500
Mails, Duster	1	6	0	0	0	0	.000
Myers, Elmer	1	3	1	0	0	0	.333
Metevier, George	1	4	1	0	0	0	.250
Miller, Walter	5	19	5	0	0	0	.263
Mitchell, William	7	27	9	3	0	1	.333
Morton, Guy	9	33	12	1	0	1	.364
Moore, Earl	2	9	4	0	0	0	.444
Rhoades, Dusty	16	64	17	3	0	1	.266
Roy, Luther	1	4	0	0	0	0	.000
Speece, Byron	1	1	0	0	0	0	.000
Steen, Bill	1	3	1	0	0	0	.333
Sothoron, Allen	2	6	2	0	0	0	.333
Smith, Sherrod	5	16	5	0	0	0	.313
Shaute, Ben	7	27	4	0	0	0	.148
Townsend, John	1	3	1	0	0	0	.333
Thielman, John	2	8	2	1	0	1	.250
Uhle, George	20	65	24	9	2	0	.369
Wright, Clarence	2	6	1	1	0	0	.167
West, James	3	9	3	2	0	0	.222
Young, Cy	7	27	6	0	0	0	.222
Totals	233	851	246	44	8	6	.289
Detroit	220	801	239	43	7	6	.298
Philadelphia	13	50	7	1	1	0	.140

COBB VS. TIGERS

Pitchers	Games	At Bats	Hits	2B	3B	HR	Pct.
Carroll, Owen	2	7	4	0	0	0	.571
Collins, Warren	1	0	0	0	0	0	.000
Gibson, Sam	3	10	4	1	0	0	.400
Holloway, Ken	2	8	3	2	0	0	.375
Sorrell, Vic	1	4	2	0	0	0	.500
Van Gildar, Elam	1	1	0	0	0	0	.000
Whitehill, Earl	2	4	1	0	0	0	.250
Totals	12	34	14	3	0	0	.411

COBB VS. YANKEES

Pitchers	Games	At Bats	Hits	2B	3B	HR	Pct.
Bush, Joe	7	26	5	1	0	0	.192
Caldwell, Ray	16	54	23	5	1	0	.426
Chesbro, Jack	9	33	12	2	1	0	.364
Cullop, Nick	2	9	4	2	0	0	.444
Doyle, Joe	3	10	2	0	0	1	.200
Ford, Russell	16	57	25	2	4	0	.439
Fisher, Ray	9	31	8	4	0	0	.256
Griffith, Clark	1	4	0	0	0	0	.000
Harper, Harry	1	3	1	0	0	0	.333
Hoyt, Waite	12	35	7	2	0	0	.200
Hughes, Tom	2	7	4	2	0	0	.571
Hogg, Bill	4	20	8	1	0	0	.400
Johnson, Henry	4	10	2	1	0	0	.200
Jones, Sam	7	28	8	1	0	0	.286
Keating, Ray	4	13	2	1	0	0	.154
Lake, Joe	1	5	2	0	1	0	.400
Love, Elmer	3	10	4	0	2	0	.400
Collins, Warren	3	7	5	2	0	0	.714
Manning, Walter	10	38	12	1	0	0	.316
Mogridge, George	13	50	14	2	1	0	.280
Mays, Carl	14	47	14	2	1	2	.298
Moore, Wilcey	1	1	0	0	0	0	.000
McGraw, Bob	1	4	1	0	0	0	.250
McHale, Marty	2	9	3	2	0	0	.333
McConnell, George	4	15	5	1	1	0	.333
Newton, Eustace	3	12	2	0	0	0	.167
Orth, Al	4	16	6	1	1	0	.375
Pennock, Herb	10	41	17	0	0	0	.415
Pipgras, George	3	11	2	0	0	0	.182
Powell, Jack	1	4	2	0	0	0	.500
Quinn, John	4	15	7	0	0	0	.467
Russell, Allan	4	14	3	0	0	0	.214
Ruether, Walter	1	4	2	0	0	0	.500
Shocker, Urban	6	20	11	1	0	1	.550
Schulz, Albert	4	13	4	1	1	0	.308
Shawkey, Bob	15	61	31	4	3	1	.506
Thomas, Myles	1	4	0	0	0	0	.000
Thormahlen, Herb	4	16	2	0	0	0	.125
Vaughn, Jim	7	27	10	3	1	0	.370
Warhop, Jack	14	60	25	5	2	2	.417
Wilson, Pete	5	14	6	0	1	1	.409
Totals	235	858	309	49	22	8	.351
Detroit	214	786	280	47	22	8	.356
Philadelphia	21	72	21	2	0	0	.292

222

COBB VS. ATHLETICS

Pitchers	Games	At Bats	Hits	2B	3B	HR	Pct.
Adams, Jim	1	5	1	0	0	0	.200
Baumgardner, Stan	2	8	2	0	0	0	.250
Brown, Carroll	3	12	4	0	0	0	.333
Bressler, Rube	1	4	3	0	0	0	.750
Burns, Dennis	3	10	4	1	0	0	.400
Bush, Joe	7	25	9	0	0	0	.360
Bender, Chief	14	54	20	1	1	0	.370
Coakley, Andy	2	7	4	0	0	0	.571
Coombs, Jack	13	42	13	2	2	0	.370
Cottrell, Ensign	1	4	0	0	0	0	.000
Coveleskie, Stanley	1	3	1	1	0	0	.333
Crabb, Jim	1	4	2	0	0	0	.500
Dygert, Jim	5	17	5	0	0	0	.294
Grove, Bob	3	9	3	0	1	0	.333
Gregg, Vean	2	9	3	0	0	0	.333
Gray, Sam	2	9	3	0	0	0	.333
Hasty, Bob	4	18	4	1	0	0	.222
Harriss, Bryan	5	20	5	0	0	0	.250
Houck, Byron	2	8	5	2	0	0	.625
Heimach, Fred	2	8	2	0	1	0	.250
Johnson, Jing	3	10	4	0	1	0	.400
Krause, Harry	10	39	13	1	0	0	.333
Kellogg, Al	1	2	0	0	0	0	.000
Knowlson, Tom	1	4	1	0	0	0	.250
Keefe, Dave	2	8	2	0	0	0	.335
Kinney, Walter	2	9	3	0	0	0	.333
Meeker, Roy	1	4	2	1	0	0	.500
Moore, Roy	1	5	2	0	0	0	.400
Morgan, Cy	1	1	0	0	0	0	.000
Myers, Elmer	10	36	12	2	1	0	.333
Nabors, John	2	9	6	1	0	0	.667
Naylor, Roleine	9	33	16	3	1	0	.485
Noyes, Win	5	19	7	1	0	0	.368
Ogden, Warren	1	4	1	0	1	0	.250
Pennock, Herb	1	5	2	0	0	0	.400
Perry, Scott	5	20	11	2	1	0	.550
Plank, Edward	33	124	37	4	1	0	.298
Quinn, John	2	8	3	0	0	0	.375
Rommel, Ed	13	46	16	3	1	1	.348
Rogers, Tom	1	3	2	1	0	0	.667
Schlitzer, Vic	1	4	0	0	0	0	.000
Schauer, Aleck	1	4	2	0	2	0	.500
Shawkey, Bob	3	11	2	0	1	0	.182
Seibold, Harry	2	8	5	2	1	0	.625
Sheehan, Tom	3	15	5	0	0	0	.333
Vickers, Rube	2	6	2	1	0	0	.333

Pitchers	Games	At Bats	Hits	2B	3B	HR	Pct.
Williams, Malcolm	1	4	1	0	0	1	.250
Wyckoff, Weldon	5	19	6	0	0	0	.316
Waddell, Rube	5	18	7	2	0	0	.389
Zinn, Guy	1	5	3	0	0	0	.600
Totals	202	759	266	32	16	2	.350

COBB VS. BROWNS

Pitchers	Games	At Bats	Hits	2B	3B	HR	Pct.
Allison, Mack	1	4	2	0	1	0	.500
Baumgardner, George	2	8	1	0	0	0	.125
Bayne, Bill	3	9	0	0	0	0	.000
Brown, Charles	2	7	2	1	0	0	.286
Ballou, Win	1	5	2	0	0	0	.400
Bailey, Bill	11	42	15	2	0	0	.359
Crowder, Alvin	3	8	0	0	0	0	.000
Dinneen, Bill	2	6	3	0	0	0	.500
Davenport, Dave	5	20	5	1	0	0	.250
Danforth, Dave	7	25	5	0	1	1	.200
Davis, Frank	11	30	8	3	0	0	.267
Gaston, Milt	3	12	4	2	0	0	.333
Gray, Sam	1	4	3	0	0	0	.750
Graham, William	5	17	5	2	0	0	.294
Glade, Fred	7	23	5	0	0	0	.217
Groom, Bob	1	5	1	0	1	0	.200
Gallia, Mel	2	7	2	2	0	0	.286
George, Bill	2	8	3	0	0	0	.375
Hoff, Chester	1	4	1	0	0	0	.250
Hamilton, Earl	13	43	13	0	2	1	.300
Howell, Harry	10	39	9	2	1	0	.231
James, Bill	3	13	3	0	1	0	.231
Kolp, Ray	2	10	3	2	0	0	.300
Koob, Ernie	1	3	0	0	0	0	.000
Jacobson, Al	7	23	6	0	0	0	.261
Lowdermilk, Grover	3	10	6	0	2	0	.600
Lake, Joe	4	16	8	0	1	0	.500
Leverenz, Walter	1	1	0	0	0	0	.000
Mitchell, Roy	3	11	5	1	0	0	.455
Maple, Rolla	2	6	1	1	0	0	.167
Nelson, Al	1	5	4	0	0	0	.800
Nevers, Ernie	1	1	0	0	0	0	.000
Ogden, John	2	7	3	0	0	0	.429
Pruett, Hub	1	2	2	0	1	0	1.000
Palmero, Emilio	1	5	4	2	1	1	.800
Plank, Edward	6	20	7	2	0	0	.350
Pelty, Barney	10	33	13	0	1	0	.394
Powell, John	15	59	20	1	2	1	.339
Rogers, Tom	4	16	7	1	0	0	.438
Rose, Charles	1	3	2	0	0	1	.667

Pitchers	Games	At Bats	Hits	2B	3B	HR	Pct.
Ray, Bob	3	10	0	0	0	0	.000
Shocker, Urban	11	40	9	3	0	1	.225
Sothoron, Allan	6	21	10	1	0	0	.476
Sisler, George	1	5	0	0	0	0	.000
Smith, Ed	1	3	1	0	0	0	.333
Spade, Robert	1	4	1	1	0	0	.250
Voight, Olin	1	4	2	0	0	0	.500
Van Gilder, Elam	12	44	14	2	0	1	.318
Wingard, Ernie	2	8	4	0	0	1	.500
Zachary, Tom	4	13	4	0	0	1	.308
Weilman, Carl	17	59	14	2	1	0	.237
Waddell, Rube	7	25	6	1	1	0	.240
Wright, Clarence	1	5	2	0	0	0	.400
Totals	228	811	250	35	17	9	.308
Detroit	215	765	232	35	17	7	.303
Philadelphia	13	46	18	0	0	2	.391

COBB VS. SENATORS

Pitchers	Games	At Bats	Hits	2B	3B	HR	Pct.
Acosta, Jose	1	5	3	1	0	0	.600
Ayers, Yancey	5	17	5	1	1	0	.294
Brillheart, Benson	1	4	1	0	0	0	.250
Burns, Bill	4	14	3	1	0	1	.214
Braxton, Garland	1	4	1	1	0	0	.250
Brown, Lloyd	1	4	0	0	0	0	.000
Boehling, Joe	8	22	11	1	0	1	.500
Coveleskie, Stan	3	10	0	0	0	0	.000
Cashion, Carl	4	17	11	0	0	1	.647
Erickson, Eric	2	5	2	1	0	0	.400
Francis, Ray	3	12	1	0	0	0	.083
Gehring, Hank	2	8	4	0	0	0	.500
Goodwin, Clyde	1	4	1	0	0	0	.250
Graham, Oscar	1	4	0	0	0	0	.000
Gray, Dolly	12	41	10	3	1	0	.268
Groom, Bob	10	38	11	0	2	1	.289
Gallia, Mel	4	15	6	0	0	0	.400
Gaston, Milt	3	9	3	0	0	0	.333
Falkenberg, Fred	4	14	4	1	0	0	.286
Hughes, Thos.	9	32	11	2	1	0	.344
Harper, Harry	5	19	7	1	0	0	.368
Hadley, Irving	6	14	5	1	1	0	.293
Johnson, Walter	67	245	82	14	3	1	.335
Kitson, Frank	3	14	5	1	0	0	.293
Lisenbee, Horace	3	9	1	0	0	0	.111
Moyer, Charles	1	4	1	0	0	1	.250
Mogridge, George	11	44	14	2	1	0	.318
Martina, Joe	2	8	3	0	0	0	.375

Pitchers	Games	At Bats	Hits	2B	3B	HR	Pct.
Otey, Bill	1	4	1	0	0	0	.250
Patten, Case	3	12	8	3	1	0	.667
Reisling, Frank	3	12	3	0	0	1	.250
Ruether, Walter	3	10	5	2	0	0	.500
Smith, Charles	4	15	8	1	0	2	.533
Shaw, Jim	10	38	11	2	0	0	.289
Schacht, Al	1	5	3	1	0	0	.600
Thurston, Hollis	1	4	1	0	0	0	.250
Townsend, John	1	3	2	1	0	0	.667
Tannehill, Jess	1	4	1	0	0	0	.250
Vaughn, Jim	1	3	1	1	0	0	.333
Walker, Ewart	3	13	8	4	1	0	.615
Wolfe, William	1	4	1	0	0	0	.250
Warmuth, Wallace	1	3	1	0	0	0	.333
Zachary, Tom	15	55	16	3	0	1	.291
Zahniser, Paul	1	4	2	0	0	0	.500
Totals	227	825	278	49	12	10	.337
Detroit	210	773	266	47	11	10	.344
Philadelphia	17	52	12	2	1	0	.231

ALL-TIME AMERICAN LEAGUE OFFENSIVE LEADERS

Batting champions come and go, but none have won a total of more individual offensive titles in the A.L. than the dozen blue ribboners listed below.

	BA	Stolen Bases	RBI's	Slugging	Runs	Hits	Total Bases	Doubles	Triples	Home Runs	Bases on Balls	Total Championships
Ty Cobb	12	6	4	9	5	8	6	3	4	1	0	58
Babe Ruth	1	0	6	13	8	0	6	0	0	12	11	57
Ted Williams	4	0	4	8	4	0	6	2	0	4	8	40
Lou Gehrig	1	0	5	2	4	1	4	2	1	3	3	26
Jimmy Foxx	2	0	3	5	1	0	3	0	0	4	2	20
Larry Lajoie	3	0	0	3	1	4	3	4	0	1	0	19

226

	BA	Stolen Bases	RBI's	Slugging	Runs	Hits	Total Bases	Doubles	Triples	Home Runs	Bases on Balls	Total Championships
Hank Greenberg	0	0	4	1	1	0	2	2	0	4	1	15
Sam Crawford	0	0	3	0	1	0	1	1	5	2	0	13
Joe DiMaggio	2	0	2	2	1	0	3	0	1	2	0	13
Tris Speaker	1	0	1	1	0	2	0	7	0	0	0	12
George Sisler	2	4	0	0	1	2	1	0	1	0	0	11
George Stirnweiss	1	2	0	1	2	2	1	0	2	0	0	11

Index

Index

232

Cooley, Dick, 43
Coolidge, Calvin, 140
Corbett, Jim, 6, 7
Coughlin, Bill, 162, 163
Crawford, Sam, 43, 56, 57, 58, 71, 129, 130, 142, 192
Criger, Lou, 98
Croke, Bill, 23, 32, 33
Cronin, Jack, 8
Cross, Monte, 57
Crusinberry, Jim, 80
Cunningham, Joe, 13, 14
Czolgosz, Leon, 6

Daubert, Jake, 88
Dean, Dizzy, 163, 164
Delahanty, Ed, 9
Dempsey, Jack, 86, 140, 166
Dickey, Bill, 205
Dillinger, John, 181
Dillon, Jack, 86
DiMaggio, Joe, 120, 121, 122, 200, 201, 211, 212
Dobie, Gil, 141
Donlin, Mike, 9, 87
Donovan, Wild Bill, 48, 49, 56, 57, 58, 160
Doyle, Larry, 88, 125
Dressen, Charlie, 73
Driscoll, Dave, 170, 171
Dugan, Joe, 143
Dygert, Jimmy, 56

Earnshaw, George, 103
Ederle, Gertrude, 141
Edison, Thomas, 6
Elberfeld, Kid, 106, 107
Ely, Bones, 8

234

235